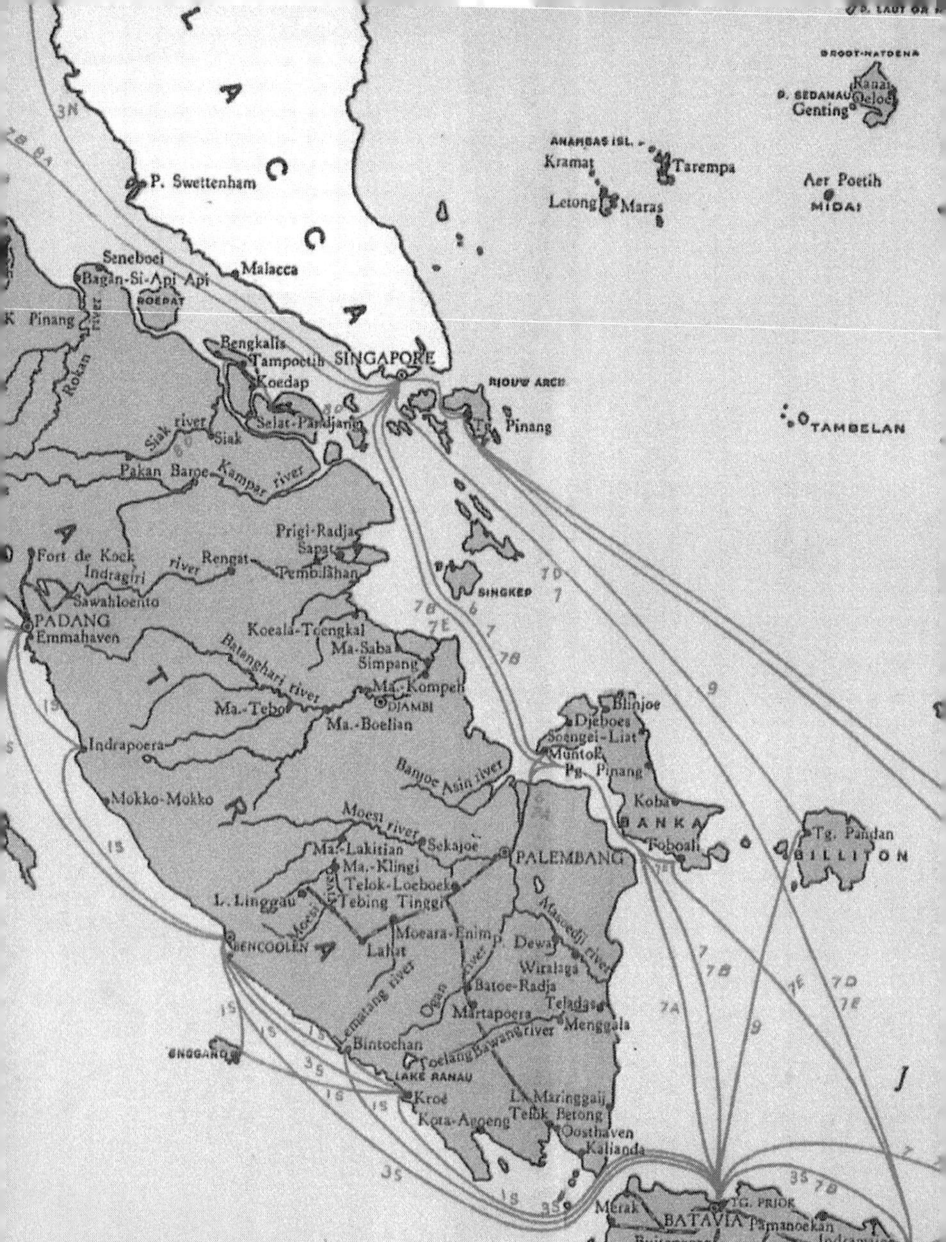

This is the official map of the KPM steamship company showing its services in the East Indies region for 1937. The map continues eastwards on the back end papers. Collingwood took this map with him on his trips around the islands, marking the routes he took himself with stippling, and pasted the map inside the back of the notebook in which he kept his Log of the journey. Map 1 in the present volume, pages 452–3, shows his journeys in a little more detail, superimposed on a modern map with modern names.

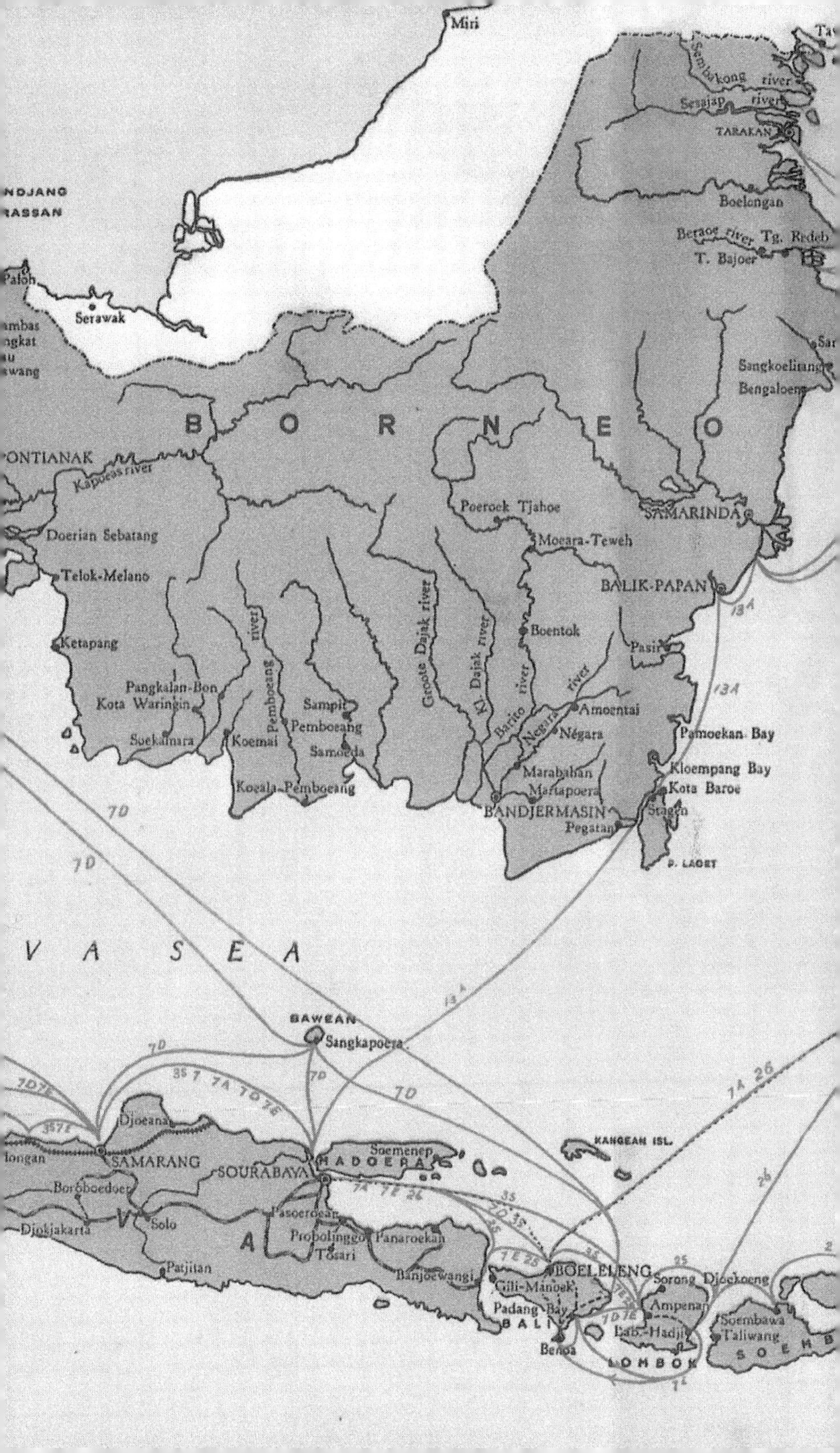

Miri
Serawak
BORNEO
PONTIANAK
Kapoeas river
Doerian Sebatang
Telok-Melano
Ketapang
Pangkalan-Bon
Kota Waringin
Soekamara
Koemai
Pemboeang river
Sampit
Pemboeang
Samoeda
Koeala-Pemboeang
Groote Dajak river
Kl. Dajak river
Barito river
Negara river
Poeroek Tjahoe
Moeara-Teweh
Boentok
Amoentai
Négara
Marabahan
Martapoera
BANDJERMASIN
Pegatan
SAMARINDA
BALIK-PAPAN
Pasir
Pamoekan Bay
Kloempang Bay
Kota Baroe
Stagen
P. LAOET
TARAKAN
Sesajap river
Boelongan
Beraoe river
Tg. Redeb
T. Bajoer
Sangkoelirang
Bengaloen
BAWEAN
Sangkapoera
KANGEAN ISL.
Djoeana
SAMARANG
SOURABAYA
MADOERA
Soemenep
Boroboedoer
Djokjakarta
Solo
Patjitan
Pasoeroean
Probolinggo
Panaroekan
Tosari
Banjoewangi
Gili-Manoek
BOELELENG
Padang Bay
BALI
Benoa
Sorong
Djoekoeng
Ampenan
Lab. Hadji
LOMBOK
Soembawa
Taliwang

R. G. COLLINGWOOD: *AN AUTOBIOGRAPHY* AND OTHER WRITINGS

'[Collingwood] helps us to look for the answers different writers give to their (not our) questions. To this end we must try to think ourselves into each writer's scheme of thought.'
John Rawls, *Lectures on the History of Political Philosophy*

'a fascinating and often brilliant book.'
Bernard Williams, *The Sense of the Past*

'[G]uaranteed to get the reader on his or her toes . . . this volume is invaluable for Collingwoodian scholarship.'
Collingwood and British Idealism Studies

'A polymath as skilled in archaeology as he was in philosophy, a staunch opponent of appeasement and an early hater of the Daily Mail. Collingwood has been my guide for many years.'
Niall Ferguson, *Civilization*

'Before I read this book there was chaos in my thoughts regarding my subject matter: having finished it, I knew perfectly well what I was going to argue for. My deepest gratitude is due to this unjustly neglected author.'
Agnes Heller, *A Theory of History, Viii*

'The new edition includes a facsimile of the first printing . . . followed by various maps and illustrations, and a mass of supplementary essays.'
Jonathan Rée, *London Review of Books*

'If these scholars have anything methodologically in common, it might be summarised as a desire to stress the historicity of the history of political theory and of intellectual history more generally. Collingwood himself expressed this commitment by demanding that we should aim to recover the precise questions to which the philosophical texts we study were designed as answers.'
Quentin Skinner, *The History of Political Thought in National Context*

'that all important "introductory" quality of Collingwood's *Autobiography* has been augmented . . . with what amounts to an accessible introduction to Collingwood scholarship.'
Christopher Fear, *History of Political Thought*

R. G. Collingwood (1889–1943) was Waynflete Professor of Metaphysical Philosophy at the University of Oxford.

David Boucher is Professor in Political Philosophy and International Relations, Cardiff University, and Distinguished Visiting Professor, University of Johannesburg. He is also Vice President of the Learned Society of Wales.

Teresa Smith is R. G. Collingwood's daughter by his second wife, Kate Collingwood. Since the 1970s she has worked closely with Collingwood scholars, and has published on R. G. Collingwood and his father, W. G. Collingwood.

R. G. COLLINGWOOD: *AN AUTOBIOGRAPHY* AND OTHER WRITINGS

With essays on Collingwood's life and work

R. G. COLLINGWOOD

Edited with an introduction by

DAVID BOUCHER

and

TERESA SMITH

OXFORD
UNIVERSITY PRESS

OXFORD
UNIVERSITY PRESS

Great Clarendon Street, Oxford, OX2 6DP,
United Kingdom

Oxford University Press is a department of the University of Oxford.
It furthers the University's objective of excellence in research, scholarship,
and education by publishing worldwide. Oxford is a registered trade mark of
Oxford University Press in the UK and in certain other countries

First published 2013
First published in paperback 2017

Published in the United States of America by Oxford University Press
198 Madison Avenue, New York, NY 10016, United States of America

British Library Cataloguing in Publication Data
Data available

Library of Congress Cataloging in Publication Data
Data available

ISBN 978–0–19–958603–5 (Hbk.)
ISBN 978–0–19–880120–7 (Pbk.)

ACKNOWLEDGEMENTS

The idea for this new edition of R. G. Collingwood's *An Autobiography* was conceived, most appropriately, in Coniston where the Collingwood family lived for many years. At the 2005 Collingwood Conference Sir Roger Bannister, former Master of Pembroke College where Collingwood was a fellow, suggested that *en route* to the full biography of one of his illustrious fellows it would be a good idea to bring out a new edition of *An Autobiography* with some additional manuscript material, and commentaries by experts in the various fields covered. We are indebted to Sir Roger for his encouragement. Peter Momtchiloff has been particularly helpful in giving the project his support and the blessing of Oxford University Press. The contributors have been wonderful to work with and we wish to express our sincere gratitude for their patience and forbearance.

Before this edition was complete Janet Gnosspelius passed away. She was the daughter of Barbara Collingwood, one of Robin's sisters. She has left behind a formidable legacy in family archives and was always ready with help and advice on all projects relating to the Collingwood family. Her indomitable enthusiasm and personality will be sorely missed. We would also like to express our thanks to our respective spouses, Clare and George, for their encouragement and support; and to George for his work on the illustrations.

All the illustrations used in this publication and in the hardback edition are now available online at http://www.rgcollingwood.uk/autobiography/images

David Boucher and Teresa Smith

CONTENTS

PART II A JOURNEY IN THE EAST INDIES 1938–1939

Commentary

LIST OF ILLUSTRATIONS

NOTE ON MAPS

NOTES ON CONTRIBUTORS

Michael Beaney is Professor of Philosophy at the University of York, United Kingdom. He works on the history of nineteenth- and twentieth-century philosophy and on conceptions of analysis in the history of philosophy. He is the author of *Frege: Making Sense* (Duckworth, 1996), and editor of *The Frege Reader* (Blackwell, 1997), *The Analytic Turn* (Routledge, 2007), and *The Oxford Handbook of the History of Analytic Philosophy* (Oxford University Press, 2013).

Anthony (Tony) Birley was professor of ancient history at Manchester (1974–1990) and Düsseldorf (1990–2002); his publications include five books on Roman Britain and biographies of three Roman emperors. He was born in 1937 at Chesterholm, now better known as Vindolanda; his father, Eric Birley, had been introduced to archaeology and to Hadrian's Wall by R. G. C. in the 1920s.

David Boucher is Professor of Political Philosophy and International Relations in the School of Law and Politics, and Distinguished Visiting Professor, University of Johannesburg. He is also Vice President of the Learned Society of Wales. He has been Chairman of the Collingwood Society since 1993 and has published widely on all aspects of Collingwood's thought. His most recent books are *The Limits of Ethics in International Relations* (Oxford University Press, 2009) and *British Idealism: a guide for the perplexed* (with Andrew Vincent, Continuum, 2011). He has edited three books by R. G. Collingwood: *Essays in Political Philosophy* (Clarendon Press, 1989); *The New Leviathan, revised edition* (Clarendon Press, 1992), and *The Philosophy of Enchantment* (with Wendy James and Philip Smallwood, Clarendon Press, 2005).

James Connelly is Professor of Politics at the University of Hull, where he teaches political theory and environmental politics. His research interests include the philosophy of the British idealists (especially Collingwood) and environmental politics and ethics. Recent publications include a second edition of Collingwood's

Essay on Philosophical Method (ed. with G. D'Oro, Oxford University Press, 2005); *Politics and the Environment: From Theory to Practice* (with G. Smith, D. Benson, and C. Saunders, third edition, Routledge, 2012); *The Withering of the Welfare State: Regression* (ed. with J. Hayward, Palgrave, 2012); *The EU as a Leader in Climate Change Policy* (ed. with R. K. Wurzel, Routledge, 2011); *The Legacy of Leo Strauss* (with A. Burns, Imprint Academic, 2010); *Anglo-American Idealism: Thinkers and Ideas* (ed. with S. Panagakou, Peter Lang, 2010).

Jan van der Dussen is Professor Emeritus of Humanities at the Open University of The Netherlands. He graduated in both history and philosophy at the University of Leiden, and got a PhD in philosophy at the same university. His publications include *History as a Science: The Philosophy of R.G. Collingwood* (Martinus Nijhoff, 1981), reissued 2012 (Springer); editor of the revised edition of R.G. Collingwood, *The Idea of History* (Clarendon Press, 1993); with W. H. Dray editor of *R.G. Collingwood. The Principles of History and Other Writings in Philosophy of History* (Clarendon Press, 1999).

Bruce Haddock is Professor of Modern European Social and Political Thought at Cardiff University. His principal publications include *A History of Political Thought: From Antiquity to the Present* (Polity, 2008), *A History of Political Thought: 1789 to the Present* (Polity, 2005), *Vico's Political Thought* (Mortlake Press, 1986), and *An Introduction to Historical Thought* (Hodder Arnold, 1980). He is also joint editor of *Evil in Contemporary Political Theory* (Edinburgh University Press, 2011), *Principles and Political Order: The Challenge of Diversity* (Routledge, 2006), *Multiculturalism, Identity and Rights* (Taylor & Francis, 2003), and *The Politics of Italian National Identity* (University of Wales Press, 2000).

Wendy James, FBA, CBE, is Emeritus Professor of Social Anthropology in the University of Oxford, and Fellow of St. Cross College. Her family roots in the Lake District fostered her interest in Collingwood; her ethnographic research in N.E. Africa has increasingly taken on a historical character. Her most recent books include *The Ceremonial Animal: A New Portrait of Anthropology* (Oxford University Press, 2003); *The Philosophy of Enchantment:*

Studies in Folktale, Cultural Criticism, and Anthropology, by R. G. Collingwood (ed. with D. Boucher and P. Smallwood, Clarendon Press, 2005); *War and Survival in Sudan's Frontierlands: Voices from the Blue Nile* (Oxford University Press, 2007, pbk. with new preface, 2009); *Early Human Kinship: From Sex to Social Reproduction* (ed. with N. J. Allen, H. Callan, and R. Dunbar, Wiley-Blackwell, 2008).

Rex Martin is Professor of Philosophy, Emeritus, at the University of Kansas and Honorary Professor at Cardiff University. His fields of major interest are political and legal philosophy, history of political thought, and philosophy of history. His books include *A System of Rights* (Oxford University Press, in paperback 1997) and the revised edition of R. G. Collingwood's *Essay on Metaphysics* which he edited, with an Introduction and additional material, for Oxford University Press (in paperback 2002).

James Patrick is Chancellor Emeritus of the College of Saint Thomas More in Fort Worth, Texas and Senior Fellow of the Walsingham Society of Dallas. He writes on early twentieth-century English intellectual history, Collingwood, Eliot, C. S. Lewis, and J. R. Illingworth, and is the author of *The Magdalen Metaphysicals: Orthodoxy and Idealism at Oxford, 1901–1945* (Mercer University Press, 1985).

Philip Smallwood is Emeritus Professor of English at Birmingham City University and Visiting Fellow in the School of Humanities at the University of Bristol. He is co-editor with David Boucher and Wendy James of R. G. Collingwood's *The Philosophy of Enchantment* (Clarendon Press, 2005). His most recent monograph, *Critical Occasions: Dryden, Pope, Johnson, and the History of Criticism*, was published in 2011 by AMS Press.

Teresa Smith is R. G. Collingwood's daughter by his second wife, Kate Collingwood, and literary executor to R. G. Collingwood and his father W. G. Collingwood. After reading Greats at Oxford, she studied social policy and from the 1970s taught in Barnett House, Oxford University's Department of Social Policy and Social Work, which she headed for ten years. Her research has focused on family policy, community development and early education, and most recently a centenary history of Barnett House.

Her publications include 'From educational priority areas to area-based interventions: community, neighbourhood and preschool', in Edwards, R. (ed.), *Researching Families and Communities: Social and Generational Change* (Routledge, 2008), and *Family centres and bringing up young children* (HMSO, 1996). She has also written on her grandfather W. G. Collingwood's travels in Iceland.

ABBREVIATIONS

for Collingwood's main works

BOOKS

RP	*Religion and Philosophy* (1916)
SM	*Speculum Mentis* (1924)
EPM	*An Essay on Philosophical Method* (1933), revised edition, edited by James Connelly and Giuseppina D'Oro (2005)
PA	*The Principles of Art* (1937)
A	*An Autobiography* (1939), revised edition (2013), edited by David Boucher and Teresa Smith
EM	*An Essay on Metaphysics* (1940), revised edition (1998), edited by Rex Martin
NL	*The New Leviathan* (1942), revised edition (1992), edited by David Boucher
IN	*The Idea of Nature* (1945)
IH	*The Idea of History* (1946), revised edition (1993), edited by Jan van der Dussen
EPP	*Essays in Political Philosophy*, edited by David Boucher (1989)
PH	*The Principles of History*, edited by William H. Dray and Jan van der Dussen (1999)
PE	*The Philosophy of Enchantment: Studies in Folktale, Cutural Criticism, and Anthropology*, edited by David Boucher, Wendy James, and Phillip Smallwood (2005)

All books are published by Clarendon Press, Oxford, with the exception of *Religion and Philosophy*, published by Macmillan.

JOURNAL

Cumberland and Westmorland Antiquarian and Archaeological Society, CWAAS

MANUSCRIPTS

Collingwood Mss in the Bodleian Library, Oxford University, Dep. Coll.

Collingwood papers in the possession of Teresa Smith [TS/reference]

INTRODUCTION: THE BIOGRAPHY OF *AN AUTOBIOGRAPHY*

DAVID BOUCHER AND TERESA SMITH

Why read Collingwood's *An Autobiography* today, more than seventy years after it was written? Or, as Stephen Toulmin put it in the introduction to the 1978 reprint, 'What is the secret of an autobiography that lasts?' (*A*, ix). Collingwood spelt out his aim in the preface: 'the autobiography of a man whose business is thinking should be the story of his thought. I have written this book to tell what I think worth telling about the story of mine' (*A*, vii). Toulmin argues that the self-told life story of an English academic working in the period between two world wars, who refused 'to use the academic life as a refuge from the larger world of politics and international affairs' (*A*, xviii), is important for us in understanding the relationship between the world of the mind and the world of action.

An Autobiography remains something of an enigma despite a great deal of speculation as to Collingwood's motives for writing it; his apparent disingenuous failure to express his intellectual debts; and the chronology of when and how the intellectual puzzles arose which he attempted to resolve. Part of the reason for its enigmatic quality is that it is almost completely cerebral, and discloses little about his life or relationships with family and friends. The anonymous reviewer in the *Times Literary Supplement* seized upon this feature of the book immediately: it is almost totally confined 'to the history of the growth of a philosopher's mind'.[1] There are, however, some basic facts that we know about it, such as when he started it and when it was completed, and the reasons he gave for writing it, as well as its immediate reception.

Collingwood's intention was to write 'a philosophical autobiography (philosophical in subject-matter)'—this from a letter written in September 1938 to Malcolm Knox, his friend and former pupil

[1] Anon, 1939. 'A Philosopher's Life: Thought in Human Affairs', *Times Literary Supplement*, 4 August, 464.

and later editor, at St Andrews University.[2] An earlier letter to Knox,[3] written shortly after Collingwood's first stroke in February 1938, shows his anxiety that he might not have time to complete his projected work: he must do less in future, and devote his time to preparing more of his writings for publication. There was also an element of mischievousness in his intention. In a later letter to Kenneth Sisam at the Oxford University Press, Collingwood wrote that he had written the book 'because I was told I was dying, and thought it time a few home truths began sitting on my lips'.[4] It seems that he particularly wanted to get at Prichard, an irascible and long-time realist antagonist. There was certainly some concern at the Press, but the general view was that Prichard could take care of himself, and if it did Collingwood any harm, then let it be on his own head.[5] Writing to his son Bill, who had obviously expressed concern about his father's remarks, Collingwood replied: 'You needn't worry about Prichard believing anything I say – nothing under any conditions would ever make him do *that*. I hope that I shall either see or hear what happens though when he reads it (in Blackwells).'[6]

Principally, however, the purpose of his autobiography was 'to put on record some brief account of the work I have not yet been able to publish, in case I am not able to publish it in full' (*A*, 118). This forward-looking intention, rather than the backward glance normally expected of autobiography, goes some way to explain why he was not as explicit about influences on him, such as Ruskin and Croce, as might have been expected. Anyone familiar with Collingwood's work, and the reviews of it even in the popular press, would be constantly alerted to such influences.[7]

Collingwood started to write *An Autobiography* on the maiden voyage of *Zenocrate*, the boat that he had built for him in 1938,

[2] Letter from Collingwood to Knox, 21.ix.38. T. M. Knox Papers, University of St Andrews.

[3] Letter from Collingwood to Knox, 23.2.38. T. M. Knox Papers.

[4] *Autobiography* file, 22 March, 1939, OUP.

[5] Letter from RWC (Chapman) to Humphrey Milford dated 28 November, 1938 Ref P.12715/RWC. [TS/GLTR091].

[6] Hotel Mataram, Djoka, Java, 19.2.39. [TS/FLTR0848].

[7] Boucher, David 1989. *The Social and Political Thought of R. G. Collingwood*, Cambridge, Cambridge University Press, 8–23.

Illustration 1. Launch of *Zenocrate* at Brentford, London, 24 May 1938. Collingwood started writing the *Autobiography* on board on 28 July, as recorded in *Zenocrate: her Log*. Photograph by Collingwood. Courtesy of Teresa Smith.

after his first stroke in February.[8] *Zenocrate* was launched on 24 May (see Illustration 1); on 29 and 30 July the log mentions 'writing autobiography'. In early September, about six weeks before sailing to the East Indies on Blue Funnel Line M. V. *Alcinous*, Collingwood visited the Oxford University Press to talk about the *Autobiography*:

> To occupy his mind, he is writing his autobiography, and wondered if it would be of any interest to us. It is a sort of commentary on his archaeological and (especially) philosophical development, and contains thoughts which he has not expressed in books, as well as explaining how he came to hold the odd views he now holds. It is destitute of all that makes autobiography saleable, and he supposed would be a dead loss, to which I demurred. He will send the MS. when it is finished.[9]

[8] Collingwood, R. G., ZENOCRATE Her Log. [TS/FDW032] 1938. *Zenocrate* is a Harrison Butler Z – 4 tonner, 22ft (6.4 metres) small off-shore sailing cruiser.

[9] Letter from Chapman at the Press to Kenneth Sisam and Humphrey Milford, ref RWC/PP 4982, OUP, 14 September 1938. [TS/GLTR071].

It is a wonder that the book got published at all given Collingwood's sales pitch. He was still working on it when he wrote to Malcolm Knox at St Andrews on 21 September. The preface, written at Coniston, was dated 2 October, and Collingwood completed the manuscript and sent it to the Press before he left for Indonesia on 22 October. In other words, he wrote *An Autobiography* in something like three months, and in the middle of this period he had a second stroke, on 28 August, on board *Zenocrate*.

The Delegates of the Press considered *An Autobiography* on 11 and 25 November, when Collingwood was in mid-voyage to the East Indies. Kenneth Sisam was charged with the delicate and unusual task of alerting Collingwood to the imminent arrival of the proofs, and somewhat elusively to intimate that the Press might not publish unless the political content of the last chapter was toned down: 'one or two of the Delegates will want to see the gallies, and may have some comments when you get back'.[10] Sisam went on to say that while he sympathized with Collingwood's views on current politics, their expression might be out of tone with the rest of the book. At the same time he sent a copy of the letter and proofs to Dr Cyril Bailey, the University Public Orator, alerting him to the line of action proposed by the Press should Collingwood 'not of his own accord tone down the most difficult passages'.[11] Collingwood received Sisam's letter on 8 February 1939. The apprehension about his reaction was in fact unnecessary: he was rather relieved that the Press was printing his book at all, despite their being 'flustered by parts of it'; he had feared that 'it might have been altogether too much for them'.[12] Collingwood was more than accommodating, given that he disagreed with Sisam's comments on the last chapter: far from being 'higher and sharper in tone', he thought it 'lower, and a piece, in fact, of soft peddling'. He nevertheless deferred to Sisam and rewrote 'the last chapter very extensively'.[13] On 23 March Collingwood wrote to his wife Ethel that he had made a lot of corrections to *An Autobiography* and would be posting it to Sisam at the Press at the earliest opportunity.

[10] *Autobiography* file, The Archives of the Clarendon Press, 18 January 1939.

[11] Sisam to Bailey, *Autobiography* file, OUP Archives, 18 January 1939.

[12] Letter to Ethel Collingwood 8 February 1939, a continuation of a letter begun on 4 February. [TS/PLTR195].

[13] *Autobiography* file, OUP Archives, 22 March 1939.

Sisam's respectful and moderate tone in his letter to Collingwood disguised the considerable disunity of the Delegates in coming to a decision; in fact, they even disputed whether they had accepted the book for publication at all. At their meeting on 11 November the Delegates expressed a variety of views. On its philosophical quality, apart from personalities, the Provost of Oriel, W. D. Ross, thought it very bad, but this was certainly a minority view countered by effusive praise about its readability and brilliance.[14] Sidgwick, a Delegate, thought the attack on Rugby offensive, and while the personal attacks were not considered good form, no one wanted to censor these views. In the general round of correspondence Arthur Norris, a Delegate, said that Prichard, whom Collingwood criticized for arriving at a position of 'complete scepticism' (*A*, 31), was not averse to giving offence and should not complain at getting a little back. Ross, while finding the attack on Prichard regrettable, thought that it would rebound on Collingwood. The Vice Chancellor of the University, and Delegate, George Stuart Gordon, thought the last ten pages impossible, and likely the product of a sick man's mind. A. D. Lindsay, Gordon's predecessor and Master of Balliol, whose anti-appeasement candidature in the Oxford by-election of 1938 Collingwood had supported,[15] and Cyril Bailey, the University Orator, expressed the view that rather than lose the book the Press should publish it.

Cyril Bailey agreed to draft a letter which was far less delicately phrased than the one actually sent. He asked Collingwood to reconsider the last chapter: it was written at a moment of crisis, and the passage of time might now persuade him to curtail or modify it. Although the meeting of 11 November had deferred a decision on the suggestion of G. N. Clark, the historian, the meeting of 25 November was mixed in its recollections as to the status of the book. The Delegates proceeded on the assumption that a decision had been deferred. Clark added weight to the mounting opinion that the last chapter should not be published as it stood. Despite protests from the Senior and Junior Proctors that the Delegates had no right to censor people's political

[14] A view that Gadamer endorsed in his German edition, translated and published in *Collingwood and British Idealism Studies*, 13, 2007: 7–15.

[15] Collingwood letter to A. D. Lindsay 20 October 1939. [TS/FLTR0839].

opinions, they decided to leave it to the 'office' to broach the subject with Collingwood. It was up to Sisam, then, to modify the tone of the earlier letter written by Bailey, which he did by hinting that the main body of the book 'gives the permanent general reflexion resulting from your life and work', whereas the final chapter dealing with the affairs of the moment was 'out of the picture'.[16]

Despite the reservations about the final chapter, the Press nevertheless went ahead with producing the galley proofs which Sisam sent to Collingwood on 18 January 1939, still leaving it open for a judgement to be made on the last chapter, pending Collingwood's revisions. Collingwood received the proofs in Batavia on 22 February, just before embarking on the voyage home, and began to work on them immediately. He got around to the sensitive issue of rewriting the last chapter on 19 March while sailing past Aden. The proofs were posted from Port Said on 22 March. In a letter to Sir Humphrey Milford dated 3 April, Sisam announced: 'Here is Collingwood which now seems to Chapman and me quite harmless. I don't think it can be held to be libellous to accuse the *Daily Mail* or Lloyd George of corrupting the public.'[17]

The reception of *An Autobiography* far outstripped Collingwood's modest expectations of interest. It is a lively and combative introduction to his thought, and still remains one of his most successful books. It received immediate and extensive reviews, none of them in less than positive tones. On its first appearance, A. L. Rowse, a fellow Oxonian renowned for his irascibility, commented that it was the most interesting book to come out of Oxford in a generation, and constituted a document for its time.[18] J. H. Muirhead, a fellow sympathizer with idealism, took it as evidence of Collingwood's recovery from illness, and expressed the view that philosophers of all schools had reason to be grateful for 'this gem of a book.[19] The *Manchester Guardian* called it 'challenging and vital'.[20] Reviewers, such as Howard Hannay, in philosophical

[16] *Autobiography* file, n.d., Archives of the Clarendon Press.

[17] Kenneth Sisam to Sir Humphrey Milford, 3 April 1939, 4609/K.S. [TS/GLTR098].

[18] Rowse, A. L. 1939. 'The Dilemma of Our Time', *Spectator*, vol. 162, 262.

[19] Muirhead, J. H. 1941. *Philosophy*, vol. XV, 89–91.

[20] A. D. R., 1939. 'Testament', *The Manchester Guardian*, 15 August, 5.

journals contended that it was 'provoking and intriguing'.[21] One of its most prominent features for most reviewers was Collingwood's rejection of the realists' alliance with natural science, and the allying of his own philosophy to history; the examples and arguments 'testify to the liveliness of Professor Collingwood's thought and to the reality of his knowledge of the two fields'.[22] An anonymous reviewer in the *Times Literary Supplement* summed up his achievement thus: 'its main trend consists in its authentic revelation of the philosophy underlying the externally remarkable union within one individual of a mastery of two disciplines which the unregenerate mind is apt to regard as divergent – speculative philosophy and historical research'.[23]

Collingwood wrote his autobiography during a period of illness, from which he gained only temporary respite. Knowing his illness was a time bomb which could explode at any time, he chose to reveal to the world the ideas that he had developed during the previous twenty years or so. In contrast with J. S. Mill, Collingwood said very little about his illness, nor about its symptoms and prognosis. He had been to see his friend and doctor Tom Nelson in the winter of 1936 about his general health and high blood pressure. He wrote to his sister Barbara in the spring of 1937 that Nelson had given him

> a very interesting lecture on the use & misuse of the human brain, & the result is that I have been doing far less work ever since, & the result of that is that my blood pressure when taken yesterday was down from about 200 to 150, which is where at my time of life it ought to be! So I am reconsidering my intention of dying apoplectically or paralytically in the Prime of Life & readjusting my ideas to the prospect of reaching a lazy old age.[24]

However, after finishing *the Principles of Art* in 1937, and before it had gone through the press he 'was overtaken by the more serious illness' which drove him to write his autobiography. In a letter to the Press in March 1938, Collingwood wrote that he had sent the *Principles of Art* to the publisher prematurely because he had a premonition of not otherwise being able to complete it, and

[21] Hannay, Howard 1941. *International Journal of Ethics*, vol. 51, 369–70.

[22] Marcham, F. G. 1941. *The Philosophical Review*, vol. L, 546.

[23] Anon, 1939. 'A Philosopher's Life: Thought in Human Affairs', *Times Literary Supplement*, 4 August, 464.

[24] R.G.C. to Barbara, no address, dated 1.iv.37. [TS/FLTR0773].

apologized for the unconscionable number of revisions to the proofs: 'Events have showed that if I had not done so the book would never have been published at all: for even if I get back to writing in a year or two I should not at that time have the heart to revise a book that had grown cold.'[25] The illness that struck him after completing a draft of the *Principles*, he wrote in the *Autobiography*, left him with little prospect of more than a few years in which to do his best work. In a letter to the Press, however, he was less pessimistic, suggesting that if he lived for another ten years, he would have time to complete his work and the *Autobiography* might be allowed to go out of print.[26]

We know now, of course, what this illness was. It was not (as Gadamer suggests in his introduction to the German edition of *An Autobiography*) a brain tumour, nor (as Knox described it, rather elliptically) a series of little explosions in Collingwood's brain.[27] Ethel, Collingwood's first wife, objected to Knox's description on the grounds that it was misleading: 'it would be better not to go into details about the blood vessels of the brain, firstly because no one can tell to within 5 years before the 1st real stroke when they actually began to go out of action and secondly because many people reading that sentence would think that the brain was affected more than it was'.[28]

The illness was a series of strokes that were the consequence of high blood pressure, a condition which also appeared to be a factor in his illness of 1932, following a severe bout of chickenpox in 1931 which he caught from his children, who had picked it up at school. The illness was followed by complications and his doctors ordered him to rest up for a year. In a letter to Knox dated 12 May 1931, we get an indication of the severity of the illness: 'I have been ill for several weeks and it's gone to my brain and made me quite unable to think . . . I hope to recover to be able to read philosophy again, but I dare say not for months yet.'[29] He thought this was also a factor in the nervous breakdown he suffered in

[25] Collingwood letter to Arthur Norrington, junior assistant secretary to the Delegates, 8 March 1938. [TS/GLTR061].

[26] R.G.C. to Kenneth Sisam, 22 March 1939. [TS/GLTR097].

[27] See Knox, T. M. 1947. 'Introduction' to the first edition of the posthumously published *Idea of History*, Oxford: Oxford University Press.

[28] Ethel Collingwood to Malcolm Knox, 10 October 1945. [TS/GLTR163].

[29] T. M. Knox Papers, St Andrews University, MS 37524/433a.

late 1931.[30] He was granted a term's sabbatical by the University, and in January and February 1932 made a journey to Italy, Sicily, and Greece, during which he experienced frequent mood swings ranging from exhilaration to melancholia. In 1934 he fell off his bicycle and broke his leg and arm, requiring six weeks in bed, and two weeks on crutches. Writing to Knox he said that his 'general health is very poor, and my heart seems to have suffered from what they call shock'.[31]

Collingwood's first stroke in 1938, which affected his left arm and left leg, but not his speech, was not unexpected. His blood pressure was often dangerously high and he seemed for many years, as his wife Ethel wrote later to Knox, to have had a premonition of his early death which drove him to work to excess in order to complete his projected endeavours.[32] He had indeed had many warnings. Ethel noted that he first started suffering from high blood pressure in 1930. In a letter to his sister Barbara of 6 February 1938, he wrote that he had been expecting a stroke for several years and that he was surprised it was not more serious. W. Kneale, the English philosopher and logician, writing to Malcolm Knox also in February 1938, remarked: 'I think everyone was much surprised when it happened, although looking back one can say that he was always rather tense as though he lived on the edge of a volcano – but perhaps even that is imagination.'[33]

His doctors recommended a year off to recuperate. Writing in March 1938, Tom Nelson noted details of his heart and blood pressure, and commented:

> Robin is a man who has when need be forced himself to work with his brain ever since he went to school. He has gradually acquired the art of putting up his B[lood] P[ressure] in order to keep his cerebral arteries going, until he has come to live continuously at a higher and higher level – until in fact he cd. not get it down to sleep. He cd. not stop his brain working. The typical so-called idiopathic hypertension. Idiopathic, my foot. And the pity of it is that he has such a good brain that it is worthy of better treatment. He has to . . . [live] for at least a year at an entirely lower

[30] In a letter to Ethel he described it as 'my nervous breakdown'. [TS/PLTR113].

[31] Collingwood to Knox, 17.iv.34, Knox archives, MS 37524/418 a-b.

[32] 10 October 1945. [TS/GLTR163].

[33] W. Kneale, Exeter College, Oxford to Malcolm Knox, Feb 18 1938. Knox papers, St Andrews, MS37525/236a-c.

level [and] will have to go slowly... He has got to get the idea of working for v. limited hours and dropping his B.P in between. He is inclined at times to say that he wd. rather cease to be than be restricted. But as I pointed out to him it may not be as easy as this. Next time he may have a more extensive lesion, and continue to live for some time with a v. 2nd class brain... I think this carried weight, because this time he says he has noticed that since the trouble he can't spell as well as he should. Frankly I can't explain this to myself, and it may be imagining on his part, but it seemed to point a moral.[34]

Collingwood suffered his second stroke on 28 August aboard *Zenocrate*, moored up in the Beaulieu River, taking refuge from particularly stormy weather which had required the coastguards rescuing him from rough seas, and aborting his prospective four-month cruise.[35] He had been painting the deck; when he awoke his face was numb and he had lost the power of speech, and lay below deck for three days before regaining the power of his legs and getting himself back to Oxford. It was a mild stroke, which nevertheless set back his recovery.[36]

His doctors now referred him to a Harley Street specialist, a Dr Stott, who explained to him that there were two types of stroke: the first, which entailed a rupturing of the artery, was generally fatal; the second, which was constrictions and spasms of the artery, was much less serious and recovery was more successful.[37] He was not confined to bed and was able to potter around in the garden; his speech remained slightly slurred and he was prone to helpless fits of giggles at anything slightly amusing.[38] According to Collingwood, his arterial specialist in London suggested spending the winter on board a ship sailing off to somewhere like Java and doing some writing each day on his next book.[39] He wrote to his cousin Charlie saying that the visit to the specialist had cheered him up considerably, and from pondering his imminent demise he

[34] Handwritten note by Tom Nelson dated 20 March 1938, from his London address, bound into Janet Gnosspelius's photocopied set of Collingwood's letters to his father dated 2.i.1931 to 29.ix.1932. W. G. Collingwood died 1 October 1932.

[35] 'Lifeboat Rescues', *The Times*, 3 June 1938, 14d.

[36] Letter from Collingwood to Barbara, no date; headed 'mild STROKE after painting on Zenocrate' in Barbara's handwriting. [TS/FLTR0832A].

[37] Letter from Collingwood to Charlie Collingwood 19.ix.38. [TS/FLTR0835].

[38] Letter from Collingwood to Barbara 5 September 1938. [TS/FLTR0833].

[39] Letter from Collingwood to Barbara 9 September 1938. [TS/FLTR0834].

was now looking forward to taking a Dutch cargo ship to the East Indies.[40]

His father had died from a stroke in 1932, but it was not until about 1940 that Robin discovered that the illness was endemic in the family. After his sister Barbara had a stroke in 1940, Collingwood wrote to her referring to it as the 'family ghost': when reading their grandfather William's diary, he had discovered that their grandmother Marie Imhoff was similarly struck down in 1860.[41]

During the time Collingwood suffered from high blood pressure there was no treatment available to control it. Surgical procedures were trialled, but were irreversible, and could precipitate dangerously low blood pressure. Sufferers were told by their doctors and specialists to rest.[42] Collingwood was, however, almost incapable of relaxing, as Tom Nelson had noted. Even during periods of recuperation he was constantly on the move, absorbing new scenery, exploring ruins and archaeological sites, writing long letters, keeping notes of what he had seen, walking sometimes twenty miles or more in the blazing heat, and continuing to write his books. This is how he dealt with his illness of 1932, by travelling in Italy and Greece; his first stroke of 1938, by sailing *Zenocrate* in rough seas; his second stroke of 1938, by travelling to the East Indies; and shortly after his return to Britain by sailing away to the Greek islands in the summer of 1939 with a group of Oxford students (see Illustration 2), during the course of which he wrote *The First Mate's Log*. During his journey of 1932 Collingwood kept a diary and sketchbook. In the letters to his father there were references to his health, and to being conscious not to overdo it. However, he exerted himself much more than one would expect from someone trying to restore his health. He wrote to his wife Ethel that he sometimes got tired and exhausted, and suffered mood swings and melancholy, referring to his 'nervous breakdown'.[43]

[40] Letter from Collingwood to Charlie Collingwood 19.ix.38. [TS/FLTR0835].

[41] Collingwood to Barbara Gnosspelius, from South Hayes, where he lived after leaving Ethel, but on Belbroughton Road paper, no date. [TS/FLTR0868].

[42] We are indebted to Sir Roger Bannister for this medical information. Damage to the three sites of the brain (L and R hemispheres and frontal lobes, affecting movement and speech and producing emotional lability) is a clear stroke pattern associated with high blood pressure. [Personal communication]

[43] Letters to Ethel Collingwood written 28 January from San Antonio in Tivoli [TS/PLTR106], and 10 February 1932 from Syracuse, Sicily. [TS/PLTR113].

Illustration 2. Collingwood as First Mate steering the *Fleur de Lys* on its voyage to Greece in 1939. Photograph by one of the crew. Courtesy of Teresa Smith.

Before sailing for Indonesia in October 1938 Collingwood wrote to Knox informing him of his intention to sail to Java after visiting St Andrews to accept his honorary degree.[44] Because of his illness he was unable to attend the July graduation ceremony, but instead attended a small ceremony on 7 October in the Parliament Hall of the University Library.[45] Knox was instrumental in providing introductions to some friends of his brother, the McMorrans of Batavia. Collingwood sailed on 22 October 1938 from Liverpool, to Batavia, Java (modern-day Jakarta in Indonesia), through the Suez Canal, on a cargo boat with a small number of passengers, the M. V. *Alcinous* (Blue Funnel Line). He wrote a log of his voyage, *Log of a Journey in the East Indies in 1938–1939*, which is printed for the first time in this volume. The commentary by Wendy James and a letter from Collingwood to his sister Barbara whilst travelling give a fuller representation of Collingwood the man—his

[44] Collingwood letter to Knox from 15 Belbroughton Road, Oxford, 21.ix.38 (Knox papers, MS 37524/425).

[45] 'Distinguished Scholars Honoured by St. Andrews University', *The Citizen*, 15 October 1938.

energy, the remarkable extent of his inquisitiveness, and the astuteness of his observational curiosity. These were characteristics that Collingwood exhibited throughout his life, and the vibrancy, fluency, and energy of the letters and the *Log* suggest that his strokes up to this point had robbed him of little of his passion, enthusiasm, intrepidness, and brilliance of mind.

Collingwood's *An Autobiography* was completed in first draft before he sailed for the East Indies. He arrived in Batavia on 20 November, where he was met by the McMorrans (Mr McMorran was manager of Lever Bros) and taken on a number of expeditions. From there Collingwood went to Bali, and through Mrs McMorran's introductions met with many of the influential ex-patriot Dutch community, including artists such as the Russian-born German artist Walter Spies (1895–1942). Collingwood took various boats around the islands, observed local burial customs, and became passionately interested in local music, dance, and art, about which he had much to say in his letters home. He did not return from Batavia to England until 5 April 1939.

While travelling to the East Indies and back he wrote *An Essay on Metaphysics*, which he began two days after sailing, and four chapters of *The Principles of History*, and as we have seen, completing the revisions and checking the proofs of *An Autobiography*, as we have seen. He also learnt Malay on board ship; by the time he reached Batavia, he was able to converse with the servants at the Hotel Daendels, for which he was very proud of himself.[46] Indeed, there were periods when visiting more remote parts when he spoke nothing but Malay. Collingwood embarked upon a gruelling schedule of expeditions and visits from the time he arrived, taking medication for angina and insomnia,[47] suffering various bouts of food poisoning, and having to endure infected insect bites on his feet.

Collingwood emerges from the commentaries in this new edition of the *Autobiography* as not only more sociable and lively than often portrayed by Collingwood scholars, and indeed by himself

[46] Collingwood letter to Ethel Collingwood begun on 20 November 1938. [TS/PLTR186].

[47] There are a number of references to his medications in the *Log*. He took soneryl (a barbiturate drug) for insomnia (e.g. *Log* 27 October 1938), and amyl nitrate for angina (e.g. *Log* 1 February 1939).

in *An Autobiography*, but also more radical—more socially and politically aware, more 'engaged', from his schooldays onwards. At Rugby he was outspoken and something of a rebel, for example opposing a motion calling socialism 'a grave national danger' and criticizing his peers for unthinking support for the conservative view.[48] As a young don at Pembroke College, he took on the post of Oxford treasurer for one of the University settlements working with poor families in London's East End, Oxford House in Bethnal Green.[49] His work for the Admiralty during World War I involved him extensively in European affairs, for example addressing the conference of Belgian students on the future of Belgium in 1919.[50] During World War II he was closely involved in welcoming Jewish refugees to Oxford, in supporting the Standing Committee for Developing Intellectual Cooperation with China, and in helping Italian academics caught up in police procedures in Oxford (this last pressure leading directly to another stroke).[51] During his 1920s and 1930s journeys in Europe he was increasingly sensitive to and critical of the growth of fascism. A good example of his awareness of the threat to democratic civilization (as he put it in his writings, notably *The New Leviathan*) was his letter to A. D. Lindsay, Master of Balliol (who stood as the anti-appeasement candidate against Quinton Hogg in the 1938 Oxford by-election), written the day before sailing for the East Indies:

> I do not think that the country has ever in all its history passed through a graver crisis than that in which it is now involved. I am appalled by the apathy with which our situation is regarded by a great many of us, and by the success which the Government has had in keeping the country as a whole from knowing the truth. Your candidature shows that the spirit of English democracy is not extinct. I hope it still survives among those who will have to vote next week.[52]

The following year he wrote, in Ruskinian tones, of how Lord Nuffield 'grinds the faces of the poor in order to make money

[48] R.G.C. to Dora no date. Autumn 1907. [TS/FLTR0180].

[49] 8 March 1914. [TS/FLTR0449].

[50] Collingwood letter to his father 9 May 1919. [TS/FLTR0536]. On his time at the Admiralty see Johnson, Peter 2012. *A Philosopher at the Admiralty: R. G. Collingwood and the First World War*, Exeter, Imprint Academic.

[51] 2 July 1940 R.G.C. to Barbara. [TS/FLTR0860].

[52] Collingwood to A. D. Lindsay 20 October 1938. [TS/FLTR0839].

wherewith to buy himself a saintly reputation as A Man Who Does SO Much Good, building hospitals and all that, while his employees rot in jerry-built houses in swamps and have no amenities of any kind whatever'.[53] All this speaks vividly of practical engagement as well as academic analysis. It is perhaps not surprising, given the politics of the times, that some of his Oxford contemporaries labelled him a Communist.

We suggest in the commentary by Boucher in this volume that Collingwood was more engaged with social reform and political thinking than is generally acknowledged. The passionate attack in the last pages of *An Autobiography* (167) on his philosophical colleagues, who professed 'a purely scientific detachment from practical affairs', grew out of a lifelong intellectual, practical, and moral context. Collingwood reminds us not only of Ruskin, but also of the work of the Victorian Oxford philosophers T. H. Green and Bernard Bosanquet, as well as Edward Caird and Henry Jones who taught generations of students that philosophy mattered in a practical and moral sense, and that engagement in the public life of social reform and politics was an honourable career.[54]

AUTOBIOGRAPHY AND COLLINGWOOD'S *AN AUTOBIOGRAPHY*

It may be something of an exaggeration to claim that the 'aim of autobiography suggests senile maunderings about the brave days of old and all the titled people the author has met',[55] but the least we expect of the author of an autobiography is to ask the questions, who am I, and how have I come to be what I am? In answering the questions it is almost impossible to avoid what Herbert Butterfield called the Whig interpretation of history, with defining moments constitutive of the self that one has become. The classics in the genre, Augustine's *Confessions* and Rousseau's *Confessions* are model exemplifications.

The autobiographer cannot avoid abstraction, but should avoid idealization in Onora O'Neill's sense of the word. To write one's

[53] R.G.C. to his daughter Ruth 30 xi 39. [TS/FLTR0858].

[54] *Autobiography*, 47–9. Caird was Master of Balliol, and Jones his successor at Glasgow. Bosanquet taught Collingwood's father, W. G. Collingwood.

[55] A. D. R., review of *An Autobiography*, *Manchester Guardian*, 15th August, 1939, p. 5.

life in full would take a lifetime, and there would be nothing to write about except the act of writing itself. Necessary abstraction, however, may easily veer towards idealization, an essentialism that is taken to be definitive of the self, to the exclusion of all else, as economics for Marx serves to explain the whole of history, and to which that history can be reduced.[56]

Collingwood's own view of the autobiographical method was given in advice to R. Q. Nelson. It is, Collingwood suggested, 'a history of your work showing how problems arose one by one and how you tackled them'.[57] In Collingwood's *An Autobiography*, although ostensibly faithful to his advice to Nelson, that is, an account of how problems arose, and of how he dealt with them, both the problems and their solutions are invested retrospectively with a peculiarly political import and significance. The act of relating his intellectual development is revelatory of a new self-understanding. The pieces of coloured glass in the kaleidoscope through which the light shines create a different pattern as they tumble into place as the pieces cascade. Whereas Collingwood's *Autobiography* may differ in many ways from the norm, it is faithful in at least one respect to the great tradition inaugurated by St Augustine. The author does not so much recount the past as recast it, as we discuss later in this Introduction.[58]

Where should we look for the model of autobiographical method that Collingwood adopted? The obvious candidates are those with which he was intimately familiar, John Ruskin, John Stuart Mill, Bennedetto Croce, and ultimately Giambattista Vico. Ruskin, because W. G. Collingwood was his secretary, and R. G. Collingwood was a great admirer of his work, evident from his 1919 lecture marking the centenary of Ruskin's birth.[59] J. S. Mill, because his autobiography is iconic of philosophical biographies, and Mill himself was the target of many of Collingwood's anti-positivist arguments. Mill was very much in Collingwood's mind at the time of writing *An Autobiography*, evident from the

[56] See O'Neill, Onora 1996. *Towards Justice and Virtue: A Constructive Account of Practical Reasoning*. Cambridge, Cambridge University Press.

[57] Collingwood letters to R. Q. Nelson, 1939–1941, Bodleian Library, Oxford, MS. Eng, lett. B. 27, fols 87–94. Dated 20.ii.40.

[58] The political aspect of his life is discussed in Boucher's commentary on Collingwood's politics in this volume.

[59] Collingwood, R. G. 1922. *Ruskin's Philosophy*, Kendal, Titus Wilson.

references in *An Essay on Metaphysics* written on the voyage from the East Indies and while correcting the proofs of *An Autobiography* (*EM*, 143, 149–53, 160–1, 165, 301–3, 318). Croce, because Collingwood himself translated his autobiography, and greatly admired the man and his work. Vico, of course, because of his immense importance for Collingwood in establishing the autonomy of history as a legitimate form of knowledge. He says of Vico: 'he was in the first place a trained and brilliant historian, who set himself the task of formulating principles of historical method as Bacon had formulated those of the scientific' (*IH*, 63).

Despite the suggestion by Collingwood's son Bill that *An Autobiography* resembles Ruskin's *Praeterita*, it is in fact an unlikely candidate. Collingwood himself suggested that 'the resemblance to *Praeterita* had escaped my notice: it is so long since I read it. Good book, if I remember rightly.'[60] Ruskin was much older than the four other autobiographers when he committed his thought to paper. Ruskin was 66, and at pains to reveal something of his personal character to complement his many books. This, of course, was not Collingwood's intention. His was at least ostensibly to shed light on the many books that he had *not* written. There is a resemblance between the two autobiographies in so far as Ruskin attributed great significance to the influence of his father and of home life at Herne Hill, but that is where the resemblance ends. Ruskin went into great detail about aspects of his life, including illnesses, emotional turmoil, and the aesthetic pleasure derived from the many places he visited, and the paintings and drawings he acquired.[61] It is from Collingwood's correspondence that we learn these details about him, not from his autobiography.

The four others wrote their autobiographies at about the same age: Mill was 47, Croce and Collingwood 49, and Vico a little older at 55 when he wrote the first part, continuing to update it for another six years.

Both Mill and Collingwood had similar motivations. Mill believed himself to be dying of consumption, and Collingwood, with more justification, feared that the increasing risk of further

[60] Letter from R.G.C. to Bill Collingwood, Hotel Mataram, Djoka, Java, 19.2.39. [TS/FLTR0848].

[61] Ruskin, John 1907, *Praeterita: Outlines of Scenes and Thoughts Perhaps Worthy of Memory in My Past Life*, three vols, London: George Allen.

strokes might lead to an early demise. For Mill, his fear impelled him to want to do three things: to silence his enemies who had said scandalous things about his twenty-one-year relationship with Harriet Taylor before their marriage; to express his intellectual debts, including those to his wife; and to write down many of the ideas that he had not yet committed to print. Mill's *Autobiography*, which he added to and revised almost up to his death in 1873, is solidly in the confessional mode of St Augustine and Rousseau. The defining moments in his life are both intellectually significant and emotionally charged. He described with disarming frankness his deep depression and mental breakdown. Upon reading Marmontel's *Memoirs*, which moved him to tears, Mill was struck by the revelation that 'the oppression of the thought that all feeling was dead within me, was gone'. He went on to say: 'I was no longer hopeless: I was not a stock or stone.'[62]

Collingwood, on the other hand, shared firmly only the third of Mill's motivations: the presentation of ideas that he had not yet put into print. Reference to his intellectual debts is scant, and his emotional life, except for his irritation at his philosophical colleagues, and anger at the current political malaise, is absent.

Croce's autobiography looks a more promising candidate in that Collingwood himself translated it in 1926 (J. A. Smith added a preface). Croce's autobiography does not have the urgency of either Mill's or Collingwood's. Having reached his fiftieth year Croce thought it an opportune time to take advantage of the pause in his spiritual life to reflect upon the road that he had travelled and was yet to traverse in his intellectual journey. It is not, he said, a book of 'confessions, nor recollections, nor memoirs', and certainly not an occasion for 'moral self-examination'.[63] Confession, he thought, alluding to St Augustine and Rousseau, whether complacent self-approbation or self-accusation and lamentation over one's misdemeanours, is simply a form of vanity based upon an exaggeration of one's self-importance. Recollections, for Croce, were related to emotions, and while the past made him both melancholy and emotional, he was unable to justify recounting such occasions

[62] Mill, J. S. 1971. *Autobiography*, edited by Stillinger, Jack, Oxford, Oxford University Press, 85.

[63] Croce, B. 1927. *An Autobiography*, translated by Collingwood R. G. with a Preface by Smith, J. A. Oxford, Clarendon Press, 19.

on paper unless he were a poet for whom these feelings provided a centre of gravity and the object of his 'best spiritual faculties'.[64] Croce excluded memoirs from his autobiography because they are a chronicle of one's life, and of the lives of those whom one's own has touched, and for which some account for posterity is deemed necessary to preserve important facts that would otherwise be lost. Since his own life had largely been devoid of such encounters, what was worth recording of his life, he suggested, was the chronology and bibliography of his written works. Like Collingwood then, Croce rejected the first and second of Mill's motivations, and appears to provide the justification that Collingwood needed for the subject matter of his own autobiography written by a person whose job it was to think. Croce maintained that in order for critics to speak more authoritatively about his work, and even to facilitate a more 'enlightened severity of judgement', he proposed to tell them what he knew of his work in case they had missed something, or had difficulty in discovering it.[65]

In reading Croce, however, we note that his conception of autobiography is quite different from that of Collingwood. Croce tells us what he was working on, and that he departed in some of his conclusions from his associates and mentors; he tells us of the events that led to changes in interest from, for example, researches into Italian and Spanish life, to a detailed study of the classic writers in economics inspired by Labriola's gift of his first essay on the materialist conception of history. Croce tells us that he read it and reread it: 'I felt my whole mind burst into flame. New thoughts and problems took root in my spirit and so overran it that I was powerless to free myself from them.'[66] We are told that he parted company with Labriola, and how that led to their estrangement, but not in what the departure consisted, or the process by which he arrived at his conclusions, let alone what his conclusions were. Croce's autobiography is in fact a commentary on how he came to develop his wide-ranging interests. He tells us how

[64] Croce, *Autobiography*, 21.

[65] Croce, *Autobiography*, 24. Incidentally, Croce takes a quite different view on boarding schools from that of Collingwood: 'I can never join in the fashionable outcry against boarding-school education or agree in thinking it better for boys to be brought up at home.' Croce, *Autobiography*, 34.

[66] Croce, *Autobiography*, 56–7.

he confronted intellectual problems presented to him by the likes of De Sanctis, Spaventa, and Hegel, that is, 'by re-enacting their intellectual drama in one's own person', but not what the results of those re-enactments were, other than that they consisted in departures which can be read in a book or article he published, and to which he refers the reader for the details. So, for example, in order to adapt Hegel for his own purposes, Croce had to criticize and dissolve him, the outcome of which was *What is Living and What is Dead in Hegel's Philosophy*, to which we are directed for the criticism and dissolution.[67]

The closest full-length analogue to the autobiographical project that Collingwood undertook was written by someone whom he admired immensely, Giambattista Vico. This genre of literature was so new that it did not yet have a name. Vico's autobiography is entitled *The Life of Giambattista Vico Written by Himself*, the first part of which was completed in 1725 with additions by the author in 1728 and 1731. The final years of Vico's life were written by the Marquis of Villarosa in 1818. The model of the kind of autobiography that seeks to trace the intellectual development and achievements of its author seems to have originated with the publication in 1728 of the first volume of a quarterly *Raccolta d' Opusculi Scientici e Filologici*. It included a proposal by Count Gian Artico di Porcía to original and creative scholars in Italy exhorting them to write their autobiographies in order to inspire young students and influence the reform of the curricula and methods taught in schools. Prospective contributors were asked to say something about the events in their lives interwoven with accurate and detailed accounts of their studies. This was to start with grammar and the merits or deficiencies with which it was taught, followed by their studies in arts and sciences, reflecting on biases and abuses or the coherence of the curriculum and soundness of methods. Omissions in the curriculum should also be highlighted. The author should then focus upon his own special area of study, outlining what he had published and what was in preparation, detailing criticisms and his responses to them, as well as giving an objective assessment of his own errors and what he regarded as defensible.[68]

[67] Croce, *Autobiography*, 97.

[68] Vico, 1975. *The Autobiography of Giambattista Vico*, translated by Fisch, Max Harold and Bergin, Thomas Goddard, Ithaca, Cornell University Press, Introduction, 2–3.

The project was ambitious and novel, mainly pedagogical; covering all the arts and sciences; having a common template; and was to include a far-reaching critical supplement to the collection.[69] Vico's *Life* was published as the exemplar of what was to be a much larger project, but nevertheless remained the only contribution to the anticipated series.

Collingwood certainly thought highly of Vico, and the Italian was very much in Collingwood's mind prior to and during the writing of *An Autobiography*. In the area of aesthetics, for example, Collingwood thought Vico's observation that poetry was the natural speech of children and savages provided the clue to the solution of all the problems of aesthetics.[70] Vico was the first, he thought, to formulate the philosophical theory of art as imagination, to which Croce and the early Collingwood himself subscribed (*A*, 138 fn.). In relation to history, writing in 1936, for Collingwood Vico's importance is that he gave a philosophical justification of the possibility of historical knowledge based upon the principle that the human mind can know what it creates, and in this respect it can be more certain of historical fact than it is of natural facts which are the creation of God and ultimately knowable only to him (*IH*, 66). While travelling to and from the East Indies, when Collingwood's own autobiography was in press, he wrote about Vico, in what was intended to be the definitive statement of Collingwood's philosophy of history. He said that anyone who had read Vico or even a second-hand account of his ideas would know that the important question to ask of any statement is not whether it is true or false, but what it means (*PH*, 15).

There are certainly similarities between Collingwood's and Vico's autobiographies. Both men were precocious children, expressed a degree of hostility towards formal education, and professed to have learnt a great deal from independent study and to have made their most original contributions in establishing the integrity and autonomy of history as a form of knowledge. Both authors take the view that the autobiography of a man whose business is thinking ought to be about his thought, that is, how he came to reach the

[69] Vico, *Autobiography*, Introduction, 4.

[70] Collingwood, R. G. 1924, *Speculum Mentis*, Oxford, Clarendon Press, 58; Collingwood, R. G. 1925. *Outlines of the Philosophy of Art*, London, Oxford University Press, 80.

conclusions he did. What Vico said about himself in the third person is equally applicable to Collingwood. Talking of his autobiography, Vico said 'Scrissela da filosofo', that is, 'he wrote it as a philosopher', by which he meant not only that it was philosophical in subject matter, but that he dealt with it philosophically.[71] Both Vico and Collingwood trace their intellectual development and highlight the significance of their achievements, investing them with a retrospective prescience. Pietropaolo contends that 'Vico the narrator, speaking in the here and now of autobiographical reflection, has no difficulty seeing that every significant episode of his past life was a sign of the future to come and the function of a truth of human nature that transcended his particularity'.[72] In Collingwood's case, each philosophical battle he fought against the realists had on reflection a political significance in his fight against fascism and Nazism.

They both were acerbic about their relative lack of recognition. Collingwood is much more reticent than Vico in confessing the intellectual sources of his inspiration. He does not mention, for example, either Vico or Croce, despite the fact that both contributed greatly to his intellectual maturation. Perhaps more tellingly, Collingwood invests his autobiography almost wholly with a political significance.[73] Vico interweaves much more of his life into his cerebral journey that ends in triumph against adversity. He was poor and passed over for positions for which he thought he was eminently better qualified than the recipients. His physical surroundings were not conducive to intellectual achievement; he lacked sponsorship, and was bitter, as he confessed, to the point of being 'choleric to a fault'.[74]

Where they differ most is in the fact that Vico accounts for his intellectual achievements, telling us how he arrived at the conclusions he had published. For the most part Collingwood tells us how he came to think what he thought, but for a different purpose. First, it was to lay before his readers ideas that he had not yet fully

[71] See Pietropaolo, Domenico 2006. '*Scrissela da filosofo*: The Life of Giambattista Vico Written by Himself', in Mathien, T and Wright, D. G. (eds), *Autobiography as Philosophy: The philosophical uses of self-presentation*, London, Routledge, 109.

[72] Pietropaolo, '*Scrissela da filosofo*', 115.

[73] See Boucher in this volume.

[74] Vico, *Autobiography*, 99.

worked out and put in print. Secondly, it was not merely a personal struggle, but a political one directed against what he thought were the pernicious and corroding influences of Oxford and Cambridge realism. Thirdly, Vico's autobiography has many of the features of the confessional genre of autobiography, in that he is frank about his failings, and effusive about his struggle, emotional and intellectual, to overcome them. Much of the emotion that permeates and animates Vico's account is absent from Collingwood's. Finally, Vico's speculative philosophy of history provides the backdrop to the account of his own achievement. Appropriately placed by providence in the intellectual milieu of his day, Vico was able to attain the reflective awareness his civilization made possible.[75] Collingwood was, of course, a critic of speculative philosophy of history, passionately opposed to the imposition of idealized patterns on the past.

Collingwood's autobiography, then, shares few of the characteristics of the exemplars he would have had to hand. It is typical in that it recasts the past in the image of his own later self-understanding, but differs in that so much of his emotional life is missing.

In studying Collingwood's *An Autobiography*, scholars have tended to focus upon his positive doctrines, such as the logic of question and answer, the theory of absolute presuppositions, and the ideas of incapsulation and re-enactment. There is a tendency to ignore, or pay scant attention to, the underlying purpose for formulating the theories, or solving the problems he set himself, and that was to counter the morally and politically corrupting influence of realism, and to make the youth of his day less vulnerable to fraudsters who duped them by purveying lies. This exemplifies his refusal to acknowledge a separation between theory and practice, and confirms his view that there were three simultaneous personae inhabiting all of his endeavours (*A*, 150–4).

Almost the whole of *An Autobiography* is infused with this purpose, and the final chapter, which so many, including the Delegates of OUP, as we saw, dismissed as an intemperate rant, was an illustration of how the realists were attempting to dupe, trick, or corrupt the consciousness of the people over Spain, Abyssinia, and

[75] See Verene, Donald, 1991. *The New Art of Autobiography*, Oxford, Clarendon Press, chapter 2.

Czechoslovakia. Realism in Collingwood's view had rendered many defenceless against governments determined to undermine democracy.

What we suggest is that Collingwood recast himself by investing the integrated succession of experiences he creates with a political import. It is quite obvious that the final chapter is overtly and strongly political, and would have been even more so had the OUP Delegates not objected, but what is less clearly understood is that each intellectual problem he encounters and works through has a political significance. Many of those who knew Collingwood were startled and disturbed by this particular pattern of recasting, especially its manifestation in the last chapter. McCallum, who wrote one of the British Academy obituaries for his friend, maintains in a letter to Malcolm Knox that: 'The transformation of the cautious and sophistical Tory that I knew to the flamboyant and anti-fascist revealed in that startled me.'[76] In truth Collingwood always had a radical bent, as we see in Teresa Smith's chapter in this volume.

His objections to both H. H. Prichard and H. W. B. Joseph, Oxford realists, were that they had become radical sceptics, the former more so than the latter. The realists, particularly G. E. Moore in Cambridge and John Cook Wilson in Oxford, attributed doctrines to thinkers that they did not hold; to Berkeley, and to Bradley respectively.

In the early part of the First World War Collingwood's archaeological work impressed upon him the importance of the questioning activity, as integral to the act of knowing, and not preliminary to it. During his time at the Admiralty Collingwood contemplated the Albert Memorial, which for many observers appeared a grotesque monstrosity. This could not have been George Gilbert Scott's intention, and led Collingwood to formulate the logic of question and answer in answer to his own question 'why had Scott done it?' (*A*, 29). Converging upon this in his philosophical studies was his emphasis on sound scholarship. Together they were prescient of what Collingwood was later more ably capable of articulating: that realism was a philosophy that erred because it neglected history. Their positive doctrine about knowledge, namely the intuitionist theory, was not compatible with what Collingwood learnt from his

[76] Knox Papers, 20 September, 1941.

own historical research, and their critical methods were ill used in refuting doctrines that were not in fact held by those to whom they were ascribed (*A*, 22–8).

At the end of the war Collingwood resumed his normal duties at Oxford, and by this time, he tells us, he was an opponent of realism. In particular he wished to refute the proposition that knowing something makes no difference to the known.[77] This was in his view a logical error entailing knowledge of what was known both before and after knowing it, which is an impossibility. More pernicious was its tendency to part company with all positive doctrines by a process of critical disintegration. In relation to moral philosophy this entailed rejecting over 2,000 years of believing that its purpose was to think out more clearly the issues involved in conduct in order to act better (*A*, 47). Prichard contended that moral philosophy was purely theoretical, focusing upon the workings of the moral consciousness, without interfering with its practice, and Russell had jettisoned ethics from the body of philosophy. The implication was fundamental. The generation of students brought up on Greenian idealism had been taught that clear philosophical thinking is essential to informing and improving conduct, whereas those exposed to realism were told that philosophical thinking is a disinterested activity with no contribution to make to practical conduct.

It was, then, the separation between theory and practice to which Collingwood objected, not least because it denied the role of the committed intellectual, and absolved philosophy of social responsibility. This separation of theory and practice, however, was not peculiar to realism. Certain strands of idealism maintained the same distinction. Hegel notoriously tells us that philosophy comes on the scene too late to influence practice, and something of the same view may be attributed to Bradley. It was, however, the realists that Collingwood had firmly in his sights, and the consequences of their doctrines and their designation of bogus philosophy on the people they taught:

> The inference which any pupil could draw for himself was that for guidance in the problems of life, since one must not seek it from thinkers or from thinking, from ideals or from principles, one must look to people who

[77] See Beaney's contribution to this volume for the argument that Collingwood misunderstood this aspect of Oxford realism.

were not thinkers (but fools), to processes that were not thinking (but passion), to aims that were not ideals (but caprices), and to rules that were not principles (but rules of expediency). (*A*, 48)

The realists had developed a flawless critical technique with which to demolish any argument. The problem was that their formulations of arguments were distortions or perversions as viewed through their own perspectives (*A*, 73). The realists were unrelenting in their negativity; they contended that a theory of knowledge was a contradiction in terms, and destroyed political theory by rejecting its very basis in the idea of a common good. The consequence was to make students contemptuous of philosophy because they were convinced that it was merely a trivial and silly game. Realists, then, transgressed all of Collingwood's golden rules; they did not satisfy themselves as to the relevance of their criticisms by reading texts historically, nor did they take pains to determine what question the author of a text was asking, but instead assumed that the questions were perennial. Their greatest crime was completely to ignore history as an example of knowledge, and to formulate their own theory of knowledge on the methodology of the natural sciences (*A*, 84–5).

What, by implication, were the realists failing to do? The First World War had demonstrated to Collingwood that the immense advances in natural science since the Middle Ages had transformed man's ability to control nature, but no comparable transformation had taken place in historical knowledge and man's ability to control human situations, of which the war was an exemplar *par excellence*. The realists' neglect of history, then, simply contributed to this malaise. What was needed was more understanding of human affairs and more knowledge of how to deal with them. History was to provide not rules of conduct but insights in helping us diagnose our moral and political problems. This required not scissors-and-paste history, with its ideal of obtaining ready-made information from the sources about a dead past, but the new kind of history of which Collingwood was an advocate. This kind of history, the re-enactment of past thoughts of a variety of different people, results in self-knowledge, that is, the realization of what one is able to think, and what one is potentially able to be and do. Self-knowledge is simply a microcosm of knowledge of the world of human affairs, and history is the science which equips us to deal with them.

Collingwood contends: 'If the realists had wanted to train up a generation of Englishmen and Englishwomen expressly as the potential dupes of every adventurer in morals and politics, commerce or religion, who should appeal to their emotions and promise them private gains which neither could procure them nor even meant to procure them, no better way of doing it could have been discovered' (*A*, 49). The realists, by dichotomizing theory and practice, were responsible for the corruption of youth, making them the potential dupes of a dishonest government. In order to counter this, Collingwood sought to reconcile theory and practice, arguing that the way a person acts is profoundly affected by the way he or she thinks.

The final chapter of *An Autobiography* is viewed as something of an aberration, an ill-tempered attack on modern politics, out of temper with the rest of the book. This was certainly how it was viewed, as we saw, by some of the Delegates of Oxford University Press. Collingwood had removed from the final chapter references to treason and insufficiently evidenced remarks on the activities of Spanish fascist troops. By the time Sisam received the corrected proofs and the substantially rewritten last chapter, Collingwood's views on British foreign policy and the conduct of the government were being echoed by *The Times*. Both Sisam and Chapman now believed that Collingwood's remarks were quite harmless, but regretted the fact that *The Times* had persuaded continental powers that 'England's promises were about as reliable as Hitler's'.[78]

Collingwood's work then, as he saw it, had a profoundly political purpose, no less than to understand better human affairs so that situations such as the First World War could be avoided. Both Collingwood's philosophical studies and his historical or archaeological studies are understood by him to be a contribution to the better understanding of human affairs. The realists, far from contributing to the better understanding required, generated perverted understandings that corrupted the consciousness of youth, making them ill equipped to obtain the knowledge of human affairs necessary to counteract the propaganda of corrupt governments. The publication of his ideas in books was for him

[78] Letter to Humphrey Milford, 3 April, 1939, OUP Autobiography file.

nothing less than a public service, that is, the dissemination of ideas that he thought 'the public would value' (*A*, 117). Both of the books that followed, *An Essay on Metaphysics* and *The New Leviathan*, are thoroughly imbued with this spirit.

This new edition of *An Autobiography* serves to provide the reader not only with greater clarity on how his ideas developed, but also with biographical glimpses, as this introduction itself has done, in order to give us a more rounded portrait. Our aim is not just to fill in the gaps, but to challenge the evidence.

Our aim here is to provide some detailed background on how Collingwood's ideas developed, from childhood onwards, and, more importantly, an analysis of how the body of his work—the 'corpus', one might say—can now be read, some seventy years after his death. Teresa Smith, on his education and childhood at home and at school, suggests a more critical and radical development which links to the 'man of action' and political engagement set out at the end of *An Autobiography* and portrayed by David Boucher in his challenge to the 'ivory tower' image commonly held of Collingwood the thinker. James Patrick's account of Collingwood's Oxford years challenges the ivory tower image in a different way, by illustrating his sociability and lively engagement in a life of music, art, writing, and friendship, as well as with his students, despite his isolation from his Oxford contemporaries after his criticism of the philosophy of the day; and Philip Smallwood continues this theme by analysing the *Autobiography* for its engagement as literature. Other chapters show why Collingwood's work continues to be relevant to us now, in any field. Tony Birley analyses some of the practical historical and archaeological puzzles Collingwood tackled and defends his approach from critics of the time, and demonstrates his importance for the survival and subsequent trajectory of Romano-British studies. Beaney, van der Dussen, Haddock, and Martin present detailed critiques of his rejection of realism, and of his lifelong work on the relationship between philosophy and history. Essentially the question is how we can say we know anything, including anything of the past. That is, Collingwood, like many of the idealists to which he has an affinity, but from which he sought a respectable distance (see Connelly in this volume), addressed the issue of the conditions of knowledge by uncovering the fundamental postulates upon which the superstructure of our thought rests. In all his enquiries,

Collingwood is furthering the frontiers of the self-understanding of the mind. But critics have questioned the authenticity of his own account of his intellectual journey, and we have addressed some of these questions in this volume. The meaning of what Collingwood meant by re-enactment; its relation to historical knowledge, including the extent to which he had a radical change of mind about the relation between history and philosophy; and the extent to which his powers of reasoning were affected by illness, are all addressed by James Connelly in his contribution.

Collingwood continues to challenge us with his insistence on critically examining the nature of evidence by making sure we are asking the right questions and using the best techniques to reach for answers. Here we try to follow his own teaching by making a fresh attempt to understand the questions he was trying to ask, and why, and to see what sort of a fist he made at answering them then and might make now.

PREFACE

THE autobiography of a man whose business is thinking should be the story of his thought. I have written this book to tell what I think worth telling about the story of mine.

Because an autobiography has no right to exist unless it is *un livre de bonne foi*, I have written candidly, at times disapprovingly, about men whom I admire and love. If any of these should resent what I have written, I wish him to know that my rule in writing books is never to name a man except *honoris causa*, and that naming any one personally known to me is my way of thanking him for what I owe to his friendship, or his teaching, or his example, or all three.

R. G. C.

CONISTON,
2 *October* 1938

PART I

AN AUTOBIOGRAPHY

AN AUTOBIOGRAPHY

By

R. G. COLLINGWOOD

CLARENDON PRESS · OXFORD

I

BENT OF A TWIG

UNTIL I was thirteen years old I lived at home and was taught by my father. Lessons occupied only two or three hours each morning; otherwise he left me to my own devices, sometimes helping me with what I chose to do, more often leaving me to work it out for myself.

It was his doing that I began Latin at four and Greek at six; but my own that I began, about the same time, to read everything I could find about the natural sciences, especially geology, astronomy, and physics; to recognize rocks, to know the stars, and to understand the working of pumps and locks and other mechanical appliances up and down the house. It was my father who gave me lessons in ancient and modern history, illustrated with relief maps in papier-mâché made by boiling down newspapers in a saucepan; but my first lesson in what I now regard as my own subject, the history of thought, was the discovery, in a friend's house a few miles away, of a battered seventeenth-century book, wanting cover and title-page, and full of strange doctrines about meteorology and geology and planetary motions. It must have been a compendium of Descartes' *Principia*, to judge by what I recall of its statements about vortices; I was about nine when I found it, and already knew enough about the corresponding modern theories to appreciate the contrast which it offered. It let me into the secret which modern books had been keeping from me, that the natural sciences have a history of their own, and that the doctrines they teach on any given subject, at any given time, have been reached not by some discoverer penetrating to the truth after ages of error, but by the gradual modification of doctrines previously held; and will at some future date, unless thinking stops, be themselves no less modified. I will not say that all this became clear to me at that childish age; but at least I became aware from reading this old book that science is less like a hoard of truths, ascertained piecemeal, than an organism which in the course of its history undergoes more or less continuous alteration in every part.

During the same years I was constantly watching the work of my father and mother, and the other professional painters who frequented their house, and constantly trying to imitate them; so that I learned to think of a picture not as a finished product exposed for the admiration of virtuosi, but as the visible record, lying about the house, of an attempt to solve a definite problem in painting, so far as the attempt has gone. I learned what some critics and aestheticians never know to the end of their lives, that no 'work of art' is ever finished, so that in that sense of the phrase there is no such thing as a 'work of art' at all. Work ceases upon the picture or manuscript, not because it is finished, but because sending-in day is at hand, or because the printer is clamorous for copy, or because 'I am sick of working at this thing' or 'I can't see what more I can do to it'. In myself I found less aptitude for painting than for literature; from an early age I wrote incessantly, in verse and prose, lyrics and fragments of epics, stories of adventure and romance, descriptions of imaginary countries and bogus scientific and archaeological treatises. A prolific habit in regard to such things was encouraged, demanded indeed, by the family custom of producing in manuscript a monthly magazine, circulated among a few friends and relations. My mother was a good pianist, and used to play for an hour every day before breakfast; sometimes in the evening as well, to a surreptitious audience of children sitting on the stairs in the dark; in this way I got to know all Beethoven's sonatas and most of Chopin, for these were her favourite composers, though not mine. But I have never been able to master the piano for myself.

My father had plenty of books, and allowed me to read in them as I pleased. Among others, he had kept the books of classical scholarship, ancient history, and philosophy which he had used at Oxford. As a rule I left these alone; but one day when I was eight years old curiosity moved me to take down a little black book lettered on its spine 'Kant's Theory of Ethics'. It was Abbott's translation of the *Grundlegung zur Metaphysik der Sitten*; and as I began reading it, my small form wedged between the bookcase and the table, I was attacked by a strange succession of emotions. First came an intense excitement. I felt that things of the highest importance were being said about matters of the utmost urgency: things which at all costs I must understand. Then, with a wave of indignation, came the discovery that I could not understand them. Disgraceful to confess, here was a book whose words were English and whose sentences were grammatical, but whose meaning baffled me. Then, third and last, came the strangest emotion of all. I felt that the contents of this book, although I could not understand it, were somehow my business: a matter personal to myself, or rather to some future self of my own. It was not like the common boyish intention to 'be an engine-driver when I grow up', for there was no desire in it; I did not, in any natural sense of the word, 'want' to master the Kantian ethics when I should be old enough; but I felt as if a veil had been lifted and my destiny revealed.

There came upon me by degrees, after this, a sense of being burdened with a task whose nature I could not define except by saying, 'I must think.' What I was to think about I did not know; and when, obeying this command, I fell silent and absent-minded in company, or sought solitude in order to think without interruption, I could not have said, and still cannot say, what it was that I actually thought. There were no particular questions that I asked myself; there were no special objects upon which I directed my mind; there was only a formless and aimless intellectual disturbance, as if I were wrestling with a fog.

I know now that this is what always happens when I am in the early stages of work on a problem. Until the problem has gone a long way towards being solved, I do not know what it is; all I am conscious of is this vague perturbation of mind, this sense of being worried about I cannot say what. I know now that the problems of my life's work were taking, deep down inside me, their first embryonic shape. But any one who observed me must have thought, as my elders did think, that I had fallen into a habit of loafing, and lost the alertness and quickness of wit that had been so noticeable in my early childhood. My only defence against this opinion, since I did not know and therefore could not explain what was happening to me, was to cover these fits of abstraction with some bodily activity, trifling enough not to distract my attention from my inward wrestling. I was a neat-fingered boy, skilful at making all sorts of things; active in walking, bicycling, or rowing, and thoroughly practised in sailing a boat. So when the fit was upon me I would set myself to make something quite uninteresting, like a regiment of paper men, or wander aimlessly in the woods or on the mountains, or sail all day in a dead calm. It was painful to be laughed at for playing with paper men; but the alternative, to explain why I did it, was impossible.

Whether it was this growing idleness that made my father send me to school, I am not sure. In any case he was too poor to pay for it himself, and my school bills (and later my Oxford bills) were paid by the generosity of a rich friend. Thus, at thirteen, I was put into a preparatory school with the aim of competing for a scholarship, and became acquainted with the treadmill on which middle-class boys in this country earn their own living by competitive examination, beginning at an age when their working-class fellow children are debarred by law from exposing themselves in the labour market. My father's friend would, I am sure, as willingly have paid two hundred pounds a year for me as one; but to myself at least it was a point of honour that I should win scholarships, if only to justify the spending upon me of all that money; and, even had it not been, the specialism which is one chief vice of English education would not have spared me. The ghost of a silly seventeenth-century squabble still haunts our classrooms, infecting teachers and pupils with the lunatic idea that studies must be either 'classical' or 'modern'. I was equally well fitted to specialize in Greek and Latin, or in modern history and languages (I spoke and read French and German almost as easily as English), or in the natural sciences; and nothing would have afforded my mind its proper nourishment except to study equally all three; but my father's teaching had given me a good deal more Greek and Latin than most boys of my age possessed; and since I had to specialize in something I specialized in these and became a 'classical' scholar.

II

SPRING FROST

In that capacity I went on, a year later, to Rugby; a school which then had a high reputation, owing (as I found out in time) to the genius of one first-rate teacher, Robert Whitelaw, a man who touched nothing that he did not adorn. Because one of my five years there was spent in his form, it would be untrue to say that my time at Rugby was altogether wasted. And there were other things. I was in the Sixth Form for three years and head of my house for two; thus for the first time I tasted the pleasure of doing administrative work, and learnt once for all how to do it. In addition to Whitelaw, whose obviously sincere assumption that you knew as much as he did stimulated his pupils to incredible feats, I worked for a time under one other good teacher, C. P. Hastings, from whom I learnt a good deal of modern history. Among those of the other masters who did not have to teach me I made a few good friends; and with my contemporaries my relations were always of the happiest.

These were benefits conferred by the school itself: others I obtained rather in spite of it. I discovered Bach, learned to play the violin, studied harmony and counterpoint and orchestration, and composed a great deal of trash. I taught myself to read Dante and made the acquaintance of many other poets, in various languages, hitherto unknown to me. These unauthorized readings (for which, in summer time, I used to perch in a willow-tree overhanging the Avon) are my happiest recollection of Rugby; but not my most vivid.

That description must apply to the pigsty conditions of our daily life and the smell of filth constantly in our nostrils. Second to that comes the frightful boredom of being taught things (and things which ought to have been frightfully interesting) by weary, absent-minded or incompetent masters; then the torment of living by a time-table expressly devised to fill up the day with scraps and snippets of occupation in such a manner that no one could get down to a job of work and make something of it, and, in particular, devised to prevent one from doing that 'thinking' in which, long ago, I had recognized my own vocation.

Nor did I get any compensating satisfaction out of the organized games which constituted the real religion of the school; for at football in my first year I suffered an injury to the knee which the surgery of those days rendered incurable. This was a crucial point in my school life. The orthodox theory of public-school athletics is that they distract the adolescent from sex. They do not do that; but they give him a most necessary outlet for the energies he is not allowed to use in the class-room. Apart from a few eccentrics like Whitelaw, the public school masters of my acquaintance were like the schoolmaster in the *Dunciad*:

> Plac'd at the door of learning, youth to guide,
> We never suffer it to stand too wide.

The boys were nothing if not teachable. They soon saw that any exhibition of interest in their studies was a sure way to get themselves disliked, not by their contemporaries, but by the masters; and they were not long in acquiring that pose of boredom towards learning and everything connected with it which is notoriously part of the English public school man's character. But they must have some compensation for their frustrated and inhibited intellects; and this they got in athletics, where nobody minds how hard you work, and the triumphs of the football field make amends for the miseries of the class-room. If I had retained the use of my limbs I should no doubt have become an athlete and stopped worrying my head about the crack of that door and what was hidden behind it. As it was, I could not reconcile myself to the starvation imposed on me by the teaching to which I was subjected; and as time went on I learnt to devote my time more and more to music and to reading in subjects of my own choice like medieval Italian history or the early French poets, not because I preferred them to Thucydides and Catullus, but because I could work at them unhampered by masters.

These habits were not undiscovered, and I became a rebel, more or less declared, against the whole system of teaching. I did not rebel against the disciplinary system, and with my housemaster (my immediate superior in the disciplinary hierarchy) I remained on excellent terms; I did not even neglect my work to the extent of incurring punishment for idleness; but my masters were quite able to discern the difference between my abilities and my performance, and were justifiably annoyed by it; especially, I seemed to notice, when they had to send up my compositions, or as we called them 'copies', to the headmaster for distinction. I could not prevent that from happening; for my plan was ca' canny, not sabotage, and I would not wilfully write bad 'copies'. But I could and did refuse to enter for the prizes which decorated the career of a good boy. To make this refusal more pointed, I would enter now and then for a prize that had nothing to do with my proper subjects of study: one for English literature, which I remember with gratitude because it introduced me to Dryden, one for astronomy, which entailed many nights with the four-inch equatorial and the transit instrument in the school observatory, one for musical theory and composition, and one (which I failed to win) for reading aloud.

The much-tried form-master of the Upper Bench made a bid for revenge when I proposed to enter for a scholarship at Oxford. He refused me leave to sit. I had no chance of winning one, he said, and he did not wish to have the school disgraced. I reported this to my father, who was an irascible man and wrote to the headmaster. My first choice was University College; to give myself another chance, I entered for a second 'group' of colleges, and thus spent two successive weeks inhabiting college rooms in Oxford. The first examination I took very seriously; in the second I decided to enjoy myself, and behaved disgracefully. In the verse paper I wrote neither Latin nor Greek, but the English verses permitted to those whose classics were shaky. In the 'general' paper I spent my whole time answering a question about Turner and another about Mozart; and what boyish nonsense I put into my essay I dare not try to recollect. But at the *viva voce* examination they asked me what I should do if I had to choose between the best scholarship in that group and an inferior one at University; and when I answered that University was my father's College and that I should go there if I was offered any scholarship at all, they did not seem like men who thought the worse of me.

But my form-master had the last word. There was a leaving exhibition confined to natives of my home county; and I told him, as the proper person, that I wished to enter for it. Time went by and nothing happened; and at last I spoke of it again. He answered that he had forgotten to send in my name and that it was now too late. So in due course that exhibition was announced with the formula 'no candidate'. This time I did not protest.

To apportion blame for mishaps is seldom worth doing. If my five years at Rugby were mainly waste, the fault lies partly with the obvious faults of the English public-school system; partly with Rugby as a bad example of that system, though among its faults I do not reckon the institution of fagging or that of government by members of the sixth form, both of which I count as virtues; partly with my father, who gave me an adult scholar's attitude towards learning while I was still a child, realizing, as I now think, what the results would be, but judging the game worth the candle; and partly with myself, for being a conceited puppy and an opinionated prig.

To show that I mean these epithets seriously, I will describe one incident of the feud between that form-master and myself. Reading to his form a note by some modern scholar, as it might be Jebb, on a passage in a Greek text, he came to the word floret, and said 'Floret? I don't believe there is such a word. Has any of you heard of it?' All the rest held their tongues, and so should I have done if I had learnt to be a proper schoolboy; but something inside me whispered 'for God's sake, speak up and put an end to this silly game of hide-and-seek'; and I said 'It means one of the little things that make up a flower of the order *compositae*; I expect he got it from Browning's description of the sunflower, "with ray-like florets round a disk-like face".' And I still remember, with bitter shame, the contemptuous tone in which I said it, and the disconcerted face with which the poor man complimented me on my learning.

Going up to Oxford was like being let out of prison. In those days, before the anthology habit infected Classical Moderations, a candidate for honours was expected to read Homer, Vergil, Demosthenes, and the speeches of Cicero more or less entire, in addition to a special study of other texts, among which I chose Lucretius, Theocritus, and the *Agamemnon*. This was not only leading a horse to the water, but (hardly less important) leaving him there. The happy beast could swill and booze Homer until the world contained no Homer that he had not read. After long years on a ration of twenty drops a day, nicely medicated from a form-master's fad-bottle, I drank with open throat. One hour a week I had to spend showing compositions to my tutor; and there were a few lectures which he had advised me to attend: otherwise my time was my own. Nor were these exceptions very serious. If I had shut myself up in my rooms for a week together, to do some work of my own choosing, my tutor would only have passed it off, when I emerged very apologetic, with an erudite but good-humoured joke. In short, I had come to a place where, even if it was not actually assumed that one had an adult attitude towards learning, at any rate one was not penalized for having such an attitude; and all I had to do was to forget my school life and let myself go.

Yet it was not quite so simple as that. The ill effects of my school years could not be removed by a mere change of environment. My long-baulked craving for knowledge was now almost morbid. I could think of nothing else. Perched in my tower in the garden quadrangle of University College, I read all day and most of the night. All the good easy social life that was going on around me I brushed aside. Even my friendships were few. Long experience of hostility between myself and the system under which I lived had made me cynical, suspicious, and eccentric; caring little for my relations with my neighbours; quick to take offence and not unready to give it. But, for all that, there were many long walks in the country, many idle afternoons on the river, many evenings spent playing and hearing music, many nights talking until dawn; and more than one lifelong friendship in the making.

When the time came to begin 'Greats' I found the same method at work. I had now two tutors, one in philosophy and one in ancient history, each demanding a weekly essay: but otherwise, apart from a little advice about lectures, I was perfectly free to arrange my own studies in my own way; and I used my freedom. When I was supposed to be working at ancient history I spent much time reading reports of excavations at Greek and Roman sites; one whole long vacation went in studying everything I could get hold of about ancient Sicily; in philosophy, where our studies were supposed to end with Kant, I managed to acquire a rough and sketchy, but first-hand, acquaintance with most of the chief writers, in English, French, German, and Italian, from that time down to the present, and once I spent several weeks reading Plato from end to end. I mention these things not in order to boast of my industry; they are a fleabite to what a very ordinary eighteenth-century student of my years would have done; but, because they were all done without the orders and mostly even without the knowledge of my tutors, as evidence of the extent to which I was left alone to work in peace. My contemporaries knew hardly more about these doings than my tutors: I was always too busy to join the societies at whose meetings undergraduates exhibited their wits and their learning to mutual admiration.

III

MINUTE PHILOSOPHERS

WHEN I began to read philosophy there in 1910, Oxford was still obsessed by what I will call the school of Green: a philosophical movement whose leader was Thomas Hill Green and whose other chief members were Francis Herbert Bradley, Bernard Bosanquet, William Wallace, and Robert Lewis Nettleship. No one has yet written the history of this movement, and I do not propose to attempt it here; but I cannot indicate the problems which I found confronting me without a few remarks on the subject.

The philosophical tendencies common to this school were described by its contemporary opponents as Hegelianism. This title was repudiated by the school itself, and rightly. Their philosophy, so far as they had one single philosophy, was a continuation and criticism of the indigenous English and Scottish philosophies of the middle nineteenth century. It is true that, unlike most of their compatriots, they had some knowledge of Hegel, and a good deal more of Kant. The fact of their having this knowledge was used by their opponents, more through ignorance than through deliberate dishonesty, to discredit them in the eyes of a public always contemptuous of foreigners. Green had read Hegel in youth, but rejected him in middle age; the philosophy he was working out when his early death interrupted him is best described, if a brief description is needed, as a reply to Herbert

Spencer by a profound student of Hume. Bradley, who knew enough of Hegel to be certain that he disagreed with his cardinal doctrines, and said so, published a series of books whose purpose is written plainly upon them: they are criticisms of Mill's logic, Bain's psychology, and Mansel's metaphysics by a man whose mind was the most deeply critical that European philosophy has produced since Hume, and whose intention, like that of Locke, was to make a bonfire of rubbish.

This movement never in any sense dominated philosophical thought and teaching in Oxford. In its most flourishing period it comprised only a few young men. Their views were always regarded with suspicion by the most part of their colleagues; and not one of them enjoyed in Oxford a long life of teaching. T. H. Green died at forty-six in 1882, after being a professor for four years. R. L. Nettleship, who was placed in the second class in 'Greats' because he 'handed out' Green's views to the examiners, perished in the Alps, at the same age, in 1892. Bosanquet, after teaching in Oxford for eleven years, left it for good in 1881, at thirty-three. Wallace was killed in an accident at fifty-three, in 1897. Bradley, though he lived in Oxford down to his death in 1924, never taught there and never sought in any way to propagate his philosophy by personal contacts. He lived a very retired life; although I lived within a few hundred yards of him for sixteen years, I never to my knowledge set eyes on him.

The real strength of the movement was outside

Oxford. The 'Greats' school was not meant as a training for professional scholars and philosophers; it was meant as a training for public life in the Church, at the Bar, in the Civil Service, and in Parliament. The school of Green sent out into public life a stream of ex-pupils who carried with them the conviction that philosophy, and in particular the philosophy they had learnt at Oxford, was an important thing, and that their vocation was to put it into practice. This conviction was common to politicians so diverse in their creeds as Asquith and Milner, churchmen like Gore and Scott Holland, social reformers like Arnold Toynbee, and a host of other public men whose names it would be tedious to repeat. Through this effect on the minds of its pupils, the philosophy of Green's school might be found, from about 1880 to about 1910, penetrating and fertilizing every part of the national life.[1]

Since the philosophy of Green's school had never been predominant among teachers, the hostility to it which was so prevalent in 1910 can hardly be called a reaction. It would be truer to describe it as representing the old academic tradition, labouring to eradicate what it had always regarded as a growth foreign to its own nature. The old stock was shooting up from below the graft, the scion dying back, and the tree reverting to its original state.

[1] The only attempt yet made to trace the history of this penetration is that of Dr. Klaus Dockhorn, *Die Staatsphilosophie des englischen Idealismus: ihre Lehre und Wirkung* (Cologne 1937), part ii.

There were still among the philosophers a few representatives of the original movement. The best of them were J. A. Smith, who had been a pupil of Nettleship, and H. H. Joachim, a close personal friend of Bradley. Each of these later became an intimate and beloved friend of my own, and I cannot think of either without gratitude and admiration;[1] but this must not prevent me from saying that they failed to avert the collapse of the school to which they belonged. The way in which this could have been done was by expounding and developing the doctrines of that school in a series of books addressed to the general public; but between them they produced only one such book, Joachim's essay on *The Nature of Truth*, whose success with the public showed unmistakably, but in vain, the demand that existed for such things. Yet, if they did not satisfy this demand, it was only because they could not. They were the *epigoni* of a great movement; and like all *epigoni* they felt that what needed to be said had been said, and need not be repeated. Often I urged them to write; and always I found that my urging was met by no corresponding impulse within themselves. They could not write, because they did not feel that they had anything to say.

The game was thus left in the hands of their opponents. These called themselves 'realists',[2] and undertook the task of discrediting the entire work of

[1] And in Joachim's case with mourning. He died soon after this chapter was written.

[2] Thomas Case (1844–1925), a leading Oxford opponent of Green's school, had written books advocating 'realism', by that name, from the 1870's onwards.

Green's school, which they described comprehensively as 'idealism' (another title explicitly repudiated by Bradley, the greatest philosopher of the school). When I say that Green's school at this time obsessed Oxford philosophy, what I mean is that the work of that school presented itself to most Oxford philosophers as something which had to be destroyed, and in destroying which they would be discharging their first duty to their subject. The question what positive views they themselves held was of secondary importance.

The leader of this school was John Cook Wilson, professor of logic. He was a fiery, pugnacious little man with a passion for controversy and an instinctive eye for its tactics; more important, an inspiring teacher, whose enthusiasm for philosophical thought I still remember with admiration and gratitude. He, too, refrained from publication; and he once explained to me his reasons. 'I rewrite, on average, one third of my logic lectures every year', said he. 'That means I'm constantly changing my mind about every point in the subject. If I published, every book I wrote would betray a change of mind since writing the last. Now, if you let the public know that you change your mind, they will never take you seriously. Therefore it is best never to publish at all.' Whether he thought that by not publishing he deceived the public into thinking that he never changed his mind, and whether he regarded this as a good thing to do, even though the public remained ignorant what his mind was, or whether he had a mind at all, I did not ask; probably because I already knew that there are two reasons why people refrain from writing books: either they are conscious that they have nothing to say, or they are conscious that they are unable to say it; and that if they give any other reason than these it is to throw dust in other people's eyes or their own.

Other sayings were more to his credit. Commenting on something I had written about Plato's *Sophist*, and led thereby to hold forth about the kind of people who disseminate error, he said, 'there are two kinds of damn fool: there are damn silly fools like X, and damn clever fools like Y; and if you're going to be a damn fool you'd much better be a damn silly one.' I am sorry I cannot think myself justified in naming the eminent contemporary philosophers whom I have called X and Y.

After Cook Wilson, the most important members of the 'realist' school were his followers H. A. Prichard and H. W. B. Joseph. Prichard was an extremely acute and pertinacious thinker, who if common report was right had on occasion been more leader than follower to Cook Wilson. At the time I speak of he had just published a book entitled *Kant's Theory of Knowledge*, in which the argument of the 'Aesthetic' and 'Analytic' portions of the *Critique of Pure Reason* were attacked from a 'realist' point of view. He used to lecture on the theories of knowledge preceding Kant's, from Descartes onward, showing how 'idealist' tendencies had been at work throughout the seventeenth and eighteenth centuries, and refuting all the theories which they had infected. Joseph, author of an *Introduction to Logic* in which a position not unlike

Cook Wilson's was taken up, lectured on Plato's *Republic*, and would hardly have repudiated the name of Platonist: for he regarded Plato as right in many at least of his views, and especially on those points with respect to which the 'idealists' were wrong. Subsequently, Prichard and Joseph tended increasingly to diverge. Prichard, developing his extraordinary gift for destructive criticism, by degrees destroyed not only the 'idealism' he at first set out to destroy but the 'realism' in whose interest he set out to destroy it, and described a path converging visibly, as years went by, with the zero-line of complete scepticism. In Joseph's case this scepticism was masked by a progressive tendency to accept Plato's doctrines as substantially true. But the scepticism was nevertheless there; or so it seemed to his pupils, one of whom once said to me, 'if the Archangel Gabriel told you what Mr. Joseph really thought about something, and you served it up to him in an essay, I'm perfectly sure he would prove to you that it was wrong'.

IV

INCLINATION OF A SAPLING

My own tutor E. F. Carritt was another prominent member of the 'realist' school, and sent me to lectures with Cook Wilson and the rest. I was thus thoroughly indoctrinated with its principles and methods. But though I called myself a 'realist', it was not without some reservations. An important document of the school, or rather of the parallel and more or less allied school at Cambridge, was G. E. Moore's recently published article called 'The Refutation of Idealism'. This purported to be a criticism of Berkeley. Now the position actually criticized in that article is not Berkeley's position; indeed, in certain important respects it is the exact position which Berkeley was controverting. In order to see this, I had only to open the article and Berkeley's text and compare them. The same thing happened with the attacks on Bradley made in Cook Wilson's logic lectures. I am sure that few of his audience took much trouble about comparing these with Bradley's text and asking how far they tallied with it. But I did; and I found that he constantly criticized Bradley for views which were not Bradley's.

I do not apologize for having felt, when young, the diffidence of youth. At forty, I should not have hesitated for a moment, if I had been attached to a school of thought whose leaders I had convicted of errors so gross on matters of fact so important, to break the attachment. At twenty-two or twenty-three I distinguished and qualified. I argued that the 'realists' professed philosophy, not history; that their business, strictly as philosophical critics, was to show whether a certain doctrine were sound or unsound, and that this they had done, on the present occasion, admirably; that their historical blunders on the question whether a certain author held that doctrine, however distressing to myself, did not affect the philosophical issue; and that I was logically bound to remain a 'realist' until I had satisfied myself either that the positive doctrines of the school were false, or that its critical methods were unsound.

These questions I did not answer until after I had taken my degree and begun to work as a teacher of philosophy. It then became clear to me, as I tried to settle in my own mind how the methods and doctrines of my 'realist' colleagues were related, that Cook Wilson's positive teaching was incapable of resisting attack by his own critical methods. If the positive teaching and the critical methods had been logically connected, that would have been fatal to both of them; but there might be no such connexion. The positive teaching might be mistaken, and the critical methods valid, or *vice versa*. To choose between these three alternatives was the problem still occupying my mind in 1914, when our academic life was broken up by war.

Meanwhile I had been half unconsciously preparing a flank attack on the same problem. When I became a teacher of philosophy I did not abandon my historical and archaeological studies. Every summer

I spent serving on the staff of some large excavation, and from 1913 onwards directing excavations of my own. This became one of the chief pleasures of my life. I had learnt how to manage schoolboys; now I had to manage labourers, to keep them well and happy, to understand their approach to our common task and help them to understand mine. At the same time I found myself experimenting in a laboratory of knowledge; at first asking myself a quite vague question, such as: 'was there a Flavian occupation on this site?' then dividing that question into various heads and putting the first in some such form as this: 'are these Flavian sherds and coins mere strays, or were they deposited in the period to which they belong?' and then considering all the possible ways in which light could be thrown on this new question, and putting them into practice one by one, until at last I could say, 'There was a Flavian occupation; an earth and timber fort of such and such plan was built here in the year $a \pm b$ and abandoned for such and such reasons in the year $x \pm y$.' Experience soon taught me that under these laboratory conditions one found out nothing at all except in answer to a question; and not a vague question either, but a definite one. That when one dug saying merely, 'Let us see what there is here', one learnt nothing, except casually in so far as casual questions arose in one's mind while digging: 'Is that black stuff peat or occupation-soil? Is that a potsherd under your foot? Are those loose stones a ruined wall?' That what one learnt depended not merely on what turned up in one's trenches but also on what questions one was asking: so that a man who was asking questions of one kind learnt one kind of thing from a piece of digging which to another man revealed something different, to a third something illusory, and to a fourth nothing at all.

Here I was only rediscovering for myself, in the practice of historical research, principles which Bacon and Descartes had stated, three hundred years earlier, in connexion with the natural sciences. Each of them had said very plainly that knowledge comes only by answering questions, and that these questions must be the right questions and asked in the right order. And I had often read the works in which they said it; but I did not understand them until I had found the same thing out for myself.

The Oxford 'realists' talked as if knowing were a simple 'intuiting' or a simple 'apprehending' of some 'reality'. At Cambridge, Moore expressed, as I thought, the same conception when he spoke of the 'transparency' of the act of knowing; so did Alexander, at Manchester, when he described knowing as the simple 'compresence' of two things, one of which was a mind. What all these 'realists' were saying, I thought, was that the condition of a knowing mind is not indeed a passive condition, for it is actively engaged in knowing; but a 'simple' condition, one in which there are no complexities or diversities, nothing except just the knowing. They granted that a man who wanted to know something might have to work, in ways that might be very complicated, in order to 'put himself in a position' from which it could be 'apprehended';

but once the position had been attained there was nothing for him to do but 'apprehend' it, or perhaps fail to 'apprehend' it.

This doctrine, which was rendered plausible by choosing as examples of knowledge statements like 'this is a red rose', 'my hand is resting on the table', where familiarity with the mental operations involved has bred not so much contempt as oblivion, was quite incompatible with what I had learned in my 'laboratory' of historical thought. The questioning activity, as I called it, was not an activity of achieving compresence with, or apprehension of, something; it was not preliminary to the act of knowing; it was one half (the other half being answering the question) of an act which in its totality was knowing.

I have tried to state the point as it appeared to me at the time. I was well enough trained in 'realist' methods to know exactly what a 'realist' would have said in answer to my statement of it. But Cook Wilson himself had said to me once: 'I will say one thing about you: you can see the obvious.' And it was obvious to me that such an answer would have been no more than an attempt to argue the hind leg off a donkey.

In my philosophical teaching I was working on a line which ultimately converged with this. From the first, I decided that one thing which Oxford philosophy needed was a background (at the time, I conceived it as merely that) of sound scholarship: such a habit of mind as would make it impossible for an Oxford-trained student to be deceived by Moore's 'refutation' of Berkeley or Cook Wilson's of Bradley. I therefore taught my pupils, more by example than by precept, that they must never accept any criticism of anybody's philosophy which they might hear or read without satisfying themselves by first-hand study that this was the philosophy he actually expounded; that they must always defer any criticism of their own until they were absolutely sure they understood the text they were criticizing; and that if the postponement was *sine die* it did not greatly matter. This did not as yet involve any attack upon the 'realists'' critical methods. When my pupils came to me armed with grotesquely irrelevant refutations of (say) Kant's ethical theory, and told me they came out of So-and-so's lectures, it was all one to me whether the irrelevance came from their misrepresenting So-and-so, or from So-and-so's misrepresenting Kant: my move was to reach for a book with the words, 'Let us see whether that is what Kant really said'.

In lecturing, I adopted a similar procedure. I had become something of a specialist in Aristotle, and the first lectures I gave were on the *De Anima*. My plan was to concentrate on the question, 'What is Aristotle saying and what does he mean by it?' and to forgo, however alluring it might be, the further question 'Is it true?' What I wanted was to train my audience in the scholarly approach to a philosophical text, leaving on one side, as sufficiently provided for by other teachers, the further business of criticizing its doctrine.

By the time war broke out in 1914 and put a stop to

all this, I had not indeed answered to my own satisfaction the threefold question stated earlier in this chapter; but I had made good progress with what I have called the flank attack upon it. I had made myself an expert in a certain kind of research, and had found out how to use it as a laboratory for testing epistemological theories. I had also established and perfected what, had I been a great artist, might have been called my 'early manner' in philosophical teaching. Working simultaneously along these two lines, I could see them tending to converge in an attack on 'realism' as a philosophy which erred through neglecting history. If I had thought it possible to forewarn the 'realists' of this attack, I should have said, 'You must pay more attention to history. Your positive doctrines about knowledge are incompatible with what happens, according to my own experience, in historical research; and your critical methods are misused on doctrines which in historical fact were never held by those to whom you ascribe them.'

A great deal of hard thinking was needed, before the vague dissatisfaction which I might have expressed in some such words as these could be focused into a clear issue. And I am not sure that I could ever so have focused it, but for the interruption of my academic life by the war. A man whose mind is always being stirred up by philosophical teaching can hardly be expected to achieve the calm, the inner silence, which is one condition of philosophical thinking.

V

QUESTION AND ANSWER

A YEAR or two after the outbreak of war, I was living in London and working with a section of the Admiralty Intelligence Division in the rooms of the Royal Geographical Society. Every day I walked across Kensington Gardens and past the Albert Memorial. The Albert Memorial began by degrees to obsess me. Like Wordsworth's Leech-gatherer, it took on a strange air of significance; it seemed

> Like one whom I had met with in a dream;
> Or like a man from some far region sent,
> To give me human strength, by apt admonishment.

Everything about it was visibly mis-shapen, corrupt, crawling, verminous; for a time I could not bear to look at it, and passed with averted eyes; recovering from this weakness, I forced myself to look, and to face day by day the question: a thing so obviously, so incontrovertibly, so indefensibly bad, why had Scott done it? To say that Scott was a bad architect was to burke the problem with a tautology; to say that there was no accounting for tastes was to evade it by *suggestio falsi*. What relation was there, I began to ask myself, between what he had done and what he had tried to do? Had he tried to produce a beautiful thing; a thing, I meant, which we should have thought beautiful? If so, he had of course failed. But had he perhaps been trying to produce something different? If so, he might possibly have succeeded. If I found the monument merely loathsome, was that perhaps my fault? Was I looking in it for qualities it did not possess, and either ignoring or despising those it did?

I will not try to describe everything I went through in what, for many months, continued to be my daily communings with the Albert Memorial. Of the various thoughts that came to me in those communings I will only state one: a further development of a thought already familiar to me.

My work in archaeology, as I have said, impressed upon me the importance of the 'questioning activity' in knowledge: and this made it impossible for me to rest contented with the intuitionist theory of knowledge favoured by the 'realists'. The effect of this on my logic was to bring about in my mind a revolt against the current logical theories of the time, a good deal like that revolt against the scholastic logic which was produced in the minds of Bacon and Descartes by reflection on the experience of scientific research, as that was taking new shape in the late sixteenth and early seventeenth centuries. The *Novum Organum* and the *Discours de la Méthode* began to have a new significance for me. They were the classical expressions of a principle in logic which I found it necessary to restate: the principle that a body of knowledge consists not of 'propositions', 'statements', 'judgements', or whatever name logicians use in order to designate assertive acts of thought (or what in those acts is asserted: for 'knowledge' means both the activity of knowing and what is known), but of these together with the questions they are meant to answer; and that a logic in which the answers are attended to and the questions neglected is a false logic.

I will try to indicate, briefly as the nature of this book requires (for it is an autobiography, not a work on logic), the way in which this notion developed in my mind as I reflected day by day upon the Albert Memorial. I know that what I am going to say is very controversial, and that almost any reader who is already something of a logician will violently disagree with it. But I shall make no attempt to forestall his criticisms. So far as he belongs to any logical school now existing, I think I know already what they will be, and it is because I am not convinced by them that I am writing this chapter. I shall not use the word 'judgement', like the so-called 'idealistic' logicians, or Cook Wilson's word 'statement': the thing denoted by these words I shall call a 'proposition': so that this word will always in this chapter denote a logical, not a linguistic, entity.

I began by observing that you cannot find out what a man means by simply studying his spoken or written statements, even though he has spoken or written with perfect command of language and perfectly truthful intention. In order to find out his meaning you must also know what the question was (a question in his own mind, and presumed by him to be in yours) to which the thing he has said or written was meant as an answer.

It must be understood that question and answer, as I conceived them, were strictly correlative. A proposition was not an answer, or at any rate could not be the right answer, to any question which might have been answered otherwise. A highly detailed and particularized proposition must be the answer, not to a vague and generalized question, but to a question as detailed and particularized as itself. For example, if my car will not go, I may spend an hour searching for the cause of its failure. If, during this hour, I take out number one plug, lay it on the engine, turn the starting-handle, and watch for a spark, my observation 'number one plug is all right' is an answer not to the question, 'Why won't my car go?' but to the question, 'Is it because number one plug is not sparking that my car won't go?' Any one of the various experiments I make during the hour will be the finding of an answer to some such detailed and particularized question. The question, 'Why won't my car go?' is only a kind of summary of all these taken together. It is not a separate question asked at a separate time, nor is it a sustained question which I continue to ask for the whole hour together. Consequently, when I say 'Number one plug is all right', this observation does not record one more failure to answer the hour-long question, 'What is wrong with my car?' It records a success in answering the three-minutes-long question, 'Is the stoppage due to failure in number one plug?'

In passing, I will note (what I shall return to later on) that this principle of correlativity between question and answer disposes of a good deal of clap-trap. People will speak of a savage as 'confronted by the eternal problem of obtaining food'. But what really confronts him is the problem, quite transitory like all things human, of spearing this fish, or digging up this root, or finding blackberries in this wood.

My next step was to apply this principle to the idea of contradiction. The current logic maintained that two propositions might, simply as propositions, contradict one another, and that by examining them simply as propositions you could find out whether they did so or not. This I denied. If you cannot tell what a proposition means unless you know what question it is meant to answer, you will mistake its meaning if you make a mistake about that question. One symptom of mistaking the meaning of a proposition is thinking that it contradicts another proposition which in fact it does not contradict. No two propositions, I saw, can contradict one another unless they are answers to the same question. It is therefore impossible to say of a man, 'I do not know what the question is which he is trying to answer, but I can see that he is contradicting himself'.

The same principle applied to the idea of truth. If the meaning of a proposition is relative to the question it answers, its truth must be relative to the same thing. Meaning, agreement and contradiction, truth and falsehood, none of these belonged to propositions in their own right, propositions by themselves; they belonged only to propositions as the answers to questions: each proposition answering a question strictly correlative to itself.

Here I parted company with what I called propositional logic, and its offspring the generally recognized theories of truth. According to propositional logic (under which denomination I include the so-called 'traditional' logic, the 'idealistic' logic of the eighteenth and nineteenth centuries, and the 'symbolic' logic of the nineteenth and twentieth), truth or falsehood, which are what logic is chiefly concerned with, belongs to propositions as such. This doctrine was often expressed by calling the proposition the 'unit of thought', meaning that if you divide it up into parts such as subject, copula, predicate, any of these parts taken singly is not a complete thought, that is, not capable of being true or false.

It seemed to me that this doctrine was a mistake due to the early partnership between logic and grammar. The logician's proposition seemed to me a kind of ghostly double of the grammarian's sentence, just as in primitive speculation about the mind people imagine minds as ghostly doubles of bodies. Grammar recognizes a form of discourse called the sentence, and among sentences, as well as other kinds which serve as the verbal expressions of questions, commands, &c., one kind which express statements. In grammatical phraseology, these are indicative sentences; and logicians have almost always tried to conceive the 'unit of thought', or that which is either true or false, as a kind of logical 'soul' whose linguistic 'body' is the indicative sentence.

This attempt to correlate the logical proposition with the grammatical indicative sentence has never been altogether satisfactory. There have always been people who saw that the true 'unit of thought' was not the proposition but something more complex in which the proposition served as answer to a question. Not only Bacon and Descartes, but Plato and Kant, come to mind as examples. When Plato described thinking as a 'dialogue of the soul with itself', he meant (as we know from his own dialogues) that it was a process of question and answer, and that of these two elements the primacy belongs to the questioning activity, the Socrates within us. When Kant said that it takes a wise man to know what questions he can reasonably ask, he was in effect repudiating a merely propositional logic and demanding a logic of question and answer.

Even apart from this, however, logic has never been able to assert a *de facto* one-one relation between propositions and indicative sentences. It has always maintained that the words actually used by a man on a given occasion in order to express his thought may be 'elliptical' or 'pleonastic' or in some other way not quite in accordance with the rule that one sentence should express one proposition. It is generally held, again, that indicative sentences in a work of fiction, professing to be that and nothing more, do not express propositions. But when these and other qualifications have been made, this can be described as the central doctrine of propositional logic: that there is, or ought to be, or in a well-constructed and well-used language would be,[1] a one-one correspondence between pro-

[1] Hence that numerous and frightful offspring of propositional logic out of illiteracy, the various attempts at a 'logical language', beginning with the pedantry of the text-books about 'reducing

positions and indicative sentences, every indicative sentence expressing a proposition, and a proposition being defined as the unit of thought, or that which is true or false.

This is the doctrine which is presupposed by all the various well-known theories of truth. One school of thought holds that a proposition is either true or false simply in itself, trueness or falseness being qualities of propositions. Another school holds that to call it true or false is to assert a relation of 'correspondence' or 'non-correspondence' between it and something not a proposition, some 'state of things' or 'fact'. A third holds that to call it true or false is to assert a relation between it and other propositions with which it 'coheres' or fails to 'cohere'. And, since in those days there were pragmatists, a fourth school should be mentioned, holding (at least according to some of their pronouncements) that to call a proposition true or false is to assert the utility or inutility of believing it.

All these theories of truth I denied. This was not very original of me; any one could see, after reading Joachim's *Nature of Truth*, that they were all open to fatal objections. My reason for denying them, however, was not that they were severally open to objections, but that they all presupposed what I have called the principle of propositional logic; and this principle I denied altogether.

For a logic of propositions I wanted to substitute

a proposition to logical form', and ending, for the present, in the typographical jargon of *Principia Mathematica*.

what I called a logic of question and answer. It seemed to me that truth, if that meant the kind of thing which I was accustomed to pursue in my ordinary work as a philosopher or historian—truth in the sense in which a philosophical theory or an historical narrative is called true, which seemed to me the proper sense of the word—was something that belonged not to any single proposition, nor even, as the coherence-theorists maintained, to a complex of propositions taken together; but to a complex consisting of questions and answers. The structure of this complex had, of course, never been studied by propositional logic; but with help from Bacon, Descartes, and others I could hazard a few statements about it. Each question and each answer in a given complex had to be relevant or appropriate, had to 'belong' both to the whole and to the place it occupied in the whole. Each question had to 'arise'; there must be that about it whose absence we condemn when we refuse to answer a question on the ground that it 'doesn't arise'. Each answer must be 'the right' answer to the question it professes to answer.

By 'right' I do not mean 'true'. The 'right' answer to a question is the answer which enables us to get ahead with the process of questioning and answering. Cases are quite common in which the 'right' answer to a question is 'false'; for example, cases in which a thinker is following a false scent, either inadvertently or in order to construct a *reductio ad absurdum*. Thus, when Socrates asks (Plato, *Republic*, 333 B) whether as your partner in a game of draughts you would prefer to have a just man or a man who knows how to play draughts, the answer which Polemarchus gives—'a man who knows how to play draughts'—is the right answer. It is 'false', because it presupposes that justice and ability to play draughts are comparable, each of them being a 'craft', or specialized form of skill. But it is 'right', because it constitutes a link, and a sound one, in the chain of questions and answers by which the falseness of that presupposition is made manifest.

What is ordinarily meant when a proposition is called 'true', I thought, was this: (*a*) the proposition belongs to a question-and-answer complex which as a whole is 'true' in the proper sense of the word; (*b*) within this complex it is an answer to a certain question; (*c*) the question is what we ordinarily call a sensible or intelligent question, not a silly one, or in my terminology it 'arises'; (*d*) the proposition is the 'right' answer to that question.

If this is what is meant by calling a proposition 'true', it follows not only that you cannot tell whether a proposition is 'true' or 'false' until you know what question it was intended to answer, but also that a proposition which in fact is 'true' can always be thought 'false' by any one who takes the trouble to excogitate a question to which it would have been the wrong answer, and convinces himself that this was the question it was meant to answer. And a proposition which in fact is significant can always be thought meaningless by any one who convinces himself that it was intended as an answer to a question which, if it had really been intended to answer it, it would not have answered at all, either rightly or wrongly. Whether a given proposition is true or false, significant or meaningless, depends on what question it was meant to answer; and any one who wishes to know whether a given proposition is true or false, significant or meaningless, must find out what question it was meant to answer.

Now, the question 'To what question did So-and-so intend this proposition for an answer?' is an historical question, and therefore cannot be settled except by historical methods. When So-and-so wrote in a distant past, it is generally a very difficult one, because writers (at any rate good writers) always write for their contemporaries, and in particular for those who are 'likely to be interested', which means those who are already asking the question to which an answer is being offered; and consequently a writer very seldom explains what the question is that he is trying to answer. Later on, when he has become a 'classic' and his contemporaries are all long dead, the question has been forgotten; especially if the answer he gave was generally acknowledged to be the right answer; for in that case people stopped asking the question, and began asking the question that next arose. So the question asked by the original writer can only be reconstructed historically, often not without the exercise of considerable historical skill.

''Sblood!' says Hamlet, 'do you think I am easier to be played on than a pipe?' Those eminent philosophers, Rosencrantz and Guildenstern, think *tout bonnement* that they can discover what the *Parmenides* is about by merely reading it; but if you took them to the south gate of Housesteads and said, 'Please distinguish the various periods of construction here, and explain what purpose the builders of each period had in mind', they would protest 'Believe me, I cannot'. Do they think the *Parmenides* is easier to understand than a rotten little Roman fort? 'Sblood!

It follows, too, and this is what especially struck me at the time, that whereas no two propositions can be in themselves mutually contradictory, there are many cases in which one and the same pair of propositions are capable of being thought either that or the opposite, according as the questions they were meant to answer are reconstructed in one way or in another. For example, metaphysicians have been heard to say 'the world is both one and many'; and critics have not been wanting who were stupid enough to accuse them of contradicting themselves, on the abstractly logical ground that 'the world is one' and 'the world is many' are mutually contradictory propositions. A great deal of the popular dislike of metaphysics is based on grounds of this sort, and is ultimately due to critics who, as we say, did not know what the men they criticized were talking about; that is, did not know what questions their talk was intended to answer; but, with the ordinary malevolence of the idle against the industrious, the ignorant against the learned, the fool against the wise man, wished to have it believed that they were talking nonsense.

Suppose, instead of talking about the world, the

metaphysician were talking about the contents of a small mahogany box with a sliding top; and suppose he said, 'The contents of this box are both one thing and many things'. A stupid critic may think that he is offering two incompatible answers to a single question, 'Are the contents of this box one *x* or many *x*'s?' But the critic has reconstructed the question wrong. There were two questions: (*a*) Are the contents of this box one set of chessmen or many sets? (*b*) Are the contents of this box one chessman or many chessmen?

There is no contradiction between saying that something, whether that something be the world or the contents of a box, is one, and saying that it is many. Contradiction would set in only if that something were said to be both one *x* and many *x*'s. But in the original statement, whether about the world or about the chessmen, there was nothing about one *x* and many *x*'s. That was foisted upon it by the critic. The contradiction of which the critic complains never existed in his victim's philosophy at all, until the critic planted it upon him, as he might have planted treasonable correspondence in his coat pockets; and with an equally laudable intention, to obtain a reward for denouncing him.

Thus, if a given doctrine D is criticized as self-contradictory because it is divisible into two parts E and F, where E contradicts F, the criticism is valid only if the critic has correctly reconstructed the questions to which E and F were given as answers. A critic who is aware of this condition will of course 'show his working' by stating to his readers the evidence on which he has concluded that the author criticized really did formulate his questions in such a way that E and F in his mouth were mutually contradictory. Failing that, a reader disinclined to work the problem out for himself will naturally assume the criticism to be sound or unsound according as he has found the critic to be, in a general way, a good historian or a bad one.

This enabled me to answer the question, left open (as I stated at the end of the preceding chapter) in 1914, whether the 'realists'' critical methods were sound. The answer could only be that they were not. For the 'realists'' chief, and in the last resort, it seemed to me, only method was to analyse the position criticized into various propositions, and detect contradictions between these. Following as they did the rules of propositional logic, it never occurred to them that those contradictions might be the fruit of their own historical errors as to the questions which their victims had been trying to answer. There was also a chance that they might not be; but, after what I already knew about the 'realists'' attitude towards history, the odds seemed to me against it. In any case, so long as the possibility existed, the methods were vicious.

All this, during my spare time in 1917, I wrote out at considerable length, with a great many applications and illustrations, in a book called *Truth and Contradiction*. I went so far as to offer it to a publisher, but was told that the times were hopelessly bad for a book of that kind, and that I had better keep it for the present. The publisher was right on both points. Not only were the times unpropitious, but I was still a beginner in the art of writing books. I had only published one. It was called *Religion and Philosophy*, and was published in 1916. It had been written some years earlier, in order to tidy up and put behind me a number of thoughts arising out of my juvenile studies in theology; and I published it because, at a time when a young man's expectation of life was a rapidly dwindling asset, I wished at any rate to leave one philosophical publication behind me, and hated (as I still hate) leaving a decision of that kind to executors.

VI

THE DECAY OF REALISM

THE War ended, I came back to Oxford an opponent of the 'realists'. I had not yet learnt the uselessness of reading papers and holding discussions on philosophical subjects; so, with the intention of putting my cards on the table, I read a paper to my colleagues, trying to convince them that Cook Wilson's central positive doctrine, 'knowing makes no difference to what is known', was meaningless. I argued that any one who claimed, as Cook Wilson did, to be sure of this, was in effect claiming to know what he was simultaneously defining as unknown. For if you know that no difference is made to a thing θ by the presence or absence of a certain condition c, you know what θ is like with c, and also what θ is like without c, and on comparing the two find no difference. This involves knowing what θ is like without c; in the present case, knowing what you defined as the unknown.

My subject was not limited to that formula. I reviewed a number of logical doctrines expounded in Cook Wilson's lectures and pointed out that they were borrowed from Bradley; and I went so far as to say that, except for this one nonsensical phrase about knowledge making no difference to what is known, 'realism' had no positive doctrines of its own at all but had stolen all that it had from the school of thought which it was primarily concerned to discredit. And I described 'realism' in consequence as 'the undischarged bankrupt of modern philosophy'.

That description might have seemed less just some years later, when the 'realist' school could point to such assets as Alexander's *Space Time and Deity* and Whitehead's *Process and Reality*. But even those great works illustrate my point. Each of them is a system of *Naturphilosophie* as the term was understood by the post-Kantians. Alexander's philosophy of nature is even more closely modelled on the *Critique of Pure Reason* than was Hegel's; in many important ways it is very much like what that 'Metaphysics of Nature' would presumably have been which Kant promised but never wrote. In Whitehead the resemblance is more with Hegel; and the author, though he does not seem to be acquainted with Hegel, is not wholly unaware of this, for he describes the book as an attempt to do over again the work of 'idealism', 'but from a realist point of view'.

Actually, however, if 'realism' means the doctrine that the known is independent of, and unaffected by, the knowing it, Whitehead is not a 'realist' at all; for his 'philosophy of organism' commits him to the view that everything which forms an element in a given 'situation' is connected with everything else in that situation, not merely by a relation of compresence, but by interdependence. It follows that, where one element in a situation is a mind, and a second element something known to that mind, the knower and the known are interdependent. This is precisely the doctrine which it was the chief aim of the 'realists' to deny.

Alexander, whose British Academy paper on *The Essence of Realism*, one of the earliest and most important documents of the school, had made just that point, did not forget it in *Space Time and Deity*; nevertheless, the main body of that noble book consists of ideas borrowed from Kant and Hegel, to which a 'realistic' façade has been attached. It is none the worse for that. Whitehead's cosmology is constructed on an anti-'realistic' principle; Alexander's is built up of non-'realistic' materials. Neither can be used as evidence that modern English 'realism' is fertile in cosmological ideas; it would be more plausible to use them as evidence that English philosophy, at any rate in the persons of two very fine philosophers, is beginning to recover from the blight of 'realism' and re-establishing contact with the tradition which 'realism' meant to break.

Different people will differ as to whether a given state of things is a blight or not. The tailless fox preached taillessness. I have already said of 'realism' that its positive doctrine was nugatory, its critical technique deadly: all the deadlier because its effectiveness did not depend on errors native to the doctrines criticized, but on a kind of disintegration produced by itself in whatever it touched. It was therefore inevitable that by degrees 'realism' should part with all positive doctrines whatever, congratulating itself at each new jettison that it was rid of a knave.

Among the first of these consequences was the attack on moral philosophy. Moral philosophy, from the days of Socrates down to our own lifetime, had been regarded as an attempt to think out more clearly the issues involved in conduct, for the sake of acting better. In 1912 Prichard announced that moral philosophy as so understood was based on a mistake, and advocated a new kind of moral philosophy, purely theoretical, in which the workings of the moral consciousness should be scientifically studied as if they were the movements of the planets, and no attempt made to interfere with them. And Bertrand Russell at Cambridge proposed in the same spirit, and on grounds whose difference was only superficial, the extrusion of ethics from the body of philosophy.

The 'realist' philosophers who adopted this new programme were all, or nearly all, teachers of young men and young women. Their pupils, with habits and characters yet unformed, stood on the threshold of life; many of them on the threshold of public life. Half a century earlier, young people in that position had been told that by thinking about what they were doing, or were about to do, they would become likely on the whole to do it better; and that some understanding of the nature of moral or political action, some attempt to formulate ideals and principles, was an indispensable condition of engaging creditably in these activities themselves. And their teachers, when introducing them to the study of moral and political theory, would say to them, whether in words or not—the most important things that one says are often not said in words—'Take this subject seriously, because whether you understand it or not will make a difference to your whole lives'. The 'realist', on the contrary, said to his pupils, 'If it interests you to study this, do so; but don't think it will be of any use to you. Remember the great principle of realism, that nothing is affected by being known. That is as true of human action as of anything else. Moral philosophy is only the theory of moral action: it can't therefore make any difference to the practice of moral action. People can act just as morally without it as with it. I stand here as a moral philosopher; I will try to tell you what acting morally is, but don't expect me to tell you how to do it.'

At the moment, I am not concerned with the sophisms underlying this programme, but with its consequences. The pupils, whether or not they expected a philosophy that should give them, as that of Green's school had given their fathers, ideals to live for and principles to live by, did not get it; and were told that no philosopher (except of course a bogus philosopher) would even try to give it. The inference which any pupil could draw for himself was that for guidance in the problems of life, since one must not seek it from thinkers or from thinking, from ideals or from principles, one must look to people who were not thinkers (but fools), to processes that were not thinking (but passion), to aims that were not ideals (but caprices), and to rules that were not principles (but rules of expediency). If the realists had wanted to train up a generation of Englishmen and Englishwomen expressly as the potential dupes of every adventurer in morals or politics, commerce or religion, who should appeal to their emotions and promise them private gains which he neither could procure them nor even meant to procure them, no better way of doing it could have been discovered.

The result of all this might have been even worse than it has been, but for the fact that the 'realists' discredited themselves with their pupils before their lessons could take effect. This self-stultification was a gradual and piecemeal business. Not only did they jettison the entire body of traditional ethics; as soon as they began work on their new brand of moral theory, whatever doctrine concerning moral action was tested, to show whether it was fit to form part of that theory, was found wanting. Another traditional philosophical science which was thrown bodily overboard was the theory of knowledge; for although 'realism' began by defining itself as a theory of knowledge pure and simple, its votaries before long discovered that a theory of knowledge was a contradiction in terms. Another was political theory; this they destroyed by denying the conception of a 'common good', the fundamental idea of all social life, and insisting that all 'goods' were private. In this process, by which anything that could be recognized as a philosophical doctrine was stuck up and shot to pieces by the 'realistic' criticism, the 'realists' little by little destroyed everything in the way of positive doctrine that they had ever possessed. Once more, I am concerned only with the effect on their pupils. It was (how could it not have been?) to convince them that philosophy was a silly and trifling game, and to give them a lifelong contempt for the subject and a lifelong grudge against the men who had wasted their time by forcing it upon their attention.

That this did actually happen any one could see. The school of Green had taught that philosophy was not a preserve for professional philosophers, but every one's business; and the pupils of this school had gradually formed a block of opinion in the country whose members, though not professional philosophers, were interested in the subject, regarded it as important, and did not feel themselves debarred by their amateur status from expressing their own opinions about it. As these men died, no one took their place; and by about 1920 I found myself asking, 'Why is it that nowadays no Oxford man, unless he is either about 70 years old or else a teacher of philosophy at Oxford or elsewhere, regards philosophy as anything but a futile parlour game?' The answer was not difficult to find, and was confirmed by the fact that the 'realists', unlike the school of Green, did think philosophy a preserve for professional philosophers, and were loud in their contempt of philosophical utterances by historians, natural scientists, theologians, and other amateurs.

The fox was tailless, and knew it. But this mental kind of decaudation, when people part with their morals, their religion, the learning they acquired at school, and so forth, is commonly regarded by the tailless as an improvement in their condition; and so it was with the 'realists'. They were glad to have eradicated from the philosophical schools that confusion of philosophy with pulpit oratory which was involved in the bad old theory that moral philosophy is taught with a view to making the pupils better men. They were proud to have excogitated a philosophy so pure from the sordid taint of utility that they could lay their hands on their hearts and say it was no use at all; a philosophy so scientific that no one whose life was not a life of pure research could appreciate it, and so abstruse that only a whole-time student, and a very clever man at that, could understand it. They were quite resigned to the contempt of fools and amateurs. If anybody differed from them on these points, it could only be because his intellect was weak or his motives bad.

The latter end of the 'realist' movement is one of those things whose history will never be written. It is a story of how the men who best understood the ideas of the original 'realists', and tried hardest to remain loyal to them, found one piece of ground after another slipping from under their feet, and stumbled from one temporary and patchwork philosophy to another in a kind of intellectual nightmare. One of them, Bertrand Russell, a gifted and accomplished writer, has left records of his successive attempts at a philosophy; but most of them are, or were, less articulate, or else struck dumb by their sufferings; and when they and their friends are dead no one will ever know how their lives were spent. What I myself know about it I shall certainly not repeat.

But if the 'realism' of my youth is dead, it has left not only a heritage of general prejudice against philosophy as such, but a partial heir. Its propositional logic, as worked out by Bertrand Russell and A. N. Whitehead, has inspired a school of thought which is continuing the good work of jettisoning whatever can be recognized as positive doctrine by reviving the old positivist attack on metaphysics. After what I have said about propositional logic, I need not pause to explain why I think that this school, with all its ingenuity and pertinacity, is only building card-houses out of a pack of lies. But I do not think that altogether a waste of time. The 'idealistic' logic, to which this school is related as Oxford 'realism' was related to the school of Green, was a confused mixture of truth and error. Mostly it was a propositional logic; but in part it was a logic of question and answer. I would rather its successors had chosen to eradicate the error and develop the truth; but they have decided to do the opposite, and I am not ungrateful. In logic I am a revolutionary; and like other revolutionaries I can thank God for the reactionaries. They clarify the issue.

VII

THE HISTORY OF PHILOSOPHY

So far as my philosophical ideas were concerned, I was now cut off not only from the 'realist' school to which most of my colleagues belonged, but from every other school of thought in England, I might almost say in the world. This did not imply social isolation. I enjoyed, in both senses of that word, the friendship and society of a great many philosophers, in Oxford and at other places in the British Isles and indeed elsewhere. I also enjoyed their philosophical conversation and liked to hear, and engage in, their discussions.

These went on with unfailing regularity. I used to meet a dozen or so of my colleagues every week in order to discuss a topic or a view propounded by one of us, and more ceremoniously a body called the Oxford Philosophical Society met on Sunday evenings two or three times a term for the reading and discussion of a paper. Once a year the thing became a debauch, in the annual joint meeting in some university town of various philosophical societies at which papers and discussions went on for days together. Such gatherings introduced one to people in one's own profession, and they were useful as showing how delightful might be the society of men whose doctrines one disapproved, or how unnecessary it was to waste time over the works of some much advertised person who had only to stand up and speak in order to proclaim himself an impostor. But these discussions serve no philosophical purpose. *Viva voce* philosophy is an excellent thing as between tutor and pupil; it may be valuable as between two intimate friends; it is tolerable as between a few friends who know each other very well; but in all these cases its only value is to make one party acquainted with the views of the other. Where it becomes argument, directed to refutation and conviction, it is useless, for (in my long experience, at least) no one has ever been convinced by it. Where it becomes general discussion it is an outrage. One of the company reads a paper, and the rest discuss it with a fluency directly proportional to their ignorance. To shine on such occasions one should have a rather obtuse, insensitive mind and a ready tongue. Whatever may be true of parrots, philosophers who cannot talk probably think the more, and those who think a lot certainly talk the less.

It was not so very unfortunate, therefore, that when I took part in these weekly arguments the problems had always to be other people's problems and the methods of handling them other people's methods; and that if I tried to raise the problems which I found especially interesting, or to conduct a discussion according to what I thought the right methods, I was met by a greater or less degree of incomprehension, or by the well-known symptoms of an outraged philosophical conscience. For these experiments very soon taught me what it was important for me to learn: that I must do my own work by myself, and not expect my colleagues in the philosophical profession to give me any help.

But this did not mean that I ceased to take part in their discussions. In another chapter I have explained that, according to my own 'logic of question and answer', a philosopher's doctrines are his answers to certain questions he has asked himself, and no one who does not understand what the questions are can hope to understand the doctrines. The same logic committed me to the view that any one can understand any philosopher's doctrines if he can grasp the questions which they are intended to answer. Those questions need not be his own; they may belong to a thought-complex very different from any that is spontaneously going on in his own mind; but this ought not to prevent him from understanding them and judging whether the persons interested in them are answering them rightly or wrongly.

This view makes it a point of honour for any philosopher holding it to take part in the discussion of problems that are not his own problems, and to help in the working-out of philosophies that are not his own philosophy. Hence, when other philosophers discussed problems arising out of distinctions I thought false, or based on principles I thought unsound, I would enter into the discussion in precisely the same spirit in which I would enter into some ancient philosophical controversy, not expecting the disputants to be interested in my problems, but very definitely requiring of myself an interest in theirs.

It was perhaps as well for me that I did not expect

other philosophers to understand me. At that time, any one opposing the 'realists' was automatically classified as an 'idealist', which meant a belated survivor of Green's school. There was no ready-made class into which you could put a philosopher who, after a thorough training in 'realism', had revolted against it and arrived at conclusions of his own quite unlike anything the school of Green had taught. So, in spite of occasional remonstrances, that was how I found myself classified. I became used to it; otherwise I might have been too much annoyed to keep that rule against answering critics which every one must keep who has work of his own to do, when one of the 'realists' (not an Oxford man), reviewing the first book in which I tried to indicate my position, dismissed it in a few lines as 'the usual idealistic nonsense'.

The book was *Speculum Mentis*, published in 1924. It is a bad book in many ways.[1] The position laid

[1] Since writing that sentence, I have read *Speculum Mentis* for the first time since it was published, and find it much better than I remembered. It is a record, not so very obscure in expression, of a good deal of genuine thinking. If much of it now fails to satisfy me, that is because I have gone on thinking since I wrote it, and therefore much of it needs to be supplemented and qualified. There is not a great deal that needs to be retracted.

About answering critics: I have never made, and shall never make, any public answer to any public criticism passed upon my work. I value my time too highly. Now and then I have thought it civil to comment briefly, in a private letter, on criticisms made by letter or on printed criticisms of which the author has sent me a copy. Such comments, of course, are not replies, and in no circumstances should I authorize their publication.

down in it was incompletely thought out and unskilfully expressed; and for most readers concealed, rather than illustrated, by a dense incrustation of miscellaneous detail. I should entirely sympathize with a reviewer who had said he could make neither head nor tail of it, or had described it as nonsense. But any one who had been intelligent enough to see what I was trying to say would have realized, had he not been grossly ignorant, that it was neither 'usual' nor 'idealistic'.

To return. This habit of following and taking part in discussions where both subject and method were other people's proved extremely valuable to me. I found it not only a delightful task, but a magnificent exercise, to follow the work of contemporary philosophers whose views differed widely from my own, to write essays developing their positions and applying them to topics they had not dealt with, to reconstruct their problems in my own mind, and to study, often with the liveliest admiration, the way in which they had tried to solve them. This power of enjoying and admiring the work of other philosophers, no matter how widely their philosophies differed from mine, was not always pleasing to my colleagues. Some of them it perhaps deceived into thinking I had no serious convictions of my own; others it annoyed, as a cowardly refusal to defend whatever convictions I had. 'I wish you'd get off the fence,' said Prichard to me once, in a voice of the liveliest exasperation, at one of our weekly discussions, when two rival theories were being canvassed (I forget what they were) both of which I regarded as based on one and the same mistake. Twenty years' familiarity with his mind had taught me that it was no use trying to explain. If I had begun, he would have broken in, and in five minutes refuted *secundum artem* everything he thought I was going to say.

This way of treating other people's thoughts, though formally deducible from my 'logic of question and answer', had been my habit long before I began working that logic out. To think in that way about philosophies not your own, as I have hinted, is to think about them historically. I dare say I was not more than six or seven when I first saw that the only way to tackle any historical question, such as the tactics of Trafalgar—I mention Trafalgar, because naval history was a childish passion of mine, and Trafalgar my pet battle—was to see what the different people concerned were trying to do. History did not mean knowing what events followed what. It meant getting inside other people's heads, looking at their situation through their eyes, and thinking for yourself whether the way in which they tackled it was the right way. Unless you can see the battle through the eyes of a man brought up in sailing-ships armed with broadsides of short-range muzzle-loading guns, you are not even a beginner in naval history, you are right outside it. If you allow yourself to think for a moment about the tactics of Trafalgar as if the ships were driven by steam and armed with long-range breech-loading guns, you have for that moment allowed yourself to drift outside the region of history altogether.

It was a doctrine of 'realism' (and this is why Prichard was so cross with me) that in this sense of the word history there is no history of philosophy. The 'realists' thought that the problems with which philosophy is concerned were unchanging. They thought that Plato, Aristotle, the Epicureans, the Stoics, the Schoolmen, the Cartesians, &c., had all asked themselves the same set of questions, and had given different answers to them. For example, they thought that the same problems which are discussed in modern ethical theory were discussed in Plato's *Republic* and Aristotle's *Ethics*; and that it was a man's work to ask himself whether Aristotle or Kant was right on the points over which they differ concerning the nature of duty.

In a quite different sense of the word, the 'realists' certainly thought that philosophy has a history. The different answers which various philosophers have given to the eternal questions of philosophy have been given, of course, in a certain order and at various dates; and the 'history' of philosophy is the study by which people ascertain what answers have been given to these questions, in what order, and at what dates. In that sense, the question, 'what was Aristotle's theory of duty?' would be an 'historical' question. And it would be wholly separate from the philosophical question, 'was it true?' Thus the 'history' of philosophy was an inquiry which had nothing to do with the question whether Plato's theory of Ideas (for example) was true or false, but only with the question what it was.

The Oxford tradition insisted upon a fine training in philosophical scholarship, the knowledge of some at least among the classical works of philosophical literature and the ability to interpret them. Under the reign of 'realism' this tradition certainly survived, and was in fact the most valuable part of an Oxford philosophical training; but it weakened almost year by year. Successive boards of examiners in 'Greats' used to complain that the standard of work on Greek philosophy was declining. When I myself examined in the middle 1920's, I found that very few candidates showed any first-hand knowledge of any authors about whom they wrote. What they knew was their notes of the lectures they had attended upon these authors, and the lecturers' criticisms of their philosophies. This decline of interest in philosophical history was openly encouraged by the 'realists'; it was one of their most respected leaders who, expressly on the ground that the 'history' of philosophy was a subject without philosophical interest, procured the abolition of the paper so entitled in the school of Philosophy, Politics, and Economics.

During the War, in the course of my meditations on the Albert Memorial, I set myself to reconsider this 'realist' attitude towards the history of philosophy. Was it really true, I asked myself, that the problems of philosophy were, even in the loosest sense of that word, eternal? Was it really true that different philosophies were different attempts to answer the same questions? I soon discovered that it was not true; it was merely a vulgar error, consequent on a kind of historical myopia which, deceived by superficial resemblances, failed to detect profound differences.

The first point at which I saw a perfectly clear gleam of daylight was in political theory. Take Plato's *Republic* and Hobbes's *Leviathan*, so far as they are concerned with politics. Obviously the political theories they set forth are not the same. But do they represent two different theories of the same thing? Can you say that the *Republic* gives one account of 'the nature of the State' and the *Leviathan* another? No; because Plato's 'State' is the Greek πόλις, and Hobbes's is the absolutist State of the seventeenth century. The 'realist' answer is easy: certainly Plato's State is different from Hobbes's, but they are both States; so the theories are theories of the State. Indeed, what did you mean by calling them both political, if not that they were theories of the same thing?

It was obvious to me that this was only a piece of logical bluff, and that if instead of logic-chopping you got down to brass tacks and called for definitions of the 'State' as Plato conceived it and as Hobbes conceived it, you would find that the differences between them were not superficial but went down to essentials. You can call the two things the same if you insist; but if you do, you must admit that the thing has got *diablement changé en route*, so that the 'nature of the State' in Plato's time was genuinely different from the 'nature of the State' in Hobbes's. I do not mean the empirical nature of the State; I mean the ideal nature of the State. What even the best and wisest of those who are engaged in politics are trying to do has altered.

Plato's *Republic* is an attempt at a theory of one thing; Hobbes's *Leviathan* an attempt at a theory of something else.

There is, of course, a connexion between these two things; but it is not the kind of connexion that the 'realists' thought it was. Anybody would admit that Plato's *Republic* and Hobbes's *Leviathan* are about two things which are in one way the same thing and in another way different. That is not in dispute. What is in dispute is the kind of sameness and the kind of difference. The 'realists' thought that the sameness was the sameness of a 'universal', and the difference the difference between two instances of that universal. But this is not so. The sameness is the sameness of an historical process, and the difference is the difference between one thing which in the course of that process has turned into something else, and the other thing into which it has turned. Plato's πόλις and Hobbes's absolutist State are related by a traceable historical process, whereby one has turned into the other; any one who ignores that process, denies the difference between them, and argues that where Plato's political theory contradicts Hobbes's one of them must be wrong, is saying the thing that is not.

Pursuing this line of inquiry, I soon realized that the history of political theory is not the history of different answers given to one and the same question, but the history of a problem more or less constantly changing, whose solution was changing with it. The 'form of the πόλις' is not, as Plato seems to have thought, the one and only ideal of human society possible to intelligent men. It is not something eternally laid up in heaven and eternally envisaged, as the goal of their efforts, by all good statesmen of whatever age and country. It was the ideal of human society as that ideal was conceived by the Greeks of Plato's own time. By the time of Hobbes, people had changed their minds not only about what was possible in the way of social organization, but about what was desirable. Their ideals were different. And consequently the political philosophers whose business it was to give a reasoned statement of these ideals had a different task before them; one which, if it was to be rightly discharged, must be discharged differently.

The clue, once found, was easily applied elsewhere. It was not difficult to see that, just as the Greek πόλις could not be legitimately translated by the modern word 'State', except with a warning that the two things are in various essential ways different, and a statement of what these differences are; so, in ethics, a Greek word like δεῖ cannot be legitimately translated by using the word 'ought', if that word carries with it the notion of what is sometimes called 'moral obligation'. Was there any Greek word or phrase to express that notion? The 'realists' said there was; but they stultified themselves by adding that the 'theories of moral obligation' expounded by Greek writers differed from modern theories such as Kant's about the same thing. How did they know that the Greek and the Kantian theories were about the same thing? Oh, because δεῖ (or whatever word it was) is the Greek for 'ought'.

It was like having a nightmare about a man who had got it into his head that τριήρης was the Greek for 'steamer', and when it was pointed out to him that descriptions of triremes in Greek writers were at any rate not very good descriptions of steamers, replied triumphantly, 'That is just what I say. These Greek philosophers' (or, 'these modern philosophers', according to which side he was on in the good old controversy between the Ancients and the Moderns) 'were terribly muddle-headed, and their theory of steamers is all wrong'. If you tried to explain that τριήρης does not mean steamer at all but something different, he would reply, 'Then what does it mean?' and in ten minutes he would show you that you didn't know; you couldn't draw a trireme, or make a model of one, or even describe exactly how it worked. And having annihilated you, he would go on for the rest of his life translating τριήρης 'steamer'.

If he had not been quite so clever, he might have known that by a careful sifting and interpretation of the evidence you can arrive at some conclusions, though certainly incomplete ones, about what a trireme was like. And by similar treatment of the evidence you can arrive at some conclusions about the meaning of words like δεῖ. But in both cases you have to approach the matter from an historical point of view, not from that of a minute philosopher; and in the conviction that whatever the Greek word in question means it will not necessarily (indeed, not probably) mean anything that can be rendered by one word, if indeed by any words, in English.

Ideals of personal conduct are just as impermanent as ideals of social organization. Not only that, but what is meant by calling them ideals is subject to the same change. The 'realists' knew that different peoples, and the same peoples at different times, held different views, and were quite entitled to hold different views, about how a man ought to behave; but they thought that the phrase 'ought to behave' had a meaning which was one, unchanging, and eternal. They were wrong. The literature of European moral philosophy, from the Greeks onwards, was in their hands and on their shelves to tell them so; but they evaded the lesson by systematically mistranslating the passages from which they might have learnt it.

In metaphysics the corresponding analysis was easy to one who had been addicted from childhood to the history of science. I could not but see, for example, when Einstein set philosophers talking about relativity, that philosophers' convictions about the eternity of problems or conceptions were as baseless as a young girl's conviction that this year's hats are the only ones that could ever have been worn by a sane woman. One heard them maintaining the 'axiomatic' or 'self-evident' character of doctrines about matter, motion, and so forth which had first been propounded by very adventurous thinkers, at risk of their own liberty and life, three or four hundred years ago, and had become part of every educated European's beliefs only after long and fanatical propaganda in the eighteenth century.

It became clear to me that metaphysics (as its very

name might show, though people still use the word as if it had been 'paraphysics') is no futile attempt at knowing what lies beyond the limits of experience, but is primarily at any given time an attempt to discover what the people of that time believe about the world's general nature; such beliefs being the presuppositions of all their 'physics', that is, their inquiries into its detail. Secondarily, it is the attempt to discover the corresponding presuppositions of other peoples and other times, and to follow the historical process by which one set of presuppositions has turned into another.

The question what presuppositions underlie the 'physics' or natural science of a certain people at a certain time is as purely historical a question as what kind of clothes they wear. And this is the question that metaphysicians have to answer. It is not their business to raise the further question whether, among the various beliefs on this subject that various peoples hold and have held, this one or that one is true. This question, when raised, would always be found, as it always has been found, unanswerable; and if there is anything in my 'logic of question and answer' that is not to be wondered at, for the beliefs whose history the metaphysician has to study are not answers to questions but only presuppositions of questions, and therefore the distinction between what is true and what is false does not apply to them, but only the distinction between what is presupposed and what is not presupposed. A presupposition of one question may be the answer to another question. The beliefs which a metaphysician tries to study and codify are presuppositions of the questions asked by natural scientists, but are not answers to any questions at all. This might be expressed by calling them 'absolute' presuppositions.

But the statements which any competent metaphysician tries to make or refute, substantiate or undermine, are themselves certainly true or false; for they are answers to questions about the history of these presuppositions. This was my answer to the rather threadbare question 'how can metaphysics become a science?' If science means a naturalistic science, the answer is that it had better not try. If science means an organized body of knowledge, the answer is: by becoming what it always has been; that is, frankly claiming its proper status as an historical inquiry in which, on the one hand, the beliefs of a given set of people at a given time concerning the nature of the world are exhibited as a single complex of contemporaneous fact, like, say, the British constitution as it stands to-day; and, on the other hand, the origin of these beliefs is inquired into, and it is found that during a certain space of time they have come into existence by certain changes out of certain others.

By degrees I found that there was no recognized branch of philosophy to which the principle did not apply that its problems, as well as the solutions proposed for them, had their own history. The conception of 'eternal problems' disappeared entirely, except so far as any historical fact could be called eternal because it had happened once for all, and accordingly any problem could be called eternal because it had arisen once for all and once for all been solved.[1] I found (and it required a good deal of hard detailed work in the history of thought) that most of the conceptions round which revolve the controversies of modern philosophy, conceptions designated by words like 'state', 'ought', 'matter', 'cause', had appeared on the horizon of human thought at ascertainable times in the past, often not very distant times, and that the philosophical controversies of other ages had revolved round other conceptions, not indeed unrelated to ours, but not, except by a person quite blind to historical truth, indistinguishable from them.

Having thus with regard to the supposed permanence of philosophical problems found the 'realist' conception of philosophical history false at every point where I could think of testing it, I turned to another aspect of the same conception: namely the 'realists'' distinction between the 'historical' question 'what was So-and-so's theory on such and such a matter?' and the 'philosophical' question 'was he right?'

This distinction was soon condemned as fallacious. I will not here explain, since the reader can easily see it for himself, how it broke down in the light of the

[1] If 'eternal' is used in its vulgar and inaccurate sense, as equivalent to 'lasting for a considerable time', the phrase 'eternal problem' may be used to designate collectively a series of problems connected by a process of historical change, such that their continuity is discernible even by the presumably rather unintelligent eye of the person who thus misuses the word, but the differences between them not so discernible.

question 'how is the so-called philosophical issue to be settled?' and the answer that it could only be settled by what I was simultaneously discovering to be the sophistical methods of 'realist' criticism. I will rather point out that the alleged distinction between the historical question and the philosophical must be false, because it presupposes the permanence of philosophical problems. If there were a permanent problem P, we could ask 'what did Kant, or Leibniz, or Berkeley, think about P?' and if that question could be answered, we could then go on to ask 'was Kant, or Leibniz, or Berkeley, right in what he thought about P?' But what is thought to be a permanent problem P is really a number of transitory problems p_1 p_2 p_3 . . . whose individual peculiarities are blurred by the historical myopia of the person who lumps them together under the one name P. It follows that we cannot fish the problem P out of the hyperuranian lucky-bag, hold it up, and say 'what did So-and-so think about this?' We have to begin, as poor devils of historians begin, from the other end. We have to study documents and interpret them. We have to say 'here is a passage of Leibniz; what is it about? what is the problem with which it deals?' Perhaps we label that problem p_{14}. Then comes the question 'Does Leibniz here deal with p_{14} rightly or wrongly?' The answer to this is not quite so simple as the 'realists' think. If Leibniz when he wrote this passage was so confused in his mind as to make a complete mess of the job of solving his problem, he was bound at the same time to mix up his own tracks so completely that no reader could see quite clearly what his problem had been. For one and the same passage states his solution and serves as evidence of what the problem was. The fact that we can identify his problem is proof that he has solved it; for we only know what the problem was by arguing back from the solution.

If anybody chooses to deny this, I will not try to convince him. Everybody who has learnt to think historically knows it already; and no amount of argument could teach it to a person who had not learnt to think historically. How can we discover what the tactical problem was that Nelson set himself at Trafalgar? Only by studying the tactics he pursued in the battle. We argue back from the solution to the problem. What else could we do? Even if we had the original typescript of the coded orders issued by wireless to his captains a few hours before the battle began, this would not tell us that he had not changed his mind at the last moment, extemporized a new plan on seeing some new factor in the situation, and trusted his captains to understand what he was doing and to back him up. Naval historians think it worth while to argue about Nelson's tactical plan at Trafalgar because he won the battle. It is not worth while arguing about Villeneuve's plan. He did not succeed in carrying it out, and therefore no one will ever know what it was. We can only guess. And guessing is not history.

A teacher who puts into his pupils' hands a philosophical text, and invites them to attend to a certain passage, may therefore say to them, 'This is a confused passage; we can see that the author was thinking about some problem or other, and we may reasonably conjecture that it was a problem somewhat like that discussed in such and such a passage by So-and-so. But he is muddled about the business, and no one can ever tell exactly what it was that worried the poor man.' He may say this; but if he does, his pupils will not greatly cherish his memory in after life. He had no business to waste their time on a passage of that sort.

Or, pointing them to a different passage, he may say, 'here our author, being neither illiterate nor idiotic (which is why I am asking you to study his works), has expressed in such a way that we can understand it a thought that was worth expressing. At first sight you cannot tell what he is trying to say. But if you will think carefully about the passage you will see that he is answering a question which he has taken the trouble to formulate in his mind with great precision. What you are reading is his answer. Now tell me what the question was.'

But he cannot have it both ways. He cannot say 'our author is here trying to answer the following question. . . . That is a question which all philosophers ask themselves sooner or later; the right answer to it, as given by Plato or Kant or Wittgenstein, is. . . . Our author is giving one of the wrong answers. The refutation of his erroneous view is as follows.' His claim to know what question the author is asking is a fraud which any one could expose by asking for his evidence. As a matter of fact, he is not basing his assertion on evidence; he is only trotting out some philosophical question of which the passage vaguely reminds him.

For me, then, there were not two separate sets of questions to be asked, one historical and one philosophical, about a given passage in a given philosophical author. There was one set only, historical. The study of Plato was, in my eyes, of the same kind as the study of Thucydides. The study of Greek philosophy and the study of Greek warfare are both historical studies. But this did not mean that the question 'was Plato right to think as he did on such and such a question?' was to be left unanswered. As well suggest that the question 'was Phormio right to row round the Corinthians' circle?' must be left unanswered because it goes outside the province of naval history, whose only concern with Phormio is to find out what he did. What lunatic idea of history is this, which would imply that it is history that Phormio rowed round the Corinthians, but not that he beat the Corinthians by doing it? Are we haunted by the ghost of Ranke, gibbering something about 'what exactly happened', and has this frightened us into forgetting that victories, as well as tactical manœuvres, are things that happen, or at any rate things that did happen before modern progress abolished them?

These ideas, except such part of them as I had already worked out before returning to Oxford, became clear to me soon afterwards. It would have been quite useless to put them before my colleagues. The 'realists', whose critical technique was flawless and whose mastery of it was perfect, would have demolished them in no time. That would not have made me give them up; for I had already analysed the principles of 'realist' criticism and knew that what it so admirably demolished was not (or not necessarily) the views it ostensibly attacked, but the critic's own perversion of these views; although the 'realist' could never distinguish between the perversion and the reality, because the perversion was simply the reality as seen through his distorting spectacles. If I had stated these ideas to the leaders of the 'realist' school, they would have said, as I have heard them say a hundred times, 'you don't mean that; what you mean is . . .' and then would have followed a caricature of my ideas in terms of 'realist' principles, with sandbags for arms and legs; all so beautifully done that I could hardly have restrained my impulse to cheer.

My job, after all, was not with my colleagues but with my pupils. According to the very ancient Oxford tradition—a tradition far older than Oxford itself—philosophy is taught by reading, expounding, and commenting on philosophical texts. Because the tradition is a living one, these texts are not those of ancient authors alone. The repertory of texts, which is nowhere printed and has no statutory sanction, is constantly changing; though it does not change very fast, and rightly, since no book is ripe for use in this peculiar way until it has become a classic. Yesterday's work of genius may have revolutionized its subject; but, even so, the best way of teaching undergraduates exactly how the subject has been revolutionized is by lecturing on the old classics and showing in your commentary how their doctrine has been modified.

Here was a field of activity which exactly suited me.

My inclinations have always led me rather towards detail than towards generalization; a general principle never comes to life in my mind except by exhibiting itself in its various special forms and in crowds of instances for each form. I did not really feel any great desire to expound the philosophical ideas I have been setting forth in these chapters, whether to my colleagues or to the public. As I have said, I tried to expound them; but when *Truth and Contradiction* was rejected by a publisher and my attack on 'realist' principles ignored by my colleagues, I felt justified in turning to the far more congenial task of applying them and thus testing them empirically. This I could now do, for several hours daily, by teaching my pupils to obey certain rules in their study of philosophical texts.

In an earlier chapter I have stated the first rule which I impressed upon my pupils, 'never accept criticism of any author before satisfying yourself of its relevance'. By now meditation on the Albert Memorial had taught me a second, namely, 'reconstruct the problem'; or, 'never think you understand any statement made by a philosopher until you have decided, with the utmost possible accuracy, what the question is to which he means it for an answer'.

These rules were never formulated in so many words. But they were exemplified by constant practice. From my return to Oxford until my becoming a professor, almost my whole teaching life as a Fellow of Pembroke College was spent in showing pupils how to read a philosophical text. It certainly interested the pupils. An undergraduate who had been merely repelled by ready-made refutations of a doctrine would grow excited when his tutor said, 'Let us see, first, that you really know what the man says, and what the question is that he is trying to answer', and books would be brought out and read and explained, and the rest of the hour would pass in a flash. And for myself it was no less salutary. Over and over again, I would return to a familiar passage whose meaning I thought I knew—had it not been expounded by numerous learned commentators, and were they not more or less agreed about it?—to find that, under this fresh scrutiny, the old interpretation melted away and some quite different meaning began to take form. Thus the history of philosophy, which my 'realist' friends thought a subject without philosophical significance, became for me a source of unfailing, and strictly philosophical, interest and delight; and for my pupils, I dare to hope, neither uninstructive nor unamusing.

But, of course, it was no longer a 'closed' subject. It was no longer a body of facts which a very, very learned man might know, or a very, very big book enumerate, in their completeness. It was an 'open' subject, an inexhaustible fountain of problems, old problems re-opened and new problems formulated that had not been formulated until now. Above all, it was a constant warfare against the dogmas, often positively erroneous, and always vicious in so far as they were dogmatic, of that putrefying corpse of historical thought, the 'information' to be found in text-books.

For in the history of philosophy, as in every other kind, nothing capable of being learnt by heart, nothing capable of being memorized, is history.

And if anybody had objected that in what I call 'open' history one couldn't see the wood for the trees, I should have answered, who wants to? A tree is a thing to look at; but a wood is not a thing to look at, it is a thing to live in.

VIII

THE NEED FOR A PHILOSOPHY OF HISTORY

My life's work hitherto, as seen from my fiftieth year, has been in the main an attempt to bring about a *rapprochement* between philosophy and history. In the preceding chapter I have described one aspect of this *rapprochement*, namely my demand that when philosophers thought about the history of their own subject they should recognize that what they were thinking about was history, and should think about it in ways which did not disgrace the contemporary standards of historical thinking. From the first, however, I saw that more than this was involved. I was also demanding a philosophy of history.

This meant, in the first instance, a special branch of philosophical inquiry devoted to the special problems raised by historical thinking. Epistemological problems, such as one might group together under the question 'how is historical knowledge possible?' Metaphysical problems, concerned with the nature of the historian's subject-matter: the elucidation of terms like event, process, progress, civilization, and so forth. But this demand for a new branch of philosophy soon developed into the demand for a new kind of philosophy. I can best explain what I meant by analogy with the new kind of philosophy which grew up in the seventeenth century.

Soon after the beginning of that century, a number of intelligent people in western Europe began to see in a settled and steady manner what a few here and there had seen by fits and starts for the last hundred years or more: namely that the problems which ever since the time of early Greek philosophy had gone by the collective name of 'physics' were capable of being restated in a shape in which, with the double weapon of experiment and mathematics, one could now solve them. What was called Nature, they saw, had henceforth no secrets from man; only riddles which he had learnt the trick of answering. Or, more accurately, Nature was no longer a Sphinx asking man riddles; it was man that did the asking, and Nature, now, that he put to the torture until she gave him the answer to his questions.

This was an important event in human history. It was important enough to divide the philosophers of the period into two groups: those who understood its importance and those who did not. The first group comprised all those whose names are now generally known to students of philosophy. The second, an immensely greater host of good men, learned men, subtle men, sleep their long night unknown and unlamented, not because they did not find a poet to praise them; few philosophers do; but because they misread the signs of the times. They did not realize that the chief business of seventeenth-century philosophy was to reckon with seventeenth-century natural science; to solve the new problems that the new science had raised, and to envisage the old problems in the new forms which they had assumed, or would assume, when refracted into new shapes through the new scientific atmosphere.

The chief business of twentieth-century philosophy is to reckon with twentieth-century history. Until the late nineteenth and early twentieth centuries, historical studies had been in a condition analogous to that of natural science before Galileo.[1] In Galileo's time something happened to natural science (only a very ignorant or a very learned man would undertake to say briefly what it was) which suddenly and enormously increased the velocity of its progress and the width of its outlook. About the end of the nineteenth century something of the same kind was happening, more gradually and less spectacularly perhaps, but not less certainly, to history.

Until then, the writer of history had been in the last resort, however he might prune and pad, moralize and comment, a scissors-and-paste man. At bottom, his business was to know what 'the authorities' had said about the subject he was interested in, and to his authorities' statements he was tied by the leg, however long the rope and however flowery the turf over which it allowed him to circle. If his interest led him towards a subject on which there were no authori-

[1] Lord Acton in his Cambridge inaugural lecture in 1895 said very truly that historical studies had entered upon a new era in the second quarter of the nineteenth century. It would be an understatement to say that since 1800 history has passed through a Copernican revolution. Looking back from the present day one sees that a much greater revolution has been accomplished than that associated with the name of Copernicus.

ties, it led him into a desert where nothing was except the sands of ignorance and the mirage of imagination.

I will not pretend that my first visit to a modern excavation (it was my father's dig at the north tower of the Roman fort called Hardknot Castle; I was three weeks old, and they took me in a carpenter's bag) opened my eyes to the possibility of something different. But I grew up in a gradually thickening archaeological atmosphere; for my father, who as a professional painter was not very successful, turned more and more as he grew older to archaeology, for which he was brilliantly gifted; and at last, during school holidays, I learnt to distinguish the relics of ancient camps and cultivations from eskers and outcrops, was entrusted with the search for prehistoric remains in unexplored districts and the surveying of them when found, and spent two seasons working as his assistant in his now classical excavation of a Romano-British village.

This and similar experiences taught me that scissors and paste were not the only foundation of historical method. All you wanted, I could see, was a sufficiently extensive and sufficiently scientific development of such work, and it would teach you, not indeed everything, but a great deal, about subjects whose very existence must remain permanently unknown to historians who believed in authorities. I could see, too, that the same methods might be used to correct the authorities themselves, where they had been mistaken or untruthful. In either case, the idea of an historian as depending on what the authorities tell him was exploded.

All this might have been got from books ever since Boucher de Perthes began grubbing in gravel-pits; and long before it entered my head it had been familiar to the readers of newspapers. But I have never found it easy to learn anything from books, let alone newspapers. When I read my friends' articles about their excavations on the middle page of *The Times*, or the beautifully illustrated handbook that tells me how to look after a certain kind of motor, my brain seems to stop working. But give me half an hour on the excavation, with a student to show me what is what, or leave me alone with the motor and a box of tools, and things go better. So these ideas about history, however elementary and commonplace they might be, were at any rate solidly acquired. I had learnt by first-hand experience that history is not an affair of scissors and paste, but is much more like Bacon's notion of science. The historian has to decide exactly what it is that he wants to know; and if there is no authority to tell him, as in fact (one learns in time) there never is, he has to find a piece of land or something that has got the answer hidden in it, and get the answer out by fair means or foul.

That was as far as my philosophy of history had got when I went up to Oxford. There the revolution in historical method which had already attracted my notice was going busily and not silently forward. Sir Arthur Evans, early in the century, had begun to give a brilliant example of the new method by unearthing and reconstructing the long history of Bronze Age Knossos. The official reaction of Oxford was to cut out of Greek history (that is, from Greek history as a subject to be taught and examined in) everything down to the first Olympiad. Next, archaeology began to invade ancient history at the other end of its time-scale. Mommsen had shown how by statistical and other treatment of inscriptions the historian of the Roman Empire could answer questions that no one had dreamed of asking. Dragendorff had classified the shapes of 'Samian' pottery, and he and others had begun to date them. It was a recently established and exciting fact that by excavation you could reconstruct the history of Roman sites not mentioned in any authority and of events in Roman history not mentioned in any book. Owing to the work of Haverfield, whose interest embraced every branch and twig of Roman archaeology, and whose skill and learning as an epigraphist were comparable, we believed, only with those of Mommsen himself, these notions had taken a firm root in Oxford and were completely transforming the study of the Roman Empire.

To the inquiring mind of youth it made a piquant contrast that Greek historical studies, in those days, were still strictly scissors-and-paste. Greek archaeology existed; had we not Percy Gardner? but it only served to adorn the tale told by the authorities, except when some bold revolutionary like D. G. Hogarth hinted that it might here and there fill in a gap. But, according to the orthodox view, the last event that had happened in Greek historical studies had been the discovery of Aristotle's *Constitution of Athens*; and the kind of thing that the undergraduate was supposed to do was to compare the two accounts of the Athenian Revolution given by Thucydides and Aristotle, and decide point by point which was the likelier to be right. And the great lecturer of the day on Greek history, E. M. Walker, was elaborately polite to archaeology in the way which only Pope has described, but lesser men can quite well understand, and weep if Atticus were he.

So Greek history was left high and dry by the tide of new methods; and for many years after this, until what I hope will be long remembered as the archonship of Alan Blakeway, it was notorious that able young men at Oxford, when devoting their lives to ancient history, specialized almost unanimously in the Roman Empire and left Greece to the scissors-and-paste men.

Haverfield himself, least philosophical of historians, cared nothing about the principles or the potentialities of the revolution he was leading. He never even seemed aware that a revolution was going on. He once complained to me that examiners in 'Greats' seemed bent on ignoring his lectures in the papers they set, and that in a general way his colleagues did not share his own attitude to history; but I do not think it occurred to him that there might be a reason for this neglect, or that differences between different historians' attitudes towards history might be worth reflecting upon.

As for the philosophers, their books and lectures

and conversations never once conveyed to me the smallest hint that any of them knew what was happening. They had inherited a tradition, dating back to the early seventeenth century, according to which the methods of natural science received the most painstaking scrutiny. It would have been considered a mark of gross ignorance in any of them not to have known something, indeed more than a mere something, about 'scientific' method, the part played in it by observation and reasoning respectively, the problems of induction, and so forth. Any of them, without special preparation, could have given an entire set of lectures on the problems of 'scientific' method. And when they discussed the theory of knowledge it was plain that, as a rule, they regarded the word 'knowledge' in that phrase as more or less equivalent to knowledge of the world of nature or physical world.

Their total neglect of history, as an example of knowledge, was to my mind all the odder because, whereas hardly any of them had ever been trained in natural science, practically all (I speak of Oxford philosophers) had read 'Greats' and therefore had undergone a course of advanced study in ancient history. Yet, in the whole literature of the 'realist' school at that time, I recollect only one passage which might even be mistaken for a treatment of history: the chapter in Joseph's *Logic* on 'The Historical Method'. When you turn it up, you find that the 'Historical Method' has nothing to do with history, but is a method used in natural science.

To say the very least of it, this gap was a discredit to

English philosophy. My 'realist' friends, when I said this to them, replied that there was no gap at all; that their theory of knowledge was a theory of knowledge, not a theory of this kind of knowledge or that kind of knowledge; that certainly it applied to 'scientific' knowledge, but equally to historical knowledge or any other kind I liked to name; and that it was foolish to think that one kind of knowledge could need a special epistemological study all to itself. I could see that they were mistaken; that in point of fact the thing they called theory of knowledge had been devised with special reference to the methodology of natural science; and that any one who attempted the 'application' of it to history found, if he knew what historical thinking was like, that no such application was possible. But perhaps I saw these things only because I knew where the shoe pinched. My head was already full of problems in historical methodology; so that, reviewing these problems one by one, I could ask myself 'what light do the accepted theories of knowledge throw on this? or on this? or on this?' and answer with certainty, every time, 'none'. It would have been unreasonable to expect a like certainty on the part of any one who had not already thought a great deal about historical method.

Even on the very modest ground that history was a form of intellectual activity on which, however inferior it might be in certainty, dignity, and utility to natural science, philosophy might do well to cast an eye, and that out of the thirty or forty professional philosophers in Oxford there would be no harm if one relegated himself to so obscure a province, it would have seemed worth my while to specialize, as I was perhaps unusually qualified for doing, in the study of historical method. Obscure provinces, like Roman Britain, always rather appeal to me. Their obscurity is a challenge; you have to invent new methods for studying them, and then you will probably find that the cause of their obscurity is some defect in the methods hitherto used. When these defects have been removed, it will be possible to revise the generally accepted opinions about other, more familiar, subjects, and to correct the errors with which those opinions are perhaps infected.

In this sense, knowledge advances by proceeding not 'from the known to the unknown', but from the 'unknown' to the 'known'. Obscure subjects, by forcing us to think harder and more systematically, sharpen our wits and thus enable us to dispel the fog of prejudice and superstition in which our minds are often wrapped when we think about what is familiar to us. The mere fact that historical methodology had been so completely neglected, at any rate in England, encouraged me to hope that by concentrating my attention upon it I might hit upon truths in the theory of knowledge which were concealed from the 'realists' by their obviously conventional and second-hand ideas about the methods of natural science.

For example, the current theories of 'scientific method' all agreed in making 'scientific' knowledge dependent on historical knowledge; though they were stated in such a way as to suggest that the writer hoped the reader would not notice it. No one, when he said that scientific knowledge depended on experiment, meant that a given scientific theory arose in a scientist's mind contemporaneously with the experiment (or rather, experiments) upon which it was based. He meant that a scientist, in framing a theory, made use of certain historical knowledge in his possession as to what experiments had been tried and what their results had been. It was a commonplace, though a concealed one, that all 'scientific' knowledge in this way involves an historical element; and it was clear to me that any philosopher who offered a theory of 'scientific method', without being in a position to offer a theory of historical method, was defrauding his public by supporting his world on an elephant and hoping that nobody would ask what kept the elephant up. It was no mere question of adding a theory of historical method to the already existing theory of 'scientific' method. It was a question of making good a defect in current theories of 'scientific' method by attending to an element in 'scientific' knowledge about which there seemed to be a conspiracy of silence, namely the historical element.

But there was more in my decision than that. In the last thirty or forty years historical thought had been achieving an acceleration in the velocity of its progress and an enlargement in its outlook comparable to those which natural science had achieved about the beginning of the seventeenth century. It seemed to me as nearly certain as anything in the future could be, that historical thought, whose constantly increasing importance had been one of the most striking features of the nineteenth century, would increase in importance far more rapidly during the twentieth; and that we might very well be standing on the threshold of an age in which history would be as important for the world as natural science had been between 1600 and 1900. If that was the case (and the more I thought about it the likelier it seemed) the wise philosopher would concentrate with all his might on the problems of history, at whatever cost, and so do his share in laying the foundations of the future.

IX

THE FOUNDATIONS OF THE FUTURE

I DID not exactly choose to spend the rest of my life on this task. By about 1919 I found that I had no choice but to do so. There was at that time a special reason, not so purely temporary as one might have hoped it to prove, why a man who felt himself able to do work of this kind should have wished to do it; and I will not deny that this reason weighed with me.

A war had just ended in which the destruction of life, the annihilation of property, and the disappointment of hopes for a peaceable and well-ordered international society, had surpassed all previous standards. What was worse, the intensity of the struggle seemed to have undermined, as if by the sheer force of the explosives it consumed, the moral energies of all the combatants; so that (I write as one who during the latter part of the war was employed in preparations for the peace conference) a war of unprecedented ferocity closed in a peace-settlement of unprecedented folly, in which statesmanship, even purely selfish statesmanship, was overwhelmed by the meanest and most idiotic passions. We had been warned some time ago, by Norman Angell, that in modern war there would be no victors in the sense that no party could be enriched by it; but we now learned that in another sense too there were no victors: no party whose morale rose superior to it; no group of statesmen who, by the end of it, had not become a mob of imbeciles, capable only of throwing away all the opportunities their soldiers had won them.

The War was an unprecedented triumph for natural science. Bacon had promised that knowledge would be power, and power it was: power to destroy the bodies and souls of men more rapidly than had ever been done by human agency before. This triumph paved the way to other triumphs: improvements in transport, in sanitation, in surgery, medicine, and psychiatry, in commerce and industry, and, above all, in preparations for the next war.

But in one way the War was an unprecedented disgrace to the human intellect. Whether it was deliberately plotted by a ring of German war-lords, as some believed, or by a ring of English trade-lords, as others believed, nobody has ever supposed that any except at most the tiniest fraction of the combatants wanted it. It happened because a situation got out of hand. As it went on, the situation got more and more out of hand. When the peace treaty was signed, it was more out of hand than ever. Fighting ended because one side was fought to a standstill, not because the situation was under control again.

The contrast between the success of modern European minds in controlling almost any situation in which the elements are physical bodies and the forces physical forces, and their inability to control situations in which the elements are human beings and the forces mental forces, left an indelible mark on the memory of every one who was concerned in it. I knew enough history to understand the force of the contrast. I knew that for sheer ineptitude the Versailles treaty surpassed previous treaties as much as for sheer technical excellence the equipment of twentieth-century armies surpassed those of previous armies. It seemed almost as if man's power to control 'Nature' had been increasing *pari passu* with a decrease in his power to control human affairs. That, I dare say, was an exaggeration. But it was a plain fact that the gigantic increase since about 1600 in his power to control Nature had not been accompanied by a corresponding increase, or anything like it, in his power to control human situations. And it was also a plain fact that the ill effects of any failure to control a human situation were more serious now than they had ever been before, in direct proportion to the magnitude of the new powers put by natural science, with divine indifference, into the hands of the evil and the good, the fool and the wise man. Not only would any failure to control human affairs result in more and more widespread destruction as natural science added triumph to triumph, but the consequences would tend more and more to the destruction of whatever was good and reasonable in the civilized world; for the evil would always begin using the engines of destruction before the good, the fool always before the wise man. I seemed to see the reign of natural science, within no very long time, converting Europe into a wilderness of Yahoos.

There was only one way in which this calamity could be averted; and only one in which, if it should occur, its effects could be repaired. European man's ability to control the forces of Nature was the fruit of three hundred years' investigation along the lines laid down early in the seventeenth century. It was the widening of the scientific outlook and the acceleration of scientific progress in the days of Galileo that had led in the fullness of time from the water-wheels and windmills of the Middle Ages to the almost incredible power and delicacy of the modern machine. In dealing with their fellow men, I could see, men were still what they were in dealing with machines in the Middle Ages. Well-meaning babblers talked about the necessity for a change of heart. But the trouble was obviously in the head. What was needed was not more goodwill and human affection, but more understanding of human affairs and more knowledge of how to handle them.

At this point in my thoughts the natural scientist would make a bid to restore his falling prestige. 'Why, yes,' said he; 'everything you have said is true; what we must have, if civilization is to be saved, is a thorough knowledge of human affairs. And that means a thorough knowledge of the human mind and its various processes, and of the different forms which these processes take in the various types of human beings. Like all genuine knowledge, this must be scientific knowledge; in a word, it must be psychology. Psychology, the science which, young though it is, has already exploded the pretensions and inherited the possessions of the old pseudo-sciences of logic, ethics, political theory, and so forth, is the saviour that the world is seeking.'

If this claim never for a moment deceived me, that is a benefit I owed to my early studies in theology. Like every one else who studied that subject in those days, I read William James's *Varieties of Religious Experience* and a lot of other books in which religion was treated from a psychological point of view. If I was profoundly shocked by the *Varieties*, that was not because some of the facts described in it were such as I would rather not hear about. They were, on the whole, amusing. Nor was it because I thought James was doing his work clumsily. I thought he did it very well. It was because the whole thing was a fraud. The book professed to throw light on a certain subject, and threw on it no light whatever. And that because of the method used. It was not because the book was a bad example of psychology, but because it was a good example of psychology, that it left its subject completely unilluminated. And in *Religion and Philosophy* I attacked, not William James, but any and every psychological treatment of religion, in a passage of which the crucial words are 'the mind, regarded in this way, ceases to be a mind at all'.

This piece of work now stood me in good stead. It was easy to see that any attempt to bring ethics within the field of psychology (and attempts of that kind had been made often enough), or to do the same with politics, would necessarily and always result in failure. As I knew very well, the plea 'do not criticize this science; it is in its infancy', rested on a falsehood. Psychology was very far from being a young science; both word and thing had been in existence ever since the sixteenth century. It was not only an old-established science, it had for centuries been a respectable and even a neighbourly one. It had been deliberately created, as any one might guess who knew enough Greek to understand its name, in order to study that which is neither mind in the proper traditional sense (consciousness, reason, will) nor yet body, but ψυχή, or such functions as sensation and appetite. It marched on the one hand with physiology, and on the other with the sciences of mind proper, logic and ethics, the sciences of reason and will. And it showed no desire to encroach on its neighbours' territories until, early in the nineteenth century, the dogma got about that reason and will were only concretions of sense and appetite. If that was so, it followed that logic and ethics could disappear, and that their functions could be taken over by psychology. For there was no such thing as 'mind'; what had been so called was only 'psyche'.

That is what underlies the modern pretence that psychology can deal with what once were called the problems of logic and ethics, and the modern claim of psychology to be a science of mind. People who make or admit that claim ought to know what it implies. It implies the systematic abolition of all those distinctions which, being valid for reason and will but not for sensation and appetite, constitute the special subject-matter of logic and ethics: distinctions like that between truth and error, knowledge and ignorance, science and sophistry, right and wrong, good and bad, expedient and inexpedient. Distinctions of this kind form the armature of every science; no one can abolish them and remain a scientist; psychology, therefore, regarded as the science of mind, is not a science. It is what 'phrenology' was in the early nineteenth century, and astrology and alchemy in the Middle Ages and the sixteenth century: the fashionable scientific fraud of the age.

These observations implied no hostility towards psychology proper, the science of sensation, appetite, and the emotions connected with them, or towards the Freudian and other forms of treatment for certain ailments, of which we were beginning to hear a good deal, and to which later I devoted a good deal of attention. At the time of which I am speaking Freud was only a name to me. But when I came to study his works I was not unprepared for the discovery that they reached a very high scientific level when dealing with problems in psychotherapy, but sank beneath contempt when they treated of ethics, politics, religion, or social structure. Nor was it strange that Freud's imitators and rivals, less intelligent and less conscientious writers whom I will not name, reached on these subjects an even lower level.

Was it possible that men should come to a better understanding of human affairs by studying history? Was history the thing which in future might play a part in civilized life analogous to that of natural science in the past? Obviously not, if history was only a scissors-and-paste affair. If historians could only repeat, with different arrangements and different styles of decoration, what others had said before them, the age-old hope of using it as a school of political wisdom was as vain as Hegel knew it to be when he made his famous remark that the only thing to be learnt from history is that nobody ever learns anything from history.

But what if history is not a scissors-and-paste affair? What if the historian resembles the natural scientist in asking his own questions, and insisting on an answer? Clearly, that altered the situation. But might he not ask questions whose answers, however interesting, were of no practical use?

The historian is a person whose questions are about the past. He is generally supposed to be a person whose questions are exclusively about the past; about a past, namely, that is dead and gone, and in no sense at all living on into the present. I had not gone very far in my study of historical thought before I realized that this was a delusion. The historian cannot answer questions about the past unless he has evidence about it. His evidence, if he 'has' it, must be something existing here and now in his present world. If there were a past event which had left no trace of any kind in the present world, it would be a past event for which now there was no evidence, and nobody—no historian; I say nothing of other, perhaps more highly gifted, persons—could know anything about it.

In order that a past event should have left in the present world a 'trace' of itself which to the historian is evidence for it, this trace must be something more than any material body, or any state of a material body. Suppose a medieval king granted certain land to a certain monastery, and suppose the charter recording the grant is preserved to this day, a brown piece of parchment covered with certain black marks. The only reason why this parchment can serve to a modern historian as evidence of the grant is because other things, besides the parchment, survive from the medieval world into the world of to-day. To take only one of these things, the knowledge of Latin survives. Other indispensable survivals, of the same general type, will occur to every reader. I will confine myself to the one I have mentioned. If the habit of reading and understanding Latin had not survived among 'clerkly' persons from the Middle Ages to the present day, the parchment could never have told the historian what in fact it does tell him. In general terms, the modern historian can study the Middle Ages, in the way in which he actually does study them, only because they are not dead. By that I mean not that their writings and so forth are still in existence as material objects, but that their ways of thinking are still in existence as ways in which people still think. The survival need not be continuous. Such things may have died and been raised from the dead, like the ancient languages of Mesopotamia and Egypt.

By about 1920 this was my first principle of a philosophy of history: that the past which an historian studies is not a dead past, but a past which in some sense is still living in the present. At the time, I expressed this by saying that history is concerned not with 'events' but with 'processes'; that 'processes' are things which do not begin and end but turn into one another; and that if a process P_1 turns into a process P_2, there is no dividing line at which P_1 stops and P_2 begins; P_1 never stops, it goes on in the changed form P_2, and P_2 never begins, it has previously been going on in the earlier form P_1. There are in history no beginnings and no endings. History books begin and end, but the events they describe do not.

If P_1 has left traces of itself in P_2 so that an historian living in P_2 can discover by the interpretation of evidence that what is now P_2 was once P_1, it follows that the 'traces' of P_1 in the present are not, so to speak, the corpse of a dead P_1 but rather the real P_1 itself, living and active though incapsulated within the other form of itself P_2. And P_2 is not opaque, it is transparent, so that P_1 shines through it and their colours combine into one. Therefore, if the symbol P_1 stands for a characteristic of a certain historical period and the symbol P_2 for the corresponding but different (and therefore contradictory or incompatible) characteristic of its successor, that successor is never characterized by P_2 pure and simple, but always by a P_2 tinged with a survival of P_1. This is why people who try to depict the characteristic features of this or that historical period go wrong if they do their work too thoroughly, forgetting that the silk of their period is in reality always a shot silk, combining in itself contradictory colours.

The idea of a living past, together with a good many others connected with it, I had completely worked out by 1920; and in that year I wrote them down in an essay of short book-length, very sparing of words and making point after point without any attempt at elaboration or explanation. It was primarily a study of the nature and implications of process or becoming. Secondarily, it was an attack on 'realism', showing how the *non possumus* of 'realists' towards a theory of history arose from their refusal to admit the reality of becoming, and from their analysis of the true proposition 'P_1 becomes P_2' into the complex of propositions 'P_1 is P_1', 'P_1 is not P_2', 'P_1 ends where P_2 begins', 'P_2 is P_2', and 'P_2 is not P_1', all of them either tautologous or false. This book, written in three days, was intended only to help the process of crystallization in my own thoughts; it would have been quite unintelligible to the general public, and I never contemplated printing it. Nobody has seen it except my friend Guido de Ruggiero, for whom I typed a copy, thinking that it might amuse him as an historian of philosophy.[1] By way of a private joke, I called it *Libellus de Generatione*, and prefixed to it a motto: 'For as the old hermit of Prague, that never saw pen and ink, very wittily said to a niece of king Gorboduc, That, that is, is: for what is that, but that? and is, but is?'

How, I asked, did these conceptions affect the question whether history could be a school of moral and political wisdom? The old pragmatic idea of history was futile because its idea of history was the scissors-and-paste idea in which the past is a dead past, and knowing about it means only knowing what the authorities say about it. And that knowledge is useless as a

[1] The original manuscript, like the only manuscript of *Truth and Contradiction*, was destroyed after I wrote this book.

guide to action; because, since history never exactly repeats itself, the problem before me now is never sufficiently like the problem described by my authorities to justify me in repeating the solution which then succeeded, or avoiding that which then failed. So long as the past and present are outside one another, knowledge of the past is not of much use in the problems of the present. But suppose the past lives on in the present; suppose, though incapsulated in it, and at first sight hidden beneath the present's contradictory and more prominent features, it is still alive and active; then the historian may very well be related to the non-historian as the trained woodsman is to the ignorant traveller. 'Nothing here but trees and grass', thinks the traveller, and marches on. 'Look,' says the woodsman, 'there is a tiger in that grass.' The historian's business is to reveal the less obvious features hidden from a careless eye in the present situation. What history can bring to moral and political life is a trained eye for the situation in which one has to act.

This may seem a small gift. Surely, some one will say, we are entitled to ask for more than that. There is not much use in showing us the tiger unless you also give us a rifle with which to shoot him. The historian will not do very much to help us in our moral and political difficulties if he only makes us see the features of the situation and does not also provide us with rules for acting in situations of that kind.

There were two things, it seemed to me, which needed to be said in answer to that. The first can be said quite shortly, but I thought it did not wholly cover the ground; for a complete answer, the second had to be said as well, and that could only be said at greater length. I will say them both.

The first is this. You want a rifle? Then go where rifles are to be had. Go to the gunsmith's. But do not expect the gunsmith to sell you a rifle which can see tigers as well as shoot them. For that, you must learn woodcraft.

In other words: if ready-made rules for dealing with situations of specific types are what you want, natural science is the kind of thing which can provide them. The reason why the civilization of 1600–1900, based upon natural science, found bankruptcy staring it in the face was because, in its passion for ready-made rules, it had neglected to develop that kind of insight which alone could tell it what rules to apply, not in a situation of a specific type, but in the situation in which it actually found itself. It was precisely because history offered us something altogether different from rules, namely insight, that it could afford us the help we needed in diagnosing our moral and political problems.

The second is this. If you are sure that the thing you are going to see in the grass is going to be a tiger, and if your only idea about tigers is that they are things to shoot, take a rifle with you. But are you sure? What if it turns out to be your own child playing Indians?

In other words: there are situations which, for one reason or another, can be handled without appeal to any ready-made rules at all, so long as you have insight into them. All you need in such cases is to see what the situation is, and you can then extemporize a way of dealing with it which will prove satisfactory. This second type of case, I thought, was of great importance in moral and political life, and I will explain as best I can, though I cannot do so very briefly, what I was thinking about it.

When I speak of action, I shall be referring to that kind of action in which the agent does what he does not because he is in a certain situation, but because he knows or believes himself to be in a certain situation. I shall not be referring to any kind of action which arises as a mere response to stimuli which the situation may contain, or as the mere effect of the agent's nature or disposition or temporary state. And when I speak of action according to rule, I shall be referring to that kind of action in which the agent, knowing or believing that there is a certain rule, applicable to the situation in which he knows or believes himself to be, decides to act in accordance with it. I shall not be referring to any kind of action in which the agent, though actually obeying a rule, is unaware that he is doing so.

In a great part of our actions we act according to rules, and that is what makes our action successful. This is because we are moving among situations of certain standard types, and trying to manipulate them so as to obtain certain standard results. Action according to rule is a very important kind of action, and the first question which any intelligent man asks, when he finds himself in a situation of any kind, is 'What are the rules for acting in this kind of situation?'

But although action according to rules is a very important kind of action, it is not the only kind. There are two kinds of occasions on which another kind is necessary. Before describing them, I will try to show that it exists.

Suppose you find yourself in a situation of a given type S; and suppose you want to obtain a result of a given type R, and there is a rule that in a situation of type S the way to get a result of a type R is to do an action of type A. You may know this rule, but how do you know it? Either because of your own experience or because of some one else's. In either case a certain body of experience has been accumulated before the rule could be known to any one. This experience must have been experience of acting in situations of the type S by persons who wanted to obtain results of the type R but did not know the rule. And their endeavours to obtain results of type R must often have been successful; otherwise the experience which led to the formulation of the rule could never have accumulated. There must, therefore, be a kind of action which is not determined according to rule, and where the process is directly from knowledge of the situation to an action appropriate to that situation, without passing through the stage of formulating a rule appropriate to the situation. And it must be very common, for a vast deal of it must go to the formulation of even the most trivial rule of conduct.

(1) The first kind of occasion on which it is necessary to act without rules is when you find yourself in a situation that you do not recognize as belonging to

any of your known types. No rule can tell you how to act. But you cannot refrain from acting. No one is ever free to act or not to act, at his own discretion. *Il faut parier*, as Pascal said. You must do something. Here are you, up against this situation: you must improvise as best you can a method of handling it.

(2) The second kind of occasion on which you must act without rules is when you can refer the situation to a known type, but are not content to do so. You know a rule for dealing with situations of this kind, but you are not content with applying it, because you know that action according to rules always involves a certain misfit between yourself and your situation. If you act according to rules, you are not dealing with the situation in which you stand, you are only dealing with a certain type of situation under which you class it. The type is, admittedly, a useful handle with which to grasp the situation; but all the same, it comes between you and the situation it enables you to grasp. Often enough, that does not matter; but sometimes it matters very much.

Thus everybody has certain rules according to which he acts in dealing with his tailor. These rules are, we will grant, soundly based on genuine experience; and by acting on them a man will deal fairly with his tailor and helps his tailor to deal fairly by him. But so far as he acts according to these rules, he is dealing with his tailor only in his capacity as a tailor, not as John Robinson, aged sixty, with a weak heart and a consumptive daughter, a passion for gardening and an overdraft at the bank. The rules for dealing with tailors no doubt enable you to cope with the tailor in John Robinson, but they prevent you from getting to grips with whatever else there may be in him. Of course, if you know that he has a weak heart, you will manage your dealings with him by modifying the rules for tailor-situations in the light of the rules for situations involving people with weak hearts. But at this rate the modifications soon become so complicated that the rules are no longer of any practical use to you. You have got beyond the stage at which rules can guide action, and you go back to improvising, as best you can, a method of handling the situation in which you find yourself.

Of these two cases in which it is necessary to act otherwise than according to rule, the first arises out of the agent's inexperience and ignorance of life. It is commonest, therefore, in the young, and in all of us when, owing to travel or some other disturbance of our regular routine, we find ourselves in unfamiliar surroundings. The second arises only for people of experience and intelligence, and even then occurs only when they take a situation very seriously; so seriously as to reject not only the claims of that almost undisguised tempter Desire, and that thinly disguised one Self-Interest, but (a tempter whose disguise is so good that most people hardly ever penetrate it at all and, if they do, suffer the sincerest remorse afterwards) Right Conduct, or action according to the recognized rules.

From this point of view I could see that any one who asked for rules, in order to obtain from them instruction how to act, was clinging to the low-grade morality of custom and precept. He was trying to see only those elements in the situation which he already knew how to deal with, and was shutting his eyes to anything which might convince him that his ready-made rules were not an adequate guide to the conduct of life.

Rules of conduct kept action at a low potential, because they involved a certain blindness to the realities of the situation. If action was to be raised to a higher potential, the agent must open his eyes wider and see more clearly the situation in which he was acting. If the function of history was to inform people about the past, where the past was understood as a dead past, it could do very little towards helping them to act; but if its function was to inform them about the present, in so far as the past, its ostensible subject-matter, was incapsulated in the present and constituted a part of it not at once obvious to the untrained eye, then history stood in the closest possible relation to practical life. Scissors-and-paste history, with its ideal of obtaining from authorities ready-made information about a dead past, obviously could not teach man to control human situations as natural science had taught him to control the forces of Nature; nor could any such distilled essence of scissors-and-paste history as had been proposed by Auguste Comte under the name of sociology; but there seemed to be some chance that the new kind of history might prove able to do so.

X

HISTORY AS THE SELF-KNOWLEDGE OF MIND

THIS chance became a probability as soon as my conception of history had advanced another step forward. This step was taken, or rather registered, in 1928, when I spent a vacation at Le Martouret, that pleasant country-house near Die, sitting under the plane-trees on the terrace and writing down as shortly as I could the lessons of my last nine years' work in historical research and reflection upon it. It is difficult to believe that so obvious a point was reached so slowly; but the evidence of my manuscripts is clear; and I know that I have always been a slow and painful thinker, in whom thought in its formative stages will not be hurried by effort, nor clarified by argument, that most dangerous enemy to immature thoughts, but grows obscurely through a long and oppressive period of gestation, and only after birth can be licked by its parent into presentable shape.

It was in my Die manuscript that I first drew the distinction between history proper and what I called pseudo-history. By that name I referred to such things as the narratives of geology, palaeontology, astronomy, and other natural sciences which in the late eighteenth and the nineteenth centuries had assumed a semblance at least of historicity. Reflection on my experience as an archaeologist enabled me to see that this was no more than a semblance. Archaeologists had often called attention to the likeness between their own stratigraphical methods and those of geology, and a likeness there certainly was; but there was a difference as well.

If an archaeologist finds a stratum of earth and stones and mortar, mixed with potsherds and coins, on the top of which is a layer of level flags, supporting more earth with potsherds and coins of a rather different type, it is easy to say that he uses these two sets of potsherds and coins exactly as a geologist uses fossils, to show that the strata belong to different periods and to date them by correlating them with strata found elsewhere and containing relics of the same type.

Easy, but untrue. For the archaeologist, these things are not stone and clay and metal, they are building-stone and potsherds and coins; debris of a building, fragments of domestic utensils, and means of exchange, all belonging to a bygone age whose purposes they reveal to him. He can use them as historical evidence only so far as he understands what each one of them was for. If in the case of one object he does not understand that, he has, as an archaeologist, no use for the object; he would throw it away, but that he hopes some one more learned or more resourceful than himself may solve the riddle. It is not only the minutiae, like pins and buttons, that he regards as expressions of purpose; he thinks of the whole building, the whole settlement, in the same way.

Before the nineteenth century, a natural scientist might have replied that the same was true of his own studies: was not every task in natural science a contribution to the decipherment of the purposes of that mighty being whom some called Nature and others God? The nineteenth-century scientist would answer quite firmly that it was not. And the nineteenth-century scientist is right as to the facts. Natural science as it exists to-day, and has existed for the best part of a century, does not include the idea of purpose among its working categories. Perhaps he is right in his theology too. I cannot think it pious to make our study of Nature depend on the assumption that the purposes of God are within our grasp; and if a palaeontologist told me that he never bothered to ask what trilobites were for, I should be glad, for the sake of his immortal soul as well as the progress of his science. If archaeology and palaeontology worked according to the same principles, trilobites would be as valueless to that palaeontologist as are to the archaeologist those 'iron implements of uncertain use' which cause him so much embarrassment.

History and pseudo-history alike consisted of narratives: but in history these were narratives of purposive activity, and the evidence for them consisted of relics they had left behind (books or potsherds, the principle was the same) which became evidence precisely to the extent to which the historian conceived them in terms of purpose, that is, understood what they were for; in pseudo-history there is no conception of purpose, there are only relics of various kinds, differing among themselves in such ways that they have to be interpreted as relics of different pasts which can be arranged on a time-scale.

I expressed this new conception of history in the phrase: 'all history is the history of thought.' You are thinking historically, I meant, when you say about anything, 'I see what the person who made this (wrote this, used this, designed this, &c.) was thinking.' Until you can say that, you may be trying to think historically but you are not succeeding. And there is nothing else except thought that can be the object of historical knowledge. Political history is the history of political thought: not 'political theory', but the thought which occupies the mind of a man engaged in political work: the formation of a policy, the planning of means to execute it, the attempt to carry it into effect, the discovery that others are hostile to it, the devising of ways to overcome their hostility, and so forth. Consider how the historian describes a famous speech. He does not concern himself with any sensuous elements in it such as the pitch of the statesman's voice, the hardness of the benches, the deafness of the old gentleman in the third row: he concentrates his attention on what the man was trying to say (the thought, that is, expressed in his words) and how his audience received it (the thoughts in their minds, and how these conditioned the impact upon them of the statesman's thought). Military history, again, is not a description of weary marches in heat or cold, or the thrills and chills of battle or the long agony of wounded men. It is a description of plans and counter-plans: of thinking about strategy and thinking about tactics, and in the last resort of what the men in the ranks thought about the battle.

On what conditions was it possible to know the history of a thought? First, the thought must be expressed: either in what we call language, or in one of the many other forms of expressive activity. Historical painters seem to regard an outstretched arm and a pointing hand as the characteristic gesture expressing the thought of a commanding officer. Running away expresses the thought that all hope of victory is gone. Secondly, the historian must be able to think over again for himself the thought whose expression he is trying to interpret. If for any reason he is such a kind of man that he cannot do this, he had better leave that problem alone. The important point here is that the historian of a certain thought must think for himself that very same thought, not another like it. If some one, hereinafter called the mathematician, has written that twice two is four, and if some one else, hereinafter called the historian, wants to know what he was thinking when he made those marks on paper, the historian will never be able to answer this question unless he is mathematician enough to think exactly what the mathematician thought, and expressed by writing that twice two are four. When he interprets the marks on paper, and says, 'by these marks the mathematician meant that twice two are four', he is thinking simultaneously: (*a*) that twice two are four, (*b*) that the mathematician thought this, too; and (*c*) that he expressed this thought by making these marks on paper. I will not offer to help a reader who replies, 'ah, you are making it easy for yourself by taking an example where history really is the history of thought; you couldn't explain the history of a battle or a political campaign in that way.' I could, and so could you, Reader, if you tried.

This gave me a second proposition: 'historical knowledge is the re-enactment in the historian's mind of the thought whose history he is studying.'

When I understand what Nelson meant by saying, 'in honour I won them, in honour I will die with them', what I am doing is to think myself into the position of being all covered with decorations and exposed at short range to the musketeers in the enemy's tops, and being advised to make myself a less conspicuous target. I ask myself the question, shall I change my coat? and reply in those words. Understanding the words means thinking for myself what Nelson thought when he spoke them: that this is not a time to take off my ornaments of honour for the sake of saving my life. Unless I were capable—perhaps only transiently—of thinking that for myself, Nelson's words would remain meaningless to me; I could only weave a net of verbiage round them like a psychologist, and talk about masochism and guilt-sense, or introversion and extraversion, or some such foolery.

But this re-enactment of Nelson's thought is a re-enactment with a difference. Nelson's thought, as Nelson thought it and as I re-think it, is certainly one and the same thought; and yet in some way there is not one thought, there are two different thoughts. What was the difference? No question in my study of historical method ever gave me so much trouble; and the answer was not complete until some years later.

The difference is one of context. To Nelson, that thought was a present thought; to me, it is a past thought living in the present but (as I have elsewhere put it) incapsulated, not free. What is an incapsulated thought? It is a thought which, though perfectly alive, forms no part of the question–answer complex which constitutes what people call the 'real' life, the superficial or obvious present, of the mind in question. For myself, or for that which at first sight I regard as myself, the question 'shall I take off my decorations?' does not arise. The questions that arise are, for example, 'shall I go on reading this book?' and later, 'what did the *Victory*'s deck look like to a person thinking about his chances of surviving the battle?' and later again, 'what should I have done if I had been in Nelson's place?' No question that arises in this primary series, the series constituting my 'real' life, ever requires the answer 'in honour I won them, in honour I will die with them'. But a question arising in that primary series may act as a switch into another dimension. I plunge beneath the surface of my mind, and there live a life in which I not merely think about Nelson but am Nelson, and thus in thinking about Nelson think about myself. But this secondary life is prevented from overflowing into my primary life by being what I call incapsulated, that is, existing in a context of primary or surface knowledge which keeps it in its place and prevents it from thus overflowing. Such knowledge, I mean, as that Trafalgar happened ninety years ago: I am a little boy in a jersey: this is my father's study carpet, not the

Atlantic, and that the study fender, not the coast of Spain.

So I reached my third proposition: 'Historical knowledge is the re-enactment of a past thought incapsulated in a context of present thoughts which, by contradicting it, confine it to a plane different from theirs.'

How is one to know which of these planes is 'real' life, and which mere 'history'? By watching the way in which historical problems arise. Every historical problem ultimately arises out of 'real' life. The scissors-and-paste men think differently: they think that first of all people get into the habit of reading books, and then the books put questions into their heads. But I am not talking about scissors-and-paste history. In the kind of history that I am thinking of, the kind I have been practising all my life, historical problems arise out of practical problems. We study history in order to see more clearly into the situation in which we are called upon to act. Hence the plane on which, ultimately, all problems arise is the plane of 'real' life: that to which they are referred for their solution is history.

If what the historian knows is past thoughts, and if he knows them by re-thinking them himself, it follows that the knowledge he achieves by historical inquiry is not knowledge of his situation as opposed to knowledge of himself, it is a knowledge of his situation which is at the same time knowledge of himself. In re-thinking what somebody else thought, he thinks it himself. In knowing that somebody else thought it, he knows that he himself is able to think it. And finding out what he is able to do is finding out what kind of a man he is. If he is able to understand, by rethinking them, the thoughts of a great many different kinds of people, it follows that he must be a great many kinds of man. He must be, in fact, a microcosm of all the history he can know. Thus his own self-knowledge is at the same time his knowledge of the world of human affairs.

This train of thought was not complete until about 1930. By completing it, I completed my answer to the question that had haunted me ever since the War. How could we construct a science of human affairs, so to call it, from which men could learn to deal with human situations as skilfully as natural science had taught them to deal with situations in the world of Nature? The answer was now clear and certain. The science of human affairs was history. This was a discovery which could not have been made before the late nineteenth century, for it was not until then that history began to undergo a Baconian revolution, to emerge from the chrysalis of its scissors-and-paste stage, and thus to become, in the proper sense of that word, a science. It was because history was still in the chrysalis stage in the eighteenth century, that eighteenth-century thinkers, when they saw the need for a science of human affairs, could not identify it with history but tried to realize it in the shape of a 'science of human nature'; which, as men like Hume conceived it, with its strictly empirical methods, was in effect an historical study of the contemporary European mind, falsified by the assumption that human minds had everywhere and at all times worked like those of eighteenth-century Europeans. The nineteenth century, likewise in search of a science of human affairs, tried to realize it in the shape of a 'psychology' in which the mental was reduced to the psychical, the distinction between truth and falsehood thrown overboard, and the very idea of a science negated, psychology itself being involved in the resulting bankruptcy. But the revolution in historical method which had superseded scissors-and-paste history by what I called history proper had swept away these sham sciences and had brought into existence a genuine, actual, visibly and rapidly progressing form of knowledge which now for the first time was putting man in a position to obey the oracular precept 'know thyself', and to reap the benefits that only such obedience could confer.

The ideas very briefly summarized in this chapter and the two preceding it were being worked out for nearly twenty years after I became a teacher of philosophy. They were repeatedly written down, corrected, and rewritten; for whenever I have had a cub to lick into shape, my pen is the only tongue I have found useful. None of these writings has ever been intended for publication,[1] although much of their

[1] Points out of them might have been published piecemeal in short articles, and now and then I did print such articles; but the only place for them was in philosophical periodicals, where they were rendered useless by the fixed determination of the persons who read such periodicals not to think about history. When I was elected to the British Academy in 1934, and was invited to contribute to their *Proceedings*, I found a more open-minded audience,

substance has been repeatedly given in lecture form; but I am publishing this short summary because the main problems are now solved, and publishing them in full is only a question of time and health.

Thinking them out was laborious, because of the method used. Every detail arose out of reflection on actual historical research, in which I had therefore to be incessantly engaged, and was tested over and over again by fresh pieces of research devised to that end. By about 1930 my health was beginning to suffer from long-continued overwork. Whether luckily or unluckily, I have never known any illness interfere with my power of thinking and writing, or with the quality of what I think and write. When I am unwell, I have only to begin work on some piece of philosophical writing, and all my ailments are forgotten until I leave off. But this does not cure them. If they are due to overwork, it may aggravate them.

They were further aggravated by my growing inability to resist involvement in various departments of University business. In this way I slaked my passion for administrative work, until I discovered that this, too, was only another arc of the vicious circle.

By this time I had in my head a great deal which I believed the public would value; and the only way of giving it to the public was by writing books. On this, therefore, I decided to spend my leisure; and planned a series, to begin with an *Essay on Philosophical Method*.

and wrote them a paper on 'Human Nature and Human History' (*Proc. Brit. Acad.*, xxii) in which some of the ideas referred to in this chapter are discussed.

This I wrote during a long illness in 1932. It is my best book in matter; in style, I may call it my only book, for it is the only one I ever had the time to finish as well as I knew how, instead of leaving it in a more or less rough state. After settling accounts with my archaeological studies in a way to be described in the next chapter, I wrote in 1937 the second book of my series, *The Principles of Art*.[1] Before it had gone through the press I was overtaken by the more serious illness which gave me both the leisure and the motive to write this autobiography; whose purpose is to put on record some brief account of the work I have not yet been able to publish, in case I am not able to publish it in full.

Henceforth I shall spend all my available time in going on with the series. I am nearly fifty, and cannot in any case hope for more than a few years in which I can do my best work. I take this opportunity, therefore, of saying that I will not be drawn into discussion of what I write. Some readers may wish to convince me that it is all nonsense. I know how they would do it; I could invent their criticisms for myself. Some may wish to show me that on this or that detail I am wrong. Perhaps I am; if they are in a position to prove it, let them write not about me but about the subject, showing that they can write about it better than I can; and I will read them gladly. And if there are any who

[1] I say nothing about the motives which led me to work at the philosophy of art, the process of training by which I qualified myself for that work, or the way in which my thoughts about it progressed during long years. A reader can find out all he needs to know on these subjects from *The Principles of Art* itself.

think my work good, let them show their approval of it by attention to their own. So, perhaps, I may escape otherwise than by death the last humiliation of an aged scholar, when his juniors conspire to print a volume of essays and offer it to him as a sign that they now consider him senile.

XI

ROMAN BRITAIN

It was necessary for the advancement of my philosophical work that I should be constantly engaged not only in philosophical studies but in historical studies as well; and in a field where I could initiate lines of research in which I could hope for the co-operation of others; a field, therefore, in which I was an acknowledged master. The field had, accordingly, to be a small one, and ripe for intensive cultivation. For this purpose Roman Britain was very suitable. Moreover, I was already committed. Haverfield, the great master of the subject, died in 1919; most of his pupils had already fallen in the War; I was left the only man resident in Oxford whom he had trained as a Romano-British specialist; and even if my philosophy had not demanded it, I should have thought myself, in piety to him, under an obligation to keep alive the Oxford school of Romano-British studies that he had founded, to pass on the training he had given me, and to make use of the specialist library he had left to the University. It was this obligation that made me refuse all offers of professorships and other employments elsewhere which I received during the years that followed the War.

My first book dealing with the subject as a whole was written in 1921, at the invitation of the Delegates of the Clarendon Press. It was a short book; I wrote it in two days; it was designed to be elementary, and it was full of faults. However, it served to lay down once for all my general attitude towards the problems, and, even more important, my general conception (partly due to Haverfield, but partly different from his) of what the problems were; it gave me a first opportunity of finding out, more clearly than was possible within the limits of a short article, how my conception of historical research was developing; and by its sale it proved the liveliness of the welcome which the public was prepared to give to that idea. Ten years later I rewrote it in an enlarged edition, and had to revise that again in 1934. In the same year I wrote the British section in Professor Tenney Frank's *Economic Survey of Ancient Rome*, and in 1935 the sections of the *Oxford History of England* on prehistoric and Roman Britain, J. N. L. Myres writing a section on the English settlements, and these together making up the first volume.

The invitations to write these two large-scale works came at exactly the right moment. I had been long enough in my laboratory; I wanted to exchange it for my study. It was time to begin arranging and publishing the lessons which all this archaeological and historical work had taught me about the philosophy of history. But I could not desert Roman Britain without saying good-bye; and a full-length book about it would not only do that, it would serve to display in a concrete form the principles of historical thinking as I now understood them.

Most of these principles were, more or less unconsciously, common ground among historians; but not all of them were generally accepted; or perhaps it would be truer to say that comparatively few were consciously recognized, and of those by no means all were generally regarded as principles by which the historian ought to stand firm through thick and thin.

For example, long practice in excavation had taught me that one condition—indeed the most important condition—of success was that the person responsible for any piece of digging, however small and however large, should know exactly why he was doing it. He must first of all decide what he wants to find out, and then decide what kind of digging will show it to him. This was the central principle of my 'logic of question and answer' as applied to archaeology. In the beginnings of archaeology digging had been done blindly, that is, without any definite question to which an answer was being sought. A landowner with intellectual interests had dug an ancient site because it was on his land; and he dug it with no problem in his head, only the vague formula 'Let us see what objects of interest we can find here for my collection', or, when the curiosity-hunger of the eighteenth-century antiquary had given way to the knowledge-hunger of his nineteenth-century successor, 'Let us see what we can find out about this site'; which is no more a 'question', as I understand that term, than are such pseudo-questions as 'What is knowledge?' 'What is duty?' 'What is the *summum bonum*?' 'What is art?' Like them, it is only a vague portmanteau-phrase covering a multitude of possible questions but not precisely expressing any of them.

In our own days, when the enlightened landowner with money to spare is an almost extinct species, excavation is organized by local societies, directed by expert archaeologists, and paid for by public subscription. Although things have changed in all these respects, they have not changed in the one that is important. Most of our digging is still 'blind' digging. The public (including persons of all grades of wealth, from rich bankers and industrialists downward) cares little or nothing for historical knowledge. If you want a lever to extract money from the public for an excavation, you must not tell them that it will yield a solution for important historical problems. Natural scientists can say that kind of thing, because after three centuries of propaganda they have battered a way for it into the public's skull. But archaeologists have to use as their lever that nostalgic self-loathing which is so characteristic of our times. 'Here is a romantic ancient site', they must say, 'which is about to be covered with revolting bungalows, hideous by-pass roads, and so forth. Give us your guineas, so that we can find whatever is to be found there before our chance is gone for ever.' Thus, instead of being chosen for excavation because it contains the solution of a burning problem, a site is excavated for non-scientific reasons, exactly as in the old days.

Other sites are excavated because the local antiquaries have long wanted to dig them but have been prevented by refusal of leave on the part of their owners. Then arises an owner who gives his consent; and the local antiquaries snatch at their opportunity, and go to the public for subscriptions while the going is good. Others, again, because they lie not in a rich man's park but in a strong antiquarian society's district; while others, in the district of a society which is either weaker or less interested in things of that special kind, lie untouched.

If historical studies were to pass through a Baconian revolution—the revolution which converts a blind and random study into one where definite questions are asked and definite answers insisted upon—the first thing to be done was to preach that revolution among the historians themselves. When I began to study Roman Britain the revolution had made a little progress, but not much. Haverfield and his colleagues of the Cumberland Excavation Committee in the eighteen-nineties had been consciously and completely Baconian in their methods. They never dug a trench without knowing exactly what information they were looking for; they knew both that this information was the next thing they needed for the progress of their study, and also that this trench would give it them. That is why they could settle highly intricate and abstruse problems at a cost of never more, and often much less, than thirty or forty pounds a year. And their successors in the north adopted and continued to apply their principles.

But in the south, when I began to frequent the rooms of the Society of Antiquaries, I found a very different state of things. Excavation was still being done according to the principles laid down by General Pitt-Rivers in the last quarter of the nineteenth century. Pitt-Rivers was a very great archaeologist and a supreme master in the technique of excavation; but as regards the problems to be solved by excavation he was for the most part (not quite consistently) in the pre-Baconian stage. He dug in order to see what he could find out. He had not applied to archaeology the famous advice of Lord Acton, 'study problems, not periods'. Among his successors, as I found, archaeology meant studying not problems but sites. The idea of excavation was to choose a site: to uncover it systematically, one piece each year, pouring thousands of pounds into the work, until it was all dug; and then go on to another. The result was that, although museums were choked with the finds, amazingly little (as it now appears) was discovered about the history of the site. The Society of Antiquaries had excavated Silchester in this style for twenty years running; and although long before the end of that time the principles of stratigraphical digging were familiar even to the general public, and the dating of strata on Roman sites by coins and pottery was a well-established practice, the Silchester excavations fixed the date neither of the town's beginning nor of its end, nor of the walls nor of the street-plan, nor of a single house or public building, nor even of any alteration carried out to a house or public building. The analysis of the bath-building into work of several different periods remains a model of its kind, except for the fact that not one of these periods was dated; so that the whole analysis is historically useless. Phases in the occupation of this or that house which can now be dated, on the evidence of parallels elsewhere, to the fourth century or even the third, were ascribed by pure guess-work to 'wandering herdsmen' of the Dark Ages.

Things have changed since then. and I will not say that they have changed because of my efforts. But I will say that, for nearer twenty years than ten, I have been preaching to my archaeological friends the duty of never digging either a five-thousand-pound site or a five-shilling trench without being certain that you can satisfy an inquirer who asks you 'What are you doing this piece of work for?' And I will say that, at first, this idea was much ridiculed by the pundits, though one or two adventurous spirits, like R. E. M. Wheeler, welcomed it from the start; that by degrees ridicule and opposition died away; and that in 1930 the Congress of Archaeological Societies, through its Research Committee, drew up a report covering every department of archaeological field-work in Britain and offering archaeologists all over the country advice as to what the problems were, in each period, upon which the experts assembled in the committee thought it desirable to concentrate. The principle of question and answer had been officially adopted by British archaeology. Since then, the London Institute of Archaeology has come into existence; and I hope that if I told the students there how that principle was received, when I began to state it at Burlington House in the twenties, they would think me not only an old bore but an old liar into the bargain.

About the future of this principle among scholars

I am, accordingly, not anxious. When the scholars have got it firmly into their heads, the public will follow suit; and when they do, we may perhaps hope that they will in time compel the Government officials responsible for looking after our ancient monuments to treat them not as objects of sentimental pilgrimage but as potential sources of historical knowledge.

But we must not allow our hopes to run very high. We are no longer living in the nineteenth century, when public opinion could influence the activities of Government officials through the medium of Parliament. Every man who is engaged in scientific work of any kind knows that it is a fundamental obligation of scientific morality to publish your results. When the work is archaeological excavation the duty is a peculiarly urgent one, because a site once thoroughly excavated is a site from which no future archaeologist will ever be able to find out anything. All archaeologists know this, and all except the official archaeologists of the British Government act accordingly. But British Government archaeologists are constantly excavating sites all over the country, at the taxpayer's expense, without publishing any reports at all. They know that they are committing the fundamental crime against their own science; because when other archaeologists speak to them about it they have their excuse ready. The Treasury will not allow them money for publication.

A second principle was that, since history proper is the history of thought, there are no mere 'events' in history: what is miscalled an 'event' is really an action, and expresses some thought (intention, purpose) of its agent; the historian's business is therefore to identify this thought.[1]

For the archaeologist this means that all objects must be interpreted in terms of purposes. Whenever you find any object you must ask, 'What was it for?' and, arising out of that question, 'Was it good or bad for it? i.e. was the purpose embodied in it successfully embodied in it, or unsuccessfully?' These questions, being historical questions, must be answered not by guesswork but on historical evidence; any one who answers them must be able to show that his answer is the answer which the evidence demands.

This was the tritest of commonplaces. But the attempt to put it consistently into practice led to some interesting results. For example, the many archaeologists who had worked at the Roman Wall between Tyne and Solway had never, I found, seriously asked themselves what it was for. Vaguely, you could of course call it a frontier defence, and say that it was to keep out the tribes beyond it. But that will no more satisfy the historian than it will satisfy an engineer if you tell him that a marine engine is to drive a ship. How did it work? Was it meant to work, for example,

[1] Some 'events' of interest to the historian are not actions but the opposite, for which we have no English word: not *actiones* but *passiones*, instances of being acted upon. Thus the eruption of Vesuvius in A.D. 79 is to the historian a *passio* on the part of the people affected by it. It becomes an 'historical event' in so far as people were not merely affected by it, but reacted to this affection by actions of various kinds. The historian of the eruption is in reality the historian of these actions.

like a town-wall, from the top of which defenders repelled attacks? Several obvious features about it made it quite impossible that any Roman soldier should ever have meant to use it in that way. No one seemed to have noticed this before; but when I pointed it out in 1921[1] every one who was interested in the subject admitted that it was so, and my counter-suggestion that the wall was meant for an 'elevated sentry-walk' was generally accepted.

A question answered causes another question to arise. If the Wall was a sentry-walk, elevated from the ground and provided (no doubt) with a parapet to protect the sentries against sniping, the same sentry-walk must have continued down the Cumberland coast, beyond Bowness-on-Solway, in order to keep watch on vessels moving in the estuary; for it would have been very easy for raiders to sail across and land at any unguarded point between Bowness and St. Bee's Head. But here the sentry-walk need not be elevated, for sniping was not to be feared. There ought, therefore, to be a chain of towers, not connected by a wall but otherwise resembling those on the Wall, stretching down that coast. The question was, did such towers exist?

Search in old archaeological publications showed that towers of exactly the right kind had been found; but their existence had been forgotten, as generally happens with things whose purpose is not understood. Search on the ground in 1928 revealed a number of

[1] 'The Purpose of the Roman Wall', in *The Vasculum*, vol. viii, no. 1 (Newcastle-upon-Tyne), pp. 4–9.

other places where it seemed possible that others might yet be revealed by future excavation.[1]

Sometimes the attempt to work on this principle led me into trouble. I thought I could understand the strategical purpose of the Tyne–Solway Roman Wall easily enough. As completed by the chain of signal-stations on the Cumberland coast, it would have been very difficult to turn at either end; and if in addition to sentries on the look-out for enemy concentrations beyond it there were compact striking-forces in its attached forts, ready to march out and break them up, it would make a very efficient line of frontier defence. But when I asked my Scottish colleagues (or myself for that matter) the same question about the Forth–Clyde Wall, I got no answer. Sir George Macdonald, the acknowledged king of Scottish archaeologists, published the splendid second edition of his *Roman Wall in Scotland* in 1934; but my question is not asked there, nor even answered by implication. In the *Oxford History of England* I tried at least to state it and to point out some of the conditions for any possible solution. I even suggested a solution of my own. It was not well received by my friends over the Border. Whether they were right to reject it I do not know. But I do know that I was right to ask the question, and that it has got to be answered.

The principle applies not merely to archaeology, but to every kind of history. Where written sources are used, it implies that any action attributed by the

[1] 'Roman Signal-stations on the Cumberland Coast', in *Cumb. and West. Antiq. Soc. Trans.* xxix (1929), 138–65.

sources to any character must be understood in the same way. Julius Caesar, we are told, invaded Britain in two successive years. What did he do it for? The question is hardly ever asked by historians; and I can remember none who has tried to answer it scientifically, that is, by means of evidence. There is, of course, no evidence to speak of except that contained in Julius Caesar's own narrative. There he never says what he meant to effect by his invasions of Britain. It is the fact of his silence that constitutes our chief evidence as to what his intention was. Whatever he meant to bring about, his intention was one which he decided to conceal from his readers. In the light of a general acquaintance with the *Commentaries*, the likeliest explanation for this concealment was that whatever his purpose had been he had failed to achieve it. I then compared the strength of his expeditionary force with that of the army sent over by Claudius, nearly a century later, and this settled it. Caesar must have intended no mere punitive expedition or demonstration of force, like that of his German expedition in 55, but the complete conquest of the country. Once more, this view of mine may be mistaken; but future historians will have to reckon with the question I have raised, and either accept my answer or produce a better one.

People who do not understand historical thinking, but are obsessed by scissors and paste, will say: 'It is useless to raise the question, because if your only information comes from Caesar, and Caesar has not told you his plans, you cannot ever know what they were.' These are the people who, if they met you one Saturday afternoon with a fishing-rod, creel, and camp-stool, walking towards the river, would ask: 'Going fishing?' And I suppose that if they were serving on a jury when some one was tried for attempted murder because he had put arsenic in his wife's tea on Monday, and cyanide of potassium in her coffee on Tuesday, and on Wednesday broke her spectacles with a revolver-bullet, and knocked a piece out of her right ear with another on Thursday, and now pleaded not guilty, they would press for his acquittal because as he never admitted that he meant to murder her there could be no evidence that he did mean to.

A third principle was that no historical problem should be studied without studying what I called its second-order history; that is, the history of historical thought about it. This, too, was a pretty obvious remark. No undergraduate would write his tutor an essay on the battle of Marathon without first finding out what other people had said about it. If he did this preliminary work well, the result would be a history of research on Marathon. It would recount the different 'theories' that had been put forward, and would show how one of them had been abandoned owing to the 'difficulties' it entailed, and how another had arisen out of the attempt to remove those difficulties. By degrees second-order history, or the history of history, seemed more and more important to me; finally it took definitive shape as the conception into which I resolved that of 'historical criticism' in all its forms. Just as philosophical criticism resolved itself into the history of philosophy, so historical criticism resolved itself into the history of history.

In describing these researches into historical method, I am taking most of my examples from archaeology (that is, history in which the sources used are 'unwritten' sources, or, more accurately, are not pre-existing narratives of the events into which the historian is inquiring). But this is not because my results did not equally apply to history whose sources are 'written'. The reason I am talking so much about archaeology is that in archaeology the issue raised by the project of a Baconian revolution is unmistakable. When history is based on literary sources the difference between scissors-and-paste or pre-Baconian history, where the historian merely repeats what his 'authorities' tell him, and scientific or Baconian history, where he forces his 'authorities' to answer the questions he puts to them, is not always quite clear. It becomes clear enough on occasion; for example, when he tries to get out of his authorities' the answer to a question which they did not expect a reader to ask (as when we try to get out of an ancient writer answers to economic and demographic questions), or when he tries to get out of them facts which they wished to conceal. On other occasions it sometimes does not leap to the eye. In archaeology, however, it is obvious. Unless the archaeologist is content merely to describe what he or some one else has found, which it is almost impossible to do without using some interpretative terms implying purpose, like 'wall', 'pottery', 'implement', 'hearth', he is practising Baconian history all the time: asking about everything he handles, 'What was this for?' and trying to see how it fitted into the context of a peculiar kind of life.

For this reason archaeology has provided a wonderfully sensitive method for answering questions to which not only do literary sources give no direct answer, but which cannot be answered even by the most ingenious interpretation of them. The modern historian wants to ask all kinds of questions which are at bottom statistical questions. Was the population of a certain country at a certain time dense or rare? Was it increasing or diminishing? What did the people look like, or rather what different physical types were there among them, and which type predominated? What did they trade in, and with whom, and to what extent? Could they read and write, and how much? For Graeco-Roman antiquity, or even for the Middle Ages, no attempt to answer these questions on the basis of contemporary literary sources is of the smallest value. They are statistical questions, and the sources out of which you would be trying to answer them were written by men who were not statistically minded. For a writer under the Roman Empire the statement 'the population is diminishing' is not a statement about population statistics, it is a statement about some way in which he feels, like the statement so often made by writers of letters to the newspapers: 'We do not have such fine summers as we did when I was young.' Imagine a future meteorologist trying to compile an account of climatic changes from these letters, in the absence of meteorological statistics, and you will see the uselessness of the traditional demographic studies in ancient history.

If you want to answer statistical questions you must have statistical evidence. And that is something the archaeologist can provide when his work has attained a certain volume. In England, where Roman archaeology has gone forward incessantly in most parts of the country ever since the seventeenth century, there is a gigantic bulk of material from which many questions of this kind can be answered, if not conclusively, at least within a reasonable margin of error. In 1929, when thanks to the bold initiative and unwearying toil of O. G. S. Crawford—to whom future generations can never sufficiently realize their indebtedness—this material was plotted on the Ordnance Map of Roman Britain, it occurred to me[1] that it could be treated statistically and, when thus treated, used as a basis for an estimate of the total population of Roman Britain. I put it at half a million. There was a deluge of comment and criticism, partly in print, partly in letters. The only critics who gave me any reason to take them seriously urged that my figure was too low. I am now convinced that it was, and would advance it to a million. None of my critics demanded more than a million and a half. If the discrepancy between these figures appears large, let me remind the reader that three different historians, working from literary sources, have estimated the population of Roman Gaul at three million, six million, and thirty million respectively.

[1] 'Town and Country in Roman Britain', *Antiquity*, iii. 261–76.

In the same paper I tried to answer another statistical question, or group of questions, of a more complicated kind. What proportion of the inhabitants of Roman Britain were town-dwellers and country-dwellers respectively? And how did these proportions vary at different times during the period of Roman rule? This implied (1) a statistical survey of all the known Romano-British towns, directed to ascertaining their total population; and (2) an historical survey of the same, directed to ascertaining how that population increased or decreased at different times. Silchester was, and still is, the only such town whose entire surface has been covered by excavation, but it gave me no data for (2), and even its data for (1) were discounted by a certain difference of opinion as to whether the excavators had or had not found numerous dwellings not marked on any of their plans. My only reliable data were therefore derived from later diggings at Caerwent and Wroxeter. In both cases evidence had been found, though its full bearing had not been previously understood, that the development of the town had reached a peak early in its history, followed by a very long period of stagnation and progressive depopulation and decay. I argued that what was true of these towns might possibly prove true of the rest, and that in any case an economic historian would expect some such history, because the population implied by the size and character of these towns at their greatest extent was so disproportionate to the entire population of the country that their prosperity must have been unstable, and their origin due to a somewhat short-sighted policy of urbanization carried through in a doctrinaire spirit by the central government. Questions of this kind about Roman Britain had never been asked before, and some people apparently thought it would have been better if they had not been asked then. But subsequent excavation on Romano-British towns has justified my questions and on all essential points has confirmed my answers.

I will quote one other illustration of the way in which my principles of historical methodology led me to an entirely new treatment of archaeological material.

Haverfield had shown, as everybody now knew, that there had been a 'Romanization' of Britain: that a civilization of Celtic type had been replaced by one of the 'cosmopolitan' pattern to be found, with local differences but not very important ones, in any province of the Roman Empire. In the matter of arts and crafts, for example, Celtic fashions had been followed with a high degree of artistic talent before the Roman conquest. After the conquest, these were shortly replaced by Roman provincial fashions. There was also, Haverfield pointed out, a 'Celtic Revival' towards the end of the period and after it. This, too, was by now a matter of common knowledge.

This was puzzling. If a kind of cultural steam-roller had flattened the Celtic taste out of the Britons, and they had learnt to adopt the taste of the Roman Empire, why should they go Celtic again three centuries later? And indeed how could they? When once a tradition has died, how can it come to life again, except through the rise of archaizing fashions, which in this case we may safely rule out? If by (say) 1920 English peasants had stopped singing modal folk-songs, and had taken instead to hearing dance-music on the wireless; and if no one had written their songs down and preserved them in libraries; would it not be very odd to find their descendants beginning to sing modal folk-songs again round about the year 2200?

In 1935, when I was writing my part of the *Oxford History of England*, the problem had lately become a fashionable one, and many first-class archaeologists had tried to solve it. Their attempts fell into three classes.

First, there were those who regarded the case as a perfectly normal one of survival. The tradition of Celtic design, they suggested, had never been broken. True, we lacked evidence for this. There were, indeed, objects dating between A.D. 150 and 300 which bore patterns in the Celtic manner, but they were very few and could not be taken to prove the continued existence of a school of Celtic decoration. But all these were of metal. Celtic designs might very well have survived in common use among textile-workers and wood-carvers, and been reintroduced from them into the trades whose products have come into our hands and made us talk of a Celtic revival.

This attempt was sound, in so far as it was based on the sound principle that revival implies survival. But it ended in failure, because the evidence of survival was not forthcoming, and no historian is entitled to draw cheques in his own favour on evidence that he does not possess, however lively his hopes that it may hereafter be discovered. He must argue from the evidence he has, or stop arguing.

Secondly, there were those who pointed out that not all the Celts were subjected to the Roman steam-roller. Why should not the traditions of Celtic art have survived in unconquered Caledonia, and thence have re-entered Roman Britain with Pictish invaders when the frontier defence broke down? Once more, a very reasonable suggestion, but for the lack of evidence. The districts in which we have evidence for a Celtic revival are those farthest away from the frontier, and Pictland offers no models or originals out of which that revival might have grown.

Thirdly, there were those who argued that Celtic art was a product of the 'Celtic temperament', and that the Celtic temperament blossomed into artistic expression only under conditions of a certain kind. These conditions had existed at the beginning of the Roman period and again at its end; but not in between. It only remained to say what the conditions were. This argument I valued for its intriguing suggestion that the survival of a certain style in art does not necessarily depend on the survival of certain patterns in workshop practice; but its dependence on an occult entity like the 'Celtic temperament' forbade me to take it seriously. With entities of that kind we have left behind us the daylight, and even the twilight, of history, and have entered a darkness peopled by all the monsters of *Rassentheorie* and Jungian psychology. In that darkness what we find is not history but the negation of history; not the solution of historical problems, but only a heady drink which gives us the illusion of having solved them.

The unsolved problem, focusing as it did the whole problem of Romanization (what exactly does Romanization mean? What was it that really happened to people when they became what is called Romanized?) focused also for me the whole problem of art-history and indeed of what the Germans call history of culture. There seemed to be no hope of solving it unless you had first of all settled certain questions of principle. And when I turned my thoughts towards the planning of my chapter on 'Art' in the Oxford History, I deliberately set aside the particular problem until I had cleared up my mind about the principles involved.

If you want to know why a certain kind of thing happened in a certain kind of case, you must begin by asking, 'What did you expect?' You must consider what the normal development is in cases of that kind. Only then, if the thing that happened in this case was exceptional, should you try to explain it by appeal to exceptional conditions.

Now, it seemed to me possible that the difficulty in this case was an illusory difficulty, due to the fact that the nature of historical process was misconceived. As I had long ago proved in the *Libellus de Generatione*, any process involving an historical change from P_1 to P_2 leaves an unconverted residue of P_1 incapsulated within an historical state of things which superficially is altogether P_2. This, I thought, might prove the key to my problem.

Incapsulation is not an 'occult entity'. It was my name for such facts as this—familiar enough to everybody—that a man who changes his habits, thoughts, &c., retains in the second phase some residue of the first. He gives up smoking, but his desire to smoke does not thereupon disappear. In his subsequent life the desire is what I call incapsulated. It survives, and it produces results; but these results are not what they were before he gave up smoking. They do not consist in smoking. The desire survives in the form of an unsatisfied desire. If, after a time, he is again found to be smoking, that need not prove that he never left off; it may very well be because he never lost the desire, and when the reasons against satisfying the desire disappeared he began once more to satisfy it.

Without any implications as to racial temperament or a 'racial unconscious' the same kind of thing may happen in a society. If the members of a certain society have been in the habit of acting or thinking in certain ways, and if at a certain time they try to stop acting and thinking in those ways, and do their best to act and think in different ways, the desire to go on acting and thinking in the old way will probably persist. It will certainly persist, and persist in a lively form, if they were accustomed to think and act in those ways very effectively and found great satisfaction in doing so. The tendency to revert to the old ways would in that case be strong.

Now you might think that, unless some occult entity like a racial temperament or an inheritance of acquired psychical characteristics were at work, this tendency would not survive into the second generation. You might think that, even though the original converts never entirely got rid of the old Adam, their children would start fair. You might think that although the fathers had eaten a good many wild oats in their time, the children's teeth would not be set on edge. They would imbibe the new ways of thinking and acting with their mothers' milk, and feel no temptation to think or act otherwise.

Well, you would be wrong. Suppose a very warlike people, at a certain crisis in its history, turned completely peaceful. In the first generation, warlike impulses would survive; but let us suppose them sternly repressed, so that everybody behaved in an entirely peaceful manner. When the people of this generation set to work on the moral education of their children, the children would be carefully told that they must on no account indulge in the forbidden pleasures of war. 'But what is war, Daddy?' Then Daddy gives a description of war, emphasizing its wrongness, but (doubtless altogether against his will) making it very plain to his innocent offspring that war was a grand thing while it lasted and that he would love to fight his neighbours again if only he did not know that he ought not. The children are quick to understand all that. They not only learn what war is, or was, but they learn also that it is, or was, a grand thing, though of course wrong; and they carefully pass all this on to their own children when the time comes. Thus the transmission by educational means of any moral ideal which involves the outlawry of an institution or custom, and the repression of a desire for it, entails the simultaneous transmission of that desire itself. The children of each generation are taught to want what they are taught they must not have.

In time, the tradition which keeps alive the memory of the forbidden thing, and keeps alive at the same time the desire for it, may die out. Its disappearance will be greatly accelerated if the new way of thinking and acting proves to be one in which the converts find themselves successful and satisfied. In that case the 'folk-memory' (nothing occult; nothing inborn; simply the transmission by example and precept of certain ways of thinking and acting from generation to generation) of a success and satisfaction now no longer permitted will tend to fade away. Where you find the new ways of thinking and acting never displayed with more than a low degree of success, you may take it as certain that the discarded ways are remembered with regret, and that the tradition of their glories is being tenaciously kept alive.

So much for generalities. There are some who will say, 'You are talking psychology, and you ought to ask a psychologist whether what you are saying is true or not.' But I am not talking psychology, and shall not ask help from its exponents; for I regard the kind of psychology that deals with this kind of question as a sham science. I am talking history.

Applying this to the case in point, I found it possible to assert a connexion between two facts, both of them notorious, which had not previously been thought of as connected. One was the Celtic revival; the other was the badness of Romanizing British art. The badness of Romanizing British art, as I say, was notorious; but my own study of it had the unforeseen effect of removing from it the only really valuable asset with which it had been credited. Its recognized masterpiece was the famous Bath Gorgon, which scholars had tried, quite in vain, to connect with prototypes in 'classical' art. I was able to prove that the inspiration of this fine work was not 'classical' but Celtic; and at the same time I suggested that it was probably the work not of a British sculptor but of a Gaul.

The general position I have already laid down implies that the less successful the Britons were in Romanizing art, granted always their very conspicuous earlier success in art of the Celtic type, and granted also the sharp opposition between the symbolic and no doubt magical character of Celtic design and the naturalistic and merely amusing character of the 'Woolworth art' of the Roman empire, the more they were likely to cherish the memory of their own fashions and ensure that these fashions were never wholly lost to sight by the rising generation.

This was the idea which I expressed in the chapter on 'Art' in the *Oxford History of England*; a chapter which I would gladly leave as the sole memorial of my Romano-British studies, and the best example I can give to posterity of how to solve a much-debated problem in history, not by discovering fresh evidence, but by reconsidering questions of principle. It may thus serve to illustrate what I have called the *rapprochement* between philosophy and history, as seen from the point of view of history.

These books summed up the results of innumerable studies, many of which were reported in greater detail in about a hundred articles and pamphlets mostly written between 1920 and 1930. But the main bulk of my work on Roman Britain went into the Corpus of Inscriptions. Haverfield, almost immediately before his death, had decided to publish a new collection of all the Roman inscriptions (excluding those brought from abroad in modern times) in Britain; and thinking it desirable that each should be illustrated with a facsimile drawing—for he had no illusions about the value of photographic illustrations in a work of this kind—he asked me to serve as draughtsman. After his death I decided to go on with the work, and from 1920 onwards I spent much time every year travelling about the country and drawing Roman inscriptions.

The detailed knowledge of the subject which I acquired, and the practice in deciphering inscriptions, many of them extremely difficult to read, were invaluable to me. But the inscriptions themselves were not of very great service to my Romano-British studies. The use of epigraphic material is a magnificent exercise for an historian just beginning to shake himself free from the scissors-and-paste mentality, which is why it developed in so wonderful a manner in the late nineteenth century; but the epigraphic historian as such can never be wholly Baconian in spirit. Regarded as documents, inscriptions tell you less, under critical scrutiny, than literary texts; regarded as relics, they tell you less than archaeological material proper. And on the questions which I particularly wanted to ask, it happened that inscriptions threw hardly any light. I felt, therefore, that by my work on Romano-British inscriptions I was rather building a monument to the past, to the great spirits of Mommsen and Haverfield, than forging a weapon for the future.

XII

THEORY AND PRACTICE

IN addition to the *rapprochement* between philosophy and history, whose earlier stages I have already tried to describe, I was also working at a *rapprochement* between theory and practice. My first efforts in this direction were attempts to obey what I felt as a call to resist the moral corruption propagated by the 'realist' dogma that moral philosophy does no more than study in a purely theoretical spirit a subject-matter which it leaves wholly unaffected by that investigation.

The opposite of this dogma seemed to me not only a truth, but a truth which, for the sake of his integrity and efficacy as a moral agent in the wider sense of that term, ought to be familiar to every human being: namely, that in his capacity as a moral, political, or economic agent he lives not in a world of 'hard facts' to which 'thoughts' make no difference, but in a world of 'thoughts'; that if you change the moral, political, and economic 'theories' generally accepted by the society in which he lives, you change the character of his world; and that if you change his own 'theories' you change his relation to that world; so that in either case you change the ways in which he acts.

The 'realist' attempt to deny this could, no doubt, be defended with some plausibility, so long as a clean cut could be made between philosophical and historical thinking. It could be admitted that the way in which a man acts, in so far as he is a moral, political, economic agent, is not independent of the way in which he thinks of the situation in which he finds himself. If knowledge as to the facts of one's situation is called historical knowledge, historical knowledge is necessary to action. But it could still be argued that philosophical thinking, which has to do with timeless 'universals', is not necessary.

Arguments of this kind were no longer even worth refuting, once I knew that 'realism' was completely astray as to the nature of history, and that consequently any 'realist' argument based on the distinction between history and philosophy, or 'facts' and 'theories', or 'the individual' (which some 'realists' miscalled 'the particular') and 'the universal', must be regarded as suspect. Immediately after the War, therefore, I began to reconsider in detail all the familiar topics and problems of moral philosophy, including under that head the theory of economics and that of politics, as well as that of morals in the narrower sense, on the principles which by now were controlling all my work.

In the first place, I subjected these topics and problems to what I called an historical treatment, insisting that every one of them had its history and was unintelligible without some knowledge of that history. Secondly, I attempted to treat them in another way, which I called analytic. My notion was that one and the same action, which as action pure and simple was a 'moral' action, was also a 'political' action as action relative to a rule, and at the same time an 'economic' action as means to an end. The problems of moral theory, in the broader sense of the word moral, could thus be divided into (*a*) problems of moral theory in the narrower sense, that is, problems concerned with action as such; (*b*) problems of political theory, that is, problems concerned with action as the making, obeying, or breaking of rules; and (*c*) problems of economic theory, or problems concerned with action as the procuring or non-procuring of ends beyond itself.

There were, I held, no merely moral actions, no merely political actions, and no merely economic actions. Every action was moral, political, and economic. But although actions were not to be divided into three separate classes—the moral, the political, and the economic—these three characteristics, their morality, their politicality, and their economicity, must be distinguished and not confused as they are, for example, by utilitarianism, which offers an account of economicity when professing to offer one of morality.

These were the lines on which I treated the subject in my lectures of 1919. I continued to lecture upon it yearly during almost the whole remainder of my life at Pembroke College, with constant revision. The scheme I have just described obviously represents a stage in my thought at which the *rapprochement* between history and philosophy was very incomplete. Any reader who has understood the earlier chapters of this book can see for himself how I modified it as time went on.

The *rapprochement* between theory and practice was equally incomplete. I no longer thought of them as mutually independent: I saw that the relation between them was one of intimate and mutual dependence, thought depending upon what the thinker learned by experience in action, action depending upon how he thought of himself and the world; I knew very well, too, that scientific, historical, or philosophical thinking depended quite as much on 'moral' qualities as on 'intellectual' ones, and that 'moral' difficulties were to be overcome not by 'moral' force alone but by clear thinking.

But this was only a theoretical *rapprochement* of theory and practice, not a practical one. I still conducted my daily life as if I thought that the business of that life was theoretical and not practical. I did not see that my attempted reconstruction of moral philosophy would remain incomplete so long as my habits were based on the vulgar division of men into thinkers and men of action.

This division, like so much that nowadays we take for granted, was a survival from the Middle Ages. I lived and worked in a University; and a University is an institution based on medieval ideas, whose life and work are still hedged about by the medieval interpretation of the Greek distinction between the contemplative life and the practical life as a division between two classes of specialists.

I can now see that I had three different attitudes towards this survival. There was a first R. G. C. who knew in his philosophy that the division was false, and that 'theory' and 'practice', being mutually dependent, must both alike suffer frustration if segregated into the specialized functions of different classes.

There was a second R. G. C. who in the habits of his daily life behaved as if it had been sound; living as a professional thinker whose college gate symbolized his aloofness from the affairs of practical life. My philosophy and my habits were thus in conflict; I lived as if I disbelieved my own philosophy, and philosophized as if I had not been the professional thinker that in fact I was. My wife used to tell me so; and I used to be a good deal annoyed.

But underneath this conflict there was a third R. G. C., for whom the gown of the professional thinker was a disguise alternately comical and disgusting in its inappropriateness. This third R. G. C. was a man of action, or rather he was something in which the difference between thinker and man of action disappeared. He never left me alone for very long. He turned over in his sleep, and the fabric of my habitual life began to crack. He dreamed, and his dreams crystallized into my philosophy. When he would not lie quiet and let me play at being a don, I would appease him by throwing off my academic associations and going back to my own part of the country to address the local antiquarian society. It may seem an odd form of 'release' for a suppressed man of action; but it was a very effective one. The enthusiasm for historical studies, and for myself as their leader in those studies, which I never failed to arouse in my audiences, was not in principle different from the enthusiasm for his person and his policy which is aroused by a successful political speaker. And sometimes this third R. G. C. woke right up; for example, on a day soon after the beginning of August 1914, when a crowd of Northumberland coal-miners, full of patriotic fervour, saw what they imagined to be a German spy on 'the old Roman camp' up the hill, and took appropriate action.

The third R. G. C. used to stand up and cheer, in a sleepy voice, whenever I began reading Marx. I was never at all convinced either by Marx's metaphysics or by his economics; but the man was a fighter, and a grand one; and no mere fighter, but a fighting philosopher. His philosophy might be unconvincing; but to whom was it unconvincing? Any philosophy, I knew, would be not only unconvincing but nonsensical to a person who misunderstood the problem it was meant to solve. Marx's was meant to solve a 'practical' problem; its business, as he said himself, was to 'make the world better'. Marx's philosophy would necessarily, therefore, appear nonsensical except to a person who, I will not say shared his desire to make the world better by means of a philosophy, but at least regarded that desire as a reasonable one. According to my own principles of philosophical criticism, it was inevitable that Marx's philosophy should appear nonsensical to gloves-on philosophers like the 'realists', with their sharp division between theory and practice, or the 'liberals', such as John Stuart Mill, who argued that people ought to be allowed to think whatever they liked because it didn't really matter what they thought. In order to criticize a gloves-off philosophy like that of Marx, you must be at least enough of a gloves-off philosopher to think gloves-off philosophizing legitimate.

The first and third R. G. C.s agreed in wanting a gloves-off philosophy. They did not want a philosophy that should be a scientific toy guaranteed to amuse professional thinkers safe behind their college gates. They wanted a philosophy that should be a weapon. So far, I was with Marx. Perhaps all that stood in the way of a closer agreement was the second R. G. C., the academic or professional thinker.

My attitude towards politics had always been what in England is called democratic and on the Continent liberal. I regarded myself as a unit in a political system where every citizen possessing the franchise had the duty of voting for a representative to parliament. I thought that the government of my country, owing to a wide franchise, a free press, and a universally recognized right of free speech, was such as to make it impossible that any considerable section should be oppressed by government action, or that their grievances should be hushed up, even if a remedy for them could not be found. I thought that the democratic system was not only a form of government but a school of political experience coextensive with the nation, and I thought that no authoritarian government, however strong, could be so strong as one which rested on a politically educated public opinion. As a form of government, I thought its essence lay in the fact that it was a nursery-garden where policies were brought to maturity in the open air, not a post office for distributing ready-made policies to a passively receptive country.

These I thought very great merits; greater than those of any other political system yet devised, and worth defending at all costs against people who, because they wished to hoodwink the citizen and enforce upon him ready-made policies devised by some irresponsible cabal, untruthfully accused it of being 'cumbrous' and 'inefficient'. I knew, of course, that Marx had denounced it as a fraud, whose business was to throw a semblance of legality over the oppression of the workers by the capitalists; but although I knew that such oppression existed and was to a great extent legalized, I thought that the business of a democratic government was to eradicate it.

I did not think that our constitution was free from faults. But the discovery and correction of these faults was the function of governments, not of individual voters. For the system was a self-correcting one, charged with amending its own faults by legislation. It was also a self-feeding one. Members of parliament were chosen by the voters from among themselves; higher grades in the system were filled from among the members of parliament; and thus, so long as the individual voters did their political duty by keeping themselves adequately informed on public questions, and voting in accordance with their judgement as to where on any given occasion the good of the nation as a whole was to be sought, there was little danger that their representatives would be insufficiently informed, or insufficiently endowed with public spirit, to do their work creditably. And owing to the majority vote it did not matter if a few, at any stage, were ignorant or misguided. So long as the majority were well enough informed and public-spirited enough for what they had to do, fools and knaves would be out-voted.

The whole system, however, would break down if a majority of the electorate should become either ill informed on public questions or corrupt in their attitude towards them: by which I mean, capable of adopting towards them a policy directed not to the good of the nation as a whole, but to the good of their own class or section or of themselves.

In the first respect, I became conscious of a change for the worse during the eighteen-nineties. The newspapers of the Victorian age made it their first business to give their readers full and accurate information about matters of public concern. Then came the *Daily Mail*, the first English newspaper for which the word 'news' lost its old meaning of facts which a reader ought to know if he was to vote intelligently, and acquired the new meaning of facts, or fictions, which it might amuse him to read. By reading such a paper, he was no longer teaching himself to vote. He was teaching himself not to vote; for he was teaching himself to think of 'the news' not as the situation in which he was to act, but as a mere spectacle for idle moments.

In the second respect, I became aware of corrupting influences rather later. The South African settlement of the Campbell-Bannerman ministry was a fine exhibition of the principles in which I believed, and a proof that I was not wrong in thinking them to be the principles of English policy. The social legislation of its successor, Asquith's first ministry, was such as I could not but approve. But the way in which it was advertised, by promising voters 'ninepence for fourpence', was the negation of those principles. Mr. Lloyd George became to me a landmark, second only to the *Daily Mail*, in the corruption of the electorate. During the first quarter of the present century, each of these corrupting influences underwent enormous development.

After the War the democratic system was threatened by two powerful rivals. There were two elements in that system, one of which was inherited by each rival. On a Lockian basis of private property the democratic tradition had erected a system of representative institutions designed to promote the good of the nation as a whole. But there existed, on paper since Marx formulated it, and in terms of political fact since the Russian revolution, a system having the same end but a different starting-point. The Socialists (I use the term as implying Marxian Socialism) agreed with the democratic tradition in aiming at social and economic betterment for the entire people, but proposed to achieve this aim through the public ownership of 'means of production'. Then came Fascism in Italy and National Socialism in Germany, which agreed with the democratic tradition in making private property their first principle; but in order to preserve it they abandoned, not only the political institutions of democratic government, but also the aim of social and economic betterment upon which those institutions had been directed.

The real breach between the democratic tradition and the Socialists was not on a point of policy but on a point of fact. No one, I think, would deny that modern European society is divided into people whose energies are focused on owning things, and people whose energies are focused on doing things. Let these be called capitalists and workers respectively. All capitalists do things, and all workers own things; but this does not obliterate the distinction. If what is vital to a man is his ownership of certain things, while his engaging in certain activities is relatively unimportant, he is a capitalist, however much he does. If the contrary, he is a worker, however much he owns.

Between these two 'classes' in modern European society, the Socialists held that there was in existence a 'class war', and that parliamentary institutions only disguised this war and did not overcome it. The democratic tradition maintained that parliamentary institutions acted in such a way as to dissipate any tendency to class war by means of free speech and open discussion. Fascism on this point agreed with Socialism; though its mouthpieces, pursuing their declared policy of deceit, denied it. But whereas Socialism hoped to end the class war by a workers' victory leading to the abolition of class distinctions, Fascism hoped to perpetuate it by a capitalist victory leading to the permanent subjection of the workers. National Socialism is only the local German variety of Fascism.

Fascism could best be understood as a capitalist Socialism: a system in which the machinery of Socialism had been turned upside down in order to connect it up with a different prime mover, namely, the desire of capitalists to remain capitalists. In order to gratify this desire they were glad to pay blackmail to the Fascist state far in excess of any taxation and control ever devised by parliamentary government. In Socialism, the prime mover was the desire for the whole nation's social and economic welfare. By comparison with this, the motive power of Fascism was not respectable, and had to be disguised. It was therefore concealed beneath a cloak of international hatred and jealousy.

Actually, Fascism was not compatible with international hatred. It was based not on the idea of nation but on the idea of class; and had it been honest, it would have answered the Communists' Manifesto with the call, 'Capitalists of the world, unite.'

But Fascism was not capable of honesty. Essentially an attempt to fight Socialism with its own weapons, it was always inconsistent with itself. There was once a very able and distinguished philosopher who was converted to Fascism. As a philosopher, that was the end of him. No one could embrace a creed so fundamentally muddle-headed and remain capable of clear thinking. The great exponents of

Fascism have been specialists in arousing mass-emotion; its minor adherents, tacticians and plotters.

Knowing all this, and thinking that in spite of some corrupting influences the true democratic tradition still existed in my own country, I rejected Socialism on the ground that the parliamentary system was still working well enough to perform its proper function of an antiseptic against class war; rejected Fascism as an incoherent caricature of Socialism's worst features; and stood by the democratic tradition.

'It was the Spanish ulcer', said Napoleon, 'that destroyed me.' I had travelled over large parts of Spain in 1930 and 1931, and in the latter year had seen revolutionary movements everywhere going on. They were being conducted in the most orderly fashion. My friends and I never saw or heard of a single act of violence, or a single piece of evidence that such acts had been done. In one town we watched what we took for a religious festival, at which children in white were singing while their elders looked on, respectfully interested and perfectly quiet. Later, in a wine-shop, with the wireless relaying evensong from Canterbury cathedral, we asked our fellow drinkers what the festival was. 'Festival?' said they. 'That was the Revolution.'

Our friends used to write from England expressing fears for our safety among the atrocities by which, the newspapers told them, the revolution was being accompanied; at the mercy of the bloodthirsty Communists in their war against religion. But there were no atrocities; no Communists to be seen or heard of, only democratically minded men at work establishing a parliamentary government; no war against religion, only a clean sweep of the old political domination by ecclesiastical and military bosses, while the Church itself, as one saw in every town, carried on its religious functions undisturbed, its buildings and its personnel in no way interfered with.

At the time, I thought it no more than comical that the English newspapers should be so ill informed about what was going on in Spain. It did not occur to me that another explanation was possible. I do not know which is the right one. Either it was a mere coincidence that this epidemic of journalistic ignorance prepared the way for the policy by which, later on, the larger part of the British press (acting, one cannot but suspect, under government instructions) deliberately deceived its readers as to the character of the Spanish republic; or else that policy was already working, and those instructions presumably issued, by 1931.

A few years later, the Spanish civil war began. It was a rebellion of the deposed military bosses against the democratic régime that had supplanted them: the rebellion of a nation's army against that nation's people and their properly constituted government; properly constituted, that is to say, according to English ideas. Every Englishman who had any faith in the English political tradition would, if he knew the truth, wish to help the Spanish government against the rebels. And very little help was needed; only a fair field. If the government could once extemporize and equip an army, the rebels' fate was sealed.

The British 'National' government prevented this from happening. It adopted, and enforced on certain other nations, a policy of 'non-intervention', which meant forbidding the introduction into Spain of men to fight and munitions to fight with. Now, if in a certain country the army is in rebellion against an unarmed government, which is trying to arm in its own defence, no great penetration is needed in order to see that an embargo against the importation of arms into that country is an act of assistance to the rebels. People in England saw that their government, under its 'non-intervention' mask, was intervening, and very energetically, on the rebels' side; so to keep them quiet a press campaign began, repeating the stories about Communism and atrocities for whose falsity a few years earlier I could vouch. It was successful. People who believe in the English political tradition do not like Communists and do not approve of atrocities. Sympathy for the Spanish government wilted visibly. No doubt, people said, it was only our 'non-intervention' humbug that was enabling the rebels to make headway against the government; but did one really want the government to win?

Everybody knew that the rebel leader was a tool of the Italian and German dictators; and that these, whatever lip-service they gave to 'non-intervention', were feeding him constantly with men and munitions. Everybody knew that in doing so they had altered the strategic situation in the Mediterranean, from the

British point of view, very greatly for the worse. But if anybody hinted at these things, the British 'National' government answered, 'Trust us; we know what we are doing; we have given you peace.' This, once more, was successful. The electorate was willing to put up with almost anything so long as war was averted. But no evidence was produced, either then or later, that it had been. No evidence was produced that either or both of the dictators bullied the British government into adopting the 'non-intervention' policy by threats of war. No evidence was produced that their own notorious refusal to abide by that policy was covered by threats of the same kind. No evidence was produced that the British government would have endangered peace by simply refraining from those actions by which, legally or illegally, it forbade its nationals to enlist in the Spanish government's service.

No evidence of these things was produced; and they were things which, certainly, no one would have believed at the time, and no one ever will believe, without evidence, and conclusive evidence, adduced to prove them. But so dense was the atmosphere of concealment in which the 'National' government had wrapped its policy for many years (beginning with the empty rodomontades of Ramsay MacDonald, who seemed to say so much and never said anything at all; and going on with the 'con-man' methods of Mr. Baldwin, who seldom said anything except what an honest man he was and how completely every one could trust him) that no one expected the government spokesmen even to say these things, let alone produce evidence for them. Nothing was definitely said, but a great deal was hinted.

But though nothing was said, much was done. Failing any statement of the 'National' government's policy, I found myself obliged to infer their policy from the evidence of their actions. This was not difficult. For any one accustomed to interpret evidence, their actions admitted only one explanation. They wanted the rebels to win, and wanted to conceal this fact from the electorate. They knew that the rebels could not win without help from themselves, so they gave that help. They knew that the rebels could not win without grave damage to British interests, so they sacrificed those interests.

Why were they so anxious for the rebels' success? Not because of 'the Communist menace', for although my old friend the *Daily Mail*, a keen supporter of the 'National' government, and now as ever a keen worker in the cause of corrupting the public mind, habitually referred to the Spanish government as 'Red', that is, Communist, the government knew as well as the *Daily Mail* did that republican Spain was not a Communist state but a parliamentary democracy, and that Señor Negrin's cabinet, for example, contained only one solitary communist, who was included after his party had joined in the general declaration of loyalty to democratic principles. The Spanish civil war was a straight fight between Fascist dictatorship and parliamentary democracy. The British government, behind all its disguises, had declared itself a partisan of Fascist dictatorship.

At the beginning of 1938, when this became clear to me, I formed no opinion as to how far individual members of that government knew what they were doing. Fascism, I repeat, is a muddle-headed business. I found it easy to believe that the 'National' government's policy of truckling to the Fascist powers, and of refusing to tell the country what they were doing, need not have arisen from that government's clear comprehension of its own aims, coupled with a clear understanding of their detestableness in the eyes of the country, and resulting in a clear decision that the country must be deceived. It might arise from imbecility of will and weakness of intellect, combined with certain sneaking admirations and certain unexamined timidities, a defective sense of responsibility, and a feeble and sometimes inoperative regard for the truth. If any one in 1937, or even early in 1938, had said to the prime minister, with a reminiscence of Dr. Johnson's repartee to the Thames waterman, 'Sir, your government, under pretence of inability to defend the national interests, is conducting a Fascist revolution', I dare say the prime minister would have denied the charge with all the sincerity that he possesses.

The events of 1938 taught me nothing about the 'National' government that I did not know already. I began the year in the expectation of two developments: an open clash between the prime minister and the principles of parliamentary government, and a more flagrant repetition, somewhere else, of the Spanish formula: aggression by a Fascist state, rendered successful by support from the British government under cover of a war-scare engineered by that government itself among the British people.

The first expectation was realized in the early summer, when in open defiance of the rules of parliamentary privilege a concerted attempt was made by members of the cabinet to suppress parliamentary criticism of the government's already notorious inefficiency in carrying out the rearmament programme, by threats of prosecution under the Official Secrets Act against Mr. Duncan Sandys, the member of parliament who had dared to criticize. The matter was discreetly hushed up in the government newspapers; but every one who had access to the facts knew that it meant war between a Fascist cabinet and the parliamentary constitution of the country it was ruling.

The second expectation was realized during the Czechoslovakia crisis in September, when the British prime minister flew successively to Berchtesgaden, Godesberg, and Munich, returning every time with orders in his pocket from the German dictator in obedience to which he changed the country's policy behind the back of parliament, and even of the cabinet.

To me, therefore, the betrayal of Czechoslovakia was only a third case of the same policy by which the 'National' government had betrayed Abyssinia and Spain; and I was less interested in the fact itself than in the methods by which it was accomplished: the carefully engineered war-scare in the country at large, officially launched by the simultaneous issue of gas-masks and of the prime minister's emotional broadcast, two days before his flight to Munich, and the carefully staged hysterical scene in parliament on the following night. These things were in the established tradition of Fascist dictatorial methods; except that whereas the Italian and German dictators sway mobs by appeal to the thirst for glory and national aggrandizement, the English prime minister did it by playing on sheer, stark terror.

He gained his point. At the time of writing, England has not formally bidden farewell to its parliamentary institutions; it has only permitted them to become inoperative. It has not renounced its faith in political liberty; it has only thrown away the thing in which it still professes to believe. It has not given away its Empire; it has only handed over the control of that Empire's communications to a jealous and grasping power. It has not ceased to have a voice in European affairs; it has only used that voice to further the ends of another power even more jealous and even more grasping.

This has been done not by the wish of the country, or of any considerable section in the country, but because the country has been tricked. To recall what I said on pp. 48–9, the forces which have been at work for nearly half a century corrupting the public mind, producing in it by degrees a willingness to forgo that full, prompt, and accurate information on matters of public importance which is the indispensable nourishment of a democratic society, and a disinclination to make decisions on such matters in the public-spirited frame of mind which is a democratic society's life-blood, have 'trained up a generation of Englishmen and Englishwomen' to be the dupes of a politician who has so successfully 'appealed to their emotions' by 'promises of private gain' (the gain of personal safety from the horrors of war) that they have allowed him to sacrifice their country's interests, throw away its prestige, and blacken its name in the face of the world, in order that he should glare out from his photographs with the well-known hypnotic eyes of a dictator.

It is not the business of this autobiography to ask how completely the country has in fact been deceived, or how long the present degree of deception will last. I am not writing an account of recent political events in England: I am writing a description of the way in which those events impinged upon myself and broke up my pose of a detached professional thinker. I know now that the minute philosophers of my youth, for all their profession of a purely scientific detachment from practical affairs, were the propagandists of a coming Fascism. I know that Fascism means the end of clear thinking and the triumph of irrationalism. I know that all my life I have been engaged unawares in a political struggle, fighting against these things in the dark. Henceforth I shall fight in the daylight.

The index to *An Autobiography* in the 1978 edition with an introduction by Stephen Toulmin follows. An updated index of *An Autobiography* has been incorporated into the main index beginning on page 557.

INDEX

compiled by Patricia Utechin

COMMENTARIES

I

R. G. COLLINGWOOD'S CHILDHOOD: HABITS OF THOUGHT

TERESA SMITH

The purpose of this chapter is to illuminate the influence of Collingwood's childhood on his later intellectual development, through a commentary on the first two chapters of *An Autobiography*, which describe Collingwood's home life and school years before going on to Oxford. Many puzzles remain about the *Autobiography*. Scholars have criticized Collingwood's own account of his life as polemical (particularly in the later chapters). Others have called it incomplete (the absence of discussion of the influence of Ruskin, one of the greatest of Victorian thinkers, to whom Collingwood's father, the artist and archaeologist W. G. Collingwood, was secretary until Ruskin's death in 1900, seems curious). He has also been accused of bad faith (for example, in his account of his schooling at Rugby). The first charge is taken up by later commentators in this new edition of *An Autobiography*. The second and third are explored here.

This chapter draws on material which has been little used so far by Collingwood scholars.[1] It explores Collingwood's childhood, boyhood, and schooling, the context of his family and parents' friends—writers, painters, historians, and archaeologists—and the influence particularly of his father and of Ruskin, as the setting for the development of habits of thought and action throughout his life. The task is to interweave the chronology of Collingwood's youth—his childhood at home in the Lake District (1889–1902) at Gillhead and then in Coniston, and his schooldays, first at the preparatory

[1] Material includes the Collingwood/Altounyan archives held in Abbot Hall Museum and Art Gallery, Kendal, and the Kendal Record Office; manuscripts in the Bodleian Library, Oxford; the Ruskin Museum in Coniston; and letters in the author's possession. Thanks to James Arnold, Vicky Slowe, and especially Zillah Scott.

school Charney Hall in Grange-over-Sands on the Cumbrian coast (1902–1903) and then Rugby School (1903–1908)—with themes that reflect his later life and work: the nature of evidence, his 'critical eye' and independence of spirit, the combination of intellectual and practical skill, his views on education.

1. COLLINGWOOD'S EDUCATION

1.1 Home and School

Most autobiographies start chronologically, with the writer's family and early childhood. Collingwood's, as 'the story of his thought', starts with his education; and this commentary chapter follows his order. The first sentence of *An Autobiography* (*A*, 1) sets the scene: 'Up to the age of thirteen I lived at home and was taught by my father.' We learn that he began Latin at four and Greek at six with his father (by the time he went to Rugby he was fluent in both French and German as well),[2] his lessons in history 'illustrated with relief maps in papier-mâché made by boiling down newspapers in a saucepan'. He also taught himself 'the natural sciences' from books and practical application, read through his father's library and those of his friends, 'wrote incessantly', listened to his mother playing the piano 'for an hour every day before breakfast', and watched his parents and other professional artists at work. The last taught him a lesson crucial for his later development, which

> some critics and aestheticians never know to the end of their lives, that no "work of art" is ever finished, so that in that sense of the phrase there is no such thing as a "work of art" at all. Work ceases upon the picture or manuscript, not because it is finished, but because sending-in day is at hand, or because the printer is clamorous for copy, or because "I am sick of working at this thing" or "I can't see what more I can do to it." (*A*, 2)

William M. Johnston, in *The Formative Years of R. G. Collingwood*, published in 1967, suggested that Collingwood's education

[2] Collingwood's grandmother, Marie Imhoff, came from Thurgau in Switzerland. His father was thus half-Swiss, and a German speaker from childhood. Collingwood and his sisters spent many holidays with their Swiss relations (Altounyan, T. 1990. *Chimes from a Wooden Bell: A Hundred Years in the Life of a Euro-Armenian Family*. London: I.B. Tauris and Co, Ltd., 41ff.).

was 'more akin to that of John Stuart Mill than to the training afforded by any elementary school, then or now'.[3] While this may be a fair comment, Collingwood was not required to follow such a rigorous curriculum and punishing work schedule as was Mill by his father. The second sentence of *An Autobiography* makes clear the difference (*A*, 1). 'Lessons occupied only two or three hours each morning; otherwise he left me to my own devices, sometimes helping me with what I chose to do, more often leaving me to work it out for myself.' The similarity lies rather in the training in habits of work. Mill, by working 'at the same table as his father throughout his childhood', was 'directly provided with a very specific notion of what men did: they worked hard, with that work consisting of reading and writing'.[4] In the same way, as his own and his father's letters make clear, Collingwood learnt habits of work from his father from an early age by imitating his reading and writing and accompanying him on sketching and archaeological expeditions.

Some details of Collingwood's home schooling survive. Two examples from his father's letters will suffice. In July 1896, when Collingwood was seven, father and son made an expedition to Furness Abbey (this followed an excursion organized the previous September by the Cumberland and Westmorland Antiquarian and Archaeological Society (CWAAS), of which W. G. Collingwood was a member): 'the steam train to Furness Abbey, where we spent 4 hours, & I drummed it well into the boy – who is to write an essay on the abbey tomorrow'. Collingwood's 'essay' survives as a little booklet: it begins with a sketch plan of the abbey as frontispiece, and the text opens thus: 'At Furness Abbey off the Barrow road the first thing you come to is a gate. Near the railway station is another gate. Furness Abbey is built in a valley with trees on each side (see plan).' This we might call Collingwood's first record of a site visit; the style (aged seven) is much the same as his later excavation reports.[5]

[3] Johnston, W. M. 1967. *The Formative Years of R. G. Collingwood*. The Hague: Martinus Nijhoff, 6.

[4] Reeves, R. 2007. *John Stuart Mill, Victorian Firebrand*. London: Atlantic Books, 18.

[5] See Collingwood's report of his first independent excavation, Papcastle in 1912, *CWAAS*, NS XIII, 131–41.

Seven months later, in February 1897, W. G. Collingwood wrote again to his wife, this time about Collingwood's lessons with his elder sister Dora, aged ten:

> Robin & Dora thought they had very interesting lessons today. They were set to pick out of the map of England all the names in -Chester &c. (Roman camps) & I made a sketch-map – joined the towns they had found – & behold! the Roman roads, with various information about why & wherefore these especial spots were chosen. I think if you could get us a couple of dozen blank maps of England (outlines without names) they would be very useful to fill up as we go on: & so make our own historical atlas.

Home schooling came to an end when Collingwood, aged thirteen, was sent to preparatory school. This, Collingwood speculated, was his father's reaction to 'growing idleness': 'I had fallen into a habit of loafing, and lost the alertness and quickness of wit that had been so noticeable in my early childhood'; an early adolescent phase described by Collingwood as the beginnings of his own lifelong task: 'I must think' (*A*, 4–5).

Collingwood's letters[6] from prep school (1902–1903) give a vivid picture of school life: they are lively and well-composed descriptions written for home consumption—games and school matches, dorm rags and tuck boxes. The letters were known in the school as 'Collingwood's Daily Epistle'. (After a visit by his mother and younger sister, he wrote: 'Of course you know all this, but I can't help writing it. My letters are my diary, you see.') The letters are full of the family's private languages and family jokes. Ogams was one;[7] Kiplingesque phraseology was another[8] (Kipling's books were read avidly by all the family). 'Mongoosing' was one example between the children; 'I gloat! I gloat! Hear me!' another; and even his father, away on archaeological excursions, wrote postcards simply urging 'Good hunting'. 'Mr Roberts is an ardent Kipling admirer . . . and confiscated the Just So's from tea to prep. last night. However, I got square with him.'

[6] Letters in the author's collection [TS/FLTR001-035A].

[7] An alphabet used by the ancient British and Irish; W. G. Collingwood was studying the script, and used it to write to Edith Mary Isaac when they were engaged.

[8] Kipling's *The Jungle Book* was published in 1894 (the mongoose's motto was 'Run and find out'; 'Good hunting' is the call of the python Kaa and Baloo the brown bear); *Stalky and Co* in 1899 ('I gloat!' is standard schoolboy talk); and *The Just So Stories* in 1902.

In September 1903, when he was fourteen, Collingwood went on to Rugby. The letters[9] from his first two years recall the tone of those from Charney Hall: racy accounts of the school; the timetable; his masters; whom he shared a study with; books; what he was working on; his developing friendships; the Cadet Corps (which he was 'not a bit keen on' but joined on his father's advice). In his first term, he reported on invitations from his masters to breakfast and tea, and discussions about his father's Icelandic work, Kipling, Ruskin, and life in Coniston (school life mirroring home concerns):

To old Mr Whitelaw's for breakfast... old Bob asked Alston minute details about the progress of Edinburgh and the state of the health of Mr Somebody's aunt's grandmother's cat's greatgrandson's owner's youngest daughter, and so on: he also asked me details about the state of agriculture and other local industries; also which part of Coniston our house was in ...; who lived at Brantwood now: and so on.

At the end of his first year, at another breakfast he met Mrs Ransome, mother of Arthur Ransome,[10] the aspiring writer whom W. G. Collingwood had befriended, and his younger brother Geoffrey, also at Rugby. Collingwood began a friendship with 'young Ransome', bicycling out with him to look at 'interesting things' such as tumuli and churches:

On Tuesday I met Ransome [i.e. Geoffrey] at c.o. [call over] and went a ride with him to Brinklow, about 7 miles out, where there are some interesting things – a big tumulus, and an old church, rather a decent Gothic one.... Next day I had a short ride, about 18 or 20 miles, as I wanted to get myself tolerably decent for stodge with the Ransomes. At 5 o'clock I turned up punctually in Old Quad and waited. After about half an hour, when the entire school must have gone past, one by one, I felt rather sick of it and went across the high to Pepperday's and laid in a large stock of post-cards for the Kid. I then returned and after waiting till 6 o'clock gave him up and consoled myself with a huge tea. After tea I was reading peaceably in my study – I think it was Tennyson or Jules Verne,

[9] Letters in the author's collection [TS/FLTR036-218].

[10] Arthur Ransome (1884–1967): see Hart-Davis, R. (ed.) 1976. *The Autobiography of Arthur Ransome*. London: Jonathan Cape; Brogan, H. 1984. *The Life of Arthur Ransome*. London: Jonathan Cape; Chambers, R. 2009. *The Last Englishman: The Double Life of Arthur Ransome*. London: Faber and Faber. Collingwood remained close friends with Arthur and his younger brother Geoffrey (1887–1918), and helped his parents sort out Geoffrey's effects after his death in the Great War in 1918.

I forget which – when I heard the voice of one of our sixth below me (my study is over the 6th-room, which looks onto the road) "Collingwood! You're wanted!" So I bolted down, and there was old Ransome [Arthur], in the weirdest hat I ever saw, and young Ransome [Geoffrey]. So we went down to Hobley's together, and stodged a second tea, nearly as big as my first and twice as sumptuous, consisting of ices and coffee and buns: and old Ransome mystified his brother with accounts of the doings of the Mongoose Club,[11] and explained to me that he was going to qualify for membership by spending the winter as 2nd mate on a Mediterranean tramp, and gave me much welcome news about the condition of my sails, boats, etc.

As at Charney Hall, there were also dorm rags, 'dorm singing' and 'dorm tossing'. 'In the evening we had a grand rag in the dorm', a fancy dress ball:

I went as Julius Caesar (in bath towels) . . . Then of course we had to have an orchestra of sorts – it was started with a tooth-glass and a hat-box . . . I have a young friend who is an Armenian[12] of small stature and enormous muscular power, and we have periodical wrestling matches. We are jolly even, but I can always last longer than he can; and last night we wrestled steadily for a full hour, and then went round the dorm to pick up the bits. It wasn't much damage: 2 jugs, a basin and a tooth-glass, and 3 beds collapsed onto the floor; no real havoc.

His father disapproved of such behaviour, but as Collingwood reminded him, it was standard for public schools of the time: 'as to your question whether I'm not too old and sedate for these amusements, I reply, you just go to a public school, and don't play games, and see what happens'.

Collingwood's football injury sustained in his first term in October 1903 (and first operated on in 1905) was, he recognized, 'a crucial point' in his school life (*A*, 8), removing him from organized games and allowing him to develop his walking and

[11] The first Christmas holidays he was home from Rugby, Collingwood read a paper to the Mongoose Club about a day in his life at school. The Mongoose Club was made up of various members of the family—his sisters Dora ('Pres in the Chair') and Barbara ('Sec') as well as Robin ('Max Simaris Howler, MMC', 'Squimpson Ratraps, MMC')—and elected favourite uncles, parents, family friends, and notables. Handwritten minutes of meetings give the flavour: 'some small speeches were made, and healths eaten'.

[12] Ernest Altounyan (1890–1962) entered Rugby at the same time as Collingwood; he later married Collingwood's eldest sister Dora.

bicycling expeditions and independent studies. Ill health was the normal lot of schools of the period: the litany in Collingwood's letters home—frequent flu, German measles ('rose rash'), measles, whooping cough—is familiar. Weak eyes, and a weak knee, however, plagued Collingwood throughout his life.[13]

When Collingwood moved up into the sixth form in 1906 in his third year, aged sixteen, the letters develop a sharper, more critical tone, often reflective and self-critical, with leaps of analysis and passion intertwined. They show clearly the continuation and deepening of his independent study: long bicycling excursions with friends to explore churches and make architectural drawings; readings of the Norse sagas, mirroring his father's interests, as well as Tennyson and Browning, and Ruskin's *Modern Painters* and *Stones of Venice*; studying music, composing, and playing. His passion for music grew to such an extent that applying to Oxford for a music scholarship was a serious possibility. By his fourth year, his letters home were filled with music lessons and practice, choir and concerts:

> It's all I have been doing. Whenever I have a spare moment, I compose, or read harmony, or sit down and play the fiddle, and so there is literally nothing else to say... when I want to express my thoughts in any other medium, I find it jolly hard: the other night – that night when it was hot, and a just full moon – I sat down to write a story; but the blessed thing wouldn't come in English: only in music. I wrote screeds of music that night, and not a single word of story – even when I'm writing letters, I have to go over what I'm going to say first on the penny whistle, and then put it down. Odd, isn't it?[14]

The later Rugby letters also show the beginning of his experimentation with style, and his growing determination to exercise independence of judgement. His critiques of the sixth form debating society Eranos, which he joined in September 1906 (he was seventeen, at the beginning of his fourth year at Rugby), provide one example of this 'critical eye' at work. In his second term of membership he proposed

[13] The former led to his rejection when applying for a commission in 1914 [TS/FLTR0464]. On the latter, see the *Log of a Journey to the East Indies* in this volume for his account of climbing mountains in 1939.

[14] A similar description of thinking in music is found in his accounts of walking to work at the Admiralty in London during World War I.

to read [a paper] about Rudyard Kipling next term, and give Eranos a stirring-round. They think he's beneath their dignity. (Eranos – excuse the digression – is the embodiment of all the qualities which I detest in human beings: chiefly exemplified in an unctuous assumption of wisdom and perspicacity, and a shut-eyed and open-mouthed awe of the Established Opinion, which makes me want to shake them. I cannot persuade them that whatever is, is not necessarily good. Last meeting (did I tell you?) I said as serenely as I could – apropos of "our mutual" Matthew Arnold – that Classicism was an attempt to express somebody else's ideas in a way unnatural and properly distasteful to yourself, because other people did. They didn't see it a bit and looked at me as if I had expressed the grave opinion that the object of scriptural inspiration was to provide a book which should supply 2000 pipelights for 10 1/2d at the S.P.C.K. [Society for Promoting Christian Knowledge]. I think incipient influenza gives one a craving to surprise people – shock them, if you like to put it that way.

In spring 1908, he was writing another paper for Eranos,

on the Devil in Literature: the title alone has given them bad fits, which was rather my object. The paper is intended to define the modern literary conception of the Devil, and to discover of what elements he is composed, and to what sources the elements can be traced: to which end I have had to read Chaldean magic, Greek and Norse mythology, and other details: and the paper also compares and contrasts the several devils of Dante, Milton, Goethe and so on. I only started it on Thursday, and I'm down to read next Sunday . . . Devil paper went off with a bang: it was about as successful as any paper I ever heard & made people talk like fun.[15]

A second illustration of Collingwood's independence of judgement is the school debates. Here is a letter to his eldest sister Dora, written in the autumn of 1907, the beginning of his final year at Rugby:

Last night I debated. The debate subject was "that Socialism constitutes a grave national danger", and I was in opposition of course. I got up and told

[15] 'The Devil in Literature: an essay upon the mythology of the Evil One': a paper read before Eranos 1908. Dep. Coll. 1/1. This paper, with its scholarly literary comparisons, and references to archaeological evidence such as Mycenaean seal gems, recalls W. G. Collingwood's analysis of Northern pre-Norman crosses as combinations of Christian and Viking symbolism (see Townend, M. 2009. *The Vikings and Victorian Lakeland: the Norse Medievalism of W. G. Collingwood and his Contemporaries*. Kendal: Titus Wilson & Son/ CWAAS, 120–38, 252–8) and also Haverfield's and W. G. Collingwood's insistence on using all sources of evidence. See also Smallwood's chapter in this volume (fn. 17).

the story of Mrs Pennington and the socialist socks, and also a dialogue which I had heard in dorm that morning:

A. What's the debate about tonight?

B. Oh, socialism or something.

A. Well, I'm surprised at anyone having the face to get up and speak for socialism!

B. Why, what is socialism?

A. Oh, I don't know.

Which I told them was characteristic of their own little minds. I also talked a great deal about morality, which was quite thrown away, and got very annoyed. Needless to say, the motion was carried. The audience evidently hadn't the face to vote for Socialism.

Collingwood's mocking comment on his peers' disregard for evidence ('It is rather amusing to be heckled by an audience none of whom have even read the book they are talking of!') reminds us of his later tutorial methods as a young don at Pembroke College (*A*, 27):

I . . . taught my pupils, more by example than by precept, that they must never accept any criticism of anybody's philosophy which they might hear or read without satisfying themselves by first-hand study that this was the philosophy that he actually expounded . . . When my pupils came to me armed with grotesquely irrelevant refutations of (say) Kant's ethical theory, and told me they came out of So-and-so's lectures, it was all one to me whether the irrelevance came from their misrepresenting So-and-so, or from So-and-so misrepresenting Kant: my move was to reach for a book with the words, "Let us see whether that is what Kant actually said."

In *An Autobiography* Collingwood was fiercely condemnatory of the split between 'the sciences' and 'the arts' (*A*, 6–14): his home schooling had equipped him equally well in classics, history and modern languages, and the natural sciences, 'and nothing would have afforded my mind its proper nourishment except to study equally all three'. But his father had given him more Greek and Latin 'than most boys of my age possessed', so it was as a classical scholar that he had gone to Rugby. He recollected the five years spent there as 'mainly waste'—a judgement on weary teachers, and the boredom of a timetable cut up into 'scraps and snippets of occupation in such a manner that no one could get down to a job of work and make something of it'. By his own account he was a rebel, spending his time on music, teaching himself to read

Dante, working on subjects of his own choice ('like medieval Italian history or the early French poets, not because I preferred them to Thucydides and Catullus, but because I could work at them unhampered by masters'), and entering for prizes (which he won) for English literature, astronomy, and musical theory and composition, which had nothing to do with the subjects he was supposed to be studying.

Written some thirty years later, Collingwood's verdict on his experience at Rugby was sharp. But we should note his analysis of the contribution by his father, 'who gave me an adult scholar's attitude towards learning while I was still a child, realising, as I now think, what the results would be, but judging the game worth the candle' (*A*, 11–12).

How far can we accept Collingwood's own account in the *Autobiography*? Inglis suggests that he was happier than his own account allows, and accuses him of bad faith at worst and poor memory at best.[16] His letters home showed close friendships with masters and boys, and time spent on studies which while not the supposed focus of his school work were at least tolerated by his masters and continued into his later intellectual interests.

It is also clear that Collingwood was warmly respected by both masters and fellow students. In a glowing reference in support of Collingwood's application in 1912 for a fellowship at Pembroke College, his housemaster W. N. Wilson wrote that during his time in Wilson's house 'he earned the respect and affection of all those with whom he came into contact, with Masters and boys, and continually developed in both power and influence'. In Collingwood's appointment as head of house when only seventeen, Wilson had passed over more senior boys, 'yet all the boys in the House fully approved of my choice which was justified by the complete success, courage and tact with which he carried out his duties'.[17]

1.2 Collingwood the Rebel?

Collingwood described himself as a 'rebel' at Rugby. So we have to ask about the nature of his rebellion. One reading of his five years

[16] Inglis, F. 2009. *History Man: The Life of R. G. Collingwood*. Princeton: Princeton University Press, 39, 45.

[17] Collingwood papers in Pembroke College, 15 May 1912; quoted in Inglis, *History Man*, 45–6.

at Rugby is that of a studious and clever student conforming to the school conventions (both formal and informal) and jumping through the usual hoops—from dorm rags, to sixth form (for three years) and head of house (for two), and on to a university career. He was a member of the school Cadet Corps and went to summer camp. He 'got religion' and was baptized and confirmed (this at a school with a long tradition of 'muscular Christianity' and public service).[18] By his own account (*A*, 7–9), he 'tasted the pleasure of doing administrative work, and learnt once for all how to do it'; he 'did not rebel against the disciplinary system', staying on excellent terms with his housemaster, and counting fagging and government by members of the sixth form as virtues. His own verdict is clear: the waste of time was not the disciplinary and governance systems of the school; rather it was the 'whole system of teaching' against which he 'became a rebel, more or less declared'.

Another reading gives a rather different picture. Collingwood brought a critical eye to even the most 'conventional' of school activities, as already shown by his comments on Eranos and the school debates. The clearest illustration is Collingwood's approach to the school Cadet Corps, with its weekly routine of march-outs and manoeuvres, drill and shooting practice. Having joined in his first year, by his second year Collingwood was enrolling his friends as members of the controversial new National Service League (NSL), founded in 1902 to press for universal military conscription ('national service') in Britain, and associated with figures such as Kipling and the Socialist George Bernard Shaw, as well as General Roberts, who was the hero of the war in Afghanistan and had led the relief of Kandahar. By his third year he had even enrolled the Corps captain in the NSL, and some of the masters, leading to Rugby's adoption of a new-style universal practice, with everyone required either to join the Corps, or to join the band, or to do drill and band practice once a week with the NSL: 'This scheme to start Monday Jan 21st 1906, thus getting ahead of ALL

[18] At Rugby, Thomas Arnold (d. 1842) created the model of a public school open to the middle classes, dedicated to ideals of public service, Christianity, and a healthy athleticism, as immortalized in Thomas Hughes' (1857) *Tom Brown's Schooldays*. Hughes and Charles Kingsley (*Westward Ho!* 1855; *The Water Babies* 1863) were associated with Muscular Christianity, a movement promoting healthy Christian activism.

schools public or private. Lord Roberts is expected to come down and "encourage" [i.e. inspect] us before long'—which he did the following month. This was hardly a conventional approach to a public school Cadet Corps.[19]

1.3 Collingwood's Education and His Own Views on Education

We also have to ask how we can reconcile the apparent discrepancies between Collingwood's account in the *Autobiography,* and his later views on education, for example, in *The New Leviathan* (*NL*, chapter XXXVII, 'Civilisation as education'), where Collingwood argues that the educational function of the family is the key to civilization, since it is the family, rather than educational specialists, that is responsible for 'civilising the children' (37.31). At first reading, Collingwood seems to be condemning the public school system as a disaster. 'If . . . the child is taken right out of the parent's hands and put unreservedly into those of the professional educator . . . the "deracination" inflicted on the child by transferring him from the hands of the parent to those of the educator must leave him emotionally disoriented for the rest of his life' (37.35). The parent, on the other hand, has the enormous advantages of being a non-specialist, and knowing the child better than any specialist. As Collingwood put it, the parent's power 'over the child enables him to make the child want to do well; his versatility in finding subjects for the child to study, or letting the child find them for himself, enables him to ensure . . . that a subject of study will be forthcoming from day to day at which, with that incentive, the child shall do well, and daily progress in the self-confidence of one that knows he can do well' (37.37). This sounds like a description of Collingwood's home schooling in his own childhood. 'The first move in our campaign against the Old Man of the Sea [the professional educator; bureaucratized education] is for every man or woman who has a child to decide in future to spend more time in its company' (37.9); 'have the child share your meals . . . have it share your bedroom . . . ; fathers, . . . don't always be thinking about doing them good and keeping them in order and all that; enjoy their company and make them enjoy yours . . . ; mothers . . . read to

[19] On the NSL, see the letter in *BMJ* April 10 1909, from Dr W. P. Herringham, a member of the NSL Executive Committee, about 'public morals'.

them out of any book they enjoy or play with them at any game they like, the sillier the better; if you are young enough to have little children you are young enough to enjoy romping with them' (37.91–94).

But Collingwood did not take the next step of advocating the abolition of professional teachers, and parents assuming the full responsibility of education.[20] Teachers should become specialists. 'There may be things a child wants to know that its parents cannot teach. Let it be sent to learn them from a professional teacher. And the parent, if it wants, can go too . . . Specialised teaching [should be] on tap for all comers who want it' (37.97–98). The 'specialism' example is that of the medical profession: 'children do not leave their homes for medical reasons to reside for half the year in a doctor's house or in a clinic. They live at home, and if they have a cold or bark their shins their parents give them first aid. If they want more, they go to a doctor' (37.99).

In *The New Leviathan*, the argument is for educational reform, and for some sort of partnership between the parent as generalist and the teacher as specialist. The *Autobiography* focused on Rugby as an example of a pedagogical system, and Collingwood found it wanting. Other aspects of the school, both formal (the governance and disciplinary structures) and informal (friendships, and his own intellectual pursuits, for which Rugby gave him considerable scope) were judged as positives rather than objects of condemnation. We should distinguish between Collingwood's critique of Rugby as a pedagogical system and his approval of its other formal and informal structures. However, as Johnston noted, it is not clear whether any established system of secondary education at the time would have satisfied the young Collingwood, who indeed recognized that as a young boy he already had 'an adult scholar's attitude towards learning'.

2. COLLINGWOOD'S CHILDHOOD AND HIS FAMILY

The lessons learnt during Collingwood's childhood are spelt out succinctly in the first two chapters of *An Autobiography*, although his family hardly feature—apart from his father. Here we sketch in

[20] As Johnston, *The Formative Years*, p. 9, suggests he did.

some family details as backdrop to the themes already outlined of his home and school learning. He was born in 1889, the third of four siblings and the only boy—Dora and Barbara, born 1886 and 1887; and Ursula, known as the Kid, born 1891. The 1891 census recorded the family living in a rented cottage in Gillhead on Lake Windermere belonging to W. G. Collingwood's childhood nurse Harriet, widow of a Windermere fisherman—parents and new baby Ursula in one cottage with servant and nursemaid, and Harriet with Dora and Robin as boarders next door. In a watercolour painted by W. G. Collingwood in 1886, Dorrie (the family's name for their mother) is pictured standing holding a baby outside the little row of cottages, with a gate and trees at the end and the road below (see Illustration 3).[21] W. G. Collingwood was working for

Illustration 3. Watercolour by W. G. Collingwood of the cottage at Gillhead, Windermere, where Collingwood was born in 1889. W. G. C. scribbled on the back, 'Dorrie's cottage, Aug 1886'. The baby in the picture is Collingwood's eldest sister, Dora, born February 1886. Courtesy of Teresa Smith.

[21] This picture has a note pencilled on its back in W. G. C.'s handwriting: 'Dorrie's cottage, Aug 1886'. The baby is therefore Dora, born six months earlier. Janet Gnosspelius recalled driving past the cottage as a young girl with her aunt

Illustration 4. Collingwood as a child at Lanehead; oil painting by his father, W. G. Collingwood, 1893. Courtesy of Teresa Smith.

Ruskin at Brantwood in Coniston, a journey by ferry across Lake Windermere and then on foot of some eleven miles each way. A few weeks after the 1891 census, the family moved to Lanehead, a much larger residence on Coniston Water, more conveniently only a few minutes walk along the lake from Ruskin's Brantwood. Collingwood, like all the family, was painted and photographed by his father in the Lanehead garden throughout his childhood (see Illustration 4).

Dora and grandmother E. M. D. Collingwood (personal communication). In *The Beautiful Furniture of the Simpsons of Kendal* (Carlisle: Bookcase, 2011), Hugh Wright describes the cottage, E. M. D. C.'s paintings of flowers on the doors (reminiscent of her flower paintings on the atrium columns at Wallington, the Trevelyans' house in Northumberland, 1895), and W. G. C.'s commissions of furniture from Arthur Simpson, who took over the cottage when the Collingwoods moved to Coniston (27–31, 213).

Collingwood had a stable childhood in a close-knit and loving family. Letters (the earliest date from when he was just over three years old) were written to his parents when they were away working or caring for elderly relatives, or to his sisters when they were away from home. These were copiously illustrated with little pencil or pen-and-ink sketches; they described home life—lessons, walks, flowers and birds, visits and presents from Brantwood and his parents' friends, family pets, making model boats and gunpowder, designing bicycle paddle boats, accompanying his father on sketching expeditions. Collingwood notes in the *Autobiography* (*A*, 3) that he

> wrote incessantly, in verse and prose, lyrics and fragments of epics, stories of adventure and romance, descriptions of imaginary countries and bogus scientific and archaeological treatises. A prolific habit in regard to such things was encouraged, demanded indeed, by the family custom of producing in manuscript a monthly magazine, circulated among a few friends and relations.

The 'monthly magazine' was *Nothing Much,* the family journal edited by Dora, which first appeared in January 1897, when Collingwood was seven. But Collingwood's writings began before that. In December 1895, when he was six, there was the first of many appearances of the imaginary Jipandland, here in five parts: 'Discoveries, Maps, A Dictionary, Alphabet and Words and Sketches' (this includes descriptions of clothes and food), and 'Stories of Japes' (the name of the inhabitants), with illustrations and a front and back cover: 'Printed & illustrated by R. Collingwood, Fin, Dec. 14.1895'. This mirrored his father's work on Norse sagas, and map-making and storytelling (W. G. Collingwood's historical novel *Thorstein of the Mere* had just been published; the book's opening illustration is of Robin as Thorstein finding Thurston-water). Jipandland made further appearances in *Nothing Much*, and as a Christmas present to his mother in 1900, in two small notebook volumes: '*A Trip to the West Jipandland Islands* by Esla Lesward [one of the young Collingwood's aliases] edited by Robin Collingwood' (the story of discovery, etc., illustrated throughout with ships, maps, diagrams of mechanical appliances, and a frontispiece). Later publications for the family were written out and bound with the usual publisher apparatus: 'I am going to write out Mr Balbus Cassel's book . . . It is going to be sermon quarto, with a vignette or two, & brown paper binding. All binding by me, one cop. to be written by Mr Cassel.'

Nothing Much's monthly instalments throughout its first year included stories by Collingwood, drawings and jokes, as well as stories and poems by W. G. Collingwood (many published later as *Coniston Tales*).[22] In 1900, volume IV had a bumper issue for Christmas, described by Collingwood in a letter to Dora (who was away from home staying with her Swiss relatives): 'the Xmas N.M. is something special this year. It contains: Title-page by Ma; Dick Hayton, a long detective story, 10 pages, by Me; "Timothy and Tottles, a poem" by Aunty Ruthie... Then there's a poem... by Pa, and an article on the Feeding of the Hens written and illustrated by Kid, and another pome, an epilog, by Pa. Good fatty of a number.' Two years later, Collingwood was writing another instalment of 'Dick Hayton', as well as an account of a three-and-a-half day mountain trek with his father on Helvellyn and Striding Edge; and a paper (read to the Mongoose Club) about climbing Weatherlam amongst the icicles.

Collingwood's detective story foreshadows his interest in the genre as archaeologist/historian qua detective.[23] In *The Idea of History*, the chapter on historical evidence has a section titled 'Who killed John Doe?' Collingwood analyses a crime scenario in order to point out the similarities between the nature of the questions the detective and the historian must ask themselves, and the nature of the evidence they use to answer those questions:

> The hero of a detective novel is thinking exactly like an historian when, from indications of the most varied kinds, he constructs an imaginary picture of how a crime was committed, and by whom. At first, this is a mere theory, awaiting verification, which must come to it from without. Happily for the detective, the conventions of that literary form dictate that when his construction is complete it shall be neatly pegged down by a confession from the criminal, given in such circumstances that its genuineness is beyond question. The historian is less fortunate. (*IH*, 243)

[22] Published in 1899 and dedicated 'To the Editor of "Nothing Much: a Monthly Magazine." It was owing to your encouragement that these sketches were attempted; and it is by your help and permission that they are now reproduced from your pages.'

[23] Quotations from *IH*, 243 and 266–82. See also *PA*, 86 for detective stories as literature.

The 'indications of the most varied kinds' mean 'anything... which is used as evidence', and in the John Doe story 'include such things as the existence of certain footprints in certain mud, their number, position, and direction, their resemblance to prints produced by a certain pair of shoes, and the absence of any others; the absence of mud on the floor of a certain room' (*IH*, 280); and so on and so on. Which means, in short, 'you can't collect your evidence before you begin thinking', as Collingwood reminds us with a reference to Poirot and Sherlock Holmes: 'thinking means asking questions..., and nothing is evidence except in relation to some definite question' (*IH*, 281).

The end of the second volume of *Nothing Much* in 1898 had a 'Tail-Piece, which Daddy won't sign', intended as a Christmas 'signing-off'. This is worth quoting in full for the four children's half-wry skit, half-sending-up view of the family's idiosyncrasies:

> We don't go in for prizes, and none of us go to schools
> We haven't got no principles, and we don't know nothing of rules
> But we scribble a bit, and sketch a bit – 'the Rabs take after their Pa'
> We're a dilettante family, we are, we are, we are.
>
> We don't do it for money, and we don't do it for praise
> We do it because we like it, and we're glad of the laugh we raise
> Laugh with us then, or at us – we ain't particular –
> We're a highly casual family, we are, we are, we are.
>
> Daddy he says it's practice, but he mostly pretends it's rot,
> I don't think he can be proud of us – he generly says he's not.
> It's Nothing Much, you understand, and it doesn't go very far;
> We're an unsatisfactory family, we are, we are, we are.
>
> So here's our second volume, all our numbers nicely bound
> Wishing a Merry Christmas and a happy New Year all round;
> But to say we'll do it another year would be saying too much by far;
> We're a dis-tinctly unpromising family, we are, we are, we are.

We can see that the 'inside story' from family records of Collingwood's home life is one of busy, lively activity with his sisters and friends—sailing, writing and drawing, making things, photography (see Illustration 5 for an example). The oft-quoted 'external source' is Arthur Ransome, who wrote about the Collingwoods in his autobiography, and turned Dora's family into the famous

Swallows and Amazons.[24] Ransome's idyllic account shows Collingwood's mother playing the piano every day before breakfast and then painting, his father writing, his three sisters working at their painting or sculpture; and sailing expeditions in the afternoon in Swallow—as Ransome wrote, 'the first of a long dynasty of Swallows in my sailing life'. In the evening 'there were stories'—Collingwood's mother reading 'from Jacob's four volumes of

Illustration 5. Peel Island, Coniston Water, by R. G. Collingwood, 1906. Given to his mother for her 59th birthday, September 1906 (recorded on the back). Courtesy of Teresa Smith.

[24] Ransome wrote an alternative version of the origins in his 1958 author's note to later editions. Local families had yet others: see e.g. Marshall, P. 1991. *Where It All Began: The Origins of Swallows and Amazons*. Byfleet.

English Fairy Tales . . . I can still hear the eerie threat she used to put into the voices of the Hobyahs . . . "Hobyah! Hobyah! Hobyah! Tear down the hemp-stalks, eat up the old man and woman, and carry off the little girl." '[25] And Ransome would tell one of the Anansi spider stories he had learnt from his friend in Chelsea, the Jamaican artist Pixie. (Collingwood wrote 'Anancy' letters to his family—this became another private language alongside Kipling.) The Collingwoods were Ransome's adopted and adoptive family; they were the first to take his writing seriously, and inevitably he fell in love with both the elder sisters; so in considering this idyllic picture we should make allowance for the rose-tinted spectacles of memory.[26]

Although Lanehead and the Lakes remained the Collingwoods' dream throughout their lives, the reality was more fractured. Collingwood's childhood at home was also rather darker than the picture sketched in the *Autobiography* and by Ransome and others. The family was always short of money, as Collingwood noted in the *Autobiography* (*A*, 5);[27] particularly so after the death of Ruskin in 1900. (This was one of the reasons for W. G. Collingwood taking a university post in Reading in 1905.) Collingwood's school and university fees were paid for by 'the generosity of a rich friend' (he also won scholarships); his father's diaries and account books show this to be Miss Emma Holt, of the Liverpool shipping line Lamport and Holt, who lived for part of the year at Tent Lodge in Coniston, close to Lanehead. Both adults and children were constantly on the move. Caring for elderly relatives was a continual demand. Throughout the 1890s Collingwood's mother went to stay in Maldon in Essex to look after her frail parents, sometimes taking some of the children with her; she and W. G. Collingwood took it in turns to visit Bristol to look after his father,

[25] Jacobs, J. (ed.) 1894. *More English Fairy Tales*. London: David Nutt, 118–25. The lines quoted were inscribed inside the front cover of one of Collingwood's copies of Hobbes' *Leviathan*.

[26] Ransome's account in his *Autobiography* is followed by Wakefield in his unpublished booklet on Lanehead and the Collingwoods, held at the Ruskin Museum in Coniston. Inglis, *History Man*, follows Wakefield in his account of Collingwood's childhood (ch. 1).

[27] See Knox's obituary of Collingwood, quoted in Johnston, *The Formative Years*, 5.

William Collingwood, until he died in 1903. They both also travelled for work; E. M. D. Collingwood was becoming well known as a portrait painter. The children were growing up fast; in 1900, Dora, aged fourteen, went to stay with the Austrian-Swiss uncles, followed later by Barbara; and from 1902, Collingwood was away at school apart from the holidays. By 1903 Dora and Barbara were in London as art students studying in Cope's studio, and Ursula was at boarding school, also requiring termly fees.

A letter from W. G. Collingwood to his wife around this time reveals the problem of making a living as an artist away from London. It set out both his uncertainty about his own career and his hopes for his children, as well as his recognition of the development of his wife's work, and anxiety about the wisdom and costs of staying in Coniston:

> The wind-up of your letter ... is curiously in line with what I have been thinking a good deal about. We shall never have these girls at home again and Ursula too will flit before long. Robin has gone! Your work is broadening out, and can be better done in London. Is the time coming when we must move? Could we get a little house in Bedford Park or a flat in Kensington for the money it costs to keep the girls in town? – either leaving Lanehead altogether, or else finding somebody to take it off our hands for part of the year?

Dora, her father's confidante, recorded some of this anxiety and movement in her diary for September 1903, after her grandfather's death. It was settled the family should try to move 'to London this year; but no house found yet and no tenant for Lanehead. This is the thin end of the wedge that will break us away from Coniston'; 'it is better to be in London [where one] must work and learn'; whereas in the country one is 'apt to become a fossil'. But 'it would be a great mistake to cut off all our connections here ... and all the things that Pater has been working at all these years ... The Coniston people are very fond of Pater ... they all think the world of him ... ' The Severns (Joan Severn was Ruskin's cousin and had looked after him at Brantwood) offered to lease them their house at Herne Hill in London for the winter. In January 1904 Dora recorded the new year's plan: 'the Kid is going to Dulwich [College] as a boarder; Robin of course to Rugby'; Dora to Austria with her mother. The Collingwood parents 'are to live in a small flat in Chelsea/Kensington [this was Editha Mansions, found by

Arthur Ransome]. All settled next day.' Lanehead was leased; Collingwood's letters record him in April 1905, the spring holidays, travelling north from Rugby by train and bicycle, in two inches of snow, to stay with Miss Holt at Tent Lodge and to pay a call on the tenants. The summer saw the family back in residence, for picnics and sailing and *What Ho!*, the final reprise of *Nothing Much*, Collingwood on crutches after his knee operation.

Autumn 1905 saw another change, when W. G. Collingwood took up an appointment at University College, Reading, first as Master of the Art Department, later as Professor in Fine Art (he stayed until 1911), and the family moved again, to Reading, Dora and Barbara continuing their art training in his department. Once again the pattern was to be Christmas in Reading or London, with the summer, and sometimes the spring, in the north. And so it continued, throughout Collingwood's life, with the family sometimes in the Lake District, sometimes in London, and sometimes abroad, split by work, marriage, or war.

This sketch of Collingwood's childhood family shows the combination of practical skill and activity and continuous intellectual endeavour that was characteristic throughout his life. We are reminded of his student Tom Hopkinson's comment[28] that while teaching as a young don he mended his son's lead toy soldiers and made his own beehives; and of his own description in *The First Mate's Log* of making an azimuth when sailing in the Mediterranean with a group of Oxford students in 1939.[29] This juxtaposing of the practical and the intellectual, the traditional and the innovative, is brilliantly illuminated in Collingwood's comment on the arts and the practical sciences in *The New Leviathan* chapter on 'The essence of civilisation': 'Consider knots. The life of every sailor, the catch of every fisherman . . . depend on knowing that a knot you have tied will not come untied until you set out to untie it, and will quickly come untied when you do.' (*NL*, 36.35)

[28] Tom Hopkinson, editor of *Picture Post* 1940–1950, later *Drum* in South Africa; see Hopkinson, Tom 1982. *Of This Our Time: A Journalist's Story*. London: Hutchinson, 85 and 301.

[29] Collingwood, R. G. 1939. *The First Mate's Log of a Voyage to Greece in the Schooner Yacht Fleur de Lys in 1939*. Oxford: Oxford University Press, 12, 22–4.

3. INFLUENCES ON THE YOUNG COLLINGWOOD

3.1 His Father, W. G. Collingwood

Although the family is absent, W. G. Collingwood appears on a number of occasions in the *Autobiography*. The memory and the debt were fresh in Collingwood's mind even some forty years later. He dedicated his first major book, *Speculum Mentis*, published in 1924, 'to my first and best teacher of art, religion, science, history and philosophy', adding in his own working copy ':- W. G. Collingwood from R. G. Collingwood'. Nothing could be plainer.[30]

So what influences can we discern from his father during this period? W. G. Collingwood was described as 'artist' on Collingwood's birth certificate. In the 1891 census he was listed as 'artist (portraits and figures) and writer', with 'sculp[tor]' written in above. In the 1901 census (Collingwood was twelve), he was listed as 'artist and author', with 'sculp[tor]' again written in above; his wife was listed as 'artist [and] sculp[tor]'; she was also elected a member of the Society of Miniaturists. For W. G. Collingwood, however, there was always a tension between art and academia. As a classics student in Oxford during the 1870s (he gained a first class classics degree in 1876), he was introduced by the painter Alfred Hunt, one of his father's friends, to Ruskin, then Oxford's Professor of Fine Art,[31] and became one of his undergraduate circle, attending his lectures and classes, joining breakfast parties in his rooms, and taking part in his projects (for example, the Hinksey road-digging project to teach undergraduates the value of hard physical labour). He decided to train as an artist after leaving Oxford, and went to work under Legros at the Slade, meeting well-known artists such as Burne-Jones whose son he tutored, while nevertheless continuing with his father's encouragement to apply (though unsuccessfully) for academic posts, and also to work for Ruskin when he moved to Brantwood in the Lake District. By the mid-1880s, with his marriage and move north to the Lake District to consolidate his work for Ruskin, he was

[30] Douglas Johnson, 1994 also takes this view: 'W. G. Collingwood and the beginnings of the Idea of History', *Collingwood Studies I*, 1–26.

[31] Ruskin was known as 'the centre of all artistic interests in Oxford, and even more as "Professor of Things in General"'. See Collingwood's obituary of his father in *The Times*, 3 October 1932.

exhibiting annually at the Royal Academy, and in 1889, shortly after his son's birth, was suggesting to his wife that keeping on a studio in London would pay for itself as well as the rent for the Gillhead cottage. He was already becoming a central figure in Lake District art, literature, and history, joining the CWAAS in 1887 (he became a member of Council in 1896 and editor of its *Transactions* in 1900, and organized many of its excursions),[32] and making friends with key figures in the Arts and Crafts movement, such as Arthur Simpson. By the time Collingwood was born, his father was recognized as the chief exponent of Ruskin's work, much in demand up and down the country as a lecturer on art, mountains, mountain drawing, and geology,[33] with a number of publications, and a developing interest in archaeology and excavation, and in Norse influences in the Lake District.

Collingwood's early involvement with his father's preoccupations is clear from his own youthful writings as well as his father's letters and diaries. This started with W. G. Collingwood's work as an artist and his studies of Scandinavian art and literature. In 1894/1895, when Collingwood was five, W. G. Collingwood was working on Norse place names in the Isle of Man and the Lake District,[34] and drafting and redrafting ideas for his historical novel *Thorstein of the Mere: A Saga of the Northmen in Lakeland*, dedicated to his son. This was published in 1895 with hand-drawn maps, and an elaborate cover and frontispieces with line drawings of animals and birds and flower lacings. W. G. Collingwood wrote to his wife in 1894 and 1895: 'Rob has been reading proofs of Thorstein – and is now writing the travels of Thorstein, for himself'; 'he says no, thank you to the proposal to write a letter, & would rather draw. "Thorstein" and "Raineach" have been killing

[32] Townend, *The Vikings and Victorian Lakeland*, 218ff. W. G. C. was elected President in 1920. The CWAAS was W. G. C.'s normal route for publishing his studies in Lake District history (he published in the *Transactions* virtually every year), and worked on CWAAS matters in partnership with his son throughout his life.

[33] W. G. C. and his wife had both exhibited in Arthur Simpson's exhibition at Kendal in 1886. In 1887, as part of the Oxford University extension lectures in Coniston, W. G. C. asked Arthur Simpson to lecture on wood-carving while he taught the minerals class: Renouf, J. 2004. *The Lake Artists Society: a Centenary Celebration. Ambleside, Cumbria: The Lake Artists Society*, 13.

[34] 1894. 'Some Manx names in Cumbria', *CWAAS* XIII, 403–14.

wolves and doing tremendous adventures.' A pen-and-ink sketch by his father dated 'May 28 "95"' shows 'Robin reading "Chronicle"' on Thorstein in train'—the first of the book reviews—totally absorbed.

The death in 1896 of William Morris, whose translations of Icelandic sagas, retellings such as *The Earthly Paradise* (1868–1870), and visits to Iceland in 1871 and 1873, had kindled Victorian interest in Old Norse and Scandinavian matters, prompted W. G. Collingwood's collaboration with the Icelander Jón Stefánsson: first in November 1896 to begin work on a translation of the *Kormaks Saga*, and then in the summer of 1897 on a three-month journey to Iceland to study and paint the saga sites. During those months W. G. Collingwood wrote extensive and copiously illustrated letters home to his family, produced hundreds of watercolour paintings and ink sketches of Iceland, and took a collection of photographs which is now recognized as a unique historical record of Iceland at that time.[35] It was against this background of his father's quickening interest in Scandinavian matters from the early 1890s onwards that the young Collingwood began writing his Jipandland stories and contributing to the family chronicle *Nothing Much*.

Collingwood continued to draw on his father's work on Scandinavian literature and archaeology in later life. In 1936 he joined the Folklore Society and began to lecture on folklore, recalling his childhood readings and drawing on folk stories to invent 'a new kind of archaeology'. He was fascinated by sagas and Old Norse throughout his schooldays, contributing papers to Eranos on

[35] Collingwood, W. G. and Stefánsson, J. 1899. *A Pilgrimage to the Saga-Steads of Iceland*. Ulverston: W. Holmes; Hannesson, H., Björnsson, Á. S., Björnsson, B. Th., and Gnosspelius, J.B. 1988. *Fegurð Íslands og fornir sögustaðir*. Reykjavík: Bókaútgáfan Örn og Örlygur hf. See <http://www.mbl.is/greinasafn/grein/24154/> for details of the *Fegurð Íslands* book. Most of W. G. C.'s original paintings and sketches, and his photographs, are in the archives of the National Museum of Iceland in Reykjavík; some material, including the original hand-written letters, is in Abbot Hall Museum and Art Gallery, Kendal and in the archives of the R. G. Collingwood Society, Cardiff University. See Smith, T. 2013. 'Why did W. G. Collingwood go to Iceland in 1897?' in Lea, M. J. and K. R. (eds). 2013 *W. G. Collingwood's Letters from Iceland: Travels in Iceland 1897 by W. G. Collingwood and Jón Stefánsson*. Cardiff: R. G. Collingwood Society/Collingwood Icelandic Pilgrimage 2012.

Norse sagas, and naming his secret place for private reading Igdrasil, one of the most potent symbols in Norse mythology: the 'world tree', which contains the source and history of all life, stretching up to the heavens and down to the underworld (*A*, 8). Here is a letter to his mother written in the summer of 1906, at the end of his third year at Rugby, when he was seventeen:

> the week having been fine I was prompted by the anniversary on June 11 to go down to Aganippe (the anniversary is Thomas Arnold's last visit to the place where he bathed every day, the day before his death[36]) and found it good. Therefore with Garratt I repaired thither today. It was a sultry day, rather dull and breezeless, and we couldn't walk far: so I suggested books and Aganippe.... It is a stretch of the Avon 200 yards long, still and deep, and wider than usual here: and thick trees overhang and shelter it completely ... We searched for a tree, and found the very thing. It was a venerable poplar, overhanging the Avon. It was hollow till 10 feet up, where it ended in a sort of little platform out of which diverged its tall branches. And in the middle of the platform was a hole. Garratt first ascended by the outside (nearly falling into the river en route): I, deciding both to explore a new way and not to fall in, climbed into the hollow, and by a judicious bit of chimney-sweeping[37] reached the hole.... Once up, we were above the river at a good height, with heaps of room and as comfortable as you please: so we read and talked till it was so late that we had to run for chapel. We decided that the retreat had to be christened something: so we considered the trees of history for a precedent: but the only one that seemed to be satisfactorily named was Igdrasil: so Igdrasil our tree was forthwith named.

Collingwood was also deeply influenced from an early age by his father's growing expertise as an archaeologist. In the *Autobiography* (*A*, 80) he recounts that his first visit to 'a modern excavation' was to his father's dig 'at the north tower of the Roman fort called Hardknot Castle; I was three weeks old, and they took me in a carpenter's bag'. This was in spring 1889, when his father was excavating with Henry Swainson Cowper.[38] W. G. Collingwood's interest at this time was 'to paint the camp, and if possible to paint it restored', which would require 'some rough survey of the

[36] Aganippe was the nymph of a mountain spring in Greek mythology.

[37] This is a reference to rock-climbing in the Lake District; 'chimney-sweeping' is a technique for climbing up a narrow cleft or gulley.

[38] See *CWAAS* XII, 1893: 28–33 and 275–438 for excavations of the Roman fort at Hardknott in 1889, 1890, and 1892.

remains'. He exhibited one of the resulting pictures, 'The Last of the Romans in Cumberland: Destruction of Hard Knott Camp (End of the 4th Century AD)', at the Kendal Arts, Crafts and Loan Exhibition in 1891, and also prepared a report on the excavations, with maps, drawings, and plans; the watercolour frontispiece was used by Collingwood as the frontispiece to his book on Roman Britain published in 1923.

Throughout his childhood Collingwood went digging and surveying with his father. Three letters written in April 1903,[39] when he was fourteen and still at Charney Hall (note the schoolboy slang),[40] give the flavour of these expeditions, when the young Collingwood was his father's walking companion, learning accurate observation through hard application on the ground. The first is to his mother:

We walked hard to Red Bank and both nearly expired ... and ate apple pasty ... Then we ploughed up Dunmail Raise and it was fearful hot and rounded the head of Thirlmere and came to the bracelet place under Rough Crag – a most awful steep place. A tiny path, nowhere more than about 1ft wide, wound round the very edge near the top, and following that we came suddenly to a little platform – precisely above where the bracelets were – and there was a small cave there ... There are little cut stone steps leading up out behind the platform ... We got in about quarter to 9 most awful tired and footsore both of us, and ate mutton chops and about a quart of tea apiece. This morning we went about 8 to Derwentwater Castle and there were two navvies ready to begin. They dug about 12 or 18 feet of trenches without finding anything whatsoever, and then found 1 small fragment of pot – just exactly like the sort bread is riz in ... At last one of them lit upon the very most vilely built walls you have ever seen, and simultaneously – the people's midden-stead! ... tons of old pot ... great chunks of Whitehaven anthracite and a girt lump of Borrowdale wad! ... and they found a 18th century saucer and claypipe, together with more unmistakeable evidence that the place is a 18th century farmhouse. Isn't it a beastly suck?

The story for the following day was continued in a letter to the Kid, his younger sister Ursula:

We have just had breakfast and have to go down to the lake to sketch and help Mr Hodgson survey ... The digging is all done, and the men paid

[39] I am grateful to Dr Townend for dating these letters (personal communication).

[40] E.g. girt = great; nowt = nothing; nobbut = nothing but; suck = shame, cheat.

off – really very decent navvies – and so we have just to amuse ourselves and do odd jobs, like overlooking Canon Rawnsley's diggings - which Mr Marshall thinks are nobbut rabbit-holes . . . It was a beastly suck for Mr Hodgson, he came up panting and perspiring to survey, all the way from Carlisle, and there was nowt but an old farmhouse and a few lumps of slag when he got here. Tom Crosthwaite the tenant supposes "they" were trying to smelt some very bad iron-ore which occurs near by, and gave it up in despair, and let their house fall down. We tried another place for the castle, but that was nobbut a peat-moss with some clearing-stones shied into it. So then we paid off the men and came back here.

The third letter continued again to his mother:

Meanwhile Pater is doing a sketch and I am writing. Thanks to Mr. Hodgson we didn't do much yesterday: I went up Skiddaw by my wild lone in a blizzard. To begin with, Mr. H. wanted me to help him survey the Lord's Island house . . . I held tape-ends and he went about with the other end . . . Then we went up to see the Canon, but he was in bed, . . . so we went back to our lodgings, sent Mr. H. to his hotel, picked up our traps and departed to examine terraces and suchlike on the lower flank of Skiddaw. They were 4 steps, as it were, cut out of the side of the hill, nobbut cultivation terraces with a ruined farmhouse by them. I left Pater to sketch them, and to wait for Mr. H., and proceeded up Skiddaw.

The first of these letters refers to W. G. Collingwood's investigations at Thirlmere following the find in December 1902 of two late Celtic or early Iron Age bracelets by workmen digging for road-mending material.[41] The other two letters refer to excavations in Derwentwater by some of the key figures in the CWAAS, Canon Rawnsley and Mr Hodgson, together with W. G. Collingwood, at Lord's Island just below Keswick, and Castlerigg, on the hill above it.[42] Throughout these years Collingwood would have seen his father writing papers for publication in the *CWAAS Transactions* (W. G. Collingwood took over as editor from 1900), and editing reports by archaeological and antiquarian friends and colleagues. Haverfield, elected Camden Professor of Ancient History in Oxford in 1907 and claimed as the chief figure in Romano-British studies at the time, was a familiar figure in archaeological excavations in the north at least fifteen years earlier.

[41] 'Two bronze armlets from Thirlmere', *CWAAS* NS IV, 1904: 80–4.
[42] 'The home of the Derwentwater family', *CWAAS* NS IV, 1904: 257–87.

Haverfield first saw the work of the CWAAS at Hardknott Castle in 1892, and joined the Cumberland Excavation Committee in 1894, working on Hadrian's Wall for the following ten years to solve problems of its date and construction.[43] W. G. Collingwood was listed as a participant on one of Haverfield's digs in 1902.[44] Collingwood as an undergraduate in Oxford knew Haverfield well, but he would already have been exposed as an adolescent to Haverfield's methods and thinking about the nature of archaeological evidence. Commenting on the state of Romano-British studies in 1911, Haverfield urged that 'the chief work to be done in Roman history [is] to wring life and blood out of stone . . . Art and epigraphy are old and familiar subjects for the Roman historian to embrace. We have now to go further to forms of archaeology which lack the written element natural to inscriptions and the language inherent in pictures'—'potsherds, fibulae and house ground plans'.[45] This is markedly similar to the insistence of W. G. Collingwood and his son on archaeological excavation to solve historical problems, as well as their practice of drawing on the widest range of sources.

From the beginning of his Rugby school years, Collingwood's father involved him more deliberately. In September 1903 (Collingwood was about to start at Rugby), father and son travelled together to the Hebrides, to prepare for the CWAAS field trip planned for May 1904 (when Collingwood's letters from school referred to the family staying on Iona). In August 1904, father and son travelled together again, this time to Norway. Collingwood kept a diary of the trip, which he read later to the family, and referred to this journey in one of his letters home from Rugby in December 1904: he had been to a lecture about mission work in Kashmir, and compared the slides with Norway: 'such splendid trees in valleys by big rivers, with tall peaks over all – a little like Briksdal in Norway I thought; only everything magnified enormously . . . I have been round to the "Art Museum" where they have a lot of beautiful things lent by S. Kensington[46] – mediaeval

[43] See Birley's contribution in this volume.

[44] *CWAAS* NS III, 1903: 331. See also Freeman, P. W. M. 2007. *The Best Training-Ground for Archaeologists: Francis Haverfield and the Invention of Romano-British Archaeology*. Oxford: Oxbow Books, 271.

[45] Freeman, *The Best Training-Ground for Archaeologists*, 232–3.

[46] The South Kensington Museum, renamed by Queen Victoria the Victoria and Albert Museum and graced with a new building by Aston Webb, 1899–1909.

arms, & a few Viking swords – not nearly so decent as the Bergen ones, but rather good.'

As Collingwood grew older, he worked for his father. In the summer holidays at Lanehead in 1905, he was copying drawings for his father's slides: 'I have had my new patent camera out in the garden, and photographed Dora picking roses . . . I have copied a huge lot of drawings (of Norse devils chiefly – most demoralising) to make slides for Pater – and the camera does that sort of work capitally.'

Working as colleague with his father was to continue throughout W. G. Collingwood's life. In the spring holidays of 1907, when Collingwood was eighteen, we find him mapping sites across Westmorland by bicycle for his father:

> I am extremely pleased to hear that our joint efforts have resulted in something worth the trouble. . . . We both derived an incalculable amount of instruction, and a fair quantity of amusement, as well as vexation, out of the expedition: and we learnt a marvellous lot about the ways of ordnance maps. . . . Between Grange Hall and Muddy Gill (to take one example) there was one gill of vast proportions to get through, and there were walls to climb . . . at 8.30 P.M. we discovered that the Shap-Kendal road was completely laid for its first 6 miles with new unrolled granite . . . occasion [ing] 10 punctures at the rate of one to every half-mile: but after the first few miles it was simply glorious rushing down limitless (or apparently so) hills with not a soul in sight, and all dark but for a star or two, a moonlit cloud in the east, and our lamps which made the faintest glow. . . . I arrived home rather before 11.30. My poor front tyre is just a collection of shreds of rubber, with handkerchiefs tied round it at intervals to keep it together: but I hadn't the cheek to add 'new tyre' to my list of expenses.

Finally, in September 1907, and again in 1908 before going up to Oxford, Collingwood worked as his father's assistant on his excavation of the Romano-British village of Ewe Close near Crosby Ravensworth.[47]

What may we conclude that Collingwood learnt from his father's work? Five things stand out here.

First, Collingwood acknowledged his father's teaching. When *Thorstein* was reissued in 1929 (with considerable rewriting by his father), he requested that the original dedication should stand on the grounds that the book had been 'his first lesson in history'.[48]

[47] *CWAAS* NS VIII, 1908: 355–68; IX, 1909: 295–309.
[48] Townend, *The Vikings and Victorian Lakeland*, 61–2.

Second, as Douglas Johnson suggests, there are parallels between Collingwood's conception of 're-enactment', that is, 'getting inside' the person's mind in order to understand the problem to be solved—*The Historical Imagination* was the title for his 1935 professorial inaugural lecture—and his father's imaginative reconstructions in the historical pictures and novels that accompanied his archaeological and topological investigations, as *Thorstein* accompanied his publications on mapping Norse names (although later on Collingwood was to be severely critical of the historical veracity of W. G. Collingwood's novels).

Third, in his own work Collingwood followed his father's practice of drawing on all available sources in order to understand a particular historical problem. His father had drawn on the literary evidence of the Scandinavian sagas to pinpoint saga sites in Iceland, and Norse mythology to understand the iconography and trace the typology of stone crosses and other remains across Cumbria, Yorkshire, and Northumberland. Later on, in similar fashion, Collingwood drew on his knowledge of folklore to invent 'a new kind of archaeology', and his knowledge of Greek and Roman literature, his precise drawing and mapping of inscriptions and archaeological finds such as pottery and brooches across England and Europe, and his documentation of sites not only through excavation but also statistically,[49] in order to understand history and culture.

Fourth, he was already wrestling with the question of what kind of evidence can be used in order to answer what kind of question, as can be seen from the later analysis in the *Autobiography*. It is not likely the young Collingwood reached this level of enquiry, but his letters from Rugby demonstrate that he had already learnt the importance of being clear about what his sources were saying and not saying, and that when you discussed a book, a picture, or a church, you had actually read and looked at what you were discussing and had thought about what the author, painter, or stonemason was trying to say or do.

Finally, in Collingwood's account in the *Autobiography* of his youthful training in archaeology alongside his father there are signs of the later 'question and answer' method:

[49] See Collingwood's reference (*A*, 135) to Crawford, O. G. S. 1929. *Air-Photography for Archaeologists*. London: HMSO.

I grew up in a gradually thickening archaeological atmosphere: for my father, who as a professional painter was not very successful, turned more and more as he grew older to archaeology, for which he was brilliantly gifted; and at last, during school holidays, I learnt to distinguish the relics of ancient camps and cultivations from eskers and outcrops, was entrusted with the search for prehistoric remains in unexplored districts and the surveying of them when found, and spent two seasons working as his assistant in his now classical excavation of a Romano-British village. (*A*, 80)

This comes in the chapter in the *Autobiography* on his developing thinking about the philosophy of history. Later, in the chapter on Roman Britain, he described Haverfield and the Cumberland Excavation Committee as 'consciously and completely Baconian in their methods. They never dug a trench without knowing exactly what information they were looking for; they knew both that this information was the next thing they needed for the progress of their study, and also that this trench would give it them' (*A*, 124).

Illustration 6. Glass plate photograph by Collingwood of burial urns excavated by W. G. Collingwood from a burial circle on Banniside Moor, Coniston. See *CWAAS* NS X, 1910, pp. 342–54. Courtesy of Teresa Smith.

Both father and son were part of the new critical approach to evidence through archaeology. The annual reports in the *CWAAS Transactions* provide abundant examples of rigorous 'question and answer', well illustrated by W. G. Collingwood's terse comment on his excavation of a burial circle on Banniside Moor above Coniston: 'it is worth noting that simple inspection and conjecture were valueless in the attempt to explain the site, whereas a few days' digging solved the problem'.[50] There is more than a hint here that Collingwood's later 'question and answer' method was germinating in his early training.

3.2 John Ruskin

Ruskin does not appear in Collingwood's *Autobiography*. This seems an odd omission. Collingwood's father was Ruskin's biographer and right-hand man, called him 'my best friend and kindest patron' and described himself as 'private secretary to Ruskin', meaning 'doing anything from making models of mountains and crystals to looking up authorities and dealing with rough copies and proofs'—'a Jack-of-all-trades'.[51] The Collingwood family was intimately bound into Brantwood and its concerns during the first ten years of the young Robin's life, until Ruskin's death in 1900.

Collingwood himself did not refer to Ruskin in his work until his centenary lecture, *Ruskin's Philosophy*, delivered in Coniston in August 1919. But we can look for earlier evidence of Ruskin's influence. Scholars such as McCallum and Johnston have argued that Ruskin's influence was indirect, mediated through his father: the 'idea of a broad and many-sided intellectual culture'; the emphasis on personal experience and practice in art, geology, natural science as the basis for writing,[52] and the independence of mind—in McCallum's words, Ruskin's 'individual and unorthodox approach . . . to many of the philosophical and political ideas of the day'.[53] It would hardly be surprising if W. G. Collingwood

[50] 'An exploration of the circle on Banniside Moor, Coniston', *CWAAS* NS X, 1910: 342–54. Urns, beads, and flints were photographed by R. G. Collingwood (see Illustration 6).

[51] Townend, *The Vikings and Victorian Lakeland*, 34.

[52] Johnston, *The Formative Years*, 18 and 28ff.

[53] McCallum, R. B. 1944. 'Robin George Collingwood 1889–1943', *Proceedings of the British Academy* XXIX. London: Humphrey Milford, 1.

had the key role as mediator during Collingwood's childhood and schooldays. Collingwood's school letters demonstrate, however, that he was already studying Ruskin for himself. Even in his first term at Rugby, as his form master commented, Collingwood 'could beguile the hours of work by giving recitations from Ruskin'. In his third year, Collingwood, then aged sixteen, was studying Ruskin on ornament; exploring churches with his friends and trying to interest them in Ruskin's writings on art and architecture; visiting churches to study and draw the architecture; and reading Ruskin's *The Stones of Venice*.

Collingwood was clearly applying Ruskin's lessons. When he criticized his colleagues in the sixth form's debating society Eranos for passing judgement on books they had never read, he referred to the 'embarrassingly analytic methods of Ruskin'. Collingwood was sufficiently intrigued by the meetings to describe them in detail in his letters, as in the following to his father:

> Well, I must stop shortly: but I must just mention a rather interesting paper read at Eranos-meeting tonight. It was entitled "The Greek spirit in Tennyson and Browning", and the reader, after first entirely failing to define the Greek spirit, proceeded to prove that Tennyson had none of it, and Browning all. This was a revelation to me: I never imagined the possibility of proving the presence of a thing whose existence you weren't sure of. I suppose that comes of being brought up on the embarrassingly analytical methods of Ruskin. I tried to define the Greek spirit as one of repose, restraint and conservation as opposed to the Teutonic spirit, of inquiry, growth and superabundance: I don't know whether I was right.

What did Collingwood mean by Ruskin's 'embarrassingly analytical methods'? We may find a clue in the art historian Kenneth Clark's introduction[54] to Ruskin's *Praeterita*. Here he describes Ruskin's drawings of Venice, Verona, and Abbeville, made during journeys between 1858 and 1880, as

> some of the most beautiful architectural drawings ever executed . . . In looking at them we begin to understand Ruskin's repeated claim that his chief merit was his power of analysis: by which he meant not scientific analysis (for, like the Brahmin, he would have destroyed all microscopes),

[54] Ruskin, J. 1949. *Praeterita*. London: Rupert Hart-Davis; Kenneth Clark's introduction, xviii.

but the power of scrutinising an object so patiently and so perceptively that he could reveal something of its true character which a hastier inspection, however adroit, would overlook.

In *Praeterita*, Ruskin himself described his obsession with precise observation thus:

on fine days, when the grass was dry, I used to lie down on it and draw the blades as they grew, with the ground herbage of buttercup or hawkweed mixed among them, until every square foot of meadow, or mossy bank, became an infinite picture and possession to me, and the grace and adjustment of growing leaves, a subject of more curious interest to me than the composition of any painter's master-piece. The love of complexity and quantity before noticed as influencing my preference of flamboyant to purer architecture, was here satisfied.[55]

So what did Collingwood draw from Ruskin, whether directly through his own study, or indirectly through the influence of his father? To start with, there is Johnston's view that Collingwood received a 'Ruskinian education' from his father: 'R. G. Collingwood did not dream up the ideal of a many-sided intellectual life: he inherited it.'[56] We recall Knox's comment that Collingwood 'was in fact one of the most learned men of his generation'.[57] Secondly, we should remember that he was not just interested in book-learning, but, like Ruskin, was immensely skilled practically, and determined to link theory and practice. Tom Hopkinson,[58] one of his students at Pembroke College in the early 1920s, wrote of his 'capacity for relating abstract speculation to everyday happenings': 'His breadth of knowledge was the subject of many anecdotes, a knowledge by no means confined to academic subjects. In discussion he could explain a point by making a quick drawing, taking a musical instrument down and playing it, or with a reference to the morning's newspapers.'

Here we should note Collingwood's insistence, in his 1919 centenary lecture *Ruskin's Philosophy*, on the juxtapositioning of Ruskin's lack of philosophical 'book-learning' with his powers of analytic observation:[59]

[55] Ruskin, *Praeterita*, 199.

[56] Johnston, *The Formative Years*, 28.

[57] T. M. Knox quoted in Johnston, *The Formative Years*, 28.

[58] Hopkinson, *Of This Our Time*, 85.

[59] *Ruskin's Philosophy*. Chichester: Quentin Nelson, 42–3.

> Ruskin . . . flung his whole mind into the new movement of thought . . . never worried by the care of making ends meet, flying through the air of thought with the freedom and security of a Tintoret angel . . . I say he was philosophically the best-equipped mind of his generation. Book-learned in philosophy he was not; but he was no great believer in book-learning. He once laughed at "foolish readers" who doubted the truth of his economic views because he said he had never read books on political economy. "Did they suppose," he asks, "I had got my knowledge of art by reading books?"

Johnston[60] also shows how both Collingwood's and his father's notion of 'the historical imagination' was foreshadowed in Ruskin's own writing on the 'imagination' and 'purpose' of the 'actor in history', as set out in his Oxford lectures in 1872:

> remember always that the most important part of the history of man is that of his imagination. What he actually does, is always in great part accidental; it is at best a partial fulfilment of his purpose; and what we call history is often . . . merely a record of the external accidents which befall men . . . It is therefore a true historian's work diligently to separate the deed from the imagination.

This 'typically Ruskinian insight' is recalled in Collingwood's 1936 lecture *Human Nature and Human History* and in the *Autobiography* (*IH*,205–31 and *A*, 70 and 112–13). Here we have Nelson's battle plan at Trafalgar: we have to reconstruct the actors' processes of thought, their calculations and their strategies to make full sense of their actions:

> How can we discover what the tactical problem was that Nelson set himself at Trafalgar? Only by studying the tactics he pursued in the battle. What else could we do? Even if we had the original typescript of the coded orders issued by the wireless to his captains a few hours before the battle began, this would not tell us that he had not changed his mind at the last moment, extemporised a new plan on seeing some new factor in the situation.

Again it is worth revisiting Collingwood's centenary lecture on Ruskin. We can see the juxtapositioning of what Collingwood calls Ruskin's 'modernism', his intense concern 'for science and progress, for political reform, for the advancement of knowledge and

[60] Johnston, *The Formative Years*, 25ff.

for new movements in art and letters', with 'his imaginative sympathy with the past', 'an imaginative, historical appreciation of a past which he recognised as past, which he admired but never worshipped ... [recognizing] that the mediaeval ideals of art and life ... were wholly unsuitable for solving the problems of modern life'. Here perhaps we can see reflections of Collingwood himself—'the mind that sees the unity of things' that Collingwood himself aspired to, the connections between the practical and the theoretical, and the seeds of 'the historical imagination'.

4. CONCLUSION

We leave Collingwood on the brink of Oxford. In December 1907, he travelled there to take the entrance examinations, and back to Reading when they were finished. Dora's diary for Saturday, 21 December, recorded the family's excitement when the news arrived that he had won the top scholarship at University College, his father's old college:

> We had a rather painful day yesterday & went to bed at last ... Suddenly at about 7 there was a wild peal at the bell & the Kid, who had been out to get a paper burst in, shouting something ... I knew it was good news from her voice. We leapt out of bed and tore downstairs shouting "what?!!" "Robin's top of the list – got the first Univ. Scholarship." "Hurrah – where is he? Where is he?" The conquering hero was in his bath, so we all sat on the stairs in the dark outside the bathroom door & drank tea which Alice brought us, & the Kid read out the list by the light of the hall gas.

In conclusion, what are we to make of Collingwood, aged nineteen, at the end of his schooldays? The evidence shows a highly intelligent and intellectual young man, with strong passions and friendships amongst adults and peers, deeply interested in music, art, photography, literature, religion, and the natural sciences, eager to practise all of them, with a critical eye and independent spirit, fiercely articulate, acknowledging his Ruskinian heritage learnt through his father of accurate observation and critical reading, already an able organizer of people, and already with the habits of hard work (and perhaps the later insomnia) that were to last his lifetime.

Alan Bennett, in his play *The Habit of Art* about W. H. Auden and Benjamin Britten, makes Auden say that as a poet he has the 'habit of art'.[61] What else should we say of Collingwood at the time he went up to Oxford to his father's old college, except that he had acquired and was practising the habits of thought, work, and practical engagement taught to him by his father in the tradition of Ruskin?

[61] Bennett, A. 2009. *The Habit of Art*. London: Faber and Faber, 47.

2

THE OXFORD MAN

JAMES PATRICK

R. G. Collingwood's *Autobiography*, published in 1939, began with a paragraph-long preface in which he warned readers that the work was focused narrowly on his philosophy: 'The autobiography of a man whose business is thinking should be the story of his thought.' But the philosopher had come up to University College at nineteen in the high summer of Edwardian optimism; won a First in Greats; secured a fellowship at Pembroke; brought his bride Ethel Graham home to Oxford and reared their children Bill and Ruth in its neighbourhood; attained the high honour of the Waynflete Professorship; and left Oxford only when, in the shadow of the coming political storm, ill health made his work impossible. Throughout these Oxford years there ran a history that was more than the history of his thought, the history of a man unscarred by cynicism who loved life, nature, music, God, old churches, his family, his students, archaeology, and, most of all, the romance of thinking. The background against which Collingwood's autobiography was played out was Oxford, the university and the city.

In his attachment to John Ruskin, William Gershom Collingwood had taken his family to Lanehead, the house at the entrance of the lane leading to Ruskin's Brantwood on Coniston Water, where Robin would spend his boyhood sailing, learning the piano and violin, and puzzling over Kant, but when Robin Collingwood went up to University College in 1908, he was taking the Collingwood name home. The Collingwoods had belonged to Oxford for four generations. When Robin went to tea with Miss Hyde in March 1911, 'She reminisced cheerfully about my great-grandparents, and I acquired a considerable knowledge of my family.'[1]

[1] R. G. C. to unnamed 12 March 1911 [TS/FLTR 0333]. Miss Emma Hyde of 7 South Parks Road was one of seven daughters of Thomas Edward Hyde, clothier, who had been in Oxford since 1861.

The great-grandparents Miss Emma Hyde remembered were Frances Collingwood, the daughter of his twice-great-grandfather Samuel Collingwood (1762–1841), printer to the university at the Clarendon Press, and her husband (and cousin) Samuel Collingwood of Deptford and Greenwich (1786–1852). Samuel's son William Collingwood (1819–1903) was born in Greenwich but schooled in Oxford at the house of his cousin James Hinton and under the eye of Samuel the printer, who lived in St Giles at the time of his death in 1841. William, destined for a scholarship at Christ Church, which he declined because he scrupled at the Thirty-Nine Articles, left Oxford for Liverpool but his son, Robin's father William Gershom Collingwood (1854–1932), would return to take a First in Greats at University College in 1876.[2]

So when Collingwood was taken around his father's college in September 1908 to choose among thirty-eight sets of rooms, the Collingwood name was returning to familiar ground. 'I have got the top rooms in the tower between the High and the inner quad: high and light and fairly cheap', he wrote to his father. But there was a difficulty: 'An ordinary little piano will not get up the stairs, so I have got no ordinary one. It is a weird little creature about the size of a spinet.'[3] Two days later (October 11) Robin wrote to his mother, whom as a boy at Lanehead 'sitting on the stairs in the dark' he had heard play Beethoven and Chopin, noting that as he wrote he heard 'Beethoven sonatas going on, on the "club piano", the Pastoral (D Minor andante to be exact)'. His determination to lift a piano up the tower stairs signalled a love of music that had caused him to consider coming up on a music scholarship, and throughout his Greats years music would be his avocation. On 25 September he wrote to his father, 'I was booked for the union concert on Wednesday: and of course Monday and Tuesday went into rehearsal for that. I was playing in a Bach trio and a Purcell chamber sonata. On Sunday I heard [Schumann's] piano quartet and it is really good. I played viola in the Mozart trio (for a charity concert).' The business of university life was Aeschylus, Cicero, and logic in Michaelmas Term and Theocritus and Lucretius in

[2] Paper on William Collingwood, written by W. G. C. [TS/FDW068].

[3] R. G. C. to W. G. C., 9 October 1908 [TS/FLTR 0223]. R. G. C. remembered the tower room with affection (*A*, 13).

the next. He wrote to his father on 24 January, 'I find that I have to read 1/3d of Demosthenes . . . before the end of the term: so I have been attacking him with unwonted vigor. But the music is the stuff for keeping one alive.'

The love of music nourished at Lanehead on Coniston Water belonged to a happy childhood lived among a family he deeply loved: his father and mother (Pater and Mater in his college letters; Dearest Daddy and Dearest Mama in his own middle age); his sisters Barbara, Ursula (the Kid or Sossie in his correspondence), Dora (Beetle in the letters). He also brought from Lanehead an imagination vivified by the beauty of the lakes and a Ruskinian love for the natural world. He wrote to his mother of his first Oxford spring:

> I am waiting breathlessly for spring every day. I assure you I watch the crockets on St. Mary's day by day for them to burst into green! The birds have been expecting it for about a fortnight–and sing improvisations about it. I have come to the conclusion that bird-singing, so far from being a mere natural shouting is a highly developed art: of course different birds develop it along different lines. Larks for instance sing recitatives in what you might call florid counterpoint in one part: robins sing real melodic phrases in plain-song, on a proper diatonic scale of sorts. However I am too frantically busy to write a treatise.[4]

Robin Collingwood also brought from Rugby a Church of England Christianity that would, like a stream sometimes submerged, sometimes in flood, mark his works from *Religion and Philosophy* (1916) to 'Fascism and Nazism' (1940).[5] He had been baptized at Rugby

[4] R. G. C. to E. M. D. C., March 1909 [TS/FLTR 0235].

[5] Oxford in 1908 was still conventionally Christian, with many clerical dons and a residuum of required chapel attendance. The diary Collingwood kept as a young don records his churchgoing (e.g. 12 April 1914, *et passim*). He tells us his parish church in Kensington during his Admiralty stint in London was St Mary's Abbot. In the university Collingwood was among the group of lay dons that included Michael B. Foster and C. S. Lewis whose members identified themselves with Church of England Christianity, the heirs of the 'via media' Newman had proposed in the 1830s as it had been developed by Benjamin Webb and John Mason Neale in the 1860s and 1870s and by *Lux Mundi* authors such as Charles Gore and John Richardson Illingworth between 1880 and 1914. Neither an Anglo-Catholic admirer of Rome nor a rationalist adherent of the Modern Churchman's Union, Collingwood might have been considered by his Oxford contemporaries (in then-current taxonomy) a liberal Catholic. His dislike of Protestantism is evident in the praise he offered the monks of Santorini on his visit in 1939, when he suggested that

on his own initiative in 1905 (when he had taken the name George, an act that remained controversial in the family), and then confirmed in 1906.[6] In this perhaps the influence of his grandfather William, whose evangelical convictions had taken him from the staid Congregationalism of his youth to the more fervent Church of the Brethren, and who had lived until Robin was fourteen, would have counted for something. At Rugby confirmation would have been a rite of passage characteristic of a culture fed by the Christian high-mindedness of Thomas Arnold. Robin thought chapel a great success when the hymns were good and the readings were Genesis 1

the monks might 'rise up in judgment against his own world and against the protestantism and secularism and utilitarianism of which it is so proud'. *The First Mate's Log of a Voyage to Greece in the Schooner Yacht Fleur de Lys in 1939* (1940, Oxford University Press), reprinted 1995, Bristol, England: Thoemmes Press, 153. On this occasion the crew and the monks found that their detestation of popery formed a common bond. Collingwood associated Romanism and neo-scholasticism, which he detested, denying (like his mentors John Alexander Smith and Clement C. J. Webb) that St Thomas had proposed any system, although he spent Christmas morning 1919 'Happily reading Thomas Aquinas in College' [TS/FLTR 0548]. See Patrick, James 1985. *Magdalen Metaphysicals*, Macon, Georgia: Mercer University Press, 140–2. In a letter to de Ruggiero (22 November 1922) Collingwood praised English theologians for abjuring 'neo-thomism, pragmatism, and such stuff'. On 16 January 1927 he wrote to de Ruggiero explaining the English church-chapel landscape and implying that the English were a church-going people, an opinion Ethel caused him to correct in a postscript. The same letter implies his participation in the parish council.

[6] Rugby School Chapel Register, 4 July 1905, 27 March 1906. R. G. C.'s great-grandfather Samuel the printer enthusiastically supported the British and Foreign Bible Society. See 1979. *The Oxford University Press and the Spread of Learning: An Illustrated History, 1478–1978*, Oxford, at the Clarendon Press, 38, 51, 52, and his son William, R. G. C.'s grandfather, was a member of the Brethren, a title descriptive of several pietist, evangelical groups, who in tandem with a successful career as a landscape painter had been a preacher and a writer of books such as 1905. *The Bible Its Own Evidence*, Kendal, England: T. Wilson. Infant baptism as practised in the Church of England would have been no part of the tradition of the household of W. G. Collingwood's youth, so it is not surprising that he would have neglected the then culturally commonplace baptism of his four children. Robin's baptism and confirmation at Rugby would have had about it a tone of modest rebellion, and when describing his funeral in Coniston in 1943 his sister Barbara still felt that his having taken the name George at the time of his baptism derogated family tradition: 'He had an unpolished coffin, and on the plate was the only name he came into the world with, Robin Collingwood (by my instructions).' Barbara Gnosspelius Diary, 12 January 1943; personal communication from Janet B. Gnosspelius, 22 February 1984.

and Revelation 21, the dramatic beginning and yet more dramatic end of the Biblical story. In October 1905 he wrote to Ursula:

> We went to church, as it was harvest thanksgiving day – we went and it was a communion service. I wish I could give you some idea of it: It was – I can't think of a word to express it, but it was too much for me and I could do hardly anything but weep the whole time. . . . The whole service is so very impressive it makes one feel so near, that the emotion of it is almost too strong.[7]

When his friend Harold Broadbent died, Robin wrote again to Ursula, 'The first thing I did was to turn to my Bible for there is no trouble that St. John cannot cure, and opening at random the first verse I saw was "If you loved me you would rejoice because I said 'I go to your father and my father.' " It hurts to lose a friend, and it hurts worse to see other people hurt, but it is really all right.'[8]

These are the words of a romantic boy, and in his undergraduate years there is more than a touch of John Betjeman's wandering from church to church in search of architectural splendours. Robin once visited Salisbury Cathedral five times in one day, and of a visit to Warrington he wrote, 'Today I have been church-hunting—we got to our church, surveyed its exterior (a tempting, decrepit, Gothic sandstone thing, decently begargoyled and sculpted) and found to our unbounded disgust that it was locked!'[9] But there was something deeper, something that if it did not effloresce into a vivid piety, did mature into a steady intellectual conviction, something Edwardian Church of England to the core, always

[7] R. G. C. to 'my dearest Sossie', October 1905 [TS/FLTR 0099]. He corresponded frequently with Ursula about religion. This letter continues: 'How I could have stood it if I had taken the whole thing [that is, the whole communion] I can't think. Please read the service through some time, though that really can't show you anything of the feeling that accompanies the time when you first hear it—when you hear the low voice "take and eat this in remembrance that Christ died for thee", you really want to sink into the earth the presence of God seems so near. You must come with me next holidays.' This openness to emotion is the adolescent anticipation of the mature Collingwood's reading of Eliot's *Waste Land* in the concluding pages of *Principles of Art* as a poem depicting 'a world where the wholesome flowing water of emotion, which alone fertilizes all human activity, is dried up'.

[8] R. G. C.'s reference to the death of Harold Broadbent is in a letter to Ursula of 1906.

[9] R. G. C. to Ursula, 23 October 1910 [TS/FLTR 0309]; R. G. C. to E. M. D. C., 19 November 1905 [TS/FLTR 0113]; R. G. C. to Sossie, Advent 1905 [TS/FLTR 0112].

anti-Roman, that never faded. In his maturity, while he never dealt successfully with the idea of revelation as understood by traditional theologians such as Charles Gore (whom Collingwood knew and admired), the Christian religion became a presupposition which made him consider it the foundation of thought and the essential steam of civilization, all to the bemusement of his critics.[10] It was as though the evangelical religion of his great-grandfather Samuel of Greenwich (1786–1852) and his grandfather William (1819–1903)—whose booklets John Ruskin kept by his chair—rejected by the freethinking William Gershom Collingwood, had discovered an intellectual form in Robin Collingwood.[11]

Life at university was a feast of ideas. 'Perched in my tower in the garden quadrangle of University College I read all day and most of the night' (*A*, 13). And there were like-minded friends who would accompany him throughout the Greats years, among them Arthur Cockin, Frank Craddock, and Colin Eddison. He wrote to Barbara on 8 May 1909:

> I believe I never before in my life stayed in bed until after nine. It was all the fault of the Old Firm (which name is attached unofficially to a Society for Nocturnal Discussion of the Universe consisting of Arthur, Colin, Frank and me). Its meetings have been so frequent and lengthy lately that this morning when Harry called me, nature rebelled. The Old Firm is a desperate institution because it seldom meets before ten or eleven and you can't work off a really pretty point of metaphysics, even without many digressions, until about two.[12]

[10] Collingwood, R. G. 1940. 'Fascism and Nazism', *Philosophy* 15: 169. T. M Knox thought Collingwood, having rejected realism as stupid, might have gone on to erect his philosophy on the foundation of human credulity (*IH*, xvi). Critics have sometimes concluded that Collingwood could neither locate religion successfully in his philosophy nor forego a lifelong conviction of its importance. Alan Donegan described Collingwood's conviction that there was 'in Christianity something which compelled his veneration while eluding his ardent attempts to define it', 1962. *The Later Philosophy of R. G. Collingwood*, Oxford: The Clarendon Press, 307. Collingwood knew Bishop Gore as an undergraduate, recorded hearing his sermons, and reviewed Gore's *Philosophy of the Good Life* in Eliot's 1931, *Criterion*.

[11] John Ruskin valued William Collingwood's religious pamphlets. Ruskin's rejection of the church and advocacy of a simple Bible religion would have reinforced the Free Church, evangelical tone of the Lanehead household.

[12] Frederick Arthur Cockin (1888–1969) was the best friend of Collingwood during his undergraduate days, sharing his interest in music, scholarship, conversation, and

And there were his tutors, Arthur Poynton, E. F. Carritt, and G. H. Stevenson. 'It must have been on Tuesday evening that the excellent Stevenson came to call after Hall. He was very amusing. He discussed German opera, and Roman antiquities (especially Corstopitum) and Ibsen, and Bernard Shaw, and modern French fiction.' But Carritt was the principal influence. Deep in the study of the first Epistle of St John, he wrote to his mother, 'St. Paul is a child to this stuff. Carritt is invaluable here. He is one of the cleverest young greats-dons in Oxford, and has quite the subtlest mind I have met.'[13] In 1912, at the end of Robin's university years, Carritt would consider him his best pupil after A. D. Lindsay, then already established at Balliol, and Collingwood would justify his tutor's confidence.

By May of his first year he could write to Barbara that Gilbert Murray had noticed him and asked his name, and when Hilary Term of his second year got under way, he wrote to his father (24 April 1910), 'I have got the Conington College Prize for "Latin Scholarship" in the Virgil, Cicero, and Lucretius of the long vac.' And his studies pleased: 'I have quite an interesting set of lectures: the *Republic* and Herodotus of course: Carritt on moral philosophy and Hogarth on Aegean civilization.' And just one week later he wrote to Barbara: 'Would you believe that I got full marks on my logic paper? That's where real profundity of intellect comes in, of course. Also full marks for Lucretius, which I believe is highly unusual. . . . I got 11 a's altogether, which is decent,

the church. Collingwood thanked him (with his tutor Carritt and S. G. Scott) in the preface to *Religion and Philosophy* and reviewed the Thirty-Nine Articles with Cockin prior to Cockin's ordination in Southwark Cathedral, which Collingwood attended (see his diary for 8 July, 19 September 1915). The diary, begun in 1912, attests that the friendship was maintained with some intensity throughout the period 1908–1920 (e.g. 13 June, 17 September, 1913; 21 April, 3, 7, June, 10 July, 1914; 30 October 1915). Cockin was Bishop of Bristol and a much published author of theology for the laity. Such interests and friendships made it not quite unreasonable for Pembroke to have sought assurances in 1912 that Collingwood did not intend to take holy orders. See footnote 22.

[13] R. G. C. to W. G. C., 6 June 1909 [TS/FLTR 0255]; R. G. C. to E. M. D. C., 12 May 1909 [TS/FLTR 0250]. Edgar Frederick Carritt (1876–1974), interested early in Benedetto Croce, took up realism about 1910. Arthur Blackburne Poynton (1867–1944), University College fellow and tutor, later bursar and dean, lecturer in classics. George Hope Stevenson (b. 1880) tutored and lectured in ancient history.

though one short of Arthur's last year.' Thus completing Mods with a flourish, he established a reputation as a student whose promise would not be overlooked in the common rooms. Philosophy had become part of life: 'Sorry, I can't keep Aristotle out of my letters.'[14]

When Collingwood began to read philosophy in 1910, Oxford philosophy was set to become the battleground he described thirty years later in the *Autobiography*. The influence of the Kantian-Hegelian school identified with Thomas Hill Green would run from 1880 to about 1914, but in 1910 the coming names in philosophy were, as Collingwood wrote in the *Autobiography*, obsessed with destroying this influence. The autumnal representatives of the idealism of Green were John Alexander Smith and Harold H. Joachim, while the Wykeham Professor of Logic, John Cook Wilson, and his satellites H. A. Prichard and H. W. B. Joseph, politely seconded by Collingwood's tutor E. F. Carritt, led the assault. The intractable nature of the differences that divided the schools and the acerbic quality that would later lie in wait beneath the surface of the debate were not yet evident in 1910, but that battle and his participation in it, first as an acolyte of the realist school and then as its determined opponent, would be the background of Collingwood's Oxford years.

His interest in archaeology blossomed. On 19 November 1910 Collingwood 'called on Professor Myres and told him I wanted to take up archaeology for greats, and would he tell me what to do. So he smiled sweetly through his gold spectacles and stroked his black beard and dictated a list of forty-one books in various languages.' A year later, presumably having read at least some of this bibliography, Robin wrote to his father, 'We had a jolly lecture on Wednesday from Forster, who is doing Corstopitum. Haverfield presided and asked me to lunch to meet Forster: and between them they invited me to go there this summer and lend a hand. It seems exactly the chance I want for a start.' Thus began the love affair

[14] R. G. C. to Barbara, 1 May 1909 [TS/FLTR 0250]; R. C. G. to W. G. C., 24 October 1910 [TS/FLTR 0265], 24 April 1910 [TS/FLTR 0287]; R. G. C. to Barbara, 1 May 1910 [TS/FLTR 0290]; R. G. C. to W. G. C., 14 November 1909 [TS/FLTR 0268]. Gilbert Murray (1866–1927) was newly appointed (1908) Regius Professor of Greek. David George Hogarth (1862–1927), who had excavated on Crete and Melos, was a scholar of the Near East and after 1909 Keeper of the Ashmolean Museum.

with archaeology and the long friendship with Francis Haverfield that ended only with his death in 1919.[15]

But philosophy made the dearer claim. On 29 January 1911 he wrote to his father:

I have done little beyond a sort of Jameson raid into the territory of Transcendentalism, where I enjoyed myself so much that I am engaged in returning for a longer stay. I think a lot of what they say about Kant's style is absurdly exaggerated—or else the translators have been remarkably efficient—for I have won through a good lump of the *Critique* without any practical hitches, and find it great fun. Now I am devouring the *Prolegomena to Any Future Metaphysic.*

And two weeks later: 'I am becoming rabid about Kant. He is a perfect darling.... Of course his theories may be wrong here and there, but they are about the best in existence all the same.' Never one to confuse enthusiasm with accomplishment, he wrote to Barbara (22 February), 'If I am going to escape getting a fourth in Greats I shall have to learn 250 times as much in the next year as I have in the last. And that is embarrassing.'[16] Carritt was still his philosophic guide. On 19 February 1911 Collingwood and Cockin called on the Carritts at Boars Hill, 'a sort of Garden City for dons', where they met Mrs Carritt, 'a wood nymph,... smoked, ate in the drawing room, and took our leave in time to pound the four miles into Oxford for evening chapel'. On 12 March Collingwood reciprocated with an invitation to dinner in his college, and by his last year the Carritts had become Edgar and Winifred. Robin would be godfather to the Caritts' son Noel, a familiarity that would make Collingwood's gradual defection from the realist fold during the years 1917–1920 poignant.[17]

His Rugby religion persisted. On 7 November 1909 Robin described Charles Gore, the popular Bishop of Birmingham, to Dora: 'He has a huge voice pitched in the very bottom of the bass

[15] R. G. C. to W. G. C., 19 November 1910 [TS/FLTR, 0315], R. G. C. to W. G. C., 3 February 1911 [TS/FLTR0323]. John Litton Myres (1869–1954) was a distinguished archaeologist. Robert Henry Forster (1867–1923) collaborated with F. J. Haverfield in excavations at Corstopitum.

[16] R. G. C. to W. G. C. 29 January 1911 [TS/FLTR 0322], R. G. C. to W. G. C. 12 February 1911 [TS/FLTR 0326], R. G. C. to Barbara 22 February 1911 [TS/FLTR 0330].

[17] R. G. C. (letter begins 'Darling'), 19 February 1911 [TS/FLTR 0327], R. G. C. to W. G. C. 12 March 1911 [TS/FRTR 0333].

octave, and is altogether charming', and 20 March 1911 was 'an exciting day winding up with a sermon by Gore'. On 23 May 1910 he wrote to his father, 'I went to lunch with the [William] Temples, which was very amusing: we discussed all sorts of things from Welsh disestablishment, the budget, Socialism, Chesterton and GBS to rock climbing.'[18] Collingwood knew the varieties of Church of England religion that would survive into the interwar years and their Oxford standard bearers; he had visited the Cowley fathers, icons of the Anglo-Catholic movement, and found plain chant intriguing, but neither Pusey House nor St Mary Magdalene, the Oxford centres of Tractarian Anglo-Catholicism, show up in his diary.[19] Collingwood was sympathetic to the Church of England orthodoxy of Charles Gore, and he would treat Gore's thought with respect, but from early on in his Oxford career, labouring to construct a philosophy of the Christian religion, Collingwood was drawn to the rationalizing theology that lay along a line joining the radical thought of Burnett Hillman Streeter, who finally declared the miracles to be psychological, and the more guarded thought of William Temple, gently modernist, if at all.[20] On 22 November 1921 he wrote to his fellow Crocean Guido de Ruggiero that English theologians erred in refusing to distinguish between mythological form and idealistic content. The approach of Streeter, fellow of Queens College from 1905 to 1933 and a stalwart of the Modern Churchmen's Union,

[18] R. G. C. to E. M. D. C., 20 March 1911 [TS/FLTR 0276], R. G. C. to W. G. C. 23 May 1910 [TS/FLTR 0296]. Collingwood reviewed sympathetically Gore's *Philosophy of the Good Life* in Eliot's *Criterion* 10 (1930–1931): 560–2. Gore roiled Oxford in 1911 by deposing J. M. Thompson, the Magdalen College chaplain, for doctrinal irregularities. See Patrick, *Magdalen Metaphysicals*, xxv–xxvi, 19–20. William Temple left Oxford for the pastoral career that would culminate in his tenure as Archbishop of Canterbury from 1942 to 1944.

[19] 'Went to Cowley this morning, where they have the weirdest services.... But the clever thing about plainsong is that one can join in and sing away' (R. G. C., January 1909 [TS/FLTR 0233]). Collingwood had read Newman, whom he praised for having resolved the problem of his special science into a historical problem (*Speculum Mentis*, 53), but the manuscripts and correspondence display no interest in the lingering influence of Tractarianism.

[20] The divergence of Collingwood's thought from the immanentist rationalism of Streeter's Group is illustrated by the contrast between the treatment of theology in *SM* as a form of thought and the last half of Streeter's *Reality* (1927), titled 'Life Force, Absolute, or God'.

tended to reduce Christian revelation to philosophical or psychological principles. The attraction for Collingwood of The Group, sometimes called the Cumnor Circle, lay in the fact that with the publication of its manifesto *Foundations* in 1912, it was established as the only group in Oxford seriously interested in exploring the relation between idealism and Christianity, a project that appealed to Collingwood, who from *Religion and Philosophy* (1916) to *Speculum Mentis* (1924) argued that religion, specifically the Christian religion, was a system of thought, not to be explained as merely psychological.[21] There would be none of the Biblical piety of his grandfather, or of the Rugby boy, but rather a settled intellectual conviction that the ideas he considered fundamental to Christianity could be stated as philosophic presuppositions that rightly served as foundations of the good life and of the civilization he valued.

A lover of Kant, Hegel, and conversation, who could not keep Aristotle out of his letters, was bound never to leave Oxford willingly, so the decision of May 1912 was no surprise, nor was

[21] The Group, inspired principally by Burnett Hillman Streeter (1874–1937), was founded 1 October 1910, and included R. Brooke, R. G. Parsons (1882–1948), chaplain of University College 1907–1911, W. H. Moberly (1881–1974), fellow of Lincoln, N. S. Talbot (1879–1943), A. E. J. Rawlinson (1880–1964), James Moffat (1870–1944), G. K. A. Bell (1883–1958), Bishop of Chichester, William A. Pickard-Cambridge, Ronald Knox, and N. P. Williams (1883–1943). The Group spanned a Church of England spectrum that included modernists or soon to be modernists such as Streeter and Parsons, and liberal Catholics, dons less enthusiastically modernist, interested in tradition and somewhat given to ritual concerns, such as R. Brooke and A. E. J. Rawlinson. Ronald Knox was a member before the publication in 1912 of *Foundations*, the work of seven Oxford dons, a group largely coterminous with the Streeter Group. Knox, who was not represented in *Foundations*, subsequently wrote *Some Loose Stones* and began his journey to Roman Catholicism. Collingwood was too junior to have contributed to *Foundations* in 1912, but he maintained his association with the Group through the 1920 and 1930s. Theological modernism, represented in Anglicanism by members of the Group (among others), in English Catholicism by George Tyrrell and (perhaps) von Hügel, and in English Protestantism by R. J. Campbell, considered religion a kind of misunderstood philosophy and sought to reduce its mythological content to philosophy. Streeter's Cumnor Group is not to be confused with the Oxford Group, later called Moral Rearmament, to which Streeter lent his support in his later years. For Collingwood's participation in the Group see his diary (e.g. 30 June 1914, 16 December 1915, 29 January 1920, 21 January 1921), an interest that continued into the 1930s. Patrick, *Magdalen Metaphysicals*, xxvi, 100.

his success. On 16 June, with Frank Barry and Pickard-Cambridge, Collingwood was interviewed at Pembroke, and asked if he would likely take orders sometime soon or marry rapidly.[22]

Despite this piquant demur: 'I wouldn't pledge myself on either point,' Collingwood was duly elected to a Pembroke fellowship and appointed lecturer in philosophy and classics. Collingwood was given a room with an oriel window overlooking St Aldate's church. At dinner the Pembroke fellows shook hands solemnly, then drank the new fellow's health. His return to Coniston on 7 July was a triumph.

On the cusp of his passage into Pembroke, the Wykeham Professor of Logic, Cook Wilson, whom he had asked to write Pembroke on his behalf, invited Collingwood to call. He wrote to his father:

> After preliminaries he began discussing my essays. "Now mark you," he says, cocking an eye at me over the corner of his beard, "I don't expect you or anyone else to understand Plato at your time of life. But nine philosophers out of ten never understand him as long as they live and you are the tenth. There are heaps of people who can make a name by writing paradox, but you have a gift that most philosophers would give their ears for—you can see the obvious." I remember a great deal more that he said, but per sample you may see why I refrain from writing it down. One thing he said was, "I told the Pembroke people that I'd never seen an undergraduate's work showing more concentration, combined with more power of writing." I think that's enough quotation. Then he went on to give me advice worth gold on how to read Plato, and how to interpret Aristotle: And he discussed all our more distinguished contemporaries with a fluency and point that would have startled them. There was one man only [Bosanquet] he spoke of with unreserved admiration. Most of them he described as 'mere windbags'—'paradox mongers'—'a charming fellow, you know, but a sophist'—'if you're a fool you may be a clever fool like—or a silly fool like—' mentioning two names of professors with reputations.

Collingwood never forgot this introduction to the gossipy, political aspect of academic life that had been hidden behind common room doors from an undergraduate much taken up with the architectural society, friendship, his music, philosophy, archaeology,

[22] R.G.C. to Ethel Graham, 16 June 1912 [TS/FLTR 0383]. Frank Russell Barry (1890–1962) did take orders, becoming Bishop of Southwell. William A. Pickard-Cambridge (1879–1957) lectured in philosophy at Pembroke 1912–1913. Robert Nigel Carew Hunt (1890–1959), Merton College, B. A., B. Litt., became a successful author and an expert on Communism and Socialism as political theories.

and general happiness. The paper Cook Wilson had in hand (Collingwood tells us in the *Autobiography*) was his essay on Plato's *Sophist*. Whatever else Wilson intended to accomplish with this combination of truth, welcome advice, flattery, and knowingness, his remarks, like the flattering comparison with A. D. Lindsay that Carritt offered the Pembroke fellows on Collingwood's behalf on 31 March 1912, were intended, consciously or unconsciously, to keep Collingwood in the realist camp. Twenty-six years later, when he wrote the *Autobiography*, Collingwood twice cited this incident, in detail in the chapter 'Minute Philosophers', refusing in 1938 as in the 1912 letter to his father to name the objects of Wilson's disapproval (*A*, 20, 26).[23]

Thus initiated into the conversation of alliances and oppositions and secure in his Pembroke fellowship, Collingwood turned to the matter of writing. He assured Barbara on 12 November 1912:

> As for the philosophy of religion, I keep going at it, but only reading, not writing just now. You can't write in term, with all your pupil's work cutting holes in your thoughts. . . . But I'm plowing away at Hegel's Philosophy of Religion, which is an immensely great work. . . . I get more and more convinced of the necessity for the work; there are very few people here who really see where the difficulties lie and want to tackle them—plenty of good theologians but of the historical rather than the metaphysical kind. And most current philosophy of religion is bilge. You read William James if you want to see.

In the fall of 1912 the new Pembroke tutor began a diary that would be maintained until 1922, which catalogues the full life of a popular don: lunch and a walk with B. H. Streeter on 14 October, Streeter again on the twenty-first. A philosophy tutors' meeting on 25 November, and dinner with (C. C. J.) Webb at the vice-chancellor's on 3 December, on 9 June 1913 the Aristotelian Society and dinner with J. A. Smith, then on 21 June beginning work on the *De Anima* lectures. During the summer of 1913 Collingwood finished his translation of Croce's *Philosophy of Giambattista Vico*. He received Croce's corrections on 27 October and between 16 and 20 December read the *Estetica*. In the years before he left Oxford for London and the Admiralty his lectures were 'The Theory of Knowledge', 'Philosophy of Religion', and the *De Anima*, the last attended by the

[23] A. D. Lindsay to the Pembroke electors, Pembroke College, Oxford Papers; R. G. C. to W. G. C. 16 June 1912 [TS/FLTR 0383].

American T. S. Eliot, sent to Collingwood on the recommendation of his tutor H. H. Joachim.[24] Before war put a caesura to university life, Collingwood was a favourite of the older dons. Although a protégé of Carritt and in his own words to Gilbert Ryle a 'Cook Wilson realist' before the war, he had come to share Professor Smith's interest in the Italians and enjoyed both his and Harold Joachim's approval.[25] On 30 January 1915 there was dinner with the pragmatist F. C. S. Schiller and the realists Prichard and Russell at Corpus Christi, and the next day dinner with Hastings Rashdall and attendance at Prichard's 'very fine' lecture on Russell.[26] By 1913 Collingwood was friendly with John Alexander Smith, since 1910 the Waynflete Professor of Moral and Metaphysical Philosophy and as such the doyen of Oxford idealists. Collingwood accompanied Smith, whose interest in Benedetto Croce he shared, to the Aristotelian Society dinner and to the theatre in Soho, and his exhaustive notes taken at Smith's 1915 Hibbert Lectures, 'The Nature of Spirit and Its life', suggest that Collingwood had developed something of a disciple's regard for Smith's thought.[27]

The collapse of European politics into the Great War in August 1914 ended the Edwardian idyll into which Collingwood had

[24] Patrick, James, 2000. 'Eliot and the New Idealism: Poetry and History at Oxford, 1914–1915', *Collingwood and British Idealism Studies* 7: 5–7.

[25] The specific occasion of Collingwood's interest in Croce's philosophy is difficult to know. Croce was well received at the International Congress of Philosophy in 1908, and J. A. Smith had developed an interest in Croce's thought before he discovered his works in Naples in 1909, quickly learned Italian, and became a disciple. Smith, J. A., 1917–1918. Review of *The Philosophy of Benedetto Croce: The Problem of Art and History by H. Wildon Carr, Hibbert Journal* 16: 503; Smith to Collingwood, 30 January 1938, J. A. Smith Papers, Magdalen College Archives. R. G. C. to Ryle, 9 May 1835, Dep. Coll. 26/3.

[26] The increasingly uncomfortable, finally combative, nature of Collingwood's relation to Oxford philosophers grown sympathetic to Cook Wilson's realism and its successors after the 1920 Aristotelian paper, and especially after *Speculum Mentis,* developed against the background of his personal popularity between his election to Pembroke in 1912 and 1926, when Collingwood was appreciated as not only bright but as affable and companionable. The friendship with Schiller, whom R. G. C. called good company despite his dislike of Schiller's pragmatist philosophy, continued (see his diary, 24 October 1920). Collingwood attended Smith's Hibbert Lectures, 'The Nature of Spirit and Its Life', on October 19 and 29.

[27] 30 November 1915 (see his diary), and took sixty-six pages of synopses, Dep. Coll. 1–32. See also his diary for 11 July, 13 August 1917.

moved in 1908, and the colleges began to empty. He wrote to his father on 11 October that the men in Pembroke were 'practically all in the O. T. C. And all the rest will be drafted off 5 or 6 months hence with commissions. I may as well also confess that I applied to people for a commission in the event of the college not needing me after June and have been rejected about eyes.' In 1916 Collingwood left Oxford for the Naval Intelligence Department of the Admiralty in London, where he would work until 1919, usually spending a day or two each week at Pembroke, where he continued his work as tutor. With no responsibility for lectures, he was able to complete *Philosophy and Religion*, described in the *Autobiography* as the culmination of his juvenile studies in theology, which was published in 1916. On 13 August 1917 he began 'Truth and Contradiction', a critique of propositional logic intended as the opening salvo of a campaign against the realist position. Despite a positive assessment by the popular idealist philosopher Henry Jones, who called the book 'a "contribution" and step forward' and its author 'a college don from head to toe', who 'has something real to say', the manuscript was declined by Macmillan, and Collingwood would not make another book-length attempt to exposit his philosophy until *Speculum Mentis*, published in 1924.[28]

Collingwood found his work at the Admiralty, mostly with maps, easy and pleasurable. He took his love of music to London. 'I've had an orgy of writing music lately—wrote four songs in 2 days', he wrote to his mother on August 28, 1916, although a year later (28 July 1917) he found that 'even music writing is getting crowded out'. The birds of Kensington, not to be outdone by Oxford, made a delightful orchestra, whose tunes he recorded in musical notations.[29] At the end of his London stay Collingwood sang Parry's Jerusalem with a choir of five hundred others in Trafalgar Square.[30]

Collingwood's gift for friendship did not fail in London. He had recruited his father and his sister Barbara for the Admiralty, and as

[28] See R. G. C.'s diary, 13 August 1917; *A*, 42, 74. Collingwood wrote [*A*, 99], 'the only manuscript of "Truth and Contradiction," was destroyed', but the second chapter is in Dep. Coll. For Henry Jones's reader's comment see Macmillan Archives, 3 Series, vol. 1911–1921, fols 114–15. Published in *EPP*, 229–31.

[29] TS/FLTR0515, TS/FLTR 0523.

[30] TS/FLTR 0536.

the universities emptied dons found the Royal Geographical Society in Kensington, where maps were made and interpreted for the Naval Intelligence Service, a good wartime billet. There Collingwood met Samuel Alexander, 'an original old creature' with 'a weird metaphysic of his own', and worked alongside Oxford colleagues Hastings Rashdall, whom he knew from The Group, and H. J. Paton, his near contemporary, another young idealist who chose to buck the realist trend.[31] There the Collingwoods also knew Evelyn Underhill, later famous for her writings on mysticism, with whom Barbara and Robin were 'on easiest and happiest terms'. As a contribution to a symposium with Underhill, Collingwood would write 'Can the New Idealism Dispense with Mysticism?' in 1923.[32]

Collingwood returned to Oxford a published author, an avowed opponent of the realists, and a married man. He had met Angus Graham of Skipness in Argyle as an undergraduate, and had visited the family in Scotland, where he met Angus's sister Ethel and fell in love: 'I never knew I could be so happy.' On 19 September 1919 the newlyweds moved into 5 Fyfield Road; Robin wrote to Ursula, 'Lord, what a business it is getting into a house.'[33] Collingwood took up his duties, tutoring at Pembroke and offering lectures: 'The Ontological Argument' in Hilary Term 1920, 'Theory of Knowledge' in Trinity Term 1921 and 'De Ruggiero' in Michaelmas Term, not realist topics. Still the golden boy, his diary records a busy round of teas, with the Stevensons on 14 November, the Josephs the next day, and on the 20th with (R. H.) Lightfoot, newly elected a fellow of Lincoln, and then with him to a Joachim lecture.

The chronology of Collingwood's abandonment of realism is documented in the *Autobiography*, where he associates his doubts with his meditations on Gilbert Scott's Albert Memorial during his time at the Admiralty. A more detailed account would discover

[31] TS/FLTR0522 W. G. C. to R. G. C. 12 July 1917; Wallace, Stuart 1988. *War and the Image of Germany: British Academics 1914–1918*, Edinburgh: J. Downey, 238–9.

[32] 1923, *Proceedings of the Aristotelian Society*, Suppl. vol. 3: 161–75.

[33] R. G. C. to Dora Altounyan [TS/FLTR 0530], 19 March 1918. Collingwood had known Angus Graham as an undergraduate, and his diary from 1912 records frequent meetings to work on archaeological matters. R. G. C. to Ursula, 20 September 1919 [TS/FLTR 0541].

the beginnings of his change in philosophic allegiance no later than his sixty-six pages of notes on J. A. Smith's Hibbert Lectures of 1915, include the unpublished 'Truth and Contradiction', and find clear exposition in the manuscript *Libellus de Generatione*, written in July 1920 at Skipness.

My relation to the New Realism may be worth a word or two. I was brought up in it, in the first flush of its success at Oxford, and as a pupil of that brilliant and stimulating teacher John Cook Wilson. I think I entered rather deeply into its spirit. I wrote a book working out some of its principles; and found it incapable of dealing with some fundamental difficulties. This led me to close criticism of its methods and results, and finally to complete abandonment of, at least, the letter. At the same time I look back on my apprenticeship to it with gratitude.[34]

The *Libellus* was intended as the manifesto of Collingwood's new philosophy, and he was eager to put his position before his colleagues. On 4 November 1920 he wrote to de Ruggiero:

I am to read a paper to the Oxford Philosophy Society at the end of November on the collapse of modern realism, which is the first occasion I have had to put my views before the professors and tutors in philosophy here. It comes at the right moment, when most people in Oxford who were realists are giving up their old position and the younger men have broken away from that school, so it may be that I shall find some people willing to listen to me. If that is so, I shall think about publishing the *Libellus*.

A few of the younger dons had broken away from the Cook Wilson school or resisted the appeal of its popularity, but only a few.[35] As it happened the *Libellus* was never published and not many were willing to listen. One, however, was, and after he had

[34] 'Libellus', 1, Dep. Coll. 28.

[35] The younger men who rejected realism in the early twenties would have been considered exponents of the New Idealism, the philosophy of the School of Green vivified by the thought of Croce and Gentile. In 1923 Collingwood was assumed to be its spokesman in 'Can the New Idealism Dispense with Mysticism?'; but in the 1924 preface to *Speculum Mentis*, he rejected the title with vehemence. The grand old man of the New Idealism was John Alexander Smith. See Coates, Adrian, 1929. 'The New Idealism of Professor J. A. Smith, and the Question of Meaning', *A Skeptical Examination of Contemporary British Philosophy*, London: Brentano's Ltd, 163–87. Others whom contemporaries might have considered part of this movement were H. J. Paton, H. Wildon Carr, Alfred Hoernlé, and G. R. G. Mure. 'J. A. Smith in fact provided the one breath of fresh air among our seniors, with his interest in Croce.' Mabbott, J. D. *Oxford Memories*, Oxford: Thornton, 74.

read his paper, J. A. Smith invited him to join the Deipnosophic, a philosophers' dining club, eclectic in membership, in which Smith and H. H. Joachim were commanding voices.[36]

The paper read before the Philosophical Society in November 1920, welcomed by Smith and Joachim, was viewed with reserve by the powerful Prichard–Joseph connection, and the change of views was the fulcrum of Collingwood's Oxford life, an incident to be recited in the *Libellus* in 1921, recounted for the undergraduates of the Pembroke Philosophical Society in 1924, in his 1935 correspondence with Gilbert Ryle, and fulsomely in the *Autobiography*.[37] In one evening in November 1920 Collingwood had gone from being something of a university favourite to being a figure of controversy, so that four years of undergraduate success and eight years of donnish popularity would be followed by two decades of relative isolation, punctuated only by the success of the *Essay on Philosophical Method* in 1932. The realists understood that no small matter was at stake. When Gilbert Ryle wrote his 'Fifty Years in Philosophy' he noted that the great achievement of positivism had been freeing logic from the human mind and its psychology.[38] If this could be done, the road to a philosophy based upon mathematics lay open. If not, if logic were entangled with human knowing, the path led back to Green and Plato, to the moral concerns G. E. Moore and Bertrand Russell wished to segregate into a philosophically irrelevant subjectivity.

[36] On the early Smith–Collingwood friendship see Collingwood's diary (e.g. 9 June 1913, 19, 29 October, 30 November 1915, 11 July 1917). Brand Blanshard wrote of Smith, 'Few remember him now, but for a time early in the century he was the most respected philosophy don in Oxford', Schlipp, Paul Arthur, ed. 1981. *The Philosophy of Brand Blanshard*, La Salle, IL: Open Court Press, 29. C. S. Lewis wrote in the preface to his *Allegory of Love* that to live on the same staircase with J. A. Smith was 'in itself a liberal education'. Webb remembered him as 'that brilliant scholar, that master of discourse, the variety, originality, and suggestiveness of whose conversation will ever be treasured'. The Deipnosophic, its name an allusion to Athenaeus of Naucratis' *Learned Banquet*, included Smith, Joachim, C. C. J. Webb, W. D. Ross, and H. A. Prichard. See Clement C. J. Webb Journals in the Bodleian Library, 5 June, 11 October 1924 [MS. Eng.misc.e.1167]; 16, 29 January, 11 June 1925 [MS. Eng. Misc. d.1117]; 6 March 1930 [MS. Eng. misc. d.1122].

[37] 'Libellus', Dep. Coll.; Minutes of the Pembroke Philosophy Society, 60th meeting, 14 June 1923, Dep. Coll.; R. G. C. to Gilbert Ryle, 9 May 1935, Dep. Coll.

[38] Ryle, Gilbert, 1976. 'Fifty Years in Philosophy', *Philosophy* 51, 376.

To have lost one of the brightest scholars and most attractive personalities in the university, Carritt's brightest pupil and a self-professed disciple of Cook Wilson, if not overtly to the *retardataire* idealists at least to a critical anti-realism, was a not inconsiderable disappointment. The reaction was quick, creating a wall of silence of which Collingwood would complain throughout his Oxford career; he wrote to Guido de Ruggerio, 'No one seemed very interested.' But he remained closely in touch with European philosophy and continental affairs throughout his life, as is clear from other contributions in this volume (and see Illustrations 7 and 8).

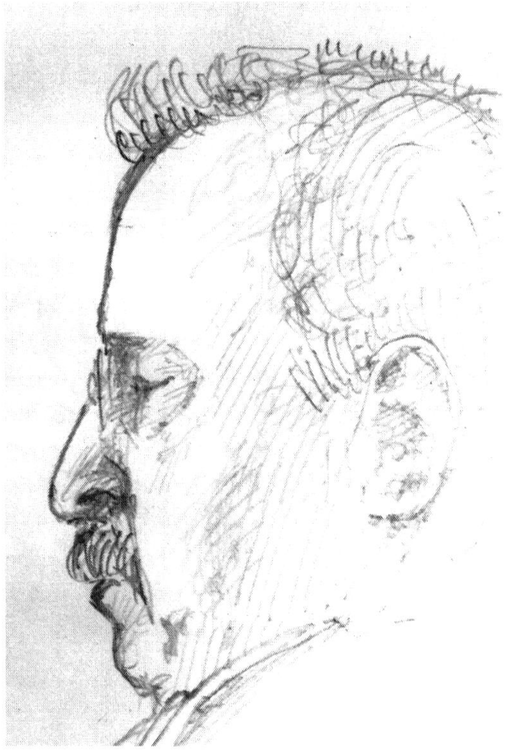

Illustration 7. Benedetto Croce, drawn from life by Collingwood at the International Philosophical Congress, September 1930. (Notebook XXIV, R. P. Wright Collection, Sackler Library, Oxford).

Illustration 8. Albert Einstein receiving an honorary doctorate of science, 23 May 1931, drawn from life by Collingwood. (Notebook XXIV, R. P. Wright Collection, Sackler Library, Oxford).

His reputation as a teacher grew among undergraduates, however, as it fell among university philosophers: 'I find myself beginning to make some kind of mark. Not among my elders and contemporaries so far as I can see, but among the undergraduates. They seem to find something to interest them in the things I say.'[39]

[39] R. G. C. to de Ruggiero, 20 March 1921, Dep. Coll.

My work, he would write in the *Autobiography*, 'was not with my colleagues but my students' (*A*, 71). Only months before the fateful paper was read, he had organized the Pembroke College Philosophical Society, a society destined to meet, usually weekly in term, for 165 sessions, the account of most meetings signed by the president, usually Collingwood, occasionally by students, T. M. Knox and Tom Hopkinson, then Pembroke undergraduates, among them. The inaugural meeting on 11 June 1920 had been attended by just twelve founders, and throughout its recorded life, from June 1920 to 15 August 1929, the meetings, held at first on Thursdays, then later on Fridays, in the president's rooms attracted a typical attendance of perhaps seven, occasionally falling to four and sometimes rising to include a dozen undergraduates. The demanding schedule would encourage members to lapse by missing several meetings but the lapsed would then routinely be re-elected. The tie that bound the society was obviously admiration for the president, which the minutes always tempered with good humoured irony, as at the 122nd meeting:

> The President delivered an address on the theory of knowledge. After outlining the particular question which occupied the Ancient, Medieval and Modern philosophers and indicating the debts owed by those of the last class who were not Scotsmen to those who were, the President reviewed the development of the theory of knowledge and the contributions made to it by Locke, Berkeley, Hume and Kant and others. Here he would have finished, but at the request of Mr. Hopkinson he continued and gave a brief outline of the nature of the work present day philosophers are doing. Of this address it need only be said that it proved of great value to new and old members of the society alike, and that in it the President surpassed his usual high standard of excellence. As an example of the salutary effect of the address upon the Society it may be recounted that one of the most hardened lapsers of the society was heard to declare that "If only I had heard all that at the beginning of his philosophical studies, what a difference."

Hopkinson was Tom Hopkinson, later a distinguished journalist and Professor of Jounalism at University College, Cardiff. Collingwood was his Pembroke tutor, and in his own biography Hopkinson explained Collingwood's appeal as a lecturer:

> His breadth of knowledge was the subject of many anecdotes. In discussion he could explain a point by making a quick drawing, taking a musical

instrument down and playing it, or with a reference to the morning's newspapers. This wide range of knowledge, his capacity for relating abstract speculation to everyday happenings, and his wit, which was not contrived but a matter of immediate response, had made Collingwood's lectures so popular that they could no longer be held in Pembroke and had to be transferred to a college with a larger hall, where they were attended by many who were not studying philosophy but came simply for enjoyment.[40]

Through his work as tutor and lecturer, Collingwood would influence undergraduates such as Hopkinson in unrecorded ways. Others would perpetuate his thought and influence in a scholarly way: T. M. Knox, John Coatman, and at least one American, the political philosopher Willmoore Kendall.[41]

The college had become his life. The house the Collingwoods had taken in September 1919 on Fyfield Road, in near north Oxford, was exchanged in November 1921 for Stapleton's Chantry, a large house in North Moreton, a village outside Oxford, and then, when the children were school age, back to 15 Belbroughton Road. R. B. McCallum thought Collingwood's habit of spending four nights in the college and three at home kept him away from the sociabilities of Oxford and contributed to the perception that he was 'remote and mysterious', and his frequent absences encouraged the disapproval of Homes Dudden, the Master of Pembroke. Just after the move to the Chantry he wrote to de Ruggiero, 'I come out from Oxford for Sunday, and generally once again in each week.'[42]

The publication of *Speculum Mentis* in 1924 marked the watershed in Collingwood's university career. It was a book that picked up the threads dropped by Green and was perhaps the last work by an Oxford philosopher that unguardedly assumed a view of life rooted in the European past and offered system in a philosophical

[40] Hopkinson, Tom 1982. *Of This Our Time: A Journalist's Story, 1905–1950*. London: Hutchinson, 85–6. The minutes of the Pembroke Philosophical Society are in Pembroke College Archives, with microfilm in the Dep. Coll. (MS facs. c. 147/1–2).

[41] On Kendall see Patrick, *Magdalen Metaphysicals*, 154–6.

[42] Collingwood to de Ruggiero, 22 November 1921, Dep. Coll; McCallum, R. B. 1943. 'Robin George Collingwood', *Proceedings of the British Academy* 19: 465.

climate that increasingly considered systematic philosophical thought impossible, but for Collingwood (he tells the reader in the preface) deliberate renunciation of this ideal represented 'the degradation of philosophy to a game, one of the most stupid and tedious games'. Thus *Speculum Mentis* was written not for philosophers but for the ordinary journeyman in art, philosophy, and religion, and written in 'English that a well-disposed and intelligent reader will understand if he tries'. The argument assumed that religion, like history and art, could be treated philosophically. In the beauty of its diction and the aspirations of the argument, if in nothing else, *Speculum Mentis* is a great book. Its author, ever optimistic, wrote to de Ruggiero in November 1924, 'I find that *Speculum Mentis* is exciting a good deal of attention . . . and is regarded as possibly opening a new movement in English Philosophy . . . . As T. H. Green was to Kant and Hegel, so is R. G. C. to Croce.'[43]

But the book did not move Oxford. In 1927 he again wrote to de Ruggiero: 'The official philosophy of the day is the realism of Moore and the rest; a very bad philosophy it is, in my opinion, as in yours, but it prevails at present, and those who dispense with it are either abused or merely neglected. The *Journal of Philosophical Studies* barely condescended to notice *Speculum Mentis*, [mentioning] it only in a few contemptuous lines of review, and other philosophical periodicals here have treated it in the same way.' Croce had written a perceptive review in *Critica*, but 'no reviewer here has treated it as a serious philosophical statement to be treated seriously'. The interests of realism, now the coming philosophy, ably represented by G. E. Moore's *Journal of Philosophy*, had decided that Collingwood's philosophy was no philosophy at all.[44]

Certainly one of the causes of the discomfort of many Oxford philosophers with Collingwood's thought was his conviction that religion, the Christian religion specifically, was properly an object of philosophic study, a position maintained in the face of the growing consensus that propositions, better pseudo-propositions, about God and theology were merely emotive. From his baptism at

[43] *SM*, 10; R. G. C. to de Ruggiero, 16 November 1924, Dep. Coll.

[44] R. G. C. to de Ruggiero, 16 November 1924. *An Autobiography* was given a patronizing review by an American professor: Marcham, F. G. 1941. Review of *An Autobiography*, by R G Collingwood, *Mind* 50 January–December, 546.

Rugby in 1905; in his first book, *Religion and Philosophy* (1916); *Speculum Mentis*, its superscript taken from St Paul with religion named one of the forms of experience; to the natural theology of the 1939 manuscript that became *The Idea of Nature* (*IH*, 87–8, 156–7); the defence of the ontological argument in the *Essay on Metaphysics;* and the claim of the 1942 essay 'Fascism and Nazism' that Christianity is the 'steam' that drives and defines Western civilization, the Christian religion, usually understood as presuppositions having intellectual content, was embedded in Collingwood's thought in a way that contributed to his marginalization, secured more directly on purely philosophic grounds, by the increasingly dominant realist school. He preached his first lay sermon on 6 May 1917, probably at Holy Trinity, Sloan Street, and what was perhaps his last at St Mary's, the university church, on 5 May 1935.[45]

Collingwood was, as he wrote to de Ruggiero on 4 October 1927, 'more and more conscious of being an outlaw'. He was still arguably the most interesting philosopher in Oxford; his paper for the Aristotelian Society in 1925 he judged 'a success: the largest meeting for years, they said, and very interesting and on the whole friendly discussion'.[46] Archaeology, which took him away from philosophy as such and away from the university, was satisfying, as was his work as a Delegate of the Oxford University Press after 1928, but apart from older professors whose influence was almost visibly fading, and a contemporary or two such as H. J. Paton, Collingwood would be ignored by the philosophical smart set in the university. He was never without friendship and encouragement. J. A. Smith supported Collingwood in the university from a first mention of Collingwood's translation of Croce in 1916 to a letter of 1938 thanking Collingwood for doing his thinking for him; and C. C. J. Webb praised Collingwood in print, beginning with his review of *Religion and Philosophy* in 1917.[47] Perhaps

[45] The 1917 sermon is referenced in TS/FLTR0517. The 1935 sermon, 'Rule Making and Rule Breaking', is in Dep Coll.

[46] R. G. C. to W. G. C. 24 March 1925 [TS/FLTR 0582].

[47] Paton, whom Collingwood called 'my friend' (see his diary, 10 March 1914), wrote that he and Collingwood were the only survivors among the idealists. Paton, H. J. 1956. 'Fifty Years of Philosophy', *Contemporary British Philosophy*, series 3, ed. by Lewis, H. D., London: Allen & Unwin, 345; Webb, C. C. J. 1917, Review of *Religion and Philosophy* by R. G. Collingwood, *Oxford Magazine*, 1 June: 281–2;

Collingwood had believed his career as a philosopher would be a continuation of the long midnight talks with Cockin and tea-time discussions with Stevenson and Carritt. In the preface to *Speculum Mentis* he had written: 'I do not expect a critic to spare his blows: I only say "strike but hear me".' But on the questions Collingwood considered paramount he was shouting to an audience of the deaf, their silence perhaps to some degree spiced with envy. Collingwood was filling lecture halls when attendance was supererogatory. Clement Webb, who reviewed Collingwood's books favourably and followed Collingwood's career in his diary, recorded in March 1926 A. E. J. Rawlinson's comment that Collingwood was 'very full of pride of intellect'; to which Webb answered, 'He is, of course, a man of most extraordinary gifts and accomplishments.'[48]

Shaken by his inability to gain a hearing for his philosophy, on 22 November 1928, Collingwood wrote to de Ruggiero: 'I have at present no very high opinion of *Speculum Mentis*.' He was in search of success, and success in the University of Oxford took the form of publication and a professorship. Until the eruption of *Principles of Art* (1938), the *Autobiography* (1939), and the *Essay on Metaphysics* (1940) he would publish no more acerbic criticisms of the realists, and assume none of the optimism of *Speculum Mentis*. He had applied for the professorship of Moral Philosophy in 1927, but a man twenty years older 'who richly deserved it' was elected.[49] Collingwood's interest in the Cumnor Group would persist; he would be a modest professorial asset to the university chaplaincy, appearing in the pulpit of St Mary's at the behest of his friend, the chaplain Arthur Cockin in May 1935 with his lay sermon titled 'Rule Making and Rule Breaking'.[50] The last

Review of *The Idea of History*, 1945, by R. G. Collingwood, *Journal of Theological Studies* 4: 25. Webb called the *Essay on Philosophical Method* 'one of the most remarkable and original among the philosophical books recently published in England'. Webb, C. C. J., 1936. 'Nature and Grace', *Journal of Theological Studies* 37: 113.

[48] Clement C. J. Webb Journals, 11 March 1926 [Bodleian Library Ms.Eng. misc. d. 1119]. The pacific Webb, disappointed by the 'megalomania' he, in common with most of Oxford, found in the *Autobiography*, still called Collingwood's career 'brilliant' (11 January 1943 [Ms. Eng. Misc. e. 1182]).

[49] The post went to H. A. Prichard.

[50] Patrick, *Magdalen Metaphysicals*, 100.

mentions of 'spirit' and 'spiritual', those markers of Edwardian idealism, occurred in *Speculum Mentis*, and the long involvement with Croce would lapse with the *Britannica* article of 1929, to be revisited only in the posthumously published *Idea of History*.[51] The published articles would be about history, philosophy, science, and art. 1928 was the year of the Die manuscript, the beginning of the *Idea of History*. Collingwood had begun to reimagine his work as having been from the first an attempt to find a rapprochement between history and philosophy, a project first evinced in an article of 1920 titled 'Croce's Philosophy of History', which began with the sentence: 'An alliance between philosophy and history is no new thing in this country.' But Oxford philosophers were no more interested in his philosophy of history than they had been in *Speculum Mentis*: 'I find that my own attempts to introduce a slender thread of historical thought [are] met with blank refusal.'[52]

Success came with the publication of the *Essay on Philosophical Method* (1933), solid evidence of original scholarship, a work that abjured an eristic, anti-realist edge; 'I have written it in a much chaster and less exuberant style than *Speculum Mentis*.' The book was appreciated with various degrees of enthusiasm by a broad spectrum of reviewers, among them colleagues such as the pragmatist F. C. S. Schiller, H. W. B. Joseph, H. H. Joachim, and J. A. Smith as well as philosophic allies such as Charles Hartshorne and Samuel Alexander (*EPM*, xxxvii).[53] Assisted by the influence of J. A. Smith, Collingwood would succeed in 1935 to the Waynflete Chair of Metaphysical Philosophy that Smith had resigned. 'From a worldly point of view,' he wrote, 'a professorship at Oxford may

[51] Collingwood mentions Croce in *Principles of Art* only once, somewhat disapprovingly, at 46n. In *Speculum Mentis* 'spirit' is still used (153, 309) as a substantive, in the metaphysically grand, quasi-theological sense of Smith's 'The Nature of Spirit and Its Life'. See note 26. In Collingwood, R. G. 1928. *Faith and Reason*, London: George Benn, 'spiritual' is an adjective (p. 7) and the 'scientific spirit' (p. 9) refers to an enthusiasm or an approach.

[52] *Hibbert Journal, 1920–21*. 19: 263–78; R. G. C. to de Ruggiero, January 1931, Dep. Coll.

[53] R. G. C. to the Clarendon Press, 9 March 1933; *An Essay on Philosophical Method*, 2005; edited with an introduction by James Connelly and Giuseppina D'Oro. Oxford: Clarendon Press, xxxvii.

be regarded as the culmination of a career and arrival at the head of one's profession.'[54]

The correspondence in 1935 with Gilbert Ryle that followed upon Ryle's review of the *Essay on Philosophical Method* in an article in *Mind* titled 'Mr. Collingwood and the Ontological Argument' perhaps assuaged Collingwood's disappointment that although the realists would strike, they would not answer. After 1920, in the wake of his anti-realist profession, Collingwood had not complained that he was isolated socially, and he had long known that his philosophy often failed to please; it was the tendency of the realists simply to ignore or patronize his thought that troubled most. But at last the realists answered. Ryle introduced his article with the acknowledgement 'at once that I intend to be destructive only'.[55]

In the exchange of letters that followed in May 1935 Collingwood wrote:

> I was brought up as a good Cook-Wilson realist (we did use that label, freely, before the war) and since rebelling against that creed I have been moving toward a position based on what is for me, almost an axiom (evidently not for you) that the old dichotomy of idealist-realist is as out of date as the Gilbertian Liberal-Conservative is in politics.... It seems probable to me that the fundamental point at issue is concerned with the way in which we answer the question, 'What is a universal?'

Ryle, Collingwood maintained, meant by calling universals a class that 'whenever we make a statement (assent to a proposition) about "all x" we are really making n statements about the n instances of x which exist.... I am disposed to think that what makes a number of things instances of a class is their common possession of some common nature and that this common nature (the so-called universal) is the *ratio essendi* of the class as such.'

[54] Tomlin, E. W. F. 1958. 'The Philosophy of R. G. Collingwood', *Ratio* 1: 117: R. G. C. to Barbara, 29 March 1935 [TS/FLTR 0753]. The benign reception of the *Essay on Philosophical Method* evoked a wistfulness: 'In England it has seemed to attract the attention of only a few, but those few are all people whose opinion is important.... My books pass peaceably into oblivion and thus far have not shown any sign of resurrection. I do not know what I would do if a second edition of *Speculum Mentis* were wanted.' R. G. C. to De Ruggerio, 7 February 1934, Dep. Coll.

[55] Ryle, Gilbert, 1935. 'Mr. Collingwood and the Ontological Argument', *Mind* 44, Jan–Dec: 137–8.

Ryle was, Collingwood pointed out, a nominalist.[56] Cook Wilson had said in 1912 that Collingwood had the gift of being able to see the obvious.

After his professorship—his inaugural of 28 October 1935 was titled *The Historical Imagination*—Oxford then had nothing more to offer, and there would be no more books until the *Principles of Art* in 1938. In the interval there would be Collingwood's involvement with psychology, fifty sessions of analysis, of which J. D. Mabbot wrote, 'I fear it did him serious harm. I thought at the time it had increased the introverted, defensive side of him, and I feel sure it added to his later breakdown.'[57]

Beginning with the essay 'Man Goes Mad' in 1936, Collingwood was deeply troubled, one might almost say obsessed, with the seeming willingness of the European civilization he loved to destroy itself, a project he found mirrored intellectually in what he considered the ravages of realism and reflected politically in the rise of fascism and the inability of British democracy to mount an effective challenge. In *Principles of Art*, Collingwood faulted Freud with encouraging irrationalism, mocked Professor I. A. Richard's theory of language, and extolled Eliot's *Waste Land*, the central image of which, the decay of civilization under the influence of that dissociation of sensibilities, was taken up in *Principles of Art* as corruption of consciousness.

The stroke of January 1938 encouraged Collingwood to make the *Autobiography*, in the words of the preface, *un livre de bonne foi*, a confession of the ideas that framed his deepest convictions while setting him outside the popular march of the philosophy of Prichard and Ryle. Its preface dated October 1938, the *Autobiography* was the belated counter-attack of the School of Green. Smith and Joachim were the best philosophers in Oxford and Joachim's *The Nature of Truth*, first published in 1906, the second edition of which Collingwood was then seeing through the press, was the exemplary philosophical work.[58] *Speculum Mentis*, written in

[56] Collingwood to Ryle, 9 May 1935, Dep. Coll.26/3.

[57] Mabbott, J. D. 1986. *Oxford Memories*, Oxford: Thornton, 76.

[58] *A*, 18. The judgement was deliberate; G. R. G. Mure remembered that after Smith's death in December 1939 Collingwood had told him that 'now Joachim and J. A. were dead there were no philosophers left who were any good', Mure to the author, 23 January 1973. See Collingwood's preface to Joachim, H. H. 1939. *The Nature of Truth*, Oxford: Oxford University Press, iv–v.

1924 but repudiated in 1928 as a work of which he had 'no very high opinion' was rehabilitated as 'better than I remembered', containing 'not a great deal that needs to be retracted' (*A*, 56).[59] When, after much hesitation, the *Autobiography* was published, Oxford was stung. R. B. McCallum, Master of Pembroke, wrote in 1943 that Collingwood's friends regretted its publication and H. W. B. Joseph sniffed that surely not *all* realists had encouraged the idea that moral philosophy was useless. However, A. L. Rowse called it 'the most interesting book that has come out of Oxford for some time'.[60]

The *Autobiography* began with attempts to straighten out matters philosophical and historical rooted in Collingwood's thirty years in the university, to settle long-standing intellectual scores and provide at least clues to the direction of his thought; it ended with a response to the destruction of Europe encouraged, so he believed, by British politicians and newspapers. Collingwood reiterated in the *Autobiography*, the draft of which had been begun just weeks after the annexation of Austria in March 1938, the first sentence in *Speculum Mentis*: 'All thought exists for the sake of action.'

Collingwood saw that the successive governments of Baldwin and Chamberlain had edged ever closer to toleration of continental fascism, until the national government was unwilling to act against Mussolini in Ethiopia or against German occupation of Austria and dismemberment of Czechoslovakia in March 1939. In the background was the war in Spain, which Collingwood construed, perhaps naively, as a straightforward and outrageous example of the abandonment of popular democracy to authoritarian dictatorship. Sir Oswald Mosley's British Union of Fascists had won a quarter of the votes in the London County Council elections of 1937; and a considerable body of British opinion, not without advocates in Oxford, thought Hitler's anti-Bolshevism should

[59] R. G. C. to De Ruggerio, 20 March 1921, Dep. Coll.

[60] McCallum, 'Robin George Collingwood': 467; Joseph, H. W. B. 1939. Review of *An Autobiography* by R. G. Collingwood, *Oxford Magazine* 58:1, 28 October: 34; Rowse, A. L. 1939, Review of *An Autobiography* by R. G. Collingwood, *Spectator* 463, July–December: 262. In 1975 Rowse considered Collingwood one of two Oxford men of genius belonging to the interwar years, 1975. *Oxford in the History of England*, New York: G. P. Putnam's Sons, 242–4. See the Introduction to this volume.

earn him a free hand in Central Europe, and that in the face of growing Nazi power wisdom ought not rule out compromise.[61]

It is not difficult to see that one as steeped in European history as Collingwood might conclude that the government of Britain, tolerating all the while the tendency of the popular press to pander rather than to educate, had acted in bad faith (*A*, 155). In summer 1938 Duncan Sandys, a territorial army officer also in Parliament, was threatened with military discipline for pointing out that the anti-aircraft defences of London were inadequate, which was interpreted in the *Autobiography* as a blow struck against England's safety by a pusillanimous government. On 30 September 1938 Chamberlain returned from Germany proclaiming peace with honour. The preface to the *Autobiography* was dated 2 October, and eight days later Germany occupied the Sudetenland. The last chapter of the *Autobiography,* 'Theory and Practice', ended with the words: 'All my life I have been engaged unawares in a political struggle, fighting against these things in the dark. Henceforth I shall fight in the daylight.' That meant opposing fascism wherever he found it, and soon, enticed by Collingwood's praise of Marx as a fighting philosopher in the *Autobiography*, Oxford buzzed with the rumour that Collingwood had become a Marxist, the beard newly acquired on the cruise to Java in 1938–1939 being taken as sufficient proof.[62]

In the last sweet summer of peace Collingwood paid his final debt to the proposition that his work was not with his colleagues but his students, sailing with eight undergraduates in the yacht *Fleur de Lys* to the Aegean. He returned to Oxford in August 1939, just in time for the invasion of Poland on 1 September and Britain's declaration of war. Perhaps he remembered another war and his desire in 1915 to get something into print for posterity. Now there was not only the pressure of impending war but the fact of his deteriorating health. Since the publication of the *Essay on Philosophical Method* in 1933 he had made prodigious efforts to

[61] Appeasement, not without some cause, was associated with the All Souls high table, although only eight members of the group that met in 1937 and 1938 to consider ways of maintaining peace were fellows of All Souls. See Dutton, D. J. 2006. Review of *Appeasement and All Souls*, edited by Sidney Aster, Cambridge: Cambridge University Press, for the Royal Historical Society, 2004, *English Historical Review* cxxi, 492, June: 963–4.

[62] Journals of Clement Webb, 18 February 1939 [Ms. Eng. Misc. e. 1175].

bring his thoughts into publishable order. From August to September 1934 Collingwood worked at what would become the heart of *The Idea of Nature*. Lectures that would become the *Idea of History* belonged to 1935 and 1936. *Principles of Art* was published in 1938, and in February 1939 he began work on the 'Principles of History'. *The Essay on Metaphysics*, at least the first draft, was completed before April 1939. The works not yet published would be revised, but the shape of his thought was complete, and on 18 October, back from his Aegean adventure and settled into his professorial duties, Collingwood proposed to the press that his works be issued as a series in three parts, Philosophical Essays, Principles, and Studies in the History of Ideas, which proposal was accepted (*IH*, 1993, ix).[63]

When the *Essay on Metaphysics* was published in 1940, it distanced Collingwood yet further from the positivists and the psychologists, from the Oxford that had come to be. The *Essay* was a running defence of positions, adumbrated in the *Autobiography*, that belonged to a tradition of European thought which lay outside the scope of the new positivist philosophy that had grown from the realist root. In it Collingwood argued not the existence of God but for the reasonableness of belief in God against philosophical sceptics and for the efficacy of reason against irrationalism. His experience of Freudian analysis had given him grounds for lambasting psychology as a pseudo-science of thought, first in the *Principles of Art*, then in the *Autobiography* and the *Essay on Metaphysics*.[64]

In 1941 Collingwood's Oxford life was drawing to a close. His marriage of twenty years was at an end. Joachim had died in 1938 and Smith had gone in December 1939. His failing health could no longer sustain his professorial duties. He left the Oxford to which he had come as a boy of eighteen in 1908, first to Streatley in Berkshire and then returning to his native Coniston. At Lanehead there would be a final chapter, having its own measure of happiness and difficulty, but Collingwood would always be remembered as an Oxford philosopher. T. M. Knox, a student then a colleague from Pembroke days, appointed to edit his works by the Oxford

[63] Dep. Coll. 17.

[64] *PA*, 77n, 171n; *A*, 93–5; *EM*, 81–142; Mabbott, *Oxford Memories*, 76; Patrick, James, 1995. 'Fighting in the Daylight: the Penultimate Collingwood, 1937–1941', *Collingwood Studies* 2: 79.

University Press, published the third part of Collingwood's planned series, *The Idea of History*, and the *Idea of Nature*, which he had left unfinished. *The Idea of History* gained Collingwood's thought an international reputation, but in the university he was not easily forgiven. Collingwood had persisted in advocating a philosophy that younger men considered a scandal more than a mistake. He had violated the canons of the expert by loving many things. He possessed the magnanimity that some of his critics lacked. Collingwood was quick to express gratitude for the pre-war influence of Cook Wilson, as in the opening paragraph of the 'Libellus' of 1920. A. J. Ayer had been the particular target of Collingwood's criticism in *Principles of Art* and the *Essay on Metaphysics*, but once in Blackwells, when Gilbert Ryle overheard H. W. B. Joseph and H. A. Prichard complaining that Ayer's *Language, Truth, and Logic* had found a publisher, Collingwood, who stood nearby, turned to them with, 'Gentlemen, his book will be read when your names are forgotten.'[65]

Collingwood had somehow made it to the top of the very slippery professional pole without the help of the realists. The Oxford that would not answer came to view him as an anomaly in whom it was impossible not to see the outlines of greatness. With the perfect irony that history so often displays, Gilbert Ryle, upon his return to Oxford from the war in 1945, was elected Collingwood's successor. In his inaugural Ryle undertook good-heartedly to honour his predecessor, describing Collingwood's interests admiringly and praising his literary style.[66] When A. J. Ayer, the object of 'The Suicide of Positivistic Metaphysics' in the *Essay on Metaphysics*, who had succeeded to Cook Wilson's Oxford chair in 1959, published his *History of Twentieth Century Philosophy* in 1982, he felt duty bound to include a chapter on Collingwood, treating him in a broadly sympathetic tone but still concluding that Collingwood's philosophy was unintelligible, his philosophy of history incredible.[67] Finally Collingwood's philosophy, like the ontological argument he defended, assumed the character of a

[65] Ayer, A. J., 1977. *Part of My Life*, London: Collins, 166.

[66] Ryle, Gilbert, 1959. 'Philosophical Arguments', A. J. Ayer, ed., *Logical Positivism*, Glencoe, Illinois: Free Press, 327–8.

[67] Ayer, A. J., 1982. *Philosophy in the Twentieth Century*, New York: Random House, 191–2.

putative mistake, one that, no matter how often rebutted, would not go quietly into philosophical oblivion. But with its broad humane themes, its insistence on the inescapably historical context of knowledge, and its critical view of what by 1940 had become philosophical orthodoxy, Collingwood's thought lay in wait around every corner for its old adversaries.

3
COLLINGWOOD'S CRITIQUE OF OXBRIDGE REALISM

MICHAEL BEANEY

1. INTRODUCTION

R. G. Collingwood's *Autobiography* is an intellectual autobiography. As he states in the preface, 'The autobiography of a man whose business is thinking should be the story of his thought.' In chapter 1 we are already introduced to key themes in Collingwood's philosophy. He reports that he received his first lesson in what he came to regard as his own subject, the history of thought, when he found a copy of Descartes' *Principia*, which taught him that 'the natural sciences have a history of their own, and that the doctrines they teach on any given subject, at any given time, have been reached not by some discoverer penetrating to the truth after ages of error, but by the gradual modification of doctrines previously held; and will at some future date, unless thinking stops, be themselves no less modified' (*A*, 2). The idea expressed here was fundamental to Collingwood's philosophy. Let us refer to it as his historicist principle. As we will see, it underlies his critique of realism.

The principle is also reflected in Collingwood's account, still in chapter 1, of his growing realization that his calling in life was to think. All he felt at first was a general intellectual unease, but as he learnt later, it was only when solutions to problems had developed sufficiently that he was able to recognize what the problems were (cf. *A*, 4–5). This also goes to the heart of his conception of philosophy, a conception he so elegantly articulated in his *Essay on Philosophical Method* of 1933. Here what Collingwood takes as his starting point is what has come to be known as Meno's paradox—the dilemma that Plato poses in the *Meno* concerning the supposed futility of seeking knowledge. Either we know what we are searching for, or we do not. If we do, then there is no point searching; if we do not, then we will not know what to search for (cf. *Meno*, 80e). Socrates' response is to argue that there is indeed a sense in which we already know what we are searching for—and hence can recognize it when we find it. What we have implicitly are 'true opinions', and what learning does is bring these to consciousness by connecting them and 'tying' them down, turning them into knowledge proper, a process that Socrates calls 'recollection' (cf. *Meno*, 97e–98a).

In chapter 1 of the *Essay* Collingwood essentially endorses Socrates' response:

> in a philosophical inquiry what we are trying to do is not to discover something of which until now we have been ignorant, but to know better something which in some sense we knew already; not to know it better in the sense of coming to know more about it, but to know it better in the sense of coming to know it in a different and better way – actually instead of potentially, or explicitly instead of implicitly, or in whatever terms the theory of knowledge chooses to express the difference: the difference itself has been a familiar fact ever since Socrates pointed it out. (*EPM*, 11)

Following Collingwood himself (*EPM*, 105, 161), let us call the principle involved here 'the Socratic principle'. In the *Essay* Collingwood teaches us to 'recollect' this principle by connecting it with his doctrines of the overlap of classes and the scale of forms. But we can also see it implicit in his remark in chapter 1 of his *Autobiography* that it is only when he has worked on a problem for a while that he begins to know exactly what it is. It is also illustrated at the narrative level in his account of how 'the problems of my life's work were taking, deep down inside me, their first embryonic shape' (*A*, 5).

2. MINUTE PHILOSOPHERS

Like the historicist principle, the Socratic principle lies at the heart of Collingwood's critique of realism. Indeed, the two principles are related: the Socratic principle might be seen as the epistemological correlate of the metaphysical, historicist principle. For if scientific (and philosophical) doctrines have a history, then it is natural to suppose that understanding them, too, has a temporal dimension. Chapter 3 of Collingwood's *Autobiography* is entitled 'Minute Philosophers', a term he employs to satirize the views of the realists who were active in Oxford during the 1910s. As it becomes clear in chapter 4, Collingwood attacked realism on the grounds that it 'erred through neglecting history' (*A*, 28).

The term 'minute philosophers' ('*minuti philosophi*') was used by Cicero at the end of his essay 'On Old Age' to refer to those philosophers who denied the immortality of the soul. The term was taken up, most famously, by George Berkeley in his book, *Alciphron, or the Minute Philosopher*, published in 1732. In section 10 of the first dialogue, minute philosophers are described as freethinkers who diminish 'all the most valuable things, the thoughts, views, and hopes of men: all the knowledge, notions, and theories of the mind, they reduce to sense; human nature they contract and degrade to the narrow low standard of animal life, and assign us only a small pittance of time, instead of immortality'. Alciphron himself, on the other hand, as the freethinker Berkeley was depicting (and criticizing), is happy to count himself as a minute philosopher. Since 'the best eyes are necessary to discern the minutest objects', Alciphron remarks, a minute philosopher is someone with 'distinguished perspicacity'.

Although Collingwood makes no reference to Berkeley's *Alciphron*, the Oxford realists would surely have recognized the allusion to the work of one of their greatest idealist foes. No doubt they would have regarded themselves as having 'distinguished perspicacity', while Collingwood saw them as diminishing 'all the most valuable things'. The ambiguity of 'minute' may also have been deliberately exploited. We might capture this by saying that, on Collingwood's view, the realists behaved as if philosophy could be pursued by simple acts of critical judgement and immediate intuitions of truths—acts and intuitions that could be completed in just a minute, as it were—without having to understand the history of what it was they were criticizing or apprehending.

Collingwood begins chapter 3, however, by mentioning the work of what he calls the school of Green—led by T. H. Green (1836–1882) and including F. H. Bradley (1846–1924), Bernard Bosanquet (1848–1923), William Wallace (1843–1897), and R. L. Nettleship (1846–1892). He denies that this school can be described as Hegelian (*A*, 15), and notes that Bradley repudiated the title of 'idealist' as well (*A*, 19). It has sometimes been called 'neo-Hegelian' to distinguish it from (true) Hegelianism, but despite Bradley's repudiation, I think 'British idealism' is the best term to use. At any rate, it is preferable to 'the school of Green', which suggests that the dominant influence was Green rather than Bradley, who is now generally agreed to be the central figure. Collingwood himself calls Bradley 'the greatest philosopher of the school' (*A*, 19)—'a man whose mind was the most deeply critical that European philosophy has produced since Hume' (*A*, 16). Bradley was certainly the main target of the realists—both in Oxford and Cambridge—who reacted to British idealism.

Collingwood says virtually nothing about the specific doctrines of the British idealists, merely mentioning instead their influence on those students of Greats who subsequently entered public life. At the time he went to Oxford, the influence of British idealism was waning, a demise that was only hastened by the relative dearth of books offering any accessible account of the central ideas of the movement. The only such book that Collingwood notes as having come out of the school was Harold Joachim's essay, *The Nature of Truth*, which was published in 1906.[1] In its preface, Joachim admits to having been greatly inspired (though not uncritically) by both Bradley and Bosanquet as well as by Hegel. It is perhaps surprising that Collingwood does not mention Bradley's work. Both *The Principles of Logic*[2] and *Appearance and Reality*[3] may have been published in the previous century, but Bradley was still writing well into the twentieth century, publishing a series of papers in the journal *Mind*, for example, which were collected in *Essays on Truth and Reality*.[4] But perhaps Collingwood did not count this as accessible enough.[5] Although Collingwood's concern

[1] Joachim, Harold H., 1906. *The Nature of Truth*, Oxford, Oxford University Press; 2nd edn, 1939.

[2] Bradley, F. H., 1883. *The Principles of Logic*, Oxford, Oxford University Press.

[3] Bradley, F. H., 1893. *Appearance and Reality*, Oxford, Oxford University Press.

[4] Bradley, F. H., 1914. *Essays on Truth and Reality*, Oxford, Oxford University Press.

[5] Collingwood had written an essay on Bradley, 1933, 'The Metaphysics of F. H. Bradley: An Essay on "Appearance and Reality" ', which was published for the first time in 2005, in the revised edition of *An Essay on Philosophical Method*, rev. edn, ed. J. Connelly and G. D'Oro, Oxford, Oxford University Press: 27–52; but this, too, is not mentioned in the *Autobiography*.

in chapter 3 is merely with Oxford philosophy, it should also be noted that idealism was still flourishing outside Oxford.

The dearth of books by the British idealists, according to Collingwood, left the field open for the realists. Among the Oxford realists, Collingwood identifies the leader as John Cook Wilson (1849–1915) and mentions two of his followers, H. W. B. Joseph (1867–1943) and H. A. Prichard (1871–1947). In his lifetime Cook Wilson published only on mathematics and ancient Greek philosophy.[6] But as the Wykeham Professor of Logic from 1889, he lectured regularly on logic and epistemology, and after his death in 1915, these lectures were edited by A. S. L. Farquharson and, together with various letters and occasional philosophical pieces, published as *Statement and Inference*, in two volumes, in 1926. Collingwood writes of Cook Wilson's resistance to publishing, on the grounds that he kept changing his mind (cf. *A*, 19), and it is true that Cook Wilson continually rewrote his lectures. But he does seem to have wanted to make his views on logic available to a wider audience than his Oxford colleagues.[7] Although *Statement and Inference* had not been published in the period about which Collingwood is speaking in chapter 3, it had certainly appeared by the time he wrote the *Autobiography* itself; yet he makes no mention of this. With over 1000 pages, *Statement and Inference* is a major work. Collingwood may not have read it all, but its publication was a significant event in the Oxford of his academic life.

Collingwood's criticism of Cook Wilson's attitude towards publication reflects a deeper disagreement between the two about the nature of thought, which brings out what lies at the root of Collingwood's critique of realism. In accord with the Socratic principle, Collingwood saw his philosophical writing as a matter of gradually working out his ideas, getting clearer and clearer about the problems that occupied him. There was no assumption of a final state of perfect understanding to be captured in a definitive statement or theory; what was important was the process of thinking itself, pursued and expressed *through* writing. Presumably he felt that writing for publication was the best way to focus the mind, and that the resultant publication could help and stimulate others to

[6] See the list of published works in Wilson, John Cook, 1926. *Statement and Inference*, 2 vols, Oxford, Clarendon Press, I: lxvi–lxxii.

[7] Cf. e.g. Cook Wilson, *Statement and Inference*, II: 870.

develop their own thoughts. Cook Wilson, on the other hand, in accord with his realist principles, held that truth is independent of human knowledge, in the sense that what is true is not affected by being known to be true. Furthermore, according to Cook Wilson, we come to know what is true—where knowledge is possible—through acts of immediate intuition. Presumably, then, until he had intuited a truth clearly and distinctly, and had found the definitive statement that captured this intuition, Cook Wilson was reluctant to go public with his views. As he once remarked, 'the (printed) letter killeth and it is extraordinary how it will prevent the acutest from exercising their wonted clearness of vision'.[8]

In Collingwood's (published) writing, there is a clear sense of *development* in the thoughts that are expressed, and Collingwood seems not to have suffered (unduly) from the feeling that later elaborations of an idea required going back and 'correcting' its initial formulation. To have done so, on Collingwood's view, would have risked undermining those later elaborations—obscuring their nature and motivation. Initial formulations could be left as vague or potentially misleading, in the knowledge that they would be clarified later, or could be clarified as occasion demanded. This is the Socratic principle at work in his own methodology.

While there is clearly development in Collingwood's philosophy, however, he never admits to anything as drastic as a *change of mind*. Even when he confesses, at the beginning of chapter 4, to having gone through a realist phase, he notes that he had reservations about realism even then. His aim is to show how growing awareness of the internal contradictions in realism helped shape his own views. Indeed, his whole *Autobiography* is an attempt to demonstrate the natural development of his philosophy, in accord with principles—and in particular, the historicist and Socratic principles—that gradually became clearer and clearer to him.

In this respect, it is instructive to compare Collingwood's autobiography with that of Bertrand Russell (1872–1970). Russell revels in his rebellion against British idealism at the turn of the twentieth century, and in his later abandonment of the extravagant realism that this rebellion initially fostered.[9] As in the case of

[8] Cook Wilson, *Statement and Inference*, II: 871.

[9] Russell, Bertrand, 1959. *My Philosophical Development*, London, George Allen and Unwin: chs 1, 5; 1975, ch. 6.

Cook Wilson, Collingwood is scornful of Russell's changes of mind. He speaks of the records that Russell left of 'his successive attempts at a philosophy', and writes of the realists in general as stumbling 'from one temporary and patchwork philosophy to another in a kind of intellectual nightmare' (*A*, 51). Of course, unlike Cook Wilson, Russell had little anxiety at all about publishing,[10] so there is no necessary connection between realism and reluctance to publish. Perhaps Collingwood felt that Russell *should* have been more reluctant. At any rate, he attacks both Cook Wilson and Russell for their intellectual stumblings, for which he holds their realism as ultimately responsible.

Cook Wilson is not the only realist that Collingwood criticizes in the chapter on 'Minute Philosophers'. He also mentions Prichard and Joseph. Prichard was White's Professor of Moral Philosophy at Oxford from 1928 until he retired in 1937, but Collingwood does not discuss Prichard's views on ethics in this chapter (he attacks them later, in chapter 6, 47–8). Instead, he notes Prichard's realist critique of Kant in *Kant's Theory of Knowledge* (1909) and Prichard's supposed progression towards complete scepticism (cf. *A*, 20–1). This latter charge is unfair: Prichard did indeed move to a more subjectivist position in ethics, but it was not a form of complete scepticism. Although there were changes of mind, no doubt provoking Collingwood's scorn, Prichard remained an 'intuitionist' in both ethics and epistemology, believing that basic principles were to be intuited as self-evident. The problem was that he was a pluralist about these basic principles, opening the door to his later subjectivism.[11] Nevertheless, just because of this, Prichard would undoubtedly count as a 'minute philosopher'; certainly, he lacked that historical self-consciousness upon which Collingwood placed such emphasis (cf. *A*, 57–9).

As far as Joseph is concerned, Collingwood mentions his *Introduction to Logic* and his work on Plato. His book on logic was first published in 1906 and a revised edition (of some 600 pages)

[10] Perhaps the only notable exception is Russell's *Theory of Knowledge* manuscript, which he abandoned in 1913 due to Wittgenstein's criticisms.

[11] For an account of Prichard's ethics, see Dancy, Jonathan, 2010. 'Harold Arthur Prichard', *Stanford Encyclopedia of Philosophy*, online at <http://plato.stanford.edu/entries/prichard/>.

appeared in 1916.[12] It is essentially a textbook of traditional logic. There is an account of terms, judgements, and inferences (syllogisms), in accord with the standard Aristotelian division, followed by discussion of induction and scientific methodology, along Millian lines. Joseph makes no attempt to consider the mathematical logic that was then emerging, in Britain, in the work of Russell and others, which was to revolutionize logic. By the time of the second edition, he recognizes its existence, but curtly dismisses it for making 'the error of representing either all thinking as a kind of mathematics, or all thinking as class-thinking, and mathematics as merely a special sort of class-thinking'.[13] The book was influenced by Cook Wilson (acknowledged especially in the preface to the second edition), but from the early 1910s Joseph began to criticize Cook Wilson's brand of realism, and as Collingwood rightly says, came to regard himself as primarily a follower of Plato. In granting a fundamental role to our supposed powers of immediate apprehension, however, he shared at least some of the epistemological views of the other 'minute philosophers', views which take centre stage in the next chapter of Collingwood's *Autobiography*.

3. INCLINATION AND INTUITION

Chapter 4 of Collingwood's *Autobiography* is entitled 'Inclination of a Sapling', a reference to his initial—though qualified—acceptance of realism. He reports that his tutor, E. F. Carritt (1876–1964), himself a realist (and a student of Prichard's), had sent him to the lectures by Cook Wilson and the other realists. Collingwood writes that he was thus 'thoroughly indoctrinated' with the principles and methods of realism (*A*, 22). His only reservation concerned the realists' lack of regard for historical fact. Collingwood mentions Moore's critique of Berkeley's idealism and Cook Wilson's critique of Bradley's idealism: in both cases, he remarks, the views criticized are not the views that Berkeley and Bradley, respectively, actually held. At the time, though, he accepted that the realists were concerned with philosophy, not history, and that the important point was whether the doctrines they criticized were indeed false or not, regardless of who held them.

[12] Joseph, H. W. B., 1916. *An Introduction to Logic*, 2nd edn, Oxford, Clarendon Press; 1st edn. 1906.

[13] Joseph, *Introduction to Logic*: 228; cf. viii.

After his degree, however, Collingwood reports that he became aware of a conflict between the realists' positive principles and their critical methods, and this left him with three options: to reject realism because of the conflict, to endorse the principles but not the methods, or to endorse the methods but not the principles—assuming, in these latter two cases, that the principles and methods could be legitimately separated. Collingwood does not spell out the conflict; he simply remarks that 'Cook Wilson's positive teaching was incapable of resisting attack by his own critical methods' (*A*, 23). What Collingwood had in mind here is made clear in the chapter that follows. As he characterizes it, the essence of the realist's critical method is 'to analyse the position criticized into various propositions, and detect contradictions between these' (*A*, 42). Applied to realism itself, Collingwood then seems to think, such a method soon detects contradictions between its own constituent propositions—and he presumably saw Cook Wilson's (and Russell's) own frequent changes of mind as evidence of the instability of realist views.

In chapter 4, however, Collingwood does not say which of the three options he ended up taking. He reports instead on his 'flank attack' on the problem (*A*, 23, 28), introducing what he calls in the next chapter his 'logic of question and answer' (*A*, 37). His main idea is that 'knowledge comes only by answering questions', an idea he says he learnt from his archaeological research on the history of Roman Britain: 'what one learnt depended not merely on what turned up in one's trenches but also on what questions one was asking' (*A*, 24–5). It is this idea that he claims the realists fail to recognize in talking 'as if knowing were a simple "intuiting" or a simple "apprehending" of some "reality"' (*A*, 25). Such talk can indeed be found in the work of the Oxford realists, and in particular, Cook Wilson[14] and Prichard.[15] But as Collingwood remarks, similar views are expressed by the Cambridge realist

[14] Cook Wilson, *Statement and Inference*, II: chs 1, 14. As the editor of his work notes, Cook Wilson nowhere defines 'apprehension', but seems to use the term for what he earlier called 'recognition': 'the immediate cognizance of the object and conviction of its being' (78). For discussion of Cook Wilson's conception, see Marion, Mathieu, 2000. 'Oxford Realism: Knowledge and Perception', Parts I and II, *British Journal for the History of Philosophy*, 8: 299–338 (Part I), 485–519 (Part II), §2.

[15] See e.g. Prichard, H. A., 1906. 'Appearances and Reality', *Mind*, 15: 223–9.

G. E. Moore (1873–1958)[16] and the Manchester realist Samuel Alexander (1859–1938).[17] In the light of what Collingwood goes on to say, though, perhaps the best illustration would be Russell's much-quoted remark in his preface to *The Principles of Mathematics*: 'The discussion of indefinables—which forms the chief part of philosophical logic—is the endeavour to see clearly, and to make others see clearly, the entities concerned, in order that the mind may have that kind of acquaintance with them which it has with redness or the taste of a pineapple.'[18] Russell did indeed conceive 'acquaintance' as an immediate 'intuiting' or 'apprehending' of some 'reality'. In his 1911 paper 'Knowledge by Acquaintance and Knowledge by Description',[19] for example, he defines it as follows:

> I am *acquainted* with an object when I have a direct cognitive relation to that object, i.e. when I am directly aware of the object itself. When I speak of a cognitive relation here, I do not mean the sort of relation which constitutes judgment, but the sort which constitutes presentation. In fact, I think the relation of subject and object which I call acquaintance is simply the converse of the relation of object and subject which constitutes presentation. That is, to say that S has acquaintance with O is essentially the same thing as to say O is presented to S.[20]

The view that Russell expresses here can be seen as encapsulating the realist conception that Collingwood criticizes: 'The questioning activity, as I called it, was not an activity of achieving

[16] See e.g. Moore, G. E., 1903. 'The Refutation of Idealism', *Mind*, 12: 453, where Moore claims that 'I am as directly aware of the existence of material things in space as of my own sensations.'

[17] See e.g. Alexander, Samuel, 1914. 'The Basis of Realism', *Proceedings of the British Academy*, 6: 283, where Alexander writes that 'mind and its object are two separate existences connected together by the relation of togetherness or compresence'.

[18] Russell, Bertrand, [1903], 1937. *The Principles of Mathematics*, Cambridge, Cambridge University Press, 2nd edn: v.

[19] Russell, Bertrand, 1911. 'Knowledge by Acquaintance and Knowledge by Description', in Russell, Bertrand, 1917. *Mysticism and Logic*, London, George Allen and Unwin: 152–67. Originally published in *Proceedings of the Aristotelian Society*, 11: 108–28.

[20] Russell, 'Knowledge by Acquaintance': 152. Cf., Russell, Bertrand, *The Problems of Philosophy*, 1912 repr. 1967, Oxford, Oxford University Press: 25, where Russell writes that 'we have *acquaintance* with anything of which we are directly aware, without the intermediary of any process of inference or any knowledge of truths'.

compresence with, or apprehension of, something; it was not preliminary to the act of knowing; it was one half (the other half being answering the question) of an act which in its totality was knowing' (*A*, 26). He goes on to say that he knows how a realist would respond to this, but refrains from telling us. A clue to the answer, though, is contained in the very title of Russell's 1911 paper. For Russell would say that 'knowledge by acquaintance' is only one form of knowledge, the other form being 'knowledge by description'. An object is known by description, he says, 'when we know that it is "*the* so-and-so", i.e. when we know that there is one object, and no more, having a certain property' (1911, 156). We need not be acquainted with the object in order to have such knowledge, according to Russell; indeed, non-acquaintance is the rule in cases of knowledge by description.

It is not hard to see how such a conception leaves space for the questioning activity. A statement of the form 'The *F* is a *G*' might well be given as an answer to the question 'What is a *G*?'. There need be no apprehension of the *F* here, and the knowledge expressed by the statement clearly has complexity. What Russell would nevertheless insist is that, at the ultimate epistemological level, there must be acquaintance with the relevant objects (universals or particulars). In accord with his theory of descriptions, 'The *F* is a *G*' is analysed as 'There is one and only one *F* and whatever is an *F* is a *G*.' If this is the fully analysed form of the statement, according to Russell, then we must have acquaintance with the logical constants (which fill out the logical structure of the statement) and the concepts *F* and *G* (not the object denoted by 'the *F*', as there may be none: this is one of the points of the theory of descriptions).[21]

Collingwood fails to address the issue of whether, at some ultimate level, we have acquaintance with objects. We might agree with him that at higher levels, there are questioning activities essentially involved, but Russell would argue that questioning itself must presuppose acquaintance with objects at the ultimate level. The point is general. The questions asked must themselves make sense, and at some point we must reach a level of understanding or

[21] The theory of descriptions was first presented in Russell, Bertrand, 1905. 'On Denoting', *Mind*, 14: 479–93. The best account is in Russell, Bertrand, 1919. *Introduction to Mathematical Philosophy*, London, George Allen and Unwin: ch. 16.

cognitive access to reality that cannot be seen as itself an answer to a question. This brings us to the logic of question and answer.

4. THE LOGIC OF QUESTION AND ANSWER

Collingwood's 'logic of question and answer' is one of the most well-known but also controversial elements of his philosophy. In chapter 5 of his *Autobiography*, which is simply entitled 'Question and Answer', Collingwood claims to have developed the main ideas during World War I, when he was working for the Admiralty. Walking past the Albert Memorial every day led him to ask what George Gilbert Scott, the architect, had been trying to do. What were the questions to which Scott's design was the answer? Collingwood also mentions his work in archaeology, which had impressed on him 'the importance of the "questioning activity" in knowledge' (*A*, 30). This led him to reject what he calls the 'propositional logic' of his contemporaries. Truth and falsehood, he claims, belong not to propositions but to question-and-answer complexes. A proposition is always an answer to a question, and both its meaning and truth value are relative to the question it answers (cf. *A*, 33–5).

Collingwood says that he first wrote all these ideas out in 1917, in a book entitled 'Truth and Contradiction'. It was offered to a publisher but rejected (*A*, 42–3, 74), and Collingwood reports that the manuscript was subsequently destroyed (*A*, 99). It turns out, though, that one chapter has survived, and we also have a reader's report on the book.[22] Neither suggests that Collingwood had developed anything at the time that might be called a '*logic* of question and answer', however; and this is confirmed when we look at *Speculum Mentis*, published in 1924. In chapter 3, there is a

[22] Collingwood, R. G., 1917. 'Truth and Contradiction', chapter 2, unpublished manuscript, Bodleian Library; Jones, Henry, 1918. '[Reader's Report on 'Truth and Contradiction']', in Collingwood, 1989. *Essays in Political Philosophy*, ed. D. Boucher, Oxford: Clarendon Press, pp. 230–1. Cf. Martin, Rex, 1998. 'Collingwood's Logic of Question and Answer, its Relation to Absolute Presuppositions: a Brief History', *Collingwood Studies*, 5: 127–9; Connelly, James, 2003. *Metaphysics, Method and Politics: The Political Philosophy of R. G. Collingwood*, Exeter: Imprint Academic, p. 116.

section entitled 'Knowledge as Question and Answer'. Here there is criticism of the 'crude empiricist' view that 'knowledge is composed wholly of assertion', as Collingwood puts it. Against this, he writes: 'People who are acquainted with knowledge at first hand have always known that assertions are only answers to questions' (*SM*, 77). Question and answer, he goes on to say, are inseparable 'moments' in the process of knowledge (*SM*, 80). But there is no mention here of propositions, propositional logic, issues of meaning and truth value, or of any new 'logic'.

If we look at the two other main books published between 1917 and 1939, namely, the *Essay on Philosophical Method* (1933) and *The Principles of Art* (1938), then we find no reference at all to the idea of question and answer. So it hardly seems as important as Collingwood makes out. In fact, the first talk of a '*logic* of question and answer' occurs in the *Autobiography* itself, which is certainly surprising if the *Autobiography* is meant to be read as a record of his thought, with chapter 5 reporting his thinking around 1917. So is Collingwood being disingenuous in claiming that he had written all this out in 1917 (*A*, 42)?[23]

In defence of Collingwood, we might appeal to his own Socratic principle and suggest that it was only much later that he appreciated exactly what the problem was that he had been thinking about while communing with the Albert Memorial and that the ideas he is talking about were only in embryonic form at the time.[24] As the previous two chapters make clear, Collingwood had been thinking his way out of Oxbridge realism, and the idea of the interdependence of question and answer came to crystallize for him his fundamental objection to realism. This still leaves Collingwood open to the charge of being misleading, at the very least, in suggesting that

[23] Martin, 'Collingwood's Logic of Question and Answer, its Relation to Absolute Presuppositions', 126–9 considers whether the 'all this' refers to the ideas of the whole of chapter 5 or just to those of the two preceding pages. I am in no doubt that Collingwood meant the former. I agree with Martin that 'we have no firm basis whatsoever for concluding that Collingwood had developed a *logic* of question and answer in 1917' (129).

[24] It might be noted here that there is no talk of the Albert Memorial in any of the surviving letters that Collingwood wrote at the time, so one even wonders how much of this story was a later reconstruction. I am grateful to David Boucher for this information.

the ideas were more fully worked out than they actually were; but he was writing in good faith in seeking to explain his objection.

If this is so, however, then there is an irony of which there is no indication at all in Collingwood's account. For the logic of question and answer has roots in the very philosophy that it was supposedly directed against—in Oxbridge realism itself. Even today this is scarcely appreciated, although that is due far more to the obscurity into which Oxbridge realism, especially of the Oxford variety, has now fallen than to any suppression of influences on Collingwood's part.[25] The key figure here is John Cook Wilson, whose *Statement and Inference* can be regarded as the Oxford realist's textbook on logic. Part II of this work is entitled 'Statement and its Relation to Thinking and Apprehension', and Cook Wilson begins by discussing the notions of apprehension, judgement, knowledge, and belief. Chapter 4 is called 'The Distinction of Subject and Predicate in Logic and Grammar', and it is here that Cook Wilson appeals to what becomes the central idea of Collingwood's logic of question and answer.

Cook Wilson's main concern is to establish that what counts *logically* as the subject and predicate of a statement depends on the question which the statement is intended to answer. Take Cook Wilson's own example, the sentence 'That building is the Bodleian.' If the question is 'What is that building?', then 'that building' counts as the subject (as indeed we might take it grammatically to be). On the other hand, if 'Which building is the Bodleian?' is the question, then 'the Bodleian' is the subject, logically speaking. Cook Wilson's point is therefore very simple: statements (sentences as used on a given occasion) are answers to questions, and we need to know the question before we can determine the logical analysis.[26] In fact, this basic idea is by no means original to Cook

[25] This is not to suggest that Oxbridge realism was the only influence on Collingwood's idea of question and answer. As Collingwood himself notes (*SM*, 77; cf. *A*, 30), the basic idea goes back to Socrates and was implicit in Bacon's conception of the scientist's interrogation of nature, for example. There may also have been important contemporary influences, such as from Evans-Pritchard's work on the Azande, operating from the mid-1930s (as Wendy James has pointed out to me in discussion). See Connelly's contribution to this volume. My focus here is only on Collingwood's relationship to Oxbridge realism, which I nevertheless do think was central in the development of his idea of a *logic* of question and answer.

[26] Cook Wilson, *Statement and Inference*, I: 117–20.

Wilson. It can be found earlier in the work of G. F. Stout (1860–1944), for example. Educated at Cambridge, Stout taught there until 1896, when he moved to Aberdeen and then Oxford, before becoming Professor of Logic and Metaphysics at St Andrews, where he stayed until he retired in 1936. In his *Analytic Psychology* of 1896, in a section on 'The Subject–Predicate Relation', Stout writes:

> All answers to questions are, as such, predicates, and all predicates may be regarded as answers to possible questions. If the statement 'I am hungry' be a reply to the question, 'Who is hungry?' then 'I' is the predicate. If it be an answer to the question, 'Is there anything amiss with you?' then 'hungry' is the predicate. If the question is, 'Are you really hungry?' then 'am' is the predicate. Every fresh step in a train of thought may be regarded as an answer to a question.[27]

Collingwood would surely have come across the idea from at least Cook Wilson, and while he may have forgotten this by 1939, one might also suggest that he was deliberately taking this idea from Oxbridge realism to turn against them—whether in an act of Hegelian synthesis or just as a mischievous dig. Whatever his motivation, however, we must recognize that, in doing so, he generalized it to such an extent that it threatened to undermine the rest of his philosophy. For according to Collingwood, it is not just the identification of subject and predicate that depends on the question which the statement answers, but the very meaning and truth value of the statement. Yet even when one and the same sentence, such as 'That building is the Bodleian', is used to answer more than one question, there may still be something that the corresponding statements have in common. This is what the traditional logician calls its 'content' or the 'proposition' it expresses.

[27] Stout, G. F. 1896. *Analytic Psychology*, 2 vols, London, Swan Sonnenschein, II: 214. The idea is developed further in his later work. In his Gifford lectures from 1919 and 1921, for example, posthumously published in 1952 (Stout, G. F. *God and Nature*, ed. A. K. Stout, Cambridge, Cambridge University Press), Stout characterizes a proposition as one of a group of alternatives that share a certain presupposition (102–4). The act of judging, Stout writes, 'is always preconditioned by an interrogative attitude of mind' (1952, 276). For discussion of Stout's views, see Schaar, Maria van der, *Stout's Theory of Judgement: From Psychology to Philosophy*, Basingstoke, Palgrave Macmillan, 2013. I am grateful to Maria van der Schaar for these references to Stout's work.

Collingwood, of course, wants to reject 'propositional logic'. He formulates its central doctrine, which he calls 'the principle of propositional logic', as follows: 'there is, or ought to be, or in a well-constructed and well-used language would be, a one-one correspondence between propositions and indicative sentences, every indicative sentence expressing a proposition, and a proposition being defined as the unit of thought, or that which is true or false' (*A*, 35–6). Now this was certainly a view that Russell held,[28] but it is not obligatory. Gottlob Frege (1848–1925), the founder of modern (propositional and predicate) logic, for example, did not hold it.[29] We need to distinguish this principle from a more basic principle, which I shall simply call the principle of logic: every sentence, as used on a given occasion to express a thought, has a content that can be expressed by a different sentence on a different occasion.

This principle can be regarded, rightly, as an absolute presupposition of logic. For it is essential to logic that we be able to transform one sentence into another in order to better express its 'content'—whether we are attempting to say what is 'really meant' or just to exhibit or clarify the logical relations it has with other sentences (as used on given occasions). Frege was clear about this. In one of his most famous papers, he wrote: 'we must not fail to recognize that the same sense, the same thought, may be variously expressed . . . If all transformation of the expression were forbidden on the plea that this would alter the content as well, logic would simply be crippled; for the task of logic can hardly be performed without trying to recognize the thought in its

[28] See e.g. Russell, Bertrand, 1918. 'The Philosophy of Logical Atomism', in *Logic and Knowledge*, ed. Marsh, R. C. 1956, London: George Allen and Unwin: Lecture 2, 197–8; and for discussion, see Hylton, Peter, 1990. *Russell, Idealism, and the Emergence of Analytic Philosophy*, Oxford, Clarendon Press; 2013. 'Ideas of a Logically Perfect Language in Analytic Philosophy', in *The Oxford Handbook of the History of Analytic Philosophy*, ed. M. Beaney, Oxford, Oxford University Press, pp. 908–25.

[29] This is controversial, and at least needs qualification. But all I will note here is that Frege undoubtedly held that one and the same 'content' or 'thought' can be analysed in different ways. Cf. the quote in the next paragraph. For fuller discussion of this, see Beaney, Michael, 1996. *Frege: Making Sense*, London, Duckworth: esp. ch. 8.

manifold guises.'[30] Cook Wilson, too, endorsed the principle. Although he regarded the identification of subject and predicate as depending on our *apprehension* of content (and hence as relative to the question asked), the content itself he saw as an 'objective fact' that could be described by different statements.[31]

The principle of logic is presupposed by Collingwood himself in his use of the Socratic principle. For in coming to know better something we already know, there must be some content in common. Indeed, this content is individuated in the process of coming to know it better.[32] There need be no definitive articulation of this content, so we can agree that the principle of propositional logic is false. But the falsity of this principle does not imply the falsity of the principle of logic, despite the impression that Collingwood sometimes gives in advocating his new logic of question and answer. Even if an assertion of a proposition *P* and an assertion of its apparent negation *not-P* are answers to different questions (cf. *A*, 42), they may still contradict one another at the level of content, so that there is value in the realist's method of analysis.

Shortly after completing the *Autobiography*, Collingwood wrote some notes for his new logic.[33] These are brief, and were never developed further, but what Collingwood is gesturing towards is a theory of speech acts rather than a new logic. Not only is this not incompatible with propositional (and predicate) logic, but its successful development requires such a logic (presupposing the distinction between semantics and pragmatics that we now take for granted). Collingwood's own ideas about a logic of question and answer were suggestive, but there remained tensions and confusions that were never resolved.[34]

[30] Frege, Gottlob, 1892. 'On Concept and Object', in *The Frege Reader*, ed. M. Beaney, Oxford, Blackwell: 184, fn. G.

[31] Cook Wilson, *Statement and Inference*, cf. e.g. I: ch. 7.

[32] The principle of logic is also presupposed in Collingwood's doctrine of re-enactment and his conception of 'eternal objects' as what can be 'apprehended by historical thought at any time' (*IH*, 218). On the importance of this for Collingwood, see Haddock's contribution to this volume.

[33] Collingwood, R. G., 1939. 'Notes for an Essay on Logic', in *EM*, 422–7.

[34] For a more detailed diagnosis of what goes wrong in Collingwood's appeal to a logic of question and answer, see Beaney, Michael, 2005. 'Collingwood's Conception of Presuppositional Analysis', *Collingwood and British Idealism Studies*, 11, No. 2: 41–114, esp. §§ 2.7–2.9, where I distinguish two notions of 'proposition', one the traditional logician's notion and the other a speech act notion.

5. REALISM AND KNOWLEDGE

The principle of logic might be taken to presuppose an even more basic principle, the epistemological/metaphysical principle that knowing makes no difference to what is known.[35] For if we come to know a content better in improving the sentences that express it, then we must presuppose that this content remains constant. For if it were changed when we come to know it better, then how could we claim that we know *that content* better? Yet this is the principle that Collingwood attacks in chapter 6 of the *Autobiography*, entitled 'The Decay of Realism'. He describes it as Cook Wilson's central positive doctrine, and the only positive doctrine that realism could count as its own.

Collingwood reports that he read a paper after the war in which he argued that this doctrine was meaningless:[36]

> I argued that any one who claimed, as Cook Wilson did, to be sure of this, was in effect claiming to know what he was simultaneously defining as unknown. For if you know that no difference is made to a thing θ by the presence or absence of a certain condition *c*, you know what θ is like with *c*, and also what θ is like without *c*, and on comparing the two find no difference. This involves knowing what θ is like without *c*; in the present case, knowing what you defined as the unknown. (*A*, 44)

The immediate point to make about this is that it only establishes, at best, that no one could claim to *know* that knowing makes no difference to what is known. This might suggest that the doctrine should simply be taken as an absolute presupposition of realism, for which no arguments can be given. One might have expected Collingwood to be sympathetic towards this suggestion, but he is not the relativist that his conception of absolute presuppositions is often taken to imply.[37] One can indeed criticize

[35] In *The Nature of Truth* Joachim calls the assumption that 'experiencing makes no difference to the facts', which he finds in Russell's and Moore's work, 'the fundamental postulate of all Logic' (1906: 33, 36). Collingwood was editing the second edition of the book at the time he was writing the *Autobiography*. It was published in 1939, a year after Joachim's death (cf. *A*, 18, fn. 2). Collingwood acknowledges his debt to Joachim's work in two places (*A*, 18, 36).

[36] For details of the event itself (which took place in November 1920) see Patrick's contribution to this volume.

[37] See e.g. Collingwood, 'Notes for an Essay on Logic': 394–5. For defence of this view of Collingwood, see Beaney, 'Collingwood's Conception of Presuppositional Analysis'.

someone else's absolute presuppositions, and Collingwood certainly felt no inhibition in doing so in the present case. The fact that he does criticize it also shows that we cannot take seriously his claim that the doctrine is meaningless; if it were meaningless, then it could not function in the kind of argument that Collingwood offers (which attempts to derive a contradiction from the supposition that it is true). The claim that a doctrine cannot be known to be true does not imply that it is meaningless.[38]

What, then, of the argument itself? The condition *c* that Collingwood has in mind is the condition of being unknown. Clearly, one cannot know something that is unknown at the time one knows it. That is indeed a logical contradiction. But assume, for the sake of argument, that in coming to know something, one knows that no change was made to it in the process. (Think of cracking open a nut and discovering the kernel inside, where one knows that cracking open a nut does not alter the nature of the kernel itself.) Of course, such an assumption is unproblematic if the realist doctrine were true, so the critic of realism might object that this simply begs the question. But all we need is a single plausible case to establish the *possibility* that in coming to know something, we know that it did not alter in the process. That is enough to show that there is no logical contradiction in the idea that we can know that knowing makes no difference to what is known. Collingwood's argument is not the knock-down argument he seems to suppose.

We might agree with Collingwood, though, that the Oxford realists never provided a knock-down argument *for* their doctrine. In fairness to the realists themselves, however, it is not clear that they ever claimed to have done so. Following Collingwood's own advice to look carefully at the texts when a charge of contradiction is being levelled, consider the following remarks by Cook Wilson:

> Now we must know something about knowledge, and we know when we reflect that the very idea of it is incompatible with any such *action* upon, or *suffering* in, the object known. You can no more act upon the object by knowing it than you can 'please the Dean and Chapter by stroking the dome of St. Paul's'.... Obviously if we 'do anything to' anything in

[38] A verificationist would beg to differ, and although Collingwood may have flirted with verificationism in writing the *Essay on Metaphysics* just a year later, I do not think that that was his considered view. Again, for further discussion of this, see Beaney, 'Collingwood's Conception of Presuppositional Analysis'.

knowing, it is not done to the object known, to what we know, for that simply contradicts the presuppositions of the act of knowledge itself.[39]

These remarks occur in a letter to Prichard, in whose work we find an even more explicit statement of the doctrine:

Knowledge unconditionally presupposes that the reality known exists independently of the knowledge of it, and that we know it as it exists in this independence. It is simply *impossible* to think that any reality depends upon our knowledge of it, or upon any knowledge of it. If there is to be knowledge, there must first *be* something to be known. (*Kant's Theory of Knowledge*, Oxford, Clarendon Press: 117)

Given the role that the idea of presuppositions comes to play in Collingwood's philosophy, the use that both Cook Wilson and Prichard make of it is significant. On their view, knowledge *presupposes* that knowing makes no difference to what is known. To deny this is to deny the very nature of knowledge itself. There can be no argument for this, since any argument would rest on premises that would need to be known, begging the question as to the nature of knowledge. Knowledge and apprehension are *sui generis* and indefinable. All one can do is get someone into a position whereby they can apprehend or intuit this presupposition.[40] Cook Wilson thought that if you genuinely know something, then you know what this involves: 'The consciousness that the knowing process is a knowing process must be contained within the knowing process itself.'[41] The idea is problematic, but not meaningless or straightforwardly self-contradictory.[42]

The basic idea here also informed Prichard's ethics. In his paper 'Does Moral Philosophy Rest on a Mistake?', published in 1912, to which Collingwood alludes (*A*, 47), Prichard argued that it was a mistake to seek a single overarching principle of morality from which to derive particular obligations; rather, the grounds for each of our obligations can be discerned in our very apprehension of it.[43] The idea is as problematic in ethics as it is in epistemology, not

[39] Cook Wilson, *Statement and Inference*, II: 802.

[40] Cf. e.g. Cook Wilson, *Statement and Inference*, I: 38–9, 98ff.; II, 803–4; Prichard, *Kant's Theory of Knowledge*, 124.

[41] Cook Wilson, *Statement and Inference*, I: 107.

[42] For a critique of Cook Wilson's views, see Marion, 'Oxford Realism, Knowledge and Perception': 307–16.

[43] Cf. Cook Wilson, referring to Aristotle: 'the principle lives only in the particulars', *Statement and Inference*, I: 43.

least because of its appeal to the conception of apprehension Collingwood criticizes in chapter 4 of the *Autobiography*; but these problems do not, I think, have their source in the central realist doctrine itself.

Is there not an obvious sense in which knowing does make a difference to what is known? In coming to know something, whether it is an object, fact, proposition, or whatever, that something acquires a property that it did not have before, namely, that it is now known by me. The standard response to this is to distinguish between essential and non-essential properties, or between internal and external relations. The property of being known by me is not an essential property of that which I know; so the realist doctrine should at least be qualified: knowing makes no essential difference to what is known. Another way to put this is to say that, in general, the relation between knower and known is external rather than internal. Now at the time Collingwood is talking about in criticizing the realists, there was a vigorous debate about the nature of relations, in which the leading figure on the idealist side was Bradley and the leading figure on the realist side was Russell.[44] Collingwood does not mention this debate at all; what it shows is that idealism was by no means as dead and that realism was by no means as unchallenged at the time as Collingwood suggests.

How, then, might the debate between the realist and the idealist be resolved? An answer can only be gestured at here, but the starting point, once again, is the Socratic principle. For (to state the obvious) in coming to know something, something must be taken as the same, in one sense, and something must be seen as changing, in another sense. It seems right to talk of the process of knowing as *presupposing* that something is identified as constant: this is what we come to know, even though our knowledge grows. Sometimes this is expressed by distinguishing between the object and content of knowledge: the object remains the same while the

[44] The problem of relations was central in Russell's rebellion against British idealism, and there were idealist responses to Russell. See e.g. some of the papers in Bradley, *Essays on Truth and Reality*; Bradley, F. H., 1924. 'Relations', in *Collected Essays*, Oxford, Oxford University Press, 1935, pp. 629–76; Joachim, *The Nature of Truth*, ch. 2. For an account of this debate, see Candlish, Stewart, 2007. *The Russell/Bradley Dispute and its Significance for Twentieth-Century Philosophy*, Basingstoke, Palgrave Macmillan: esp. ch. 6.

content is refined in coming to know something better. Some such distinction is clearly needed; there are various ways in which this can be developed. I think Collingwood himself provided one such way in his *Essay on Philosophical Method*, and it is both surprising and disappointing that he does not discuss this in the *Autobiography*, especially since, in the only mention he does make, he describes it as his 'best book in matter' (*A*, 118). Perhaps his animus against realism clouded his judgement in the *Autobiography*; it certainly prevented him from giving the more nuanced critique that I think could be mounted on his behalf, which accommodated elements of realism that Collingwood himself had absorbed.[45]

6. CONCLUSION

In the penultimate paragraph of chapter 6 of his *Autobiography*, Collingwood remarks that the end of the realist movement 'is one of those things whose history will never be written' (*A*, 51). Collingwood had in mind its disintegration into 'a kind of intellectual nightmare' (*A*, 51). More than seventy years later, it is clear that this prophecy has turned out false. Within the analytic tradition itself, whose early founders Collingwood criticized, there has been an historical turn, as at least some of those trained in that tradition have been led to investigate its historical and philosophical foundations.[46] Cambridge realism has received far more attention than Oxford realism, or indeed, non-Oxbridge realism, but even here there have been historical accounts.[47]

[45] I have identified a source of the idea of a logic of question and answer in Oxbridge realism, but it might also be noted here that the Socratic principle, too, can be found in Cook Wilson's work; see e.g. *Statement and Inference*, I: 44–5.

[46] The historical turn can be dated as having properly got going around 1990, with works on Moore by Baldwin, Thomas, 1990, *G. E. Moore*, London, Routledge, and on Russell by Hylton, Peter, 1990. *Russell, Idealism, and the Emergence of Analytic Philosophy*, Oxford, Clarendon Press, and Griffin, Nicholas, 1991. *Russell's Idealist Apprenticeship*, Oxford, Clarendon Press. On the historical turn generally, see Beaney, Michael, ed., 2013. *The Oxford Handbook of the History of Analytic Philosophy*, Oxford, Oxford University Press, and Reck, Erich, ed., 2013. *The Historical Turn in Analytic Philosophy*, Basingstoke, Palgrave Macmillan.

[47] On Oxford realism, see esp. Marion, 'Oxford Realism', and Travis, Charles and Kalderon, Mark, 2013. 'Oxford realism', in Beaney, *The Oxford Handbook of*

Collingwood's sense that there was something wrong in the realism of his Oxbridge contemporaries, however, has proved right. While his attack on the doctrine that knowing makes no difference to what is known leaves something to be desired, he correctly identified their appeal to 'apprehension' and 'intuition' as problematic. I have argued that Collingwood was wrong to reject the new logic that Russell did so much to establish, although he was right to criticize what he called 'the principle of propositional logic'. The 'logic of question and answer' that he hoped would replace existing logic was too poorly conceived to take seriously, although the basic idea of question-and-answer complexes has certainly been influential.

In the *Autobiography*, Collingwood exaggerates his opposition to realism, for reasons that are political rather than philosophical, as the final chapter, in particular, makes clear. As I have tried to show here, there is continuity as well as opposition, in accord with Collingwood's own historicist and Socratic principles, which provide unity in the development of his philosophy. In the hastily written works of his last few years, when he knew that he may not live much longer, there are caricatures and exaggerations, loose formulations and weak arguments. But as Cook Wilson had once said to him, he had the gift of seeing the obvious (cf. *A*, 26), and he had a good nose for what was wrong in a philosophical doctrine or theory. When the story of realism does indeed emerge from the accounts that are now being written, Collingwood will have his own rightful place in it.[48]

the History of Analytic Philosophy, pp. 489–517; and on other forms of realism, see e.g. Nasim, Omar W., 2008. *Bertrand Russell and the Edwardian Philosophers*, Basingstoke, Palgrave Macmillan.

[48] Talks based on drafts of this chapter were given at the Collingwood conference in Montreal in October 2007, at the conference organized by the Centre for the Study of British Idealism at Hull in December 2009, and at the workshop on the *Autobiography* held in Oxford in July 2010. I am grateful to the participants for discussion, and especially to David Boucher, James Connelly, Wendy James, Sharon Macdonald, Rex Martin, and Teresa Smith for detailed comments.

4

COLLINGWOOD AS ARCHAEOLOGIST AND HISTORIAN[1]

TONY BIRLEY

For four months I have been deep in historical studies, and there I find myself among friends and willing collaborators; the return to philosophy means a return to a work in which I become more and more conscious of being an outlaw.

(Letter to Guido de Ruggiero, 4 October 1927, quoted from van der Dussen *History as a Science*: 192).

It may now be hoped that a tropic sun has restored him, at least for a part of the year, to the more substantial and mundane studies that are (for us) his proper realm.

(R. E. M. Wheeler, review of *Roman Britain and the English Settlements*, 87).

R. G. Collingwood, long the brilliant and dearly loved leader of Romano-British studies.

(Eric Birley, 'Britain under the Flavians: Agricola and his predecessors', *Durham University Journal* 38. no. 3 (June 1946): 79–84, reprinted in Birley, E. 1953. *Roman Britain and the Roman Army. Collected Papers*: 10–19, at 19).

[1] Dussen, Jan van der 1981. *History as a Science: The Philosophy of R.G. Collingwood*. The Hague: Nijhoff: esp. 201–53, 404–12, covers this theme at much greater length than can be attempted here. The 1981 edition is cited throughout. The 2012 edition (Dordrecht: Springer) was not available to the writer. Since 1981, publication on Roman Britain has swelled enormously. See e.g. Mattingly, D. J. 2006. *An Imperial Possession. Britain in the Roman Empire, 54 BC–AD 409, Penguin History of Britain, I*. London, Allen Lane: 541–80; and more can now be said about the reception of Collingwood's work; cf. also Freeman, P. W. M. 2007. *The Best Training-Ground for Archaeologists. Francis Haverfield and the Invention of Romano-British Archaeology*. Oxford, Oxbow Books: esp. 537–58.

It has not seemed necessary or desirable to supply chapter and verse for every statement in this contribution; cf. in particular the chapters by Teresa Smith and Jan van der Dussen in this volume. For their comments on an earlier draft I am grateful to Paul Bidwell, Robin Birley, Duncan Campbell, James Connolly, Philip Freeman, Stephen Leach, and the editors. Remaining errors are my own.

1. INTRODUCTION

R. G. Collingwood is still a potent name in Romano-British studies, nearly seventy years after his death. His passion for the subject, surprising at first sight for a philosopher, had started early, his father being an active antiquary; and he soon became involved in excavation. After Francis Haverfield, the great authority on Roman Britain, died in 1919, Collingwood, who had been his pupil, volunteered, in addition to his duties as a teacher of philosophy, to fill the gap: to lecture on Roman Britain and also to continue Haverfield's project for a new corpus of inscriptions. 'Obscure provinces, like Roman Britain, always rather appeal to me,' he wrote in his *Autobiography* (*A*, 86); and this was to be the 'laboratory' for his work on the philosophy of history (*A*, 121). Further, regular returns to his home country, in the hinterland of Hadrian's Wall, 'to address the local antiquarian society', were a kind of 'release' for the 'suppressed man of action' (*A*, 151). All the same, he took it very seriously and became the inspiring leader of that branch of archaeology and history. Towards the end of his life his outspoken views in the last chapter of the *Autobiography*, then, even more so, his separation, divorce, and remarriage, in 1941–1942, upset some of those close to him and lay behind the misleadingly critical view of his achievement published by Ian Richmond. That criticism was long influential, but it can be explained and rebutted (see section 5). Collingwood is still regularly cited as co-author of the *Roman Inscriptions of Britain* (*RIB*), on which he had worked for over fifteen years, although the first part was not published until 1965, the second not until the 1990s. His *Archaeology of Roman Britain* (1930) and *Roman Britain*, the greater part of Volume I in the *Oxford History of England*, *Roman Britain and the English Settlements* (1936, 2nd edn 1937), remained standard works for over thirty years, until his views required modification in the light of steadily increasing information. More important is the fact that his theory of question and answer is now standard practice.

His two professions, as philosopher and historian,[2] were sometimes difficult to reconcile with one another; the remarks to de

[2] Or three, if one divides the second into archaeologist and historian, as van der Dussen, *History As Science*, 201–2: while admitting that archaeology and history

Ruggiero in 1927 suggest that at times he felt more comfortable in the latter. Twelve years later, for his close friend Wheeler, archaeology, 'the more substantial and mundane studies', rather than metaphysics, were his 'proper realm', to which he should be restored. To be sure, his first interest in philosophy was excited at the age of eight by finding, and trying in vain to understand, a copy of Kant's *Theory of Ethics* (*A*, 3 f.), and his 'first lesson in what I now regard as my own subject, the history of thought, was the discovery, in a friend's house . . . of [what] must have been a compendium of Descartes' *Principia*' (*A*, 1). All the same, he grew up, in the Lake District, 'in a gradually thickening archaeological atmosphere'. His skills as a draughtsman (see Illustrations 9 and 10 for examples) and his earliest experiences in archaeology were owed to his father, W. G. Collingwood, an accomplished artist and active excavator. During school holidays, he

was entrusted with the search for prehistoric remains in unexplored districts and the surveying of them when found, and spent two seasons [1906 and 1907] working as his [father's] assistant in his now classical excavation of a Romano-British village [Ewe Close]. This and similar experiences taught me that scissors and paste were not the only foundation of historical method. All you wanted . . . was a sufficiently extensive and sufficiently scientific development of such work, and it would teach you, not indeed everything, but a great deal, about subjects whose very existence must remain permanently unknown to historians who believed in authorities. (*A*, 80)

Here was the germ of his theory of question and answer:[3]

I had learnt by first-hand experience that history is not an affair of scissors and paste, but is much more like Bacon's notion of science. The historian must decide exactly what it is that he wants to know; and if there is no authority to tell him . . . he has to find a piece of land or something that has got the answer hidden in it, and get the answer out by fair means or foul.

'cannot be sharply divided, especially in Collingwood's own practice', he insists that they are not the same. But cf. Collingwood's own account in *A*, e.g. 120 (quoted later); 130: 'The principle [of question and answer] applies not merely to archaeology, but to every kind of history'; 133: 'I am taking most of my examples from archaeology (that is, history in which the sources used are "unwritten" sources, or, more accurately, are not pre-existing narratives of the events into which the historian is inquiring).'

[3] Set out fully in *A*, 122–38.

That was as far as my philosophy of history had got when I went up to Oxford. (*A*, 81)

He went up in 1908, when he was 19, to read Mods and Greats. Through his father, who had been editor of the Cumberland and Westmorland Society's *Transactions* since 1900, he must already have met Francis Haverfield. From 1894 to 1903 that

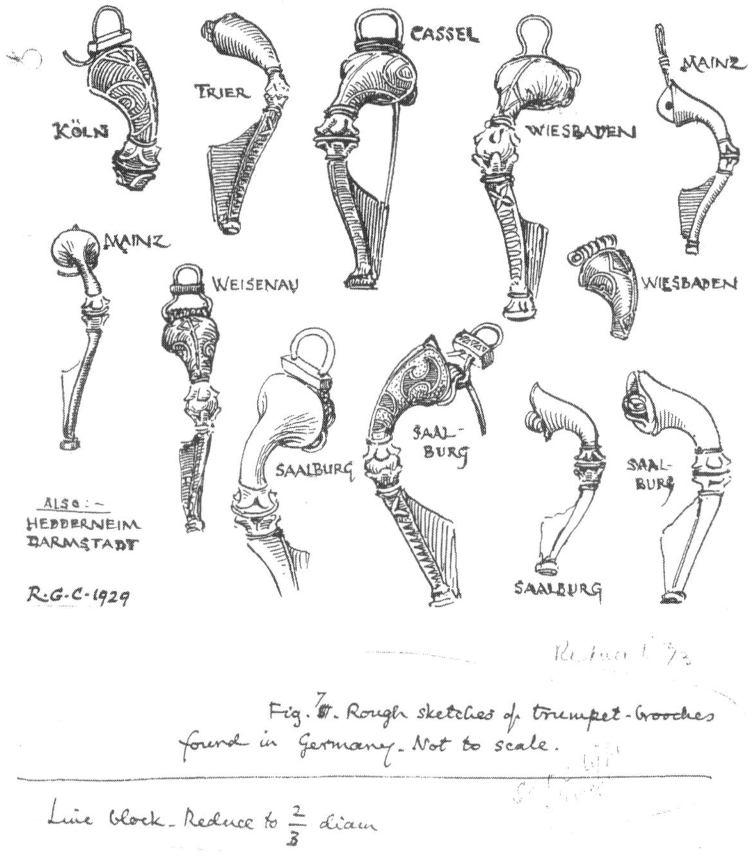

Illustration 9. Collingwood's archaeological sketchbooks I: sketches of Roman brooches for a proposed volume classifying the different designs and their significance. R. G. C. 1929. (Item 15, Box 14, R. P. Wright Collection, Sackler Library, Oxford).

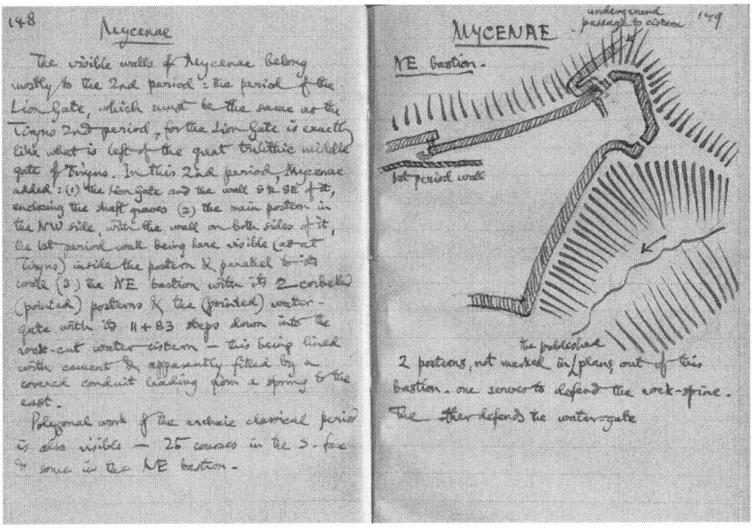

Illustration 10. Collingwood's archaeological sketchbooks II: field notes on Mycenae, pp. 148–9 in his notebook on travels in Italy, Sicily, and Greece January–April 1932. Courtesy of Teresa Smith.

scholar, already the leading expert on Roman Britain, had led the excavations along Hadrian's Wall for the Cumberland Excavation Committee, and in 1902 W. G. Collingwood had participated in them himself.[4] Haverfield had taught at Oxford since 1892, when his *Ephemeris Epigraphica* VII came out, a supplement to the *Corpus Inscriptionum Latinarum* volume on Britain's Roman inscriptions. Before that he had been in contact with the great Theodor Mommsen for nearly ten years and in 1907 became Camden Professor of Ancient History. As Collingwood saw it,

[4] Haverfield's excavations were regularly published in the *Cumberland and Westmorland Antiquarian and Archaeological Society's Transactions* (hereafter *CWAAS*). Freeman, *The Best Training-Ground*: 538 by oversight (as he confirms by personal communication) gives the year that W. G. C. took part as 1903 and mistakenly states that R. G. C. was also involved. On Haverfield's life and career, see Freeman, *The Best Training-Ground*: *passim*; cf. also the obituary by Macdonald, G. 1920–1921, 'Haverfield, 1860–1919', *Proceedings of the British Academy*, 9: 475–91; conciser but full of detail.

Mommsen had shown how by statistical and other treatment of inscriptions the historian of the Roman Empire could answer questions that no one had dreamed of asking. Dragendorff had classified the shapes of 'Samian' pottery, and he and others had begun to date them. It was a recently established and exciting fact that by excavation you could reconstruct the history of Roman sites not mentioned in any authority and of events in Roman history not mentioned in any book. Owing to the work of Haverfield, whose interest embraced every branch and twig of Roman archaeology, and whose skill and learning as an epigraphist were comparable, we believed, only with those of Mommsen himself, these notions had taken a firm root in Oxford and were completely transforming the study of the Roman Empire. (*A*, 82)

In 1911 and 1912 Collingwood joined the excavations at Corbridge sponsored by Haverfield;[5] and in 1912 directed a short dig himself, at the Roman fort of Papcastle in Cumberland.[6] From there he evidently planned to go to Wroxeter, presumably to join Bushe-Fox's excavations.[7] In summer 1913 he directed the dig at Ambleside, with Haverfield, in the Roman fort at the head of Lake Windermere. He dug at Ambleside again, as sole director, in 1914 and 1915. He had a fourth and final season in 1920, after returning from his work in the Admiralty Intelligence service; all these 'explorations' were reported punctually and in full.[8]

By 1920 he had taken on much wider responsibilities for Roman Britain. As he described the situation in retrospect:

[i]t was necessary for the advancement of my philosophical work . . . to be engaged in historical studies as well; and in a field where I could initiate

[5] Freeman, *The Best Training Ground*: 410 n. 71.

[6] 1913. 'Report of the excavations at Papcastle, 1912', *CWAAS*[2] 13: 131–41.

[7] In a letter to her mother on 23 June 1912, his sister Ursula, who was assisting him at Papcastle, mentioned that 'Robin . . . will be very hard up until January', but that there were various sources of funds for him, including 'Univ. Coll. £10 for Wroxeter'. (Unpublished; text kindly supplied by James Connolly.)

[8] Haverfield, F. J. and Collingwood, R. G. 1914. 'Report on the exploration of the Roman fort at Ambleside', *CWAAS*[2] 14: 337–44; Collingwood, R. G. (with Professor Haverfield), 'Report on the exploration of the Roman fort at Ambleside, 1913, with a preliminary report of explorations in March and April 1914 (with L. B. Freeston)', *CWAAS*[2] 14: 433–65; Collingwood, R. G., 'The exploration of the Roman fort at Ambleside: Report of the second year's work (1914)', *CWAAS*[2] 15 (1915): 1–62; 'The exploration of the Roman fort at Ambleside: Report of the third year's work (1915)', *CWAAS*[2] 16 (1916): 57–90; further, 'Explorations in the Roman fort at Ambleside (fourth year 1920) and at other sites on the Tenth Iter', *CWAAS*[2] 21 (1921): 1–42.

lines of research in which I could hope for the co-operation of others; a field, therefore, in which I was an acknowledged master. The field had, accordingly, to be a small one, and ripe for intensive cultivation. For this purpose Roman Britain was very suitable. Moreover, I was already committed. Haverfield, the great master of the subject, died in 1919; . . . I was left the only man resident in Oxford whom he had trained as a Romano-British specialist; and even if my philosophy had not demanded it, I should have thought myself, in piety to him, under an obligation to keep alive the Oxford school of Romano-British studies that he had founded, to pass on the training he had given me, and to make use of the specialist library he had left to the University. (*A*, 120)

An initial result was the joint article 'Roman Britain in 1921 and 1922', in *Journal of Roman Studies* 11 (for 1921; not published until 1923), by Collingwood and Margerie Venables Taylor, Haverfield's former secretary, who was to work for the bequest (on which see section 3). The article carried an appeal for information for the 'new *corpus* of Roman inscriptions in Britain'; the annual survey articles became a regular feature of *JRS*.

2. HADRIAN'S WALL

Collingwood was soon actively engaged with Hadrian's Wall, which had so long preoccupied Haverfield and about which questions still had to be answered. The same volume of *JRS* that carried the first survey article contained his history of the problem; and in a short paper in a Newcastle periodical he had tackled a fundamental aspect. As he summed it up later (*A*, 128 f.):

The many archaeologists who had worked at the Roman Wall . . . had never, I found, seriously asked themselves what it was for . . . How did it work? Was it meant to work, for example, like a town-wall, from the top of which defenders repelled attacks? Several obvious features about it made it quite impossible that any Roman soldier should ever have meant to use it that way. No one seemed to have noticed this before; but when I pointed it out in 1921 every one who was interested in the subject admitted that it was so, and my counter-suggestion that the wall was meant for an 'elevated sentry-walk' was generally accepted.[9]

[9] Referring to his 1921 paper, 'The purpose of the Roman Wall', *The Vasculum. The North Country Quarterly of Science and Local History* 8: 4–9; cf. summaries in Collingwood, R. G. 1923. *Roman Britain*. Oxford, Clarendon Press, 30ff.; revised

This interpretation long held the field, albeit sometimes rejected, recently in quite emphatic terms—some specialists now argue strongly that the Roman army did need to use the Wall as a fighting platform and that it had the weaponry to do so.[10]

'A question answered causes another question to arise', he goes on:

> If the Wall was a sentry-walk, elevated from the ground and provided (no doubt) with a parapet to protect the sentries against sniping, the same sentry-walk must have continued down the Cumberland coast . . . to keep watch on vessels moving in the estuary . . . here the sentry-walk need not be elevated . . . There ought, therefore, to be a chain of towers, not connected by a Wall.

A short ground survey in 1928, after search in older publications, confirmed the hypothesis. The mile-fortlets and towers along the Cumberland coast have ever since been treated as an integral part of the Wall system (see Illustration 11), and ever more intensively investigated.[11] One may note that in 1922 Collingwood conducted a short trial excavation at the Cumbrian fort of Burgh-by-Sands, his only dig on the Wall itself[12] (though his close involvement with Wall research continued throughout the 1920s and beyond).

edn 1932: 32ff. Collingwood, R. G. 1936. 'Roman Britain', in Collingwood, R. G. and Myres, J. N. L., *Roman Britain and the English Settlements*. Oxford, Clarendon Press: 131 f.

[10] Collingwood's view was accepted e.g. by Birley, E. 1961. *Research on Hadrian's Wall*. Kendal, Titus Wilson & Son: 67 f.; Breeze, D. J. and Dobson, B. 1976. *Hadrian's Wall*. Harmondsworth, Penguin, 4th edition, 2000: 39 f., largely unchanged in later editions; Breeze, D. J. in Bidwell, P., ed. 2008. *Understanding Hadrian's Wall*. Kendal, Titus Wilson: 1 ff. For criticism, Bidwell, P. 2005. 'The System of Obstacles on Hadrian's Wall: their extent, date and purpose', *Arbeia Journal*: 53–75. Bidwell, P. 2008. 'Did Hadrian's Wall have a Wall-walk?', in Bidwell, ed. 2008: 129–43; Hodgson, N. 2009. *Hadrian's Wall 1999–2009. A Summary of Excavation and Research Prepared for the Thirteenth Pilgrimage of Hadrian's Wall, 8–14 August 2009*. Kendal, Titus Wilson: 42–50 reviews recent argument.

[11] Collingwood, R. G. 1929. 'Roman signal-stations on the Cumberland coast', *CWAAS*^{2} 29: 138–65; see e.g. Birley, *Research on Hadrian's Wall*: 126 ff.; Breeze, D. J. 2006. *J. Collingwood Bruce's Handbook to the Roman Wall*, 14th edition. Newcastle upon Tyne, Society of Antiquaries of Newcastle upon Tyne: 373 ff.; Hodgson, *Hadrian's Wall 1999–2009*: 158–67.

[12] 1923. 'Explorations at the Roman fort of Burgh-by-Sands', *CWAAS*^{2} 23: 2–12. His next (and for a long time his last) excavation was in 1926 at a Roman fort in Wensleydale, North Yorkshire: Collingwood, R.G. 1928. 'Excavations at Brough-by-Bainbridge in 1926', *Leeds Philosophical Society Proceeedings* 1.6: 261–84.

Illustration 11. R. G. C., Miss Fair, and W. G. C. at Walls Castle, Ravenglass, on the Cumbrian coast, September 15, 1927, photographed by Mr H. R. Hulbert (as recorded on the back of the photograph). Courtesy of Teresa Smith.

His article on the Wall problem, and one by F. G. Simpson and R. C. Shaw on the Vallum,[13] prompted the Director of the *Reichs-Limeskommission*, Professor Ernst Fabricius, to write a review, of which he sent an offprint to Collingwood. He had just drafted the article 'Limes' for Pauly-Wissowa, the great encyclopedia of *Altertumswissenschaft*, and was still baffled by the Vallum—for which there is no parallel on any other Roman frontier—and its relationship to the Wall system.[14] The ten-year programme of the Cumberland Excavation Committee had been intended to solve the puzzle; but uncertainty continued. In his letter of thanks, Collingwood stressed his belief that the Vallum was Hadrianic—although he was still wedded to the notion of a 'Vallum frontier' with associated forts, supposed briefly to have preceded the stone Wall, also Hadrianic.

I am far too familiar with the difficulties and chances of error in this kind of work, to be offended by your criticisms or to regard them otherwise than as sincerely helpful. But may I venture to make you what we call a sporting offer? Come to England and dig wherever you like, along the Limes, to test the views which you have challenged... Or, if that is impossible, at least come to England and let us show you the ground, and prove by our welcome how much we value your friendship and co-operation.[15]

In June 1928, Fabricius did come, and the University of Durham conferred an honorary doctorate on him. He was then taken for four days along Hadrian's Wall by Collingwood, R. C. Bosanquet, and F. G. Simpson; met Sir George Macdonald to visit the Antonine Wall and other Roman sites in Scotland; back in England he was shown more of Hadrian's Wall and visited excavations in

[13] Simpson, F. G. and Shaw, R. C. 1922. 'The purpose and date of the Vallum and its crossings', *CWAAS*[2] 22: 353–433.

[14] See Fabricius, E. 1923, 'Neue Arbeiten über die britannischen Limites', *Germania* 7: 79–89. Discusses Collingwood, R. G. 1923. 'Hadrian's Wall. A history of the problem', *Journal of Roman Studies* 11: 37–66, Simpson, F. G. and Shaw, R. C. 'The purpose and date of the Vallum', *CWAAS*[2] 22: 353–433 as well as three other recent publications. See further Fabricius, E. 1926. 'Limes', *Realencyclopädie der classischen Altertumswissenschaft* 13.1: cols. 572–671, at 615–34; at 633, note * he thanks Collingwood and others.

[15] Letter of 25 January 1925 in Fabricius *Nachlass*, Universität Freiburg-im-Breisgau Archiv.

progress, with a day at Birdoswald. Collingwood summed up the visit's significance:

> Not a small part of this was that we made the acquaintance of a singularly charming man, imperturbable by rain and storm and fatigue, overflowing with kindness and cheerfulness, and carrying his load of learning with the modesty of a boy. But the real importance of his visit was not a matter of personalities. The work of the last 20 years on the Wall has been done by men almost wholly cut off not only from the international exchange of archaeological ideas, but even from the main stream of English archaeology. For most of that time—1907 to 1924—it was done on the individual initiative and responsibility of these men; for although the local antiquarian societies of which they were members made important contributions to the cost of the work, they did not in any sense initiate, direct or criticise it.

In the previous century foreign scholars (he named Mommsen, Huebner, and von Sarwey) had cooperated with archaeologists working on the Wall and after that the work was largely in the hands of Haverfield. But when Haverfield's involvement with the Cumberland Excavation Committee ended,[16] work on the Wall 'ceased to enjoy any real publicity ... there are probably not a dozen persons resident in London who have the remotest idea of what has been done ... in the last twenty years'. Those working on the Wall had badly needed contact with experts: Fabricius 'came to us bearing all the credentials of his record and position, the chief authority in the world on the Roman frontier system'. He was heard to comment during his visit that: '"in Germany we have no excavations so scientific as yours". Such recognition is the only kind of success that scientific workers can greatly value ... Through the visit of Professor Fabricius, the work done on the Wall in the last twenty years has made contact with the main stream of European learning and has been accepted as an integral part of that stream.'[17] In 1929 the Newcastle Antiquaries' *Proceedings* reported Fabricius' letter to the Principal of Armstrong College,

[16] See Freeman, *The Best Training-Ground for Archaeologists*: 249 ff. for details of Haverfield's involvement with that committee, the visit by General Otto von Sarwey in 1893, and Haverfield's correspondence with Mommsen.

[17] Collingwood, R. G., Bosanquet, R. C., and Simpson, F. G. 1928. 'Professor Fabricius' visit. Reception Committee's Report', *Proceedings of the Society of Antiquaries of Newcastle upon Tyne*, 4th series, 3: 280–6.

expressing deep appreciation of the reception that was given him . . . and of the pains taken to enable him to become acquainted with the results achieved by recent Roman Wall research . . . 'The excavations have been conducted with the utmost care and discretion, and have completely satisfied all the technical requirements which are nowadays demanded of such a work. But the unusually high value of these explorations is due to the genuinely scientific manner in which they have been undertaken and carried out.' Dr. Fabricius concludes by paying a warm tribute to the skill of our member, Mr. F.G. Simpson.[18]

Apart from the value of Collingwood's interpretation of the Wall's purpose and function, and his creation of the numbering system for its parts, it was judged in 1961 that 'he did perhaps even greater service to mural studies by putting Simpson into touch with Fabricius'.[19] In 1929 Fabricius' *Assistent*, Dr Kurt Stade, joined the excavation at Birdoswald directed by Simpson, with the assistance of Ian Richmond and Eric Birley. On his own visit Collingwood just missed witnessing the discovery of two important building-inscriptions, one Severan, the other of the Tetrarchy. These led the excavators, with Collingwood's approval, to re-date the Wall's history: instead of the first period being ended by destruction soon after 180, this was amended to *c.* 197; likewise, the end of period II was now put in 296, rather than earlier in the third century. Like much else from those years, the dating is now generally abandoned.[20]

18 *Proceedings of the Society of Antiquaries of Newcastle upon Tyne*, 4th series, 4 (1929): 52.

19 Birley, *Research on Hadrian's Wall*: 68; cf. 70–7 on the numbering system, originally worked out by Collingwood, R. G. 1930. 'A system of numerical references to parts of Hadrian's Wall and the structures along its line', *CWAAS*[2] 30: 108–15, and Collingwood, R. G. 1930. 'Hadrian's Wall: a system of numerical references', *Proceedings of the Society of Antiquaries of Newcastle upon Tyne*, 4th series, 4: 179–87.

20 Richmond, I. A. and Birley, E. with a note by F. G. Simpson, 1930. 'Excavations on Hadrian's Wall in the Birdoswald-Pike Hill sector, 1929', *CWAAS*[2] 30: 169–205; Collingwood, R. G. 1931. 'Hadrian's Wall: 1921–1930', *Journal of Roman Studies*, 21: 38; Collingwood, R. G. 1932. *Roman Britain*, revised edition, Oxford, Clarendon Press: 36f., 41; Collingwood, R. G. and Myres, J. N. L. 1936. *Roman Britain and the English Settlements*. Oxford, Clarendon Press: 155 f.; 277; cf. Birley, *Research on Hadrian's Wall*: 250 f. Breeze, D. J. 2003. 'J. Collingwood Bruce and the study of Hadrian's Wall', *Britannia* 34: 13, suggests that 'The Wall-periods theory governed thinking on the Wall and forced its history into a straight-jacket which lasted for forty years.' All the same, the theory was already challenged

Collingwood was very active in the 1930 Wall Pilgrimage, compiling the *Book of the Pilgrimage*; and was preparing a new, ninth edition of Bruce's *Handbook*. In the first footnote to his 1931 article on 'Hadrian's Wall 1921–1930' (*JRS* 21: 36–64), he commented on that in *JRS* 11, which 'contains much that I should now alter . . . later discoveries modify one's reading of texts and facts already known'. He praised those responsible for the work:

> first and foremost Mr. F.G. Simpson, who has done more than any other one person to lay down the lines on which archaeological study of the Wall must proceed, and to bring about all the advances . . . made . . . during the present century. [He names nine others, to whom he was also] indebted, through conversation and correspondence, for much that has gone to the making of this paper. My own part . . . has been that of an interested spectator, with whom the workers have always been willing generously and without reserve to discuss their hypotheses, their methods, and their results.[21]

Collingwood—like all then working on the Wall—still believed that Hadrian's initial plan for the frontier line in Britain had been, as expressed in his first book on Roman Britain, a series of forts,

> connected with a broad and flat-bottomed ditch running from fort to fort right across England; not a military earthwork, for its design and choice of ground make it quite impossible to treat it as a defensive fosse, but an indelible and unmistakable line . . . to mark where the civil government of Rome ended and her military occupation of hostile territory began: for Hadrian's forts were planted on the northern margin of this ditch . . . which English antiquaries call the Vallum.

in the 1960s, and it is now generally agreed that there is no evidence for the view that there were three separate destructions by invaders, each of which supposedly affected all or most of the sites along the Wall (and many in the hinterland): see especially Hodgson, N. 2008. 'After the Wall-Periods: what is our historical framework for Hadrian's Wall in the twenty-first century?', in Bidwell, ed., *Understanding Hadrian's Wall*: 11–23.

[21] Cf. Birley, *Research on Hadrian's Wall*: 65 ff. for further tribute to Simpson, for whom Collingwood was 'the interpreter to the outside world . . . also the master-planner of financial and moral support for that work . . . and the diplomat who saw to it that what needed doing was not only done but also published promptly'. Note *A*, 127 and Collingwood, R. G. 1933. 'An introduction to the prehistory of Cumberland, Westmorland and Lancashire north of the Sands', *CWAAS*^{2} 33: 198 for his views on publication of excavations; cf. van der Dussen, *History as Science*: 224–5.

The 1932 edition had more detail, but the basic picture was unchanged. However, by 1935, when he wrote his part of *Roman Britain and the English Settlements*, further excavation had brought clarity at last: the stone wall came first, then the forts, finally the Vallum.[22]

Apart from his work in philosophy in the 1920s, including a book of over 300 pages,[23] he might well be thought to have had enough to do in vacations with drawings for *RIB*—over 300 in 1922 and 1923. But in addition to his first book on Roman Britain, he published a good deal more on Roman sites in that decade, and in 1929 wrote *The Archaeology of Roman Britain* (see section 4).[24]

His posthumous reputation was to suffer from the treatment in the *Proceedings of the British Academy* obituary. The separately printed pamphlet version was reviewed by Isobel Henderson, the ancient historian and Fellow of Somerville College, a friend of Collingwood and of his first wife.

> Collingwood's polymathy was not a mere *tour de force*: it was the practice of his belief in the unity of knowledge, a belief abandoned by the modern world for reasons which were illustrated in Collingwood's own failure. The failure is not concealed in this justly balanced record. Mr. Richmond shows with truthful understanding how the metaphysician could sometimes distort the archaeologist's view . . . His enduring work, it would seem, is the British volume of *CIL*: a stark monument for so versatile a mind, but one which any man could be proud to have left.

[22] Collingwood, *Roman Britain*: 26 f.; Collingwood, *Roman Britain*, 2nd edition: 25–9; Collingwood, 1936. *Roman Britain* in *RBES*: 124–39; see Birley, *Research on Hadrian's Wall*: 119–22 for the elucidation of the relationship, chronological and physical, between Wall and Vallum. Collingwood's explanation of the Vallum as a financial frontier manned by customs officers never caught on. The present *communis opinio* is that it was 'a means of defining the limit of the military zone . . . the second-century equivalent of barbed wire': Breeze, *J. Collingwood Bruce's Handbook*: 86.

[23] Collingwood, R. G. 1924. *Speculum Mentis*; cf. Bibliography in McCallum, R. B., Knox, T. M., and Richmond, I. A. 1944, 'Robin George Collingwood 1889–1943', *Proceedings of the British Academy*, 29: 474–5 for other substantial items, as well as his translations from the Italian of works by de Ruggiero (there misspelt 'da' Ruggiero) and Croce.

[24] The Bibliography of Collingwood's archaeological and historical writings given by Richmond 1944: 481–3 suggests that Freeman, *The Best Training-Ground*: 557 slightly exaggerates: 'But most of Collingwood's articles were usually no more than ten to twelve pages long', although many of his articles were of course quite short. Note also his *A Guide to the Roman Wall*, 32 pp., with 4 maps, and *A Guide to the Chesters Museum*, 52 pp., with 2 plates, both Newcastle upon Tyne 1926.

Comment on Richmond's supposedly 'truthful understanding' is offered later.[25] But first some detail is needed on Collingwood's 'enduring work', *Roman Inscriptions of Britain* (I), eventually published in 1965, under the names of Collingwood and R. P. Wright.

3. *ROMAN INSCRIPTIONS OF BRITAIN*

A special feature of *RIB* is the 'facsimile drawing'.

> Haverfield, almost immediately before his death [30 September 1919], had decided to publish a new collection of all the Roman inscriptions . . . in Britain and thinking it desirable that each should be illustrated with a facsimile drawing—for he had no illusions about the value of photographic illustrations in a work of this kind—he asked me to serve as a draughtsman. After his death I decided to go on with the work, and from 1920 onwards I spent much time every year travelling about the country and drawing Roman inscriptions. (*A*, 145)[26]

As explained by Wright in the Preface to *RIB* (I), Haverfield left Oxford a substantial bequest, whose administrators[27] 'made the editing of the future work, to be styled *The Roman Inscriptions of*

[25] McCallum et al., 'Robin George Collingwood', *Proceedings of the British Academy*, 29, reviewed in *Journal of Roman Studies* 35 (1944): 148 by M. I. Henderson, referring especially to Richmond, I. A., 'Appreciation of R.G. Collingwood as an archaeologist', *Proc. Brit. Acad.*: 476–85 (14–23 of the pamphlet version). Here it may be mentioned that in his obituary of Macdonald, written slightly earlier, Richmond wrote that 'on his [Haverfield's] passing the mantle fell upon Macdonald'; he did not mention Collingwood. Richmond, I. A. 1941, 'Sir George Macdonald', *Archaeologia Aeliana*[4] 19: 181. Cf. *A*, 120, quoted earlier.

[26] Shortly before his death Haverfield hoped to involve M. I. Rostovtzeff, a refugee from the Russian revolution, in *Roman Inscriptions of Britain*, but this came to nothing: Macdonald, G. 1920–1921. 'F. Haverfield 1860–1919', *Proceedings of the British Academy*, 9: 13; van der Dussen, *History as Science*: 206 and n. 89; Freeman, *The Best Training-Ground*: 201 f. Cf. also Richmond, I. A. 1960. 'Roman Britain, 1910–1960', *Journal of Roman Studies* 50: 175. 'The very high quality of Collingwood's inherited powers of draughtsmanship inspired Haverfield with the idea of a new work, *The Roman Inscriptions of Britain*, which should reproduce to scale an objective line-drawing of each stone, together with a text and critical apparatus.' The earliest drawings 'by R. G. C.' in *Roman Inscriptions of Britain* are dated 1921.

[27] Cf. Todd, M. 2003. 'The Haverfield Bequest: 1921–2000 and the study of Roman Britain', *Britannia* 34: 35–40; Freeman, *The Best Training-Ground*: 432–5; 597.

Britain, a primary claim on their funds. . . . Between 1921 and 1929 and again in 1936 Collingwood carried through the scrutiny, drawing, and fair-copying of most of the inscriptions on stone and other materials.'

In his Report as University Lecturer in 1932 Collingwood wrote that the project was 'begun in 1920 and planned to take 20 years; every inscription to be illustrated with a drawing made by myself. . . . The drawings made have risen from about 600 to about 1100. The whole material has been arranged and indexed.'[28] In *Roman Inscriptions of Britain* it is noted who had made each drawing, and in which year: this shows that from 1921 to 1929 Collingwood had drawn almost 1,000 inscriptions. When *Roman Inscriptions of Britain* (I), covering inscriptions on stone, was published it had reached a total of 2,400. Of these just over 500 are described as 'now lost', 'sought in vain', or not drawn for some other reason; 75 were drawn by C. W. Baty and a few more by others; the drawing of just under 900 was 'by R. G. C.'; most of the rest were drawn by Wright. A good many of Collingwood's drawings of graffiti and the like would not be published until the 1990s, in *RIB* II.[29]

In 1936, he was now Waynflete Professor of Metaphysical Philosophy, and his fieldwork on *RIB* was nearing completion. He made his final set of drawings of inscriptions (well over 100) that year, when an announcement headed 'The Roman Inscriptions of Britain' appeared in *Antiquaries Journal*:

It was Haverfield's intention to issue a new *corpus*, and before his death he . . . had secured the services of our Fellow Mr. R.G. Collingwood as draughtsman and assistant. Since then Mr. Collingwood has been continuing the collection of material, and now finds himself in sight of the

[28] Cited from van der Dussen, *History as a Science*: 234 n. 91.

[29] About 100 more stone inscriptions were found between 1938, when he finally stopped drawing inscriptions, and the end of 1954, the cut-off point for inclusion in *Roman Inscriptions of Britain*. van der Dussen, *History as a Science*: 221 slightly exaggerates: '[n]early all are illustrated with drawings, the majority of them made by Collingwood'. In *Roman Inscriptions of Britain* II, R. G. C. is credited with some 75 from the 1920s, of graffiti, etc.; about 40 more in the 1930s, making only 115 out of over 5,000—but the cut-off point for *Roman Inscriptions of Britain* II was more than thirty years later than for *Roman Inscriptions of Britain* I. Little more than a fifth of the 5000 had been found or published when R. G. C. ceased work. Note also *Roman Inscriptions of Britain* II. i, p. 88: '[s]ome drawings made by R.G.C. in the thirties cannot be found'.

end ... But there remains the final and necessarily laborious task of searching for inscriptions that have been overlooked. For assistance in this final clear up, an appeal is being made to all readers of this *Journal* to send information about any Roman inscription with which they are acquainted, in a place where it is likely to have eluded search hitherto, either to the editor of the new *corpus* (Professor R.G. Collingwood, 15 Belbroughton Rd, Oxford) or to one of the three collectors who have undertaken to assist in special districts.[30]

In October 1938, a few weeks after writing the Preface to his *Autobiography*, and on the eve of his departure to the East Indies, Collingwood selected an assistant to help him as Junior Editor to complete *RIB*: rather than one of the three 'collectors' named in 1936, it was Richard Wright (1908–1992), Lecturer (from 1932) in the Durham Classics Department.[31] In 1941, when his health deteriorated further, he gave Wright sole responsibility, including for the annual reports in *JRS*. It all took a lot longer than expected: for one thing, Wright himself suffered serious ill health in the later 1940s; he delivered his text, in holograph, and drawings to the Press in 1960, with a Preface dated 11 November—because of printing delays, the Press altered '1960' to '1964'.[32] Wright expressed 'my deep appreciation of the honour which R. G. Collingwood paid me in inviting me to share the task of editing. Secondly I am greatly indebted to him for the expert guidance which he found the energy to afford me for two years despite his serious illness.'[33]

[30] For southern England, C. E. Stevens; for everything north of the line joining Gloucester and the Wash, E. B. Birley; for Wales, V. E. Nash-Williams, 1936. *Antiquaries Journal*, 16: 326.

[31] As Stephen Leach kindly informs me, on Collingwood's return to Oxford from the East in 1939 'he was going back and forth to the Clarendon Press – taking in drawings and making blocks'.

[32] Richmond, 'Roman Britain, 1910–1960': 175, clearly knew that *Roman Inscriptions of Britain* I was ready—'a publication by Mr. R.P. Wright is shortly to be expected'; date changed: Tomlin, R. S. O. *Roman Inscriptions of Britain* I^2: p. 751.

[33] *Roman Inscriptions of Britain* I: viii. The Indexes to *Roman Inscriptions of Britain* I did not appear until 1983. *Roman Inscriptions of Britain* II, on the *instrumentum domesticum*, came out in eight fascicules between 1990 and 1995, still bearing the names of Collingwood and Wright (who died in 1992), but edited by S. S. Frere (who promptly compiled the index) and others, notably R. S. O. Tomlin. The latter in 1995 produced the *addenda* and *corrigenda* for *Roman Inscriptions of Britain* I^2. *Roman Inscriptions of Britain* III (covering stone inscriptions found between 1955 and 1986), edited by Tomlin, Wright, and M. W. C. Hassall,

In *The Archaeology of Roman Britain* Collingwood wrote:

The value of inscriptions as historical material is so great that it can hardly be exaggerated . . . they are contemporary and authoritative documents, whose text if legible cannot be corrupt, and whose cumulative value, in the hands of scholars accustomed to handling them in the mass, is astonishing. They are the most important single source for the history and organization of the Roman Empire.[34]

In the Bibliography to *Roman Britain and the English Settlements*, this was nuanced:

For every part of the Roman Empire, Britain not excepted, inscriptions constitute a source of high importance. In Britain, however, their distribution is curious and gives rise to some difficulties. Throughout the lowland zone they are relatively rare; in the highland zone they are extremely common. The result is that for every aspect of the life of the frontier armies . . . they give us voluminous evidence; for the more civilized parts of the country they give us very little indeed, and this is one of the reasons why archaeology is so overwhelmingly important as a source of information on the general life of the people . . . A complete new *corpus* of Romano-British inscriptions is in preparation. (p. 464)

In his *Autobiography*, he took a rather negative view:

the main bulk of my work on Roman Britain went into the Corpus of Inscriptions . . . The detailed knowledge of the subject which I acquired, and the practice in deciphering inscriptions, many of them extremely difficult to read, were invaluable to me. But the inscriptions themselves were not of very great service to my Romano-British studies. The use of epigraphic material is a magnificent exercise for an historian just beginning to shake himself free from the scissors-and-paste mentality, which is why it developed in so wonderful a manner in the late nineteenth century; but the epigraphic historian as such can never be wholly Baconian in spirit. Regarded as documents, inscriptions tell you less, under critical scrutiny, than literary texts; regarded as relics, they tell you less than archaeological material proper. And on the questions which I particularly wanted to ask, it happened that the inscriptions threw hardly any light. I felt, therefore, that by my work on Romano-British inscriptions I was rather building a

appeared late in 2009 (without an Index). Cf. Birley, A. R. 2011. '*RIB* III in its historical context', *Journal of Roman Archaeology* 24: 679–96 with more on the history of *Roman Inscriptions of Britain*, bibliographical details, and (at 690–6) 'Partial Indexes'.

[34] Collingwood, 1930. *Archaeology* of *Roman Britain*, 162.

monument to the past, to the great spirits of Mommsen and Haverfield, than forging a weapon for the future. (*A*, 145 f.)

Examination of Collingwood's other main works helps to explain this change of emphasis.[35]

4. COLLINGWOOD'S MONOGRAPHS ON ROMAN BRITAIN

Summarizing his main works on Roman Britain, Collingwood registers first *Roman Britain*, written in 1921, 'in two days', revised ten years later and again in 1934. In that year:

> I wrote the British section [over 100 pages] in . . . Frank's *Economic Survey of Ancient Rome* [*ESAR*] and in 1935 the sections of the *Oxford History of England* on pre-historic and Roman Britain [*RBES*] . . . The invitations to write these two large-scale works came at exactly the right moment. I had been long enough in my laboratory; I wanted to exchange it for my study . . . But I could not desert Roman Britain without saying good-bye. (*A*, 120f.)

He does not here mention *The Archaeology of Roman Britain*, but it deserves discussion.[36] In the Preface, dated 'January 14th, 1930', he explained that: 'Romano-British studies . . . only lately have become a branch of scientific archaeology . . . the special literature grows in bulk', much of it 'highly technical, repulsively unintelligible to the general reader', and inaccessible to the inquiring amateur, student, and foreign scholar; it was now 'impossible even for the best-equipped expert in this country, to work with the necessary books round him, or even to consult them at all.' It was time for someone to digest this material. 'So elementary a book ought to have been easy to write; but it has not proved to be the case . . . elementary and simple ideas were just what no one seemed

[35] Comparing the statements from 1930 and 1936 with the *Autobiography*, van der Dussen, *History As A Science*: 407 fn. 99 finds it 'difficult to explain these striking differences in judgment on a subject on which Collingwood had worked for so many years'. He does not note Collingwood's 1936 caveat about the very different frequency of inscriptions in the highland and lowland zones, perhaps a partial explanation of the 'differences in judgment'. Collingwood's increased emphasis on art is another (see what follows and n. 38).

[36] For more detail than is possible here: van der Dussen, *History As A Science*: 213–20, with nn. 53–92.

previously to have worked out.' He did his best, thanking friends for help: Sir George Macdonald on the Antonine Wall, H. Mattingly on coins, T. Davies Pryce on Samian pottery, and F. G. Simpson on Hadrian's frontier. The book was almost 300 pages long, with 68 illustrations in text and 8 plates; and '[t]he illustrations, except for the photographs and four or five others, have been drawn by myself'. It at once became a standard work, eventually revised by Richmond and reissued, four years after the latter's death.[37] Reviewing the new edition, Wheeler wrote at length about the old one:

> I saw much of Robin when he was writing the book. For him, with his essentially broad habit of thought, it seemed at first a trifle off-beat that he should immerse himself in so much museum-like detail at the expense of his more specific interests in the diverse fields of professional metaphysics, the wide movement and meaning of history, and the intriguing puzzledom of epigraphy, to say nothing of his periodical journeyings up and down Roman Britain.... In many ways he was by nature a survivor from that long and distinguished line of amateurs—in the fullest and best sense of the term—who for three centuries or more had sustained the study of British antiquities as an inevitable and engrossing duty of the educated mind. The true end of this line had been marked by the brief but powerful transit of Pitt Rivers... But Pitt Rivers had died in 1900, and now it was 1930 and time for a receptive mind like Collingwood's to get his details right, along modern lines. In the process, he might help other aspirants into new, often ill-sorted, knowledge; but that admirable motive, I felt sure at the time, was incidental to a primary mission to organize his own thinking.[38]

Roman Britain and the English Settlements appeared early in 1936, a second edition, with a few corrections, in 1937, when volume III of *ESAR* came out, in which Collingwood's part occupies over 100 pages. In 1934, 1937, and 1939 his short sections on Roman Britain were published in the *Cambridge Ancient History*, X–XII. One can find a reason for Collingwood's negative view of inscriptions in the previous pages of his *Autobiography*, on 'Romanization' and the 'Celtic Revival' in the late Roman period. He explains the latter phenomenon by his theory

[37] It was edited by Richmond's former assistant, D. R. Wilson.

[38] Wheeler, R. E. M. 1969. 'Review of Collingwood and Richmond 1969', *Antiquity* 43: 239.

of 'incapsulation' (his preferred spelling), summed up as follows: 'This was the idea which I expressed in the chapter on "Art" in the *Oxford History of England*; a chapter which I would gladly leave as the sole memorial of my Romano-British studies, and the best example I can give to posterity of how to solve a much-debated problem in history, not by discovering fresh evidence, but by reconsidering questions of principle' (*A*, 144 f.).

On the art of Roman Britain he was trenchant: '[O]n any Romano-British site the impression that constantly haunts the archaeologist, like a bad smell or a stickiness on the fingers, is that of an ugliness which pervades the place like a London fog: not merely the common vulgar ugliness of the Roman empire, but a blundering, stupid ugliness that cannot even rise to the level of that vulgarity.'[39] Over forty years on, Richard Reece quoted this judgement with approval.[40]

Wheeler's review of *RBES* was delayed long enough for him to refer to both the first and the second editions.

> So long is it since this review was written that, even in a shortened form, I have surrendered it to an importunate editor . . . actuated by one persuasive thought: here is an opportunity to tell something of the debt which, on every sort of ground, the post-Haverfield generation has owed to Robin Collingwood . . . And now . . . I find it difficult to write. The idiom of a review is not apt for the appreciation of that warmth and vitality and contemplative humanity that are woven into the fabric of Collingwood's scholarship, of Collingwood's whole outlook on life. His friends and pupils are familiar with these qualities and have for two decades found

[39] Collingwood and Myres, *Roman Britain and the English Settlements*: 250.

[40] Reece, R. 1979. 'Romano-British Interaction', in Burnham, B. C. and Kingsbury, J., eds, *Space, Hierarchy and Society. Interdisciplinary Studies in Social Area Analysis*. BAR International Series 59, Oxford, BAR: 237 ff. on 'Collingwood's . . . theory of encapsulation, in which Celticism somehow went underground in the products of Roman Britain. I now think I understand this idea, and, since it has mystified all students to whom I have tried to impart it, my new interpretation may at once serve to reinstate Collingwood, and say something about Romano-British interaction of a very delicate nature as well.' Another thirty years on, David Mattingly, stern critic of the concept of 'Romanization', quoted the same passage in *Roman Britain and the English Settlements* with approval. Mattingly, D. J. 2011, *Imperialism, Power and Identity: Experiencing the Roman Empire*. Princeton and Oxford, Princeton University Press: 22–3. It is perhaps no coincidence that Collingwood's comments about the badness of Romano-British art were made not long before he wrote *The Principles of Art*, 1937. Oxford, Clarendon Press.

an inspiration in them. When, not long ago, after illness, he gave away his archaeological books and threatened permanent withdrawal to the thin air of a metaphysical Arvernus, the sense of loss was immediate and deadening. It may now be hoped that a tropic sun has restored him, at least for a part of the year, to the more substantial and mundane studies that are (for us) his proper realm.[41]

In the second edition Collingwood

> has mostly set aright those factual errors which are the easy and inevitable prey of the punctual reviewer... with periodical revision this book will long remain the standard survey of its subject... [But] Mr. Collingwood has adopted a personal and subjective attitude towards History that must either be accepted or rejected by the reader at the outset; it admits no compromise. He interpolates motives, builds characters, constructs episodes with a liberality or even licence that is great fun, but is liable to shock the pedant. Fact and speculation stand shoulder to shoulder, no documents are cited, the innocent student may know not with what voice his author speaks. Mr. Collingwood's feet are on the mantelpiece, he enjoys himself and his reader with him.

Detailed criticism of the early chapters followed, the defects being 'to some extent inherent in the subjective method of interpretation... Caratacus, Classicianus... become fit stuff for Shakespearian drama rather, perhaps, than for the Oxford History of England'. But he praised the later part: 'From chapter viii onwards it were difficult to find anything but admiration for his sober, workmanlike survey, and his fluid prose.'

When Richmond turned to *Roman Britain and the English Settlements* in his 'Appreciation', he began on Wheeler's lines: 'To those learned in the subject, this book is possibly the most stimulating that Collingwood ever wrote.' Then came the reservations: 'The general reader, however, may discover too late that it has one major defect. It does not sufficiently distinguish between objective and subjective, and combines both in a subtle and apparently objective presentation. There are, in fact, many points in which his text goes far beyond the evidence, or ventures into realms where evidence is deceitful upon the weights.' He gave some 'striking examples': theories on Hadrian's Wall and Vallum, the founding of the York *colonia*, and King Arthur and his Knights

[41] Wheeler, R. E. M. 1939. Review of Collingwood and Myres, *Roman Britain and the English Settlements*, *Journal of Roman Studies*, 29: 87.

after Roman rule ended—'Bury himself, whose extravagancies Collingwood had severely castigated, perpetrated no bolder flight of fancy than the last.' A strange remark followed: 'Again, political passion led him at least once to disregard abounding evidence. Hating fascism, he subjected Agricola to systematic denigration, despite the abundant evidence of his competence and energy.'[42]

The alleged 'systematic denigration' can only refer to one long sentence:

> For all Tacitus's praise, he [Agricola] remains a somewhat unattractive character: an able man, evidently, both in the field and in administration; a man of sound judgement, and incorruptible; but cold, calculating, obsequious to authority, yet grudging in his submission; incapable of inspiring enthusiasm like Cerialis or reverence like Frontinus; in his last years, after a longer term of office than most, a man with a grievance, resenting his recall, living in gloomy retirement for safety's sake, and nursing his spleen.[43]

In 1946, Eric Birley, immediately after demobilization, firmly rejected Richmond's attack (without naming him):

> It will be seen that my estimate of the governorship of Agricola tallies substantially with that arrived at by R. G. Collingwood, long the brilliant and dearly loved leader of Romano-British studies; but I would not have it thought that the foregoing study represents nothing more than the tribute of *pietas* to the memory of a writer whose estimate of Agricola has lately been impugned. The literary evidence here surveyed leaves no room for any other interpretation, as long as Roman Britain is studied in its true perspective, as one of many provinces in the Roman Empire, in a period when the *Schwerpunkt* of military activity lay on other frontiers, nearer to the heart of the empire.[44]

[42] Richmond, I. A., 1944. 'Appreciation of R. G. Collingwood as an archaeologist', *Proceedings of the British Academy* 29: 478.

[43] Collingwood and Myres, *Roman Britain and the English Settlements:* 114 f. Oddly enough, in his article, 'Gnaeus Iulius Agricola', 1944, *Journal of Roman Studies* 34: 34–45, Richmond has no comments about Collingwood's views.

[44] Birley, E. 1946. 'Britain under the Flavians: Agricola and his predecessors', *Durham University Journal* 38, no. 3: 79–84, at 84; reprinted in Birley, E. 1953. *Roman Britain and the Roman Army. Collected Papers.* Kendal, Titus Wilson: 10–19, at 19. For later work on Agricola, cf. e.g. Hanson, W. S. 1987. *Agricola and the Conquest of the North.* London, Batsford, revised edition 1991; Birley, A. R. 2005. *The Roman Government of Britain.* Oxford, Oxford University Press: 71–95; Wolfson, S. 2008. *Tacitus, Thule and Caledonia. The Achievements of Agricola's Navy in their True Perspective.* BAR British series 459. Oxford, BAR.

Richmond not surprisingly omitted *RBES* from the bibliography of his Penguin *Roman Britain* (1955). His Preface alludes to his strictures on *RBES*: he himself treated 'the subjects upon which evidence rather than conjecture holds the field'. Richmond's book originally appeared just before he became the first Professor of the Archaeology of the Roman Empire at Oxford; it had several revised reprints, but was too brief to be a replacement for *RBES*. That came in 1967: Sheppard Frere's *Britannia*, a book of 432 pages, with 32 pages of plates (*RBES* had not been allowed any), published a year after Frere succeeded Richmond (who died in October 1965). Meanwhile, in 1961 the Editor of the *Oxford History of England*, Sir George Clark, had offered a revealing sidelight: 'When the late Professor Collingwood's masterly contribution on Roman Britain was published one of the other contributors remarked rather tartly: "He gives the impression that we know more about Roman Britain than about any subsequent period." '[45]

A. L. F. Rivet's review of Frere opened by warning about the dangers of *RBES*, to which the new book would be the proper antidote.

> Collingwood set out with perfect lucidity what happened in Roman Britain, why it happened, and how it could not possibly have happened otherwise.... No other full-scale account was available—the nearest was Haverfield's Ford Lectures... Again, it was the first volume of the Oxford History of England, a series which rapidly established itself as authoritative and soon became a necessary part of any educated man's furniture. And finally there was the sheer beauty of the prose (it is surely one of the most compulsive works ever written) and the intellectual stature of the author; curiously, criticism of Collingwood's philosophy has seemed to increase rather than to diminish respect for him as an historian. But even Collingwood was the prisoner of his age, and precisely because of his brilliance this means much more than that he was not aware of facts which have since come to light... it means also that all of Collingwood's wider conclusions need to be re-tested against the whole body of the evidence as it stands today. At present—again because of its brilliance—his work is not merely out-dated but dangerous... To clear the mind completely of Collingwood is almost impossible for anyone who has read him (even more so for anyone who heard him lecture), but the attempt

[45] In *The Times* of 15 November 1961, quoted by van der Dussen, *History as a Science*: 248 f. with n. 286.

needs to be made, and it can only be made by someone who has had to face up critically, iconoclastically even, to the basic evidence. In this respect Professor Frere, the reinterpreter of Verulamium, is supremely well qualified.[46]

Rivet several times compares the new book with *RBES*: on prehistory, 'Frere himself has contributed substantially to the knowledge and is thus much better qualified than Collingwood to deal with it, but he does not fully solve the problem' (247); but he is criticized for the 'resurrection of the hoary old myth that "city-life was alien to the Celts as it was to the Germans"... Collingwoodism at its worst' (249). It may be added that Frere disputed Collingwood's interpretation of art.[47]

Rivet had already attacked Collingwood on another front, in 1958: mainly relying on an excavation in Wiltshire by G. Bersu, he called into question the very existence of 'native villages' in Roman Britain, to which Collingwood had devoted a good deal of space.[48] Rivet's view became the new orthodoxy, followed widely, including by the present writer.[49] Yet before long 'work reported at the... 1965 conference on Romano-British rural settlement restored the *status quo*, showing that in the south of England at least, nucleated villages associated with traditional native field systems were to be found'.[50] This was hardly noticed for some time; but in recent years Collingwood on villages has been to a large extent rehabilitated.[51]

[46] Rivet, A. L. F. 1969. Review and discussion of S. S. Frere, *Britannia: A History of Roman Britain*. London, Routledge and Kegan Paul, in *Journal of Roman Studies* 59: 247.

[47] Frere, S. S. 1967. *Britannia. A History of Roman Britain*. London, Routledge and Kegan Paul: 315.

[48] *Roman Britain and the English Settlements*: 209–14, 221–5; contrast Rivet, A. L. F. 1958. *Town and Country in Roman Britain*. London, Hutchison University Library: ch. 5—citing Bersu, G. 1940. 'Excavations at Little Woodbury, Wiltshire I. The settlement as revealed by excavation', *Proceedings of the Prehistoric Society*, new series 6: 30–111. Cf. nn. 46–8 and 66.

[49] Birley, A. R. 1964. *Life in Roman Britain*. London, Batsford: 83: 'neither in the pre-Roman nor in the Roman period does the village appear to have been a common form of organisation. Many sites previously identified as villages are now seen to have been settled by only one family group.'

[50] Applebaum, S. 1972. 'Roman Britain', in Finberg, H. P. R. ed., *The Agrarian History of England and Wales*. Cambridge, Cambridge University Press: 51.

[51] Against Rivet: Hingley, R. 1989. *Rural Settlement in Roman Britain*. London, Seaby: 2, 11, 122, 124, 128–9, and esp. 190 f., n. 35; Mattingly, *An Imperial*

Not long before Frere's *Britannia* became the new 'standard work' on Roman Britain, *Roman Inscriptions in Britain* (I) had at last been published—twenty-five years later than Collingwood had hoped—in 1965. Even more significant for the future of research was the new periodical, *Britannia. A journal of Romano-British & kindred studies*, 'hived off' from *JRS* in 1970, largely through Frere's initiative.[52] The 'official' replacement in the *Oxford History of England* came in 1981: Peter Salway was given a whole volume, now labelled 1a, and allowed 500 pages more than Collingwood.[53] He found the task daunting.

> Collingwood's brilliance made his book all things to all men . . . By 1936 . . . a series of distinguished students . . . had brought order to the subject. The main outlines of political, military, and social history seemed established, with promise that further research would fill in more details and settle outstanding problems. The pattern was indeed so firmly set that in the 1950s it remained still largely unchanged. For these twenty years it was possible to conceive of definitive accounts of the period, as indeed Collingwood's largely remained . . . We are now [1980] in a period when there is

Possession. Britain in the Roman Empire, 54 BC–AD 409: 353 ff., esp. 357 f., 375; Hingley, R. 2007. 'The Roman Landscape of Britain: From Hoskins to today', in Fleming, A. and Hingley, R., eds, *Landscape History After Hoskins, I*. Macclesfield, Windgather Press: 101–12.. My acceptance of Rivet's view and the pages on Little Woodbury (81–3) were excised from revised editions of Birley, *Life in Roman Britain*, esp. that of 1981, and villages rehabilitated, 84 f.

[52] Stray, C. 2010. 'Patriots and Professors: a century of Roman Studies, 1910–2010', *Journal of Roman Studies* 100: 21–23; Frere, S. S. and Goodburn, R. 2010. 'Britannia 40 years: Roman Society 100 years', *Britannia* 41: 33–35. Collingwood and his contributions to *Journal of Roman Studies* are mentioned only in passing by Stray, 'Patriots and Professors': 9; but not at all by Taylor, M. V. 1960. 'The Society for the Promotion of Roman Studies', in her brief history of the Roman Society's first fifty years—although she recalls, 130, 'the publication in the *Journal* of an annual survey of Roman discoveries in Britain' (without naming the authors, herself and Collingwood), as one of two 'more effective' ways of recruiting much needed new members for the Society, the other being the institution of Student-Associates.

[53] Salway, P. 1981. *Roman Britain*. Oxford History of England, now 1a. Oxford: Clarendon Press (who does not treat art) has xxxii+824 pp. and 14 maps, compared with Collingwood's xv+324 pp., plus 15 pp. of Bibliography, 6 maps and an index shared with Myres. The new version of *The English Settlements*, now 1b, was written, remarkably enough, by the same author as in 1936, J. N. L. Myres. It appeared in 1986, when Myres was over eighty: with xxxii+248 pp., it has some 100 pages more than in the first edition (and its own index).

no agreement on many major issues and, perhaps much more important, no possibility that all aspects of the subject can ever be comprehended by one historian.

He added a personal note:

One of the problems of Romano-British studies has been the emotional commitment of many of its practitioners, whether to 'pro-Roman' or 'anti-Roman sentiments' or to favourite theories within the subject. There has also been, outside this circle, a curious prejudice against Romano-British studies, as if they were in some way not quite intellectually respectable, though whether this was because of a distaste for the Romans themselves or belief that the subject was too well comprehended and therefore 'easy', I cannot say.[54]

In 1987, Frere commented that 'Collingwood dominated Romano-British studies in the 20s and 30s; and because he could write English like an angel his views had an astonishing influence'.[55] Twenty years later, Philip Freeman wrote that 'to judge from the number of laudatory references to him, Collingwood continues to exert a powerful influence on Romano-British studies'.[56] But he then writes: 'Haverfield might have had students, Collingwood did not'—overlooking Richmond, Eric Birley, C. E. Stevens, and C. F. C. Hawkes.[57] He claims that Collingwood's

work, originally undertaken as an act of *pietas*, was secondary to his other interests... his engagement with the subject progressively diminished, first in terms of actual research, then in the teaching he offered, then

[54] Salway, *Roman Britain*: vi, vii, viii.

[55] Frere, S. S. 1988. 'Roman Britain since Haverfield and Richmond'. A lecture delivered in All Souls College 23 October 1987. *Alan Sutton History and Archaeological Review* 3: pages not numbered (6 pp.): 1.

[56] Freeman, *The Best Training-Ground*: 558.

[57] Eric Birley and C. F. C. Hawkes both offered two papers on 'Roman Britain' as an optional extra subject in their Finals for *Literae Humaniores* in 1928; both were placed in the First class—taught by Collingwood. He thanks Birley and Stevens in his 1929 paper (Collingwood, R. G. 'Roman signal stations on the Cumberland coast', *CWAAS*[2] 29: 149) for help with the Cumberland coast field survey; praises Richmond and Birley in his 1931 paper ('Hadrian's Wall'); and thanks Birley and Stevens along with his father, M. V. Taylor, and R. E. M. Wheeler, for reading the proofs of *The Archaeology of Roman Britain*. London: Methuen, 1930: vii. In his Preface to *Roman Britain and the English Settlements*, Stevens is singled out for his discussions of agrarian problems (1936: vii). On Birley and Richmond, cf. Birley, *Research on Hadrian's Wall*: 68.

merely to the production of textbooks, enduring as some of them have become.... Based on his fieldwork, had Collingwood realized that Romano-British archaeology was not an intellectually meaningful discipline or period? [If so] then it is not especially explicit in his written work but is manifested more by his retreat from the subject from the late 1920s, a withdrawal that was otherwise explained by his curtailment of activities through illness.[58]

In the light of his continued involvement with the Wall, with drawing inscriptions, and the composition of *The Archaeology of Roman Britain*, not to mention revising his *Roman Britain*, one cannot accept that 'his engagement progressively diminished'; nor was he retreating from the subject 'from the late 1920s'. As for illness, this did not affect him seriously until 1931–1932 (*A*, 118). Under Haverfield, Freeman continues, Roman Britain 'had failed to put down roots within the teaching for *Literae Humaniores*. That failure persisted under Collingwood and in fact deteriorated as his commitment to the subject waned.' After Haverfield's death the subject was 'relatively moribund in its progress in spite of the credit and adulation afforded R.G. Collingwood'.[59]

He saw his contribution to *Roman Britain and the English Settlements*, written in 1935, as his 'goodbye' to Roman Britain (cf. *A*, 121, quoted earlier).[60] But he had a final season's fieldwork drawing inscriptions in 1936; and the announcement in *Antiquaries Journal* that year shows his continued commitment. In January 1937 he chaired a discussion on 'Roman Britain as a subject of teaching': his summing up and the eight speakers' differing views are recorded in *Journal of Roman Studies*—the most positive was Ronald Syme, it may surprise some, who 'urged the study of the subject'.[61] But it had never caught on at Oxford. Haverfield's hope

[58] Freeman, *The Best Training-Ground*: 587 ff.

[59] Freeman, *The Best Training-Ground*: 597, 600.

[60] In the Preface, dated 14 January 1936, he thanks 'the University of Oxford, which, by creating for me the post of University Lecturer in Philosophy and Roman History, gave me for many years together encouragement and opportunity to pursue the studies whose results, having now vacated that position, I offer to it and to the public'.

[61] Anon., 1937. 'Report on the discussion on Roman Britain as a subject of teaching' held on 12 January 1937. *Journal of Roman Studies* 27: 251–3. As an undergraduate Syme may have attended Collingwood's lectures on Roman Britain; he went on the Wall Pilgrimage in 1930, knew Fabricius well, and wrote sections on wars and frontiers in *Cambridge Ancient History* X and XI.

that his bequest would be used to support a Lectureship or Readership in the subject was not fulfilled.[62] Salway's comments on 'a curious prejudice against Romano-British studies, as if they were in some way not quite intellectually respectable', were quoted earlier. As a Cambridge graduate, he perhaps did not grasp the reason. From the nineteenth century onwards, well into the second half of the twentieth, 'ancient history' at Oxford ended with the death of Trajan, 8 August AD 117; and 'modern history' (the term 'mediaeval' was not used) began with Diocletian's accession, 20 November 284. The years in between—so important for Roman Britain—were a kind of black hole. Not by chance: ancient history in *Literae Humaniores* was geared to classical literature; and apart from some of Juvenal's *Satires* (and perhaps, in Ronald Syme's view, Tacitus' *Annals*), no 'classical' Latin was written after Trajan's reign. For this reason alone, attempts to cultivate interest in Roman Britain in general, and in particular Hadrian's Wall, were bound to fall on stony ground. The full-time ancient historians at Oxford in the years from 1920 to 1935 were no doubt happy to leave Roman Britain to a philosopher, who was also an accomplished pupil of Haverfield and particularly interested in the Wall.[63] Times seemed to change when Richmond became first holder of the Chair of the Archaeology of the Roman Empire. All the same, during his tenure Roman Britain was not given much attention. His successor Sheppard Frere drove the subject ahead from 1966 onwards—but it still had no place in the Greats syllabus; and his successors in the new Chair had no interest in Roman Britain. It is true that the recently retired Camden Professor of Ancient History, Alan Bowman, is best known for his work on the Vindolanda writing tablets; but conveniently for the Greats syllabus (now slightly extended), they are almost all of Flavio-Trajanic date.

[62] Freeman, *The Best Training-Ground*: 434–5.

[63] Freeman, *The Best Training-Ground*: 436 aptly cites the review of Haverfield's *The Romanization of Roman Britain*—by his favourite pupil, G. L. Cheesman: in his view, the study of archaeology and Roman Britain in particular was 'nothing but an intricate mass of technical detail, in which none but specialists can find their way, and from which no conclusions of general interest are likely to emerge'. Cheesman, G. L. 1913. Review of F. Haverfield, 1912. *The Romanization of Roman Britain*, 2nd edition. Oxford, Oxford University Press: 102.

The Vindolanda tablets are only one item in the changed landscape of Romano-British studies. There have been all kinds of further discoveries, for example of ancient rural settlement, now seen to have been much more intensive, thanks to air photography and geophysics. University departments of archaeology have proliferated and while Roman Britain has a reduced profile within them, the subject at the same time attracts enormous public attention in other spheres. Of course, Collingwood's views can be corrected or need modifying, on numerous pages in *Roman Britain and the English Settlements*. Nonetheless, for the author of the fullest recent study of Roman Britain it was one of two 'historiographical milestones that I have particularly enjoyed visiting'.[64]

5. EXCAVATION AND FIELDWORK

As a tailpiece, Richmond's 'Appreciation' needs some further comment:

> His attitude to excavation was profoundly influenced by the selective method of excavation, introduced and perfected by F. G. Simpson on Hadrian's Wall; and the first lesson which he drew from these methods, that excavations should be conducted with specific problems in mind upon sites likely to provide an answer, was salutary and useful. But Collingwood's corollary, that to pose a problem permitted its answer to be predicted, was a product of the study rather than of the field.[65]

This criticism of his supposed 'corollary' was shown by van der Dussen to be unfounded,[66] but repeatedly crops up.[67] In discussing Collingwood's own excavations, Richmond made the

[64] Mattingly, *An Imperial Possession*: 541. The other milestone was Rivet, *Town and Country in Roman Britain*, 1964 edn.

[65] Richmond, I. A. 1944. 'Appreciation of R. G. Collingwood as an archaeologist', in McCallum et al., 476–85 (14–23 of offprint).

[66] Van der Dussen, *History as a Science*: 207, 218.

[67] E.g. Breeze, D. J. 2003. 'John Collingwood Bruce and the study of Hadrian's Wall', *Britannia* 34: 13: 'On Hadrian's Wall . . . we can clearly see the disadvantages of Collingwood's question-and-answer approach . . . once the answer was determined, the whole problem can be placed on one side as "solved".' He is unaware of van der Dussen, *History as a Science* (see previous note). Breeze further believes that Collingwood's approach led to a closing down of research on the Wall. For another view, cf. Hodgson, *Hadrian's Wall 1999–2009*: 5–51.

unjustified claim that his 'planning of the excavation at Bainbridge left much to be desired. To examine the headquarters building in isolation, relating it neither to stratification within the fort nor in turn to the history of the rampart, was in fact to miss the opportunity of even a preliminary survey of the fort's history'.[68] In fact, Collingwood also cut trial trenches through the south rampart and the commanding officer's house and completely excavated the east gate. He had hoped to continue the excavation for several more years; but the landowner withdrew permission.[69]

Then came Richmond's most damning criticism:

> Still less fortunate was his excursion into pre-history at King Arthur's Round Table, near Penrith. There he had made up his mind in advance what he was to find and found it with fatal precision. When the writer, one of his oldest friends and admirers, came to translate the German report upon a second examination of the site a year later, it was sad and inexorable reading, a very verdict of Nemesis. Granted that Collingwood was then physically ill and bedevilled by complicated private and professional entanglements, one had nevertheless the feeling that he had fallen into a pit of his own digging . . . This was high tragedy, the remorseless fate of those whose brilliance illuminates many fields but not with steady light and, conversely, not with steady perception.

Much of this is simply untrue: one can hardly call this dig an 'excursion into pre-history' in view of his long survey article a few years earlier on the prehistory of the north-western counties, and he had not 'made up his mind in advance'—he made a suggestion in 1936, when visiting the site,[70] which he tested in 1937; the

[68] Richmond, 'Appreciation of R. G. Collingwood as an archaeologist', 479.

[69] As well as the report by Collingwood 1928, 'Excavations at Brough-by-Bainbridge in 1926', *Leeds Philosophical Society Proceeedings* (Lit. and Hist. Section) 1: 261–84, there is a detailed account in *The Yorkshire Post* of 14 September 1926, for a copy of which I am indebted to Stephen Leach. He also informs me of letters in the site record revealing 'a mysterious falling out between Collingwood and Dr J. L. Kirk'. Kirk had begun the excavation in 1925, with the landowner's permission, which was only 'a personal one to Kirk', and the landowner was unwilling for it to continue.

[70] Prehistory of north-western counties: Collingwood, R. G. 1933. 'An introduction to the prehistory of Cumberland, Westmorland and Lancashire north of the Sands', *CWAAS*[2] 33: 163–200. His suggestion in 1936: Simpson, G. 1998. 'Collingwood's latest archaeology misinterpreted by Bersu and Richmond', *Collingwood Studies*, 5: 109, with n. 1, citing *CW*[2] 37 (1937) 190–1, which reports his comments when visiting the site in summer 1936: 'Merely as a suggestion, he hazarded the

'second examination' of the site, by Bersu, was not 'a year later', but in 1939 (a year after Collingwood's report appeared); in 1937 Collingwood was not 'physically ill'—his two strokes followed in 1938, which is why he could not have a second season—nor was he then 'bedevilled' by 'entanglements'. As for Bersu's interpretation, this is itself open to question.[71] Of course, Collingwood, by his prompt publication, had put his head above the parapet. Had he behaved as Richmond himself was not seldom to do, his few weeks' digging at King Arthur's Round Table might never have been published at all, and might have been buried in oblivion. All the same, it is clear to the present writer that Collingwood's report on this excavation, and hence his reputation as a field archaeologist, was wrongly impugned.[72] Remarkably, some may feel, it is still

theory that we might have here "a miniature Avebury", and that excavation might possibly reveal the former existence upon the site of a stone circle or of a wood circle.'

[71] See Simpson, 'Collingwood's latest archaeology' for a detailed defence of Collingwood's excavation methods and conclusions, with, at 113–16, well-founded criticism of Bersu's own work at the Round Table (also at 117 noting that his interpretation of Little Woodbury is to some extent no longer valid). It is a pity that Simpson's paper is not better known to students of prehistoric and Roman Britain. Recently (November 2011) Paul Bidwell writes (personal communication): 'I have compared the reports by Collingwood and Bersu . . . and find it difficult to believe that all of the internal features which Collingwood claimed to have found were of natural origin. The site is on river gravels which are certainly very difficult to dig. Collingwood was aware of these problems and acknowledged the help of skilled excavators on his team, including K. S. Hodgson, who had much experience of prehistoric sites.' Further, as Stephen Leach kindly tells me, a report on the site in the *Manchester Guardian* (19 July 1937) mentions that 'the postholes contained charcoal'. He comments: 'That would tip the balance more in favour of postholes rather than animal holes'—Bersu, G. 1940. 'King Arthur's Round Table. Final report including the excavations of 1939', *CWAAS*[2] 40: 169–206, dismissed the holes found by Collingwood as made by mice, rabbits, or other creatures rather than by posts. Collingwood's letter to Ethel 31 December 1938 is very supportive of R. E. Porter's proposal that Bersu conduct the dig. [TS/PLTR194].

[72] Cf. Collingwood, 'An introduction to the prehistory of Cumberland': 198: 'A dig whose results are not published is a dig whose results are lost to the world, which therefore ought never to have been undertaken.' Richmond was no paragon, when one considers his unpublished excavations, notably Inchtuthil, where he excavated for fourteen seasons, 1952–1965; the full report was published by others in 1985. As for Hod Hill, published with the help of others a few years after his death, the trenchant review by Wheeler, R. E. M. 1968. 'Review of I. A. Richmond's Hod's Hill', *Antiquity* 42: 149–50 aroused a storm of protest in the same volume of *Antiquity*: 292–5. Wheeler gave an unrepentant reply: 295–6.

difficult to discuss all this dispassionately. Strong feelings remain.[73] Sometimes one feels that it is perhaps better not to air certain memories in public: 'You are walking over fires hidden beneath treacherous ashes.'[74]

Collingwood as an archaeologist is now mainly remembered in academic circles at home and abroad because of his skill at recording and interpreting inscriptions, eventually published as *RIB*. But he deserves to be thought of as a field archaeologist as well: it is absurd not so to describe one who not only directed excavations, but carried out his own surveys, drew the plans, took the photographs, and produced magnificent illustrations and classification of small finds, notably for his handbook of 1930. Research and publication in British archaeology have expanded enormously since he wrote, especially from the 1960s onwards. Numerous details in Romano-British history and archaeology have been subject to drastic revision, in some cases repeatedly, after strenuous debate, particularly when new evidence has come to light. A few have been mentioned earlier, but it would serve no useful purpose to list all of those items where Collingwood's interpretation must be rejected (or indeed can be upheld or reinstated)—after all, a good many pages in later standard works are also now regarded as mistaken or obsolete. More significant is the fact that his 'question and answer' approach to excavation is now enshrined as public policy. Under the Ancient Monuments Acts of 1979 permission to excavate scheduled monuments in Great Britain requires Scheduled Monuments Consent, administered by English Heritage, Cadw (for Wales), and Historic Scotland. Applicants for the SMC must demonstrate that they have a genuine research strategy, aimed at answering specific research questions, which are, further, relevant to the wider research strategy for the region or subject, and that their excavations will advance the state of knowledge.

[73] Richmond's view, discussed earlier, was shared by some others, clearly affected by personal considerations. The immensely influential M. V. Taylor was 'very distressed and disgusted' when Collingwood left his first wife (as reported in September 1941 by someone who knew her)—this doubtless explains her failure to mention him in her retrospective article, Taylor, 'The Society for the Promotion of Roman Studies'. I prefer the recollection of him by his close friend and contemporary, Wheeler, 'Review of Collingwood and Richmond 1969', quoted at n. 38.

[74] *incedis per ignes | suppositos cineri doloso* (Horace, *Odes* 2.1.7–8—to Asinius Pollio, who was writing a history of Rome's Civil War).

This requirement perfectly matches Collingwood's question-and-answer approach (whether or not the framers of the Act were aware of this). Furthermore, the excavation report must be published within a stated time limit after the expiry of the SMC, which will otherwise not be renewed. This too is a principle that Collingwood repeatedly reasserted.

5

COLLINGWOOD'S PHILOSOPHY OF HISTORY IN THE YEAR OF HIS *AN AUTOBIOGRAPHY*

JAN VAN DER DUSSEN

Discussing Collingwood's last works, Stefan Collini comments that 'had he died in 1938, his publications and his institutional position might well have ensured that his name was as familiar to later generations as that of such comparable luminaries as, say, H. H. Joachim or J. A. Smith'.[1] There is some truth in this observation, since Collingwood's fame is indeed primarily based on the books he published or prepared for publication from 1938: *An Autobiography*, *An Essay on Metaphysics*, *The New Leviathan*, and the posthumously published *The Idea of Nature* and *The Idea of History*, both being prepared by Collingwood for publication in revising his lectures on these subjects in 1940.[2] In all these books, one could say, a specific view on the relation between philosophy and history was elaborated. The only exception is *The New Leviathan*, but this book was written in reaction to the outbreak of the war.

Of these books *An Autobiography* was the first one to be published. Collingwood wrote it in the summer of 1938 and offered the manuscript to Oxford University Press before he sailed to the Dutch East Indies on 21 October 1938. On his voyage to and from this country and during his stay there he worked at three books:

[1] Collini, Stefan 1999. 'When the goose cackled. The discovery of history and the world beyond the walls: how Collingwood wrote his last works', *Times Literary Supplement*, 27 August: 3–6, there 3. Parts of this article are reprinted in the chapter on Collingwood, in: Collini, Stefan 2006. *Absent Minds. Intellectuals in Britain*, Oxford, Oxford University Press: 331–49. The passage quoted is on 334 but 'comparable' was omitted.

[2] For *The Idea of History* this only holds for the first four parts, and not for the Epilegomena.

An Essay on Metaphysics,[3] *The Principles of History*,[4] and *An Autobiography*.[5]

Since these books were written at the same time it is no surprise to find connections between them. In *An Autobiography*, for instance, Collingwood briefly discusses his theory of absolute presuppositions (*A*, 65–8), and in *The Principles of History*, when criticizing psychology as the 'science of human nature', he refers in a footnote explicitly to *An Essay on Metaphysics* (*PH*, 84), whereas in the latter book the logic of questioning is discussed as well. But, as we will see, in *The Principles of History* various themes are discussed that are also referred to in *An Autobiography*.

Of the three books by Collingwood on the philosophy of history—*The Idea of History*, the unfinished *The Principles of History*, and *An Autobiography*—the last is not merely the only one published during his life, but also, one could say, in certain respects the most informative. This claim is of some importance, since Collingwood's reputation as a philosopher of history is almost exclusively based on *The Idea of History*, his *An Autobiography* being accordingly underestimated.[6] It should be noticed that this is inappropriate and even misleading: *The Idea of History*, as posthumously edited by Knox, would not have been published in this form by Collingwood himself. This in particular pertains to the patchwork of essays put together by Knox in the Epilegomena of the book. Since it is especially this part of *The Idea of History* that has attracted most attention, being the starting point of most of the debates on Collingwood's philosophy of history, one could maintain with hindsight that this has contributed to a misleading

[3] Its first draft was written on the ship sailing to the Dutch East Indies, and Collingwood also worked at it from 23 February 1939 and during the return trip.

[4] Parts of it were written during the stay at the island of Java, from 9 to 23 February 1939.

[5] Collingwood received its proofs on 22 February 1939. He worked at it afterwards and rewrote the last chapter on the return trip. He sent the corrected manuscript to Oxford University Press on 25 March 1939 from Port Said.

[6] Toulmin, however, claims that '[c]hapters X and XI of the *Autobiography* are a better statement of Collingwood's historical principles . . . than the longer and more complex essays in *The Idea of History*' (Toulmin, Stephen 1978, 'Introduction' to *A*, xviii), and Salas declares that '[t]here is no better introduction to Collingwood's historical principles than that given by Collingwood himself in *An Autobiography*'. Salas, Charles G., 1987. 'Collingwood's Historical Principles at Work', *History and Theory*, 26: 53–71, there 53.

perspective on his ideas on the subject. Hence there is every reason to correct this perspective by paying attention to the views developed by Collingwood on the philosophy of history in his more reliable and authoritative works: *An Autobiography* and the unfinished manuscript of *The Principles of History*, which he authorized for publication.

I. COLLINGWOOD AS A PHILOSOPHER, ARCHAEOLOGIST, AND HISTORIAN

The reason for emphasizing the importance of *An Autobiography* for assessing Collingwood's philosophy of history is not only that the subject is all-pervasive in the book, but, in particular, since it explicitly explains how his activities as a philosopher, archaeologist, and historian were closely interrelated. Since it has almost exclusively been philosophers who have written about Collingwood's philosophy of history, his work as an archaeologist and historian and its influence on his philosophy of history have not had the attention they deserve.

Archaeologists, on the other hand, have likewise disregarded Collingwood's philosophy of history. As one of them, Ian Hodder, observes, '[o]verall, Collingwood's theoretical and philosophical writings were ignored by archaeologists', and 'his views on history were largely discounted in archaeology until the present day'.[7] But this has apparently changed, since Hodder also notes that 'Collingwood is currently at the centre of archaeological debate'.[8]

Since philosophy, history, and archaeology are quite different studies, with disciplinary aims of their own, it is understandable that a scholar such as Collingwood, who not only combined the three fields of study, but also explicitly developed views interrelating them, is not easily apprehended. His scholarly endeavours were perhaps too uncommon, one could say, to be plausible. This was

[7] Hodder, Ian 1995. 'Of Mice and Men: Collingwood and the Development of Archaeological Thought', in Boucher, David, Connelly, James, and Modood, Tariq, eds, *Philosophy, History and Civilization. Interdisciplinary Perspectives on R. G. Collingwood*, Cardiff, Wales University Press: 364–83, there 374, 364.

[8] Hodder, 'Of Mice and Men', 364. See, for instance, Browning, Margot 1995. 'A Baconian Revolution: Collingwood and Romano-British Studies', in Boucher, Connelly, and Modood, *Philosophy, History and Civilization*: 330–63.

not only the case during his life, but was in fact also his fate afterwards. For it is noticeable how parochial divisions within the scholarly world have thwarted a proper understanding of Collingwood's philosophy of history.

What is more serious, however, is that these scholarly divisions have even obscured a proper assessment of Collingwood's work in the specific fields of interest to him; he has been criticized for not limiting himself to one field, suggesting that this impaired his contributions to those fields. The archaeologist P. W. M. Freeman, for instance, characterizes Collingwood's work in archaeology as 'an intellectual exercise', 'a case study for much of his general theorizing on history', and as being 'secondary', and 'at least peripheral' to his other interests.[9]

Likewise, the philosopher of history Frank Ankersmit expresses the curious claim that '[p]erhaps Collingwood never developed a historical awareness because he was an archaeologist rather than a historian'.[10] He is apparently ignorant of the fact that Collingwood not only is the author of a standard work on Roman Britain, the first volume of *The Oxford History of England*,[11] but also extensively published on the most varied subjects related to Roman Britain. But it is of course equally absurd to suggest that an archaeologist would by definition lack historical awareness.

It is rather odd, to put it mildly, to see how Collingwood is blamed by an archaeologist for primarily being a theorist of history, and by a theorist of history for being rather an archaeologist, both suggesting that Collingwood's supposed 'real' interest impaired his contributions to the other fields concerned.

The fact that Collingwood was not only well versed in three fields of study, making important contributions to each of them,

[9] Freeman, P. W. M. 2007. *The Best Training-Ground for Archaeologists. Francis Haverfield and the Invention of Romano-British Archaeology*, Oxford, Oxbow Books: 588, 589, 590.

[10] Ankersmit, Frank 2007. 'Danto's Philosophy of History in Retrospective', in Danto, Arthur C., *Narration and Knowledge*, New York, Columbia University Press: 364–93, there 393. Besides this, Ankersmit expresses a rather curious view on Collingwood's contribution to the theory of history, saying that 'no one [sic] . . . can fail to be disappointed by the shallowness of *The Idea of History* and its absence of sensitivity to the real interest in and about the past' (393).

[11] Collingwood, R. G. and Myres, J. N. L. 1936. *Roman Britain and the English Settlements*, Oxford, Oxford University Press.

but also used them in developing a philosophy of history of his own, is indeed a remarkable achievement. But this accomplishment is to this very day insufficiently apprehended, the proper assessment of his work being in fact still impeded by parochial scholarly divisions. The best way to correct this is to take *An Autobiography* seriously, for it is particularly this book that makes clear how philosophy, history, and archaeology are closely entwined in Collingwood's thought. For a proper understanding of Collingwood's philosophy of history it is therefore in fact of more importance than *The Idea of History*.[12]

This is especially the case with the two pivotal themes of Collingwood's philosophy of history, the logic of question and answer and the re-enactment doctrine, which are discussed in *An Autobiography* within the context of archaeological and historical practice. In the following, both subjects will be dealt with.

2. THE LOGIC OF QUESTION AND ANSWER

For many decades the re-enactment doctrine has attracted most attention in the discussions on Collingwood's philosophy of history. With hindsight this is to be deplored, especially because of the incorrect methodological interpretations that have been given to it. But it has also resulted in attention being diverted from the logic of question and answer, the central theme of Collingwood's historical methodology.

The logic of question and answer is related to various themes within Collingwood's methodology of history: the way evidence should be used, the rejection of 'authorities' and scissors-and-paste history, and the emphasis on the autonomy of historians. But in a more general sense it also implies a theory of knowledge and enquiry, as well as a theory of hermeneutics, while in *An Autobiography* a theory of truth is also based on it. Although the subject had already been discussed by Collingwood in a specific context in *Speculum*

[12] This especially holds for the first edition of *The Idea of History* (see also note 6). For in the revised edition (1993) some important essays are added. In one of them ('Outlines of a Philosophy of History', dated 1928) an exposition is given of the re-enactment doctrine, but frequently references are also made to historical and archaeological studies, *IH*, 426–96.

Mentis,[13] it is extensively and systematically dealt with in *An Autobiography*.

In this book the logic of question and answer is linked with the philosophical principles of Bacon and Descartes (*A*, 25, 30, 37), with Plato, Kant, and Socrates added (*A*, 35). But with regard to the methodology of history Collingwood attached most value to Bacon's principles, since at various places he refers in this connection to 'a Baconian revolution' (*A*, 115, 124, 133).

Writing about the development of the science of history, Collingwood also speaks of a 'Copernican revolution'. In *An Autobiography* this is referred to only once in a footnote, saying that 'since 1800 history has passed through a Copernican revolution' (A, 79). But in his inaugural lecture 'The Historical Imagination' Collingwood also refers to a Copernican revolution in the theory of history (*IH*, 236, 240). This is done, however, in the context not of the logic of question and answer, but of the emphasis put on the self-authorizing position of the historian against traditional authorities. The idea of a Copernican revolution in history is therefore a more general concept than the one of a Baconian revolution in this field, the latter being part of the former. It exemplifies, one could say, a scale of forms as explained by Collingwood in his *An Essay on Philosophical Method*; the Baconian revolution embodies its generic essence in both kind and degree and by opposition and distinction.[14]

Referring to his logic of question and answer, Collingwood says in an often quoted passage that he used his archaeological experience as a 'laboratory of knowledge' (*A*, 24). In the following the nature of this archaeological experience and its background will be discussed, since it is primarily this aspect that is emphasized by Collingwood, rather than the philosophical theories of Bacon or Descartes. It is rather curious, of course, that a philosophical theory is based on the experience of a specifically 'unphilosophical' science such as archaeology. But the way this is done by Collingwood in *An Autobiography* is one of its most interesting and challenging features.

[13] *SM*, 76–80.

[14] Collingwood says of Bradley's *The Presuppositions of Critical History* that 'in it the Copernican revolution in the theory of historical knowledge has been in principle accomplished' (*IH*, 240).

3. THE HAVERFIELD–MOMMSEN LINK

In his *An Autobiography* Collingwood refers on several occasions to Haverfield, his teacher in both ancient history and archaeology. Collingwood had a great respect for Haverfield (1860–1919), who was from 1907 Camden Professor of Ancient History at Oxford. He calls him 'the great master of the subject', and says that he thought himself 'in piety to him, under an obligation to keep alive the Oxford school of Romano-British studies that he had founded' (*A*, 120). What Collingwood in particular appreciated was Haverfield's practice of 'scientific' digging, that is, digging with specific questions in mind, rather than what Collingwood calls 'blind' digging (*A*, 122–3). Collingwood considered this a (Baconian) revolution in archaeology, but he is not consistent about Haverfield being conscious of it. For at one point he says that 'Haverfield himself, least philosophical of historians, cared nothing about the principles or the potentialities of the revolution he was leading', whereas he maintains elsewhere that 'Haverfield and his colleagues . . . had been consciously and completely Baconian in their methods' (*A*, 83, 124).[15]

For a proper understanding of the nature of the revolution in archaeology as practised by Haverfield it is necessary to refer to another scholar, who played a prominent part in Haverfield's career, the German ancient historian Theodor Mommsen (1817–1903). Freeman calls him 'the most brilliant culmination of the development of *Altenwissenschaft*', and 'the catalyst for a revolution in writing about Roman ancient history in this country and throughout Europe'.[16] The revolution he brought about concerned the new types of evidence he explored, in particular epigraphy and numismatics, and the way they were used in his writings on Roman history. In epigraphy Mommsen is especially known for his monumental *Corpus Inscriptionum Latinarum*, and as a

[15] It is interesting to note that this aspect of Haverfield's work was also mentioned by Collingwood twenty years before in a commemorative speech on the occasion of Haverfield's death at a meeting of the Society of Antiquaries, saying that 'he did much to inaugurate the era of scientific investigation which has replaced, in Romano-British archaeology, the cruder methods of the last generation'. 1919. *Proceedings of the Society of Antiquaries of Newcastle-upon-Tyne*, 3rd ser., vol. ix, no. 9: 117–18, there 118.

[16] Freeman, *The Best Training-Ground for Archaeologists*, 125, 126.

historian for his *Römische Geschichte* in five volumes, the fourth of which never appeared, however.

The fifth volume of Mommsen's *Römische Geschichte*, which appeared in 1885, dealt with the Roman provinces, including a chapter on Roman Britain. Haverfield was much impressed by Mommsen's work, and was in close contact with him, in particular concerning the *Corpus Inscriptionum Latinarum*, to which he contributed on invitation by Mommsen. After Mommsen's death Haverfield eventually decided to work on a separate project of *Roman Inscriptions of Britain*,[17] and after his death the administrators of the Haverfield bequest commissioned Collingwood.[18]

In a commemorative article on Mommsen, Haverfield gives a most laudatory account of his accomplishments, saying that 'in Mommsen alone, since Gibbon, the imaginative and the critical really met, and Mommsen surpassed Gibbon in his critical faculty'.[19] On the *Corpus Inscriptionum* he observes that it 'has given to learning not only a new field of research, but a new method of scientific inquiry . . . With the inscriptions a new world opened . . . A stimulus was given to historical inquiry such as nothing but some great discovery can give to scientific work.'[20]

In a later article Haverfield pays tribute to Mommsen in the same vein. But it is interesting to note that after maintaining that '[h]e added at one stroke a huge body of evidence to the resources of the Roman historian', he makes the observation that '[n]ow it is becoming possible to advance from inscriptions to the uninscribed'.[21]

[17] Richmond suggests that Collingwood played a role in this decision, saying that '[t]he very high quality and accuracy of Collingwood's inherited power of draughtsmanship inspired Haverfield with the idea of a new work, *The Roman Inscriptions of Britain*, which should reproduce to scale an objective line-drawing of each stone, together with a text and critical apparatus'. Richmond, I. A. 1960. 'Roman Britain, 1910–1960', *The Journal of Roman Studies* 50: 173–91, there 175.

[18] Freeman, *The Best Training-Ground for Archaeologists*, 304. For a description by Collingwood of his involvement in *The Roman Inscriptions of Britain*, see *A*, 145–6.

[19] Haverfield, F. 1904. 'Theodor Mommsen', *The English Historical Review* 19: 80–9, there 81.

[20] Haverfield: 88.

[21] Quoted in Freeman, *The Best Training-Ground for Archaeologists*, 197. In his earlier article on Mommsen, Haverfield maintains that 'he did not often advance into the regions of the uninscribed. From letters on stone or coin he could extract abundant meaning: he cared less for the unlettered relics of Italian *terramari* or Gaulish villas'. Haverfield, 'Theodor Mommsen', 86.

By the time Haverfield wrote these words he was himself in fact already realizing, both in theory and practice, the advance from inscriptions to the uninscribed. That is, he organized excavations in order to obtain other types of material evidence for constructing history. Whereas Mommsen was epoch-making in the scientific study of non-literary evidence, confining himself to epigraphy and numismatics, the important contribution by Haverfield was that he expanded this approach to archaeology in general, including objects as diverse as potsherds, brooches, and forts.

4. THE NATURE OF COLLINGWOOD'S LABORATORY OF KNOWLEDGE

The Haverfield–Mommsen link shaped the context in which the young Collingwood worked as an archaeologist[22]—and as a philosopher too, for it was this capacity that made him acutely aware of the principles involved. When this context is taken into account, the idea of a Baconian revolution gets its proper purport, for the innovations to the study of history realized by Mommsen were indeed considered revolutionary, by both his contemporaries and later generations. The principles of this revolution were subsequently put into practice by Haverfield in the wider field of archaeology. But it was a revolution in the making, a pervasive theme in Collingwood's *An Autobiography*.

The concept of a Baconian revolution is in the first instance conceived by Collingwood in the context of certain developments in archaeology, then applied to the study of history in general, ultimately being crystallized into the logic of question and answer. Though based on Collingwood's archaeological experience, the concept is coined by him as a philosopher. It is a concept with complexities of its own, indeed—like the concept of a Copernican revolution—a philosophical concept as explained in *An Essay on Philosophical Method*.

[22] The influence of his father, W. G. Collingwood, should be mentioned in this connection. For Collingwood notes that he 'grew up in a gradually thickening archaeological atmosphere', referring to his father as being 'brilliantly gifted' for archaeology. *A*, 80. See Smith in this volume.

As said earlier, the Baconian revolution in history can be seen as part of the Copernican revolution in this field. The latter displays a certain development exhibiting a logic of its own. The starting point is that the traditional literary sources used by historians (Collingwood's 'authorities') are unsatisfactory for the study of history in a more advanced stage.[23] This problem can be obviated, at least partially, by using archaeological evidence. '[I]t would teach you,' Collingwood says, 'not indeed everything, but a great deal, about subjects whose very existence must remain permanently unknown to historians who believed in authorities' (*A*, 80). Collingwood recognizes the revolutionary nature of this new approach as practised by Mommsen, saying that he 'had shown how by statistical and other treatment of inscriptions the historian of the Roman Empire could answer questions that no one had dreamed of asking' (*A*, 82).

Mommsen's principle of using archaeological evidence for history was subsequently extended to excavations in search of all types of evidence. Within archaeological excavations, however, Collingwood made a distinction he considered crucial, namely between 'complete' and 'selective' excavations. The difference between these two types of excavations is dealt with in *An Autobiography* (*A*, 122–7), but is for the first time explained in his article 'Hadrian's Wall: 1921–1930'.[24]

It is no coincidence that in writing on the research done on Hadrian's Wall the principle of selective excavation is put forward. For the sheer size of the Wall makes it impossible, Collingwood maintains, to excavate it according to 'the methods current among professional archaeologists'. These methods were aimed at excavating certain sites, Collingwood says, giving the ones of Silchester, Housesteads, and Corbridge as examples. To apply these 'ordinary' methods of excavation to the Wall would be useless, he argues, since '[t]he excavation of Silchester took twenty years; at that rate, to excavate the Wall would have taken two thousand'.[25]

[23] It should be noted that this problem is particularly urgent for the history of Roman Britain, its literary sources being scanty.

[24] Collingwood, R. G. 1931. 'Hadrian's Wall: 1921–1930', *The Journal of Roman Studies* 21: 36–64.

[25] Collingwood, 'Hadrian's Wall: 1921–1930', 37.

It was therefore the nature of Hadrian's Wall which compelled archaeologists to change over to the alternative type of selective excavation, its essence being that in contrast to 'complete' excavation only specific ones were carried out, aimed at finding answers to specific problems related to the Wall. In his article Collingwood says that '[i]t is chiefly to Haverfield that we owe this method'.[26]

It is a moot point whether Haverfield may indeed be considered the father of the method of selective excavation. What can be said, anyhow, is that the archaeologist F. G. Simpson (1882–1955), Collingwood's lifelong associate in archaeology and a close friend, was the first to put this method into practice. It was he who, using this method, definitely proved in 1911 (together with J. P. Gibson) that the stone Wall was built by Hadrian and not Severus.[27] In an obituary of Collingwood, the archaeologist I. A. Richmond (1902–1965)—a pupil of Collingwood—says that '[h]is attitude to excavation was profoundly influenced by the selective method of excavation, introduced and perfected by F. G. Simpson on Hadrian's Wall'.[28]

In an article on the research done on Roman Britain,[29] Richmond gives a most interesting and detailed description of the method of selective excavation. Commenting upon the issues of 1903 that faced the archaeologists of Hadrian's Wall, he says:

To abandon this problem for the time being seemed the proper course, and at this very moment the first steps were being taken, by J. P. Gibson and F. G. Simpson, to work out a new technique, often since described as selective excavation, which was in course of time to master the question. It is important to realize the purely empirical nature of the method. Briefly, the procedure was to select for examination that structure whose position in relation to others would enable it either to subsume them as belonging to the same structural series, or, conversely, to furnish a definable contrast with some other element. The operative criterion was the fact . . . that archaeological material of the Roman period, in the form of coins, pottery, and other classifiable objects, could in itself

[26] Collingwood, 'Hadrian's Wall: 1921–1930', 38.

[27] The way this was done is described by Collingwood in an article on the problem of Hadrian's Wall, in a paragraph with the telling title 'The Period of Scientific Excavation'. Collingwood, R. G. 1921. 'Hadrian's Wall: a History of the Problem', *The Journal of Roman Studies* 11: 37–66, there 61–2.

[28] Richmond, I. A., 1943. 'Appreciation of R. G. Collingwood as an Archaeologist', *Proceedings of the British Academy* 29, 476–80, there 478.

[29] See note 17.

provide a date, varying in sharpness of definition but in good conditions very close, which could put the structure into its historical context... The intellectual attraction of these methods was to have some interesting results in other fields than Hadrian's Wall.[30]

It is interesting to notice that this description by Richmond of the principles involved in selective excavation can be seen as an illustration of what Collingwood means by calling archaeology his 'laboratory of knowledge'. For one may find in it certain notions of Collingwood's logic of question and answer, such as the importance of asking specific questions and their relation to empirical evidence. It is also telling that Richmond speaks of 'the intellectual attraction of these methods'. But for Collingwood these attractions were not confined to archaeology ('other fields than Hadrian's Wall'), but considered by him to be relevant not only for historical research in general, but even to be characteristic of science. The intellectual attraction of the methods of selective excavation as described by Richmond is equivalent to Collingwood's notion of the Baconian revolution, as the basis for his logic of question and answer. Or, the other way round, as Collingwood puts it referring to the method of selective excavation: 'This was the central principle of my "logic of question and answer" as applied to archaeology' (*A*, 122).

5. COLLINGWOOD'S ELABORATION OF HIS LABORATORY OF KNOWLEDGE AS A THEORY OF ENQUIRY AND HISTORICAL UNDERSTANDING

'The reason I am talking so much about archaeology,' Collingwood says, 'is that in archaeology the issue raised by the project of a Baconian revolution is unmistakable' (*A*, 133). By qualifying his archaeological experiences with the metaphor of a 'laboratory of knowledge' Collingwood indicated that he extended the principles involved to a wider context and other fields, the latter being incorporated in his conception of a logic of question and answer. As said earlier, this concept includes various aspects and is related to various themes within Collingwood's methodology of history.

[30] Richmond, 'Roman Britain, 1910–1960', 174.

The most unambiguous aspect of the relevance of the logic of question and answer to the study of history is one that can literally be transferred from the archaeological laboratory of knowledge: the conception of the Baconian approach as a theory of enquiry. It is Collingwood's prominent theme in 'Historical Evidence', declaring that Bacon's phrase, to 'put Nature to the question' 'is also . . . the true theory of historical method' (*IH*, 269), and that 'the questioning activity . . . is the dominant factor in history' (*IH*, 273). This activity is famously illustrated with Collingwood's detective story 'Who killed John Doe?' (*IH*, 266–8), which is subsequently analysed (*IH*, 270–3, 275–6). In order to be meaningful, the questioning activity must meet certain requirements, however. Three of them, especially relevant to the study of history, are dealt with by Collingwood: questions must 'arise' (*A*, 37), they must be put in the right way (*A*, 122), and their relation to evidence must be evident (*IH*, 278–82).

Looking for evidence is a hallmark of empirical knowledge. It is therefore interesting to see how Collingwood elaborates in the chapter 'Postulates of Empirical Thought' in *An Essay on Metaphysics* his view on empirical knowledge, providing a philosophical vindication of his logic of questions and answer (*EM*, 273–81).

Starting from Kant's 'categories of modality'—the notions of possibility, actuality, and necessity—Collingwood maintains that in the activity of scientific research these should be conceived as a methodological distinction between three stages in it. Concentrating on the modalities of actuality and possibility he says: 'When a scientist describes something as actual he means that it has been observed . . . When he describes it as possible he means that it is being looked for; that is, that the question whether it is actual is a question that is being asked' (*EM*, 274). The latter, 'the principle of possibility, that there are possible objects of perception which as yet have not been perceived', is, Collingwood argues, as a 'postulate of empirical thought' 'an absolute presupposition of all science in so far as science implies the organized and systematic asking of questions', referring to it as 'the Baconian doctrine' (*EM*, 275).

But the principle of possibility as an absolute presupposition of all scientific thought proves to be operative in various ways. For Collingwood makes the qualification that '[d]ifferent kinds of scientific thought are possible according as the centre of gravity in a particular piece of research lies in observing or in questioning'. He adds to this in a note an interesting and intriguing observation: 'I say this with the more confidence because it is a matter of personal experience to me that in historical and archaeological research . . . the difference between the two attitudes is sufficiently clear to divide researchers into two camps. There has been a kind of war between these two camps, in which I have taken part' (*EM*, 276).

It is obvious that reference is made here to the distinction between on the one hand 'blind' digging and 'complete' excavations, and on the other 'selective' excavation based on specific questions, as elaborated in *An Autobiography*. Since Collingwood simultaneously speaks of historical research, one wonders what he was referring to as the 'wrong' approach. Most probably it is the ideas of both historical 'facts' and 'authorities'.

Collingwood's criticism of the scientific approach concentrating on the activity of observing instead of questioning is couched in an attack on positivism. 'According to the positivists,' he observes, 'facts are things which present themselves to our senses. According to modern science, from Bacon onwards, facts are things which give us answers to our questions', adding to it that 'it is a crucial difference on a matter of fact with regard to the procedure of scientific research' (*EM*, 277).

The vindication of the validity of the logic of question and answer for scientific research, as argued in *An Essay on Metaphysics*, is a philosophical reflection on Collingwood's elaboration of his archaeological laboratory of knowledge as a theory of enquiry. As such it is a telling illustration of the interaction between his work as a philosopher, archaeologist, and historian.

The logic of question and answer is a theory of enquiry which gives emphasis to determining answers to specific questions, and in this respect it is forward looking. As such it is part of the activity of the historian (history *a parte subjecti*) and directed towards the future. The logic of question and answer is also relevant, however, to the object studied by the historian, that is, the past as history *a parte objecti*. This is a backward way of looking to the process of question and answer and related to the retrospectively determinate, whereas conceived as a theory of enquiry this process is put into practice forwardly, being prospectively open.[31] The logic of

[31] See Mink, L. O. 1969. *Mind, History, and Dialectic. The Philosophy of R. G. Collingwood*, Middletown, CT, Indiana University Press: 131–2, 138–9.

question and answer therefore covers the two dimensions of historical enquiry and historical understanding or hermeneutics.

The latter is in particular discussed by Collingwood in the chapter 'The History of Philosophy' in *An Autobiography*, asserting that 'a philosopher's doctrines are his answers to certain questions he has asked himself, and no one who does not understand what the questions are can hope to understand the doctrines', and conversely that 'any one can understand any philosopher's doctrines if he can grasp the questions which they are intended to answer' (*A*, 55). Likewise, on the occasion of his meditation on the Albert Memorial, Collingwood puts forward the rule '"reconstruct the problem"; or, "never think you understand any statement made by a philosopher until you have decided ... what the question is to which he means it for an answer"' (*A*, 74). 'To think in that way about philosophies not your own ... is to think about them historically' (*A*, 58), Collingwood says. In his discussion of Marx he presents an example of this way of thinking by asserting that he will be misunderstood if his philosophy is not seen in the context of the 'practical' problem he meant to solve (*A*, 152–3). Historical understanding as a reconstruction of the question-and-answer complex of an author is part, however, of the process of historical enquiry and should accordingly be based on evidence (*A*, 71).

6. THE RE-ENACTMENT DOCTRINE

Collingwood's theory of history as the re-enactment of the past is, besides his logic of question and answer, the other pivotal, and by far the most widely discussed, concept in his philosophy of history. It has attracted wide attention—much more than the logic of question and answer—and has spurred many debates. The reason for this is not surprising, since it is through *The Idea of History* that after World War II Collingwood became widely known as a philosopher of history, and it has in particular been the chapter on 'History as Re-enactment of Past Experience' (*IH*, 282–302) that has attracted special attention.

It should be noted, however, that this essay is part of the lectures on philosophy of history Collingwood gave in 1936, and was not meant for publication. Since *An Autobiography* was, and

Collingwood describes its purpose as 'to put on record some brief account of the work I have not yet been able to publish' (*A*, 118), it is of some interest to see how he brought the principles of his philosophy of history in it to the fore.

It is noteworthy that in contrast to the logic of question and answer, the re-enactment doctrine is not dealt with in a separate chapter, but put forward in the chapter 'History as the Self-knowledge of Mind' as a 'second proposition' of his 'new conception of history' as developed in his Die manuscript (*A*, 112, 110). There is therefore reason to suppose that Collingwood himself would probably have been surprised that in particular this aspect of his philosophy of history would arouse so much debate, and especially that it has been so often misinterpreted.

It is made clear in *An Autobiography*, however, that Collingwood considers his theory of the re-enactment of the past most important. He developed it in 1928, during a vacation spent at Le Martouret, 'that pleasant country-house near Die', and describes it as 'another step forward' in his conception of history (*A*, 107). It is most fortunate that this manuscript has been available since 1978, and in print since 1993 under the title 'Outlines of a Philosophy of History' (*IH*, 426–96). For it is indeed in this essay, written in preparation for his lectures on philosophy of history in 1928, that Collingwood develops his theory of the re-enactment of the past.

It is remarkable, however, that in *An Autobiography* Collingwood gives a picture of the 'Die manuscript' that differs completely from its real nature. For he says that in it he 'first drew the distinction between history proper and what I called pseudo-history', referring to 'such things as the narratives of geology, palaeontology, astronomy, and other natural sciences' (*A*, 107). But in the text itself this theme is only mentioned in passing, and only after an exposition has been given of the re-enactment of the past.[32] The most plausible reason why in *An Autobiography* Collingwood gives the impression that the 'Die manuscript' dealt with

[32] The passage reads: 'The birth of solar systems, the origins of life on our planet, the early course of geological history – all these are not strictly historical studies because the historian can never really get inside them, actualise them in his mind: they are science, not history, because, however much they may take the form of narrative, they are generalized narratives, accounts of how things must have happened in any world, not accounts of how things actually happened in this world' (*IH*, 445).

the distinction between history proper and pseudo-history is that at the time he wrote that book it was in particular this topic that occupied his mind. This is evidenced by *The Principles of History*, written in the same period as *An Autobiography*. For, as we will see later, in this manuscript attention is focused on the characteristics of history, as distinguished from natural science.

For a proper understanding of the re-enactment doctrine it is important to pay attention to the context in which it was developed by Collingwood. In the preface to the 'Outlines of a Philosophy of History' he refers to the underlying problem to be discussed as 'that of the relation between history *a parte subjecti*, historical thought, and history *a parte objecti*, historical fact'. 'Implicitly', he says, 'this problem is discussed and solved by the doctrine of the ideality of history: for that doctrine lays it down that historical fact, as known to the historian, is essentially relative to the thought that knows it' (*IH*, 428–9). It is in this context that the doctrine of the re-enactment of past thought is developed, explaining by this how knowledge of the past is possible (*IH*, 441–50).

In *An Autobiography*, however, Collingwood does not elaborate on the philosophical foundation of the re-enactment theory, but rather gives an illustration of it by emphasizing that in archaeology one should focus on the purpose as expressed in relics (*A*, 108–9). 'I expressed this new conception of history,' Collingwood says, 'in the phrase: "all history is the history of thought"' (*A*, 110). After this he gives as his second proposition that 'historical knowledge is the re-enactment in the historian's mind of the thought whose history he is studying' (*A*, 112).

As an example of re-enacting past thought Collingwood refers to Nelson, focusing on what is implied in understanding what Nelson meant by saying 'in honour I won them, in honour I will die with them'. He uses this example in order to discuss the aspect of different levels of thought involved in rethinking a past thought: in this case Nelson's thought and the present thought in rethinking it. The latter Collingwood calls the 'primary series' of his 'real life', to be contrasted with the 'secondary life' of Nelson's thought. Put differently, Collingwood maintains that both levels of thought represent a different question-and-answer complex: the one of the historian and the one of Nelson, the second being 'incapsulated'

(Collingwood's preferred spelling) in the first.[33] This brings Collingwood to his third proposition: 'Historical knowledge is the re-enactment of a past thought incapsulated in a context of present thoughts which, by contradicting it, confine it to a plane different from theirs' (*A*, 114).[34]

It is interesting to note that the notion of incapsulation of past thought in present thought is the only aspect of the re-enactment doctrine discussed in *An Autobiography*, but is not referred to in the earlier essay 'History as Re-enactment of Past Experience' in *The Idea of History*. Since it is a substantial element of the re-enactment doctrine and crucial for a proper understanding of it, its discussion in *An Autobiography* is therefore of special value. It is striking, however, that in discussions of the re-enactment doctrine it has not got the attention it deserves.

7. *THE PRINCIPLES OF HISTORY*

As mentioned earlier, Collingwood worked on *An Essay on Metaphysics*, *The Principles of History*, and *An Autobiography* during his trip to the Dutch East Indies. The fate of *The Principles of History* has been unfortunate, in that the manuscript was 'lost' for many decades, and was recovered only in 1995 in the archives of Oxford University Press. The manuscript had been available to Knox as editor of *The Idea of History*. But he only made use of parts of it, however, viz. the essays 'Historical Evidence' and 'History and Freedom', which were included in the Epilegomena of *The Idea of*

[33] That is, the first refers to the logic of question and answer as enquiry (history *a parte subjecti*), and the second to its hermeneutical dimension (history *a parte objecti*).

[34] Collingwood says of the problem of different levels of thought being involved in rethinking a past thought, that '[n]o question in my study of historical method ever gave me so much trouble; and the answer was not complete until some years later [that is, after 1928]' (A, 112). This statement is rather surprising, since in his essay of 1928 Collingwood presents us with the conception of incapsulation without actually using the term. '[T]o re-enact the past in the present is to re-enact it in a context which gives it a new quality. This context is the negation of the past itself', he declares, and giving the example of reading Dante he says: 'For Dante, the *Commedia* was his whole world. For me, the *Commedia* is at most half my world, the other half being all those things in me which prevent me from literally becoming Dante' (*IH*, 447).

History (*IH*, 249–82, 315–20), and the section on 'Hegel and Marx' (*IH*, 122–6).

It is fortunate that *The Principles of History* is now available in print (*PH*, 3–115). It is an interesting and important source for Collingwood's philosophy of history, providing new information about certain aspects of his views on the subject. It is therefore a valuable addition to *An Autobiography* and *The Idea of History*. The qualification has to be made, however, that it is an unfinished work, in both content and form. For only one-third of the planned book was written, and even that, far from being in a finished shape, should rather be seen as a first draft. It would therefore be far-fetched to consider *The Principles of History* as Collingwood's chief work, as he intended it to be.[35] What can anyhow be said is that we are not in the position to assess it as such. It is rather an expectation that unfortunately was not realized.

But the scheme Collingwood wrote for *The Principles of History* demonstrates that his plan for the book was ambitious. It is noticeable that various themes are mentioned that are also dealt with in *An Autobiography*. 'It starts thus: *Main* topics will include (1) a single account of the most obvious characteristics of history as a special science (2) Relations between this and others (3) Relation of history as thought to practical life. These could be Books I, II, III' (*PH*, 245). Of these three books only the first three chapters of book I were finished, while a beginning was made on a fourth chapter. In his sketch of contents Collingwood gives the following plan for book I:

> I.1. State and expound the conception of *Evidence*. Contrast this with the conception of *Testimony* and the *Scissors-and-paste history* which that implies. I. 2. State and expound the conception of *Action* (*res gestae*). Contrast this with the conception of *Process* or *Change* and the pseudo-history which that implies. I. 3. Conception of *Re-enactment*, and contrast the *Dead Past* and *Completeness*. I. 4. History as the *self-knowledge of mind*. Exclusion of other sciences of mind. (*PH*, 245)

[35] On 19 February 1939 Collingwood wrote in a letter to his son Bill from Djokjakarta (on the island of Java in the Dutch East Indies): 'As an antidote for boredom I have begun writing my next book. It is *The Principles of History* which will go down to posterity as my masterpiece. I suddenly began it, somewhat unexpectedly, as my boat was approaching Soerabaja, and spent my whole time in that damn hot town writing it as hard as I could lick.' Collingwood began writing the book on 10 February, and on the 19th he had finished more than 60 per cent of the manuscript (*PH*, 3–75).

8. OUTLINE OF *THE PRINCIPLES OF HISTORY*

As said earlier, the special characteristics of history are the main theme of *The Principles of History*, focusing on its methodological principles. It is explicitly dealt with in the first chapter entitled 'Evidence', which is well known, it being incorporated in the Epilegomena of *The Idea of History* (*IH*, 249–82). In the second chapter on 'Action' it is claimed that the object of historical knowledge is *res gestae*, and more specifically the thoughts expressed in it: 'actions in which reason, in a high or a low degree, reason triumphant or reason frustrated, wise thought or foolish thought, is not only at work but recognizably at work' (*PH*, 47). In this connection, in the section 'Evidence and Language' an interesting expansion is given of the discussion of evidence in the first chapter. Collingwood argues that evidence should not so much be seen as perceptible things, but as having the nature of language or a notation of language. In reference to this he makes the distinction between what a piece of evidence 'says' and 'what it means', the latter being inferential and the true aim of historical knowledge.

In the following sections attention is paid to the difference between studying natural events and human actions. Discussing the views of, among others, Alexander and Whitehead on the 'historicity' of nature, Collingwood argues that this position should nevertheless be sharply distinguished from history proper. The gist of his argument is expressed as follows: 'Chronology, yes; developments of the age-old idea that nature is essentially process or event, by all means; but history, no . . . [A]nyone who has ever worked intelligently at history knows that it is never about mere events, but about actions that express the thoughts of their agents' (*PH*, 61–2).

As in *An Autobiography* (*A*, 108), Collingwood illustrates this distinction with the stratigraphical methods used in geology and archaeology (*PH*, 62).[36] With regard to archaeology he refers, as in *An Autobiography* (*A*, 127–8), to the principle of looking for the thought-side of archaeological objects, giving the example of 'triangular slabs of clay with a hole in one corner', which should be '"read" . . . as a piece of language' (*PH*, 66).[37]

[36] See also *IH*, 212.

[37] In line with his criticism of the custom of 'blind' digging in *A*, 122–4, Collingwood again rages against this practice, saying 'that no archaeologist ought even to be

Under the heading 'Nature and Action' Collingwood deals in the third chapter extensively with the relation between history and natural science.[38] In this chapter Collingwood gives a most critical assessment of the influence of natural science on the study of history, especially paying attention to the pretensions of natural science as they have developed since the eighteenth century. In combination with its intellectual authority this has led to the position of 'pupilage', as Collingwood calls it, traditionally occupied by history in relation to natural science.

This is an often recurring and well-known theme in Collingwood's philosophy of history and referred to by him as a form of positivism, naturalism, or pseudo-history.[39] The way Collingwood discusses in depth the troublesome relation between history and natural science in *The Principles of History* is especially valuable since it provides a useful background to the references made to instances of positivism or naturalism in *The Idea of History*.[40] But it is also in line with the position taken in *An Autobiography* emphasizing the distinction between history proper and pseudo-history (*A*, 107).[41]

In his preparatory notes for *The Principles of History* Collingwood makes a distinction between two forms of what he calls 'historical naturalism': '(a) *substituting* natural facts for the historical facts about which one is trying to think (losing the distinction between them altogether), or else (b) *superordinating* natural facts to

allowed to excavate at all unless, when he is deciding to work at a certain site, he can answer the question "what historical problems lead you to that site, why do you think you can solve them there, and how exactly do you mean to go about it?" '(*PH*, 65).

[38] Collingwood diverges with this from his original plan for the book. For in the 'scheme' for *The Principles of History* he mentions as the subject of chapter 3 the conception of re-enactment. What is dealt with in this chapter is in line, however, with the declared project of treating in the first book 'the most obvious characteristics of history as a special science'.

[39] Though Collingwood is in particular known for underlining the specific characteristics of history, it is notable that he emphasized certain uniformities between history and natural science. The most important one is the Baconian approach of the logic of question and answer.

[40] An example is Collingwood's criticism of the positivistic approach of Toynbee's *A Study of History* (*IH*, 159–65).

[41] But, as has been argued earlier, Collingwood wrongly projected this position into the 'Die manuscript'.

historical facts, as the causes of which these historical facts are the effects' (*PH*, 235). These two forms of historical naturalism are worked out at length in two separate sections entitled 'The Science of Human Nature' and 'Nature as Environment'.

In the first one Collingwood focuses on the pretensions of psychology as the science of thought. This subject is also extensively discussed in *An Essay on Metaphysics* (101–32), on which he worked at the same time.[42] As in *An Essay on Metaphysics* Collingwood ardently repudiates the claim of psychology to be the science of thought. The argument he concentrates on is the absence of the criteriological aspect in this approach, it being in Collingwood's view a crucial aspect of thought.[43]

The following section on 'Nature as Environment' deals with the second form of naturalism. The question raised by Collingwood is how the influence of the natural environment on civilizations should be conceived. He argues that this influence is never a direct one, but always depends on 'what man makes of nature by his enterprise, his dexterity, his ingenuity, or his lack of these things' (*PH*, 93). The characteristics of the environment determining the characteristics of a civilization are therefore only 'conferred upon it by the people whose conduct they determine' (*PH*, 94).

On second thoughts, however, Collingwood qualifies this position. For it is still based on the idea that one of two interacting terms is nature as it is in itself, and he wants to deny that in this sense nature 'can ever be detected by the historian as a factor influencing the course of history' (*PH*, 95). To illustrate his position more pointedly he therefore discusses in more general terms, in which nature is not concerned, the idea of 'brute force' which is supposed sometimes to play a role in human affairs. He gives the example of an army of a small nation being crushed by an army of a large one and consequently being 'forced' to surrender. The point Collingwood wants to stress is that, in such a case, it is not the

[42] In a note Collingwood refers to it, saying: 'I do not choose to repeat or supplement here the evidence for the bankruptcy of modern "psychology"... which I have already adduced in my *Introduction to Metaphysics*' (*PH*, 84). The title *Introduction to Metaphysics* was the working title.

[43] Collingwood means that the elements of success or failure and truth or error are always implied in thought. They should therefore be taken into account by the sciences investigating thought. It is discussed in *EM*, 109–11, and also in *PA*, 171.

situation 'in itself' which determines the surrender of those said to be forced, but the way it is conceived. For 'knowledge that the situation is what it is' should therefore be read 'belief that the situation is what in fact they believe it to be', he maintains. 'Here at last we get down to hard facts as the historian understands hard facts', Collingwood concludes; 'the phrase hard facts, in the mouth of an historian, refers to the facts of how certain human beings on certain occasions think' (*PH*, 96).

Collingwood's criticism of historical naturalism can be seen as an elaboration of his thesis that all history is the history of thought. In the next section on 'Freedom', however, he draws an interesting conclusion based on the preceding ones. For he claims that his argument makes clear that history is free in two respects: the actions it studies are free in the sense of not being determined by natural conditions, and historical thought is free in the sense of not being dependent upon natural science. 'The so-called problem of human freedom solves itself,' Collingwood concludes, 'the moment history becomes a science' (*PH*, 109).

The section on 'Freedom' was included by Knox in *The Idea of History*, and is therefore well known. But since its line of thought relies on the preceding sections of *The Principles of History* it does not properly belong in the Epilegomena, and the essence of its argument is hardly intelligible in that context.[44]

9. THE ABSENCE OF THE RE-ENACTMENT DOCTRINE IN *THE PRINCIPLES OF HISTORY*

In discussing *The Principles of History* there is one aspect that deserves special attention, namely the absence of the conception of re-enacting the past. No reference is made to it—to the surprise, and also disappointment, of Collingwood scholars. This is quite intelligible, especially since the re-enactment doctrine is by far the most debated subject of Collingwood's philosophy of history. What explanation can be given for this puzzling omission?

As explained earlier, Collingwood developed his re-enactment theory in 1928 within the context of his conception of the ideality

[44] The first two paragraphs of 'History and Freedom' (*IH*, 315) were written by Knox and are inadequate as an introduction.

of history, implying the inseparability of history *a parte subjecti* and history *a parte objecti*. In his subsequent discussions on the re-enactment doctrine, however, Collingwood never again referred to his conception of the ideality of history, most probably because he simply took it for granted. It had played a part, one could say, in the 'context of discovery' of the dual conceptions of the re-enactment of the past and history being the history of thought, and therefore not in need of further discussion. But it is quite possible that the same holds for the re-enactment doctrine itself. That is, that it was taken for granted by Collingwood, and that he subsequently only focused on its repercussions for the study of history. It is striking, anyhow, that this is his approach in *An Autobiography*. For there, with the exception of the aspect of the incapsulation of past thought, the re-enactment of the past is simply put forward as a principle and not explained, as Collingwood does with the logic of question and answer. The argument that in 'History as Re-enactment of Past Experience' in the Epilegomena of *The Idea of History* the re-enactment doctrine is explicitly discussed does not hold, since this essay was only part of Collingwood's lectures on the philosophy of history of 1936 and was not meant for publication.[45]

It is particularly this essay, however, that has aroused debate on the re-enactment doctrine. This could not have been foreseen by Collingwood, of course, and more specifically, he could not have foreseen the type of critical questions that would posthumously be raised about the re-enactment doctrine. What has often been insufficiently taken into account in the comments on Collingwood's re-enactment doctrine is the approach advocated by him, that in order to understand a theory one should focus on the questions it was meant to answer.[46] It should be noticed, though,

[45] Collingwood had definite ideas about the publication of his manuscripts and would not have been happy with the publication of 'History as Re-enactment of Past Experience' as it stood—especially if one takes into account that even his 'Outlines of a Philosophy of History', in which the re-enactment doctrine is properly explained, was not meant for publication.

[46] This approach was practised for the first time, however, in the 1950s by A. Donagan and W. H. Dray. They (rightly) argued that the re-enactment doctrine should be seen as answering the philosophical question of how historical knowledge is possible, and not as a methodological prescription for acquiring historical knowledge. Donagan, Alan 1956. 'The Verification of Historical Theses', *Philosophical*

that this has only really been made possible by the availability of the 'Outlines of a Philosophy of History', which provides the most systematic and extensive discussion of the re-enactment doctrine. The unfamiliarity with this essay has therefore contributed to most misunderstandings of this doctrine.

As said before, there is a striking discrepancy between the way the dual and interrelated theses of the re-enactment of the past and all history being the history of thought are put forward in 'Outlines of a Philosophy of History' and in *An Autobiography*: whereas in 'Outlines' re-enactment is the starting point from which the thesis of history as the history of thought is derived, in *An Autobiography* it is the other way around. This means that at the time of writing *An Autobiography* and *The Principles of History* Collingwood apparently had changed his mind on the relation between the theses of the re-enactment of the past and all history being the history of thought. Though in the original 'context of discovery' the re-enactment of the past had been primordial, this subsequently changed and the thesis of all history being the history of thought acquired that status. This does not mean, however, that Collingwood did not consider the re-enactment doctrine that important anymore. But he apparently no longer considered it a *problem* and took it more or less for granted. It is striking, anyhow, that though the re-enactment of the past is put forward in *An Autobiography* as an important principle, it is not discussed there, apart from the aspect of the incapsulation of past thought, and neither is it discussed in *The Principles of History*.

But the question remains why Collingwood in his 'scheme' for *The Principles of History* mentioned the conception of re-enactment as the third chapter of the first book, but did not realize it. A possible explanation is that the term re-enactment is simply used here as a shorthand for the dual theses of all history being the history of thought and the re-enactment of past thought. For in his 'Notes on Historiography', written in preparation for *The Principles of History*, Collingwood writes: 'I have . . . insisted that all history is the history of thought, and that the historian knows a past

Quarterly 6: 193–208; Dray, W. H., 1957. 'R. G. Collingwood and the Acquaintance Theory of Knowledge', *Revue Internationale de Philosophie* 11: 420–32; and Dray, W. H., 1958. 'Historical Understanding as Re-thinking', *University of Toronto Quarterly* 27: 200–15.

thought by re-enacting it in the present' (*PH*, 244). That is, he describes both theses as a unity, re-enacting being the implication of history being the history of thought.[47]

Taking this into account, the fact that in chapter 3 the subject of all history being the history of thought is dealt with,[48] whereas in the 'scheme' the conception of re-enactment is mentioned as its subject, becomes less puzzling if it is seen as a way of referring from the implication (re-enactment) to what is presupposed (history as the history of thought). But this relation holds the other way around as well. That is, the way the thesis of history being the history of thought is discussed has its implications for the theory of re-enactment; the latter is in this way also indirectly discussed.

It may be observed that the question why the re-enactment theory is not explicitly discussed in *The Principles of History* becomes less relevant if it is realized that it is quite understandable that Collingwood, in discussing in this work the principles of history, focuses on its specific object and the methodological principles involved, but not on the distinct philosophical questions related to the re-enactment of past thoughts. The latter questions, one could say, did not arise within the context of a treatise that is primarily focused on the methodological principles of history and their repercussions. In this connection the aspect of the specific object of history, *res gestae*, being the history of thought, is emphasized again and again in *The Principles of History*. Since thoughts are not objects and can only be known in re-enacting them, the latter is simply presupposed as being the way by which past thought is known and consequently taken for granted.

10. THE PRESENCE OF THE RE-ENACTMENT DOCTRINE IN *THE PRINCIPLES OF HISTORY*

The argument that the conception of re-enactment of past thought is indeed present, though implicitly, in Collingwood's discussion of history being the history of thought is illustrated by various passages in chapter 2 of *The Principles of History*. In discussing the idea that in understanding an action historians should aim at the

[47] After the passage quoted, Collingwood asserts that '[a]s so re-enactable' 'it is neither a condition of the past's being historically knowable nor a consequence of its being historically known, but the same thing as its being historically known' (*PH*, 244–5).

[48] The subject is more explicitly dealt with, however, in chapter 2.

thought embodied in it and, more specifically, what was 'meant by it', Collingwood refers to Diocletian's Edict of Prices and the revocation by Louis XIV of the the Edict of Nantes. In order to make these into historical knowledge, Collingwood argues, 'we must "read" it, that is, find out what Diocletian or Louis meant by it; then (and this is the special business of the historian) we must interpret it as implying that he envisaged the situation in which he found himself in a certain manner' (*PH*, 50). Likewise, he says of a charter of Henry I that a historian 'must decide what it means, that is to say, what Henry I was "driving at" when he issued that charter: how the king envisaged the situation he was dealing with, and how he intended that it should be altered' (*PH*, 51).

In 'History as Re-enactment of Past Experience' in *The Idea of History* Collingwood's well-known example of reading the Theodosian Code is phrased in a remarkably similar way, saying that the historian 'must envisage the situation with which the emperor was trying to deal, and he must envisage it as that emperor envisaged it . . . Thus he is re-enacting in his own mind the experience of the emperor; and only in so far as he does this has he any historical knowledge . . . of the meaning of the edict' (*IH*, 283).

It is noteworthy indeed how in *The Principles of History* and 'History as Re-enactment of Past Experience' almost the same phrasing is used, Collingwood speaking of 'envisaging the situation' and the way it should be dealt with as being part of historical knowledge. The only difference is that in *The Principles of History* no reference is made to re-enactment, the example being given as an illustration of history being aimed at action embodying thought, whereas in 'History as Re-enactment of Past Experience' no reference is made to the latter aspect, the example being given as an illustration of what re-enactment is like. In other words, what is implied in one case is made explicit in the other and vice versa. This difference is related to the context within which the examples are used: in the first case a treatise on the principles of history and in the second a lecture on the re-enactment of past thought as part of lectures in the philosophy of history.

The foregoing examples of passages from *The Principles of History*, relevant for the conceptions of history as the history of thought and the re-enactment of past thought, were not known before its publication in 1999. But there is one passage in this work that was known and has occasioned many critical comments. It is part of the section 'Freedom', included by Knox in *The Idea of History*. The passage concerned reads: 'All history is the history of thought; and when an historian says that a man is in a certain situation this is the same as saying that he thinks he is in this situation. The hard facts of the situation, which it is so important for him to face, are the hard facts of the way in which he conceives the situation' (*IH*, 317). It is followed by the example of a man who is afraid to cross the mountains because he is frightened of the devils in them; Collingwood's point is that it is irrelevant for a historian to call this superstition.

This position has been widely criticized for its disregard of objective conditions playing a part in history. Without going into the various arguments that have been put forward, the distinction made by W. H. Dray between objective and subjective rationality is relevant in this connection, asserting that Collingwood adheres to a subjective conception of rationality.[49] Referring to the passage concerned in *The Idea of History*, L. O. Mink gives an important comment from another perspective, saying: 'Natural facts, one may say, always enter historical explanation only in the mode of indirect discourse; that is, if "*p*" is a proposition describing natural fact, then historical discourse proper never contains statements of the form "*p*" but only of the form, "It was known that *p*," "It was believed that *p*," "X said to Y that *p*," and the like.'[50]

Mink is certainly right in this contention. But it should be noticed that the principle he refers to not only holds for historians, but is a well-known doctrine in the philosophy of language and semantics, known as 'indirect speech', 'propositional attitudes', or 'oblique contexts'. It was developed by the German logician Gottlob Frege in his famous article 'Über Sinn und Bedeutung' of 1892.[51] Frege develops in this article the thesis that in a main sentence that refers to a subordinate one containing a thought as its reference, it is not the latter's truth value that is at issue, but the sense of the thought concerned. This is exactly the point made by Collingwood too: he claims that what is at issue in referring to

[49] Dray, W. H., 1995. *History as Re-enactment: R. G. Collingwood's Idea of History*, Oxford, Clarendon Press: 116.

[50] Mink, *Mind, History, and Dialectic*: 171–2.

[51] Translated in Beaney, M., ed., *The Frege Reader*, Oxford, Blackwell: 151–71.

someone being in a certain situation is the sense of the thought about it involved and not a supposedly 'objective' situation or condition.[52] Since this position is crucial for both Collingwood's theory of all history being the history of thought and the re-enactment doctrine, it should rather be seen as in line with an important and generally accepted doctrine in semantics, instead of implying a supposedly contentious position.

Unfortunately *The Principles of History* was never finished. But the part of it Collingwood left us is nevertheless of great value. He extensively deals in it with the specific characteristics of history, discussing its object and methods in their mutual relation. This approach is in line with the picture of history given in *An Autobiography*. The pivotal theme of this book is, one could say, to express the importance of history, not only for a proper understanding of the past, but also for understanding society, both of which were highly relevant for practical life. That Collingwood projected 'Relation of history as thought to practical life' as the subject of the last chapter of *The Principles of History* bears witness to the great value Collingwood attached to this theme. It can be seen as the pinnacle of his philosophy of history and it is no coincidence that this is also the subject of the last chapter of *An Autobiography*. It can also be seen as part of the project of 'a new philosophy which will be a philosophy of history in the wide sense, i.e., a complete philosophy conceived from an historical point of view' (*IH*, 7).

The outbreak of World War II made Collingwood decide to concentrate on subjects he considered more directly relevant to the current situation. Though history played a part in them, Collingwood was unable to develop his specific thoughts on the philosophy of history because of the severe circumstances he was confronted with. But the last chapter of *An Autobiography* gives a hint of the direction his thoughts might have taken. And this was precisely the declared aim of that book.

[52] For the relation between Collingwood's re-enactment doctrine and Frege's theories, see Dussen, Jan van der 1995. 'The Philosophical Context of Collingwood's Re-enactment Theory', *International Studies in Philosophy* 27: 81–99.

6

THE HISTORICITY OF THOUGHT

BRUCE HADDOCK

Collingwood claims emphatically in his *Autobiography* that his 'life's work hitherto, as seen from' his 'fiftieth year, has been in the main an attempt to bring about a *rapprochement* between philosophy and history' (*A*, 77). Commentators have broadly endorsed that view, while remaining deeply divided about its implications. From Knox's controversial introduction to the original version of *The Idea of History*, down to the recent reissue of *An Essay on Metaphysics*, there has hardly been a settled view of the significance of his 'historicist turn' for a wider estimate of his thought (*IH*, *EM*). If it is a 'historicist turn', what are the implications for moral and political theory? And in a broader context, how should we, doing the best we can in a public culture even more profoundly aware of conceptual pluralism, regard the normative bearing of the past on our attempts to do our own thinking?[1]

These are very deep questions that Collingwood raised in beguilingly straightforward fashion. They have formed the basis of much tortured discussion of methodological questions in the history of ideas since the 1960s. If we hear rather less of these debates today, it is certainly not because the points at issue have been effectively settled. If anything, exhaustion has set in, with philosophers and historians going their separate ways, much as they did in the past. In these circumstances, it is timely to go back to Collingwood's formulation of the issue. The discussion is very much the centrepiece of the *Autobiography* (see, especially *A*, chs 7–10: 53–119). In true Collingwoodian fashion, we should establish as clearly as we can exactly what he was claiming.

[1] See Floyd, Jonathan and Stears, Marc, eds, 2011. *Political Philosophy versus History? Contextualism and Real Politics in Contemporary Political Thought*, Cambridge, Cambridge University Press, for a full discussion of the state of the debate in contemporary theory.

In itself, this is by no means a straightforward task. Collingwood's life was tragically cut short, and there is obvious evidence of desperate hurry in the formulation of ideas in his very late work. We cannot avoid asking ourselves how he might have taken these ideas forward had he had the time. Most importantly of all, however, reflection on his work, again in true Collingwoodian style, might signally help us to sort out our own thinking on these vexed questions.

Collingwood's primary concern in these central arguments of the *Autobiography* is to show that the dominant realist critique of historical knowledge simply misses the point. The realists suppose that historical knowledge is impossible because historians cannot gain access to the past to check the veracity of the (more or less plausible) accounts they have managed to put together. So much the worse for history, we might say. But if history goes to the wall, much of our ordinary understanding of moral and political life goes with it, so the damage is much deeper than the failure of a discipline. All thinking involves recollection and imaginative projection, key facets of historical thought of any kind. If history is not to be trusted, it follows that we should have no confidence in our own minds. What passes for thinking might better be described as a series of happenings in our heads, very much along the lines of the prevalent modes of psychology that Collingwood castigates in the *Autobiography*. Securing a basis for historical knowledge is thus much more than a historical task for Collingwood. Our ability to think critically is at stake, and with it our capacity to assume responsibility for our actions.

Collingwood thus addresses two related problems that most of his contemporaries (and indeed successors) kept strictly separated. He wants to defend history as a discipline, conducted in an appropriate way, but also to claim that proper historical discipline and awareness can anchor us in the myriad engagements of practical life. This is a tall order, not least in our own day, where academic specialization has made the mutual support of disciplines for a thriving public culture much more difficult to discern.

What needs to be noted here is the audacity of Collingwood's ambition. He may have bitten off more than he, or anyone else, could possibly chew. When we look at the reception of his ideas (among philosophers and historians rather than Collingwood specialists) it is the reform of history as a discipline that is most often noticed. We have to be aware, however, that there is always a wider dimension; and whatever we want to say about his disciplinary contribution should (at least) be compatible with the larger project.

Collingwood encapsulated his distinctive position in the dictum 'all history is the history of thought', but what constitutes a thought is not entirely clear (*IH*, 215; *A*, 110). At one (very basic) level, he equates thought with the activity of asking and answering questions. In his celebrated 'logic of question and answer', dealt with in more detail by Michael Beaney in this volume, he denies that a propositional logic can ever make sense of intellectual engagement, since what we do when we are thinking is to seek answers to questions that puzzle us (*A*, 29–43). What we mean cannot be separated from the attempt to answer questions. Even the most simple utterance, if it is worth expressing, will settle some query in our mind's eye. Obviously, we know what we are asking ourselves. Understanding other people's utterances presupposes that we are aware of the questions they are asking.

Whether the logic of question and answer is actually a logic is, of course, a controversial matter in its own right. Collingwood presents it as a method for understanding actions and utterances, at any time, in any place. And, certainly, read in this way, his position has had a massive influence on the history of ideas in particular. But other questions suggest themselves, which Collingwood hints at, but does not effectively resolve. Understanding answers to specific questions is one thing. Yet something might have to be presupposed in order to ask questions at all. The simple fact that we can talk to each other might presuppose assumptions that cannot be reduced to a logic of question and answer, no matter how construed. The issue of intelligibility might have to be addressed in significantly different terms.[2]

Under the rubric 'all history is the history of thought' Collingwood runs together two quite distinct ideas. One is the stress on thinking and doing as problem-solving activities in determinate situations. We are confronted with difficulties (practical or theoretical) and try to resolve them. The attempt to establish universal

[2] See Davidson, Donald, 1984. *Inquiries into Truth and Interpretation*, Oxford, Clarendon Press, especially chs 1 ('Theories of Meaning and Learnable Languages'), 9 ('Radical Interpretation'), and 13 ('On the Very Idea of a Conceptual Scheme').

laws of physics, for example, can be understood only as a set of responses to determinate questions that arise. What these questions are is a matter of history. We can synthesize them cleverly, and even state the answers in propositional form. The propositions, however, are not free-standing. If they mean anything at all, they are answers to specific questions. Propositions, at best, are a form of shorthand. At worst, as in *Principia Mathematica*, they are no more than 'typographical jargon', and effectively an obstacle to understanding, or so Collingwood claims (*A*, 36).

The other side of Collingwood's doctrine of thought is less often noticed, but much more controversial philosophically, and arguably more significant in relation to his moral and political theory. The fact that we can understand past thought, indeed any thought, commits us to a view of the universality of thought, despite Collingwood's insistence on thinking as a determinate activity. He is quite unequivocal on this point. He notes that while 'thoughts are no doubt themselves events happening in time', nevertheless 'there is another sense . . . in which they are not in time at all' (*IH*, 217). He endorses Whitehead's view of a 'right-angled triangle' as 'an eternal object', but insists on extending the idea to (for example) 'the Roman constitution and the Augustan modification of it' (*IH*, 218). The fact that an idea 'can be apprehended by historical thought' makes it an 'eternal object' (*IH*, 218). He states this as a necessary condition of understanding, arguing that 'time makes no difference to it in this respect, just as it makes no difference to the triangle' (*IH*, 218). These views surely complicate a casual historicist reading of Collingwood's later thought, though they may be compatible with a historicism of a rather more complicated kind. At the very least, they should alert us to a range of problems if we assimilate Collingwood too readily to (currently fashionable) social constructivist theories of thought. And it is clear from the text of the *Autobiography* that an 'eternal' reading of thought is central to his critique of scepticism.

Collingwood denies categorically that a historian's task is simply to present a plausible account from the perspective of agents. He is surprisingly harsh in his dismissal of Dilthey's notion of empathetic identification in *The Idea of History*, arguing that psychological sympathy can never be precise enough to serve as a basis for knowledge (*IH*, 171–5). We can picture someone's position for ourselves, exercising our largest sympathies, but we still can't be sure that we have grasped an agent's perspective. Many contemporary historians would be content to say that we get as close as we can, given the state of the evidence. If knowledge of this kind lacks the precision of logic, so much the worse for logic, at least in the historical domain.

Collingwood is much more demanding. He claims that 'the historian of a certain thought must think for himself that very same thought, not another like it' (*A*, 111). This is a tall order even in the history of philosophy or mathematics, where the task is to re-enact a highly self-conscious engagement. But even here it is not clear what identity adds to the thought that we have understood an idea for our own purposes. And, of course, Collingwood is perfectly well aware that our purposes are not the same as an agent's.

Most commentators are content to allow that Collingwood has set the bar too high here. He may have specified an appropriate regulative idea, but it would be a very unusual exercise in historical reconstruction that gave us good grounds for supposing that we had grasped the very same thought. But the issue was clearly important to Collingwood. It is almost as if the *rapprochement* between philosophy and history requires philosophical precision in historical work. This is a decidedly odd view, and many of Collingwood's admirers strive hard to show (from the evidence of the manuscripts especially) that he can't possibly have meant it. Yet in the *Autobiography* he says 'no question in my study of historical method ever gave me quite so much trouble' (*A*, 112). He is clear that re-enacting is not the same as acting; and invokes a standard conception of context to portray (for example) the difference between Nelson and his historians. This, in itself, is not a complicated thought, so we must assume that we have not grasped its full significance for Collingwood. Reading between the lines of what is otherwise a limpid account, Collingwood almost lapses into outmoded idealist language (identity in difference), in a text in which he is especially guarded about any identification of his own thought with idealism.

The identity of thought is thus a central but puzzling notion for Collingwood. He sidesteps what might be assumed to be a core question in logic, contending that for all practical purposes a logic of question and answer is sufficient to keep our thinking moving forward. The link between theory and practice, we must remember, is as important to him as the *rapprochement* between history and philosophy (*A*, 147–67). In the *Autobiography* he concentrates, instead, on methodological implications. He highlights, in particular, the doctrine of a 'living past', stressing continuity in change as ideas are adapted to new situations (*A*, 98). He refers also, frustratingly for an earlier generation of commentators, to the two destroyed texts (*Libellus de Generatione* and *Thought and Contradiction*) in which he had worked through these ideas formally. Happily a copy of the *Libellus* still exists, and is available among Collingwood's papers at the Bodleian Library.[3] Intriguingly for the purposes of this chapter, Collingwood rejects in the *Libellus* the false contrast between philosophy as a pursuit of universal truth and history as an amassing of detailed information. He claims, instead, that history and philosophy 'are opposite moments which never exist apart' and should properly be held in 'concrete synthesis'.[4] His emphasis throughout, however, is on reality as process of becoming, and not on the practice of history. Revealingly, too, he describes the work as a defence of 'absolute empiricism', endorsing Hume's critique of naïve realism, but without lapsing into a 'subjectivism' that he sees as a standing temptation even in the work of the contemporary Italian idealists he so admired.[5]

It is surely revealing, in an autobiography conceived as a sketch of work that he had not been able to complete, that the formal defence of a position that remained central to his thought should seem so unimportant to him. This tells us a lot about the distance, in terms of both style and substance, that he felt separated him from his contemporaries. He records, for example, that the *Libellus* was 'very sparing of words', making 'point after point without any attempt at elaboration or explanation' (*A*, 98–9). He was plainly not prepared to defend his views against possible objections. And while he describes the manuscript as 'an attack on realism', we can

[3] Collingwood, R. G. '*Libellus de Generatione*: An Essay in Absolute Empiricism', unpublished manuscript, Dep. Coll.

[4] Collingwood, *Libellus:* 75.

[5] Collingwood, *Libellus:* 1. Chapter two of *Truth and Contradiction* has also been recovered, though sadly the rest of the text is still missing. A copy of a highly perceptive reader's report by Henry Jones is available in *EPP* Oxford: Clarendon Press: 229–31.

see that he does not engage in a critique of actual realists, involving argument and counterargument.

We can treat Collingwood's avoidance of direct controversy as a personal trait, separable from his body of ideas, but not the urgency of tone that is a feature of the late works.[6] Collingwood's worry is that confused thinking generates confused action. Thinking, after all, makes a difference to what is known and done. In relation to moral and political thinking, the link between thought and action is direct, at least in Collingwood's view. Despite his ultimate faith in the ability of human beings to think clearly, there is an unmistakeable mood of anxiety and foreboding in the *Autobiography*, especially in the (toned-down) final chapter. The titles of some of the manuscripts are striking ('Man Goes Mad', *PE*, 305–35). The thought that a position as narrowly 'academic' as logical positivism should be construed as a threat to civilization is breathtaking.[7] Collingwood had taken Hegel's dictum to heart (philosophy is 'its own time comprehended in thoughts'), but is much more direct than Hegel in attributing the woes of civilization to philosophical error.[8]

Getting historical method right is thus much more than a matter of setting the record straight. In order to act effectively, we have to have a clear idea of ourselves as historical creatures, responding well or ill to the problems that confront us. We apply criteria when we act, and our criteria may be woefully inadequate. What worries Collingwood most is that we should lose sight of ourselves as thinking creatures, treating our thoughts almost as if they are images that simply flash by. The philosophical point of history is that it provides the best possible record of ourselves as agents engaged in problem solving. For Collingwood we are creatures who do things, not creatures to whom things just happen. His concern is that reductionist theories of thought (he is especially scathing in his criticism of psychology in the *Autobiography*) serve to undermine the critical capacity that should be our primary resource (*A*, 92–5).

[6] Most especially evident in *NL*.

[7] The final paragraph of *EM*, 343, continues to surprise.

[8] See Hegel, G. W. F. 1991. *Elements of the Philosophy of Right*, ed. Allen W. Wood, Cambridge, Cambridge University Press: 21.

It is not entirely clear how this wide redemptive agenda should be connected with the narrow reading of question-and-answer logic that has dominated debate about the significance of Collingwood's legacy. And it must be said that the way he presents his case does not always help a balanced reading of his contribution. His critique of the fallacy of perennial wisdom was taken up with enthusiasm in the revisionist debate on approaches to the history of ideas in the 1960s and 1970s. Anachronism was presented as the cardinal error for any historian. On this reading, Collingwood is a pioneer in a methodological revolution that barely made an impression in his lifetime.

To cite Collingwood as a revisionist in these terms is not, of course, mistaken. It is simply that his wider philosophical purpose is not sufficiently noticed. Yet, as with most authors, he has contributed in some measure to the misreading of his work. The emphatic tone of the *Autobiography*, in particular, but other late works too, presents ideas in the boldest possible terms, without supporting qualification. The tirade against political philosophers, trawling the history of political philosophy for the best account of a conception of the state, is a case in point. He comes close to ridiculing the idea that we can compare and contrast Plato's *Republic* and Hobbes's *Leviathan* in order to glean the best of their thinking. He insists that 'the nature of the state in Plato's time was genuinely different from the nature of the state in Hobbes's' (*A*, 61). In some sense, we all know this, yet continue to see a point in reading contrasting accounts of political experience alongside each other. Collingwood, too, grants that both texts are, in some unspecified way, 'concerned with politics' (*A*, 61). He warns us against the obvious error of supposing that a *polis* is the same as 'the absolutist state in the seventeenth century', but that is not the mistake the seekers of perennial wisdom were making, even in Collingwood's day (*A*, 61).

The real problem is deeper, and Collingwood is fully aware of it. Whatever Plato or Hobbes might have thought about perennial wisdom, their texts were not direct attempts to disclose it. They were troubled by problems generated by the political thought and experience of their own day, and sought means of sustaining political stability on defensible terms. They disagreed, of course, about how that might be attained, and what assumptions should best be invoked in order to persuade their contemporaries. Their concerns were different. Very different conceptions of a relevant public signally affected the style and substance of their work. Yet it would be very odd to deny altogether that they were both addressing *a* problem of political obligation. I use the indefinite article; some of the philosophers Collingwood had in mind might have been tempted to use the definite article. If anything hinges on that, it needs to be carefully explained. At the very least, it is clear that only one side of the argument was picked up in the revisionist debate on the history of ideas that gathered momentum in the 1960s. In an obvious sense, Plato and Hobbes were responding to the specific dilemmas that their circumstances had thrown up, but they were also contributing to a wider process of conceptual change, evident only in retrospect, that continues to shape our view of political order.

Collingwood himself was clear that though a primary objective of understanding is to set specific answers to specific questions, he always maintained that re-enacting past thought remained a critical engagement. He insists, and never wavers from the thought, that re-enactment 'is not a passive surrender to the spell of another's mind' (*IH*, 215). Re-enactment 'is a labour of active and therefore critical thinking' (*IH*, 215). Given his stress on the significance of grasping other people's questions, the form of that critical thinking is not obvious. A critical historian will, of course, have to work to establish precisely which questions a given thinker or agent had asked himself. That is a technical matter. Collingwood's view of critical thinking is much broader, involving, he maintains, the entire context of a historian's knowledge, and, in 're-enacting' an idea, a historian 'criticizes it, forms his own judgment of its value, corrects whatever errors he can discern in it' (*IH*, 215).

This is a very broad brief indeed, and cannot be accomplished in terms of a narrowly conceived logic of question and answer. Establishing what someone was trying to do sets us off on the right track. After that we are very much on our own, assessing formal consistency, implications, and even wondering whether a thinker has asked himself the right questions. This is very much critical reading as it has always been done, from Plato's day down to our own, with variations informed by the cultural, moral, and political obsessions of a period.

This creates problems for Collingwood only if we read him in the narrowest of methodological terms. Like so many great thinkers, especially in the history of political philosophy, he was responding to what he saw as a deep crisis in the culture of his day.[9] He treats the trials and tribulations of contemporary politics as symptoms of a deeper malaise in European civilization. Philosophers, historians, a reflective class more broadly, had taken a wrong turn in their portrayal of what it is to be a thinking creature confronting an uncertain future. Whatever merit we might see in Collingwood's analysis, and it would be out of place to go into full detail here, his claim is that actual thinkers had gone astray, broadly portraying political and moral thinking as (at best) passive adaptation rather than active engagement.[10] My point here is not that Collingwood's view should necessarily be endorsed, that is a matter for continuing discussion, rather that his view of the practical implications of intellectual choices makes normative argument indispensable. And normative argument can be conducted well or ill.

When Collingwood addresses these issues directly, it is often in the broadest possible terms. The discussion of barbarism in *The New Leviathan*, for example, is deeply revealing, but very unusual as a piece of philosophical argument (*NL*, 342–87). The assertive tone suggests a man in a desperate hurry to get core elements of his thought across in a period of personal and political crisis. To equate barbarism with 'hostility towards civilization' begs a host of questions (*NL*, 342). And Collingwood's examples of barbarism (the Saracens, the Albigensian Heresy, the Turks, and the Germans) are tendentious, telling us a good deal about the depth of his feelings, but giving us very little to work with philosophically or historically. Similarly the essay 'Fascism and Nazism' reads like a personal lament for intellectual failures stretching back to the Enlightenment and beyond (*EPP*, 187–96). It is important for us to note how we read these works. Most of us will try to read through the alarmist tone to get to the considered thought beneath,

[9] See Haddock, Bruce 2008. *A History of Political Thought: From Antiquity to the Present*, Cambridge, Polity Press, for a wider account along these lines.

[10] For full discussion see Boucher, David 1989. *The Social and Political Thought of R. G. Collingwood*, Cambridge, Cambridge University Press, and Connelly, James 2003. *Metaphysics, Method and Politics: The Political Philosophy of R. G. Collingwood*, Exeter, Imprint Academic.

committed to clarifying an issue that Collingwood may have left shrouded.

If Collingwood's broad worries about the well-being of British and European culture intensified in his last years, the claim that theory should guide practice was an abiding concern from his earliest works. He opened *Speculum Mentis* with the categorical contention that 'all thought exists for the sake of action' (*SM*, 15). He presents a properly conceived philosophy as therapy for a troubled civilization in that text, seeking a remedy for present discontents. 'We are wrecks and fragments of men,' he announces, obsessed with the specialized compartments of our lives such that we cannot appreciate the wonder of being alive (*SM*, 35). His ideal is a 'complete and undivided life', where the different facets of experience are mutually supportive (*SM*, 36). Philosophy can nurture awareness of a 'unity of mind', comparable, at least in principle, with the institutional fabric of medieval society in Collingwood's view, but with the added benefit of technical expertise that was simply not attainable in the medieval period.

What he sought in the *Autobiography* and *The New Leviathan* was very much along these lines, though Europe's prospects had signally deteriorated over the last generation. Philosophy as therapy is deeply unpopular today, not least because sub-disciplinary specialization has gone so much further since the 1930s, but the fact that Collingwood vested (perhaps desperate) hopes in philosophical redemption sheds intriguing light on some of the technical issues in his philosophy that have proved to be so intractable.

The conception of thought as an 'eternal object', for example, puzzling in the context of the alleged historicism of his later work, is taken for granted in *Speculum Mentis*. What he hopes to present, he says disarmingly, is 'the essence of every great philosopher's teaching' (*SM*, 13). It has always been assumed that the strictures against a pursuit of perennial wisdom in the *Autobiography* were directed against just such a view. Yet Collingwood's comment on *Speculum Mentis* in the *Autobiography* is revealing. He notes that 'it now fails to satisfy me ... because I have gone on thinking since I wrote it', and that 'much of it needs to be supplemented and qualified' (*A*, 56). But, significantly, 'there is not a great deal that needs to be retracted' (*A*, 56). At the very least, this suggests that we should look again at Collingwood the methodologist, and think more patiently through the doctrine of re-enactment and what it might require conceptually.

These issues take us to the heart of Collingwood interpretation, and cannot be resolved effectively here. A great deal hinges on precisely how we view Collingwood's intellectual development. Plainly a critical edition of the *Autobiography* will contribute to that assessment, but key questions may well require a full intellectual biography before we can move forward confidently.[11] Controversy has always surrounded Collingwood's claim that metaphysics is a 'historical science' (*EM*, 49–57). Detailed comment on *An Essay on Metaphysics* would be out of place here, but we need to be very careful how we interpret Collingwood's central claims about 'absolute presuppositions'. It is one thing to assert that metaphysics is a matter of establishing precisely 'what absolute presuppositions have been made on certain occasions', and quite another to suppose that this makes styles of reasoning in different periods radically incommensurable (*EM*, 49).

Doubtless this issue will continue to generate controversy in the years ahead. Rex Martin's introduction to the new edition of *An Essay on Metaphysics* and his contribution to this volume surely set us along the right lines, but much more detailed work remains to be done. Collingwood insists that 'every statement that anybody ever makes is made in answer to a question' (*EM*, 23). This is an unqualified claim, applicable to thinking in any conceivable presuppositional context. A historical science of metaphysics, Collingwood style, thus leaves open a logical enquiry into forms of thinking at a more abstract level, a meta-metaphysics, as it were. That is very much how logic has developed post-Tarski and Quine, and it is hard to see how Collingwood could object to it. Traditional metaphysical questions might have to be dealt with rather differently, as Collingwood suggests, but the claim about incommensurability of meanings would have to be dropped. Collingwood is actually talking about historical misunderstanding at a more mundane level, where we simply pick up the wrong end of a stick.

Note, too, that one of Collingwood's major themes, the link between monotheism and the emergence of modern science, hardly

[11] Inglis, Fred 2009. *History Man: The Life of R. G. Collingwood*, Princeton, Princeton University Press, gives an account of the personal context.

looks as if it is simply one possible conceptual view among others. For all Collingwood's worries about an exaggerated scientism, he never questions the astonishing tangible achievements of modern science. To retreat from science would be to embrace conceptual barbarism, as if, as thinking creatures, we could knowingly endorse a manifestly inferior conceptual scheme. He does not hesitate to describe a wilful retreat from reason as barbarism in *The New Leviathan*. We may not be happy with this way of making the point, but everything he says in the *Autobiography* and *The New Leviathan* suggests that a great deal more is at stake than the emergence of a different way of seeing the world.

We get much less close analysis of moral and political confusion from Collingwood than we might want, but his position is emphatic, even dogmatic, in the literal meaning of the word. In 'Fascism and Nazism', he asserts, without qualification, that 'the vital warmth at the heart of a civilization is what we call religion', and that 'civilization dies because the people to whom it belonged have lost faith in it' (*EPP*, 187). These look like causal claims, though Collingwood makes no attempt to show why we should grant his view. I do not say that he is necessarily wrong about this, rather that we cannot be sure what he is claiming. The examples he cites in the text are illustrative, persuasive no doubt to (at least some) contemporaries who share his concerns, yet they are beside the point to anyone who does not. He treats 'liberal or democratic principles' as 'a function of Christianity' (*EPP*, 195). He thus interprets the crisis of European politics in the 1930s as, first and foremost, a crisis of religion. Italian fascism, he says, 'is a function . . . of the pre-Christian paganism which has survived under the toleration and protection of Italian Christianity'; while in Germany 'pagan survivals have always been extremely vigorous' (*EPP*, 195). Whether these views are helpful is not the issue here. What we should note is his insistence that only strong religious sentiment enables peoples to conceive of a notion of 'absolute value' (*EPP*, 187). And relentless criticism of religion, from the Enlightenment onwards, has deprived European cultures of an inestimable grounding. Collingwood does not put the point so bluntly, but it is hard to resist the conclusion that the Enlightenment was a moral and political mistake, despite its obvious power to change the shape of the modern world. Whatever else we have here, it is a lament for things gone badly wrong.

The point to stress from the perspective of this chapter is not Collingwood's specific thesis, but the practical seriousness of intellectual error and confusion. Collingwood's stance on the historical contingency of values must thus be read alongside his warnings against sleepwalking into an irrationalist future. The fact that Collingwood's work has been taken up so much more by philosophers of history than political philosophers has left us with a significantly unbalanced picture of the man and (especially) his late work. Some of his contemporaries, Knox most obviously and prominently, have regretted both the tone and content of the late writings, distancing themselves from both the historicist implications of *An Essay on Metaphysics* and the strident critique of irrationalism in the *Autobiography* and *The New Leviathan*. Knox asks himself in his preface to his edition of *The Idea of History* if 'a hostile critic might have asked Collingwood whether his own historicism was at bottom any less irrationalist or any less prejudicial to civilization than the philosophies he so unsparingly attacked'.[12] Within Knox's terms of reference, based on a reading that largely discounts the late works, that puzzle is difficult to resolve. And while Knox's view has been widely (and rightly) challenged, especially in relation to editorial decisions, very little sustained work has focused specifically on the paradox he highlights.

Nor can the matter be settled within the limits of this chapter. My concern has been to look again at certain themes in Collingwood's work that he stresses in the *Autobiography*. Philosophers especially, but all of us to some degree, have separated the technical discussion of philosophy of history in chapters 7–10 from the anguish of the final chapter. Yet we can find no indication in Collingwood's writings that he ever saw the *rapprochement* between philosophy and history as other than a practical matter. In this, in some sense, we have been following Collingwood himself as he distinguished between philosophy of history in the narrow sense, focusing on 'the philosophical problems created by the existence of organized and systematized historical research', and the wider question of the impact of historical awareness on our sense of ourselves, what Collingwood calls 'a complete philosophy conceived from an historical point of view' (*IH*, 6–7).

[12] See Knox's preface to his edition of Collingwood, *IH*, xxiii.

Here, again, we are victims of the sub-disciplinary specialization that Collingwood so deplored. When Alan Donagan, W. H. Dray, Patrick Gardiner, and others engaged with Collingwood, it was because they used his thought in order to press ahead with their own work.[13] Their interests were more technical and limited than Collingwood's, but their achievements are tangible, signally advancing discussion of questions of history among analytical philosophers.

The wider question of history's significance was barely taken up by philosophers at all. Certainly political philosophers in the 1950s and 1960s showed little interest in what we might call civilizational critique. Collingwood specialists have done sterling work in presenting us with a more balanced picture of the philosophy, though very much in terms of the historical record of his life and thought. Results in this sphere, too, have been very good indeed. When I first read Collingwood over forty years ago, the secondary literature was decidedly limited, with little awareness of the significance of the unpublished manuscripts. Happily, those days are behind us, but there is still work to be done in resolving tensions in the late work.

We can no longer claim, however, that gaps in the Collingwood record are preventing proper assessment of the work. What we need, surely, is philosophical engagement with issues, not simply specialist studies, though such studies are always welcome. And here, at least, there are promising signs. There is now much more widespread recognition of the complex relationship between our capacity to make normative judgements and the contexts in which those judgements arise. This has been generated by practical problems thrown up in our experience of living in deeply pluralist societies in a context of global interdependence, quite as much as awareness of the variety of historical paths that have led peoples and cultures to their current positions. Intriguingly, however, the conceptual issues are strikingly similar. In both the historical and practical spheres, we are confronted with the demands of difference, where agents see their world in radically different ways, and

[13] See Donagan, Alan 1962. *The Later Philosophy of R. G. Collingwood*, Oxford, Clarendon Press; Dray, W. H. 1957. *Laws and Explanation in History*, Oxford, Clarendon Press; and Gardiner, Patrick 1952. *The Nature of Historical Explanation*, London, Oxford University Press.

the need, in the practical sphere at least, to decide what to do next in problematic situations. Understanding how other people deal with these issues, Collingwood would say, deepens our understanding of what it is to be an agent ourselves. Diversity obliges us to make judgements, despite the fact that we are more aware than ever before of the historical weight behind different views of the world. It would be tempting to fall back on capacious description of the varieties of experience we encounter, much as a historian might suppose normative judgement to be somehow beyond his professional concern. In practical contexts, however, we have to think through deep differences in order to sustain complex, and changing, schemes of social cooperation. Direct experience of these (very ordinary) situations has had a clear impact on our approach to moral and political philosophy. And it takes us back to some of the difficult questions Collingwood was addressing in his last years.

The dilemma for Collingwood scholars is that we do not have anything in the late writings that can properly be regarded as a definitive statement of his views on these issues. *The New Leviathan*, very much a war book, though full of absorbing material that could have been worked up in a number of different directions had he had time, reads like a synthesis of work in progress, reduced to bare bones. It cannot stand in the canon of 'great texts' in political philosophy, though as commentators and critics, we often find ourselves striving to take the arguments forward. From the text as we have it, too much in the way of supporting argument is missing for comfort.

One way of making best sense of the late political writings is to distinguish between values and arguments, much as we have to presuppose common patterns of argument across different constellations of absolute presuppositions in *An Essay on Metaphysics*. In interpretative terms this is clearly risky business, too close to Croce's radically reconstructive treatments of Vico and Hegel to be entirely convincing.[14] But if we are interested in Collingwood as a 'living' philosopher (and how else would he have wanted to be read?), we have very little choice.

[14] See Croce, Benedetto 1967. *La filosofia di Giambattista Vico*, Bari: Laterza, first published, 1911, and Croce, Benedetto 1967. *Saggio sullo Hegel e altri scritti*, Bari, Laterza.

Here I can do no more than encourage future generations of scholars to take philosophical engagement with Collingwood's work seriously. There are tantalizing hints in writings throughout his career of what he might have been able to achieve in political philosophy if his priorities had been different. The seminal essay on 'Political Action' of 1928–1929, for example, invites us to look at political thought in terms of patterns of order. He shifts attention away from something as historically contingent as forms of the state, and asks questions instead about thought and action that inform the imposition of order in any context. What we get clear about in this sort of exercise is not the relative merits of particular forms of order (state, *polis*, empire, etc.), but the thinking that shapes a political world. He insists that 'the business of sound theory, in relation to practice, is not to solve practical problems, but to clear them of misunderstandings which make their solution impossible' (*EPP*, 94). The stress is on thinking clearly, whenever and wherever we might be situated.

Collingwood speaks of political action as 'the imposition of order', yet maintains that we are never confronted with an orderless situation (*EPP*, 102). Normative justifications of order change with circumstances, and may be well or ill conceived. Arguments may be construed as self-interested, naïve, reckless, utopian, etc., and may never command universal support. Controversy is an integral dimension of political thought and action. What is crucial, according to Collingwood, is that relations in a political community should be regarded as reciprocal. 'Only a free agent can obey,' he insists; 'only one who is conscious of himself as a source of independent political energy can recognize that energy in another, and co-operate with it' (*EPP*, 103). Of course, agreement can be forged on all number of terms, and may very well be wrongheaded. That is why normative argument is inescapable. If most of us happen to see political order as a direct reflection of order in the cosmos, we are likely to settle on rather different terms of cooperation from transactional individualists, each pursuing a narrowly conceived advantage. Where there are sharp differences in world view within a community, doubtless it will be harder to attain a workable consensus. We need to take actual contexts into account when we assess specific proposals. But, note, modelling what is going on at a further remove serves a philosophical purpose. Whatever we might want, we are trying to establish mutually acceptable ground rules, among other things. The supposition that, at least at some level, reciprocity must prevail, limits what can plausibly be proposed. Being clear about what we are doing will not guarantee neat and easy solutions; but it will save us from some of the follies of confusion.

As philosophers, we can ask ourselves where these ideas might take us, and that will involve hard thinking of our own. We may start with Collingwood, and end up in a position that might be described as Collingwoodian, without the benefit of chapter and verse. Throughout the *Autobiography* Collingwood exhorts us to nurture a culture of critical thinking, precisely because we always find ourselves having to adapt to unforeseen events. Our thinking may be situated, even parochial, but a commitment to critical thinking remains a universal value.[15]

[15] I am grateful to contributors to this volume for comments on an earlier version of the chapter, and especially to David Boucher for detailed suggestions, advice, and help.

7
FROM METHOD TO METAPHYSICS

REX MARTIN

1. INTRODUCTION

The notion of fundamental presuppositions, organizing principles of knowledge or of practice, has a long and important history in R. G. Collingwood's thought. These are things that he had talked about for much of his career, had done so from at least as early as his lecture on Ruskin, in 1919.[1] The notion of such organizing principles had developed over time in the course of Collingwood's thought and was given its most extensive statement, and its definitive formulation, in his *Essay on Metaphysics* (1940).[2] In the present chapter I try to put Collingwood's treatise on metaphysics in context by sketching out some of the main contributions made in his writings in the 1930s—in particular in his *Autobiography*—to the development of his distinctive idea of fundamental presuppositions.

In *Metaphysics* Collingwood makes two important and controversial claims. (1) The actual practice of science (be it natural or historical or social science) always has certain determinate organizing principles (fundamental or absolute 'presuppositions',

[1] A paper delivered at the Ruskin Centenary Conference in Coniston, 8 August 1919. The address was published as *Ruskin's Philosophy*, Kendal, T. Wilson, 1922. For a very helpful survey of Collingwood's discussion of fundamental presuppositions, from his first writings up through the early 1930s, see Connelly, James 2003. *Metaphysics, Method and Politics*, Exeter, Imprint Academic: 115–41, at 115–23. Connelly suggests, in the section on relativism in his chapter in the present volume, that Collingwood's conception of absolute presuppositions was significantly influenced by Evans-Pritchard E. E., 1937. *Witchcraft: Oracles and Magic Among the Azande*, Oxford, Oxford University Press (a book which Collingwood had read pre-publication in his role as a delegate of the Press). See also Wendy James's contribution in the present volume.

[2] *EM*, edited by Rex Martin. All pages references to *EM* will be to this particular edition.

Collingwood called them). These presuppositions are inseparable parts or ingredients of an ongoing and complex nest of practices aimed at knowledge and understanding. (2) In an important sense, these presuppositions are themselves always historically located.

The *Essay on Metaphysics* contends, then, that the main business of metaphysics is to identify (and formulate) these fundamental principles and to assess their adequacy. Collingwood did not regard the outcome of this metaphysical project to be merely reportorial. Rather, Collingwood envisioned an element of critical assessment as part of the proper task of metaphysics. He indicated this by introducing the term 'criteriological', by which he meant 'self-critical' or critical on internal standards (see *EM*, 108–9, 111, 115–16; in *EM*, 142, he identifies metaphysics as criteriological).

Accordingly, I would be reluctant to regard Collingwoodian metaphysical statements (formulations of fundamental presuppositions) as essentially *descriptive* in nature. These statements of metaphysics are more accurately viewed, I believe, as analytic constructs, as rational reconstructions of presuppositions which can be shown to ground scientific practice and understanding in a given period.

2. SOME PROBLEMS IN METAPHYSICS

Several of the points Collingwood raised in his *Essay on Metaphysics* are problematic. In this section I will take up some of the main questions and main issues that recur, again and again.

(a) One question that comes up with some frequency is how, in Collingwood's scheme of things, we can account for changes in the basic views (in the presuppositions) of a given science. In particular, the question persists whether these changes are, given the way Collingwood describes them, reasoned changes (as opposed to irrational or sub-rational ones). These questions are pressing, in particular, because the presuppositions that inform and guide scientific enquiry are, in Collingwood's view, often things the practitioners of a given science were initially unaware of, or are aware of only dimly (see *EM*, 26, 43, 48n).[3]

[3] These questions were originally raised by A. D. Lindsay, one of the pre-publication readers of *Metaphysics* for Oxford University Press. For Collingwood's

The key thing, I think, in getting hold of the problem at hand is to see that Collingwood embeds these presuppositions in ongoing scientific practice. The foundational and governing presuppositions of a given system of knowledge are objective standards and conventions to which people conform when they frame and evaluate knowledge claims or hypotheses, when they 'automatically' follow a narrative or a proof, and so on. Absolute presuppositions constitute the nature of our understanding within a particular universe of discourse and they govern the enquiry we undertake and the explanations we give there in individual cases.

Science tries to find things out and to explain them, and since its methods and findings are public and depend heavily on experimental testing for results and on mutual criticism within the community of practitioners, the changes that do occur in scientific practice (and in the findings and explanations offered there) reflect, at a fairly high level, standards of critical enquiry and of public rationality.

It is through such changes in scientific practice that change can occur in the organizing presuppositions themselves. Indeed, where the presuppositions of a science are unconsciously held, they can only be changed *indirectly*, by changes in scientific culture and practice itself. But these changes in scientific culture and practice can be adjudged to be based, in large measure (but not exclusively), on experiment and criticism and on time-tested disciplinary standards, arguably on rational standards; accordingly, the resultant changes that occur in the ingredient presuppositions (once we become aware of them) can be adjudged, in that same train, to be well founded. There's no good reason to deny this.

Suppose, though, a scientist (or a philosopher) takes the trouble to lay out some of the regnant ingredient presuppositions relatively clearly and to suggest significant changes or reformulations that should be made regarding them (as Einstein did in a series of famous papers, early in the last century). It doesn't follow that things will be significantly different here from what has already

direct response to Lindsay's criticisms, see *EM*, 48n. For further detail regarding Lindsay's criticism and Collingwood's response, see Editor's Endnote C, *EM*, 350–5. These same issues were raised again later by Toulmin, Stephen 1972. *Human Understanding: The Collective Use and Evolution of Concepts*, Princeton, NJ, Princeton University Press: 52–84, esp. at 74–8, 82–3.

been said. Einstein's bold conjectures didn't become presuppositions of an ongoing science overnight; rather, they had to be incorporated into the existing body of scientific practice and theory. Again, the changes in the governing presupposition(s) will not be made directly, as they would in the writing of a new law or constitution; rather, they will occur indirectly and often gradually, as a result of changes that have been introduced and incorporated into scientific culture and practice.

(b) In the Editors' Introduction to Collingwood's treatise on method it is said (p. cxii) that, though the fundamental presuppositions of science are revisable, these presuppositions cannot be subject to empirical tests that might serve to refute them.[4] Collingwood's views on the refutation (or confirmation) and on the truth status of fundamental presuppositions in the various sciences in fact underwent significant change in the 1930s. Let me chart the main phases.

Collingwood delivered two lectures at Balliol College in 1934 as part of a lecture series under the overall title 'The Nature of Metaphysical Study'. The second of the two lectures is important as perhaps Collingwood's first explicit statement, certainly his most extended one (before the *Essay on Metaphysics*), of the idea that metaphysics is peculiarly concerned to identify and to state and to clarify the main organizing principles actually present in the natural science of its own day. In this same lecture, Collingwood said as well that the task of metaphysics so conceived is to prove the truth of these background 'assumptions'.[5]

But in Collingwood's British Academy Lecture of 1936, he denied that one could 'prove' any such presupposition to be 'true'.[6] This same theme was repeated in an important sketch of

[4] *EPM*, edited by James Connelly and Giuseppina D'Oro. All pages references to EPM will be to this particular edition.

[5] See 'The Nature of Metaphysical Study' (hereafter: NMS) in the Bodleian collection of Collingwood MSS in dep. 18.2, at folio pp. 17–19. The concluding paragraphs of the first Balliol lecture and the entire second lecture, things previously unpublished, are printed in *EM*, 356–78, and the folio page numbers of the lecture(s) are printed there in bracketed bold numbers.

[6] This lecture, entitled 'Human Nature and Human History', was delivered in May 1936 and is reprinted in full in *IH* (originally published, posthumously, in 1946 by Oxford University Press under the editorship of T. M. Knox). See the current edition of *IH*, edited (with an introduction) by Jan van der Dussen, pt. V, ch. 1: 205–31, at 229–30 (esp. 230).

the main argument of the *Essay on Metaphysics*; in this sketch (written in January of 1938) Collingwood again denies, contrary to the Balliol lecture of 1934, that the governing principles of a natural science can themselves straightforwardly be described as true, let alone that they can be *proven* to be so. Or proven false, for that matter.[7]

Late in the summer of the same year (1938) in which he wrote this sketch, Collingwood wrote his *Autobiography*. And that autumn, on board ship (sailing to the East Indies), Collingwood wrote the first draft of the *Essay on Metaphysics* (that is, the first draft of Parts I and II and the essay on Kant in Part III).

In both the sketch of 1938 and in the *Metaphysics* Collingwood put forward the view that every system of enquiry—every science—has some foundation, which is from the standpoint of the practices in that enquiry logically ultimate. It is these background foundations that Collingwood referred to as fundamental or absolute presuppositions. There is, his argument continued, no clear way in which presuppositions such as these could be determined to be true or false. It is difficult to see what fact of the matter or state of the world they could be referred to in order to determine their truth value. Further, as absolute they presuppose nothing in the universe of enquiry they govern; whereas all of our network of relevant knowledge claims, by which we do determine truth or falsity in that domain, for example, by going to the facts of the world, already presuppose them. So, clearly, we cannot take the way in which we could determine, to be true or false, a statement *within* the universe of discourse organized by a fundamental presupposition to be the same as the way in which we could then determine that presupposition itself to be true or false.

[7] This sketch, previously unpublished, was entitled by Collingwood 'Function of Metaphysics in Civilization'. It is found in the Bodleian collection of Collingwood MSS in dep. 19.7. 'Function' begins in mid paragraph (as it were) in a mini essay concerned with British constitutional history. Despite this abrupt and curious beginning (on folio 29), it quickly becomes apparent that in this manuscript we have an initial sketch of what later became Part I of the *Essay on Metaphysics*. The piece is printed in *EM*, 379–421 (and the folio pages numbers of the sketch are printed there in bracketed bold numbers). The relevant folio page, which I draw on here, is 44. It should also be noted that, in the sketch (on folio 48), Collingwood repudiated his earlier use of the term 'assumption', preferring instead to use such terms as 'presupposition' and 'principles'. See also *EM*, 413 and 420–1 for further editorial adumbration.

In Collingwood's view, there simply is no way, no possible method, whereby we could *verify* (that is, confirm or disconfirm) that fundamental principles of scientific enquiry are true.[8] For verification itself always rests on presuppositions and some presuppositions, then, must necessarily escape its reach. Indeed, if we were concerned to verify a *basic* presupposition, it will be presupposed in any relevant process of verification, including any process of verifying *it*.[9] To speak of verification (empirical or otherwise) here is senseless; verification in such a case simply cannot do its job; it is out of the question. This is Wittgenstein's argument; it is also Collingwood's.[10]

Collingwood was not using the notion of verification here in the same way that the logical positivists of his day did. For them it followed that any statement, if it's not true by definition (so to speak) and not empirically verifiable either in practice or in principle, would be meaningless; it would be a pseudo-statement, one that lacked literal significance altogether.

Collingwood was neither looking for an *empirical* way to verify fundamental presuppositions nor denying they were meaningful because he couldn't find one. He was doing something radically different. Collingwood was looking at basic presuppositions systemically, taking account of the role they played within systems of enquiry, and arguing that given this role they couldn't be verified

[8] For an example of the problems, ultimately insuperable, involved in verifying (confirming or *dis*confirming) something like a fundamental presupposition (such as the schema of inference used in history in explaining actions by reference to such things as intentions and motivations of agents), see my book 1977, *Historical Explanation: Re-enactment and Practical Inference* (hereafter: *HE*), Ithaca, NY: Cornell University Press: chs 9 and 10, esp. 190–6.

[9] 'The method [of verification] will always involve two terms: a) It will involve ascertaining certain *facts*, b) it will involve presupposing certain principles. Granted these two terms, the verification will consist in what is rather rhetorically called "appealing" to those facts, which means arguing *from* those facts, *according* to those principles, to the proposition itself or its contradictory' (*EM*, 404, at folio 42; see also folio 43 and 44). It is on this understanding of verification that Collingwood says 'there is no possible method of verifying a metaphysical proposition' (*EM*, 407, at folio 44; also *EM*, 401, at folio 41).

[10] See here Wittgenstein, Ludwig *1972*. *On Certainty*, ed. Anscombe G. E. M. and Wright, G. H. von. tr. Paul, D. and Anscombe, G. E. M. New York, Harper and Row. For elaboration on this point, see my book *HE*, 198–214, esp. 203–10.

at all, certainly not in the way that the statements governed by these basic presuppositions could be verified.[11]

I have here interpreted Collingwood as saying that metaphysical principles—absolute presuppositions—are distinct from *historical* statements about absolute presuppositions. The historical statements can be true or false; one can assert that a certain presupposition governed scientific enquiry at a given time, and this assertion can be true or false (see *EM*, 54–5). But the presuppositions themselves—were they to be separated out from the complex of questions, propositions, and subordinate presuppositions they organize, were they to be formulated, and then *asserted* on their own—are not confirmable as true or false. There's simply no way to determine them (to 'prove' them, as Collingwood says in the *Idea of History*) to be true or false. Indeed it becomes difficult to identify even a sense in which they could be true or false—when they are removed from their moorings *within* a system of enquiry.

This is the consistent line Collingwood took, in the 1938 sketch and in the *Metaphysics* itself. And the clearest evidence that he hadn't bought into logical positivism was that he affirmed throughout that basic presuppositions were both useful and *meaningful*—in their role of guiding scientific enquiry—even though they were not and could not be verified, *empirically* or otherwise.[12] The place to look in order to find models or sympathetic examples of Collingwood's idea that basic presuppositions couldn't be verified would be, then, not logical positivism, which he criticized and totally rejected, but rather strong philosophical critics of that doctrine, like Wittgenstein or Quine.

(c) Some commentators have in effect claimed that there is an *essential* relationship between fundamental presuppositions, on the one hand, and Collingwood's logic of question and answer

[11] The language of 'verification', which Collingwood uses here, he no doubt took over from Ayer, A. J. 1936. *Language, Truth and Logic*, London, Gollancz, New York, Oxford University Press. The idea expressed here is not a new idea for Collingwood (an idea to be found only in 1938 or thereafter) but is clearly expressed in his British Academy Lecture of 1936 (as cited in note 6). Indeed, the British Academy Lecture (with its denial that one could 'prove' any such presupposition to be 'true') relied on the same key term that Collingwood had used earlier in 1934 in NMS.

[12] See here *EM*, 42–3, 146–53, 162–71, 193–4; 'Function of Metaphysics' in *EM*, 379–421, at folio 39–45, esp. 41–4; and, interestingly, *EPM*, at 166–7.

(understood as a logic of meaning and truth), on the other.[13] My discussion of Collingwood to this point has not taken account of this claim. But, if the claim is sound, my discussion of Collingwood's notion of absolute presuppositions would have to be given a quite different slant, and interpreted in the light of the logic of question and answer.

The argument from the logic of question and answer can be set out, briefly, in five steps.

1. All statements are answers to questions, and that which is stated (that which can be true or false) can be called a proposition (*EM*, 23–5; *A*, 31–3, 39).[14]
2. Every question involves a presupposition (*EM*, 25).
3. Some of these presuppositions stand 'relatively to one question as its presupposition and relatively to another as its answer' (*EM*, 29 (for the matter quoted), 40; *A*, 66; Collingwood calls presuppositions of this sort 'relative' presuppositions).
4. But some of these presuppositions, while presuppositions of given questions, are never answers to any question (*EM*, 31–2; *A*, 66; these Collingwood calls 'absolute' presuppositions).
5. Accordingly, absolute presuppositions are not propositions; and they are *logically* incapable of having truth values (*EM*, 32, 162; *A*, 66–7).

The structure of this argument is substantially the same in the *Essay on Metaphysics* as it was in the *Autobiography*. There is a point-by-point overlap at almost every step. And in each of these works Collingwood tied the meaning of statements in with the questions to which they were answers (*A*, 31, 33, 39; *EM*, 24–5).

I would grant, then, that the logic of question and answer, understood as a logic of meaning and truth, was integral to the actual *explication* of fundamental presuppositions in chapter 4 of the *Metaphysics*. But it was not a happy device. For, though that

[13] These commentators take the logic of question and answer as the sole or main ground for Collingwood's idea of absolute presuppositions. See e.g. Mink, Louis O. 1987. *Historical Understanding*, ed. Fay, Brian, Golob, Eugene O., and Vann, Richard T. Ithaca, NY, Cornell University Press: 269–70; Code, Lorraine 1989. 'Collingwood's Epistemological Individualism', *Monist* 72: 542–67, at 544.

[14] All references by page to *A* are to the page numbers in the present volume.

explication provided a handy way for removing truth value from these presuppositions, it also had the effect of removing meaning from them as well. The very reason Collingwood used to deny that such presuppositions can be true or false (viz. that they are not answers to questions) would also be reason to deny that they are propositions in any sense or even that they are meaningful statements.

But this won't do. The things Collingwood called absolute presuppositions of science were necessarily conceived by him to be *meaningful*. For, if absolute presuppositions were not meaningful, then they could not be supposed (by anyone who thinks about them) or be presupposed (in some sort of logical relationship) by inferior propositions, or be reasoned to and assessed by metaphysicians in their attempts to determine the grounds of scientific enquiry and explanation. And, as I've already suggested, there are alternative ways (both in the 1938 sketch and in the *Essay on Metaphysics* itself) by which Collingwood could make and did make his point about our inability to 'prove' truth values in the case of such presuppositions, and could do so without suffering the untoward results one gets from relying on the logic of question and answer.

Besides this very fundamental issue, there's another problem with Collingwood's logic of question and answer. In a recent rereading of the *Autobiography*, I noted—to my surprise—a very curious thing. At the very point (*A*, 66–7) where Collingwood introduced, for the first time, his term 'absolute presupposition' (and in this first introduction the word 'absolute' was single-quoted), he referred *six* times to such presuppositions as *beliefs*. Now, beliefs are propositional attitudes; so the point I'm making here, about presuppositions as meaningful (and about sameness of content as between suppositions and propositions), is reinforced by this point about beliefs.[15]

[15] The point I've just made about sameness of content as between suppositions and propositions is taken from Collingwood's 'Notes on Logic'. These notes, previously unpublished, were written during Collingwood's return voyage from the East Indies (in 1939) in the last few pages of a notebook on Malay phrases and grammar that Collingwood was keeping; the title I have cited was given to this particular set of notes by Collingwood himself. (The notebook can be found in the Bodleian collection of Collingwood MSS in dep. 30.) These notes are printed at *EM*, 422–7 (and the folio page numbers of these jottings on logic are printed there in bracketed bold numbers). The relevant folio pages, which I refer to here, are 18–19.

These considerations all add up to and support the claim that absolute presuppositions are propositions. Collingwood offered no sound and principled basis for denying that they were. What he says here about presuppositions as beliefs is not compatible with the logic of question and answer.

Collingwood's *Autobiography* was completed late in the summer of 1938 (and the preface was dated 2 October 1938), just before he set sail for the East Indies during which voyage he completed Part I of the *Metaphysics*.[16] The logic of question and answer (understood as a logic of meaning and truth) was one of the direct legacies conferred by Collingwood's *Autobiography* on his *Metaphysics*. That legacy can, I think, be turned aside without loss.[17]

I have in the discussion in this section quickly canvassed some of the main problems and questions that have occupied and sometimes troubled readers about Collingwood's view of metaphysics. There is one question I've saved for last. It is whether Collingwood's position was, as his first editor (T. M. Knox) and many others have claimed, radically historicist and ultimately deeply relativist, if not downright sceptical. I'll take this issue up in the next section.

3. PROGRESS IN SCIENCE

Collingwood's strong endorsement of progress in science (which he expressed and defended both in *The Idea of History* and in *An Essay on Metaphysics*) should indicate that he is not committed to

[16] The completion of *An Autobiography* and the beginning of Collingwood's draft of Parts I and II of the *Metaphysics* were separated, literally, by only a few weeks. And throughout the period of Collingwood's stay in the East Indies, and his sea voyages going and returning, work on the *Metaphysics* and correspondence about and work on the *Autobiography* (including his reading of the proofs of *A*) were intertwined, as described in the log he was keeping. See my discussion of the composition of the *Metaphysics* in my Editor's Introduction (*EM*, xv–xxi). Collingwood's 'Log of a Journey in the East Indies' (1938–1939, found in the Bodleian collection of Collingwood MSS in dep. 22.7) is published for the first time in the present (revised) edition of the *Autobiography*.

[17] For further discussion, see my article 1998, 'Collingwood's Logic of Question and Answer, its Relation to Absolute Presuppositions: A Brief History', *Collingwood Studies* 5: 122–33. See also the discussion in section 4 of Michael Beaney's chapter in the present volume.

either relativism or historicism in any negative or deleterious way. Collingwood believed that one of the competing accounts within scientific practice, say, within biology (Darwin vs the idea of fixed species) or within physics at a given time in its history (e.g. Einstein vs Newton), can be assessed as better than another, from within the perspective afforded by that practice.

What we don't have yet is a clear understanding of Collingwood's criteria for determining any such progressive improvement. Here I suggest we turn to one of his less frequently cited pieces, the short essay on progress (dating from 1936) that comes at the end of his *Idea of History* (see *IH*, Part V, section 7, 321–34). There Collingwood, talking about historical progress generically, identified two principal criteria (at *IH*, 329).

> If thought in its first phase [at some first stage], after solving the initial problems of that phase [criterion 1], is then, through solving these, brought up against others which defeat it; and if the second solves these further problems without losing its hold on the solution of the first [criterion 2], so that there is gain without any corresponding loss, then there is progress.

He then proceeded to apply this analysis of progress (in the sense of improvement over time) specifically to natural science (see *IH*, 332–4).

What is important about Collingwood's criteria is that they are called on and their content is built up in the historical process of science itself. Presumably the experience, the 'history', of engaging in science at a given time with respect to specific disputes (e.g. Darwinian vs pre-Darwinian biology, Einsteinian vs Newtonian physics), itself provides the relevant *concrete* criteria in terms of which an assessment can proceed.

These criteria make it possible to say—about two contemporaneous but competing theories within a science, or about two stages in the development of one and the same science—that science is better done by one of these theories or at one of those points than it was by or at the other. Einsteinian physics is adjudged to mark an improvement because it can handle all the data that Newtonian physics successfully incorporates (satisfying criterion 1) but it can solve some problems that Newtonian science simply can't solve (criterion 2). What happens, in short, is that the same sorts of non-controversial instances can still be handled in the progressive form of science but that the problem cases require as well the introduction of new categories and new theories which can solve the problems and deal with such problem cases on a continuing basis (see IH, 324), but 'without any corresponding loss'.

Collingwood did not restrict his discussion of scientific progress to the natural sciences. It is clear that he regarded history and archaeology, sciences that he worked in himself as a first-hand contributor, as progressive in the same way, and in accordance with the same criteria. (See, for example, *A*, ch. 8, concerned principally with archaeology, and his 1936 British Academy Lecture, concerned principally with history, and reprinted in *IH*, at 205–31.)

Absolute presuppositions, the metaphysician's ostensible subject matter, cannot be divorced from the methods, the theories, and the thematics of the sciences they ground and with which they are, ultimately and intimately, bound up. Thus, these basic principles—as determinate presuppositions, as ingredients (often implicit), of going sciences—are in a historical process of development simply because the given science that they ground is itself involved in such a process.[18]

It stands to reason, then, if we can compare pre-Darwinian to Darwinian biology (or Newtonian to Einsteinian physics or scissors-and-paste to scientific history) on the point of the betterment in knowledge and explanatory power of the one over the other, that we can treat the ingredient absolute presuppositions (the ground forms reached through philosophical analysis) of each pair as at least *involved* in this same progressive process. We have a licence, then, to make explicit and to take a look at the grounding presuppositions in each case, to see how the one that belongs to successful science might actually have contributed to this improvement and the other, as belonging to the less successful scientific programme, might have made a negative contribution, or have been unresponsive, on this same point.

Thus, where this can be done, we can assess one ingredient set of fundamental presuppositions as marking an improvement over another. Not absolutely, but only within the developing practice that the two shared in. Indeed, the very criteria by which we make

[18] The term 'process of development' I take from Collingwood; see *IH*, 162.

such judgements are found in that same process of historical development (see *IH*, 333–4).[19]

That Collingwood regarded absolute presuppositions per se as capable of standing in a relationship of progressive improvement (within a process of development) is beyond doubt, in my view. For example, he regarded the presupposition of the science of history at an earlier stage (the presupposition that there is a constant and common human nature) as inferior to the basic presuppositions characteristic of re-enactment in present-day history (though he did not make very clear what these latter presuppositions are).[20] And he regarded the monotheistic presuppositions of classical science as superior to the polytheistic ones of an even earlier proto-science.[21]

One main role of metaphysics, in Collingwood's view, is the essentially comparative and normative (or 'criteriological') one that I have been describing—the task of *assessing* progress, the task of showing, where it can be shown, that improvement has occurred as between contemporaneous scientific theories or between theories occupying two different stages in a historical process of scientific development and differentiation. In this role of assessing, with special attention paid to organizing presuppositions, metaphysics is indispensable to science, where science is understood to be itself an ongoing self-critical enterprise (see *EM*, 224, 343).

[19] For additional discussion by Collingwood on progress, besides *IH*, 321–34, see *EM*, 65, 94–6, 342–3; *NL*, 64–5 (sections 9.44–9.48). It should be noted, though, that two things, A and B, can exist within roughly the same historical process, in the course of which A has changed into B, without satisfying the criteria for progress. This was the case that held, Collingwood thought, between the 'body politic' as conceived by Plato and, later, by Hobbes (see *A*, 61–2).

[20] For Collingwood's idea of progress in the absolute presuppositions of the discipline of history, see *IH*, Part V, section 1, and *A*, 115–16. See my book *HE*, chs 1 and 2, for discussion of Collingwood's critique of the idea of human nature (itself an absolute presupposition of the incipient social sciences being developed in the seventeenth and eighteenth centuries). Louis Mink is quite right, then, (in his book *Historical Understanding*, at 265) to see Collingwood as offering a criticism and revision of that particular absolute presupposition.

[21] For Collingwood's discussion of monotheism as in a progressive relationship to polytheism, and of each as an absolute presupposition of physics, see *EM*, Part III, section A (at *EM*, 185–227). For further discussion see Connelly, James 1997. 'Natural Science, History, and Christianity . . . ', *Collingwood Studies* 4: 101–32.

4. FROM METHOD TO METAPHYSICS

Some scientific theories will actually confront one another (as the Ptolemaic and the Copernican theories of celestial movement, especially as to the relation of sun and earth, did in debate at the time of the Renaissance), but then one theory would gradually give way to the other. And this process repeats itself at later junctures. Thus, though the Newtonian or the Einsteinian theory never directly confronts the Ptolemaic, they nonetheless belong to the same process of scientific development. For these theories take full account of the Copernican revolution, while going beyond it as well.

In science the actual confrontation between theories is not between *all* the relevant theories but, rather, only between those standing in an immediate predecessor–successor relationship. And the topmost (or ultimately dominant) scientific theory in a process of development, then, usually comes far down the road (and with little direct overlap between it—say Einsteinian cosmology—and its much earlier predecessor forms, such as Aristotelian physics or Ptolemaic astronomy).

Much scientific enquiry is driven by the finding out of new things, often aided by new techniques and by technological innovations. The idea that all the instances of competing theories are the same, or can be assumed to be the same, simply won't hold for scientific theories, even for closely contemporary ones and certainly not for theories widely divided by time or by a paradigm shift.[22]

In finding new instances (instances that differ in *kind* from earlier instances), scientific theories often have to come up with new explanations or even new models of explanation. And gaps may then appear in the explanatory capacities of a given theory. An older theory, for example, might well confront problems 'which defeat it' and a newer and revisionary one might well deploy new explanations (or new models of explanation) which solve 'these further problems without losing its hold on' the solutions that the earlier theory had achieved. This process is ongoing. It is

[22] The term 'paradigm shift' is Thomas Kuhn's. See his 1996 *The Structure of Scientific Revolutions*, 3rd edition enlarged, Chicago, IL, University of Chicago Press (which includes an important Postscript, dated 1969).

driven by *critical* confrontations at its points of contemporary 'overlap' and then by carefully reasoned and experimentally checked cumulative development as time goes by. So the profile of the various reigning scientific theories, even theories of the same ostensible subject matter, will become increasingly differentiated and even disjoined over long stretches of time.

The principal concern of the *Essay on Metaphysics* is science and the history of science. The task of the metaphysician is to attempt to identify and assess the organizing presuppositions of science, at one time (the present, say) and then another (the recent past, say). This task is in sharp contrast with the 'logical' or 'conceptual analysis' model propounded in the *Essay on Philosophical Method*, where *all* the competing conceptions (each an interpretation of one and the same concept) simultaneously confront one another and modify one another on a point-by-point basis, once we reach the culminating focal stage. Here the instances of all these competing conceptions overlap completely, so that the extension of any one conception is identical to that of any other. This assumption of a wholesale overlap of classes (which Collingwood made in chapter two of the *Essay on Philosophical Method*), however useful it might be in the interpretation of a given concept, simply will not allow for the very thing that inevitably happens in a paradigm shift or over longish stretches of time in human history.

Collingwood has embedded scientific practice and its grounding presuppositions within historical processes of change—of coming to be, modification, and disappearance over time. Thus, the distinctive features of science, as a historically embedded and ongoing practice, cannot be captured by the 'method' of Collingwood's essay on method. And this is true whether the science we're interested in is a natural science or a historical one.

Collingwood's two main metaphysical treatises (the *Essay on Philosophical Method* and the *Essay on Metaphysics*) are very unlike, then, in some ways. They are quite different in aim; nonetheless, their main philosophical results are compatible and exhibit significant similarities.

The notion of cumulative development is central to each treatise. Each envisions a process of mutual criticism and mutual modification, such that the end result (though it is not necessarily the final result) is in continuity with what went before. What results is the building up of a particular series of criticisms and modifications which can then be 'summed up' into a complex body of materials which can be given a comprehensive and relatively coherent formulation.

In the one case (the one emphasized in *Method*) the formulation of cumulative development takes shape as a 'scale of forms' in which competing interpretations of a common concept are arranged in an ascending order so as to give the clearest account, at the culminating point, of the main elements contained in the organizing concept, and of the real character of its instances (up to that point). Many concepts that we are familiar with contain multiple dimensions (and thereby allow for competing interpretations of how these dimensions are best arranged). The *Essay on Philosophical Method*, with its emphasis on contested concepts, gives us a careful and valuable account of the sense in which the process of contestation is cumulative and it gives us a definite notion of the kind of progress aimed at.[23]

Progress here means reaching a better understanding of a contested concept by resolving the conflict between its competing interpretations. A successfully achieved scale of overlapping forms gives us the outline of how we can come to a progressively better understanding of such contested concepts. Understanding here represents, if you will, a notion of logical or conceptual development, a notion of progress in that sense.[24]

The *Essay on Metaphysics* affords us a careful and valuable account of how sciences, as disciplines or practices ongoing over time, may be able to provide cumulative theories, theories that cover an expanding range of instances, including instances of new kinds, with ever more fine-grained and effective explanatory capacities. Progress in science means advancement and improvement *over time* in finding new things out, without losing grip on what has already been found out, and explaining all these matters satisfactorily or, in the favoured case, more satisfactorily.

[23] The term 'contested concept' is adopted from Gallie, W. B., 1968. 'Essentially Contested Concepts' in his *Philosophy and the Historical Understanding*, 2nd edn, New York, Schocken Books: 157–91, esp. 161 and 168.

[24] For a quick account of what a successful scale of forms analysis amounts to and of the main doctrines of *EPM*, emphasizing the first hundred pages or so of that treatise, see my review 2005, of the new edition (2005) of *EPM*, in *Collingwood and British Idealism Studies* 11.2: 179–90, at 183–5.

Collingwood's emphasis on identifying and assessing the adequacy of the presuppositions of given sciences at given times is closely tied in with this account of progress.[25]

Even though the two programmes (that of *Method* and that of *Metaphysics*) are different in aim, they can work together. The two programmes can be mutually supportive of one another; there is nothing incompatible between them.

The *Essay on Philosophical Method* is not only an ancestor of sorts to the *Essay on Metaphysics*; the two bear a pronounced family resemblance, as I've just sketched. The frequent attempt to draw deep contrasts between the two treatises (amounting to a real incompatibility between them or to a 'radical conversion' in Collingwood's thought) is, I think, misplaced.[26]

5. THE OWL OF MINERVA

The writing of *An Autobiography* and of the *Metaphysics* were very close in time and, indeed, overlapped. And the claim of a 'radical conversion' in Collingwood's thought (happening somewhere in the mid 1930s and separating the *Essay on Philosophical Method* from his later writings) is even less plausible in the case of the *Autobiography* than it is for his *Metaphysics*.

Collingwood begins his *Autobiography* with the idea that 'the autobiography of a man whose business is thinking should be the story of his thought' (Author's Preface, first sentence). What prompted Collingwood to undertake this autobiographical task is something that invites speculation. He mentions ill health as providing both motivation and the time to do such a book (see *A*, 117).

The final chapter of that book provides yet another hint of what had moved Collingwood to write his autobiography. Collingwood had lived through the period of World War I, serving in the Admiralty Intelligence Division in London (see *A*, 29). In 1938,

[25] See also Bruce Haddock's discussion, in his contribution to this volume, of the 'tangible achievements of natural science' and the need to avoid radical incommensurability across theories, both of these themes found in Collingwood.

[26] The notion of a 'radical conversion' is the idea, widely held, that after 1936 Collingwood adopted the very views which he had explicitly repudiated earlier. See James Connelly's discussion of the radical conversion hypothesis in his contribution to this volume.

less than twenty years after World War I had ended, the calamitous spectre of World War II haunted Collingwood's thoughts and stimulated him to write (and rewrite) the concluding chapter, the most controversial part of the book.

Whatever the motivating background, the professed aim of his *Autobiography*, Collingwood tells us, was to provide a 'short summary' of his work to date and to 'put on record some brief account of the work I have not yet been able to publish, in case I am not able to publish it in full'. And here he makes clear that he proposes to spend all his 'available time in going on with the series' he began with the *Essay on Philosophical Method* in 1933, adding that he is now 'nearly fifty, and cannot in any case hope for more than a few years in which I can do my best work'.[27]

What with the retrospective and reflective tone of much of the book (not unexpected in an autobiography), the sense of momentary pause (of being between things), and the intimation of culminating projects to be undertaken after the brief pause (and starting off from work already accomplished or underway), one is naturally drawn to recall Hegel's famous metaphor of the owl of Minerva, which spreads its wings only with the falling of dusk.[28] It is appropriate then to ask, given Collingwood's 'short summary' of his own thought and of work he planned to do, how much does he anticipate in the *Autobiography* the things he was to write (beginning literally in weeks) in the *Essay on Metaphysics*.

There are, in fact, several things in *Metaphysics* that surprise us, even after we survey the foundation laid in *Autobiography*. In *Autobiography* Collingwood made a strong case for saying that just as 'the chief business of seventeenth-century philosophy was to reckon with seventeenth-century natural science' (*A*, 78), so the 'chief business of twentieth-century philosophy is to reckon with twentieth-century history' (*A*, 79, see also 88). One might well be surprised then to see how much of *Metaphysics* was given over to

[27] See *A*, 116–19, for the important programmatic discussion I've summarized here. Collingwood turned fifty the next year, in February 1939.

[28] The metaphor is developed at the very end of the preface to Hegel's *Philosophy of Right* (originally published in 1821). The context of Hegel's metaphor suggests that the owl is not beginning its flight at dusk but, rather, ending it then and settling onto its perch, for a time. The editors of the present edition of the *Autobiography* suggested 'The Owl of Minerva' to me as the title of the present chapter; I have used it instead as the title of its final section.

natural science and to the history of science (and of philosophy and theology).

Collingwood, in the *Autobiography*, identified his *Essay on Philosophical Method* as the jumping-off point in the series of books and other writings that he planned next to turn his hand to. Collingwood, however, provided almost no detail, regarding the content or themes of *Method*, in what he said in his *Autobiography*. Moreover, the notion that something on the subject of metaphysics might constitute part of a *continuing* series with what he'd said in *Essay on Philosophical Method* was not spelled out in the *Autobiography*.[29] So the *details* of connection that I have sketched and that others have sketched, between these two treatises, would also be something unanticipated on the basis of one's reading of what Collingwood had said in his 'short summary' of his own thought and work in *Autobiography*.

The *Autobiography* has several chapters devoted to issues in logic (*A*, ch. 5) or to issues in what might be called general philosophy. In this book we do find highly critical remarks aimed by Collingwood at the philosophers (denominated 'Realists') who were among his tutors at Oxford and who, in his view, dominated philosophy there and at Cambridge during the time he was a lecturer and a professor at Oxford. (See *A*, chs 3, 4, 6, 7 and, for Collingwood's sharply critical summing up of their legacy, see 166–7; for further discussion of Collingwood on 'Oxbridge' realism see the chapter by Michael Beaney in the present volume.)

Curiously, though, what is missing in the *Autobiography* is *any* real discussion or even mention, by name, of logical positivism.[30] I was very struck by this in a recent rereading of *Autobiography*. So, this is a third point, and perhaps the major one, where we could not—from the discussion of philosophy in the 1930s in the *Autobiography*—anticipate the important bearing that logical

[29] For additional evidence that Collingwood saw continuity between *Method* and *Metaphysics*, see Editor's Endnote A, in *EM*, 344–8, esp. 347.

[30] Collingwood does say that propositional logic, as worked out by Russell and Whitehead, 'has inspired a school of thought which is continuing the good work of jettisoning whatever can be recognized as positive doctrine by reviving the old positivist attack on metaphysics' (*A*, 52). The phrase 'a school of thought' may here be an oblique reference to the logical positivists, but the 'old positivist attack' is a clear reference to the nineteenth-century positivism of Mill and others. And this is literally *all* we get on the logical positivists in Collingwood's *Autobiography*.

positivism might have on what Collingwood had to say about metaphysics.[31]

But there is, of course, one point at which an important theme of the *Essay on Metaphysics* can be anticipated from what Collingwood had said in his *Autobiography*. I mean Collingwood's argument (in *EM*, ch. 4) that absolute presuppositions are not propositions and that they cannot have truth values, let alone be *proven* to be true or false. This argument was anticipated in the *Autobiography* in Collingwood's presentation of the logic of question and answer (*A*, ch. 5 and pp. 66–7). Indeed, the argument in *Metaphysics* maps the one in *Autobiography* almost point by point, as I showed earlier. But I also suggested that this argument, based on the logic of question and answer (understood as a logic of meaning and truth), was not a good argument and had, I suggested, serious and unwanted consequences for Collingwood's account of fundamental presuppositions.

The criticism just mentioned concerned *one* line, the main line, of Collingwood's discussion of the logic of question and answer. This particular line of discussion envisioned questions and answers as arranged in a hierarchical order: (i) propositions (answers) at the bottom, so to speak, (ii) superintended by questions, which in turn were (iii) superintended by presuppositions, (iv) some of which were presuppositions that were not answers to *any* question; these superordinate presuppositions, the last or highest in the hierarchical series, were called by Collingwood *absolute* presuppositions.

But there was another line that Collingwood took in his discussion of the logic of question and answer. This second line did not exhibit the simple sort of hierarchical ordering that I've just laid out. Moreover, in this second line, it is mainly the issue of truth and falsity that is in play; meaningfulness is not a primary issue, and is assumed throughout.

[31] Collingwood did, however, in his 1938 sketch entitled 'Function of Metaphysics' (written before the *Autobiography*) discuss logical positivism; see *EM*, 398 (at folio 39) and for more extensive discussion see *EM* 401 (folio 41, at the date) continuing on in *EM* 402–13 (folio 42–7 (esp. 44–5)). And of course Collingwood discussed both positivism and logical positivism in the *Metaphysics*, esp. in ch. 14 (Mill and positivism) and in ch. 16 (Ayer and logical positivism); see also *EM*, 5, 19, and ch. 34.

Here, jumping off from his denial that 'a proposition . . . defined as the unit of thought [is] that which is true or false' (*A*, 36), Collingwood goes on to say, 'What is ordinarily meant when a proposition is called "true" [is this:] the proposition belongs to a question-and-answer complex which as a whole is "true" in the proper sense of the word' (*A*, 38; see also 37).[32] The idea here is that a complex of statements and answers and suppositions is the basic unit of thought; 'each question and each answer in a given complex had to be relevant or appropriate, had to "belong" both to the whole and to the place it occupied in the whole' (*A*, 37). It is the *whole* complex, made up of these elements, that is the proper subject, and the venue, of judgements about truth or falsity.[33]

Something like the notion of such a complex has been entertained by such eminent and diverse thinkers as Pierre Duhem and Willard V. O. Quine. They are ordinarily taken to say that a belief (say, a scientific hypothesis) belongs to a whole scheme of beliefs and suppositions; the totality of these beliefs and suppositions constitute the basic unit of discourse. Thus, the test of a given hypothesis is in effect a test of the whole scheme; where called for, adjustments can be made throughout the entire scheme (any part of which is revisable in principle).[34]

Collingwood did add one interesting wrinkle to his idea of a complex of statements and questions when he revisited that idea

[32] Collingwood did not, however, make sufficiently clear what he meant by '"true" in the proper sense of the word'.

[33] A complex of statements and questions and suppositions can be true *as a whole*—though not necessarily true in each of its parts.

[34] For helpful discussion, see Hesse, Mary 1970. 'Duhem, Quine, and a New Empiricism', in *Knowledge and Necessity*, Royal Institute of Philosophy Lectures, vol. 3, London, Macmillan, New York, St. Martin's Press: 191–209; and see Gillies, Donald 1998. 'The Duhem Thesis and the Quine Thesis', in Curd, Martin and Cover, J. A. (eds). *Philosophy of Science: The Central Issues*, New York, Norton: 302–19. See Quine, W. V. O., 1980. *From a Logical Point of View*, 2nd revised edition, Cambridge, MA, Harvard University Press (1st edition 1953) and 1960. *Word and Object*, Cambridge, MA, MIT Press. Jonathan Gorman makes a careful attempt to bring Quine's holistic views into the context of historiography and the philosophy of history in ch. 4 of his 2008 book, *Historical Judgement*, Montreal and Kingston, Canada, Ithaca, NY, McGill-Queens University Press: esp. at 139–63. Collingwood's idea of absolute presuppositions is mentioned in passing here, but no reference is made to Collingwood's idea of a (true) complex of beliefs and suppositions.

one further time at the very conclusion of his discussion of absolute presuppositions in the *Autobiography*. Here he said that 'the beliefs of a given set of people at a given time concerning the nature of the world are exhibited as a single complex of contemporaneous fact, like, say, the British constitution as it stands today' (*A*, 67). What I find interesting about this example is the suggestion that the complex isn't made up simply of questions and answers and presuppositions. Rather, if the British constitution is the model for our 'beliefs' about the 'nature of the world', then the whole in question is more like a complex institutional arrangement or practice that would extend over not just the usual question-and-answer stuff, fundamental presuppositions included, but also over ways of doing things, expectations, constitutive rules, and so forth.[35]

The idea of such a complex whole could be grafted onto and integrated with the account given earlier of science as a system of enquiry, as a complex arrangement or practice designed to find things out and then explain them. It would then nest very nicely into one of the main themes of the *Essay on Metaphysics*.

Practices as a whole are not typically called true (or false) but, rather, sound or unsound, effective or ineffective (given what they're trying to do). And so we would want to say about science as a complex practice. It is, at its best, a sound practice when the statements of the facts it finds are credible and the explanations it offers are convincing (in ways that can be critically and experimentally tested), and where it raises questions that can lead to new enquiry, which may give us both new and well-confirmed results but also revisions and even rejections of old findings and of existing beliefs. But if our explanatory practices or investigations should prove inadequate, in any of a variety of ways, then we change what we do.[36]

Collingwood's idea of a whole comprising 'the beliefs of a given set of people at a given time concerning the nature of the world... exhibited as a single complex of contemporaneous fact'—his idea of a scientific *practice* as centring on a complex of beliefs and

[35] Besides what he had said in *A* there are two other joinings, in Collingwood's writings, of the British constitution with metaphysical presuppositions—one very brief (*EM*, 77) and the other more extended. The latter is found in 'Function of Metaphysics' (at *EM*, 379–80, at folio 29).

[36] For more on this point, see my discussion in *HE*, at 210–13, 240.

suppositions—would provide one very valuable extension into *Metaphysics* of an interesting and fruitful idea from the *Autobiography*. But this idea, found in the *Autobiography*, was *not* in the later work.

We could take this then as yet another example of *Autobiography* failing to anticipate the developments in thought that Collingwood made in *Metaphysics*. But we could equally take it as a lost opportunity to steer the logic of question and answer away from perilous shoals, and to head it into open water and in a promising direction.[37]

[37] *A* and *EM*, though close in time and with some overlap in content, are quite different books. My point in section 5 has not been to suggest discrepancies between them (for they are not drafts or versions of the same project). Rather, my concern here has been to ask how much of *EM* was anticipated in the earlier book, given that *A* had, avowedly, mentioned or developed important programmatic features respecting Collingwood's future work.

8

COLLINGWOOD AND EUROPEAN LIBERALISM

DAVID BOUCHER

Liberalism is one of those evaluative descriptive terms whose mention evokes among many Western intellectuals feelings of approval and warmth. Throughout the latter part of the twentieth century and the early years of the twenty-first, Anglo-American political theory defined itself in terms of the concept of liberalism. Scarcely a book went through the press on a wide variety of political issues that did not include the concept in its title, or in some way invoke, develop, or address 'liberal principles'. Our leading political philosophers graced the bookshelves with such titles as *The Modern Liberal Theory of Man*; *Multicultural Citizenship: A Liberal Theory of Minority Rights*; *Political Liberalism*; *Justificatory Liberalism; The Liberal Archipelago*; and more recently, reflecting the general trend among theorists to encompass the long-neglected international dimension, *A Liberal Theory of International Justice*.[1] Such books extolled the virtues of freedom, an open society, and manner of acting and thinking deemed to be far superior to any alternatives so far available, so powerful in its persuasiveness that it reached its self-congratulatory epitome after the fall of the Berlin Wall in Francis Fukuyama's *The End of History and the Last Man*.[2]

[1] Gaus, Gerald F. 1983. *The Modern Liberal Theory of Man*, London and Canberra, Croom Helm; Kymlicka, Will 1995. *Multicultural Citizenship: A Liberal Theory of Minority Rights*, Oxford, Oxford University Press; Rawls, John 1995. *Political Liberalism*, Princeton, Princeton University Press; Kukathus, Chandran, 2003. *The Liberal Archipelago: A Theory of Diversity and Freedom*, Oxford, Oxford University Press; Altman, Andrew and Wellman, Christopher Heath 2009. *A Liberal Theory of International Justice*, Oxford, Oxford University Press.

[2] Fukuyama, Francis 1993. *The End of History and the Last Man*, London, Penguin Books.

Despite the many attempts to define it, the concept remains elusive, tolerating a wide variety of views to be encompassed under its auspices, ranging from the extreme libertarianism of the nineteenth-century libertarian eccentric Herbert Spencer, to the collectivist radicalism of his near contemporaries L. T. Hobhouse and J. A. Hobson. Stephen Toulmin has described liberalism as an historical population of ideas, not all of which are logically or inextricably related, allowing for both unity and diversity.[3] Its history has been chequered and its travails many, testimony to its character as an achievement rather than an endowment.

European liberalism is perhaps even more amorphous than its British counterpart, and has certainly had a more turbulent history, forged in the face of constant threat. In this respect its challenges have a closer analogy, for example, to the Taiwanese struggle for freedom and democracy after forty years of military rule by Chiang Kai Shek and his successors, than with British liberalism.[4]

There is much in European liberalism that is non-political with a general emphasis upon freedom, morality, and justice, and a tendency among some of its leading twentieth-century exponents not to define it, but instead to characterize it by reference to its history. This is particularly true of the Italians Benedetto Croce and Guido de Ruggiero and the Spaniards Miguel de Unamuno and José Ortega y Gasset, all of whom fought for its principles against a rising tide of fascism.[5] Ortega y Gasset is representative of them when he contends: 'Liberalism – it is well to recall this today–is the supreme form of generosity; it is the right which the majority concedes to minorities and hence it is the noblest cry that has ever resounded this planet.'[6]

[3] Toulmin, Stephen 1972. *Human Understanding*, Vol. One, Princeton, Princeton University Press.

[4] Roy, Denny 2003. *Taiwan: A Political History*, Ithaca and London, Cornell University Press.

[5] Unamuno, Miguel de 1921. *The Tragic Sense of Life in Men and Peoples*, translated by John Ernest Crawford Flitch, London, Macmillan; Ortega y Gasset, José 1993. *The Revolt of the Masses*, New York, Norton, first published in Spanish in 1930; Ruggiero, Guido de 1927. *European Liberalism*, translated by Collingwood R. G., London, Macmillan; Croce, Benedetto 1941. *History as the Story of Liberty*, translated by Sylvia Sprigge, New York, Norton.

[6] Ortega y Gasset, *Revolt of the Masses*, 76.

The emphasis tends to be not upon positive and negative freedom, but instead on the more inclusive concept recognized by McCallum and Feinberg. Negative and positive freedom are not two distinct types of freedom. On the contrary, McCallum contends, it is one concept which has three related elements each of which has a referent comprising (i) a statement about an agent (ii) who is constrained or unconstrained (iii) to do a particular act or to be a particular something.[7] Put succinctly: 'X is free from Y to do or be Z.' Freedom is never either/or, negative or positive, but always simultaneously both. For example, to be free *from* hunger requires being free *from* certain obstacles—social, agricultural-economic, political—which when absent renders me free *to* stave off hunger by the acquisition of food. While there is one concept of liberty or freedom, there are many conceptions of it, for instance, freedom as the absence of impediments; as the availability of choice; possessing a certain power, or having a certain status, etc.[8]

I want in this chapter to explore R. G. Collingwood's conception of liberalism in relation to the sources that inspired him, and the context in which he developed his ideas. Cambridge realism in the guise of Bertrand Russell, G. E. Moore, and the early Ludwig Wittgenstein, and the Oxford realism of John Cook Wilson, H. H. Prichard, E. F. Carritt, and W. D. Ross had come to prominence during his formative years. Collingwood's work, as the *Autobiography* attests, is a sustained engagement with and rejection of realism. He rejected realism and its outgrowth, logical positivism, and looked for inspiration in continental philosophy in the Hegelian tradition. Collingwood looked to Hegel, but more importantly to the Italian idealists, Gentile, Croce, and de Ruggiero, and purported to go beyond idealism and realism in logic, metaphysics, and moral philosophy.

In these respects Oakeshott, Collingwood's near contemporary, remained more faithful to the idealist heritage. Both, however, early in their careers, wrote books that were firmly in the Absolute idealist tradition. Collingwood's *Speculum Mentis* and Oakeshott's

[7] McCallum, Jr., Gerald C. 1967. 'Negative and Positive Freedom', *Philosophical Review*: 334. Cf. Fienberg, Joel 1992. *Rights, Justice and the Bounds of Liberty*, Princeton, Princeton University Press: 5.

[8] Gray, Tim 1990. *Freedom*, London, Macmillan.

Experience and Its Modes[9] explored the different modes or forms of experience which constituted different worlds of ideas in terms of which we order experience. Oakeshott and Collingwood had very different conceptions of the relationship between theory and practice. For Oakeshott, practice was a separate mode of experience and distinct from, and immune to, the theoretical intrusions from the other modes, and from philosophy itself. For Collingwood, however, all theoretical problems begin in the world of practice, and return to it. Each of his forms of experience has both theoretical and practical overlapping features. Collingwood argues, for example, that 'in every field of activity there is a theoretical element, in virtue of which the mind is aware of something; there is a practical element in virtue of which the mind is bringing about a change in itself and in its world'.[10]

Collingwood held very different political views from Oakeshott and saw himself as a liberal in the European sense. He was opposed to the class-based politics of socialism, but not to state interventionist policies that eradicated inequalities and which provided equalities of opportunities. I have suggested elsewhere that Collingwood's political views did not shift radically to the left, and despite accusations to the contrary by such commentators as Joseph Needham, Collingwood always was and remained a liberal in the continental sense, by which he meant not classical laissez-faire liberalism, but the sort of liberalism espoused by T. H. Green and L. T. Hobhouse, and particularly that of Guido de Ruggiero, whose *European Liberalism* Collingwood translated in 1927, and that of the Spaniard Miguel de Unamuno, whose *The Tragic Sense of Life in Men and in Peoples* he recommended to Macmillan, who published it in 1921 (*EPP*, Introduction 1–51).[11]

[9] Oakeshott, Michael 1933. *Experience and Its Modes*, Cambridge, Cambridge University Press.

[10] Collingwood, R. G. 1964 [1925], *Outlines of a Philosophy of Art*, reprinted in *Essays in the Philosophy of Art*, ed. Donagan Alan, Bloomington, Indiana University Press: 50.

[11] Also see Boucher, David 1989. *The Social and Political Thought of R. G. Collingwood*, Cambridge, Cambridge University Press: chapter 5. The correspondence of R. G. Collingwood recently made available by his daughter Teresa Smith makes Collingwood's connection to European liberalism clearer, especially in relation to Miguel de Unamuno.

During the course of translating de Ruggiero's book, Collingwood wrote to the author on 2 September 1926 confessing that: 'The political principles expounded and implied are at every point my own, and expressed with a justness and completeness that leave me nothing to do but express my complete agreement.' We may take it, then, that Collingwood's summary of these principles in the translator's preface to *European Liberalism* was a characterization of the principles to which both men subscribed. These principles include constitutional liberty and representative government, based on the assumption that men are free and that their acts spring from their own personalities without coercion. Liberalism is not something possessed at birth; it is rather an achievement and not a gift. Finding inspiration in T. H. Green, de Ruggiero argued that: 'Men are not born free, they become free by means of society and the State.... This is the great distinction between the liberal conceptions of the eighteenth and nineteenth centuries. The one places liberty at the beginning, the other at the end, of the historical process.'[12] In addition, he maintains that 'men are not born free but become free. This applies both to the life of the individual and to the historical life of humanity.'[13]

The principles are gradually acquired through the self-conscious possession or development of personality by the exercise of discipline and the deliberate cultivation of progress in moral action. The function of a liberal state is to facilitate the individual's self-discipline to assist in the attainment of moral progress, rejecting the opposite extremes of forcing upon the individual a project for which he or she is ill prepared, or of leaving that person alone, 'depriving him of that aid to progress which a political system, wisely designed and wisely administered can give'.[14] De Ruggiero's conclusion was optimistic for the prospects of liberalism against the hostile forces of continental illiberalism. It is the conviction that reasonableness in the long run defeats its enemies, and that in the conflict of tendencies and ideas the most rational survive. Ortega y Gasset was to echo this faith in liberalism in 1930 when he argued that liberalism had greater vitality than

[12] Ruggiero, Guido de 1927. *The History of European Liberalism*, translated by Collingwood, R. G., Oxford, Oxford University Press: 32.

[13] de Ruggiero, *European Liberalism*, 354.

[14] de Ruggiero, *European Liberalism*, ix.

anti-liberalism and had proved itself victorious time and time again. It was for him endangered by the rise of mass man, and without minimizing the immensity of the task he believed that liberalism could triumph.[15] Political liberty in the long run would never fail because it is 'inevitably a part of the very substance of European life, and will be returned to when its presence is truly required, in the hour of grave crisis'.[16]

In *An Autobiography* Collingwood reaffirms his commitment to liberalism at a time when it was subject to even greater dangers than those perceived by de Ruggiero and Ortega y Gasset. Collingwood proclaimed that he had always been a liberal in the continental sense, and what translates as democratic in the British context. For him this entailed a universally acknowledged right to free speech; an obligation of each citizen to vote, informed by a sound political education facilitated by the dissemination of a wide variety of views expressed in a free press (*A*, 153). In this context the *New Leviathan* constitutes a study in the development of rational consciousness by which freedom develops, morality progresses, and liberal principles inform political decisions which will eventually win out against fascism and Nazism. Collingwood saw the rise of fascism and Nazism first-hand during his various travels to the continent of Europe, and also was aware of developments within Italy from his correspondence with de Ruggiero.

Collingwood was also, however, an admirer of the actualism of the early Gentile, who later became the philosopher of fascism, and the allusion to his philosophy in *The New Leviathan* may make his renunciation of the Italian in *An Autobiography* appear disingenuous. This, I think, would be a mistake. Collingwood never accepted Gentile's position uncritically. In the 'Libellus de Generatione' of 1920, which Collingwood sent to de Ruggiero as a gift, Collingwood refers to Gentile's dialectic of *pensante* (the act of thinking) and *pensato* (the content of thought). For Gentile the *pensante* is outside time in that it creates *Pensato*, the content of thought. The product of *pensante* always happens in time. Collingwood criticizes Gentile for taking up a position similar to that of Spinoza, that is, of identifying the *pensante* with the pure act of

[15] Ortega y Gasset, *Revolt of the Masses*, 104. Cf. 94–6.
[16] de Ruggiero, *European Liberalism*, 441.

thought, in which all experience is reduced to thought, and in particular philosophical thought.

By 1923 Collingwood was adopting a more favourable view of Gentile. Collingwood argues that the mind which originates change itself is at once inside and outside time. Collingwood argues: 'as the source and ground of change, it will not be subject to change; while on the other hand, as undergoing change through its own free act, it will exhibit change'.[17]

Collingwood emphasized, more than Gentile did himself, the historical character of the Italian's philosophy. Collingwood maintains that reality is history, and that history is the knowing mind become conscious of itself. It is by being self-conscious of this history that mind has a history at all. Collingwood contends that 'Gentile's philosophy is a "metaphysic of knowledge", that is to say, a philosophy which never loses sight of the question "how do we come to know what we know?".'[18]

His position, however, continued to develop. In 1926 he writes to de Ruggiero: 'For myself, I am trying to clear up my conception of History – helped greatly, but not wholly satisfied, by both Croce and Gentile, and developing further the view expressed in *Speculum Mentis*. And always pursuing the study of history itself.'[19] In fact, he came to view Gentile's position as little more than a 'fossilized or arthritic version' of Croce's.[20] What Collingwood objects to is the implication of an eternal present which creates its own past, an abstraction, which does not take the past up into itself but instead defecates one out of itself. Gentile concentrates his attention on the epistemological problems of the historian creating the past and forming his own perspective of it, while completely neglecting to address the relation of the perspectives to each other. This is, for Collingwood, a form of subjective idealism which wholly overlooks the problem of development,

[17] Collingwood, R. G. 1968. 'Can the New Idealism Dispense with Mysticism?', in *Faith and Reason: Essays in the Philosophy of Religion* by Collingwood, R. G., ed., Rubinoff, Lionel, Chicago, University of Chicago Press: 275.

[18] Collingwood, 'Can the New Idealism Dispense with Mysticism?', 274.

[19] Letter from R. G. Collingwood to Guido de Ruggiero, 18 August 1926.

[20] Collingwood, R. G. 1999. 'Notes Towards a Metaphysic' (1933–1934), in *The Principles of History and Other Writings in the Philosophy of History*, ed. Dray, W. H. and Dussen, W. J. van der, Oxford, Oxford University Press: 127.

'with the result that Fascist thought, egocentric and subjective, can rightly be called by Croce *antistoricismo*'.[21]

De Ruggiero's thought, as encountered in *European Liberalism*, was much more conducive to Collingwood's way of thinking than either Croce's or Gentile's. For de Ruggiero, the foundational principle of liberalism is the repudiation of all reductionist interpretations of human action. In their place is the assertion of spiritual freedom in which individual consciousness and the expression of the self develop unimpeded. Only free persons, autonomous intelligent human agents, are capable of acknowledging and recognizing the possession of freedom by others.[22] By the pure act of thinking, the human mind creates the experience of which it is conscious. De Ruggiero's 'actualism', in contrast with that of Giovanni Gentile, emphasizes the spiritual development of the individual, not in terms of dominating others by subordinating their wills, but in terms of the liberation of the self from internal passions and external constraint.

The emphasis upon the historical character of mind is reiterated by Collingwood in *The New Leviathan*: 'Man as mind *is whatever he is conscious of being*.' In other words, 'mind is "pure act", so that *what mind is* resolves itself without residue into the question *what mind does*' (*NL*, 7, §1.84 and 61, §9.17.). This should not be taken as an endorsement of Gentile, who takes an extreme view of what in different forms found expression in many idealists. Henry Jones, for example, suggested that: 'A thing is what it does.... A thing that does nothing *is* nothing. Strip an object of its activities, and see what remains: You will find nothing.'[23]

In his private correspondence Collingwood expressed his views both about fascism and Gentile, although he was constrained by de Ruggiero's view that the cause of Italian anti-fascism would be harmed by foreigners openly critical of the government from outside.[24] Writing to Ethel, his first wife, from Terminio Hotel, Napoli, on what he thinks is 5 February 1932, Collingwood

[21] Collingwood, 'Notes Towards a Metaphysic', 128–9.

[22] de Ruggiero, *European Liberalism*, 357.

[23] Jones, Henry 1922. *A Faith That Enquires*, the Gifford Lectures 1920–1921, London, Macmillan: 242. In *Speculum Mentis* Collingwood refers to Henry Jones as 'one of our most eminent philosophers', 73–4.

[24] Letter to Ethel dated 2 February 1932 from Albergo e Ristorante della Stella. [TS/PLR108].

commented on the rise of fascism and the demonstrations that he witnessed in Formia: 'beastly town and all full of loutish Fascist demonstrations, brass band and banners, sending off cruisers to Shanghai'. Later that same month, in a letter to Isobel Munro, Collingwood dismisses fascism in general and Gentile in particular. Collingwood contends that: 'the most obvious and incontrovertible item in the count against Fascismo is that it has killed its own philosophy absolutely dead—if you doubt it read Gentile's *Filosofia dell'arte* and blush'.[25]

Two years before he wrote this, Collingwood holidayed in Spain with his wife Ethel and Isobel Munro. On his return he compiled an extensive travelogue comprising a series of letters he sent to his father, in which he exquisitely describes the landscape, architecture, and Roman remains. He says little of the politics, other than to comment on his perception of Spain as historically fragmented. He contends that Spain is more of a geographical expression than a political organism, and lacks a central focus, which Madrid singularly failed to provide. He speculates that this must be the reason why its modern history has been a series of despotisms, both political and religious. Autocrats and inquisitors seemed to do what they liked with the country because it lacked a national unity. It is this very lack of unity, however, that contributed to the failure of the imposition of their various projects.[26] Five days later, on 22 October, he returned to the subject of politics while reflecting upon the importance of the University of Salamanca and Miguel de Unamuno in restoring freedom to Spain.

Miguel de Unamuno was a Spanish Basque poet, dramatist, and novelist, but it was largely as a discursive prose writer that he was known in Britain. He was a political radical who campaigned for social justice and international freedom, and who was dismissed from his position as Rector of Salamanca in 1914 for his political views. The Spanish dictator Miguel Primo de Rivera had him exiled to the Canary Islands in 1924, but the restriction was lifted amid an international outcry. He returned to Spain in 1930, the year that Collingwood visited. In 1931 he was elected to the

[25] To Isobel Munro from the British School in Athens, 29 ii, 1932. [TS/PLR123].

[26] Collingwood ms., 1930: Vol I 41-2. [TS/PLR113]. Vol II Photographs [TS/PHT258].

reconstituted Spanish Parliament where he was as rigorous an opponent of the Second Republic as he had been of de Rivera. His reputation as a fighter for freedom was so well known in England that he gained honorary degrees from the Universities of London, Oxford, and Cambridge in 1936. Collingwood's observation on de Unamuno demonstrates without doubt his longstanding commitment to the principle of freedom, and of social liberalism. He commented to his father on 22 October that the University of Salamanca interests him because:

> it had been involved in recent events of importance through its connexion with a man of whom I had long known. There is a philosopher of some distinction in Spain, Miguel Unamuno; and several years ago I was the means of having his chief work translated into English. It impressed me very deeply, not as a contribution to philosophical science, but as the expression of a *forma mentis* which I took to be Spain at its best – a way of looking at things which one might nickname *hidalguesque*, on the analogy of gentlemanly. Later, when the Dictatorship came in, Unamuno was banished because (like so many philosophers) he believed in freedom and objected to being told what he must think, and say and do. This summer he returned from banishment and appeared in Salamanca, where those decent quiet undergraduates gathered round him and began a movement which has now led to the restoration of constitutional government.... it was in these cloisters that Unamuno had worked for the freedom of the Spanish people, and that, in its way, deserves to be remembered alongside of the events which drove Marmont out of Salamanca in 1812 and freed Spain from the French.

The book that Collingwood was instrumental in getting translated and published was *The Tragic Sense of Life in Men and Peoples*, originally published in Spanish in 1913, and published in English by Macmillan in 1921. The introductory essay by S. de Madariaga sums up what was characteristic of de Unamuno, but which may also be said to epitomize his fellow Spaniard Ortega y Gasset, the Italian de Ruggiero, and the Englishman R. G. Collingwood. All three were men of strong passions. Strong passions, de Madariago contends, 'urge man to action'.[27] It is these strong passions that impelled Collingwood to profess his sympathy for gloves-off philosophers fighting against those who philosophized behind college gates for the amusement of fellow philosophers, in *An Autobiography* (1939); to fight

[27] Unanumo, *Tragic Sense of Life*, xi.

against irrationalism by defending metaphysics in the face of a peril that threatened European civilization in *An Essay on Metaphysics* (1940); and to make evident what was at stake against the forces of barbarism during World War II in *The New Leviathan* (1942).

De Unamuno's work of modernist experimentation was a reflective, discursive commentary that meets few of the requirements of rigour or consistent argument, but which is nevertheless evocative of the spirit of freedom that drew Collingwood towards de Ruggiero's *History of European Liberalism*. Between 1923 and 1929 de Unanumo wrote a series of newspaper articles decrying the corruption of the governments of the Restoration political system (1875–1923), and Primo de Rivera after the coup d'état of 13 September 1923. He characterizes European civilization as exhausted in the face of onslaughts from Communism and dogmatic socialism against individualism and spirituality throughout the continent.[28] De Unamuno pleads for a rediscovery of deeper European values in the spiritual roots of its peoples. If Europe was to be saved it needed to be reinvigorated by a religious renaissance. In essence, this entailed what Gerald Gauss has identified as a common feature of the principal modern liberal thinkers, namely a reconciliation between 'the pursuit of individuality with sociality and membership in a community'.[29] It was such a reconciliation that Collingwood strived to bring about by suggesting that the values that lay at the heart of European civilization were those of the Christian religion, and whether one was religious or not, the values that underpinned the sanctity of the individual, and social responsibilities towards our neighbours, are derived from the spiritual beliefs of Christianity which were threatened by the excessive utilitarianism of the age, in which emotions and superstition were derided and expunged by utilitarian instrumental reasoning.[30] Indeed, this was one of the impassioned pleas of de Unamuno's *Tragic Sense of Life*, that is, for giving priority to passion over rationality, faith over reason.

[28] Unamuno, Miguel de 1996. *Political Speeches and Journalism* (1923–1929), ed. Roberts, G. H., Exeter, University of Exeter Press: 3–9.

[29] Gauss, Gerald F. 1986. *The Modern Liberal Theory of Man*, London and Canberra, Croom Helm: 3–4.

[30] See, for example, Collingwood, 'Fascism and Nazism', 170–1.

In his political speeches de Unamuno discusses liberalism in much broader than ideological terms. His understanding of liberalism, because of its religious roots, is both spiritual and individualistic, emphasizing not just the rights, but also the duties of the citizen. Politically liberalism was for him, as it became for Collingwood, a method in which political parties and individual citizens engage in debate in the formation of public opinion.[31] Like de Ruggiero in Italy, and the social liberals in England, such as T. H. Green, Henry Jones, and L. T. Hobhouse, de Unamuno rejected dogmatic class-based socialism, but favoured that kind which worked for a more just, fairer, and less corrupt liberal state. Indeed, he praises the Party Secretary of Partido Socialista Obrero Español (PSOE), Pablo Iglesias, for striving towards the achievement of a more socially responsible state. This kind of socialism is almost indistinct from liberalism as he understood it, and was one to which all social liberals could subscribe. Indeed, that was how Croce and de Ruggiero understood it in common with many of their British counterparts. Croce acknowledged that socialism had made a positive contribution to the advancement of liberalism by enabling liberalism in the public eye to escape from its identification with economic freedom.[32] There could be no compromise between liberalism and socialism at the level of ideals, but at the level of political practice liberalism could learn from socialism. Both Croce and de Ruggiero abhorred Communism and authoritarian, or mechanical, socialism based upon pernicious class divisions. The kind of socialism of which they strongly approved was the kind that taught liberalism that abstract formulations and declarations of individual rights and duties often vindicated the power of the strong over the weak. To make such declarations of rights a reality for everyone they had to be accompanied by positive sanctions. De Ruggiero contended that, 'by following the action of Socialism for the improvement of wages and the general condition of the working classes, Liberalism has had occasion to see how groundless were the arguments by which employers justified their stubborn resistance'.[33] Croce took

[31] De Unamuno, *Political Speeches and Journalism*, 39–40.

[32] Croce, Benedetto 1934. *History of Europe in the Nineteenth Century*, translated by Furst, Henry, London, Allen and Unwin: 313.

[33] De Ruggiero, *European Liberalism*, 394.

England as an example of how socialism had become absorbed by liberalism. Even the Fabians, he maintained, were liberal in spirit.[34]

All three are committed to developing education to facilitate debate and independence of mind in order to question and challenge the prevailing dogmas of the day. De Unamuno is in fact an advocate of the free formation of public opinion, and the development of a more just society in which that can be attained in the context of a parliamentary system of government, itself responsive to public opinion.[35]

At the time of writing his *An Autobiography* in 1938 and 1939, events in Europe clearly threatened the ideals of democracy and liberalism that Collingwood cherished. He wrote to *The Times* to complain of the complacency of his Oxford colleagues, and visited the Labour Party headquarters to try to persuade its leaders to reject appeasement. The appeasement policy of the prime minister, in his view, was likely 'to make a European War inevitable'.[36]

There were many people in Oxford disillusioned with the foreign policy of the prime minister, Mr Chamberlain, and who believed that he either did not have a foreign policy, or that he was concealing his intentions from the nation and from the cabinet because he feared that he would not get its support. Appeasement, it was believed, was a threat to British democracy, and simply postponed the same fate for Britain as that of Czechoslovakia. There was evidence that the British government was not seeing to it that even the humiliating conditions of the settlement were being respected by Germany. A. D. Lindsay, the Master of Balliol, put himself forward as the voice of anti-appeasement in the 1938 Oxford by-election, in opposition to the Conservative Quintin Hogg. Although a member of the Labour Party, Lindsay offered himself as the Independent Progressive Candidate representing all those from whatever party who were profoundly disturbed by the government's foreign policy. He had the support of both the Oxford Labour and Liberal parties, who agreed not to field candidates.

[34] Croce, *History of Europe in the Nineteenth Century*, 309.

[35] De Unamuno, *Political Speeches and Journalism*, 46.

[36] Letter to T. M. Knox 21.ix.38. Knox papers, St Andrews University, MS 37524/425.

Collingwood pledged his support to Lindsay in a letter of 20 October, just before he sailed to the East Indies to recuperate from his series of strokes. What was he actually supporting? Lindsay's election address accuses the government of failing to respect the principles of the League of Nations in acting collectively, with both Russia and smaller nations, to resist aggression. He accuses Chamberlain of undermining British democracy by failing to tell the British people what his foreign policy was, or even if he had one. Lindsay advocates a foreign policy of rebuilding the League of Nations and adhering to its principles, while not being against either Bolshevism or fascism, but strongly pro-democratic. The government should negotiate with those who threaten war, while at the same time cooperate with all powers, including Russia, that work for peace. He also maintained that there should be no ratification of the Anglo–Italian agreement unless there was a complete withdrawal of intervention in Spain.[37]

On the domestic front his policy was one of rearmament, with the emphasis upon defence from air attack, and ensuring a truly national policy designed to abolish unemployment. He was confident that rearmament on the scale required could be achieved without undermining democracy or essential liberties. State control could be sensitive to democracy as long as trade unions and local government were 'taken into co-operation and into the full confidence of the government'.[38]

Collingwood must have received this election address just before he left for the East Indies, but he also will have been familiar while writing *An Autobiography* with the discontent in Oxford among Labour and Liberal supporters with Chamberlain's foreign policy and the collusion of the press in it. In his letter to Lindsay, Collingwood makes it clear that he is appalled by the apathy with which many in Oxford viewed the situation, and of the success of the government 'in keeping the country as a whole from knowing

[37] The agreement concerned good neighbour relations in Africa, the evacuation of Spain, and the Naval Treaty of London, 16 April 1938. The Naval Treaty of 25 March 1936 was designed to limit the growth of naval armaments until the expiry of the treaty in 1942. The Italians had declined to sign the second naval treaty because of the outcry over the invasion of Abyssinia.

[38] Lindsay, A. D. 1938, *Oxford By-election campaign leaflet*.

the truth'.[39] He applauds Lindsay's candidature for keeping the spirit of democracy alive.

Those of Collingwood's friends, and colleagues among the Delegates of Oxford University Press, who were by no means unanimous, and who were alarmed at Collingwood's apparent newly found political commitment, must also have been opponents of Lindsay, who in effect shared many of Collingwood's views, along with a considerable number of Labour and Liberal party members who supported a popular front. Collingwood's friends and colleagues, indeed, were the complacent ones who would have supported appeasement, and opposed rearmament. Indeed, as Stephen Toulmin delicately suggests, Oxford philosophers did not acquit themselves well in standing up to fascism.[40]

It was in this political climate, one that threatened European civilization, that Collingwood put aside a project that he saw as the culmination of his life's work in the philosophy of history, *The Principles of History*, and was impelled instead to write the *New Leviathan*, which he described as his contribution to the war effort. It was in fact an expression of his faith in European liberalism and its ability to defeat the forces of irrationalism. It is an intensely politically committed work in which he wants to make self-conscious what was at stake in the war.

While writing the *New Leviathan* after the start of World War II, Collingwood spent some time in London, sending Ethel, his wife, occasional postcards, but on 1 October 1940 he decided to send her a letter, written on the back of discarded pages from the *New Leviathan* manuscript. It seems to be this trip to London that confirmed for him that liberalism will in the end win out against fascism because of the resolve of the British people. He had previously questioned the resolve of liberalism in his article on 'Fascism and Nazism',[41] but now had come to share Croce's optimism. Croce's position is summed up in the title of one of his best-known books, *History as the Story of Liberty*, in which he contends that 'we always tend towards liberty and work for it even when we seem to be working for something else; liberty is realised in every

[39] Collingwood, Ms, 20 October 1938.

[40] Toulmin, Introduction to *An Autobiography*, xix, 1972 edition.

[41] Collingwood, R. G. 1940. 'Fascism and Nazism', *Philosophy*, 15: 172–3.

thought and in every action that has the character of truth, poetry and goodness'.[42]

Collingwood remarks that before he went to London he thought that there was an outside chance of Mr Chamberlain returning to the office of prime minister and surrendering to Hitler, but now he had experienced the destruction, and the inability of the bombing to prevent the British from going about their business. He says that he now thinks the war will go on until Hitler is smashed, but he did not think that the German people would overthrow him, despite his failures, because they were a people too cowed to rise against him. 'They are a pack of good for nothings anyhow, or Hitler would never have been able to stay in the saddle since 1933: ten good Germans, if there had been ten good Germans, would have shot him years ago.'

World War II represented a clash between the forces of barbarism and civilization. For him, barbarism was not a development out of savagery, but instead a reaction against civilization, that is, an attempt to retard or destroy the freedom of will attained through the socializing and civilizing processes. This is in contrast with the general tendency to view savagery, barbarism, and civilization on a developmental scale, exemplified by Lewis H. Morgan and Edward Tylor.[43] They were reacting against the regression theory, that is, the argument that peoples begin in civilization and regress to barbarism and savagery. Collingwood's position is distinct in that he sees savagery, not in any pejorative sense, leading to civilization, and that barbarism is in fact an attack on civilization. José Ortega y Gasset is more typical of the crisis theorists in this respect when he considers Bolshevism and fascism a regression to barbarism and primitivism.[44]

Like de Unamuno, Collingwood takes his own personal experience to be representative of the experience of European civilization in general, and through a process of 'taking soundings' in his own mind he articulates the principles that would triumph over fascism and Nazism. He accounts for how the European mind has

[42] Croce, *History as the Story of Liberty*, 232.

[43] See Boucher, *Social and Political Thought of R. G. Collingwood*, 196–206.

[44] Ortega y Gasset, *Revolt of the Masses*, 92–4. He contends, nevertheless, that the uncivilized tendencies are a product of modern civilization, which bestows the gifts without the realization of the history, the pain, the toil, that has led to the achievements we take for granted. See 101–2.

developed to the level of consciousness of freedom, first through capricious choice in which the reason for what is chosen is not apparent, to the levels of rational choice which he calls practical reason.[45] These levels are utility, right, and duty, all of which are characteristic of a certain type of action, and each affords a different answer for why one chooses to do something. First, because it is useful; second, because it is the right thing to do; and third, because it is my duty. Utility is action according to means and ends, in which neither the means nor end is fully determinate, and in which the justification of the end is absent. Right is regularian in that it is action according to a rule, but in any concrete situation a variety of rules may be applicable and may be in conflict with each other. Action according to rule does not tell you which rule to follow. Only dutiful action is determinate and lacks the residue of caprice that the others display. Dutiful action is individual action in that given the sort of person I am and the sort of circumstance in which I find myself there is only one thing I could do, that is my duty. Freedom, then, in Collingwood's theory is equated with freedom of choice, but not the choice to do anything I wish unimpeded, but the choice to choose what is consistent with the principles he develops.

Ortega y Gasset had emphasized the relationship between duty and history, while at the same time disparaging natural rights as passive, the generous gift of fate presented to everyone. The life of effort, however, entails excelling oneself, exceeding what one is by

[45] Before the level of rational action the mind develops through many stages. First-order consciousness is represented by feelings and their emotional charges which Collingwood argues are the appanages of mind. They are merely registered indiscriminatingly without differentiation. Feelings are what the mind has, consciousness is what it is. The second level of consciousness is achieved by selectively attending to feelings, and it is the level at which conceptual thought and appetite overlap. At the third level of consciousness the mind becomes capable of propositional thinking which overlaps with desire. The fourth level is attained by acts of will, able at first to make capricious choices and distinguish between good and evil. The development of mind through the three stages of practical and theoretical rational consciousness gradually eliminates caprice. Each of the practical levels has its counterpart in theoretical forms of rational consciousness. Utility produces a vision of the world that is teleological, epitomized by Greco-Roman natural science; right contributes to a view of the world that sees nature in terms of conformity to laws; and duty, the highest form of practical reason, finds its theoretical expression in historical explanation.

determining one's obligations and duties.[46] For Collingwood, the linking of history as the highest level of theoretical reason and the highest level of practical reason, duty, was designed to respond to and transcend the problems of 'Realism' and 'Idealism'. Collingwood's moral philosophy is both normative and descriptive. Normative in the sense that duty is presented as the highest form of good in human action, and descriptive in that history provides the content of duty uniquely for each individual in the circumstances with which he or she is confronted. In other words, the freedom in duty for Collingwood is to be able to think out what I ought to do in a situation by considering everything concretely and rationally to the fullest extent, and at the same time to perform the action myself. Duty, then, is fully particularized, but in addition the range of what the agent has to consider is extensive. The agent must consider everything that is relevant to the situation. Collingwood argues that 'it is my duty, not only to do this act but to make myself into the right kind of person to do it'.[47] Furthermore, 'it is my duty to determine myself as a will, i.e. to act in such a way that in acting I take entire responsibility not only for acting thus and not otherwise, but for acting at all'.[48]

We saw earlier how McCallum argued that the distinction between negative and positive liberty was premised upon a false assumption that they constituted two different types of freedom. Much of the confusion about freedom, McCallum maintained, resulted from the tacit assumption that one was either 'free or not free *simpliciter*'.[49] Collingwood does not commit this error. For him there are different kinds of freedom, but they are not separate species of a genus. Freedom is a philosophical concept which includes within itself a unity, or overlap of differences in kind with differences in degree. Each kind of freedom is both negative and positive. Positively it is freedom to do certain things; negatively, it is freedom from certain compulsions. Collingwood puts his position succinctly: 'Freedom of the will is, positively, *freedom to choose*; freedom to exercise a will; and negatively, freedom *from*

[46] Ortega y Gasset, *The Revolt of the Masses*, 64–5.

[47] Collingwood, R. G. 'Lectures on Moral Philosophy', ms., Bodleian Library, Oxford. Collingwood Papers, DEP 7, fol. 114.

[48] Collingwood, 'Lectures on Moral Philosophy', fol. 116.

[49] McCallum, 'Negative and Positive Freedom', 328.

desire; not the condition of having no desires, but the condition of not being at their mercy' (*NL*, 13.25).

Freedom is not a matter of either/or; it is not a matter of absolutes, but of degrees. To choose an action capriciously is to choose, but the choice embodies the generic essence of freedom to a low degree. In comparison with utilitarian choice, the level above it, capricious choice is irrational. Each form of practical reason, utility, right, and duty, exhibits less capriciousness than the form it supersedes, and is more rational, embodying the generic essence of action, namely goodness, to a higher degree.

Collingwood claims not only to be modifying Hobbes's *Leviathan* by bringing it up to date, but also to be transcending the social contract theories of Hobbes, Locke, and Rousseau. The mistake they make, he suggests, is that they see society and the state of nature as separate entities with the former always on the verge of degenerating back into the latter. The social contract is that moment which converts the state of nature into society. In Collingwood's view every community has a non-social and a social element, and socialization is a continuous process of converting the non-social into the social. It is the social community, or ruling class in the body politic, which determines at what stage and at what level of competency those in the non-social community qualify for the transition. In an aristocratic system of rule, for example, the bar may be set unrealistically high, whereas in a democratic system the bar may be set too low. Politics is essentially a dialectic rather than an eristic process in which parties representing these two elements act, in the case of the democratic tendencies as the forces of progress, whereas the aristocratic represents a necessary brake upon potentially too rapid and radical change. Politics is a dialectical process between progressive and negative or retarding forces. For Collingwood, the pre-eminent feature of liberalism is the dialectical resolution of all political problems, and in this respect it has demonstrated that it is the true heir to the dialectical method.[50] Regulating the conversion process from the non-social to the social community is a dialectic process between those who wish to hasten the process and those who wish to slow it down.

[50] Collingwood, R. G. 2005. 'Man Goes Mad', in *The Philosophy of Enchantment*, ed. Boucher, David, James, Wendy, and Smallwood, Philip, Oxford, Oxford University Press: 318 and 325.

Socialization is for Collingwood a process that goes on within the body politic, and has its counterpart in the civilizing process that takes place at the level of relations among bodies politic. A social relationship is, for Collingwood, inextricably tied to consciousness of freedom. To be socially conscious is to be conscious of freedom. This means that a society requires of its members that each is conscious of himself or herself as being free, with the concomitant realization that the same freedom they see in themselves is also possessed by every other member. The members of a society share a social consciousness. They possess a will. Hence society requires the attainment of a rational will since without it there can be no society, merely a community.[51]

For the European liberal, socialization and civilization are processes which are characterized by the gradual elimination of force in our relations with others, which is a result of our consciousness of freedom and recognition that others are also in possession of this capacity. Ortega y Gasset, for example, argues that 'civilisation is nothing else than the attempt to reduce force to being the *ultima ratio*' and rejecting the proclamation of violence 'as *prima ratio*, or strictly as *unica ratio*'.[52]

For Collingwood, the reduction of force first occurs in our attitudes to each other within the body politic, but which we are often unable to extend to others in different bodies politic. When we are unable to recognize ourselves in others outside our body politic we deny their human and rational status and treat them as part of the natural world, and force characterizes our relations with them. Through continuous contact and commerce we come to see in others outside our body politic possessors of the same capacities as ourselves, capable of exercising the same degree of freedom of choice. The civilizing process is one that not only pertains to relations among members of the same body politic, and between members of different bodies politic, but also in our relation to nature. Ruthless exploitation of nature, and a disregard for the ecosystem, is itself destructive of civilization. Being civilized

[51] Collingwood, *The New Leviathan*, 20.1–20; 20.61–2; 20.9–94. Also see Collingwood, R. G., 'Rule-making and Rule-breaking' sermon preached in St Mary's the Virgin's Church, Oxford, 5 May 1935. Collingwood papers, Bodleian Library, Oxford, Dep. Coll. 1, fol. 10.

[52] Ortega y Gasset, *Revolt of the Masses*, 75.

entails having an intelligent attitude to nature, what Collingwood calls intelligent exploitation. In other words, a civilized relationship with the environment is one of sustainable development.

The state, then, has an important role to play in that it removes the obstacles to the elimination of force. In so far as significant inequalities of wealth result in unequal relations, especially in the employer and employee relationship, force, whether physical or psychological, is endemic in the relationship. The state, then, is necessarily interventionist in that its role is to assist the elimination of force in social relations. Redistributive justice is part of the civilizing process. Barbarism, in so far as it is a reaction against civilization, uses force to suppress the development of consciousness to the level of rational choice, and seeks instead to suppress the exercise of the faculty of choice by means of psychological and physical violence.

CONCLUSION

Using material previously unavailable in the archive of Mrs Teresa Smith, it has been suggested that Collingwood drew a good deal of inspiration from European liberalism, and this is somewhat at odds with his admiration for the actualism, or actual idealism, of Giovanni Gentile. Even though he owed a considerable debt to Gentile, for example, in the formulation of his logic of question and answer, Collingwood could not condone the fascist conclusions that Gentile drew from his philosophical theory of the will, which saw wills in conflict with each other and compelled to dominate those of others. Collingwood's theory of the will necessarily implied mutual respect for the freedom of will, without which there could be no society or civilization. In this regard he echoes the liberalism of Miguel de Unamuno, Ortega y Gasset, Guido de Ruggiero, and to a lesser extent Croce's less expansive understanding of the history of liberty. This chapter also demonstrates what it meant for Collingwood to endorse A. D. Lindsay's candidature in the 1939 Oxford by-election.

9

COLLINGWOOD CONTROVERSIES

JAMES CONNELLY

To write a worthwhile autobiography you need either the wisdom of an Augustine or the shamelessness of a Rousseau or the confidence in one's own self-knowledge of a Collingwood.

Interview with Alasdair MacIntyre, *Cogito*, Vol. 5, No. 2, 1991, 68.

1. INTRODUCTION

George Santayana refers to Collingwood's *Autobiography* as written on 'Crocean lines, strangely conceited but instructive'.[1] In many ways it is undeniably both. Conceit is a necessary part of its purpose: anyone writing an autobiography has to believe in the value of what they have to say. In Collingwood's case, the book is a triptych comprising intellectual autobiography, political intervention, and a glimpse into the yet to be written: such a book is bound to appear to be conceited. No conceit, no autobiography.

An Autobiography is a work full of controversies, some overt (especially the political), some covert (mostly the philosophical). It has been charged with being highly selective, omitting people and influences. This leads not only to the charge of wilful concealment of influences and the implied accusation of plagiarism, but also to the charge that Collingwood either concealed (or was unaware of) fundamental changes of mind.

In his Preface, Collingwood writes that 'The autobiography of a man whose business is thinking should be the story of his thought. I have written this book to tell what I think worth telling about the story of mine.' This seemingly innocuous statement, together with his claim that an autobiography 'has no right to exist unless it is *un*

[1] McCormick, John 1987. *George Santayana, A Biography*, New York, Alfred A. Knopf: 396.

livre de bonne foi' and that he never names a man 'except *honoris causa*' in fact provokes the reader into consideration of how those who are named are treated and why some are never named at all. It also prompts reflection on what is 'worth telling', given that much of great potential interest is left unsaid. The book focuses on what Collingwood thinks now ought to be told, for reasons of political or philosophical urgency, and what led up to this. What is left unsaid is not considered unworthy of attention, but is easily available elsewhere. And this restraint has a positive consequence. The fact that the *Autobiography* is no litany of publications and influences is one of the secrets of its success; the others include its brilliant and incisive writing. However, undeniably, some felt aggrieved by its harsh criticisms, whilst others believe that its paucity of reference to influences and interlocutors was an attempt to conceal the source of his doctrines. In sum, the *Autobiography* both conceals and reveals, and both revelation and concealment have caused controversy. It is a work of revelation not in spilling private or professional secrets, but in its being a visible record in near real time of Collingwood's self-understanding. Thus the palpable resonance of 'history as the self-knowledge of mind' arising from the reader's sharing this self-knowledge as it is enacted on the page. He reveals himself as he understands himself and it culminates in the dramatic final utterance that 'I know that all my life I have been engaged unawares in a political struggle, fighting against these things in the dark. Henceforth I shall fight in the daylight' (*A*, 167).

An Autobiography is highly selective and to that extent partial: indeed, Collingwood himself both declares and explains this by writing that its purpose is 'to put on record some brief account of the work I have not yet been able to publish, in case I am not able to publish it in full' (*A*, 118). Although there is abundant evidence that Collingwood took care to reread his works and consult his papers in writing the book, nonetheless it is written from a distinct vantage point and with a distinct purpose in mind, not only as a record of his thinking (and its direction), but also as an illustration of the unity of theory and practice and as a warning against false philosophies and false politics.

Despite its omissions the *Autobiography* is generally accurate. The omissions are not seriously or materially misleading and, more to the point, they are also obvious. Collingwood highlighted what he chose to highlight for good reason and he made no commitment to telling anything other than what he thought worth telling. Of course there are controversies of authenticity, veracity, and provocation. The last covers both philosophical and especially non-philosophical issues. The key issues, philosophically, are matters of omission and matters of interpretation, and change of doctrine. Collingwood records that he has 'gone on thinking' but tends not to record particular changes of view.

The five controversies discussed in this chapter are bad faith, relativism, political radicalism, re-enactment, and idealism. The first is the charge that Collingwood deceived the reader as to his influences and affinities; the second is the claim that he underwent a 'radical conversion' to historical relativism; the third concerns his purported move to the radical left; the fourth concerns the correct interpretation of re-enactment in historical knowledge; the final controversy is the extent to which it is correct to identify him as an idealist.

2. *HONORIS CAUSA?*

Collingwood's acerbic comments on his colleagues, both in particular and in general, were no secret, and revealed a frustration that grew over many years when he found that his philosophical life was less congenial than his archaeological life. But this does not mean that he was unconscientious in his Oxford academic life. He was a frequent giver of papers to the usual clubs and societies, including undergraduate societies in Oxford (both philosophical and literary) and he engaged in philosophical correspondence with philosophers including Joseph, Schiller, Prichard, Alexander, Croce, Mabbott, de Ruggiero, Smith, and Ryle. But he did not spare his words when he recalls his exasperation with his colleagues, especially Joseph and Prichard. And these words were personal, philosophical, and political in their claim that the 'minute philosophers' were propagandists of a coming fascism.[2]

[2] The appellation 'minute philosophers' (from Berkeley's *Alciphron, or the Minute Philosopher*) was employed by Collingwood and J. A. Smith for a number of years. In a letter to Smith in 1932 Collingwood writes that 'if you and I are to be

He blamed them and their contemporaries (e.g. Russell) for promoting a philosophy which divorced theory from practice, for denying the common good, and ultimately preparing the ground for fascism. However, despite the acerbity of these remarks, Collingwood's dealings with his colleagues had at least the surface appearance of courtesy.

Collingwood rarely pinpointed links or continuities in his philosophical work. A partial exception is *An Autobiography*, although some absences are rather conspicuous, for example its failure to acknowledge any debt to Croce or Gentile. Croce is not mentioned at all, even though Collingwood translated his book on Vico in 1913 and later his *Aesthetics*, *Autobiography*, and various articles. He acknowledges his debt to Croce in private correspondence, and also explains why his name is 'mentioned . . . hardly at all; but that is in accordance with a method of writing which I inherit from a long line of English philosophers, and it will not disguise from you, or from anyone else who knows anything of the subject, the closeness of the relation which connects my thought with your own'.[3] This may all be so, but it hardly explains why, in accordance with the principle of *honoris causa* Croce's name was not mentioned in the *Autobiography*. In correspondence with Gilbert Ryle in 1935, he again states that he mentions names only *honoris causa*, and that his 'usual practice is to refrain from naming persons who have committed (in my opinion) what I regard as fallacies'.[4] This accounts for the absence of Croce's name from *Philosophical Method*, where (for example) in chapter III Collingwood expounds and criticizes the main principles of Croce's logic as fallacious, but it does not explain why in the *Autobiography* he denounces the 'realists' by name; least of all can it explain why there is no mention of Croce's name on those occasions where Collingwood obviously agreed with him or was indebted to him. Again, Gentile is criticized but not named in chapter III of *Philosophical Method* and he is heavily

fellow-conspirators against the régime of the minute philosophers we ought, I suppose, to indulge in a certain amount of conspiratorial correspondence' (Letter to J. A. Smith, 27/6/32, J. A. Smith papers, Magdalen College, Oxford, MS JAS I 22).

[3] Letter to Croce on 20.4.38, Biblioteca Benedetto Croce, Naples.

[4] Letter to Gilbert Ryle, 9.5.35, MS Eng let d194 (reprinted in *EPM*, revised edition, 2005).

criticized without being named in the *Autobiography*.[5] But it is clear that Collingwood learnt a lot from Gentile (Croce went so far as to complain that Gentile's influence vitiates *Speculum Mentis*)[6] and also that he carried on learning from Gentile after Gentile joined the Fascist party in 1923.[7] The reference to Gentile in the *Autobiography* is inescapable: 'there was once a very able and distinguished philosopher who was converted to fascism. As a philosopher, that was the end of him. No one could embrace a creed so fundamentally muddle-headed and remain capable of clear thinking' (*A*, 158). The natural inference is that there could be nothing of interest in Gentile's post-fascist writings: 'the most obvious and incontrovertible item in the count against Fascismo is that it has killed its own philosophy absolutely dead – if you doubt it read Gentile's *Filosofia dell'arte* and blush'.[8] But in a later review of Gentile's 'The Transcending of Time in History', Collingwood remarks of its leading idea that 'This is an important idea, and I believe a true one.'[9] Here he is willing to judge Gentile's work in philosophy separately from his politics, and to judge it good, thereby belying his judgement a year later that no fascist could think straight.[10] If Collingwood learned not only from Gentile's pre-fascist writings but also from late post-fascist writings, why is he so reluctant to say so? H. S. Harris regards Collingwood's silence about Italian influence as deliberate concealment, and goes on to say that 'we cannot grant, therefore, that his *Autobiography* is, as he pretends, *un livre de bonne foi*'.[11]

[5] *A*, 158.

[6] Croce, B. 1996. 'In Commemoration of an English Friend, a Comparison in Thought and Faith', in *Collingwood Studies*, 3: 178.

[7] See Harris, H. S. 1960. Introduction to Gentile, G., *Genesis and Structure of Society*, Urbana: University of Illinois Press. Harris detects the influence of Gentile not only in *Speculum Mentis*, but also in *The New Leviathan*; see also Harris, H. S. 1981. 'Gentile's "*The Reform of Hegelian Dialectic*": *an Introductory Note*', *Idealistic Studies*, 11: 187–8.

[8] Letter to Isobel Munro, 29/2/32 [TS/PLR123].

[9] Review 1937, *Philosophy and History: Essays presented to Ernst Cassirer*, *English Historical Review*, 52: 141–6.

[10] It is clear that he was personally and politically wary of Gentile, see Connelly, J. 1995. 'Art Thou the Man?', in *Philosophy, History and Civilization*, ed. Boucher, D., Connelly, J., and Modood, T., Cardiff, University of Wales Press: 92–114.

[11] Harris, Introduction to G. Gentile, *Genesis and Structure of Society*: 15 and footnote.

The *Autobiography* contains little reference to the contents of Collingwood's earlier works, and this goes together with an almost complete absence of comment on his own terminology. For example, he writes of *Philosophical Method* as his 'best book in matter; in style, I may call it my only book' (*A*, 118), but he says nothing of its content, and its central theme—the scale of forms—receives no mention.[12] The puzzle dissolves, however, if we adopt the view that Collingwood wrote each book or article as a *piece d'occasion*, tailoring it to his present audience and refusing to be shackled by premature identification with any particular school and the knee-jerk dismissal which frequently accompanied it. His keen awareness of this can be seen in his reference to the reviewer (a non-Oxford realist) who dismissed *Speculum Mentis* in a few lines as the 'usual idealistic nonsense' (*A*, 56).[13] He became increasingly wary of employing any philosophical idiom which stood between him and his readers or allowing them the easy option of dismissal by association; and he resented being labelled, especially when the label bestowed was 'idealist' or 'new idealist'. This is apparent throughout the 1930s and especially in *An Essay on Metaphysics*, where he knew that he would not be listened to if he wrote in the idealistic idiom: he therefore chose to play the logical positivists on their own pitch and try to beat them at their own game.[14] This was not without consequence: he invented new terminology and this, together with the lack of cross-reference, sometimes obscured the relationship between his books.

3. RELATIVISM AND THE RADICAL CONVERSION HYPOTHESIS

It has long been asserted that Collingwood's thought was subject to a 'radical conversion'. But such a conversion is nowhere recorded in the *Autobiography*. The claim that there was a conversion, together with the fact of its being unrecorded by its author, led directly to the view adopted by T. M. Knox (and in a more

[12] Except perhaps implicitly on 148–9.

[13] The philosopher reviewer has not been traced.

[14] See Connelly, J. 1997. 'Natural Science, History and Christianity: the Origins of Collingwood's Later Metaphysics', *Collingwood Studies*, 4: 101–32.

refined form by Alan Donagan)[15] that not only was there a change of view, but that in failing to record it the *Autobiography* was inaccurate and possibly deceitful. This is a false inference, but to appreciate this one has first to disentangle the philosophical issue of the implications or commitments entailed by Collingwood's philosophical statements from the autobiographical issue concerning whether he himself thought there had been a change in doctrine. There are three possibilities: no change (hence nothing to remark); a change unperceived by Collingwood himself (inviting the charge of inaccuracy, but not of an attempt to deceive); and conversion to a relativistic historicism of which Collingwood was aware but did not acknowledge (inviting the charge of deception).

Lionel Rubinoff was the originator of the term 'radical conversion hypothesis', which he coined in order to repudiate it. In *Collingwood and the Reform of Metaphysics*,[16] Rubinoff sought to show that Collingwood's thought developed through the elaboration of themes already present in the early works, principally *Speculum Mentis*. His central thesis is that the later philosophy is a dialectical outcome of the earlier philosophy. He argues that Collingwood's thought is 'not characterised by a radical conversion from "idealism" to "historicism" ' but that the rapprochement he set out to accomplish in 1916 was achieved in *Speculum Mentis* and *An Essay on Philosophical Method* and subsequently applied to the interpretation of philosophical problems in his later writings.[17] A fellow-traveller in rejecting the radical conversion hypothesis was Louis Mink in *Mind, History and Dialectic*, although he laid greater emphasis upon *The New Leviathan* than *Speculum Mentis*.[18] Both agree in rejecting the claim that Collingwood became a historical relativist, denying the possibility of transhistorical truth and asserting that each epoch of human thought was bounded by a set of absolute presuppositions beyond the reach of rational criticism. In the *Autobiography* we find, for instance, the defence of an historical approach to the history of philosophy and political

[15] See Knox, T. M. 1962, Preface to *IH* and Donagan, A. 1962. *The Later Philosophy of R. G. Collingwood*, Oxford, Clarendon Press.

[16] Rubinoff, Lionel 1970. *Collingwood and the Reform of Metaphysics*, Toronto, University of Toronto Press.

[17] Rubinoff, *Collingwood and The Reform of Metaphysics*: 24.

[18] Mink, Louis 1969. *Mind, History and Dialectic*, Bloomington, University of Indiana Press.

thought which appears to relativize thought and theory to its context of utterance, and a sketch of the doctrine of metaphysics as the science of absolute presuppositions later developed in *An Essay on Metaphysics*.

In his preface to *The Idea of History*, Knox saw Collingwood's thought peaking in *An Essay on Philosophical Method*, and thereafter declining. He grouped his writings into three: (1) *Religion and Philosophy* and *Speculum Mentis*; (2) *An Essay on Philosophical Method*, *The Idea of Nature*, and the bulk of *The Idea of History* (these were, in Knox's estimation, the best, typified by a balanced view in which philosophy and history were understood as related but distinct categories); (3) *An Autobiography*, *An Essay on Metaphysics*, and *The New Leviathan*, all marred by historicism and scepticism. He regarded *The Principles of Art* as akin in part to the second group, in part to the third.

For Knox, Collingwood betrayed philosophy by absorbing it into history, and he found himself 'compelled to believe that his philosophical standpoint radically changed between 1936 and 1938' (*IH*, xi). He is thus forced to question the reliability of the *Autobiography* because it fails to record any change in Collingwood's philosophical standpoint, and also regards as 'hardly credible' Collingwood's claim that he had elaborated his doctrine of absolute presuppositions before composing *An Essay on Philosophical Method* (*IH*, x).

Knox saw Collingwood's later years as a tragedy, and his changed philosophical views as a symptom of that tragedy in which a great mind had lost possession of itself. In a letter to Ethel Collingwood, he wrote:

> You say that the preface is 'melancholy'. I agree. But to me the last few years of Robin's life are the greatest tragedy I have personally known. And I cannot help the gloom in what I have written. But I have tried to show to others far less appreciative of him than I was and am that they undervalue his best work and certainly do not realise how great his potentialities were. I hesitated upon being so strongly critical of his later work, but I look again at a letter I had from him at the beginning of the war in 1939 when he thanked me for steady and persistent criticism; and I feel sure that a frank statement, like that I have written, is what, in his best years, he would have wished.[19]

[19] Letter to E. Collingwood, 13.10.45 [TS/GLTR164].

Knox saw himself as holding the later Collingwood to standards that he himself would have wished to be judged by. In a review of Mink he wrote that 'there was quite a definite change in him shortly after 1936, a change visible not only to me but equally to others who knew him well'.[20] It is, of course, impossible to gainsay evidence from personal acquaintanceships, but what exactly does it prove? We may accept that there was a distinct change in Collingwood's personality, but this does not address the philosophical question of whether there was a radical shift in philosophical standpoint between 1936 and 1938.

Knox believed that Collingwood 'suppressed' the original conclusion to *The Idea of Nature*, and replaced it by a conclusion in line with his later 'historicism' (*IH*, x). This is doubly false: first there is no evidence that Collingwood 'suppressed' the conclusion. In fact the conclusion changed to bring *The Idea of Nature* in line with *The Idea of History* in his projected series of *Studies in the History of Ideas*; to have Collingwood's own cosmology appended to his historical survey of cosmologies would have been an intrusion; and it would also have upset the balance of the series. Secondly (as some reviewers noted)[21] the conclusion to *The Idea of Nature* simply repeats the transition from Science to History found in *Speculum Mentis*, a book of which Knox generally approved. Knox also accuses Collingwood of inconsistency: he wrote of *An Essay on Metaphysics* that it:

> professes not to expound the author's own metaphysical ideas, but to explain what metaphysics is 'and always has been'. If so, then, on his own principles, it can hardly be a work of history; and indeed the argument of a crucial chapter 'On Presupposing' is set forth *more mathematico;* even if this were only a matter of form, the argument can still not be made into an historical one... Philosophy would thus seem to have resisted absorption into history at the very time when its absorption was being proclaimed. (*IH*, xii)

This objection only makes sense on the prior supposition that the later writings do in fact proclaim the absorption of philosophy by history. If Knox is wrong on this, the contradiction vanishes: if the later writings are not historicist there is no occasion for surprise

[20] 1971 Review of L. Mink, *Mind, History and Dialectic*, *Mind*, Vol. 70: 150.

[21] For example, Webb, C. C. J. 1945. Review of *The Idea of Nature*, *Journal of Theological Studies*, 46: 251.

when we discover passages incompatible with historicism; indeed, such passages become witnesses for the defence rather than the prosecution.

It might be worth taking a closer look at what Collingwood says in the passages cited as evidence in Knox's preface to *The Idea of History*. What does Collingwood mean when he writes that 'Philosophy as a separate discipline is liquidated by being converted into history' (*IH*, x)? Surely the important word here is 'separate'? It is philosophy as a separate discipline which is rejected: what we have then, is an overlap between philosophy and history. The attempt to maintain philosophy and history as separate disciplines is what in *Philosophical Method* is called the 'fallacy of precarious margins'. This consists in assuming that 'the overlap which has already affected a certain area of the class in question can be trusted not to spread, and that beyond its limit there lies a marginal region in which the instances exhibit only one of the specific forms, uncontaminated by the presence of the other' (*EPM*, 48). This fallacy Collingwood avoided by maintaining throughout *Philosophical Method* the cross-fertilization of philosophy and history; the question that now arises is whether in his later works Collingwood committed the opposite fallacy of 'identified coincidents' (*EPM*, 49). This consists in the view that because two concepts overlap therefore they are identical. Did Collingwood commit this fallacy? In a letter to de Ruggiero concerning *The Principles of Art* he writes of the science of mind as history—but a special kind of history: 'The absorption is mutual: the product is not philosophy based on history nor history based on philosophy, it is both these things at once', and that: 'the problem of "the nature of art" should become the problem of the nature of *modern* art; and the solution of this problem is the historical problem (but philosophical as much as historical) of the genesis of modern art.'[22] For Collingwood philosophy and history were inseparable: philosophy if it was to be concrete had to be historical, and this implied not the absorption of the one into the other, but overlap.

Again, Knox quotes Collingwood as saying:

St. Augustine looked at Roman history from the point of view of an early Christian; Tillemont, from that of a seventeenth-century Frenchman;

[22] Letter to de Ruggiero, 21.10.38, Bodleian Library.

Gibbon, from that of an eighteenth-century Englishman; Mommsen, from that of a nineteenth-century German. There is no point in asking which was the right point of view. Each was the only one possible. (*IH*, xii)

This is taken by Knox to be historical relativism. But it depends on how one interprets the phrase 'point of view'. If we take it to mean that the thought of historians and their conclusions are determined in every detail by their epoch and situation, the charge would stand. However, if it is the assertion that every historian works within an inherited framework of problems and solutions, it is far less threatening. It is the difference between what Stephen Toulmin calls relativism and relationism.[23] And, further, there is nothing in the passage quoted by Knox that Collingwood does not assert in his 1930 pamphlet on the *Philosophy of History*. There we find a frank recognition of the inescapability of historians possessing a point of view together with the comment that 'the attempt to eliminate this "subjective element" from history is always insincere – it means keeping your own point of view while asking other people to give up theirs – and always unsuccessful. If it succeeded, history itself would vanish.'[24] Either one claims that Collingwood was an historicist in 1930 or one has to accept that (on this evidence, which Knox takes to be decisive) there was no conversion. It would seem, therefore, that Knox's explanation of what he sees as the unsatisfactory nature of Collingwood's later work is irrelevant as it is neither discontinuous with the earlier, nor internally inconsistent, in the way he supposes.

Knox proffered illness as an explanation of the philosophical failings he identified, but this fails on its own terms, for the dates do not fit. To give a key example. Knox had a high regard for *An Essay on Philosophical Method*, which he considered a philosophical classic, separated from the later work both by philosophical merit and also in being written pre-illness. This is false. Collingwood was ill from April 1931 for a year; he began to write *Philosophical Method* in November 1932 and completed it in June 1933. Thus the *Essay* was written *after* a period of serious illness. However, this illness was not a stroke, but chickenpox and attendant complications, and if the claim is that strokes (unlike other

[23] Toulmin, Stephen, 1972. *Human Understanding*, vol. I, Princeton, Princeton University Press.

[24] *The Philosophy of History*, Historical Association, 1930.

illnesses) undermine their victim's judgement, then one would expect any objectionable views to be expressed only after Collingwood's first stroke in early 1938. However, Knox is committed to the view that the change of mind took place between 1936 and 1938, that is, prior to his first stroke, but while his health was deteriorating. Knox regards Collingwood's strokes as an intensification of his illnesses (*IH*, xxi). It is difficult to make the facts fit the claim, especially as Knox did not maintain that with the ever greater impact of illness, Collingwood's judgement steadily and progressively deteriorated, with the later works all being affected equally.[25] On the contrary, he affirms that:

> The *Autobiography* outlines an interesting logic of question and answer which has already begun to be noticed by contemporary logicians. The *specimina philosophandi* in the *Essay on Metaphysics* are brilliant essays in the history of thought. *The New Leviathan* gives some hint of the fruitfulness of applying to ethics the method expounded in 1933, and the value of its sustained defence of our civilized way of life has been recognized even by reviewers not very favourably disposed to Collingwood's other books. (*IH*, xxii)

Knox, then, does not regard the later books as uniformly bad, and he has considerable sympathy for the book *most* affected by Collingwood's strokes, *The New Leviathan*.[26] If Collingwood's judgement was impaired in writing the later books, why is it that the *Autobiography* and *Metaphysics* were more seriously affected than *The New Leviathan*? No satisfactory answer is possible given the initial assumption that illness can somehow be blamed for what Knox finds objectionable in the later writings.[27]

In his advocacy of the radical conversion hypothesis, Donagan agrees with Knox that the *Autobiography* and *An Essay on Metaphysics*

[25] Sir Roger Bannister, a neurologist, suggests that Collingwood's IQ would have been so high that even if he lost 20 per cent of his capacity, he would still be far more intelligent than most.

[26] Knox, T. M., 1968. Gifford Lectures, published as *Action*, London, Allen and Unwin. The book draws both on the approach and content of *NL*: see 45 and 51n.

[27] Collingwood considered *The New Leviathan* to be the only one of his books possibly affected by illness. He wrote that 'Part 3 is in manuscript, having been written just before my last stroke. Part 4 which is typed, was written after my stroke and removal to Streatley. If there are any signs of battiness in the whole work, they will occur in Part 4, which should for that reason be looked at with especial care.' Letter to Clarendon Press, 6.8.1941, Clarendon Press, Archives.

marked a shift to historicism, but revises his account significantly. He agrees that Collingwood underwent a 'radical conversion' between 1936 and 1938, but he disagrees with Knox on both the explanation and the division of the later writings into the 'non-historicist' and the 'historicist'.[28] First, he argues that illness may affect a person's judgement in such a way as to cause him to mistake bad reasons for good, but will not cause a change of mind for no reason at all. He suggests, therefore, that we identify Collingwood's reasons, even if they might appear inadequate to us or would have appeared inadequate to Collingwood himself when in good health.[29] He argues that in *The Principles of Art*, Collingwood came to conclusions concerning the nature of thought incompatible with the position laid down in *Speculum Mentis* and *An Essay on Philosophical Method* and that he could no longer accept the possibility of a non-abstract ontology of the kind propounded in *Method*.

In Donagan's view, the writings from *The Idea of Nature* (begun in 1934) onwards contain no major reversal of doctrine, excepting that of the nature of philosophy and its relation to history.[30] Donagan also rejects Knox's division on the grounds that, whatever may be true of the *Autobiography* and the *Essay on Metaphysics*, it is not at all clear that when Collingwood wrote *The New Leviathan* he still subscribed to the view that philosophy could be converted into a purely historical enquiry.[31] His alternative interpretation was this: by 1932 Collingwood had planned a series of books. On the completion of the first in the series, *Philosophical Method*, he wrote *The Idea of Nature* and the bulk of *The Idea of History*. In 1937 he wrote *The Principles of Art*, the second in the series. The theory of conceptual thinking developed there was incompatible with the conception of philosophy advanced in *Method*, and he therefore reconsidered that conception in the *Autobiography*, *Essay on Metaphysics*, and *Principles of History*. He then returned to his series, polishing *The Idea of Nature* and writing *The New Leviathan*. Donagan concludes that Collingwood's major philosophical work—*The Idea of Nature*, *The Idea*

[28] Donagan, *The Later Philosophy of R. G. Collingwood*: 12 ff.

[29] Donagan, *The Later Philosophy of R. G. Collingwood*: 12.

[30] Donagan, *The Later Philosophy of R. G. Collingwood:* 12.

[31] Donagan, *The Later Philosophy of R. G. Collingwood*: 16.

of History, *The Principles of Art*, and *The New Leviathan*—forms a largely consistent whole which should not be divided into historicist and non-historicist groups. *The New Leviathan* showed that the 'historicist' conception of philosophy satisfied him as little as did the 'idealist' conception of *Philosophical Method*.

Donagan's interpretation is more subtle than Knox's, but concurs on the major claim that between 1936 and 1938 Collingwood radically changed his mind on the relation of philosophy to history. Concurrence on this also generates the conclusion that the *Autobiography* is 'beyond doubt untrue' in that it (amongst other omissions) fails to record the radical change in his philosophical standpoint.[32] Some of the debate concerns the compatibility (or otherwise) of *An Essay on Philosophical Method* and *An Essay on Metaphysics*. Collingwood did not take them to be incompatible, for otherwise why would he have later directed that they be regarded as volumes I and II in his series of 'Philosophical Essays'? It is evident that there are few points of continuity between the terminology employed in the books, and this makes analysis both more difficult and more contentious. However, many commentators deny that there is incompatibility between the two, regarding them as complementary, as does Martin in this volume. If they are, then the claim of a 'radical conversion' as supposedly demonstrated by the differences between the two essays (the contents of *Metaphysics* being adumbrated in the *Autobiography* and contemporaneous with its composition) falls and we are compelled both to take the *Autobiography* more seriously as an historical document, and also to abandon the Donagan/Knox line.[33]

3.1 The Temptations of Relativism

Although Collingwood underwent no radical conversion, this is not to deny that he felt the pull of relativism and saw its attractions.[34] How could it be otherwise for a sensitive historian with an

[32] Donagan, *The Later Philosophy of R. G. Collingwood:* 1.

[33] See, for example, Mink, *Mind, History and Dialectic*; Rubinoff, *Collingwood and the Reform of Metaphysics*; Connelly, J. 2003. *Method, Metaphysics and Politics: The Political Philosophy of R. G. Collingwood*, Exeter: Imprint Academic; Vanheeswijck, G. 1996, *Over Metafysica*, Kampen, Kof Agora; Martin, R., Introduction to the revised edition of *An Essay on Metaphysics*.

[34] See Gellner, Ernest 1974. 'Thought and Time, or the Reluctant Relativist', in *The Devil in Modern Philosophy*, London, Routledge.

interest in anthropology? Appreciating relativity may seem only a step away from adopting relativism: but the step is vital and it has to be shown that it has been made before the charge of relativism can come into play. Collingwood was alive to this and sought a position which did justice to both the unchanging and changing elements in knowledge and experience. His views on philosophical method are an attempt to expound this. To be satisfied with differences in degree alone implies a single unilinear scale; to be satisfied with sheer difference is to abandon the search for unifying principles, and would be relativism. Collingwood developed a conception of method which encompassed both difference in degree and in kind, thereby avoiding both absolutism and relativism.

Thus, the opponent of the 'radical conversion hypothesis' can readily admit that Collingwood was much exercised by the relativity of thought and action in history, archaeology, and anthropology. How far this went can be seen in comments made to the child psychologist Margaret Lowenfeld:

> I am really *very much worried* about the point I have raised . . . We all know what kind of world it is to which you refer as the reality (or objective reality) world. But what exactly is its *title* to the name reality? I am haunted by a suspicion that it has none except the fact that adult members of modern European society (or rather, the "educated classes" of that society) are agreed to treat it as real; that (in other words) it is the *conventional* world of a particular historically-determined culture. It is *not* the world of adult human beings *as such*: not, e.g., of modern Indians & (educated) medieval Europeans.[35]

This appears to be teetering on the edge of a relativism which is only a step away from a sort of nihilism. The temptation was clearly strong. The passage was written when Collingwood had been working extensively on anthropology and folklore, had joined the Folklore Society and attended its meetings, engaged in correspondence with Brenda Seligman on issues of kinship and taboo, and written a book-length manuscript on anthropology.[36] It is also clear that a strong influence was exerted by Evans-Pritchard's *Witchcraft, Oracles and Magic Among the Azande*, which he read in manuscript and was probably the first person to quote in print. In *The Principles of Art* he quotes the passage: 'Let the reader

[35] Letter to M. Lowenfeld, 19.5.37, Lowenfeld Archive, Cambridge.
[36] See *PE*.

consider any argument that would utterly demolish all Zande claims for the power of the oracle. If it were translated into Zande modes of thought it would serve to support their entire structure of belief.'[37] Again, the relativist temptation is clear.

Another clear example of a recognition of the dangers of relativism, but coupled with a refutation of relativism (and hence a denial that his own position was committed to relativism) can be found in 'What Civilisation Means', written in 1940. He steers a course between 'historical monism' and 'historical pluralism' and argues that:

> the present-day conception of the relation between civilization and barbarism is that any given society at any given time has its own standard of civilized life, and thinks of itself as civilized in so far as it recognizes that standard, and of other societies as barbarous in so far as they do not. The attempt to be a civilized European is an attempt to live one kind of life; the attempt to be a civilized Chinaman is an attempt to realize a life of another kind. It is not surprising that Europeans think Chinamen barbarous and that Chinamen think the same of Europeans. Each rightly thinks that the other when judged by his standard, fails to satisfy it. The question with regard to any given society, then, is not how high it stands in the scale of civilization, for there is no one scale; still less whether it is just civilized or just barbarous, for every society is civilized, or it would not be a society: but in what way it is civilized. And, from the point of view of any one civilization, any other is merely one of the innumerable forms of barbarism. (*NL*, 489)

This seems to indicate Collingwood's acceptance of relativism, but he invokes his principles of philosophical method to escape the danger, without giving up either the diversity or the unity of civilization. He acknowledges that:

> This may seem a dangerous option. It may seem to imply that for any given society the proposition 'we are civilized' has a sense peculiar to that society, for 'civilized' has no constant meaning in such propositions; the definition of civilized conduct varies from society to society, and in any given society from time to time, in such a way that every society thinks its own present way of behaving civilized and the others barbarous. This is called 'historical relativism', and is rightly regarded with suspicion, because it really amounts to denying what it professes to explain. It amounts to denying that there is any such thing as an ideal of civilized conduct: not

[37] Evans-Pritchard, E. 1937.Oxford, Clarendon Press: 319–20; *PA*, 8n.

merely that there is one single ideal valid for all societies and all times, but that there are many ideals each valid for one society at one time. (*NL*, 489)

He then provides a solution which is rooted in a conception that civilizations differ in both degree and in kind, and cannot be placed on a scale differing merely in degree. Collingwood's conception of the scale of forms was developed in *An Essay on Philosophical Method* and partly exemplified in *The New Leviathan*. The only satisfactory conclusion is that Collingwood, although tempted by what was plausible in relativism, saw its dangers and avoided them.

4. POLITICAL RADICALIZATION

Although in his final year at Rugby and his undergraduate years at University College the young Collingwood was a Socialist—arguing in favour of it in debates and informal discussions—the adult Collingwood was regarded by his contemporaries as a conservative and a Tory. His own remarks at the time certainly indicate an urge to distance himself from Socialism. In 1920 he remarked to de Ruggiero that 'I am glad that you did not go to the last meeting . . . it would have been very painful to you. Mr. C. E. M. Joad (who seems to be not a philosopher but a socialist) made me more ashamed of my country than I have ever yet been.'[38] Writing to his father in 1931, shortly after the general election which returned the national government, he remarked that

the election has proved that even at this stage in its history the English people can't be bribed by panis et circenses; and it's very comforting to see that the "working" man and "working" woman will vote against the people who pose as their friends and for the people who promise them lower doles, higher prices, and solvency. We shall see whether the promises are redeemed; but if a country gets the government it deserves, this electorate ought to get a good one.[39]

This clearly fits his Pembroke colleague R. B. McCallum's description of him as a 'cautious and sophistical Tory'. And yet in the final pages of the *Autobiography* his voice is as strident as a Hyde Park radical—all the more so for apparently having realized

[38] Letter to de Ruggiero, 2.10.20, Dep. Coll. 26.
[39] Letter to W. G. Collingwood, 29.10.31 [TS/FLTR0618].

that he had hitherto been duped. He comments that his 'attitude towards politics had always been what in England is called democratic and on the Continent liberal' (*A*, 153). This is not, of course, necessarily incompatible with a conservative disposition. In the book he records no change of view in political beliefs; rather he records a gradual awakening to the mendacity of the government. Whether it mattered that this government was a Conservative government in all but name is a separate matter. What mattered were tendencies in the modern world and the government as a willing victim of these tendencies. Hence his 1936 essay 'Man Goes Mad', in which he writes passionately about contemporary politics, war, and the destruction of the countryside. *The Principles of Art* reveals the same sense of moral and political urgency. In 1938, on the eve of his departure to the Dutch East Indies, he wrote to A. D. Lindsay, supporting his candidature as anti-appeasement candidate standing against Quintin Hogg (later Lord Hailsham) in the Oxford by-election.[40]

The last chapter of the *Autobiography*, an outspoken attack on the government of the day, was naturally the subject of disapproving Oxford gossip. McCallum commented that *An Autobiography* 'was regretted by most of his Oxford friends. It revealed amongst other things a sharp change in his political outlook which swung suddenly from conservatism to radicalism, a change legitimate enough in itself, but requiring a much better rationalization than he gave himself in the last chapter of the book.'[41] For many the only explanation was alien influence. McCallum, like others, attributed the change to the influence of Kathleen Edwardes, who was to become his second wife:

[40] He wrote to Lindsay, expressing his support: 'I am leaving for the East tomorrow; But I cannot go without sending you my deepest good wishes for your success in your candidature. I do not think that the country has ever in all its history passed through a graver crisis than that in which it is now involved. I am appalled by the apathy with which our situation is regarded by a great many of us, and by the success which the Government has had in keeping the country as a whole from knowing the truth. Your candidature shows that the spirit of English democracy is not extinct. I hope it still survives among those who will have to vote next week.' 20.10.38 Lindsay Papers, Keele University Library. Also see Boucher in this volume on what Collingwood was committed to in supporting Lindsay.

[41] McCallum, R. B. 1943. 'Robin George Collingwood', *British Academy*, 29: 467.

It was said that she was a 'communist', i.e. a person of radical and socialistic views. To her influence was attributed the change in his political views displayed in the last (political) chapter in the *Autobiography*. The transformation of the cautious and sophistical Tory that I knew, to the flamboyant anti-fascist revealed in that book startled me. It was not that I disapproved of the change in general but the revelation of what Collingwood considered historical evidence with regard to the Spanish republic shocked me deeply. I then heard that there was an Influence at work and the change had affective as well as intellectual inspiration.[42]

One of the curiosities is the extent to which the whole affair threw many contemporaries quite off balance, with sharply polarized responses typically conflating the personal, the political, and the academic. Some went so far as to regard his sporting a beard on return from the Dutch East Indies as evidence for his conversion to the political left. Others, such as Ian Richmond, found evidence of his politics in his analysis of historical evidence: 'political passion led him at least once to disregard abounding evidence. Hating Fascism, he subjected Agricola to systematic denigration.'[43]

Others, upon reading *An Autobiography*, read rather more into Collingwood's politics than the evidence there allowed. Joseph Needham, whom Collingwood had known for several years, wrote that 'The only criticism which occurs to me is that marxism is brought in somewhat abruptly on p. 152. For those who have any eyes to see, many earlier remarks lead up to it, e.g. pp. 50, 61, 95 & 148, but just a single sentence or paragraph would have supplied the connection.'[44] Needham seemed almost desperate to find Marxism in the text—although Collingwood plainly does not endorse Marxism. What the final chapter reveals is disenchantment with, and denunciation of, the government, not the erection of an ideological alternative. However, it is true that Collingwood was taking an interest in Marxism at this time. He informed Chadbourne Gilpatric, the prime mover of the Mediterranean sailing adventure narrated in *The First Mate's Log*, that:

[42] McCallum, R. B. letter to T. M. Knox, 20.9.41 (St Andrews University Library).

[43] Richmond, I. A 1943. 'Appreciation of Collingwood as an Archaeologist', *British Academy*, 29: 478. See Birley in this volume for a rebuttal of this view.

[44] Needham, Joseph, letter to R. G. Collingwood, 14.1.40, inserted into Collingwood's own copy of the book in the possession of Teresa Smith.

I have a very short article coming out... giving my present diagnosis of Fascism & Nazism. I gave a diagnosis in the *Autobiography*, but that was wrong. I tried there to give an account of them in Marxist terms, as class-war phenomena; but it was wrong. I now see them as *religious* phenomena; outcrops of pre-Christian religion in revolt against Christianity and therefore against civilization, which (as we understand it) is a corollary of Christianity. When I wrote the *Autobiography* I was being a good deal impressed by Marxist ideas, but since then I have studied Marx & Marxism a bit more closely and now I can see just where they get off. A statement of the case against Marxism will, of course, have to go into the *New Leviathan*.[45]

This implies that he flirted with Marxism; it also implies that his real intellectual engagement with Marxism was *after* writing the *Autobiography*, not before, and that he rejected it.[46]

4.1 Theory, Practice, and the Realists

Another indication of political radicalism in the *Autobiography* is Collingwood's intemperate blaming of the Oxford realists for their approach to political and moral theory. He might have been provoked into this by the recent appearance of John Plamenatz's *Consent, Freedom and Political Obligation*.[47] In his preface, Plamenatz made his realist affiliations clear in thanking Moore, Prichard, Carritt, and Ross for their help or influence. One of his aims was 'to show that there could not exist any such thing as a good which was common to several persons at once, at least not in the sense required by Green and others who think like him'.[48] In *An Autobiography* Collingwood remarks that the realists destroyed political theory 'by denying the conception of a "common good", the fundamental idea of all social life, and insisting that all "goods" were private. In this process, by which anything that could be recognized as a philosophical doctrine was stuck up

45 Letter to Chadbourne Gilpatric, 17.2.40 (in possession of Peter Johnson).

46 For more on Collingwood's political thought see *EPP* and Boucher, D. 1989. *The Social and Political Thought of R. G. Collingwood*, Cambridge, Cambridge University Press, and Connelly, *Metaphysics, Method and Politics*.

47 Plamenatz, J. P. 1938. *Consent, Freedom and Political Obligation*, Oxford, Clarendon Press. Collingwood was one of the editors of the series in which the book appeared.

48 Plamenatz, *Consent, Freedom and Political Obligation*: 97.

and shot to pieces by the "realistic" criticism, the "realists" little by little destroyed everything in the way of positive doctrine that they had ever possessed' (*A*, 49).

Lest it be thought that Collingwood moves too quickly in making the connection between the realist theory of knowledge and their denial of any relation between theory and practice (*A*, 44, 147) it should be noted that the link between epistemological realism and ethics and political theory is made explicitly by Plamenatz in his rejection of Green's thesis that rights are constituted by their recognition within a community. Plamenatz objects that this amounts to recognition creating its own object and that Green, both in epistemology and in political theory, 'confuses knowing and making, for he says that there is no right but thinking makes it so' (*A*, 90). Plamenatz and his master Prichard could not accept the idea of mind creating its object, even social facts such as rights. The *locus classicus* of the realist attitude can be found in Prichard's claim that:

> knowledge is essentially discovery, or the finding of what already is. If a reality could only be or come to be in virtue of some activity or process on the part of the mind, that activity or process would not be 'knowing', but 'making' or 'creating' ... This presupposition that what is known exists independently of being known is quite general ... it is equally presupposed that knowing in no way alters or modifies the thing known. We can no more think that in apprehending a reality we do not apprehend it as it is apart from our knowledge of it, than we can think that its existence depends on our knowledge of it.[49]

Against this background, Collingwood's linking of the realist attitude in epistemology to their views in political theory and ethics (even if intemperate and overstated) makes sense.

5. RE-ENACTMENT AND METHODOLOGICAL INDIVIDUALISM

The *Autobiography* is often (and rightly) considered the neatest and most succinct exposition of Collingwood's philosophy of history. However, its summary presentation there, together with the text later published as *The Idea of History*, laid him open to the

[49] Prichard, H. A. 1906. *Kant's Theory of Knowledge*, Oxford, Clarendon Press: 118–19.

criticism that he is both a methodological individualist (the view that all historical explanation ultimately resides in discerning individual intentions) and committed to an occult doctrine of historical re-enactment resting on Cartesian dualism. A related issue is whether the doctrine of re-enactment is intended to be an historical method or a description of the conditions of epistemological success.

Much hinges on the interpretation of the claim that 'all history is the history of thought' (*A*, 110). If this is taken to refer, as it was by some, to the re-enactment of individual intentions by historians possessing an occult ability to intuit their thought, it certainly looks implausible. But let us examine this more closely. First, it is quite clear that Collingwood was never a Cartesian dualist. Careful inspection of his writings from *Religion and Philosophy* to *The Principles of Art* and *The New Leviathan* attest to that. There are, however, passages in the *Idea of History* and the *Autobiography* where he refers to the 'outside' and 'inside' of events, the 'outside' being what can be described in bodily terms and the 'inside' what can be described in mental terms. This, if taken literally, could indicate a Cartesian view. Would the metaphor be taken literally? In the post-war, and post-*Concept of Mind* (published by Gilbert Ryle in 1949) philosophical world it certainly could be. Notable commentators who took this view included the otherwise sympathetic W. H. Walsh in his influential *An Introduction to Philosophy of History*,[50] and Patrick Gardiner, whose *The Nature of Historical Explanation* was very influential on the development of philosophy of history in the 1950s and 1960s. Commentators such as Gardiner foisted on Collingwood the view that historical understanding was a form of telepathy, 'an intuitive capacity to apprehend the mind of an historical agent that transcended ordinary modes of cognition'. This view he retracted many years later, but by then it had poisoned the wells of interpretation for a generation or more.[51] The counter-attack was led by W. H. Dray, and later Jan van der Dussen and the old view is now thoroughly discredited. However,

[50] Walsh, W. H. 1951. *An Introduction to Philosophy of History*, London, Hutchinson.

[51] Gardiner, P. 1996. 'Collingwood and Historical Understanding', in O'Hear, A. ed, *Verstehen and Humane Understanding*, Cambridge, Cambridge University Press: 112.

there are still influential adherents of the old interpretation (Quentin Skinner, for example) who although close to Collingwood in many ways, refuse to accept the notion of re-enactment. Skinner states that: 'we can surely never hope to abolish the historical distance between ourselves and our forebears, speaking as though we can spirit away the influence of everything that has intervened, empathetically reliving their experience and retelling it as it was lived'.[52]

This is a good point to address the controversy of whether re-enactment is intended to be a method or an epistemological account; that is, whether it should be taken as an epistemological analysis of what occurs in a successful act of historical thought or whether it should be taken as a prescription for doing history. Although the consensus has come down firmly on the side of the first interpretation, it cannot be denied that Collingwood often talks in a way as to suggest that historians should put themselves in the shoes of those they study, see the world through their eyes, and think the way they thought. But comments of this sort are unexceptionable if interpreted as heuristic devices; the point is that this should not be confused with re-enactment. Re-enactment, if successful, is an achievement; it is what happens when we know a thought historically. If we know a thought historically then we have rethought its content and in that respect there is identity between knower and known.

Collingwood was primarily concerned with the content of an act of thought, with its meaning, rather than with its psychological components. Taken in this way a thought can be rethought without any commitment to identity of the thinkers of the thoughts: what is rethought is the content, not the psychological background of its utterance or expression. Thus, he distinguishes between thought in its immediacy and thought in its mediation, meaning by the latter the propositional content of a thought: 'the argument simply as itself, starting from these premisses and leading through this process to this conclusion ... is what I call the thought in its

[52] Skinner, Q. 2001. 'The rise of, challenge to and prospects for a Collingwoodian approach to the history of political thought', in Castiglione, D. and Hampsher-Monk, I. eds., *The History of Political thought in National Context*, Cambridge, Cambridge University Press: 185. See Boucher's criticism of Skinner's argument in *PE*.

mediation' (*IH*, 301). The key point is that 'because it is a thought and not a mere feeling or sensation, it can exist in both these contexts without losing its identity, although without some appropriate context it could never exist' (*IH*, 301) and, irrespective of whether we affirm, deny, or refute the thought, it is still 'the same argument and the act of following its logical structure would be the same act' (*IH*, 301–2).

A corollary of the doctrine of re-enactment, with its apparent emphasis on individual acts of thought, is that it led some to assert that Collingwood was a methodological individualist. For Donagan, he was 'a methodological individualist in the strongest sense of the term'.[53] For Dray, however, Collingwood saw history as a study of 'an essentially social subject-matter'.[54] For Collingwood the choice between methodological individualism and methodological collectivism was in many ways a false one. He has no difficulty in discussing both individual and corporate minds. He is careful not to reify society but equally careful not to reduce it to atomized individuals. And this carries over into his understanding of history. He seeks to account for individual thought and intention whilst never divorcing it from its social, cultural, or historical context. He elaborates the notion of a point of view and accounts for collective fundamental beliefs in his doctrine of absolute presuppositions which are not individual possessions so much as corporate possessions. The charge of being a methodological individualist is therefore to be resisted: but it does not, of course, require us to be uninterested in individuals in history. On a related point, in his archaeological work, Collingwood frequently has recourse to the identification of collective patterns of thought and behaviour as well as statistical forms of evidence.[55]

6. CONCLUSION: BEYOND IDEALISM?

Collingwood is often labelled an idealist. Was he? Nowhere in the *Autobiography* does he admit that he was. I shall suggest in this

[53] Donagan, *Later Philosophy of Collingwood*, 206.

[54] Dray, W. H. 1995. *History as Re-Enactment*, Oxford, Clarendon Press: 171.

[55] See Dray, *History as Re-Enactment*, ch. 5, and Dussen, J. Van der. 1981. *History as a Science*, The Hague, Nijhoff. Also *PH*, where Collingwood addresses this issue directly.

final section that he knew what he *wasn't*. Looking back, he remarks that in the 1920s:

> any one opposing the 'realists' was automatically classified as an 'idealist', which meant a belated survivor of Green's school. There was no ready-made class into which you could put a philosopher who, after a thorough training in 'realism', had revolted against it and arrived at conclusions of his own quite unlike anything the school of Green had taught. So, in spite of occasional remonstrances, that was how I found myself classified. (*A*, 56)

He clearly resented the label and sought to distance himself from it. This was not because he was unaware of his affinities, but because he resisted the presumption that what was common to those labelled in the same way was more important than their differences. This is very clear in his comments about Bradley who he clearly saw (as commentators frequently did not) repudiated Hegel and was quite different from Green. If we rephrase the question and ask whether Collingwood was sympathetic to idealism, the answer is that he certainly was, but became increasingly reluctant to admit it in print. After the mid-1920s he rarely identifies as an idealist, whereas before that time he frequently did. In *Speculum Mentis* he repudiates the title of 'New Idealist, referring to it as "silly" ' (*SM*, 13). In 1935 he wrote to Ryle, asking 'why presume me an idealist? I have nowhere in this essay or any other publication or lecture so described myself, and I do not see why you should attach the label to me without giving some reason. I am afraid I resent both the label and the irresponsible manner of attaching it.'[56] This shows very clearly his later reluctance to be pigeonholed: but it is at odds with his professed adherence to idealism in 1923 in 'Croce's Philosophy of History' and 'Can the New Idealism Dispense with Mysticism?' (although in the latter he does question the term 'new idealism' itself). The truth seems to be that he realized, by the time of writing *Speculum Mentis*, that tactically it paid better dividends to avoid the label 'idealist'. The price he paid, of course, was striking out on his own in a philosophical world in which one was presumed either a realist or an idealist. Later, by the mid-1930s, the divisions had shifted, with

[56] See the Collingwood–Ryle correspondence in *EPM* (revised edition, 2005).

the rise of logical positivism and the analytic school, but this did not help Collingwood at the time as he was regarded by the new generation as old-fashioned. It no longer mattered whether he was realist or idealist, as *both* were in the process of being superseded. Besides, he could hardly deny that he was known as a follower of Croce, Gentile, and de Ruggiero, having worked with and translated a number of their works. Equally, he was associated with J. A. Smith and H. H. Joachim (the second edition of whose *The Nature of Truth* he was editing as he wrote his *Autobiography*). The passage quoted earlier shows that he accepted how he would be labelled, but at the same time he struck out on his own, seeking to appeal to a different audience. In *Speculum Mentis* he wrote that 'I want my position to stand on its merits rather than on names of great men cited as witnesses for its defence' (*SM*, 13). Hence he dressed his thought in different language on different occasions as he thought appropriate. He does not rely on the traditional language of idealism, even where it can plausibly be maintained that he was arguing within the idealist tradition.

The key to Collingwood's *Autobiography* lies in what he opposed. He opposed the realists and said so. He opposed their epistemology and ethics and their repudiation of the relation between theory and practice. His argument against the realist doctrine that 'knowing makes no difference to what is known', was not an argument for idealism, or for the claim that knowing *does* make a difference. As he says, the formula was meaningless and properly understood applies equally to the claim that knowing makes a difference and that it does not.[57]

Positively Collingwood sought to develop his own position, irrespective of label. In his lectures on realism and idealism in 1935 he referred to his position as 'objective idealism', acknowledging affinities with the thought of Hegel and Whitehead. But his use of the term signifies little: in 1933 he noted that 'the controversy between the two [realism and idealism] as theories of knowledge, [has] by now played out in a kind of stalemate'.[58] The conclusion to draw is that the *Autobiography* provides an

[57] See Beaney's discussion of this issue in this volume.

[58] Cosmology Notebook A, 10, Dep Coll. 18/3. Original in the Clarendon Press Archives.

accurate account of his philosophical development, within its self-imposed limits. It vividly demonstrates both his frustration with the philosophical world he found himself thrown into and also his determination to escape it by developing and publishing his own positive views irrespective of fashion.

10

COLLINGWOOD'S *AUTOBIOGRAPHY* AS LITERATURE

PHILIP SMALLWOOD

In the final analysis . . . the prerogative of autobiography consists in this: that it shows us not the objective stages of a career—to discern these is the task of the historian—but that it reveals instead the effort of a creator to give the meaning of his own mythic tale.

Georges Gusdorf

1. COLLINGWOOD'S *AN AUTOBIOGRAPHY* AND LITERARY FORM

If 'It is difficult for a man to speak long of himself without vanity,' as David Hume believed, then anyone opening on first acquaintance *An Autobiography* of R. G. Collingwood could not miss the combined modesty and ambition of the traits which transform this work of philosophy, of self-fashioning, and of historiography into a narrative text of unambiguous literary quality. Collingwood's *An Autobiography* is short and rigorously depersonalized, but is also a frankly self-assertive volume that forms a first-person 'mythic tale', or in the words of the philosopher Alasdair MacIntyre, a 'narrative concept of selfhood'.[1] The work intimates a literary consciousness that the author does not willingly bring to the fore, but which projects the personality of the writer onto the screen of literary form; it suggests Collingwood's eminent command of

[1] MacIntyre, Alasdair 1984. *After Virtue: A Study in Moral Theory*, 2nd edn. Notre Dame: University of Notre Dame Press: 217. Correspondence held in the Oxford University Press archive relating to the prospective sale of the rights to *An Autobiography* reveals that MacIntyre at one time proposed to write an Introduction to a new edition of the work.

self-narrativization, and the consequent eloquence of his silences.[2] I have in mind here the unusual clarity, wit, and expositional force of *An Autobiography*, which has been thought the most readable of Collingwood's works. This chapter examines how the specifically literary value of Collingwood's text encourages attention to the dynamics of the intellectual life; but I also wish to suggest the breadth of the literary experience that informs the self-narration, and to illuminate the heroic intensity and tragedy of the creative life of writing that helped bring Collingwood's career to an early close. In the process I commend to the practice of literary history in general the theory of historical change expressed in condensed form in the pages of *An Autobiography*. I suggest one overshadowed application of this theory and its European analogues.

But rather than being the exclusive province of the literary critic, *An Autobiography* will also suggest how literary expression is linked to other dimensions of textual meaning. Collingwood's *An Autobiography*, writes Peter Johnson, is 'a literary text appearing in the public world as a political act', and Johnson quotes in this same analysis Hans-Georg Gadamer's remark from the Introduction to the German translation of Collingwood that the book 'has something of the narrative power of fiction; it is a novel about the passion for thinking, about the inter-penetration of thought and living'.[3] With a similar sense of the combination of thought, fiction, and self-narrative, Donald Phillip Verene has placed Collingwood's *An Autobiography* in the distinguished line of Vico, Rousseau, Hume, and Nietzsche, drawing attention to its

[2] Reviews of *An Autobiography* appeared under the heading 'Thought in Human Affairs' in the *Times Literary Supplement*, 5 August 1939: 464; in the *Manchester Guardian*, 15 August 1939: 5; by Crossman, R. H. S. 1939. 'When Lightening Struck the Ivory Tower: R. G. Collingwood', *New Statesman and Nation*, 17: 222–3; by Hannay, H. A. 1941. *International Journal of Ethics*, 51: 369–70; by Lamprecht, Sterling, P. 1939. *Journal of Philosophy*, 36: 717–18; by Marcham, F. G. 1941. *Philosophical Review*, 50: 546; by Muirhead, J. H. 1940. *Philosophy*, 15: 89–91; and by Rowse, A. L. 1939. 'The Dilemma of Our Time', *Spectator*, 163: 262.

[3] Johnson, Peter 1995. 'Intention and Meaning in R. G. Collingwood's Autobiography', *Collingwood Studies*, II: *Perspectives* (1995): 13, 18. The German translation appeared as *Denken. Eine Autobiographie*, Eingel. v. H.-G. Gadamer, übers. v. H. J. Finkeldei, Stuttgart: K. F. Hoehler Verlag, 1955. An English translation of Gadamer's Introduction by G. Barden and N. McCormick, presented by James Connelly, has appeared in *Collingwood and British Idealism Studies*, 13, no. 1 (Spring 2007): 5–15.

'hallmarks . . . as a philosophical idea' and has suggested that 'autobiography is philosophically important because it is the transformation into literary form of the process of self-reflection that is present as a process natural to any individual'.[4] Much has been imparted regarding autobiographical meaning by the leading post-structuralist theorists of recent years, including Barthes, Derrida, and De Man.[5] All have fared better than Collingwood within the community of anglophone literary criticism; but how far Collingwood extends the possibilities of the form, and how far he was drawing with more accessible humanity on the literary experience of the life that he wrote, I try to explain in what follows.

The classic statement on the art of writing the life of the self was made in the eighteenth century in exceptionally eloquent terms by Samuel Johnson:

> The writer of his own life has at least the first qualification of an historian, the knowledge of the truth; and though it may be plausibly objected that his temptations to disguise it are equal to his opportunities of knowing it, yet I cannot but think that impartiality may be expected with equal confidence from him that relates the passages of his own life, as from him that delivers the transactions of another.[6]

The narrative of the self, then, will have the potential to reproduce the authenticity of the historical narrative, but may give a carefully edited-down (one might say quintessential) account of the truth of a life. There is a teasing poise of fact and of fiction. Both constituents have in recent years come to enjoy renewed prominence within the field of literary studies, and to suggest the critical relation between historical and autobiographical narrative modes. Thus has the doctrine of deconstruction, for example, focused on

[4] Verene, Donald Phillip 1991. *The New Art of Autobiography: An Essay on the Life of Giambattista Vico Written by Himself.* Oxford: Clarendon Press: 48, 77. In the Introduction to the present volume David Boucher suggests the specific influence on Collingwood of the autobiographies of Mill, Ruskin, and Croce and suggests that Vico was most influential.

[5] See Barthes, Roland 1975. *Roland Barthes par Roland Barthes.* Paris: Éditions du Seuil; Man, Paul De 1984. 'Autobiography as De-Facement', in *The Rhetoric of Romanticism.* New York: Columbia University Press: 67–81; Bennington, Geoffrey and Derrida, Jacques 1993. *Jacques Derrida*, Chicago: Chicago University Press.

[6] Johnson, Samuel 1759. 'Idler', No. 84. See *The Yale Edition of the Works of Samuel Johnson*, vol. 2: *The Idler and The Adventurer*, ed. Bate, W. J. Bullitt, John M., and Powell L. F., 1963, New Haven and London: Yale University Press: 263.

the nexus of life and text, at the same time that feminist humanism has done much to reanimate the writing of individual female lives. Yet other critics and critical movements have reacted against the anti-biographical instincts of American 'New Criticism',[7] have breathed new life into the study of the authorial experience, and inspired reflection on the circumambient social and cultural context of literary work. Considerable influence has been exerted by experiments in 'postcolonial' theory which insist on the importance of distinctive racial histories. In resistance to the notorious concept of the 'death of the author', these innovations come as a departure from the grand imperial narratives imposed by nineteenth-century historical forms and ramified by later examples of 'Grand Theory'.[8]

In the wake of such Theory, and theories, Collingwood's *An Autobiography* stands out as a text of personal witness and an effort of self-re-enactment, a quest or pilgrimage (the making of a 'choice of life', in Samuel Johnson's terms), encapsulating the story of a philosophical career. The volume is one of Collingwood's few published works not in the philosophical genre, but nevertheless puts into practice Wilhelm Dilthey's interrelation of the life course of the human individual and the world of conceptual knowledge, with the proposition that 'there never is a present: what we experience as present always contains memory of what has just been present'.[9] Yet the work also captures the transformation, leading to termination, which is of the substance of human life: 'all human Nature is always in the midst', writes Michel de Montaigne, 'betwixt being Born and Dying, giving but an obscure appearance and a shadow'.[10] This figuration of Montaigne was

[7] Collingwood's relation to this movement is not simple, and may not even be conscious. One of the valued tenets of 'New Criticism' might be thought to be the discrediting of authorial, or artist's, intention in the process of evaluating artistic, especially poetic, works; yet in the opening of chapter 5 of the *Autobiography* Collingwood reflects on his distaste for the Albert Memorial, and the potential injustice of that distaste in the light of what the artist may have been trying to do (*A*, 29–30).

[8] A common collective name for French and continental post-structuralism and its influence, particularly in the USA.

[9] *Wilhelm Dilthey: Selected Writings*, ed. Rickman, H. P., 1976. Cambridge: Cambridge University Press: 210.

[10] From the 'Apology for Raimond de Sebonde'. 1700. *Essays of Michael, Seigneur de Montaigne*, trans. Charles Cotton, 3rd edn, 3 vols, London, vol. 2: 446.

incorporated by William Shakespeare into the language of his great tragedy of *Macbeth*:

> Life's but a walking shadow; a poor player,
> That struts and frets his hour upon the stage,
> And then is heard no more. (5.5.24–6)

In Collingwood's realization of its generic potential, *An Autobiography* may doubtless do no more than relate the story of 'my life so far'—the experience of all our yesterdays up to and including the Shakespearean 'last syllable' of Collingwood's own 'recorded time' (5.5.21).[11] But Collingwood's nature and the interests which drove his professional career ahead are also revealed to readers in their seeming totality. In a narrative having a beginning, a middle, and an end, the distance in Benvenistean terms dissolves between the authorial present 'I' that narrates and the past 'I' that is the narrative subject; Collingwood's intellectual personality seems to unfold through time, its formation being a solitary journey taken to a point of consciousness that is creative and acute. This is the penultimate chapter of the whole experience which gives birth to *An Autobiography*.

In its literary aspect, Collingwood's *pièce de theâtre* turns on the divide between the past self (as related by the work) and its present (from which perspective the past can be told, and Collingwood's ambitions for the future revealed). More than most recapitulations perhaps, Collingwood's story of his own life studiedly holds at bay—as it simultaneously stirs—any appetite for curiosity about the detail of his more intimate experience. *An Autobiography* is unusually spare in its employment of anecdote, and there is, for example, no awareness of a class sense, such as might be expected in the account of an educated Englishman's life in this period. None of the domestic privacies is explored; there is an utter absence of romantic love, and no confession of love filial or parental, making for a tight-lipped representation of the self. We learn nothing of the progress of Collingwood's marital disintegration, nor gather informed clinical accounts of the causes and effects of his illness. The *TLS* reviewer of 1939 can write regretfully of the 'withdrawals of the veil, all too modest in their brevity'. Collingwood's is more purely an emotional and an intellectual voyage than any biography of him likely to be written in the

[11] See *Macbeth*, ed. Muir Kenneth 1951. London: Arden Shakespeare: 159–60.

present day, and it forms a text of mind, a fable of intellectual tenacity and a moral investigation in which the reportable facts of Collingwood's schooling, family, and acquaintance fall away as excursions into philosophy, history, and method supervene.[12] Each phase in this sequence is coincident with a stage in Collingwood's development, and the progress charted is placed in a human and emotional context by his work's passionate, manifesto-like close. Beside Collingwood's cogent attacks in other contexts on the pseudo-science of psychology, the interest of *An Autobiography* is intensely psychological.[13]

An Autobiography is the composition of an historian and a philosopher of history (alongside artistic and cultural accomplishments of equal pertinence to its making). Historical consciousness mingles with self-consciousness in its pages. Such a casting of the self into the historical mode takes precedence over forms that Collingwood *could* have embraced (such as the lofty objectivity of the epic philosophical treatise), but at this stage of his career, chose not to. *An Autobiography* therefore encourages a parallelism with biographical accounts that we might imagine. There is a combination of exemplariness, the human experience for which the individual stands, and singularity, a sense that *this* experience, that of Collingwood's own life, is unique. As the conclusion suggests, there is an element of the confessional, the 'conversion narrative' or 'coming out', as Stefan Collini describes it, in *An Autobiography*,[14] just as autobiography and memoir may overlap yet stand somewhat apart, the latter as a reflective, the former as a more assertive mode of self-memorialization. Most evidently in the drive and pace and focused brevity of the text, a degree of compulsiveness may be detected and the disinterested ethical stance may clash with the autobiographical self-promotion. We see most clearly that while the author and the subject of the narrative converge, there is a developing relation between Collingwood's

[12] For an account of Collingwood's personal circumstances see Inglis, Fred 2009. *History Man: the Life of R. G. Collingwood*. Princeton: Princeton University Press.

[13] Cf. Collingwood's characterization of psychology as 'anti-metaphysics' and 'pseudo-science' in *An Essay on Metaphysics*, ed. Rex Martin, 1998, Oxford: Clarendon Press: 101–12.

[14] See Collini, S. 2006. 'Professorial Cackling: R. G. Collingwood', ch. 14 of *Absent Minds: Intellectuals in Britain*. Oxford: Oxford University Press.

inner life and the phase of history in which he has lived. The self is, as it were, turned inside out, and is seen against the larger canvas of history's events. And yet there is no strong evidence of deep personal crisis simultaneous with (say) the international trauma of World War I: many elements of Collingwood's intellectual personality seem to develop independently of political history.

This quality of historicity reveals, then, the consciousness of being conscious which Collingwood valued as the key to the idea of history. And in this inwardness with the object of historical interest, Collingwood indulges a licensed introspection that autobiography shares with the confessional. The ability to conceive of one's life as a whole grows, we see, with the passage of life itself, and Collingwood's work has in common with influential examples of the genre the fact that his is the special kind of story, like that told by W. B. Yeats, of a man committed to the life of writing. Thus Collingwood's writing out of his personal experience is both a product and the shaping agent, and the creative energy which impels the writing evokes what such a life may sometimes be like. The self-indulgence of autobiography is excused by the urgency of the theme, while the autobiographical form captures the poignancy of the creative life, and forges the relation of writing both to the living and the dying of R. G. Collingwood.

The variety of voice adds much to the literary meaning of *An Autobiography* (written in the wake of a series of strokes that could have killed him, just prior to a recuperative tour to the Far East, and revised on the voyage home). But Collingwood's emotional relation to his past self avoids the nostalgic serenity of memoir. There is the airily diffident, or mock-diffident, barely concealing a deep pride in his unusual intellect, as when Collingwood writes about the advanced theoretical lessons on the history of natural science taught by the *Principia* of Descartes, a work Collingwood had first encountered at the age of nine. 'I will not say,' he says, implying the correspondent positive, 'that all this became clear to me at this childish age' (*A*, 2). Elsewhere in the volume we find the briskly superior,[15] the fierce, the sardonic, the passionate, and

[15] The reviewer for *The Journal of Philosophy* writes that the book has 'a quiet and intriguing charm, a touch of the whimsical, a disarming persuasiveness. It has also a haughty tone, an arrogance, or (to use an Americanism of which doubtless Professor Collingwood would disapprove) a good deal of the "I'll-tell-the-world" spirit' (717).

evidence of writing to rouse or provoke, along with a certain amount of militant platform oratory.

The experience of the past culminates in the quasi-Churchillian assessment of the present state of the nation, as here for example in a moment of autobiographical climax. With each sentence of Collingwood's sounding peroration we pause to double-take, and to consider which of the two offered alternatives is nearer the mark. The balance of clauses in successive sentences turns repeatedly on the fulcrum of the semi-colon and makes emphatic this choice:

> At the time of writing, England has not formally bidden farewell to its parliamentary institutions; it has only permitted them to become inoperative. It has not renounced its faith in political liberty; it has only thrown away the thing in which it still professes to believe. It has not given away its Empire; it has only handed over the control of that Empire's communications to a jealous and grasping power. It has not ceased to have a voice in European affairs; it has only used that voice to further the ends of another power even more jealous and even more grasping. (*A*, 166)

The pulpit, the parliamentary benches, the lecturer's podium, and the soapbox of the political orator all come to mind at such moments; but the mix of Collingwood's tones eloquently channels his thought, and it is as a moralist text which succeeds by literary means that Collingwood's distinctive mode within *An Autobiography* can best be grasped. The work draws on, and is part of, literary history, and as a literary enactment it combines an outspoken ethical commitment with the voice of a satirical tradition, and with the fire of English prophetic rebellion in the line of F. R. Leavis, D. H. Lawrence, and William Blake.[16]

2. LITERARY EXPERIENCE AND LITERARY HISTORY

The early chapters of Collingwood's *An Autobiography* catalogue the memories of a middle-aged man recalling his childhood, but they have none of the wistfulness of recollection, where nothing that can be remembered is intentionally suppressed. At the same

[16] See on this theme (apropos Collingwood) Robinson, Ian, 2001. *The English Prophets: A Critical Defence of English Criticism*. Denton: Edgeways. The same qualities of a literary tradition were noted by Gadamer in his Introduction.

time, what Collingwood does not mention in his account of his early educational experience, and the inner life of that period (containing, in the first two chapters, not a single date), can be supplemented by what he has left behind in published writings, and in the unpublished manuscripts that chart these years. We discover here Collingwood's coincident literary interests and the breadth of his reading experience. Thus 'The Devil in Literature', an astonishingly learned essay on literary treatments of Satan, was written as a schoolboy and includes a lengthy discussion of Dante. The essay picks up on the anecdote that Collingwood relates, early within *An Autobiography*, about an image from the poetry of Browning, and what he says in the same chapter of his boyhood reading: 'I taught myself to read Dante and made the acquaintance of many other poets, in various languages, hitherto unknown to me' (*A*, 7).[17] We can likewise map in greater cultural depth the period Collingwood spent as an undergraduate studying *Literae Humaniores* and Classical Greats at Oxford (from 1908) and his immediate appointment as a Fellow in Philosophy at Pembroke College, before the result of his examinations was known. To chart the development of Collingwood's inner biography we must take account of the evidence of the published works alongside the dated but unpublished manuscripts that were written during these years.

Certain juvenile manuscripts have survived from the artistically creative family environment of Collingwood's childhood.[18] Other published and unpublished productions of the first twenty-five years of Collingwood's life (up to about 1916) are a further guide to his early interests and suggest a range not represented in the severely selective approach of Collingwood's self-narrative. On the topic of his first published book, a translation of Benedetto Croce's *The Philosophy of Giambattista Vico* of 1913, Collingwood

[17] 'The Devil in Literature – an essay upon the mythology of the Evil One . . . Read before "Eranos" 1908'. ii + 40 leaves, 28–39 blank (Dep. 1/1). A discussion of the literary treatment of Satan in Dante, Milton, and Goethe, with substantial quotations in R. G. C.'s own translations. The essay is a good example of the integration of R. G. C.'s literary critical and cultural thinking at an early stage in his development. Other poets mentioned in the course of the volume include Vergil, Homer, Pope, Dryden, Catullus, Theocritus, Lucretius, and Wordsworth. There are also allusions to Johnson and Swift. See Smith, in this volume.

[18] Such pieces are preserved in the care of Collingwood's daughter, Teresa Smith. See Smith in this volume.

is silent. Amongst other achievements, he passes over almost apologetically—as if embarrassed by the best-forgotten follies of his youth—his first monograph, *Religion and Philosophy* of 1916. This, we are told, was 'written some years earlier, in order to tidy up and put behind me a number of juvenile studies in theology' (*A*, 43),[19] and echoes the theme of the manuscript of the same date, 'Lectures on the Philosophy of Religious Evolution'.[20] When Collingwood refers to his reasons for publishing the book (at the age of twenty-eight), he appeals to a personal future already sufficiently plagued by a sense of present and impending destruction, whether through sickness or through the generalized slaughter of total war. This is again a motive to urgent action, and his explanation is delivered with sardonically doom-laden humour:

> I published it because, at a time when a young man's expectation of life was a rapidly dwindling asset, I wished at any rate to leave one philosophical publication behind me, and hated (as I still hate) leaving a decision of that kind to executors. (*A*, 43)[21]

Collingwood refers fleetingly in *An Autobiography* (*A*, 42–3) to an early book, *Truth and Contradiction*, as abandoned when a publisher turned it down, but a portion of the manuscript, dated 1917, survives as chapter 2, and is clearly a source of chapter 5 of *An Autobiography* ('Question and Answer')—'a brilliant critique', according to Hans-Georg Gadamer,[22] 'of the Oxford "realist" school'. The thinking in this chapter lends itself to what would now be called a 'dialogic' conception of the present's relation to the literary past. This is, of course, at the same time, of lasting relevance to the philosophy of literary history for which Gadamer

[19] Though Collingwood accords this work an enclosed historicized compartment in his self-narrative, it in fact looks forward in all sorts of ways to his later thinking, such as that on the question of religion, as embedded in his folktale manuscripts (now published *PE*). *Religion and Philosophy* was reviewed by T. S. Eliot 1927, in the *International Journal of Ethics*, 27: 543.

[20] See Dep. Collingwood, 1.

[21] A self-dramatizing moment, perhaps. I am grateful to David Boucher for pointing out that Collingwood seems to have been extremely happy in London during the Great War, and never appears to have been in danger. His letters are full of social engagements, lunches, singing practice, concerts, and much more.

[22] Gadamer, Hans-Georg 1989. *Truth and Method*, trans. rev. by Weinsheimer, Joel and Marshall, Donald G., London: Sheed and Ward: 370.

and his colleagues in the Constance School—Hans Robert Jauss and Wolfgang Iser—are more often acclaimed.[23]

Collingwood's theory, in common with Gadamer's, teaches that there is no one-way traffic in the passage from past to present, and that the textual material with which the historian must regularly deal is perpetually volatile, for ever widening as it is reassembled in response to questions that arise from its own unique and unprecedented historical moment. Thus every work of literature, being a product of an intention to create literature as such, is historical as an answer to a question in the mind of the past author that remains unanswered in the mind of the reader in the here and now. The point has been made to good effect by Wayne C. Booth who, in his Introduction to R. S. Crane's *The Idea of the Humanities*, adapts Collingwood's thought on history to literary-historical purposes when he writes that 'one of the critic's tasks is to reconstruct the *problem*—in this case how to achieve the work itself—as it might have been faced by the author'.[24]

The marked absence of individual portraits *besides* Collingwood's in *An Autobiography*—whether personal acquaintance, mother, wife, children, or other close family, or of philosophical, critical, or literary contemporaries—is especially notable. The people that Collingwood gives an account of having known or met are at most shadowy figures, such as the unnamed master at Rugby School who made a misery of his schoolboy years. Literary critics, F. R. Leavis and William Empson amongst them, have appropriated and praised the philosophical work of Collingwood,[25] but their attention to him is not reciprocated by Collingwood's intense engagement with criticism or literary scholarship and its controversies—as might most easily have happened in the rich

[23] For details see Holub, Robert, 1995. 'Reception Theory: School of Constance', in Raman Selden, ed., *The Cambridge History of Literary Criticism*, vol. VIII: *From Formalism to Poststructuralism*. Cambridge: Cambridge University Press: 319–46.

[24] Booth, Wayne C. 1967. Introduction to Crane, R. S. *The Idea of the Humanities*, 2 vols. Chicago: University of Chicago Press: I, xvii.

[25] For a full account of literary critics' interest in Collingwood see Smallwood, Philip, 2001. '"The True Creative Mind": R. G. Collingwood's Critical Humanism', *The British Journal of Aesthetics*, 41, no. 3: 293–311, and Smallwood, Philip 2000. 'Historical Re-Construction, Literary Transmission and the Value of R. G. Collingwood', *Translation and Literature*, 9:1: 3–24.

cross-disciplinary environment to which Collingwood aspired.[26] Collingwood's admiration for T. S. Eliot's poetry, praised with unusual warmth and respect in the conclusion to the *Principles of Art* (published in the year before *An Autobiography*) is well attested. There is, however, no mention of Eliot or his poetry in Collingwood's autobiographical account of his thinking life, not even at those points in the story which bear most directly on the history of his aesthetic experience. This absence may suggest a wish to narrow his focus and to redefine the core of his expertise within professional philosophy.[27] (It is noteworthy, as an aside, that Eliot attended Collingwood's lectures on Aristotle's *De Anima*, the first he gave in full-time academic employment at Oxford, and Eliot's copious notes to Aristotle's text, mainly written in Latin and Greek, with Collingwood's commentary upon the same, survive in the John Haywood bequest of the Library of King's College, Cambridge; Collingwood's own manuscript translation and commentary on 'Aristotelis de Anima' is dated 1913.)[28]

Other work produced by the end of the Great War corresponds chronologically with the chapter on 'Question and Answer'. This includes 'Words and Tune' of 1918, an essay containing a lively discussion of music in its relation to patterns of poetical articulation, and reflecting an early musical interest, both intellectual and practical. Collingwood's passion for music is marked by the award of Earnest Newman's volume on *Musical Studies* as his 1908 'Prize for Harmony' at Rugby School. Collingwood commenced his

[26] A certain compositional policy may have come into play here: Collingwood writes in his Preface that 'my rule in writing books is never to name a man except *honoris causa*'. But such a policy would not necessarily limit the visibility of the cross-disciplinary conversations Collingwood could have had, had he been so inclined, with others of his generation via his published works.

[27] Given, for example, the parallels that exist between Collingwood's idea of history in general and Eliot's sense of a specifically literary history in his influential essay on 'Tradition and the Individual Talent' of 1921.

[28] Collingwood knew Eliot and sent him his books as they were published. A letter from Eliot to Collingwood is preserved in the collection of Teresa Smith. Most of Eliot's notes 'made during R. G. Collingwood's *explication de texte*' are entered on thin additional sheets of paper glued into the text of Eliot's copy of Aristotle and consist of Latin paraphrases of the Greek. Very few notes, dated 1911, are in English, while many offer glosses on individual Greek words or refer to sources in Plotinus or Plato.

reviewing for the *Oxford Magazine* in this wartime period,[29] though his first reviews of theoretical works on the theme of literature, specifically on texts by the English Romantics, did not appear until the mid-1920s.[30] His work on a general aesthetic theory in these years nevertheless pays much detailed respect to particularities of literary form. Such an emphasis on literature was continued in Collingwood's draft of an unpublished book, written in the mid-1930s but not printed until 2005, and apparently evolving from a series of undelivered lectures on the oral narratives of folktale and their implications for historical thought.[31] The emphasis is recalled in manuscript reflections on Shakespeare's plays and the Greek and French theatres, again in his lectures on Jane Austen's fiction of 1921 and (most probably) 1934, as well as in Collingwood's commentaries on the many examples of literary artists discussed in the *Principles of Art*.

Judged by the many allusions to literary works and figures to be found within the self-dated or dateable manuscripts,[32] an author-by-author summary of the documented literary experience, in chronological order of appearance over these early years, would include as follows—1908: Dante, Milton, and Goethe; 1918: Shakespeare's *Hamlet*, Molière, Victor Hugo, Pope's *Homer*, Goethe's lyrics, Rupert Brooke, William Blake, George Herbert, H. G. Wells; and 1921: Jane Austen, Molière, Boccaccio, Cervantes, Fielding, Balzac, Dickens, Henry James, Dostoevski, Scott, Shakespeare, Meredith, Hardy, and Charlotte Brontë. No *biographical* study of Collingwood would be complete without some account of these literary influences and experiences; but as part of the story he tells, autobiographically, these figures have few resonances, and

[29] See Collingwood, R. G, 1917–1918. Review of J. N. Figgis, *The Will to Freedom: or the Gospel of Nietzsche and the Gospel of Christ*, *Oxford Magazine*, 36: 229, and Collingwood. R. G. 1918–1919. Review of Bertrand Russell's *Mysticism and Logic, and Other Essays*, *Oxford Magazine*, 37: 129.

[30] See Collingwood, R. G. 1924–1926. Review of Annie Edwards Dodds, *The Romantic Theory of Poetry*, *Oxford Magazine*, 44: 494–5, and Collingwood, R. G. 1925–1926. Review of Crane Brinton, *The Political Ideas of the English Romanticists*, *Oxford Magazine*, 44, 497.

[31] The run of draft chapters, along with other manuscript material, was published as the core text of *PE*.

[32] See, for example, the essays printed for the first time in *The Philosophy of Enchantment*. See also Smith in this volume for references to reading in his letters.

the references to poets and creative writers (Dryden, Homer, Johnson, Lucretius, Pope, Theocritus, Vergil, Wordsworth, and Browning) occur only in passing. The dates of notes or longer reflections on various literary figures in the array of unpublished manuscripts are often not ascribed by Collingwood. In the absence of external evidence they may be mostly unascertainable.[33] But the cultural and linguistic range of Collingwood's early literary experience is evident enough, and his excursions into literature in the 1920s and 1930s round out our sense of the directions he took.

We have seen that the literary experience of the years embraced by *An Autobiography* can be interpreted in the light of his work's intrinsic literary qualities and effects. I have in mind the earlier-mentioned manipulations of tone in the volume, with its stringent selection of subject matter and effort of self-modification. Collingwood is able thereby to *produce* an experience of literariness in his reader—one that is consistent with his emphasis on links between poetry and philosophy expressed in *An Essay on Philosophical Method* of 1933. It is the philosophical thought of Collingwood, and not, that is, the matter of his experience of life, which here forms the literary and the logical substrate of *An Autobiography*.

Chapter 7 of *An Autobiography*, on 'The History of Philosophy' deals with the period in the mid-1920s when Collingwood was coming to terms with the historical nature of philosophy, and this is the decade in the midst of which he wrote the first draft of his paper for the Aristotelian Society, 'Some Perplexities about Time' (1925), with its simultaneous historical and philosophical ramifications.[34] The relation of thinking philosophically to the romantic drama which is the history of thought, where other *dramatis personae* are Collingwood's colleagues at Oxford University, is registered by the ordering in time of the phases of life, which are, as it were, chaptered or split into 'Acts'. Despite a tendency to reticence in the exact dating of events in the whole volume, time is explicitly marked by the opening formulations of successive

[33] Presently undated manuscripts that also suggest Collingwood's literary interests are 'The Electra Story', Bodleian Dep. Collingwood, 17, and 'Hieronomo and Hamlet', Dep. Coll. 17.

[34] Collingwood, R. G. 1925–1926. 'Some Perplexities about Time: with an Attempted Solution', *Proceedings of the Aristotelian Society*, 26: 146; 150. The manuscript 'first draft' of this paper is in the Bodleian Library, Dep. Coll. 18/1.

chapters. The divisions of *An Autobiography* enact life's structure and rhythms—first as an approach to the present via the past. Thus:

> Until I was thirteen years old I lived at home and was taught by my father. (*A*, ch. 1)
>
> In that capacity [of classical scholar] I went on, a year later, to Rugby. (*A*, ch. 2)
>
> When I began to read philosophy there in 1910, Oxford was still obsessed by the school of Green. (*A*, ch. 3)
>
> A year or two after the outbreak of war, I was living in London and working with a section of the Admiralty Intelligence Division. (*A*, ch. 5)
>
> The War ended, I came back to Oxford an opponent of the 'realists'. I had not yet learned the uselessness of reading papers. (*A*, ch. 6)[35]

'Until', 'later', 'still', 'after', 'ended', 'not yet', and so on, are here the operative terms in the temporal organization of *An Autobiography*—until chapter 8. Then, by a shift from the narration of completed past action and thought to a present in continuity with the past in which the action and thought have occurred, the line of time is broken. The chapter recalls the point of view in the present from which the past is being, and to that point *has* been, recollected: 'My life's work hitherto, as seen from my fiftieth year, has been in the main an attempt to bring about a *rapprochement* between philosophy and history' (*A*, 77). Here, with one of the rare uses in the volume of the word 'hitherto', the moment of telling the past in the conscious present, from which *An Autobiography* is as a whole composed, seems to assume a position external to the process whose development Collingwood narrates up to that moment. The succeeding chapter ('The Foundations of the Future') then returns us to the period at the end of the 1914–1918 war: 'I did not exactly choose to spend the rest of my life on this task [the philosophy of history]. By about 1919 I found that I had no choice but to do so' (*A*, 89). The topics of our academic investigations, Collingwood intimates, seem to be chosen for us. We are not at unfettered liberty to select them for ourselves.

Collingwood dates the crucial, revelatory or epiphanic, step in thinking about the nature of history at a point almost a decade

[35] David Boucher informs me that Collingwood was never paid for his work at the Admiralty in London, and merely given expenses. His duties at Pembroke required that he travel back to Oxford once, or later twice, per week.

later, in 1928. At that time there arrives within his mind his conception of historical thought, in appropriately autobiographical terms, as a 'self-knowledge of mind' (107). This is not the first epiphany that *An Autobiography* places on record: the drama of revelation is, indeed, formative, and we learn in the first chapter that Collingwood had at the age of eight discovered an English translation of Kant which he could not understand, but which, he nevertheless felt, was somehow, suddenly, '[*his*] business':

> a matter personal to myself, or rather to some future self of my own . . . I did not, in any natural sense of the word, 'want' to master Kantian ethics when I should be old enough; but I felt as if a veil had been lifted and my destiny revealed. (*A*, 4)

Such details in the distant past of the self, as seen from middle age, capture Collingwood's moving sense of the experience of time as part of the experience of thought. And at the end of the volume, Collingwood reminds us that an autobiography, so far as it is written by someone who yet has more life to live (though in Collingwood's case this may have been pitifully little), is at best an interim report on experience. The sense of unity in autobiography comes from a fictional control over character and narrative. This may bear comparison with the unity the novel can achieve, or as here the compactness and intensity of the Greek drama. But there is an expectation of veracity that we do not bring to fiction, and the oneness of autobiography is in its essence incomplete; insufficient to its purported aim, as the example of Collingwood's short life shows. Collingwood's *An Autobiography* suggests the sense in which a work of autobiography is inevitably a tragic tale: a verification of inescapable failure.

The volume closes in a fiercely written chapter on 'Theory and Practice'.[36] Here Collingwood gives an account of the political

[36] This was the toned down version. The initial draft of the MS appears to have deeply divided opinion amongst the Delegates of the Press, and questions were raised about potential libels contained in the final chapter and the wisdom of its political stance. A letter dated 12 November 1938 from Humphrey Milford, and held in the Oxford University Press Archive, records that 'The V.C. and the Dean said they were clear that the last 10 pages [of the MS] were impossible.' The original MS of *An Autobiography* is disappointingly not extant, but the internal correspondence within the Press allows some inferences to be drawn about Collingwood's targets, including the British press and government, the Spanish government, and the Vice Chancellor of Oxford University. See Boucher's and Smith's Introduction in this volume.

programme ahead, and announces his intention, which dates from that time, to 'fight in the daylight'. The classic work of romantic autobiography is the Wordsworthian *Prelude*; but there is little in this declaration of emotion, traditionally recollected in tranquillity, from Collingwood's personal past. Indeed, in an emphatically unromantic vein, Collingwood made reading notes on politics and governance in this year, extracted from the tragedies of Jean de Racine.[37] And if—according to the vision of the seventeenth-century poet Abraham Cowley—Collingwood knew he had 'Of little *Life* the best to make' in 1938, his ambition to 'manage *wisely* the *last stake*'[38] was conceived in assertively practical terms as a determination to carry theory into practice while civilization proceeded to crumble around him. Granted, the matter of what, exactly, 'practice' might mean in this context is not particularly clear, but such a conclusion comes out of a Collingwoodian present, in the moment of 1938, which stands on the borders of the divide between aspiration and memory, and marks a sense of spiritual rebirth and renewed self-assertion fully in accord with the mood he admired in Eliot's *The Waste Land*. The narration by R. G. Collingwood of his personal past is thereby transformed into an autobiographical discourse of penitence. The chapter retrospectively reviews the assumptions held by the tripartite persona—the 'R. G. C.'—that Collingwood constructs as the spokesman of his internal dialogue, the internal tension of which is the life of thought (150–3).

Thinking and writing are for Collingwood the authentic realm of tragic and heroic action in *An Autobiography*; they are the practical expression within modern literary civilization of the ancient heroism that once functioned to motivate the Homeric and Virgilian heroes of Collingwood's Oxford training in 'Classical Greats'. 'Fighting in the daylight' is ironic in the context of a work in

[37] In his manuscript 'Notes on various works by Racine' (1938), Collingwood examines the relationship between Racine's *Phèdre* and the politics of the monarchical state. He writes of *Athalie* as advancing a theory of constitutional monarchy designed to replace an absolutist collapse. See Dep. Coll. 17/12. In the 'Log of a Journey to the East Indies', 15 November 1938, Collingwood records that he had 'little heart for study. So read Racine'. It is possible that Collingwood's notes on Racine were made on the voyage at this time. See James in this volume for other reading by Collingwood on this voyage.

[38] Cowley, Abraham, 1681. 'Age', in *Works*, London: 34.

which so much is left out of the narrative. It means, in effect, guarding one's private opinions no longer, albeit that the feuds with the Oxford 'Realists' earlier described in *An Autobiography* imply no inordinate reticence where contestations of philosophical opinion are concerned.[39] Such a heroism may involve no blood-spilling military combat or exorbitant physical risk to the body of the person, but its creative and intellectual expenditure cost Collingwood dear in terms of his personal health, and it is in this respect an equally self-consuming course—one that leads to the deathbed completion of Collingwood's 'war effort' work: his application to contemporary conditions of the philosophy of Thomas Hobbes as *The New Leviathan* (1942). The writing of the life is one of the ways in which Collingwood's living is shaped and brought to a close; in which the effort to comprehend one's purpose in living leads to its exhaustion; and in which *An Autobiography* is also (as Paul De Man might say) an 'epitaph', or in David Hume's terms, a 'funeral oration of myself'.[40]

The text of *An Autobiography* as republished here yields, then, a record of the breadth of Collingwood's cultural experience, and includes the dimension of the literary as adjunct to a philosophical and political significance for which Collingwood has been better known. This breadth may be concealed by the animated exterior of the narrative, but can itself be brought into the light of day alongside Collingwood's recollected history of thought (in the past) and his prophesied political engagements (in the future). Collingwood's self-narrativization is embedded in literary form and its generic and stylistic context, and his work withstands analysis as a literary complex elucidated by the art of writing the self. But the leading historical notions of *An Autobiography*, as its argument widens out, can even now be fruitfully applied to the study of literary history. They are in practice applied by the theorist specifically responsible for recommending a German edition of *An Autobiography* and composing an Introduction.[41] This is, once

[39] For a discussion of Collingwood's meaning in this expression see Patrick, James. 1995. 'Fighting in the Daylight: the Penultimate Collingwood 1937–1941', *Collingwood Studies,* vol. 2, 'Perspectives', 73.

[40] See Hume, David 1778. *The History of England, from the Invasion of Julius Caesar to the Revolution in 1688*, 8 vols. London, vol. I: 21.

[41] See *Denken. Eine Autobiographie.* For Gadamer's engagement with Collingwood's 'Logic of Question and Answer', and his attempt to distinguish, as he claims

again, Hans-Georg Gadamer, who wrote of Collingwood as 'a worthy member of a tradition that included Swift and Sterne'. In continuity with this eighteenth-century tradition, Collingwood's philosophical insights are similarly sharpened on the edge of satirical powers.

The narrative, then, subserves a theory of past and present developed even as the story of its evolution is told. Thus does *An Autobiography* close the gap between his literary-aesthetic interests, as expressed in the *Principles of Art*, and Collingwood's organized expression of his historical consciousness. As a history of Collingwood's thought, *An Autobiography* has as a primary context what is unmentioned or self-concealed. But it also looks outwards to examples of Collingwood's published work that map this most intensely lived of intellectual lives. 'I have displayed myself as I was,' wrote Jean-Jacques Rousseau.[42] R. G. Collingwood cannot quite say this of *An Autobiography*; but this does not mean his account of himself is lacking in the truth of experience that belongs to a literary work.

Collingwood did not, between intended past actions and meaningful ones, see Gadamer, *Truth and Method*, 369–75.

[42] Rousseau, J. J., 1953. *The Confessions*. Harmondsworth: Penguin Classics: 17.

PART II

A JOURNEY IN THE EAST INDIES 1938–1939

Illustration 12. M. V. *Alcinous*, Blue Funnel Line, docked at Padang, Sumatra, photographed by Collingwood. See *Log* entry 17 November 1938, p. 7. Courtesy of Teresa Smith.

INTRODUCTION TO COLLINGWOOD'S *LOG*

WENDY JAMES

READING NOTES ON THE EAST INDIES: THEN AND NOW

Collingwood's travels were to Java, Bali, and lesser-known island groups then part of the Dutch colonial empire. He also visited what was then Portuguese Timor. Many place names and words in local languages, including varieties of Malay, were then spelled in the Dutch manner. With Indonesian independence in 1945, a key dialect of Malay was elevated to become the official national language, Bahasa Indonesia, or simply 'Indonesian'. There was a major reform to spelling in 1972. To assist the modern reader in transposing Collingwood's spellings to their modern equivalent in Bahasa Indonesia, we could note the following: oe becomes u, as in the Balinese town of Oeboed, now spelled Ubud; while dj becomes j, j becomes y, nj becomes ny, and tj becomes c. Place names mentioned in the *Log* have typically changed in these ways: Baloerin = Balaurin; Bedoegoel = Bedugul; Boejalali = Boyalali; Boeleleng = Buleleng; Maoemerie = Maumere.

Several place names have changed completely: thus, the capital of Java which he knew as Batavia is now Jakarta. Celebes is now Sulawesi. On Collingwood's sketch map of Karangasem and eastern Bali (see Illustration 15), the old town Karangasem has now given its name to the region, and itself is now called Amlapura. The change was almost certainly made after the 1962 explosion of the volcano Gunung Agung—the old name having become inauspicious. Some of the buildings and hotels Collingwood described on his various visits still exist, while others have disappeared; the following details on Jakarta may be of interest. The Hotel Daendels where Collingwood stayed no longer exists, though it seems to have been on Koningsplein, now Medan Merdeka ('Freedom Square' or 'Independence Square'). The hotel may have been a survival from the original 'Hotel Daendels', or perhaps been named after it—that is the official residence (in Malay, the Istana or 'Palace') of Daendels, the Governor-General from 1808 to 1811, just before the British took over. Molenvliet is today's Jalan ('Street') Gajah Mada and Jalan Hayam Wuruk. Pasar Ikan is still there and is still a 'Fish Market'.

'Old Batavia' is Jakarta Kota ('City' or 'Fort') and still has important old Dutch buildings and a nice (old) restaurant. The Harmonie Club was situated on the corner of Rijswijk (Jalan Veteran) and Rijswijkstraat (Jalan Majapahit). It opened in 1868 but was torn down in March 1985 to widen the road and make a parking lot. The Hotel des Indes opened in 1856, and in 1960 became the government-owned Hotel Duta ('legation') Indonesia. In 1971 it was torn down and replaced by the 'Duta Merlin Shopping Center'. Buitenzorg is today's Bogor; Poentjak (today, Puncak) means 'Summit' Pass. Djoka (today, Jogja) is a common short form of Jogjakarta.

In the course of his travels within the East Indies, Collingwood used the commercial route map provided by the KPM steamship company who arranged his itinerary. We reproduce his own copy of this as our Map 2, spread across the front and end covers of this volume. The dotted lines Collingwood marked on it himself as his island cruise progressed can be seen faintly on the eastern section. Here we can find many of the place names mentioned in the *Log*, common currency in the 1930s but now outdated. Map 1, which follows here, is provided to help the reader trace his route more clearly on the basis of today's place names. We are greatly indebted to Terence Crump for creating this updated guide, and to Collins Bartholomew for permission to use their base map.

The text of the *Log* is scattered throughout with reference to people simply by their initials. The first Glossary which follows was compiled by David Boucher, James Connolly, and Teresa Smith in order to help the reader identify these. The *Log* and letters quoted here are also rich in local terms; reading through, one is very conscious that Collingwood was himself enthusiastically learning 'Malay'. Terms in some of the indigenous languages of the region are also picked up here and there in the *Log*, and by no means always translated. For assistance here, we turned to R. H. Barnes, a retired Oxford colleague and specialist in the anthropology of Indonesia.

Bob Barnes also provided background on the social history of the region for these notes, and on its modern geography for Map 1. His advice and knowledge were invaluable in putting together our second Glossary on local terms occurring in the *Log*, along with their modern spellings.

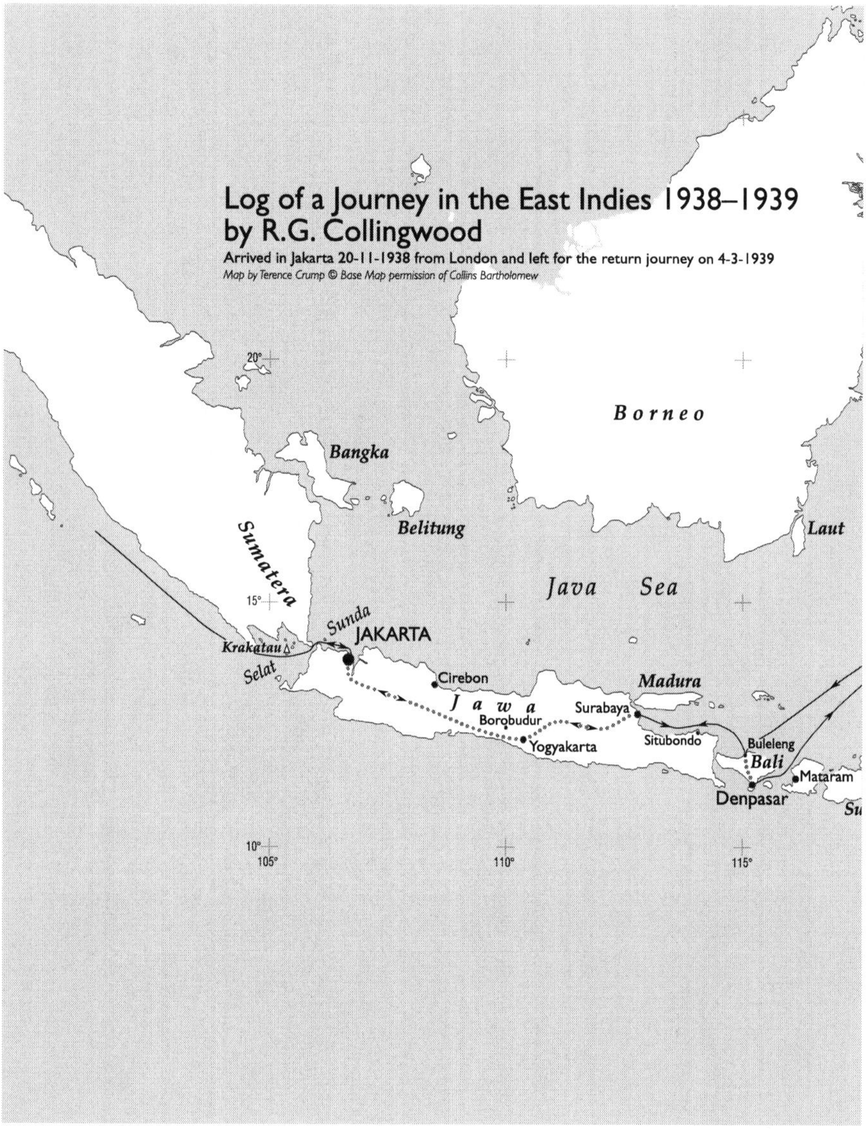
Log of a Journey in the East Indies 1938–1939
by R.G. Collingwood
Arrived in Jakarta 20-11-1938 from London and left for the return journey on 4-3-1939
Map by Terence Crump © Base Map permission of Collins Bartholomew
Borneo
Bangka
Belitung
Sumatera
Laut
Java Sea
Sunda
Selat
Krakatau
JAKARTA
Cirebon
Jawa
Madura
Surabaya
Borobudur
Yogyakarta
Situbondo
Buleleng
Bali
Mataram
Denpasar
20°
15°
10°
105°
110°
115°

Map 1

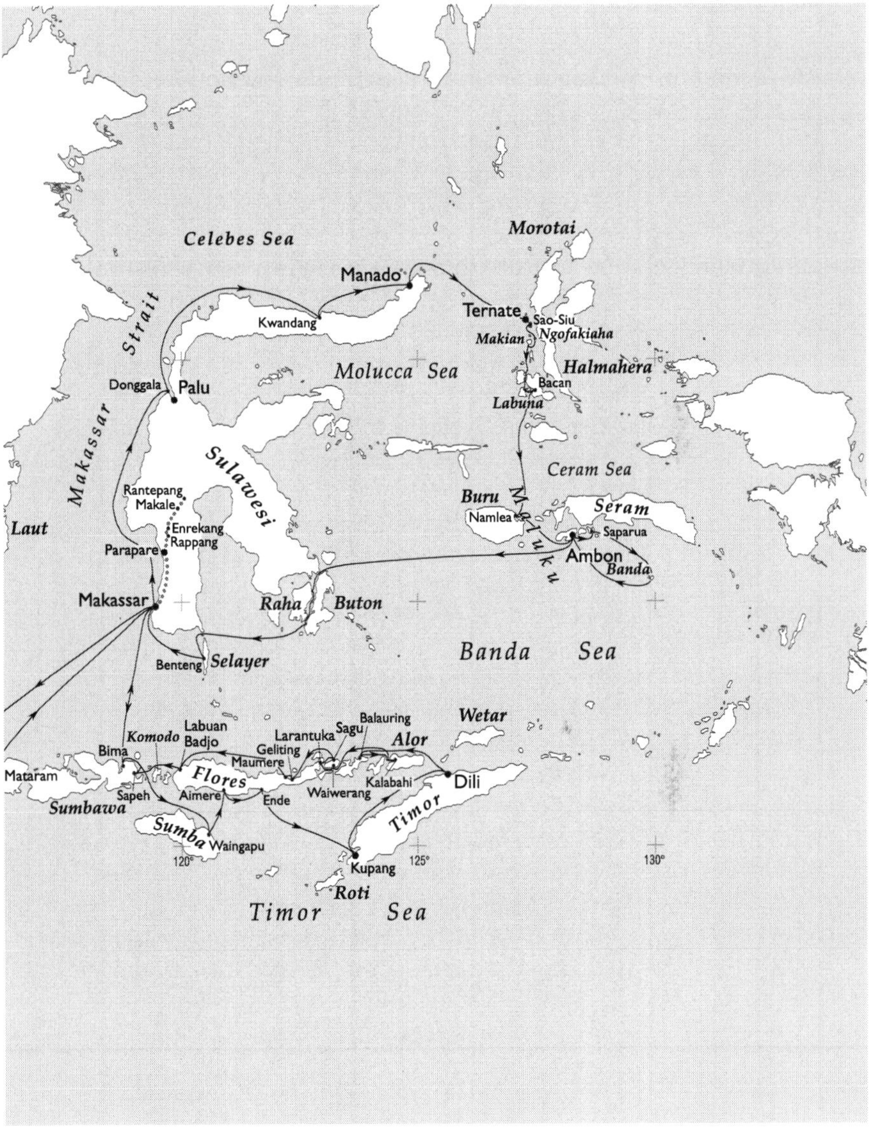
Celebes Sea
Morotai
Manado
Ternate
Sao-Siu
Makian
Ngofakiaha
Kwandang
Strait
Molucca Sea
Halmahera
Bacan
Donggala
Palu
Labuna
Makassar
Sulawesi
Ceram Sea
Rantepang
Makale
Enrekang
Rappang
Buru
Maluku
Seram
Namlea
Saparua
Laut
Parapare
Ambon
Banda
Makassar
Raha
Buton
Benteng
Selayer
Banda Sea
Wetar
Balauring
Labuan Badjo
Komodo
Larantuka
Sagu
Alor
Bima
Geliting
Maumere
Mataram
Flores
Kalabahi
Dili
Sapeh
Aimere
Ende
Waiwerang
Sumbawa
Timor
Sumba
Waingapu
120°
125°
130°
Kupang
Roti
Timor Sea

GLOSSARY 1: NAMES REFERRED TO IN THE *LOG*

AG	Angus Graham, Ethel Collingwood's younger brother, and friend of R. G. C. from undergraduate days.
BCG	Barbara Crystal Gnosspelius, R. G. C.'s elder sister, married to Oscar Gnosspelius.
BWC	Unknown
Cambridge V-C	A. C. Seward, Master of Downing College and Vice Chancellor of Cambridge University.
CG	Either Cristobel Graham, Ethel Collingwood's sister-in-law, or Cosmo Gordon, Ethel's brother-in-law, married to her elder sister Frances.
Chrystabel	Cristobel Graham, Ethel Collingwood's sister-in-law, married to her eldest brother Robert (Bertie).
DSA	Dorothy Susie Altounyan (Dora), R. G. C.'s eldest sister, married to Ernest Altounyan, from Aleppo.
EWC	Ethel Collingwood, R. G. Collingwood's first wife.
HML	Hugh Last, Camden Professor of Ancient History at Oxford.
IH	Isobel Henderson, née Munro, R. G. C.'s former student, archaeologist and friend of Ethel and R. G. C.
KENM	? Katherine Munro, sister of Isobel?
KFE	Kathleen Edwardes (Kate), R. G. C.'s second wife and mother of Teresa Smith.
KPM	Koninklijke Paketvaart-Maatschappij was a shipping company in the Dutch East Indies.
KS	Kenneth Sisam (1887–1971), Assistant Secretary and Secretary to the Delegates of Oxford University Press.
LMcM	Lilian McMorran; the McMorrans were R. G. C.'s hosts in Batavia, and Lilian's father and his wife, the van der Noordaas, were his hosts in Bali.
RWC	R. W. Chapman was Secretary to the Delegates of Oxford University Press from 1920 to 1942.
Teresa	Kate Collingwood's mother, E. F. T. Edwardes.

TMK	Malcolm Knox, Principal of St Andrews. R. G. C.'s former student and editor of *The Idea of Nature* and *The Idea of History*.
TSN	Tom Nelson, R. G. C.'s friend and doctor, based in London.
UMLS	Ursula Mavis Luard-Selby, R. G. C.'s younger sister, married to Revd R. B. Luard-Selby, who officiated at Collingwood's funeral.
URC	Ruth Collingwood, R. G. C.'s daughter by Ethel Collingwood.
WRC	Bill Collingwood, R. G. C.'s son by Ethel Collingwood.

GLOSSARY 2: LOCAL TERMS AND INTERESTING PLACE NAMES MENTIONED IN THE *LOG*

Term (R. G. C. spelling)	Modern spelling	English meaning
alang-alang		tall grass for thatching
Anak Agoeng	Anak Agung	a high-status title used within the warrior and ruling caste; also used as title for a ruling prince
Baloering	Balauring	lit. 'Base of the Elephant Tusk'
baris		ritual war dance with spears
djanger	janger	a modern musical comedy with many foreign elements, danced by boys and girls
gamboeh	gambuh	the classic technique for dramatic performances
gamelan		orchestral ensemble
goenoeng	gunung	mountain
goenoeng api	gunung api	'fire mountain', i.e. volcano
kali		ravine
kampong	kampung	hamlet, village
kebiar		a modern dance, performed by a boy dancer who interprets musical moods

ketjak	kecak	a dance with large groups of men singing in chorus, often as accompaniment to trance performances. The Monkey Dance is a famous example.
klamboeh	kelambuh	mosquito net
klapa	kelapa	coconut
Labuan Bajo		'Anchorage of Bajau Laut', i.e. Sea Gypsies (see Illustration 15)
legong		girls' dance, intricate foot-work, finger movements
pasanggrahan		rest house for passing Europeans
pasar		market
Pasar Baroe		New Market
Pasar Besar		Great Market
Pasar Ikan		Fish Market
pedanda		Balinese priest
pentjak	pencak	martial arts, war dance
poera	Pura	temple
poera dalem	pura dalem	temple of the dead, in or near burial ground
poeri agoeng	puri agung	royal palace
prahu, prau	perahu	sailing boat
'Poentjak Pass'	puncak	summit, as in 'Summit Pass'
redjang	rejang	line dance performed by a group of girls at temple festivals
rumah		house
Rumah Blanda		Dutch house (from Belanda, i.e. 'Hollandia')
rumah orang matih	rumah orang mati	dead man's house
saput		man's ceremonial outer cloth
sawah		wet rice field or fields
Tandjoeng Priok	Tanjung Periuk	'Pot Peninsula'
tempat orang		place-of-people
tempat orang matih	tempat orang mati	place-of-the-dead
tempat pesta		place-of-festival
'tida(k) tidur'		'no sleep'

Tjokorde	Cokorde	king or ruler; the Lords of Ubud bore this title but were under the suzerainty of Gianyar.
Tjokorde Istri		'Istri': spouse of a Cokorde
toekang	tukang	workman, craftsman
toekad	tukad	river
topeng		masked dance
Toradja	Toraja	indigenous peoples of central Celebes (Sulawesi)
wayang kulit		'kulit' means skin; *wayang kulit* is a shadow puppet performance using leather puppets behind a screen, seen in silhouette
wayang wong		'wong' means person; *wayang wong* is a performance acted by people

Note. Collingwood's references to 'Malay', which he himself studied in the course of his voyage, was to the lingua franca of the East Indies region at the time. One of its dialects was endorsed as the official Indonesian language of today, and exists alongside many local languages (the majority of the Austronesian family), with frequent examples of mutual influence and borrowing.

In the table, for example, the following terms are Indonesian: *gunung* (mountain), *kampung* (village), *kelambuh* (mosquito net), *kelapa* (coconut), *pasanggrahan* (resthouse), *pasar* (market), *pencak* (martial arts), *perahu* (sailing boat), *puncak* (summit), *rumah* (house), *saput* (man's ceremonial cloth), *sawah* (rice field), *tempat* (place-of-), *'tida(k) tidur'* ('no sleep'), *tukang* (craftsman), *kulit* (skin).

Terms which are purely Balinese include: *Anak Agung* (high title), *Corkorde* (ruler), *rejang* (dance), *tukad* (river).

Terms which are used in Indonesian as well as Balinese, sometimes with slightly different meanings, include: *baris* (line formation, war dance), *janger* (dance), *gambuh* (classic drama), *gamelan* (orchestral ensemble), *kecak* (dance), *legong* (dance), *pedanda* (priest), *pura* (temple), *puri agung* (royal palace), *topeng* (dance), *wayang wong* (acted performance).

A few of these terms are also used in Javanese; and the place name Balauring means 'Base of Elephant's Tusk' in Kedang.

Further information may be found in the following sources (the first two books were read by Collingwood in the course of his journey):

Covarrubias, M., 1937. *Island of Bali*. New York: Alfred A. Knopf.

De Zoete, Beryl and Spies, Walter, 1938. *Dance and Drama in Bali*. London: Faber & Faber.

Wertheim W. F. (ed.), 1960. *Bali: Studies in Life, Thought, and Ritual*. The Hague: W. van Hoeve.

LOG OF A JOURNEY IN THE EAST INDIES IN 1938–1939

R. G. COLLINGWOOD

[1]

1938. 21 Oct. Leave Oxford 12.55. Fine sunny day: at Birkenhead (5.29) went to customs for a certificate for Leica. Met by BCG. & UMLS. and dined at Queen's Hotel. Went on Board MV. Alcinous at Victoria Dock 9.30.

22 Oct. Up 6 am. Left quayside (tugs) 6.15. Dock gates opened 9.0: went out then. Foggy, dull. Dropped pilot, Holyhead, 1 P.M. Inoculated first dose TAB 2.30. Rain, dull, calm.

23 Oct. Fine day, gentle swell from W. and wind about force 3, NNE. Passed outside the Scillies (not in sight) about noon. On deck all day, in sunshine.

24 Oct. Fine day. Wind moderate to fresh, NNE; sea fairly smooth, sun bright. Crossing Bay of Biscay. Began writing Metaphysics in afternoon. Off Finistere 6 P.M. Fine clear night.

25 Oct. Fine day, warmer. Wind light NNE; sea smooth, sun bright. Off Lisbon, in sight of Cape Rocas, 8–10 AM. Saw a few steamers & one yawl. SS. Achilles (our neighbour in dock at Birkenhead) hull down behind us. At sunset passed Cape St. Vincent about 3 miles out. Much traffic, some from the Straits & some from W. African Coast.

In margin above page number [2]

Distances (from K.P.M. Dienstregeling 1939). Southampton – Port Said 3032 sea miles. S – Gibr. 1152. Marseilles – P.S. 1544. P.S. – Suez 88. S – Aden 1312. S – Padang 4728. S – Batavia 5228 (April-October course).

26 Oct. Fine day, bright sun; wind following (WNW) light. Sea calm. Entered Straits of Gibraltar at dawn. On deck 6 AM, nearing Gibraltar. Passed it at sunrise (6.30). In sight of Spanish coast; high mountains with thunder-clouds over them, all morning. After dark a distant thunderstorm perhaps 100 miles away on port bow.

27 Oct. On deck 6 AM; cloudy sky of stormy appearance, wind WSW, chilly. Flag at half mast; C. C. Lynam had died at 2.30 AM. (passenger). He had embarked for Java & Australia; had been suffering from angina pectoris which had been visibly worse the last day or two. Spent afternoon working at his papers, by Captain's request. Cloudy showery day, thunder about. Took soneryl, good result.

28 Oct. Finer, but a good deal of cloud. Wind WSW, moderate. Photographed Lynam's coffin. Passing Pantellaria 8–9 AM. At 4.0 P.M. buried him, 9 miles N. 20° E. of Cape Bon. Working, as usual, at Malay and metaphysics by spells. 1 wk [*encircled*].

29 Oct. Passed Malta 4 AM. Very fine & hot. The Captain gave me the run of the lower bridge with table & chair & I took my writing there.

30 Oct. Very fine & warm, calm. Writing all day. Sunday.

31 Oct. Very fine & calm. Hot sun. Writing all day, finished ch. 6. Clear sunset: green flash.

[3] 1 November. After going slow since about 8 P.M., arrived Port Said c. 5.30 AM under our own steam: made fast to buoys. Discharged and took in some cargo. Did not stay long enough to make it worth while going on shore. Sailed c. 12.0 & entered the Canal. Overcast day, sultry; hardly any wind. Second TAB inoculation 2 PM. Bed early, feverish. Arrived Suez 10 P.M.

2 November. Up early. Fuelling ship from oil tanker. Took 35 pilgrims on board, returning to Java. Sailed 10 AM. Overcast dark day, strongish NNE. wind. Writing metaphysics all day. Sinai in cloud.

3 November. Going down Red Sea. Passed lighthouse (?Daedalus) about noon. Finer; a good deal of sun; but overcast again by sunset. Hot, these days, but not unpleasantly so. Writing all day; finished chapters on Psychology (begun yesterday). My study on the captain's bridge once more in use, but too windy (moderate NE breeze) for comfort with papers there.

4 November. Brilliant day, hot sun, cool moderate NE breeze. Writing metaphysics all day; got to end of ch. XIII after completely rewriting X. Sea very brilliant blue, like Mediterranean. Clear sunset, green flash. Moon gibbous, ½ way through 2nd quarter. Plough well below horizon in evening. 2 wk [*encircled*].

[4] 5 November. Brilliant day, practically cloudless: head wind, moderate to light. Flying fish at the bows. Metaphysics all day & finished ch. XV. Sunset clear, but a little haze: no green flash. Passed Jebel Zebayir islands & light ho. at 5.30, sunset.

6 November, Sunday. Brilliant day. Zodiacal light seen 5.0 AM. Passed through Straits of Bab-al-Mandab 6–9 AM. Aden abreast 2.30 P.M. Gentle head wind, calm sea; flying fish; clear sunset: green flash. Arabian coast extraordinarily savage and rocky, with no sign of vegetation; precipitous sierras and towards Aden dunes. Having slept badly, no writing: working at Malay.

7 November. Brilliant day. Somaliland coast visible at 80 m. in morning. Writing all day. Coast nearer in afternoon: sandy & rocky; cliffs, rugged islands. Cape Guardafui abeam at sunset: clear sunset, green flash.

8 November. 1 AM, total eclipse of moon; up looking at it. In morning some swell; course S 8° E. (set before Guardafui, arriving at Minikoi). Wind about 2 pts. on port bow, very light. Double swell all day, from E. and S: ship moving to it a bit. Writing all day. Sea calm except for this slight swell. Cumulus clouds about the sky: sunset not clear, much colour on cirrus.

[5]

Officers of M.V. Alcinous

Captain	C Koningstein	Passengers
1st officer	A van Visure	No. 1: Steven Velds R.G.C.
2nd —	E. Broersma	
3rd —	L M Burger	No. 2: Mr & Mrs Paul, of Manado, Celebes, Armenians
Chief Eng.	J. Wezel	
2nd —	M Blokker	'Administrator' (i.e. passenger wangling an officer's cabin)
3rd —	M. Hartman	C.C. Lynam
4th —	P. Klaarwater	'Assistant Engineer' (something of the same sort)
Dokter	A Boerma	Currie

9 November. Fine day, a good deal of small cumulus about. Ship pitching gently in a long low swell from NE; wind light, NE, with small white heads in the afternoon. Mr. Wezel showed me over the engine room in the morning, right along to the shaft-tunnel. Otherwise writing all day. (3 chapters, on Kant). Passed a Blue Funnel, port to port, about 4 PM. Fine night, after a cloudy sunset. Moon, swell, ship gently pitching.

10 November. Very fine day. Small cumulus in clear sky. Slight swell from N; light breeze from NW; ship quiet, a good deal better owing to the following breeze. Bigger flying fish, up to perhaps a foot long, coloured like mackerel. Passed a French two-funnel mailboat (from Saigon) **[6]** about noon. Writing metaphysics all day, 2 chapters, finishing Kant; but much revision needed. Clear sunset, green flash. 3 wks [*encircled*].

11 November. Very fine day, fresh following breeze about NW. sea slight, white heads; ship gently rolling. Passed P & O about 10 AM; French liner about noon. Small cumulus clouds, sunset not clear. Sighted Minikoi light ½ hr. after sunset: abeam 6.30 P.M. Revising Kant all day, wrote two new chapters. Wireless reported Kemal's death.

12 November. Fine, hot. Fresh following breeze, NW. Sea slight to moderate, ship gently rolling. Cumulus clouds. Thunder-packs with rain in sight; one reached us about 6 P.M. Sunset not clear. Revising all day. Wrote new chapter XII. Revised English letter for 3rd officer.

13 November, Sunday. Fine, hot. Moderate breeze, N, morning, with slight sea; falling almost calm towards evening with smooth sea & gentle swell. Some cumulus. Sun set in a thunder-pack with fine Buddha's rays.

Revising all day; wrote new chapter XXVII (last). Back to Malay. Passed a cargo vessel in morning.

14 November. Fine: cloudy (cumulus below cirrhus and cirrho-stratus), calm, hardly any wind. Working at Malay all day; and some letter-writing. Cooler, owing to less sunshine. Sunset bright yellow underneath c-stratus, turning orange & red: green flash before the sun reached horizon, when [7] it went behind a level cloud (I have never seen or heard of this happening).

15 November. I have never seen that kind of sunset except before very wet weather, & this evidently holds good even in the tropics. Today broke dark (heavily overcast) and very wet, & stayed so. Did some Malay but in such weather (and after a bad night thanks to certain pranks of my companion) little heart for study. So read Racine.

16 November. Day broke in heavy rain. Later cleared up & began to blow: wind fresh, about W., and freshening towards evening. Rough sea, wind fresh to strong, some spray on deck. Got off our course somehow in the morning (query something about a current: they are odd hereabouts) & recovered it in the afternoon when we sighted an island – heavily wooded, rocky shores – & passed it about 3 miles to port. Revising book.

17 Nov. At dawn, entering Padang in heavy rain. Waited at anchor 6.0 – 6.30 for pilot; tied up to quay; unloaded cargo all day as fine intervals permitted. Rain more or less continuous all morning. After lunch took car with Mr. & Mrs. Paul & S. Velds & drove 13 km. round harbour, past kampong, to light ho. & then to Padang town. After dinner drove to P. town with the same & Burger & 2 engineers to the flicks, after which sat in club drinking until 1.30 AM. Argument about 'fishiology' & 'metaphyshiology' with Klaarwater. Posted letters EWC. BCG. UMLS. KFE. RWC.

[8] 4 wks [*encircled*].

18 November. Heavy rain, fair intervals. Finished unloading cargo 6 – 8.20, sailed 10.0. Weather better away from the coast; wind W. light, sea calm, some showers. Racine.

19 November. Coasting along Sumatra. Morning fair, overcast, light following wind; afternoon wet. 6 PM: passed Krakatau (now a group of 3 islands, the largest only 2600 ft high, instead of a single mountain 10,000 ft. high: beneath the former summit a hole 150 fathoms deep in sea-floor). Sunda Straits.

20 November. Sunday. Anchored in Batavia roads 2 AM. Entered Tanjong Priok 6.30 AM, berthed 7.0. Met by McMorran & driven by him to Hotel Daendels, Koningsplein east. He called for me again at 11.30 and drove me round the town (Molenvliet, Pasar Ikan, etc.) & to lunch with his wife, to meet the Rampollets. Mrs R. took me to Chinese temples afterwards, then to golf club; walked on the course, had drinks, driven home by McMorrans. Very delightful day, thanks to McMorran's hospitality. Some rain, morning; cool day.

21 Nov. Walked down to old Batavia in morning: went to Chartered Bank (to find I had forgotten my letter of indication) and to Maclaine Watson, where found my first letters from Oxford. Hot. After lunch returned by tram to bank cashed £100 = g 833. Went to Harmonie [*Club*], read papers. Haircut, bought cigars.

[9] 22 Nov. Wrote home: at 10.30 went to Uniegebouw, met the editor of Wereldnieuws, who gave me guide-book to the N.E.I., was photographed, interviewed, & shown all over the printing works including photographic & blockmaking departments and drawing-office. Then to Museum. Siesta after lunch. Walk in town before dinner.

23 Nov. Up 5.30, at 6.0 left with McMorrans & Cochrane (a consulting engineer from Bangkok) for Buitenzorg and Poentjak Pass. Dull, some rain on the way. Breakfast at the hotel on the summit. Walk to the lake in the jungle. Drove back; lunch with McM's alone, and story of their lives. Hotel: reading Vandenbosch, Dutch E. Indies. Dined with Rambonnets at a Chinese restaurant & drinks at Hotel des Indes till 12.0. Moslem New Year's Eve.

24 Nov. Moslem New Year. General holiday: natives all very much en-dimanchés, plenty fireworks. Walked out morning, bought stockings & a book, read at Club. Siesta. Lazy day.

25 Nov. Writing letters: spent morning with K.P.M. people arranging cruise. 5 wks [*encircled*]

26 Nov. To Maclaine Watson morning; found letter from home; then to Museum. Letters to EWC, TMK, KFE, BCG.

27 Nov. Sunday. Packing: lazy day. Dined at Harmonie with McMorrans, then H. des Indes until 1 AM. Hot.

28 Nov. Up 5.30. Breakfast: train (Koningsplein sta) 6.45. 2nd class to **[10]** Djokja via Cheribon. Fare 4.50 + 3.0 express supplement; lunch 1.50. A hot journey but comfortable: good carriages, good line. Lunched while crossing the divide after Cheribon: arr. Djokja 2.10: Hotel Mataram, cheap & good. Rest of day siesta, walking in town.

29 Nov. Up 7.0. At 8.0 attended office to get permit for Sultan's palace, which is only visited on Tuesdays. Visit

8.30 – 10.0. Then unwell, bad head (? touch of sun) spent most of day resting. Dull day, no sun: heavy rain in night.

30 Nov. Up 6.30. At 7.30 started in car for Borobudur. (car hire f5.50). Reached it at 9. Spent 2 hrs. seeing it, looking at all sculptures & photographing a lot. Visited 2 small temples on way back. Bright hot day (but Djokja much pleasanter climate than Batavia).

1 Dec. Went after breakfast & bought batiks from Billal Zaini, escaping with difficulty with what is left of my virtue; B.Z. explaining that tourists generally like buggery. So home rather disgusted & wrote to E.W.C. and KFE. Letter from LMcM enclosing introduction to her father in Bali: answered it & received invitation by telephone to visit her uncle near Solo on Sat.

2 Dec. Walking & photographing in town all morning. Wet afternoon, siesta & packing. 6 wks [*encircled*].

3 Dec. Up at 5. At 6.01 left by train (after breakfast) for Solo. Met there by van der Noordaa who drove me home & took me over his tobacco plantation & drying sheds & fermenting- and packing- shop. After lunch **[11]** he took me to Prambanan Temples, & home to tea. Stayed night with him & his wife outside Solo (it is between Solo & Bodjalali). Arguing about Darwinism in the evening. NB – their butterfly collection.

4 Dec. Sunday. Spent morning quietly in garden with Mrs v.d.N & baby. Early lunch, then driven to Solo & took 12.56 train for Soerabaja. Very heavy rain & thunder on the way, at Kertosono. Reached Soerabaja 5.15 and put up (by v.d.N's advice) at Ngemplak hotel. Walked in town until dark.

5 Dec. Walked into town 8 AM. To K.P.M. ordering passage: to Chartered Bank, cashed £50; to Fraser

Eaton, asking for letters (none); they to give me option on a passage home in March. Walked down river to just below Stat. Prins Hendrik (11 km. there) looking at shipping, & back. Had a pocket-book made by a Chinese leather-toekang. After siesta more walking, Pasar Besar &c. Very fine day, no rain, bright sun nearly all day. Wrote Chrystabel, Maclaine Watson.

6 Dec. Wrote TSN. Fine day, hot, slight cirrhus. Morning fixing up cruise at K.P.M. office, got tickets & paid for them, spent rest of mg. photographing native shipping down river below Roode Brug. Did nothing else this day, except siesta & sweat. Called in vain for letters at Fraser Eaton.

[12] 7 Dec. Fine, hot. Went down in vain to F.E. for letters at 9 AM: at 11 they rang up to say some had come, so went down again. Letters from EWC (25 xi) KFE (21 xi) C.G. (8 xi, ordinary mail). 2.30 P.M. left hotel by taxi for Tandjong Perak, boarded SS. Merak for Bali. Made various friends & talked until late (after sailing at 5). Hot day, very sultry in Soerabaja: glad to see the last of that town. (Soerabaja – Boeleleng = 160 m)

8 Dec. Called at 5.30, approaching Bali: breakfast at 6, ashore in K.P.M. launch 6.30 at Boeleleng. At 7.30 set off by car with 2 American women over the mountains, 113 km., summit 1400 on the north crater-rim of Goenoeng Tjatoer (NB. road well engineered in lacets cut in the deep volcanic soil, nowhere cut in rock except for the first short distance of descent) to Den Pasar. On way down stopped in a village where tooth-filing festival was going on, and listened to gamelan – about 20 performers, pentatonic scale, each composition introduced by a solo passage. A very highly-wrought and satisfying form of music. Den Pasar 11 A.M. Bali Hotel. Letter from BWC (27 Oct) – with Unicode. Afternoon, visited Elephant cave, Royal tombs, & sacred spring with Mr. & Mrs. Weiner, & saw Monkey Dance. Fine: heavy rain in night.

9 Dec. Up at 6, writing EWC. At 8 went by car to Oeboed. Found v.d. Noordaa's had been expecting me since Monday & were meaning to put me up indefinitely. Returned promising to go next day. Cloudy sultry, damp.

[13] 7 weeks [*encircled*]. Wrote KFE. Siesta. Evening: kebiar dance in front of hotel. Rain came on; dancers moved in to hotel for a kind of mumming play. This was a Topeng on a Uriah-the-Hittite theme – shortened perhaps for the tourists' sake.

10 Dec. Morning, 8.30, Legong & Djanger danced at a neighbouring village. After this, drove to Oeboed to take up residence with v.d.N's. This was the 'birthday' of the 3-months daughter of the Tjokorde in the front part of whose puri they live. He was giving a feast to celebrate. In the afternoon a great cock-fight, of which I saw about 8 rounds: then listened to his private gamelan practising. After dark, went to his house & saw the child being given its presents by the priest. A very pretty scene. (The child quite white). Then watched mumming play (Topeng) until 9.20, leaving it unfinished. Wayang kulit 12.0 – 4.0 AM, the gamelan making sleep impossible.

11 Dec. Sunday. Drove in morning to the Monkey Wood (described by v.d.N. in rather sinister phrase as 'the local Hollywood', meaning holy wood). I got a touch of sun, going without a hat; for the sun came out v. strong – Siesta. Early bed.

12 Dec. Got up with bad head & diarrhoea. Better in the course of the day. Went to Gianjar about the approaching festivities (with G. vd N and Bonnet); met Spies there. Called on the Tjokorde Istri [*last child of the last king of Ubud*] weaving on her porch. Letters from WRC (29 xi) BCG (28 xi) KFE (27 xi).

[14] 13 Dec. Letter, brought by hand from Gianjar, from EWC & URC (2 xii). Walked morning across sawahs to God's Bathing place and neighbouring poera dalem with coloured Rangda statues; drank coconuts. Read De Zoete on Balinese dance. Splendid sunset, purple mountains, green sky, gold clouds. Drove to call on Bonnicker.

14 Dec. Up early writing to EWC, URC, WRC. At 10.30 drove to Den Pasar, finished my letters in the hotel there & posted them. We lunched in hotel. I bought a roll picture, 2.25. We then drove to Sanoer & walked on the beach (coral sand); water as hot as a moderately hot (more than tepid) bath. Sunny & hot all day. Home to tea.

15 Dec. After early breakfast walked with L. to Pura Bedoegoel in the sawahs to west of here, taking Tingal as guide. Strong sun, fresh air; walked fast & enjoyably, sweating no more than reason. Then walked diagonally up to another temple (where we lost Tingal by sending him for klapa) & so home, 2 hrs. fast walking. Wrote KFE. About 5.30 drove to Pliatan where the village gamelan (reputed one of the best) was rehearsing for Gianjar competitions. A large audience. Listened with very great pleasure and admiration (NB isolated staccato chords on the full orchestra, like pizzicato chords on strings, with no raggedness at all). After dark a kebiar followed by a legong in which the 3rd girl was absent (she has developed chronic asthma & has had to give up dancing & has not been replaced) and the kebiar dancer remained on the stage to make a 3rd. A very interesting new dance-form resulted. Butterfly transformation. My hosts' dinner party, with **[15]** Balinese food, and the Oeboed children's djanger & baris. We then went to Batoean & saw Gamboeh in a very great crowd. Left about midnight (or how much later I don't know) still during the introductory solos & duets – 2 bearded men, 2 moustached men, 1 young man & the Raja were all we saw. Gamelan with bass recorders.

16 Dec. Bright morning. Walked with L to his toekang's house (Goesti Njoman of Oeboed) & saw work in progress (a gamelan in the making for Pliatan & various rather Beardsley drawings) & thence E. & first to N into the sawahs, W. across a canyon, & S. home. A 2-hour walk, in fresh and hot summer-like weather. After siesta drove N. to Sepatu (?) & walked to the sacred bathing place at a temple in the canyon below. Sawahs thereabouts (500 m. up) very fine, on slopes of even 45°. Found a note from Bonnet informing us of a ketjak at Bedulu: had tea & went, calling at Bonnicker's & picking up a party (Miss Van Wessum; the Baronin from Batavia; & men). Differences of detail between this & the ketjak (same people, same place, only leading soloist different) I saw last week. So back to B's for drinks & talk, & home; supper 10.30. bed 11.15. 8 weeks [*encircled*].

17 Dec. We left for Gianjar about 9.30, L. in dress clothes, me in white men's jacket. Went to the Controleur's house (a charming young man (but I think foolish) with pretty wife). At 10.15 we all went to the Anak Agoeng's palace (greatly decorated) shook hands & sat round a large temporary wall of bamboo & coloured paper. Champagne. The Resident (Moll) proposed the AA's health in a Malay speech. Other speeches by natives & Dutchmen all very good except the Controleur, who was very bad. Then we went across to a temporary shed in the grounds & saw **[16]** Gamboeh. Then to another shed & saw Topeng with a Redjang worked in as an episode (this extremely beautiful. Procession of 8 girls, in file, took 20 minutes to move 20 yards). Then lunch. We sat down c.1.00, & had soup, rijstafel, rum cake, fruit, coffee. Good. I sat by Spies, who told me that the orchestra we were hearing at lunch was a modification by him of the S. Bali instruments to enable them to play N. Bali music. That the composition they were playing (one of amazing rhythmical complexity & terrific bravura) was a N. Bali symphony which 2 of the players had learnt by heart in 3 days & had taught to the rest less than a week ago. That no Balinese orchestral player is ever off the beat. That all music is learnt by heart (his answer to my question whether orchestras ever extemporized seemed meant for a negative but wasn't quite clear). That they have a musical notation capable of recording themes. That now much B. music has been written down by him & others. Then we watched the processions from the various villages. At 5 there was Legong & after dark Wayang Wong, but after the processions we went home.

18 Dec. Sunday. My hosts stayed at home. I went with Walter Spies's party (Miss van Wessum) to Gianjar about 9 AM. Song competitions all day: 6 competing groups; first each played classical symphonies, then (in the same order) modern music with dance (kebiar & legong).

Songs arranged thus [*see Illustration 13*]. Karangasem had no dancer.

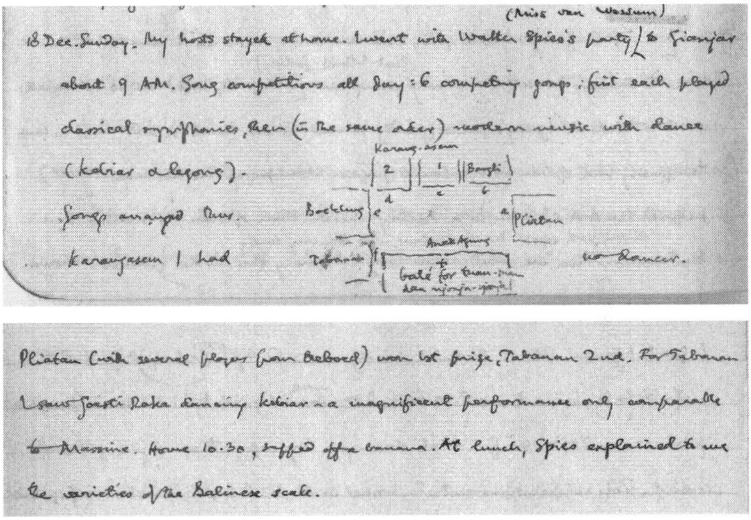

(Miss van Wessum)
18 Dec. Sunday. My hosts stayed at home. I went with Walter Spies's party to Gianjar about 9 AM. Song competitions all day: 6 competing gongs: first each played classical symphonies, then (in the same order) modern music with dancer (kebiar dancers).
Songs arranged thus. Karangasem I had no dancer.

Pliatan (with several players from Oeboed) won 1st prize, Tabanan 2nd. For Tabanan I saw Goesti Raka dancing kebiar – a magnificent performance only comparable to Massine. Home 10.30, supped off a banana. At lunch Spies explained to me the varieties of the Balinese scale.

Illustration 13. Collingwood's sketch of the arrangement of a song competition at Gianjar, Bali. Facsimile of the *Log* entry for 18 December 1938, pp. 16–17. Courtesy of Teresa Smith.

[17] Pliatan (with several players from Oeboed) won 1st prize, Tabanan 2nd. For Tabanan I saw Goesti Raka dancing kebiar – a magnificent performance only comparable to Massine. Home 10.30, supped off a banana. At lunch Spies explained to me the varieties of the Balinese scale.

19 Dec. Lazy day. Read books (Covarrubias: Djawa) lent by Bonnet. Thunder.

20 Dec. Walked with L. 8.0–11.0 AM. uphill N of Oeboed from the Tjokorde's temple at the meeting of the kalis by Tjampanan. Footpath through alang-alang, passing up to sawahs & 3 successive villages. Back same way. Fine, hot. Thunder afternoon & night. Dined with

Bonnet to meet Kidors (Swiss artists). B's boys danced pentjak on the grass. B showed modern Balinese paintings.

21 Dec. Left Oeboed after breakfast, went to stay with Bonnicker. Talked all morning, slept till 4.30, then walked through Bedulu to the old rock-carvings at Tojo Poeloeh below that village: king with long curly hair hunting the boar on horseback in centre: on sin. [*sinister*] side huntsmen carry 5 dead boars on a pole, & king rides home; extreme sin, Ganesha. Dexter side, a half-open door with seated woman inside, man with mattock on shoulder. Said to be Cx. Clothing like modern Balinese. Boar-hunt reminds me of Hellenistic work & late Rom. sarcophagi. Vigorous work. Decorative motive [*small sketch provided*] everywhere repeated. Then called on **[18]** I Goesti Njoman Sole in Bedulu, kindly received by his beautiful little wife & baby, he out: sat & talked, & were shown his work in progress, picture c. 20 x 14″ of a devil chasing a boy up a tree in a gale of wind [*see Illustration 14*]. Très-impressionnant. So home in dark. Bought 2 Sebadu figures.

22 Dec. Up 6 AM., writing EWC. At 8.30 set out with B. in his car by Pliatan up an increasingly rough road to the main Gianjar-Boeleleng road on the rim of the crater of Goenoeng Batoer. Car konked out about 5 km. before the main road (ignition) & we walked up the last 1000 ft. through very poor farmland. Car then arrived & we drove to Kintainani, turned, & so down to Bangli: there saw the magnificent temple; pedanda's son tried to sell us carvings; saw the poeri in which Kidurs are to live. Down by a secondary road to near Kloengkoeng & back to Gianjar in hot sun. Car pulling badly. Home to lunch 2 P.M. Siesta, tea, talk, supper, talk, bed (NB maggots for lunch, lizard for supper).

Illustration 14. Painting by Goesti Njoman Sole of 'Devil chasing a boy up a tree in a gale of wind'. See *Log* entry for 21 December 1938, p. 18. Courtesy of Teresa Smith.

23 Dec. Wrote K. Sisam, BCG, KFE, while Bonnicker was in Gianjar for legal business. Then at 12.0 with him to Den Pasar for car-repairs & a Chinese lunch. Bought a saput and a drawing from a visitor. Frau Kidor on the way to D.P. handed me letters from EWC. AG. DSA. Teresa. KFE. Cambridge VC. To Mengwi, watched cremation in the rain. Home (fine by now, mountains clearing) via Oeboed: tea with Bonnet; gave him f100 for Balinese modern pictures, his choice, for exhibition in England. v.d. N.'s to dinner preceded by gong & legong in the garden, **[19]** from Bedulu. 9 weeks [*encircled*].

24 Dec. Returned to v.d.N.'s for the day & night. Christmas dinner – duck, plum pudding; cigars by me.

25 Dec. Wrote Teresa, Cambr. V.C. Drove to Karangasem; called Groder, put up at the pasanggrahan [*see Illustration 15*]. Hot. Walk round town before sunset: poeri agoeng etc. Sunday.

26 Dec. Wrote K. At 7.30 after breakfast drove through mountains to Besakih & visited the temple, the metropolis of Balinese religion. 40 km each way. Remarkable sawah-complexes on steep hillsides round Selat. Photographed aqueduct over Toekad Bangka, also temple & sawahs, also temple at or near Sibetan.

27 Dec. Wrote WRC (posted at Gianjar, 28 xii). 8 AM, drove N. over pass between G. Agoeng & G. Seraja to the sea at Amed. Photographed fishing craft.

28 Dec. Returned to Oeboed for night, arriving I think about 9.30 AM. Unwell.

29 Dec. Left Oeboed 9 AM with v.d.N's; called at Gianjar post office; card from Teresa, coffee at Kintamani, lunch Singaradja; night there.

30 Dec. Up 5 AM. Boarded SS. Ophir 5.45. Overcast; heavy showers about. 10 wks [*encircled*].

31 Dec. Arr. Makasser 6.30 AM. Rain. To Empress Hotel. Wrote Lloyds Bank for £50; to Maclaine Watson & F. Eaton to forward letters c/o KPM here. Letter from EWC at Vence. Wrote EWC. Hair cut; saw Meyer about Toradja trip. Revels all night; tida' tidur [*no sleep*].

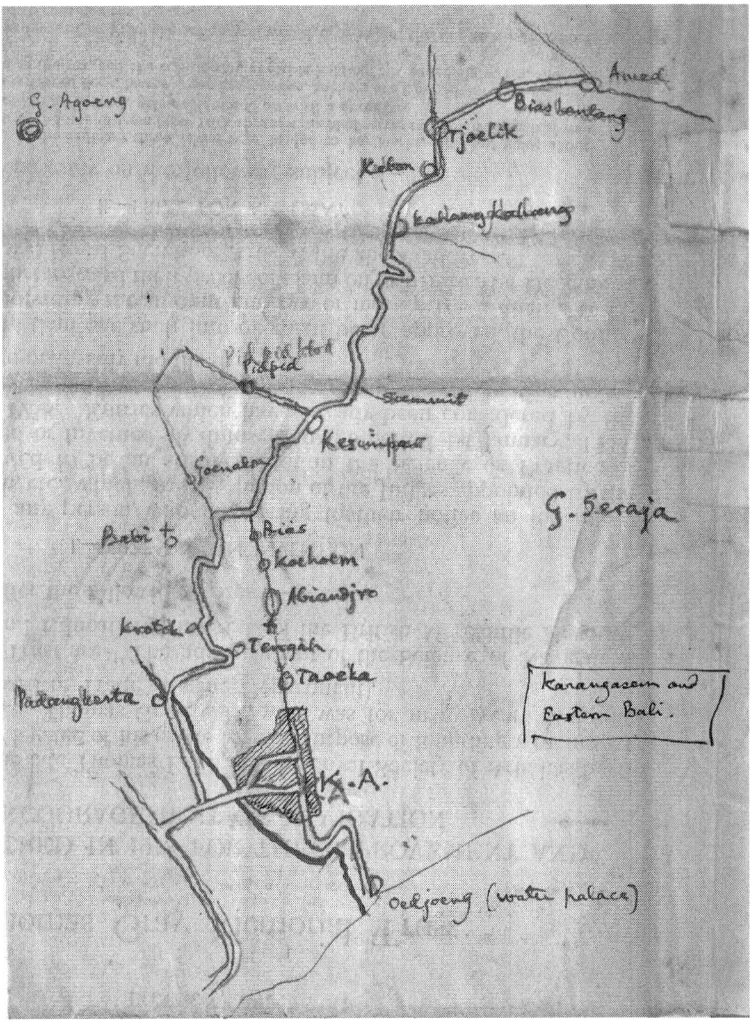

Illustration 15. Sketch map of Karangasem and Eastern Bali by Collingwood, pasted into the front of the *Log*. See *Log* entries for 25–27 December 1938, p. 19. Courtesy of Teresa Smith.

1 Jan 1939. Boarded SS. van Overstraten (4482 tons: Captain Kooper) 9 AM. Fair morning, overcast. A very little sun during the middle of the day. Sailed about 3 P. M. Coasting northwards along Celebes.

2 Jan. Dull, calm, no sun. Called 3–5 PM. Donggala, went ashore for an hour.

[20] 3 Jan. Dull, calm, no sun: wild desert coast. Called Kwandang 3–4 PM.

4 Jan. arr. Menado c. 6 AM, landed 7 AM in heavy rain. Hotel; walk in town. Wrote Kopenberg, Lilian Macmorran.

5 Jan. Waiting for ship (a day late). Unwell (diarr. & headache) in bed most of day.

6 Jan. 11 wks [*encircled*]. Fine sunny morning: walked out. Ill again afternoon. Boarded SS. van Neck 4.30 P. M, sailed about 7 (3027 tons gross). Bed at once: arrowroot for dinner. Slept after sweating.

7 Jan. Fair morning, calm, some sun. Sighted Ternate 8 AM. Wrote URC, posted on board. 12.30, transshipped to SS. van Imhoff (2980 t.); sailed 3 P.M. Called at a neighbouring island Soefifi for copra & gum copal 5-7 P.M. Full moon. Talking to H. Kern. Sunny fine day. Called Tandjong Poera 10 P.M.

8 Jan. Another call (Ngofaghisha) by moonlight 3 AM; another 6 AM at Makian (Defotalamahoe). Fine sunny morning. Among islands W. of Halmaheira; very beautiful cruising-ground. Kampong Baroe, called 4 P.M.; Batjan (Laboeha) 7 P.M. Moonrise there. Sunday.

9 Jan. Open sea once more, wind E, moderate, fair morning. Unwell. Namlea 1 P.M.

10 Jan. Entering Ambon 5 AM. on bridge. Alongside 7 AM; landed after breakfast. Walk in town & by sea with

Doctors & Kern. Rather squalid hotel. Unwell. Dull, fair. Letters from EWC. URC. Cambridge V-C. CG.

11 Jan. Boarded SS. van Rees (3000 t.) 8 AM. Called Saparua afternoon. Dull, fair.

12 Jan. Up 5 AM. nearing Banda, anchored 6.0, landed 8.0. Walking in & near town. Dull, fair.

13 Jan. Fine sunny day. 7.30, to sea-gardens in prau. Also to Mr. van Kock's nutmeg estate. 12 [*encircled*].

14 Jan. Fair day, mostly overcast. Up 5 AM., breakfast, ascended Goenoeng Api (658 m) with Dr. Dootor, Controleur of Ambon, wife of Controleur of Banda (who fell out & was sick after 200 m & had to be sent home) & 2 boys. I fell behind & only reached **[21]** c. 500 m. Back c. 10 AM. Then called on Brönsen, the local robber baron of the nutmeg trade. Fine afternoon. SS Reael arr. 5 P.M.

15 Jan. Sunday. Boarded SS. Reael (2557 t.) 10 AM. Fine, hot. Sailed noon. Writing URC. (post 20.i)

16 Jan. Called Ambon 9–3. Picked up a captain of the garrison, with great send-off. Fine, moderate breeze evening. Writing KENM. (post 20.i.)

17 Jan. Passed an island (Boeroe) at dawn. Fine, moderate breeze. Writing v.d.N.'s (post 20.i.)

18 Jan. Straits between Raha & Boeton: called at both: showery. Racine.

19 Jan. Saleier morning (photographing praus). Bonthain aftn. Passed yawl 'Fram', from Sydney for London. Showers. Racine. Wrote KFE. (post 20.i.)

20 Jan. Arr. Macassar 6 AM. On shore 7.40. Empress hotel. Letters from EWC (31.xii), KFE (22 xii), BCG (18 xii). Walk in town, hair cut. Fair, overcast. 13 [*encircled*].

21 Jan. Set out 7.30 AM by car for Toradja country in a De Soto 6, hired from H M Meyer (Cotram) with native (Malay speaking) driver; 25 km (to Maros) over flat sawah country; there encountered a transverse wall of vertical limestone & bore left into a narrowing coastal plain with sawahs for 100 km; then 25 km. between the mountains & the sea to Pare-Pare. Put up at pasanggrahan. Walk round town before lunch (ships, shops). Cranes & kingfishers in sawahs. Fishing villages. Fine; one shower. Afternoon: rest. Wrote DSA. Thunderstorm in night.

22 Sunday. Up at dawn, breakfast 6.45, start 7.15. Crossed the coastal range, of bumpy down-like hills made of boulders & detritus, into the inland depression beyond Rappang. Northwards across this towards the big mountains, which we entered **[22]** by the valley of a large but shallow river. Left this at Eurekang & started climbing steeply to the plateau. Mountains here limestone, geologically very young, much peak, crest, & precipice formation; dip generally to S. At Tondok (a few huts & a bridge over river, above the gorge & waterfall sector, i.e. definitely on the plateau) a vertical rockface 200′ high x 150 yds. long, rising from R. side of river, with a horizontal ledge cut in it 30–50 ft. above the water and full of wooden coffins, said to be Cxii. Thence to Kalosi: pasanggrahan; fine view, roses in garden, [*estimate of 5000 ft up, deleted*] really 2,500 ft. Fine, some clouds on mountains (10,000). The French ethnologist & the post-cart. Thunder & rain towards evening. Hotel-keeper's toothache.

23 Jan. Up at dawn, everything in mist, which broke as we drove up the valley & over the divide into the Toradja country & down to Makale [*see Illustration 16*]. Left

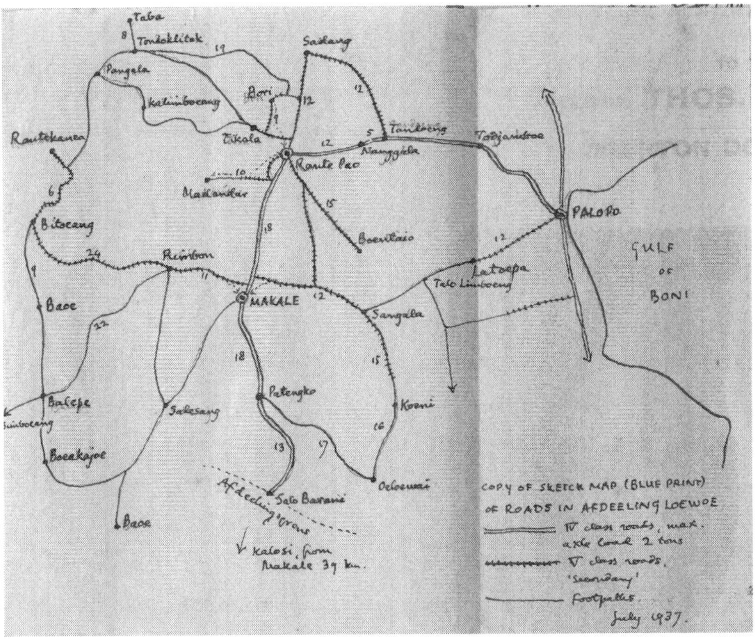

Illustration 16. Collingwood's copy of a sketch map of roads in Afdeeling Loewoe, Central Celebes, pasted into the front of the *Log*. See *Log* entries for 23–27 January 1939, pp. 22–24. Courtesy of Teresa Smith.

luggage at pasanggrahan. Below Makale (4 km. north of it, on E. of road), rock-graves with wooden dolls. More with bigger & better doll-show (photographed this), on a side-road at Lemo (E. of main road), where our car got bogged: exorbitant demands of the simple peasantry to help us out; successful appeal to village headman; car pushed uphill. To Rantepao. Valley here wide & fertile, level bottom, full of sawahs, large population. Wild jagged mountains all round (limestone, volcanic intrusions). Bori (side-road among sawahs) number Xópos [*Greek: burial chamber*], newly-cut rock chambers in hard volcanic boulders, Toradja houses (all photographed). Digging-stick in sawahs, (like an oar, iron-shod, 6 ft. long).

Note at foot of page. The following is deleted: '[NB. The place we saw was NE of Rantepao: Bori is NW: & the description doesn't correspond. I think it was a different place.]' No, it was Bori. Revisited 25.i.39 & got the topography right. It was this day or the next that I was bitten by a mosquito-like fly, causing a septic wound to develop in the left ankle and extending the sepsis to all bites elsewhere, especially right foot & left hand.

[23] 24 Jan. Drove to Sangala (13 km + back). Toradja-style church, rather depressing. Large rumah Blanda (? minister's house), natives much clothed. NB. digging stick thus [*see Illustration 17*]: –

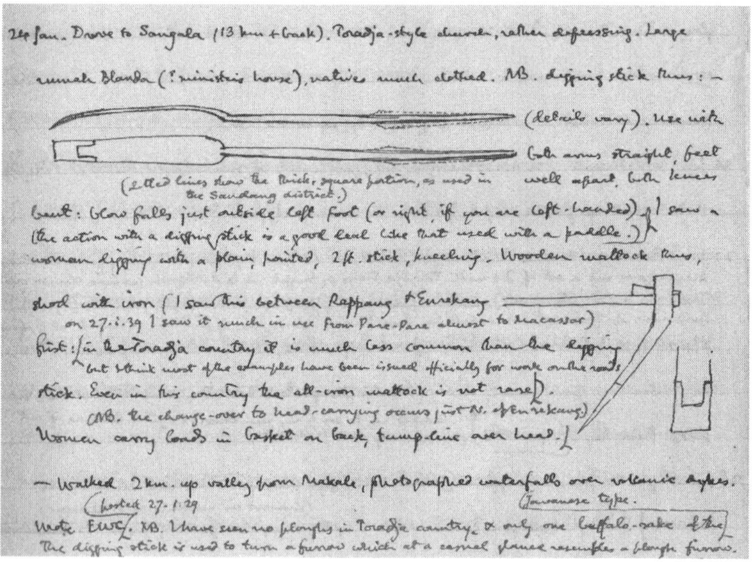

Illustration 17. Collingwood's sketches of a digging stick and wooden mattock in use in the Toradja country, Central Celebes. Facsimile of the *Log* entry for 24 January 1939, p. 23. Courtesy of Teresa Smith.

(dotted lines show the thick, square portion, as used in the Sandang district) (details vary). Use with both arms straight, feet well apart, both knees bent: blow falls just outside left foot (or right, if you are left-handed). (The action with a digging stick is a good deal like that used with a paddle). I saw a woman digging with a plain, pointed, 2 ft. stick, kneeling. Wooden mattock thus, shod with iron (I saw this between Rappang & Eurekang first: on 27.i.39 I saw it much in use from Pare-Pare almost to Macassar). In the Toradja country it is much less common than the digging stick. Even in this country the all-iron mattock is not rare (but I think most of the examples have been issued officially for work on the roads). Women carry loads in basket on back, tump-line over head. (NB. the change-over to head-carrying occurs just N. of Eurekang.)

Walked 2 km. up valley from Makale, photographed waterfalls over volcanic dykes. Wrote EWC posted 27. i.39. NB. I have seen no ploughs in Toradja country, & only one buffalo-rake of the Javanese type. The digging stick is used to turn a furrow which at a casual glance resembles a plough furrow.

25 Jan. Drove to Rantepao & thence to Nanggala: village with good street; 500 yds. further on a tempat orang matih (strongly built teak house, dead inside, horses & riders (2) on top below roof, too badly lit to photograph: a 2nd & larger house of the same kind: Xtian graves in front; Xópos hard by). NB. this burial-place though some distance from Nanggala is cheek by jowl with a little hamlet. Then to Tandoeng (passing a Xópos up on a hillside on left, 1 km. from the Nanggala turning – NB. Nanggala is not on the road, as shown on map, but S. of it) & Sandang, hence turned southward down valley of Kali Sata to Rantepao. Saw market, very large & busy – crowds of dingy-clad Toradjas selling coffee & buying elevenses – then drove to Tikala, nice little dead-house richly decorated, standing on a rock surrounded by moat (to keep the dead in): it had a **[24]** glass window through which images were visible, & in the space below it was (an older?) stone model horse and a wooden horse. Xópos close by ('tempat pesta', I was told). Newer dead-house on a higher rock close by, across the road.

26 Jan. Left Makale 7.30 AM. Fine morning, good views of mountains. Reached Pare-Pare 11.30 & put up for the night. Bracken on summit of pass.

27 Jan. From Pare-Pare to Makasser. Called on Meyer & paid him. Long conversation. Meyer gave me a set of three small Toradja trays & taught me to distinguish genuine Chinese crackle. Then to hotel (Empress). Letters from EWC (7.i, 14.i) WRC (8 Jan) B. Croce (19. xii) (with news of Momigliano's expulsion from Turin, asking me to find him a tempat at Oxford) KFE (9.i, 16. i). Finished letter to EWC; asked her to see to my remittance, & send to Batavia if not already sent to Soerabaja; wrote KFE, HML, IH. Spent evening with Potter, the Australian yachtsman, & Mrs Proctor. Mosquitoes beat the wire klamboeh; no sleep. Fine day. 14 weeks [*encircled*].

28 Jan. Up 5.30. finished & posted letter IH. After breakfast boarded ss. de Weert (1800 t.) Sailed noon, on course about S by E. Fine (showers in morning at Macassar): breeze NW, light to moderate (Potter with the Fram sailed for Soerabaja this morning). Green flash sunset, fine Buddha's rays. Moon near first quarter, fine calm starry night.

29 Jan. Sunday. Fine calm morning, approaching Sumbawa. A small, high, volcanic island (Soengghean, or Goenoeng Api, a young volcano but seemingly not active) on the port bow at sunrise. Photographed this. Into Bima, a deeply land-locked harbour with tortuous entrance. Anchored 100 yds. from the jetty. Went ashore (9.30) in ship's launch, returned 11.0. Native town a short mile inland from jetty: large pasar. Photographed men cutting down acacia tree, and praus. Sailed at 1.0. At 4.0, passing between the small **[25]** volcanic island and the shore. Fine afternoon, partly overcast. At sunset, running through the strait between Sumbawa & Komodo, past Klapa island with its (coconut-oil) light, white flash every 5″, run by 2 natives & visited by a Govt. steamer every 3–4 months. Strong tide-rips here: odd oily motion of the ship followed about 8 PM. by violent jolting in the rapids over a sunken rock-ledge. Running slow all night. Talk with Mijnheer McGillavry, asst. contr. at Bima.

30 Jan. At dawn approaching Waingapoe (leading lights). Anchored in 45 metres at 5.50. Stayed there until 8.0. Small town, 5 Europeans, Salvation Army mission & church, Controleur, small harbour containing 2 'schooners' so far as I could see from a mile away. Calm, hot, clear morning (cirrus at dawn, small cumulus later, light NW breeze got up at 8.30); mountains of Flores clearly visible at 60 miles & more. [Sumba is a low island, apparently limestone: a table-land about 500 ft. high near Waingapoe, eroded into gorges: all green in the rainy season, but at other times very arid. Low rainfall. Grows maize & breeds cattle & especially horses, of which several thousands go yearly to Java.] From 2.0 to 9.0 P.M. at Aimere, Flores (60 miles from Waingapoe). Open beach where goods & passengers are carried on coolies' backs from anchored boats. Village of about 5 houses, infested with malaria tropica. Controleur & all other Europeans live up in the mountains, which are close, rugged, & steep. Between them & the beach, parkland with Bali type cattle.

[26] 31 Jan. 5.30 AM, Ende-Bay with black sand beach; jetty with 2 hand-cranes. Went ashore at 8 for an hour, had ticket seen to by K.P.M. agent (N.B. all roads are washed away, therefore no inland trip possible, inspected market, photographed copra-loading from beach into praus (carriers wading over their heads in water when a roller came in). Nice bay, lots of klapa: young volcanic cone just behind town to ESE, and E. extreme of bay formed by an active one (solfataras in broken crater on top and whole cone covered with recent lava & cinders) which we passed on leaving. Mountains of Flores then obscured by showers.

1 Feb. Up before dawn approaching Koepang (Timor). Fine sunrise. Anchored 6 A.M. The island very mountainous to E., flat (apparently a limestone table-land) to W. Went ashore 8–9. The town ancient & tortuous, Portuguese-Chinese, with new Dutch residential suburbs behind. Market; much retail spice trade. Left leg not working well in landing & on shore: inhaled amyl nitrite, in case. Mild intoxication symptoms with retinal green patch. Here the Maduranese princess (Mevr. Gabeler) left us, my Soneryl having given her one good night. Sailed noon. Some swell in the afternoon, but sea otherwise calm: hot.

2 Feb. Morning, nearing Timor-Dilly; anchored 6.55. My feet troublesome (5 septic bites on L, 4 on R: I got them over a week ago in the Toradja country & they had been getting bad the last 4–5 days) & I stayed on shore, mostly in bed. Dilly a nice bay, yellow sand: reef all across except one narrow **[27]** entrance to W, marked by 2 buoys: large vessels must keep centre of channel. No leading lights, but a lighthouse on W. extreme of bay – useless, so far as I can see: certainly no help in entering. Plenty water in anchorage (40 metres). Very Portuguese-looking town spread out among shade-trees all round the bay. One small, mouldering steamer at anchor. Numerous inhabitants came off (in a motorboat handled in a most lubberly manner) to welcome our passengers Senhor & Senhora José de Carvalho, most affectionately. Coffee-planting the chief industry hereabouts. Europeans live up in the mountains; those just inland from the coast, 3-4,000 ft. & wooded. Sailed 2 P.M. in heavy rain. Passed to E. of Alor: on its N. coast, at dark, ran into a slight NW. swell. Began letter EWC.

3 Feb. 15 weeks [*encircled*]. Anchored at Baloerin 6.30. A crater-harbour, too deep to anchor (400 m: our cable is 120 fathom). The harbour is 2/3 of a circle 4 miles diameter: ENE of it rises a youngish volcano about 5,000 ft: W. of it, more distant, an active one, smoking; and about 25 m. away to N. another active one, isolated, rises from the sea. Photographed these two, telephoto. Very small settlement in harbour. Sailed 9.30; from N. of harbour, heights of Flores visible to W. Proceeded to Koala Bay, an inlet 35 m. long in the W. end of Alor, called after the numerous jellyfish (I saw them in some places apparently about one per cubic metre of water). People here naked & very wild (chief officer). The inlet is about a mile wide, heights 1000 ft on each side; scrub & trees; klapa on shore. Anchored Kalabahi 3.30 (small stone jetty, about 10 corrugated iron sheds & **[28]** houses; kampong, v. small, 300 yds. away). Sailed 5.30

P.M. In the evening the Chief Engineer dressed my septic bites with ointment (ichthyol-diachylon).

4 Feb. 6.0 AM anchored Waiwerang (small kampong, market sheds, KPM hut like a Border cottage, small wooden jetty & red light). A little copra. Wild volcanic country. Raised beach at 50′ on the opposite island (phot.). A few patches of maize, a few klapa. Wet morning. 8.30, to Larantoeka. Photographed Lobetobi. Sailed 11.30 through Flores Strait (NB. no light here, never was one; we passed very close to both the 2 points on which it might have stood. Sides & bottom of strait, coral rock ∴ screw piles impossible. Current in water not streaky: whorls & eddies owing to roughness of rock). Then E. to Sago Bay; around inlet, with fairsized kampong, in N. side of the same island as Waiwerang. Writing EWC. Wet evening. Full moon.

5 Feb. Sunday. 5.30 AM. anchored Geliting, small kampong in a very slight bay, in effect an open roadstead. No jetty: coolies wade. (NB these ships carry all their own coolies). 12.0 Maoemerie, a bit of a town, jetty with leading beacons, 2 boat jetties, 4–5 sailing prahus. Calm, warm day, overcast. Sailed 4.0. Wet then. Wrote BCG.

6 Feb. Running W. into a swell from NW, along coast of Flores. At 1.15 anchored at Labuan Badjo after rounding NW. corner of Flores & passing among a great many steep conical islets. Sailed 1.45. Rainy day. I can now walk a little almost without discomfort. Writing T.L.S. [*Times Literary Supplement*], B.C.G. Called Sapeh after dark.

7 Feb. 5.50 AM, anchored Bima: overcast, calm. Sailed 7.50. Wind rising all day: fresh by 2.0, strong by 4.0; W. by S. Rainy. NB practically no colour in sea under **[29]** these conditions: slight grey-blue tinge. The strong tropical blue seems to be almost all reflection from the sky. Storm force by 6: heavy rain then smoothed the heads off the waves; but a roughish night followed.

8 Feb. Fresh W wind. Berthed Macassar 9.20. Pilot brought off letters from EWC (24.i), K Sisam, KFE (27.i), Kopenbergs, Bonnet (and his parcel of Balinese drawings). Trans-shipped to van Lansberge, sailed 10.0. Posted on board this ship letters to EWC, BCG., TLS, F. de Zulueta, B Croce, Penguin. Heavy showers in morning. Butting all day into a fresh to strong wind 1–2 pts. on the starboard bow, & a rough lumpy sea. Good deal of rain. Got shoes on again (first time for a week).

9 Feb. Bright morning, wind W by S., fresh, sea less rough. Wrote sketch contents for Principles of History. Wrote Bonnet, KFE. Boat drill. Seasick passengers re-emerging. Called at Bali (not at Boeleleng on account of weather; somewhere more to the W) for passengers 9.30 P.M.

10 Feb. 16 weeks [*encircled*]. Fair morning, sea calm, wind W, light. At 7 AM. Madoera in sight to N; about abreast Sitoebondo. Landed Tandjong Perak 11.45 AM. To Chartered Bank, drew £50: to Fraser Eaton, letter from EWC & Ruth (31.i): to Ngemplak Hotel. Began writing Principles of History. Bright, hot day.

11 Feb. Bright, hot day. Went down to F. Eaton 10 A.M. for letters (WRC, G.v.d.N) writing P.H. all day otherwise.

12 Feb. Bright, hot day: thunder & rain c. 5 PM. Writing all day; didn't leave the hotel at all. Sunday.

[30] 13 Feb. Writing all morning. After short siesta walked down to Fraser Eaton. Letter KFE (3 Jan.) Also bought writing paper, 2 books (E. Sitwell, W. Steed). Packing. Hot. (All these days 82° in my room at dawn, rising to 90° in the late afternoon). Wrote K.

14 Feb. Up 5 AM. breakfast 5.30, station 6.0, took Java Limited for Djokja (6.18). Arrived there 10.35. Got last room but one at Hotel Mataram; and spent morning writing Bill. Lunch, sleep, thunder. Spent evening with Captain George Wright (China Navigation Co., Hong Kong).

15 Feb. Writing all morning & from tea, to dinner; finishing & tidying up chapter 1. Bought ichthyol-diachylon & boric ointments for my sores, as they refuse to heal. Wright left 2. PM for Bali.

16 Feb. Writing all day except siesta. 9 pp. of ch. 2. Wrote Maclaine Watson confirming passage on *Manon* 18 March, and asking for letters. Did not leave hotel.

17 Feb. Writing all day except siesta; (12 pp: too much, didn't sleep well). Only went out to buy a few cigars. 17 weeks [*encircled*].

18 Feb. Letters from Maclaine Watson, HML (enclosing Momigliano). EWC (7.2.39) K. Tired & slack this day after bad night: kept off the book. Read; wrote EWC, KFE. Dressed sores–improving, even the left heel, which however is still a nasty bit of work.

[31] 19 Feb. Sunday. Writing all day except siesta (12 pp., beginning 5 AM; by the end, not doing so well – last page bad & will have to be scrapped). Didn't go out all day. –All these days at Djokja are alike: some clouds at dawn, clear morning, rapidly turning hot: clouding over in middle of day, heavy thunder & generally heavy rain afternoon. Sometimes showers at night: a very heavy one today woke me at 4.35 AM. Wrote HML.

20 Feb. Writing most of the day. Much annoyed by uproarious fellow-guests the hotel wireless & other incessant discomforts: decided to return to Batavia the following day. Wrote 8pp.

21 Feb. Up 5 AM, writing. Went out after breakfast, haircut, bought cigars & soap. (Shops handier than at Batavia). Caught Java Express Limited at 10.30 AM. for Batavia. Comfortable journey revising MS, lunching, writing a poem. Arrived B. 5.45 & got a room next my old one at Hotel Daendels. Recovered the suit-case I had left there, unpacked it, found some things mildewed a little from the leather case of Angus's EEG. binoculars, but no serious damage. Some points in favour of being back in civilization. Have been long enough in the Dutch East Indies.

[32] 22 Feb. Went down after breakfast to Maclaine Watsons for letters–None. Discussed passage. Details of *Manon* (sailing 18 March) now doubtful; no one knew when they would be certain; as things now stand, she may not get me home in time. *Rhesus* (4 March) would get me home 4 April: booked passage in her. Wrote EWC. announcing this–Late in the afternoon received & read proofs of my Autobiography.

23 Feb. Wrote L. Macmorran, Maclaine Watson enclosing order for ticket home, K. Working at Aut. and Int. Met.

24 Feb. Letter from KFE. Working all day at Aut. & Int. Met. Right foot: last sore now seems to be healing. Left foot, all healed except the worst sore, beside tendon, Ach. Telephone from R. Macmorran to say Lilian is in Bali. New moon (not so new; about 3 days). 18 weeks [*encircled*].

25 Feb. Walked round Rijswijk in morning, bought sticking-plaster, paste (for labelling trunks), Agatha Christie Murder in Mesopotamia. Otherwise working all day at Int. Met., especially rewriting chapter VI.

26 Feb. Sunday. Int. Met. all day. Finished rewriting chap VI, almost entirely rewrote ch. VII, largely new material & quite a new idea of arrangement. All these days warm, but not really hot; practically no sun, but very little rain; temp. in cool veranda about 80°. Left heel still nasty.

[33] 27 Feb. Int. Met. all day. Revising ch. VII, ch. V. Didn't go out. Letter from EWC (17.2.39); Maclaine Watson, with ticket home.

28 Feb. Int. Met. all day. Finished revising Part I. Didn't go out. No siesta (too many noises). No sun: one short heavy shower c. 3 P.M. Wrote Chrystabel.

1 March. Int. Met. (writing a new chapter VIII) until 10 AM. Then called for by Lilian Macmorran & taken shopping at Djokjasche Kunstarbeid shop (Pasar Baroe) – reckless extravagance –then back to lunch with her & Robert, & home. Wrote EWC.

2 March. Bright sunny morning. Int. Met., working on first half of part II. Letters from KFE, BCG. Wrote BCG. Finished revising part II.

3 March. After breakfast (overcast, not hot) went down by tram to Kali Besar. Changed f176.60 for £20 at the Hong Kong & Shanghai Bank, being sent there by my friends at the Chartered. To Maclaine Watson; Rhesus sails 5.30 P.M. Left address. Bought 100 4 cent cigars on way home. 19 weeks [*encircled*].

4 March. Went out in the morning & spent the rest of my guilders. Revised I.M. part III. At 4 P.M. drove down to Tandjong Priok & went on board S.S. Rhesus. Mr. Harrison the chief Steward told me the story of his life before we were outside the breakwater; Mr. Olivant the Chief Engineer before **[34]** it was dark (we sailed 6 P.M.) washing it down with a gin; one of the midshipmen & the doctor after dinner. A friendly ship. Other passengers, Mr & Mrs Nimmins with 2 children, coming home from Macassar: Mr. Taylor formerly of Maclaine Watson & his pretty daughter, from Batavia. All North-Country people, thank God, & very sweet.

5 March. Sunday. Passed Krakatau 3 AM. Wind W., light, dying away in the course of the day; sea smooth. Warm day, airless. Sun shining through cloud-veil. Working on Met.

6 March. Wind W., very light, sea smooth. Working on Met. Hot day. Very brilliant sunset (gold to crimson) approaching Padang. Berthed there 7 P.M. Very hot noisy night working cargo: plague of copra beetles, no sleep. Full moon. Finished loading 7 AM.

7 March. Sailed 8 A.M. Hot. Wind W., very light, sea calm. Slept in morning. Slept from lunch to tea.

8 March. Wind W., light, freshening at evening, sea smooth, slight swell. Writing M. all day: completed new version of ch. VIII. Began using Captain's dressing on left heel; right one practically well.

9 March. Wind SW, moderate to fresh, sea moderate, ship rolling. Dark day, no sun, heavy showers. Working at M. all day. Ship being delayed by unseasonable weather. Young George Nimmins developed whooping-cough.

[35] 10 March. 20 weeks [*encircled*]. Fine sunny day, cumulus & cirrus but much bright sunshine. Wind W, light, sea calm. Working at M. all day. Contrary winds & resulting currents have put us a good deal behind our schedule time. Boat drill 4.30.

11 March. Very fine sunny day, cumulus: wind W. light, sea calm. Working at M. all day. Wrote EWC for Colombo air mail. Clear sunset; green flash lasting 3 seconds.

12 March. Sunday. Clear dawn: entered Colombo 6.15 AM, tied up to buoys by 6.45. Port doctor, agent

&c. on board. Began working cargo about 7.30. Hot day in harbour. Working at M. Sailed 8 P.M. Took dressing off right heel. Trouble with the lobster mayonnaise.

13 March. Very fine bright day. Wind W, light to moderate. Trouble continued, too serious to allow any work. Sun set in a cloud-bank.

14 March. Passed Minikoi 6 AM. Fine bright day, cool N wind, moderate, sea calm. Diarrhoea less acute. Working on M. Sun set in clouds.

15 March. Fine bright day, cool N wind, fresh, sea calm to moderate. Swam in bath 6 AM & 3.30 PM. Ate some food (weak from hunger, diarrhoea gone). Green flash.

16 March. Fine bright day, cool fresh N. wind. Got up 4 AM. & rewrote ch. VI. Eating again. Green flash behind a cloud at **[36]** one solar diameter above horizon.

17 March 21 weeks [*encircled*]. Fine bright day, cool light N. wind. Ship seems now to be going slower than schedule; foul bottom & contrary current. Working on M. Sun set behind narrow cloud-bars, clear air: green flash. Socotra 4 points on st. bow after sunset. Back to Autobiography.

18 March. Islands between Socotra & Guardafui abeam 7 AM; Guardafui itself visible then from bridge; abeam 9.30. (4% longer time between here & Minikoi than on the voyage out). After a bad night, did some work on Aut. & after lunch slept. Fine, hot: fresh following wind, white heads on sea. Sun set in cirro-stratus veil: no g.f. Recurrence of diarrhoea.

19 March (Sunday). Fine bright day. Wind moderate, SE. Aden passed 3.30: Penin. [*Peninsula*] 9. PM. Rewriting last chapter of Aut. Clear sunset, slight haze: g.f. dimly.

20 March. Dull morning, passing among high rocky islands at daybreak. Came out fine & hot; light following wind. Entered Kamaran 1.0 to pick up a passenger; sailed 5.0 Veiled sunset, no g.f.

21 March. Cloudless day. Light wind, S. Duplicating corrections of Aut. Bathing 12.0–1.0. Slept after lunch. Slight g.f.

22 March. Entering Port Sudan at daybreak. It is a narrow, deep creek in a bay of desert coast. Very hot in there, in spite of E. breeze. Sailed again 1.30 heading N. Sun set in clouds. Diarrhoea continuing, & stomach poor. **[37]** Packed copy of Aut. proofs to send to Oxford by air mail from P. Said, and wrote KS. Very thin new moon 6.30 PM (17 hrs. old: the newest I ever saw). Much diarrhoea on this ship: both stewards great sufferers, & the old Doctor very bad. This day I ate practically nothing.

23 March. Bright morning, running NW; strong following wind which at 10.0 suddenly changed to dead ahead bringing a sandstorm. Wrote EWC. Cold, dull, windy day. Wind veering to NNE. in afternoon: spray coming over forward between-decks. Daedalus abeam 6 P.M. to port. Met a big submarine to port at noon this day.

24 March. After a cold night, very noisy owing to the strong head wind, everything still hazy with sand, & so all day. Wrote UMLS. Cold. Everybody back in European clothes. Met Blue Funnel Diomed 10 AM. Passed Ashrafi, visible through the sand. In the afternoon, visibility better; both shores dimly visible. Wind falling about 5 PM. 22 weeks [*encircled*]. My sick stomach better.

25 March. Arrived Suez at midnight. Medical inspection. Got up about 3.30: on deck watching the stars & then the dawn. We were discharging oil with much smell. Weighed & entered the Canal at 7.30. Fine, sunny, cold day, with light N. breeze freshening & veering to NE. about 5 P.M. Went through the Canal with the tide. Reading Croce, as the last 2 days. Reached Port Said evening. Letters from EWC (2), Ruth (2), Chrystabel, KFE. Left P.S. about midnight, after coaling.

[38] 26 March. Sunday. N. 77 W. Very fine day, practically cloudless. Fresh S wind in morning, dying away afternoon, when we ran into a fair W. swell. I had a cold in the head. Playing with Principles of History.

27 March. Fine day, becoming overcast in the afternoon. Tried to begin ch. IV of Principles of History in morning – stuff wouldn't flow. Stomach worse, in fact worse than it has been yet. Very idle and uncomfortable all afternoon. Passed an Italian cargo-steamer mounting 2 guns, steering towards a Libyan port. Some swell all day. Logging 12 knots.

28 March. Fine day; strong head wind and roughish sea all day. Spent day in bed nursing my stomach & starving.

29 March. Fine day, light to moderate S. wind, sea calm to moderate, ship steady. Stayed in bed all day, ate a few poached eggs. Read the illiterate autobiography of the exhibitionistic vulgarian M. Asquith – equally revolting from a literary & from a moral point of view. Passed Malta about 8–9 AM., Pantellaria 5 P.M.

30 March. Got up after breakfast for 3 hrs. and out. Sun, cool, fresh breeze. N.W. Hazy day: African coast not visible. Still no meals, only poached eggs & some fruit. Inside easier. Chiefly reading Beatrice Webb's autobiography, very good & interesting piece of work.

[39] 31 March. Overcast day. Calm morning, hazy, African coast in sight, mountainous, 10 miles to port: at 10 AM. a fresh head wind got up bringing some rain and at times sleet: sea getting up in the afternoon. Came in to lunch & dinner. Reading B. Webb. 23 weeks [*encircled*].

1 April. Fine sunny day; fresh head wind all day. At 8 A. M., high Spanish mountains, upper half snow-covered, on the starboard beam. Felt rather better this day & tried without success to do some writing in morning. Listened in to the Boat Race. At 1.45 the German liner Columbus (cruising) overtook us. Passed Gibraltar 5.15 PM. Passed a whale, spouting, surrounded by a school of porpoises, in the Straits, also armed trawler. Stormy sunset.

2 April. Fine, sunny, calm; swell. C. St Vincent 9 AM. Afternoon overcast: wind, light to moderate, W; swell increasing. Cape Rocco, 6 P.M. Metaphysics, working on chapter IV. Passed the Birlings, 8.30 P.M. Sunday.

3 April. Dull: wind SW, fresh, sea rough. Metaphysics: finished ch. IV, working on V. Finistere 3 PM. Glass falling, sea rising, also wind. Rain toward sunset.

4 April. Finc morning: full moon setting at sunrise: wind SW, fresh, sea moderate, ship rolling deeply & easily. Metaphysics. Wind backing in afternoon to SE and falling calmer. Sun all day.

5 April. After a fine night, moon & dew, a cloudy morning, wind SE, light. Start Point abeam, about 7 miles, 8 AM.

The Log *as such ends here; but the exercise book in which it is written also includes, starting from the last page and working back, a variety of notes on recipes, tunes, cash drawn out, exchange rates and expenses incurred on the trip. A section of the official map of the KPM Line for 1937, covering the East Indies, has been cut out, folded, and pasted into the end covers of the notebook: this is reproduced as the front and back end papers of the present volume.*

COMMENTARY

A PHILOSOPHER'S JOURNEY: COLLINGWOOD IN THE EAST INDIES

WENDY JAMES

The story of a person's life has often been cast as a journey, metaphorically, almost to the point of cliché. In Collingwood's case, his life's work and the way he accounts for it have more than the *image* of a journey about them: his journeys are through very material landscapes, and are very sensual in recording impressions such as heat, wind, rain, the taste and feel of things. His encounters with other people are quite specific and circumstantial. As conventionally understood, the *Autobiography* is largely an account of Collingwood's 'thought'—in Philip Smallwood's discussion in this volume, a very self-conscious account of the thought and professional scholarly development of a liberal citizen. But even in that text, the internal experiences and thoughts of which he writes, both personal and philosophical, are often situated in specific places. We are reminded repeatedly of *where he is* when engaged in the business of writing—many of his scholarly pieces almost seem to emerge from a specific address, as letters do. His writing itself is often *about* places, from sailing on Coniston, sitting on trains, reading in the library of the Folk Lore Society in London, to walking past the Albert Memorial, and so on—not to mention the obvious case where he is writing about archaeological sites, or the ideas which they have provoked. We could even say the book is addressed directly to us, as readers, almost as a long personal letter might be. Of course, it is not a 'complete' account of Collingwood's life—as if there could ever be a complete account of anyone's. However, there are unpublished writings from the later years of his life that add further depth and colour to our picture of Collingwood the man; this is the main justification for publishing here his 'Log of a Journey in the East Indies, 1938–1939', and quoting at length from some of his often exuberant letters home. Here is no armchair philosopher. He emerges from these writings as an extraordinarily determined traveller, whose observations on the material and human world feed directly into his scholarly reflections. We see him too as a cheerful stoic in the face of physical discomfort, a warm and witty family man, and a loyal friend.

In this chapter I illustrate these themes from the *Log* itself, backed up by some of Collingwood's letters home, some of the photographs he himself took (Teresa Smith's chapter records his early use of a camera as a child), sketches he made, and a few pictures of the art and other mementos he brought back.[1] The trip was recommended on medical grounds for the sake of his health and made possible through a year's sick leave from Oxford. The text of the *Log* was obviously not written for publication—a rough and ready diary, jottings made of direction, weather, anchorage conditions, ports of call, hotels, and brief trips into the interior of various islands, sometimes by road, or by train, or on foot. But even the barest jottings were made at least for close family and friends to read; and as it unfolds, and the distance from home increases, the literary style warms up to the point where we have memorable descriptions and commentaries on the landscapes, art, and music of what we now know as Indonesia. These brief notes themselves add further colour to the portrait of what I have elsewhere dubbed 'a fieldworker's philosopher',[2] but are greatly enhanced when read in conjunction with some of Collingwood's letters, alongside the photographs he took, objects he collected, and sketch maps he made. The *Log* also records encounters with hosts, with colleagues, and fellow 'tourists', but most of all with the peoples of the islands, especially Bali, where Collingwood spent three weeks in December 1938. Collingwood's philosophy of history exhorts us to employ the 'historical imagination', something founded on the possibility of engaging, in the conscious present, the realities of other times; and this is surely complemented by his

[1] A good deal of the preliminary research on the factual background to the journey and on the relevant letters was done by David Boucher, and some research on place names and checking of the text by Rosie and Dai Blatchford. We are grateful to Teresa Smith for permission to draw on her collection of letters, photographs, and other material relevant to this crucially creative period in Collingwood's life.

[2] James, Wendy, 'A Fieldworker's Philosopher: Perspectives from Anthropology', in *PE*: lvi–xci.

treatment of travel, as a way of engaging, over geographical space, the human realities of other places.

In the closing pages of *An Autobiography*, Collingwood talks of the ancient distinction we have inherited between theory and practice, between thinkers and men of action; and of how he himself had adopted a variety of attitudes to the distinction. He writes of the 'first R. G. C.' who knew philosophically that the division was false; the second, who lived as though it was sound (while resenting his wife's pointing out the contradiction); and the third, in whom 'the difference between thinker and man of action disappeared'; he 'never left me alone for very long' and sometimes 'woke right up' (*A*, 150–2). This 'third R. G. C.' does seem to take over as Collingwood eagerly embarks on his Eastern adventure, interspersing his philosophical writing with trips around the islands and up the mountains, taking photographs, collecting objects, and engaging with the locals of all classes, especially among the Balinese. It was the first time he had experienced a non-European civilization at first hand, or indeed the contradictions of European colonial rule.

Collingwood's scrupulous notes on the six-month voyage to the East Indies record a period of focused hard work in the face of recurrent physical problems and a knowledge that he might not have many years ahead. He had already relayed an account of advice given by Dr Stott, a London consultant recommended to him by Tom Nelson, in a letter to his sister Barbara:

> He was very definite and very cheering about my case. He said that my two strokes have not been cerebral haemorrhages (which, according to him, are generally fatal and in any case very seldom pass off in such a way that the symptoms disappear) but 'arterial spasms' which though annoying and troublesome do no permanent damage to the brain. He says that nobody knows why they happen, but that in my case it was probably overwork and I mustn't do it again; but that I must on no account stop work altogether, even temporarily. He seemed to envisage me spending my winter on board ship pottering off to Java or somewhere and doing a bit of writing every day on my next book. He said that he could find no reason in my present condition or my history why I shouldn't live and work another twenty years or more.[3]

[3] Letter to Barbara Gnosspelius, 9 Sept. 1938. [TS/FLTR0834].

Reading the *Log* we feel very sharply the passage of time for Collingwood himself, as the journey extended itself over the weeks and months—each week he noted how many he had been away, encircling the number in the diary, and noting all letters received and posted off at each port of call. Without further elaboration, the *Log* might have remained unpublished in some archive, but in addition to its record of the trip as such it has considerable value for those interested in his philosophy to understand better how Collingwood actually wrote his books. There are also several interesting passages in the letters home where he reflects on his own work and career, from which I quote below.

THE EAST INDIES VOYAGE AND ITS TEXTS

1. The Outward Voyage: 21 October–7 December 1938

Embarking on his voyage to what we now know as Indonesia, Collingwood was full of confidence and anticipation. He had just taken the manuscript of *An Autobiography* to the Press (the Preface is dated 2 October). The very day before he left Birkenhead on the voyage he had written a strong letter of support to A. D. Lindsay, Master of Balliol, who as a respected left-leaning politician was standing on an anti-Munich platform in the imminent Oxford by-election. The bulk of the letter with Collingwood's political fears for the future is quoted in the introduction to this book; here we might note the opening, which adds a touch of personal warmth and optimism very much of the moment: 'My dear Lindsay, I am leaving for the East tomorrow; but I cannot go without sending you my deepest good wishes for your success in your candidature.'[4]

We sense as soon as Collingwood started out from Birkenhead on the MV *Alcinous* (21 October 1938) a mood of relaxation and enjoyment; the sheer seamanly satisfaction of passing well-known landmarks, such as Cape St Vincent—noting shipping from the West African coast—Gibraltar, and then features and landmarks he had never been near before—the Suez Canal and the Red Sea with its volcanic island lighthouse at Jebel Zubair. After Aden and

[4] Collingwood to A. D. Lindsay, 20 October 1938 [TS/FLTR0839]. See David Boucher's contribution to this volume for a discussion of Lindsay's manifesto.

then out across the Indian Ocean, the *Alcinous* eventually docked at Padang in Sumatra on 17 November (see Illustration 12, Collingwood's own photograph of the occasion, which we have used to introduce the *Log*, page 447). Along with regular notes of latitude, longitude, and weather conditions, he noted unusual sights in the sky, for example a 'green flash' at sunset (on 31 October, 4, 7, 10, and 14 November)—the last glimmer of a setting sun against a low horizon, the earth's atmosphere acting as a prism on the sinking light; and the eerie 'Zodiacal Light' (on 6 November), which may appear—most likely in an eastern sky, before dawn.

One sad event marred the opening days of the outward journey: a fellow passenger, Charles Cotterill Lynam, former Headmaster of the Dragon School in Oxford and widely known by his nickname 'Skipper', died of angina. He was buried, as he had wished, at sea, on 27 October. Then eighty years of age, he was still a keen sailor and had recently returned from a voyage to Australia. Collingwood's son Bill and daughter Ruth had been at the school, and Collingwood wrote a comforting sympathetic letter with a kind description of a dignified burial at sea to Lynam's brother, Alfred Edmund.[5] In a letter to Ethel, however, swearing her to secrecy, he relates how the burial was far from dignified. The carpenter had drilled holes in the side of the coffin, but had forgotten to drill them in the top, thus causing an air lock. The coffin floated and bumped against the side of the ship. A gloating hammer-headed shark appeared and nosed and circled the coffin, triggering near panic among the assembled passengers and crew. Fortunately the coffin sank of its own accord after a few minutes.[6]

Following this drama, Collingwood found the four weeks of the outward journey calming and productive for his work. By the next day he was working on Malay 'as usual'. He seemed to have an insatiable appetite for languages even at this stage—Teresa Smith's chapter mentions his teaching himself to read Dante at school. Tom Hopkinson, who was a student of his at Pembroke and later editor of *Picture Post*, records finding Collingwood reading

[5] This was later printed in Jaques, C. H. 1977. *A Dragon Century 1877–1977*. Oxford: Blackwell: 142–4.

[6] Letter to Ethel Collingwood, 29 October 1938. This letter was written in instalments on 26, 29, and 31 October and posted from Padang on 17 November. [TS/PLTR185].

Dante and commenting 'I didn't know you spoke Italian, sir.' The reply came back: 'Speak Italian? . . . Certainly not! Whoever can have told you that? . . . Anyone who knows some Latin can read Italian. Or Spanish too for that matter. And I don't need a dictionary because I've read Dante many times before. But talking's another thing altogether.'[7] On 29 October Collingwood was given working space on the lower bridge. This was a reward from the captain for giving a dressing-down to a particularly irritating young Dutchman who was generally making a nuisance of himself; in the same letter to Ethel Collingwood he wrote: 'For three hours I harangued that young fellow behind closed cabin doors; and next day, that is today, the Captain rigged me up a special private study, with a marble table and a cane chair, in the open air on the lower bridge, where I can do my writing.' To his sister Barbara he wrote a little later, when the voyage was well under way, of the atmosphere of the sea:

here I am sitting in pyjamas under an electric fan somewhere towards the middle of the Indian Ocean, between sunset & moonrise at 7 P.M. after dinner. I suppose we are about 9° N. Lat. and at a very rough guess about 65° E. Long. It has been getting hotter every single day since we left England, and is now quite a lot hotter than it almost ever is in that country, but it hasn't ever been hotter than comfortable. I still sleep happily in pyjamas, & under a sheet most of the night, and am always perfectly comfortable all day, in a shirt & shorts & a pair of slippers, sitting under an awning at a table that the Captain has rigged up for me on the bridge so that I can write in comfort & seclusion.

The letter then suddenly announces: 'And I have written since we left home practically a whole book, called Introduction to Metaphysics; in which please tell O. [*her husband, Oscar Gnosspelius*] that I am putting in what he says about the difficulty of making a mathematical theory of the flow of the air on the basis of the differential calculus, because that is an extremely neat point in metaphysics and most instructive.' He returns straight back to the feelings of being on board:

We have had constant fine weather, sun & light breezes every day except for 2 days after leaving Suez when it was overcast and gloomy; and I have never in my life felt so free and jolly and grand. No post, no paper, no telephone, no jobs, no responsibilities, no fellow-travellers to look after –

[7] Hopkinson, Tom, 1982. *Of This Our Time: A Journalist's Story 1905–1950*. London: Hutchinson: 94.

at least, not much... Watching the sea go by gives me the most extreme joy. We go 13 ½ knots, and that is fast enough to be a constant excitement to a bow-wave fan like me, & not fast enough to feel that the ship is being pushed, which I hate. She goes her own pace, & here forward in my cabin I can hardly hear the engine, & don't feel them shaking her at all. And I spend hours watching her lift her nose out of one swell and putting it very deliberately & deep, like a thirsty horse, into the next, and watching the bow-wave spread in a sheet of broken water & the flying fish leap clear of it. This is the most delightful thing in the world, especially by moonlight. The flying fish were at first only about the size of blue-tits, so far as I could see, but today they have taken, so to speak, a leap ahead, & have suddenly become the size & colour of mackerel.[8]

He greatly valued the privacy he had been granted on this outward journey. A sign of the professionalism with which he was approaching his arrival in the East Indies was the way he concentrated on 'Malay', the regional *lingua franca* of which one dialect is now endorsed as Bahasa Indonesia. He mentions his language work again on 6 November, and on 13, 14, and 15 November, and as we shall see later he made great use of Malay in his journeys around the islands.

Collingwood's main intellectual concern, however, during the basic calm and quiet of the outward voyage was to get well into his planned work on 'Metaphysics'; this was mentioned in the *Log* as soon as 24 October, and again on 28 and 31 October, when he noted 'Writing all day, finished ch. 6'. No doubt a little revised later on, this initial draft seems to have stood its ground as the famous chapter VI ('Metaphysics an Historical Science') in which Collingwood argues that all metaphysical propositions are historical. He wrote to his wife Ethel: 'I have now finished six chapters of the book, but I'm keeping them very short; these 6 chapters are only 10,000 words. I think it is a nice book and being at sea like this is a lovely way to write.'[9] The work continued on 2 and 3 November ('Writing all day; finished chapters on Psychology (begun yesterday)'[10]), 4 November ('Writing metaphysics all day;

[8] Letter to Barbara Gnosspelius, 10 Nov. 1938. from the M. V. *Alcinous*, 10 Nov. 1938. [TS/FLTR0840] The point about the flow of air can be found, considerably elaborated as a footnote, in the *Essay on Metaphysics*, pp. 260–1.

[9] Letter to Ethel Collingwood, 29 October 1938. [TS/PLTR185]

[10] There are three chapters on psychology in the completed book: IX ('Psychology as Anti-Metaphysics'), X ('Psychology as the Science of Feeling'), and XI ('Psychology as the Pseudo-Science of Thought').

got to end of chapter XIII after completely rewriting X'), and 5 November ('Metaphysics all day and finished chapter XV'). The next mentions are on 9 November (after being shown the engine room, 'Otherwise writing all day. (3 chapters on Kant)'), 10 November ('Writing metaphysics all day, 2 chapters, finishing Kant; but much revision needed'), 11 Nov. ('Revising Kant all day wrote two new chapters'[11]), 12 November ('Revising all day. Wrote new chapter XII'[12]), 13 November ('Revising all day; wrote new chapter XXVII (last)[13]). Despite the reference to this chapter being his last, *An Essay on Metaphysics* eventually had thirty-four chapters. After returning to his Malay studies, however, he did note on 17 November, the day before landing in Sumatra, that he was 'revising book'.

The curt entries of the *Log* are expanded in all Collingwood's letters home; they are vividly evocative of his situation on the ship, the bracing wind and the ocean, his own seamanship and love of sailing, his acute observation of his fellows on board, and his personal confidence in the journey ahead—approached not as an invalid's chance of a rest, but as a project, and an opportunity, of which he was going to make the most. He continued his general reading throughout; in a letter to his wife on 21 November he expands on this:

> My chief reading is Racine, & I have read Phèdre over & over again, and with great interest too. It is a wonderful play. Racine is very odd. All his plays (except his one comedy) are about one subject, namely the psychology of absolute monarchs. It is as if he was thinking all the time what it was like to be Louis XIV. Phèdre is not at all like the Euripides original. The Hippolytus is a study in sexual perversion . . . Euripides's moral is that you can't be abnormal in sex without paying for it in the most comprehensive & disastrous way. Racine's moral is that kings and queens are as wax in the hands of their servants, and that their lives & happiness depend on their choosing good ones.[14]

When the *Alcinous* docked at Padang in Sumatra on 17 November, where Collingwood spent a day and an evening with other passen-

[11] There are seven chapters on Kant in the published version, comprising Part IIIB of *An Essay on Metaphysics*.

[12] Ch. XII: 'A Pseudo Science Refutes Itself'.

[13] Ch. XXVII: 'Analogies of Experience'.

[14] Letter to Ethel Collingwood, 21 Nov. 1938. [TS/PLTR187] See Smallwood in this volume.

gers seeing something of the harbour and the town; it then set sail the following morning, to reach Jakarta on 20 November, the capital of Java, then known as Batavia. Appended to the notebook in which he kept his *Log*, Collingwood pasted a double-page spread map of sea-routes around the East Indies (reproduced here as front and back end covers). This had been recently published by the K. P. M. Line, with whom he made his onward bookings. We shall trace Collingwood's journey giving the modern place name alongside the older one on its first occurrence, but then follow through with his own usage. Batavia became his headquarters for the next couple of months, and he had already arranged for letters (which took about ten days from England) to be held for him there, and where possible forwarded.[15] According to a letter to Ethel Collingwood written a little later as he was arriving in Bali, he had left his 'Introduction to Metaphysics' behind in Batavia with his European clothes, ready to collect on the way home. He declared there his intention to revise the book on the homeward journey.[16]

2. *Java, 20 November–7 December 1938*

A couple of days after having arrived in Batavia and settled in to the Daendels Hotel, sitting writing at 2 a.m. (in this case, we presume letters) in the porch of his suite, open to the garden, he indicated to his daughter Ruth how easily he was slipping into the language:

I was interrupted . . . by a boy trying to sell me roses. They come around all day long, some with two baskets at the ends of a bamboo pole, thus [*drawing of the pole and baskets*] over the shoulder, some with a kind of tablecloth knotted up at the four corners which they open out on your step, and try to sell you jewellery & metal goods & haberdashery & silver & food & painted cottons & silk shawls and embroideries: and I have bought nothing whatever except a pair of wooden sandals to go to the bath in because in tropical countries you don't stand barefoot on the ground unless you want to pick up jiggers, which bore under the skin & have families there. I have to spend quite a lot of time telling these people to go away: I'm not going to start buying things yet though one boy yesterday had some wood-carvings that rather worked upon me – sort of Java-Nefertiti

[15] Letter to Barbara Gnosspelius, 10 Nov. 1938; a note added vertically up the left-hand margin of this letter. [TS/FLTR0840]

[16] Letter to Ethel Collingwood, 8 Dec. 1938. [TS/PLTR190]

affairs. One tried to sell me a whole set of silver spoons & forks with little Java-puppets on their butt-ends, like apostle spoons. "Itu wayang-kulit", says I, proud of knowing a Java puppet when I saw it & of knowing the name for it too. "No, tuan" says the boy with a puzzled expression on his choir-boyish face, "that's not a puppet, that's a silver spoon." We did not trade. I was terribly snubbed. I took refuge in "tida man" (don't want) and repeated it until the child crept noiselessly away.[17]

He had been met in Batavia by a friend of a brother of Malcolm Knox, Mr Robert McMorran, who was manager of Lever Bros in the city; he and his wife Lilian made a special point of showing him round.[18] In a letter to Knox he expressed his appreciation:

I really had no idea that there was such a thing as hospitality of the kind, and in the degree, to which it has been lavished upon me by McMorran. And my debt will continue to accumulate. The most interesting part of my travels would in any case be, of course, my visit to Bali; but the question in a place like that is whether you can get behind the façade of shows arranged for the tourists; and this has been settled for me by Mrs McMorran, whose mother and stepfather live there in a local prince's palace, the stepfather being a sculptor employed by the government to study native art; and to these people's care I am to be committed.[19]

McMorran introduced him to the Rambollets, a Dutch-Danish couple, who showed him more of the city, taking him to Chinese temples—'all exquisitely & the bigger ones astonishingly furnished with statues, carvings, porcelain, bronzes, ivories, chairs & Lord knows what. The biggest one was where we had our fortunes told.'[20] Mrs Rambollet was a journalist and editor of the local illustrated newspaper; he allowed her to photograph him and write a story. The next day, Collingwood walked down to old Batavia where among other things he collected his first batch of letters from Oxford, and went to the Harmonie Club. Of this he later wrote to Ethel:

This is a lovely building – a marble palace of the late 18th century where Raffles lived when he was governor of Java... He conquered Java in the Napoleonic Wars and governed it with great success until we gave it back

[17] Letter to Ruth Collingwood, 22 Nov. 1938. [TS/FLTR0841].

[18] Letter to Ethel Collingwood, 20 Nov. 1938. [TS/PLTR186].

[19] Letter to Malcolm Knox, 25/11/38, Hotel Daendels, Batavia, Java. The Knox Papers, University of St Andrews.

[20] Letter to Ethel Collingwood, 21 Nov. 1938. [TS/PLTR187].

to the Dutch after the war. When that happened his palace was given to the Dutch for use as a club, and I have been made a visitor member. So I sat in marble halls and read the papers – the weekly edition of the Times, with a great deal of Chamberlainisms in it and I was glad to be away from my dear native land. Then I went & got my hair cut and bought some cigars. You can get the kind of cigar which costs 1/- in England for 2^d here, so I smoke them. I am smoking one now after breakfast. It is 6 inches long and lovely.[21]

Very soon Collingwood was introduced to the editor of the newspaper *Wereldnieuws*, given the standard modern account of the Dutch East Indies,[22] and shown round the printing works, where again he was interviewed and photographed. A news item appeared shortly in the local press:

Professor R. G. Collingwood of Magdalen College in the University of Oxford has arrived in Batavia on a holiday trip to the Dutch East Indies. His specialism is philosophy, but he is also interested in history and archaeology. The British professor considers his journey of great importance in order to make a comparison between the system of government of the ancient Romans and that of the modern Dutch. He is of the opinion, as he explains, that these systems have very much in common. The Romans were bent on governing their territories in line with their existing character, without attempting to shape their inhabitants into 'fake-Romans'. As for Holland and the Indies, the professor has observed the same phenomenon.

Prof. Collingwood hopes to make contact with the authorities in the field of antiquities here, and otherwise as an interested person to 'put out feelers' in various social fields.[23]

By 25 November, Collingwood was arranging his planned cruise of the islands. He wrote to Ethel of his tentative travel arrangements:

On Monday next I leave Batavia 6.45 AM. for Djokjakarta in central Java, where there is a Sultan and where natives are still native and not gradu-

[21] Letter to Ethel Collingwood, 23 Nov. 1938; continuation of letter of 21 xi 38. [TS/PLTR187].

[22] Vandenbosch, Amry, 1933. *The Dutch East Indies: Its Government, Problems and Politics*. Grand Rapids, MI: Wm. B. Eerdmans Publishing Co.

[23] 'Prof. R. G. Collingwood: Britsch hoogleeraar op bezoek', *Java-Bode*, 22 November 1938: 9; the substance was republished the next day on the front page of *De Indische Courant*. Translation kindly supplied by Professor Jan van der Dussen.

Illustration 18. Borobodur, Java, photographed by Collingwood. See *Log* entry for 30 November 1938, p. 10. Courtesy of Teresa Smith.

ally... turning into half-caste Dutch. It is the centre of puppet-plays and native crafts, notably batik, also of Javanese nationalism. And round it are all the best remains of Hindu-Buddhist architecture... I am cutting out all visits to places that are famous for their scenery, hill-stations, places where you can get cool, & so forth. I have been working hard in the Batavia Museum and am bitten more than somewhat by native art. Perhaps a week at Djokja (as it is called for short). Then on to Sourabaya, whence I sail for Bali. In Bali I shall be looked after by Mrs. McMorran's mother & step father.[24]

Further days of sightseeing in and around Djokja included a car trip on 30 November to Boroboedoer looking at sculptures, puppet shows, temples and 'photographing a lot' (see Illustrations 18–20). Collingwood eventually boarded the SS Merak from Sourabaya on 7 December (Illustrations 21 and 22 show the quayside) and sailed for Bali.

He had already written in anticipation to Barbara:

The point about Bali is that they have stuck to their Hindu religion and art, and have produced a most extraordinarily vigorous & sensitive art

[24] Letter to Ethel Collingwood, 26 Nov. 1938. [TS/PLTR188].

Illustrations 19 and 20. Street scene and market in Djoka, Java, photographed by Collingwood. See *Log* entry for 2 December 1938, p. 10. Courtesy of Teresa Smith.

Illustrations 19 and 20. Continued.

Illustrations 21 and 22. Quayside photographed by Collingwood in Soerabaja, Java, with boats unloading and bullock carts waiting to load up. See *Log* entry for 6–7 December 1938, p. 11. Courtesy of Teresa Smith.

Illustrations 21 and 22. Continued.

which combines the delicacy of Hindu art with the fierceness of Polynesian. And it is all quite alive still. They have, for example, a ballet which is said to make the Russians look like amateurs. It is all danced by children of under 14. And their (modern) woodcarving to judge by specimens in the museum here is as good as good European medieval, which it rather resembles. I shall try to bring some home.[25]

3. Bali, 8–29 December 1938

Arriving ashore at Boeleleng on Bali early the next morning, Collingwood and some of the other tourists were off within an hour by car over the mountains. Bali was already famous for its arts, music, and festivals; and has become more so since. Collingwood's notes and letters were soon liberally sprinkled with local names and words, and he lets us know he was reading the beautifully illustrated volume of de Zoete and Spies on Balinese dance (which had just come out). In the letter to Barbara which we include as a whole at the end of this chapter, he presses her to get the volume from the library.[26] In passing a village, the party stopped to listen to the famous music of the Balinese orchestra for the first time. The brief jottings in the *Log* itself begin to fill out from this time as Collingwood sees and hears more of Balinese cultural events, but in the letters home there is even more vivid detail and explanation:

We found this village was having a tooth-filing feast, & doing it very well. Inside a mud-walled enclosure were huts richly decorated with silk hangings containing beds for the candidates; all about were people in their best clothes having frightful fun; masses of food was being cooked; and a large & expensive gamelan[27] was in full blast. A gamelan is an orchestra. This

[25] Letter to Barbara Gnosspelius, 26 Nov. 1938. [TS/FLTR0842]

[26] Letter to Barbara Gnosspelius, 23 Dec. 1938. [TS/FLTR0844] The book referred to is by De Zoete, Beryl, and Walter Spies, 1938. *Dance and Drama in Bali*. London: Faber & Faber. A copy exists in the possession of Teresa Smith, bought in a Bath bookshop. More recent accessible works on Indonesian music, dance, and cultural life, include the following: Geertz, Clifford, 1980. *Negara: The Theatre State in Nineteenth-Century Bali*. Princeton, NJ: Princeton University Press; Fox, James (ed.), 1980. *Indonesia: The Making of a Culture*. Canberra: Australian National University; Howe, Leo, 2001. *Hinduism and Hierarchy in Bali*. Oxford & Santa Fe: James Currey & SAR Press; Hughes-Freeland, Felicia, 2008. *Embodied Communities: Dance Traditions and Change in Java*. New York & London: Berghahn.

[27] For description of the 'gamelon' or the more modern spelling *gamelan* for the style of orchestra found in Java and Bali, see de Zoete and Spies, *Balinese Dance and Drama*: 6–11 and for other Balinese terms used by Collingwood, *passim*.

one was all percussion . . . It makes me enormously excited even to remember it now. They had immense control over their climaxes, and were rehearsed to perfection.

Having arrived at his hotel at Den Pasar, the party set out again to visit various special sites, including royal tombs, and Collingwood goes on to describe the Monkey Dance they witnessed that afternoon:

This was in a village about 20 km. from here. I was given a chair on top of a wall, looking down on a plot of ground in the middle of which a branched lamp-stand 6 ft high had been planted. It had ten wicks burning in oil (coconut oil). Towards sunset, young men came striding on, tucked up their clothes into the merest loin-cloths, & sat down. By degrees they formed a circle, 200 of them, enclosing 5 deep an area of 5 yards across, in the middle of which was the lamp. Then they suddenly began making monkey-noises, very faint. Then louder, waving their bodies about and jerking their hands. The noises were as carefully planned and controlled as if they had been a choir singing from short scores. Then they began using their hands. Every hand was a monkey-hand, not a human hand at all.[28]

Back at the hotel there were more dances the following evening. By the morning of 10 December he was off to see further dances in a neighbouring village, and then drove to Oeboed to stay with the van der Noordaas, the parents of Mrs McMorran. Here, among other excitements, he photographed a famous temple (Illustration 23) and witnessed eight rounds of what was already a Balinese classic—the cock fight,[29] as part of the special birthday celebrations of a daughter of the local Tjokorde—or Prince. The music of the *gamelan* orchestra kept him awake most of the night.

Collingwood's interest in folklore, folktales, and what today we could call social or cultural anthropology had deepened during the mid-1930s. He had joined the Folk Lore Society in London in 1936 and begun attending their meetings. He had little sympathy for the circle of anthropologists around R. R. Marett at Exeter College at the time—indeed, in an early letter to his father he mentioned meeting Marett among other guests at a dinner in Corpus Christi and had a little fun at his expense:

[28] Letter to Ethel Collingwood, 8 Dec. 1938. [TS/PLTR190].

[29] See Geertz, Cifford, 1973. *The Interpretation of Cultures.* New York: Basic Books, which includes his famous essay 'Deep Play: Notes on the Balinese Cockfight', pp. 412–53.

Illustration 23. Temple at Besakih, Bali, photographed by Collingwood. See *Log* entry for 26 December 1938, p. 19. Courtesy of Teresa Smith.

Marett was discoursing on Palaeolithic Man and his habits, especially the Aurignacian burial-customs – scarnitura [*stripping of flesh*] and painting bones red of course – and told the story of how the great Ambrose founding his church at Milan came upon two skeletons identified as early Xtian martyrs, their blood having been preserved and still reddening their bones . . . Voice from Bertrand Russell: Do tell me – I never hear of these strange persons without wanting to know their doctrinal peculiarities – What was the Aurignacian heresy?[30]

[30] Letter to W. G. Collingwood, from Oxford, 31 Jan. 1915. [TS/FLTR470A].

Collingwood's continuing ambivalence towards Oxford social anthropology (though he read a good deal of its literature in the Bodleian Library and as a Delegate of the Oxford University Press, eventually developing a high regard for Evans-Pritchard) is what took him to London and the Folk Lore Society.[31] His archaeological interest had always led him towards the historical significance of myths and legends, rather than to bones and stones as such, and this interest had drawn him to the theories of the anthropologists about such things and the way their meanings were transmitted over time. In his book-length manuscript on folktales and anthropology he put forward the argument that here was a new field for study, a 'new kind of archaeology' (see *PE*) and here is the key significance of his excited encounter with Balinese art and culture.

Collingwood's diary jottings, drawings, and letters not only illustrate delight at Balinese performances, but also show how carefully professional his notes were. Despite the large literature on Balinese culture since his visit, Collingwood's descriptions and suggestive comparisons stand the test of time. Towards the end of a letter of 14 December to Ethel, he addresses his daughter Ruth at length on his thoughts about folk tales, music, arts, drama, and civilization, referring to those of Greece, the Hebrides, and eastern Europe, as well as those of Indonesia, all of which he claimed to be related. Balinese music is modal, 'like European folk music'—it has no 'weird' Eastern scales. As part of a series of numbered observations starting with climate and seasons, he writes:

> (3) No reason Greek folk-music shouldn't resemble Hebridean. The Hebridean fairy-tales are just the same as those of Eastern Europe. For that matter they all reappear in India in about the 10th century, and a lot of them extend to Bali. Europe as a whole belongs to a cultural region which includes also (a) the Near East (b) India (c) Indonesia, & has infiltrations into China and, by way of Polynesia, extends to America. In Europe the culture of this region has been submerged by "modern civilization" & is what we call "folk lore". These observations have been proved for the case of fairy-tales, which as you know I have studied; I have seen for myself how they work out for plastic arts & drama; no one has yet worked them out for music, but what I have heard here convinces me that they will work

[31] For Collingwood's ambivalent relationship to the Oxford anthropologists, see Wendy James, 'A Fieldworker's Philosopher: Perspectives from Anthropology'.

out there. Balinese music is modal, like European folk music. It has our scale (I was surprised to find that, having heard a lot of balls about "Eastern" music having weird scales) but no key. That is, it is not built up on the double principle of (a) contrast between tonic & dominant harmonies and (b) modulation into different keys (these 2 principles are really the same, because modulation happens when the original dominant harmony becomes a tonic harmony). (4) I am not drawing, & I have stopped using my camera, because I have seen other tourists using theirs & it has turned me sick. But I am using my eyes, & I am also buying a few things to bring home.[32]

The *Log* itself documents in some detail Collingwood's immersion in a series of Balinese festivals, song competitions, and performances over the next ten days or so. On 21 December he went to stay with Dr Bonnicker, an elderly bachelor in the next village, a retired lawyer living in a small house on his pension, of whom we get a portrait in a letter written to Ethel the next day:

He is one of those charming old men who have the faces & minds of little boys, and he lives in the greatest and happiest intimacy with his Balinese servants & neighbours. Of an evening his half-dozen Balinese house-boys come and squat round our feet and hug the dogs and chatter in Malay with us, all looking perfectly happy & perfectly adorable. The Balinese are the sweetest & most beautiful people I have ever seen & they make friends with you on the smallest provocation, and look at you out of the kindest imaginable eyes.

He went on to report on the previous evening's entertainment:

Late at night the whole dinner party (as if going on to a night club) went to Batoean, about 7 miles away, and saw a Gamboeh, which is the oldest & most venerated of all Balinese dances – a very stylized drama accompanied by an orchestra of archaic pattern consisting chiefly of bamboo flutes or recorders 3 ft long. (I am not sure if they were recorders or flutes. If flutes, they were played as one "plays" on a key, blowing across the end. It was dark in that place, with only a few coconut-oil lamps barely illuminating the densely packed audience, and the dancers looming up out of the darkness). By about 12.30 I began dropping off to sleep on my stool: the tangle of children about my feet were already dead asleep: the Gamboeh showed every sign of going on to sunrise; & we went home.[33]

[32] Letter to Ethel and Ruth Collingwood, 14 Dec. 1938. [TS/PLR191] Much of Collingwood's work on fairy tales, and the mention here of his European/Indian comparisons in particular, has now been published for the first time in *PE*.

[33] Letter to Ethel Collingwood, 22 Dec. 1938. [TS/PLTR192].

Illustration 24. Balinese landscape: rice terraces (sawahs) photographed by Collingwood and mentioned many times in the *Log*. See e.g. entries for 15, 16, and 26 December 1938, pp. 14, 15, and 19. Courtesy of Teresa Smith.

Bonnicker escorted Collingwood over the next couple of days in explorations by car and on foot through the interior, taking photographs of the landscape (Illustration 24), visiting rock-carvings (which again reminded him of Greek and Roman works) and the homes of artists. He collected various paintings and objects en route. Bali was already famous as a tourist destination, and had already attracted a variety of artists, anthropologists, and assorted eccentrics who in some cases stayed on or even retired there. Among these, Collingwood notes in the *Log* (12 December 1938) that through the van der Noordaas he met Walter Spies, the Russian-born German artist who came to Java in 1923 and moved to Bali in 1927. At the invitation of the Prince, he had settled in the village of Oeboed, where the van der Noordaas where now living. Spies became Bali's most famous European resident in the 1930s and had distinguished visitors such as Charlie Chaplin and the conductor Leopold Stokowski. Margaret Mead, the famous anthropologist, and her husband Gregory Bateson helped Spies by testifying at his trial for homosexual practices that his 'transgressions' were consistent with Balinese culture. Collingwood may not have been aware that Margaret Mead and Bateson were probably on the island, though on the other side, when he was there; they were soon to publish a fine volume of photographs illustrating Balinese life.[34] Spies, reputedly a flamboyant character, and the Dutch artist Rudolf Bonnet—more effective at realizing projects—are claimed to have influenced the work of local Balinese artists to adopt more modern genres in order to appeal to the narrow tastes of Western tourists. Bonnet lent Collingwood a book on Bali which had become highly successful in New York and elsewhere, by the Mexican Miguel Covarrubias who had visited Bali with his wife and called on Spies in 1930, returning in 1933 to collect material for the book (see note in the *Log*, 19 December). One chapter opens with the bold claim 'Everybody in Bali seems to be an artist.'[35]

Back in Java a couple of months later, Collingwood lamented what was happening politically on Bali—he was alarmed that a recent change of government had led to a crackdown on homosexuality and the imprisonment of many of the friends he had made: 'A lot of distinguished and high-up Dutch officials have got pinched, and lots of private persons, among them my friends Walter Spies, Rudolf Bonnet, and dear old Bonnicker, the nicest man in Bali. Van der Noordaa, of course, is a virtuous married man (and a prig to boot) so he isn't involved.'

Collingwood's observations of the local street scenes, seafaring ways of life, and rural landscapes he found all over the islands are richly documented in his own photograph albums; we include a small but representative sample of them here.

Alongside his gift for making friends with the artistic set, Collingwood had a sharp eye for the social relations between local people and their European rulers and settlers. In a letter sent quite soon after his arrival in Java he comments on how the Europeans imposed themselves on the Indonesians:

[34] Bateson, Gregory, and Margaret Mead, 1942. *Balinese Character: A Photographic Analysis*. New York: Special Publications of the New York Academy of Sciences, vol. 2.

[35] Covarrubias, Miguel, 1937. *The Island of Bali*. New York: Alfred A. Knopf.

They created a situation, hereabouts, which consisted essentially in the claim that any European is a Tuan and has to be treated as such. It is a very odd thing, this idea that one entire civilization should be so related to another that any member of the first is given a title of nobility by any member of the second. It doesn't mean that either understands the other, for they don't; nor that the dominant people beat the natives at their own game and win their respect that way, for that again doesn't happen; it does mean, however, that the natives recognize the strangers as people whom they can see to be obeying a stern and exacting law, living for an idea & not for a good time, living hard & not taking things easy. And I don't think this is true any longer. I don't think the people hereabouts look up much to Europeans.[36]

Just before returning to the van der Noordaas for Christmas, 1938, Collingwood wrote various letters home on 23 December, as detailed in the *Log*. In particular, he sent a very full letter on his delight with the Balinese arts to Barbara, and to complete our portrait of his time on the island, we quote this in full at the end of this chapter. He also received a number of letters—including one from the Vice Chancellor of Cambridge University. This was almost certainly to do with the search for a successor to G. E. Moore; Collingwood was one of the electors, replying to the VC on Christmas Day (though this letter itself has not surfaced); and Wittgenstein was appointed in February 1939. Academic matters were beginning to catch up with him even more directly, as we know from the reply he received later to the letter he sent off to Kenneth Sisam at the Oxford University Press. In that reply, Sisam forewarns Collingwood that the proofs of *An Autobiography* are on the way and that a few of the Delegates would also want to read them and perhaps have comments.[37] The doubts and hesitations surfacing at the Oxford University Press are discussed in detail in the Introduction to this volume.

4. *Cruising the Islands: 31 December 1938–8 February 1939*

By 30 December Collingwood's stay on Bali was at a close; he boarded the SS *Ophir*, arriving the next day at Macassar in

[36] Letter to Ethel Collingwood, 31 Nov 1938. [TS/PLTR189].

[37] Letter from Kenneth Sisam to R. G. C. dated 18 January, 1939. [TS/GLTR096] Oxford University Press Archive, 4609/KS.

Celebes (now named Sulawesi), basing himself at the Empress Hotel. He then embarked on a double-looped cruise around the easternmost islands, taking short trips on a series of boats and observing the landscape, staying at miscellaneous hotels, visiting and sharing excursions with various people met en route. The first loop of the cruise took him along the curving coast of Celebes to its tip at Menado, where he was distinctly unwell. The onward trip southwards and eastwards was a little delayed, but he went on using his camera, recording the harbour of Ternate and local canoes as he passed through the Moluccas (Illustrations 25 and 26). By 7 January he chanced to board a local vessel called the SS. *van Imhoff*; and later made an interesting confession in a letter to his daughter Ruth:

My grandmother, you know, was an Imhoff; and when I found her coat of arms plastered up all over my new boat's saloon, I made inquiries, and found that the man after whom she was named was indeed a member of my grandmother's family (which was a great mercantile family in Bavaria in the late middle ages; Nuremberg Cathedral is choked with their tombs &

Illustration 25. Ternate harbour, photographed by Collingwood. See *Log* entry for 7 January 1939, p. 20. Courtesy of Teresa Smith.

Illustration 26. Moluccan canoes, photographed by Collingwood. See *Log* entry for 7–8 January 1939, p. 20. Courtesy of Teresa Smith.

lousy with their cockatrices) who migrated to Holland & in time became Governor-General of the East Indies.[38]

A few days into this trip Collingwood found himself on the island of Banda. He expanded with some enthusiasm in a subsequent letter to Barbara: he had found Banda Neira the loveliest place he had ever seen—'a group of 3 precipitous volcanic islands all overgrown with nutmegs and sprinkled with the ruins of the marble palaces where lived the nutmeg-planters in the good old days [Illustration 27], before some perfidious Englishman, about 1900, bought a handful of cuttings from a local traitor, planted them at Singapore (where they did very well indeed, I may say), and broke the monopoly.' Mentioning to Barbara that he stayed in a 'real 17th century hotel, vast and dignified and cool', he seems to have generally enjoyed himself, visiting delights such as the sea-gardens—'you go out in a canoe and look down at coral with real tropical fishes dodging about in it, just like the aquarium' and

[38] Letter to Ruth Collingwood, 15 Jan. 1939 [TS/FLTR0846] KPM line, a/b s.s. REAEL, Banda 15.1.39.

Illustration 27. Portico in Banda Neira, photographed by Collingwood. See *Log* entry for 12 January 1939, p. 20. Courtesy of Teresa Smith.

calling on 'the local baron of the nutmeg trade'. Moreover, 'And I climbed the local volcano, 2000ft high, and very nearly got to the top. Think of that.'[39] He photographed this volcano, of which more below (Illustration 28).

[39] Letter to Barbara Gnosspelius, 5 Feb. 1939. [TS/FLTR0847].

Illustration 28. The Goenoeng Api volcano in the island of Banda Neira, photographed by Collingwood. See *Log* entry for 14 January 1939, p. 20. Courtesy of Teresa Smith.

In the very full letter to Ruth just mentioned, written right after his time on the island, we get a more complicated picture of these experiences on Banda:

There is no agriculture whatever, unless you count small tapioca-gardens & a few banana-trees, and <u>one</u> cow kept as a pet; everybody lives directly or indirectly on the nutmeg trade. Once it was vastly profitable; no nutmegs grew anywhere else in the world, and the nutmeg lords lived in marble palaces in Banda, and those were the days. About 1900, some foul traitor sold some cuttings to a foul Englishman from Singapore . . . All the spendthrift old Dutch nutmeggers went bankrupt; and their estates were bought up by the local money-lender, who now prospers exceedingly, because Banda nutmegs are still the best in the world, and almost all of them pass through the hands of this short fat Dutchman, with a face like a film gangster's, whom I am not very proud to call my friend.

The *Log* tells us (14 January) he had attempted his climb up the nearby volcano with the Controller of Ambon (she was married to the Controller of Banda) though she gave up quite soon and he himself only reached about 500m. In the letter to Ruth we have a truly graphic description of this experience:

Another day I went up Goenoeng Api. Or rather, nearly up it. We got up at 5, all in the dark, and after eating some food were off in the dawn at 5.30. Dr John Doctor, a young Dutch civil servant, the wife of the local Controleur (a rather tubby girl in the late 20's) and myself. We crossed to the mountain in a canoe which very nearly sank beneath the weight of so many fat Europeans ... The volcano, clothed in scrub of one sort & another, rises at a uniform slope of about 30 degrees from sea to summit. It is made of cinders. 30° doesn't sound much, but if you try stacking cinders at that angle & then walk up them you will see what I mean. When we had gone up about 150 metres our young lady fell out & was sick. Not pregnancy: just heart-sickness, such as fat people out of training often produce if they start too fast up a mountain. So we sent her back, and one of our two native boys with her, to ferry her across to the mainland where I hope she went back to bed. It was not yet 6 AM. Halfway up, I found that my left foot wouldn't lift high enough to get the necessary full-length step, so I had to do all the climbing with my right leg, like Geoffrey Winthrop Young when he went up the Matterhorn with a wooden leg. This made me slow, and I fell behind. I also had to have constant rests. So the end of it was that I got 3/4 way up when the others, coming down from the top, met me; and I never got to the top at all. I didn't care; but God, how I sweated. Coming down, experience told at first; I was able to slide down that cinder heap at an appalling velocity. But the pride thus generated came before very numerous falls. When I got to where the cinders became fist-size stones, I found that my left (& partially paralyzed) ankle was literally no more use than a broken leg. Whenever I landed left foot first on a stone that rolled (that is, whenever I landed left foot first; i.e. once at every other step) the left ankle doubled up, and I went down like a shot rabbit – fortunately: for unless I had had the presence of mind to fall perfectly limp I'd have sprained the ankle. After about 100 of these falls, and the conversion of my whole carcase into a world's-record bruise collection, I decided to creep the rest of the way down, and reached the sea a very bad last of the party. But what I say is, put me on a mountain whose surface holds together, and I'll get up it; & down again too.

Fortunately for Collingwood, there seems to have been at least one doctor on board, and as he had already been feeling unwell for about a fortnight he was glad of some attention:

It has ... been useful to have a doctor in the party: he hasn't cured me, but he has found some stuff like pale pink toothpowder called MAAGPOEDER or belly-powder, made of bismuth, sold in Ambon, which damps down the symptoms & keeps me going. Apart from this I shouldn't greatly mind if I hadn't got the Doctors with me. I have to be with them almost all the time, because they have no Malay & no Dutch, and I am therefore indispensable and am, so to speak, their Jeeves (you remember the definition of Jeeves? "like what the poet johnnie said about some chappie who was always somewhere around: a guide, don't you know; philosopher if I remember rightly: and – a rather fancy-friend.") John, being a successful doctor, is an educated man & a man of the world; his Glasgow accent sits lightly on him, and he has a wide-open eye and a receptive mind which make him an amusing companion.[40]

By 20 January Collingwood was back at Macassar, where we see from the *Log* that among other things he had his hair cut.

Without the lavish hospitality he had enjoyed on Bali, and the various excitements of the recent cruising, he was left more on his own, and inevitably his letters home returned more to thoughts of own work and career. He was not in the best of health, but his commitment to making the most of the journey was undiminished. From his base at the Empress Hotel in Macassar, he arranged a number of trips by car into the interior of Celebes, and details his observations in the *Log* (Illustration 29 shows one of his landscape shots). On 24 January, a letter to Ethel mentions having spoken nothing but Malay since leaving Macassar, except for a conversation in English with a French ethnologist. The letter continues on the next day with more elaborate descriptions of his findings, for example on burial customs:

Today I have had a lovely long drive examining kampongs (that is the Malay for native villages) and studying manners & customs. When they have no nice rock-face handy to cut graves in, they build not far from the village a Rumah orang matih (dead men's house), very solid, of teak, and put their corpses inside: the hot weather seems to dry them up. In an upper story they put the wooden images, mounted on wooden horses & dressed very expensively in the best Javanese batiks. These houses are decorated like live men's houses, and very grand. Nearby, there seems always to be a group of standing stones; this is <u>not</u> a graveyard but a tempat pesta or feast-place, that is, people sing & dance & hold festivals there. I haven't seen a festival, alas. But now that we have a Professor of Anthropology you can ask him to dinner if you like & tell him you want to know what a Toradja festival is like. I found one Rumah orang matih

[40] Continuation of letter to Ruth Collingwood, 15 Jan. 1939 [TS/FLTR0846] KPM line, a/b s.s. REAEL, Banda 15.1.39.

Illustration 29. Landscape in South Celebes, photographed by Collingwood at the outset of his journey into the interior. See *Log* entry for 21 January 1939, p. 21. Courtesy of Teresa Smith.

(which they call Romatih, for short) on a small rock carefully surrounded by a moat, which I was told kept the dead men safe inside.[41]

Writing also to Barbara about this trip, Collingwood described in more detail how he spent a week in the middle of the sprawling island of Celebes, in his own hired car with his own hired chauffeur

& for a week spoke nothing but Malay. This was great fun. The middle of Celebes is wildly mountainous. It is limestone, much tilted & twisted by volcanic action and seamed with dikes of diorite or some volcanic muck or other I don't know rightly what, and mountains go up to 10,000 feet & it is quite cool. Round about dawn, at the villages up there, you get thermometer readings of 70 F. Right in the middle of these mountains there is an upland basin, very hard to get at any way you go, inhabited by very queer folk called Toradjas, & it was among them that I spent my time. They are gaunt and black and ferocious-looking and they wear a loincloth and a huge black cloak, and they grow rice in sawahs but they have no ploughs,

[41] Letter to Ethel Collingwood, 24–25 Jan. 1939. [TS/PLTR194] The 'Professor of Anthropology' mentioned is A. R. Radcliffe-Brown, the first holder of the newly-created Chair of Social Anthropology at Oxford, linked with All Souls College, and superseding the Readership held by R. R. Marett at Exeter College.

only digging-sticks, which are exactly like our oars, and you use them with both arms straight & feet well apart, so that the blow falls just to the left of your left foot, and with these digging-sticks they turn a furrow that looks just as if it had been ploughed. And they dry their corpses in the sun & then put them either into square holes cut in a vertical rock-face, of which Providence has supplied plenty in that land, or else in a very stoutly-built teak house with no doors or windows and sometimes with a moat round as well, to keep the ghosts inside. And outside these tombs they stick up almost life-sized wooden images of the deceased, realistically painted & dressed in the most expensive clothes. And near every burying-place there is a group of standing stones – not a circle, just sort of cluster – where they have their feasts in honour of the dead, & eat a great deal of buffalo & drink a great deal of rice wine and do a great deal of dancing. People who have seen these feasts assure me that they are Very Disgusting – all except a young French girl, a student of ethnology with a travelling scholarship from the Sorbonne, who said they were très-jolis.[42]

The photographs Collingwood took of these little-known Toradja ceremonial grave sites are certainly striking and of some historical value (Illustrations 30–33).[43] On 28 January, he sailed off again, on the second loop of his cruise out from Macassar, briefly visiting ports on islands such as Sumbawa and Sumba, continuing eastwards along the southern side of Flores for several days, and after Timor turning north and then back, westwards, along the north coast of Flores. On 5 February, he wrote a long letter to Barbara, describing his adventures:

Since leaving Macassar 9 days ago we have called at 12 ports, all of a greater or less degree of one-horseness, in almost as many islands – all the islands from Soembawa to Timor, inclusive, you can look them up on the map yourself, I'm not going to choke you with tropical scenery. Three days more of it & then, alas, Macassar again & so to Soerabaja once more. I say alas because it is frightful fun, this cruising, and I have a jolly little 1800 ton steamer all to myself & nobody ever speaks to me unless I want them to, and it's never uncomfortably hot and it's lovely calling at all these islands with their whacking great volcanoes and their deep sapphire harbours – no, no scenery please – and there's absolutely nothing whatever to do and nothing whatever to worry about, and it's grand. The only fly in the ointment (you will see in a minute that I chose these words with my usual

[42] Letter to Barbara Gnosspelius, 5 Feb. 1939. [TS/FLTR0847].

[43] Background information may be found in H. Nooy-Palm, *The Sa'dan-Toraja: A Study of Their Social Life and Religion*. Vol. 1, The Hague: Martinus Nijhoff, 1979. Vol. 2, Leiden: Brill, 1986.

Illustrations 30, 31, 32, and 33. Photographs by Collingwood of Toradja rock graves, dead men's houses, and feasting places, taken during his journeys in the interior of Celebes. See *Log* entries for 21–26 January 1939, pp. 21–24, and sketch map of roads in Central Celebes (Illustration 16). Courtesy of Teresa Smith.

Illustrations 30, 31, 32, and 33. Continued.

Illustrations 30, 31, 32, and 33. Continued.

care) is that about a fortnight ago, in the mountains in central Celebes, I thought that somebody was driving a rusty needle into my left ankle, and looked, & it was some nasty kind of a mosquito . . . so I put myself 3 days ago into the hands of the chief engineer, who always acts as surgeon in these little cargo-boats.

His observations on the way the boats operate go on:

All day we handle cargo in ports; all night we go busting from one port to another, among dangers (I use the word in its technical seafaring sense)

Illustrations 30, 31, 32, and 33. Continued.

that would make your hair curl; and never one chink of light to show us where we are or where there is something we had better avoid. No wonder our captain is a martyr to chronic insomnia and what is obviously nervous dyspepsia, and is paid a salary larger than the Prime Minister of the Netherlands, or rather: there is one light, just one, in all the islands east of Java. That is on Klapa Island, a little ragged vicious island lying bang in the fairway of the strait east of Soembawa, between Soembawa & Komodo. I suppose they put it there because that island really does block the channel, and you have to creep round it. Otherwise, Captains on this line are supposed to see in the dark, like cats. I believe the Dutch do this on purpose, simply to prevent foreign craft from coming into these waters. They have a perfectly sixteenth-century idea of what an empire is for – they regard it as a monopoly, just as the Portugese did, from whom they took it; and the lengths to which they will go to preserve their monopoly are most surprising. Non-Dutch commercial shipping is simply not allowed, except (under very severe restrictions) at a few ports like Batavia, Soerabaja, & Macassar.[44]

[44] Letter to Barbara Gnosspelius, 5 Feb. 1939. [TS/FLTR0847].

Even on this short trip, Collingwood's commentaries back home include sharp observations and not a few references to literary topics; the same letter continues the next day:

Another day of blessed idleness, butting all morning into a head-swell westward along the north coast of Flores, then calling for half an hour at what my friend the Chief Engineer called a "nice place; no port, no passengers, no cargo, no nothing" (thus showing a much truer view of what makes niceness in a place than the hotelkeeper's at Cáceres, who was very much puzzled to think why on earth I had ever come to his town, "porque no tiene nada"). Rain all day, and all day I have been writing... what do your think? My first & only letter to the Times Literary Supplement, explaining how far from accurate is the description of Flores strait given by Kipling in that admirable story, A Disturber of Traffic. One of his very best.[45]

The letter he mentions having sent to the *TLS* is addressed from the 'S. S. De Weert, off Flores', and posed tricky questions about the credibility of Kipling's facts in the story. Written on 4 February, it was published by the *TLS* on 11 March 1939. A few brief quotations give a sense of the whole:

Sir, – In "Something of Myself", Kipling says that in one passage of his works he has made a mistake on a point of fact. I do not know to what passage he refers; but I beg to offer a few remarks on a story which might reasonably have been mentioned in that context. "A Disturber of Traffic" is about an Englishman in charge of a screw-pile light in Flores Strait, who goes mad because the strong tidal current there makes the water "streaky" in a way that gets on his nerves. The chief accessories in the story are the volcano "Loby Toby," which shows a constant light at the end of the strait, and a native, described as an "Orange Lord" (Orang Laut), who spends his time swimming about in the sea and has webbed fingers.

Collingwood then agrees about the violence of the currents in the strait; when he came through, the velocity was five knots. 'But the water is very far from streaky... [it] flows in eddies and whorls... The surface of the water looks like a diagram of cosmic vortices in an old edition of Descartes's "Principia": just the sort of pattern which Kipling's light-keeper always longed to see by way of a change.' There was no screw-pile light in Flores Strait. Partly

[45] Rudyard Kipling, 1904. 'The Disturber of Traffic', in *Many Inventions*. London: Macmillan: 1–22.

because the strait was carved in solid rock, 'There is no light at all and never has been . . . the Lesser Sunda Islands are completely unlighted, except for one single lighthouse.' It was not thought desirable to 'facilitate visits by foreign shipping'; and Kipling showed his ignorance of the Dutch Empire when he put his imaginary light in the charge of an Englishman. Where there are lights in the East Indies, they are put in charge of 'specially trained natives', while government service is otherwise closed to all but Netherland subjects. And while 'Orang Laut' does mean 'man of the sea' it is not the name of an 'aquatic tribe' but the Malay term for a seaman. In conclusion Collingwood explains why he mentions these 'errors of fact'; it is 'in the hope that it may interest your readers to see what crimes against the realism which was Kipling's official literary programme were compatible with the production of a story which is among the best he ever wrote'. He had never heard of an Englishman visiting Flores Strait before, nor met a reader of Kipling who seemed aware of the facts he had stated. Interestingly, after Collingwood's return home, he spotted a comment from a writer signing himself 'Netherlander' in the *Straits Times* of 26 April, pointing out that it was only recently that the N. E. I. government had closed its doors to foreigners; and that this had not been the case in Kipling's time. Collingwood replied courteously and thanked 'Netherlander' through a brief follow-up letter in the *TLS* on 20 May.[46]

His letter to Barbara of 5 February continues: 'Last night the Chief Engineer did some rather drastic things to my feet, and announced that they were improving. And he was right. Today I hobble about with little pain. He says that by the time I reach Soerabaja I may play football.'

Writing on 4 and 5 February to Ethel, Collingwood tells her how he kept up his general reading despite the sores on his feet. 'All this time I have 3 books with me: (a) Racine (b) a volume of Damon Runyon stories (c) ditto, Penguin, of early and bad P. G. Wodehouse ones. I read (a) & (b) incessantly: (c) I have got bored with. I am making extensive notes on Racine's plots and Runyon's vowel-patterns, both of which interest me enormously.' The little

[46] Collingwood, letters to the *Times Literary Supplement*, 11 March and 20 May 1939.

book of Damon Runyan's stories survives; and is extensively marked up in faint pencil with comments on content, style, and recurring vowels, which clearly took up a lot of his time. One relatively decipherable comment is found on the inside cover:

> Are these stories in chronological order of writing? If so, that would explain why nos. [so-and-so] have their sting in the tail, and nos [so-and-so] a distinct wiggle in the same organ, while [so-and-so] merely hold their tails up with a self-satisfied gesture. It looks as if the author, between no. 2 & no. 14, has discovered that putting the sting of a story in its tail is a cheap method of composition, and one which must not degenerate into a habit.[47]

The letter to Ethel continues: 'then I have my diary to keep, and letters to write, especially to the van der Noordaas, to whom I promised a full account of my travels; and sometimes I sketch volcanoes, & sometimes I take photographs.' Continuing this letter on 8 February, after berthing at Macassar once again (where he was handed another set of letters from home) he updates her on the reception in Oxford of the manuscript of his 'Autobiography': 'I had also a letter from Sisam from which I learn that they are printing my autobiography but are rather flustered by parts of it, especially the last or Spanish chapter. I am relieved, because this is the first I have heard of it & wildly fancied it might have been altogether too much for them.'[48]

5. Java again, 10 February–21 March 1939

Collingwood was transferred very quickly to another ship, which set sail in poor weather for Java on the first leg of his homeward journey. By the next morning, 9 February, it was less rough; the *Log* tells us simply: 'Wrote sketch contents for Principles of History.' His mind was certainly back on academic activities; among the letters sent from this ship were ones for the *TLS*, for B. Croce, and for Penguin. They called briefly at Bali and eventually arrived at the small port of Sourabaya on Java, where Collingwood made for the Ngemplak Hotel and based himself there for four days,

[47] Runyon, Damon, 1938. *More Than Somewhat: A Series of Stories*, selected by E. C. Bentley. Leipzig: The Albatross.

[48] Letter to Ethel Collingwood, 4-5-8 Feb., 1939. [TS/PLTR195].

noting each day in his *Log* that he was writing the 'Principles of History'.[49]

On 14 February, he took the train for the major city of Djokja, securing the next to last room at the Hotel Mataram. The *Log* records that he worked at his 'Principles of History' almost every day while there, except for 18 February, after a bad night when he 'kept off the book'. That day he did, nevertheless, write a most important letter to Ethel, reflecting on his own career, scholarly writing, and lost promise as a might-have-been novelist. He says he is now in better spirits, the reason being: 'I began writing the book I have been working up to for 30 years, The Principles of History; and what's more, my very first evening here I passionately made friends with an Englishman of about 45, a sea captain now working in China, a native of Bishop Auckland'—a welcome meeting in this remote place, understandably, with a fellow-spirit from the North of England. Since getting back to Djokja, he explains to Ethel he has spent about four days writing 50 pages. He comments that:

> it is very good, very clear and mature and decisive, just what I have always hoped this book would be like, and the only trouble is my imagination is being so frisky that I have to ride it on the curb and strike out heaps of my choicest passages because the old Pegasus is cavorting around more than you'd expect any reader to stand, let alone a publisher. I have got in some priceless episodes, one a full-size detective novel, another a bogus report on the excavation of a hill-fort, both in my opinion great fun. And I find it really hard to refrain from sticking in lots of snappy dialogue between myself & various imaginary critics. This experience has shown me that I have in me the makings of a quite good novelist, hitherto repressed by the cramping effect of Academic Society. Sad isn't it? But yesterday I wrote too much and got very excited & slept badly, so today I am being very strong-minded & am not writing at all. [But the lunch bell went 10 minutes ago & my elderly friend will be fearing that something untoward has happened to me.] I don't think I ever realized before, how fatally I missed my bus when I took a job in Oxford instead of becoming a professional writer. I know why I did it, it was because I was angry with my father for being that sort of person and not being able to bring up his family in consequence; but that's neither here nor there. I know now, too,

[49] For a full discussion of the writing of *The Principles of History*, see Boucher, David, 1995. 'The Principles of History and the Cosmology Conclusion to the Idea of History', *Collingwood Studies* II: 140–74.

why I was so annoyed with Isobel [*Munro*] when she made the same wrong decision, especially after all her protestations about being a writer. But I now think those protestations were bogus. I mean, she wouldn't have been so hot about them if she had believed she was a writer. She would just have gone and written. Well, I don't see my way to changing my job now, except so far as that means doing what, anyhow, I have made up my mind to do – cut out every other sort of job so far as that is possible, and put everything I can into writing for the future.

Collingwood also mentions that he cannot now sail (from the capital, Batavia) before 18 March, and despite the advertised time of arrival it was not known when or where he would arrive in Europe: 'Certainly I shouldn't be home until about 22 April so don't expect me before that and if I don't arrive until later just sit tight. It's long odds that I should be home by the time I have to begin lecturing, on I think the 25th.'[50] He comments that he gets on very well with the natives at Djokja and likes them more and more.

Collingwood also sent a letter the next day to his son Bill, asking for news, thanking him for comments on his 'Autobiography'—and responding to Bill's comments on it with some pertinent insights of his own. On news:

I get very little, so I'm grateful for it, bloody though it is. These Dutch all think that Germany is going to blow up; they tell circumstantial stories about what things are like there when you can get behind the smoke-screen, but I don't believe anything I'm told. Without home politics I am really lost; & in these days when no definite news is allowed to leak out I have to get it by hints & inference, & you can't do that out of the country. I've just got the Penguin Special on "Britain", which has some useful stuff in it though nothing very [?] Thank you for your remarks about my Autob (or Aut., perhaps). Parts of it, as you may have noticed were rather directed towards your eye, especially the bit about schools. You needn't worry about Prichard believing anything I say – nothing, under any conditions, would ever [?persuade] him to do that. I hope that I shall either see or hear what happens, though, when he reads it (in Blackwell's). The resemblance to Praeterita had escaped my notice: it's so long since I read it. Good book, if I remember rightly.[51] As an antidote for boredom I have begun writing my next book. This is The Principles of History,

[50] Letter to Ethel Collingwood, 18 Feb. 1939. [TS/PLTR196].

[51] For background discussion of Collingwood's relationship to Ruskin and his *Praeterita*, see the Introduction to this volume.

which will go down to posterity as my Masterpiece. I suddenly began it, somewhat unexpectedly, as my boat was approaching Soerabaja, and spent my whole time in that damn hot town writing it as hard as I could lick. It will completely ruin what little reputation I have left, because in order to explain what historical evidence is I indulged my genius (in the Latin sense) by writing an original & complete detective story as a kind of episode, and then solemnly lectured on it. It is a nice detective-story, & I am surprised at myself for the ease and convincingness with which I wrote it: I feel like William Morris when he was an undergraduate at Exeter, "Well if this is poetry, it's very easy to write." The star character is the Scotland Yard man, Detective Inspector Jonathan Shufflebottom, a native of Oldham & alumnus of Manchester Grammar School. There is a blackmailer called John Doe (corpse of, first sentence) and a medical student called Richard Roe, who acts as Red Herring No. 1, and a very attractive village Woman Constable & a village Spinster, & a village Poacher, and the Rector, & the Rector's Daughter & the Chief Constable. The Rector is the murderer. John Doe was the man who seduced the Rector's now long dead wife (so the Rector's Daughter, a seven months' baby, was really John Doe's daughter, you see) and has kept her letters & now is blackmailing the Rector for her fortune, which she left to him in trust for the child... It's a nice story, but, as I say, it will be fatal for the reputation of R. G. C. as a philosopher. Who cares? I don't. When I think of the people with reputations, these days, I'd just as soon not have one.[52]

By 21 February, after an early morning session on his writing, Collingwood had taken the train again, and was back in Batavia at the Hotel Daendals, reunited with the things he had left there. His *Log* does record 'Have been long enough in the Dutch East Indies.' The next day he was able to book an earlier voyage home than expected, on the *Rhesus*, leaving on 4 March and arriving in London by 4 April.

He wrote to Ethel immediately about this and other matters, including the need to see Dr Stott again, the consultant in London he had seen before he left on the voyage. The letter was dated 22 February, which happened to be his birthday, and expresses disappointment at not getting any letters that day; it then goes into some interesting—and to fellow scholars somewhat eye-opening—details about the progress of his various writing projects. Of the 'Introduction to Metaphysics', he notes:

[52] Letter to Bill Collingwood, 19 Feb. 1939. [TS/FLTR0848].

I spent an hour looking at the book I wrote on the voyage out; it strikes me as very good indeed & hardly in need of revision at all. (Query: I know that Pope advised other people to "keep your piece nine years", but did he do it himself? I will lay quite a little 6 to 5 that he did not). My new book goes well. I have spent only nine days, not all whole days, on it, and have now written 41,000 words, which I think is one-third of the bulk of Principles of Art, which I don't wish greatly to exceed. This looks as if there would be two-thirds of Principles of History written by the time I sail. We will try to get it on the Christmas market, for historians' wives to give them as Christmas presents.

Oriented now fully to his writings and imminent voyage home, Collingwood set to work immediately at the proofs of *An Autobiography* and the manuscript of his 'Introduction to Metaphysics' (noted in the *Log* on 23 and 24 February), and then focused on the latter. On 25 February he revised ch. VI, and bought Agatha Christie's *Murder in Mesopotamia*; on 26 February he completed the revision of ch. VI and began to rewrite ch. VII, with largely new material and rearrangement; on 27 February he finished this and also revised ch. V; the next day he finished Part I, and over the next two days wrote a new ch. VIII and finished revising Part II. On 3 March he did some jobs in town; on the morning of 4 March and after a little shopping he worked again at the 'Introduction to Metaphysics', revising Part III. The same afternoon he boarded the SS *Rhesus* for the homeward voyage.

In addition to these notes made in the *Log*, we learn a little more from Collingwood's letter to Ethel written on 1 March and sent off shortly before boarding ship for home. He there made some interesting remarks about his 'Introduction to Metaphysics' and relates Agatha Christie's *Murder in Mesopotamia* to his own historical method. He says:

Almost every day I have spent on my veranda rewriting my Introduction to Metaphysics, which I am beginning to think will be a rather important book except for the one snag that nobody nowadays wants to be introduced to metaphysics. In my wicked pride, I think this book has settled the question which Kant broke himself up trying to settle – how can metaphysics become a science? and settled it in a manner which is as simple as it is conclusive & illuminating, by saying that metaphysics is a branch of history. Won't that annoy people! But it's true; and I am so clear about its truth that I can write it all out with hardly any waspishness at all. The rough draft written on Alcinous was a bit waspish in places, but re-writing is getting rid of all that.

Of Agatha Christie's book he writes that 'as an example of historical method the solution is really very fine, because there are no "clues" in the stupid old sense whatever, & the solution is done by the sheer working of what I once called Historical Imagination. The fact is that Agatha Christie's work has been raised to a new level by her getting involved in archaeology.'[53]

In a letter to Barbara, written only a couple of days before his final departure, he elaborated further on his progress and thoughts concerning the two book manuscripts and proofs of a third which he was working on.

On 9 Feb I began writing The Principles of History, which is the book I have been getting ready to write, consciously, for 25 years. I wrote it quite hard from then to 22 Feb. and wrote 40,000 words. Then I got diverted by other cares. Meanwhile I landed at Soerabaya on 10 Feb. and spent 4 very warm days there. Thermometer in my bedroom 80° at dawn, 90° at evening every day. Very busy writing. Took no interest in my surroundings at all.

He then relates how he went to Djoka on 14 February in order to 'muscle in' on a royal wedding there, and to 'see dancing & plays & hear music'. Although discouraged by the curator he had met before, he showed up—'Found that my curator friend was quite right; dilarang masuk – sorry, slipping into Malay: I mean, no admittance. So I was very happy keeping my room and writing my book and never going out at all.' He then mentions what was awaiting him on his return to Batavia:

When I got here I found the proofs of my autobiography from Oxford, and the MS of the book I wrote on board Alcinous on the voyage out. So I dropped the history book & have been working ever since on these. I have only been out once, since 22 Feb., which was yesterday when Lilian MacMorran came to take me shopping and I riotously spent £10 on fancy-priced Javanese goods – silver work & so on – at a rather unscrupulous shop called something Kunstarbeid.[54]

On the train from Djoka back to Batavia, Collingwood had produced a final surprise both for Ethel and for Barbara. For

[53] Letter to Ethel Collingwood, 1 March 1939. [TS/PLTR198].

[54] Letter to Barbara Gnosspelius, 2 March 1939. [TS/FLTR0849].

each he enclosed a poem called 'The Java Express Limited'; to Ethel he comments that he hasn't written any poetry since he was about 27, though at about 26 'I was writing a good deal of verse, mostly comic, to amuse my fellow sufferers in the Admiralty Intelligence Department.'[55] This is verifiable from correspondence written during that time. To Barbara he explains further about the poem that came to him on the train across Java:

> And on the way, the incident occurred which I have faithfully recorded in the enclosed poem. When did you last see a poem by me? I haven't written one since I was married – awful effects of matrimony! The incident began with seeing certain pale pink flowers rather like evening primroses, & then the fat was in the fire. The dialogue, as you will correctly infer, was not spoken out loud. This incident showed me that my homesickness, which I believed to be chronic but mild, was acute. Mr. Chamberlain no longer seemed to be so important... So I decided to come home as soon as I possibly could... Perhaps I shall be able to see you on your way back north, at the end of the month. Or even to rush north for a stolen week-end in May. I have only twice seen Coniston in May since 1901.

One evening Robert McMorran had confided to Lilian, in front of Collingwood, that he was planning to take her to 'the nicest place in England', by which it turned out he meant 'the Tarns'—i.e. Tarn Hows and the Coniston district generally. Collingwood therefore asked Barbara to be prepared: 'if they turn up, remember that they have been very kind indeed to me'.

The poem he referred to was sent in slightly different versions to Barbara and to Ethel; Ethel's version reads as follows:

JAVA EXPRESS LIMITED

Mile after mile the fields, harsh green,
Wheeled past the window. Yellow streams,
Brimming their banks, came pelting down
Out of the mountains dark with cloud.
The thunderous afternoon was gay
With naked boys who splashed and played,
And slender brown-skinned girls went by,
Bright-robed, between the fields of rice.
And in the dining-car alone,
A little man sat, fat and old;
His spectacles were wet with tears,

[55] Letter to Ethel Collingwood, 22 Feb. 1939. [TS/PLTR197].

The tears rolled down his grizzled beard.
'Why do you cry, mile after mile?
Little old man, why do you cry?'
'The summer lasts the whole year round,
But brings no roses. Never drought
To freeze the fields, and never cold.
But never any roses.'
So
The little man, mile after mile,
'I want wild roses' said, and cried.
R. G. C. 21.2.39

6. Homeward Voyage

On board the *Rhesus* Collingwood was glad to meet up with a further set of congenial fellow-passengers—jotting down in his *Log* 'All North-Country people, thank God, and very sweet.' As the days passed he noted working on the 'Metaphysics' on 5, 6, 8 (new version of ch. VIII), 9, 10, 11, 12, 14, 16 (rewrote ch. VI), and 17 March, at which point he went back to the 'Autobiography'. He continued working on these proofs on 18 and 19 March (reaching and rewriting the last, controversial chapter); on 21 March he was making a duplicate of corrections done, and the next day packed up a copy of the proofs to be deposited when they called at Port Sudan, for sending on to Oxford by airmail from Port Said. He had already sent a letter to Ethel from their stop at Colombo, mentioning that 'The ship is old (1911), slow, and uncomfortable; my cabin is as hot as hell, and there is no nonsense about bedsteads & running water. You have a good old bunk with drawers under it, and a basin, and the steward brings a quart jug of water before meals.' He concludes by saying, 'I am hard at work revising my Metaphysics book that I wrote on the Alcinous. I think by the time I get home I shall have made a job of it. Perhaps it will be as good as the Essay on Method; and it will certainly attract more readers. The weather is lovely in spite of head winds: sun, blue sea, flying fish, all that. Your R.'[56] Collingwood's health problems had continued to plague him throughout the journey

[56] Letter to Ethel Collingwood, 1 March, 1939. [TS/PLR199].

home, from the sore feet he originally got from hiking and from some mountain insect in Celebes to sleep and digestive problems which had also persisted for some weeks. But by 24 March he was feeling better; he noted 'Everybody back in European clothes', and then resumed his reading of Croce (see note for 25 March, as they docked at Port Said).

During the fairly quiet last lap of the voyage back across the Mediterranean, although he was still feeling unwell from time to time as we see from the *Log*, he returned to work—'playing with' the 'Principles of History' (26 March) but the next day finding 'the stuff wouldn't flow'. He notes that he was reading two autobiographies at this point—M. Asquith's, which was 'illiterate... equally revolting from a literary and from a moral point of view' (29 March) and Beatrice Webb's, 'very good and interesting piece of work' (30, 31 March).[57] By 1 April they were passing Gibraltar; he had listened to the Boat Race on the radio; and among other things, had spotted an armed trawler in the Straits. The concentration on 'Metaphysics' continued, as he worked on ch. IV (2 April), finished that and worked on ch. V the next day, returning again to the manuscript on 4 April, his last full day at sea. They docked in London on 5 April.

In the course of this whole six months' journey, Collingwood had clearly found inner resources which enabled him to make the most of any passing moments of peace and calm for his writing projects. The stimulation of the sea trips themselves and the fresh landscapes he saw obviously gave him great satisfaction, and there had been the extra excitement, after studying Malay on the outward journey, of using the language in the East Indies when he got there. The mix of Hindu, Islamic, and ancient indigenous civilization in the region, particularly the rich artistic and musical culture of Bali, was profoundly fascinating to him, and some of his detailed records are now a distinctive addition to the social and cultural archives of that island itself.

In the outline here, I have not yet indicated how Collingwood's jottings in the *Log*, to some extent, but more particularly his letters home, are punctuated by references to the rising fears of, and

[57] Asquith, Margot. 1920–1922. *The Autobiography of Margot Asquith*. New York: George H. Doran Company. 2 vols. Webb, Beatrice. 1926. *My Apprenticeship*. Cambridge: Cambridge University Press.

preparations for, war in Europe. This background no doubt, in addition to Collingwood's fragile state of health, helps explain the sense of urgency behind his commitment to making the most of the unexpected opportunities that opened up to him: and especially to pressing on with his writings. We owe to this time, and the circumstances of this journey, the bulk of what we now know as *An Essay on Metaphysics* (published 1940) and *The Principles of History* (eventually published, though not yet in the completed form the author would have wished, in 1999).

It was on the voyage too that he received proofs of *An Autobiography*, rewrote the final 'Spanish' chapter in the light of reservations that had been forwarded from the Oxford University Press, and had the proofs returned by airmail. The fear of impending war was quite explicitly a source of anxiety over getting these proofs home safely, which is perhaps why he had made copies of all his corrections. On 23 March, as he had just left his package of proofs at Port Sudan for onward delivery by air from Port Said to Kenneth Sisam, he wrote to Ethel that there was still considerable uncertainty about the date of arrival at London, not least of which because of the fear of an impending war:

> When we heard that Hitler had walked into Czechoslovakia we thought it would be war (it seemed hardly possible that even Mr Chamberlain could gloss over that) and in that case we couldn't have got through the Canal; we should either have spent the war in Suez or made for the Cape and tried to go home in a convoy. It now looks as if Mr. Chamberlain had glossed over it, & as if there would be no war: though you can't think how little nutriment one gets out of the wireless "news".[58]

We should recognize various other points where the ongoing political tension and expected war surfaced in Collingwood's commentaries from the voyage. In his letter to Ethel of 8 December (written soon after he had arrived in Bali, and already referred to earlier), he acknowledges her information about the result of the Oxford by-election (when Lindsay lost to the Conservative Quintin Hogg) and goes on to express his views of the current state of Europe. He mentions that he had been speaking to two Americans and two Italians. The Italians told him that:

[58] Letter to Ethel Collingwood, 23 March 1939. [TS/PLTR200].

Mussolini's regime is becoming more & more discredited in Italy which they ascribed to the follies of his incompetent underlings. Although they were fascists themselves & wouldn't hear a word against Benito himself. But they say "he is now tired & is being badly served by his own men." I begin to form the impression (based also on what my Dutch friends tell me about internal affairs in Germany) that the dictator states are only being kept on their legs by the execrable Chamberlain and the bloody-awful Halifax.[59]

After Christmas (with the van der Noordaas, mother and step-father of Mrs McMorran on Java), he writes that he caught an infection in a scratch on his lip which made him in his last two days in Bali irritable towards his hosts:

There were always potentialities of friction there. They are fascists & Hitler-worshippers, not out of conviction but out of defeatism; they are sure Hitler is going to conquer the world, and think only fools will try to stop him. And I found it impossible to argue with them because v.d.N. is stone-deaf & has the egotism of a deaf man: and if you do make him hear something he replies "That will I never believe. You say that: but what I think is . . . " and then you have to listen to his stuff all over again'.[60]

A little later, following a note made in the *Log* itself (27 January) about a letter from Croce asking him to find Momigliano a home in Oxford, he mentions to Ethel that he must write to Hugh Last about Momigliano, 'who Croce tells me has been chucked out of his professorship at Turin for being a Jew. How long will it be before Hitler tells Mr. Chamberlain that all Jews must be driven out of jobs in England?'[61]

Collingwood presumably never came to know of the tragic situation in which the artist Walter Spies, whom he had met on Bali, died in 1942. Along with hundreds of other Germans, he had been deported from the Dutch East Indies; Jan van der Dussen has drawn our attention to the fact that Spies was one of those imprisoned in locked cells on the SS *van Imhoff*, and with the great majority drowned as the ship was bombed by the Japanese. The *van Imhoff*, ironically, was the very ship on which Collingwood had spent a happy and productive time only three years before,

[59] Letter to Ethel Collingwood, 8 Dec. 1938. [TS/PLTR190].

[60] Letter to Ethel Collingwood, 31 Dec. 1939. [TS/PLTR193].

[61] Letter to Ethel Collingwood, 27 Jan. 1939. [TS/PLTR194] The letter from Croce is dated 19.xii.38.

noting his family links with its name, in the course of his island cruise.

7. *Postscript*

In retrospect, it does seem that Collingwood found more peace of mind and time for concentrated writing on his 1938–1939 voyage to the East Indies, well away from Europe, than he might have done had he remained at home during that period. The experiences of this voyage seem to have been a stimulus to some of Collingwood's subsequent publications and writings, to the point where one wonders whether, given more years of life, he would not have returned to that part of the world. In his late writings there are not only explicit mentions of his experiences on the voyage, for example, but his more general discussions of what is meant by 'society' and 'civilization' strike a definite chord with some of the observations made in the East Indies. For example, in the late essay 'What Civilization Means' he notes: 'An American lady whom I met in Bali on first seeing the mud-walled and grass-thatched villages of that country, asked me "How long do you think it would take to civilize these people?" but a few hours later when she had heard a Balinese orchestra and seen Balinese dancing, was sorry she had spoken.'[62] Some passages in *The Principles of History* were clearly written on the voyage; we read in one place, for example, 'In Java where I am writing . . . ' and there is a discussion of Javanese agriculture, which though involved in various 'superstitious' notions, is nevertheless practically very successful (*PH*, 97).

Collingwood's engagement with the people of the East Indies, especially Bali, went far beyond that of an ordinary tourist. His curiosity had an intensity more that of an anthropologist—and of a very open kind, his notes reflecting an empathy with the 'natives' and the sophistication of their civilization well ahead of his times. The range of his enthusiasms and practical interests in these later years of his life and travels reflects those of his earliest years, as described by Teresa Smith in this volume. It is often remarked that *An Autobiography* is basically 'cerebral', an account of the way

[62] Collingwood, R. G. 1992, 'What "Civilization" Means', printed as Appendix 2 to *NL*, revised edition, 1992: 485.

a philosopher's thought developed; but we gain a more rounded picture of Collingwood, the whole man, from his accounts of the voyage to the East Indies, and in particular his letters home. These writings help document a life which had a profound degree of coherence, of directed activity and continuity of practical achievement, even though it was so sadly to be cut short.

A LETTER FROM BALI TO HIS SISTER BARBARA GNOSSPELIUS, 23 DECEMBER 1938

R. G. COLLINGWOOD

Bedulu, Bali, 23.xii 38[1]

My darling Barbara, your letter of 28 Nov. reached me in this island nearly a fortnight ago, and I have not had time to answer it yet. I have been staying with friends, and my times & seasons have consequently been arranged for me, and arranged rather full. And Bali is a place where the visitor has to keep going, out of sheer greed, unless he is to miss something good. I'll try to tell you very shortly what it is like. It is about 100 km. from N to S by 200 from E to W. In the N. & E is a group of volcanoes from 7000 to 10,000 ft. high. All the rest of the island is made of volcanic stone and of soil, very rich & deep, washed down from these volcanoes. It slopes down abruptly on the N and more gently on the S., but everywhere rather steeply, so that there is no level ground; the southern plain is tilted sufficiently for all the very numerous parallel watercourses to have cut themselves into ravines generally 100–150 ft. deep. Steep where they are cut in the soil & vertical where they are cut into the soft tufa beneath it. It is therefore easy travelling on a N-S line along the intermediate ridges, but almost impossible to travel on a E-W line, except in the few places where the ravines have been bridged, either with native bamboo structures which

[1] Letter from R.G.C. to his sister Barbara [TS/FLTR 0844].

swing rather when you walk across them or with suspension bridges by the Dutch. The soil is hugely fertile. It is almost all given over to rice, grown in flooded sawahs engineered & irrigated with great skill. The population is very dense, and lives in villages uniformly planned in a most civilized way, on a scheme of square blocks separated by streets at right angles. Each village is a self-governing community, rather like a Greek city-state, and (like the Greeks) the Balinese go in for clubs to an astonishing extent. A Balinese house is a group of little mud-walled buildings that serve mainly to sleep in, all contained within a high mud wall; but people spend most of their time out of doors, foregathering with their friends in the unwalled buildings which are their club-houses. Producing their food takes very little time, and they have vast quantities of leisure. Much of it they spend in cock-fighting, but no inconsiderable quantity goes into music, dancing, acting, sculpture, drawing, metalwork, & so forth. Their music is orchestral. The Balinese orchestra is a percussion orchestra consisting of (a) batteries of circular brass gongs, each containing 10 gongs (b) things like the stone musical instrument in your Museum, but with metal bars instead of stones, and underneath each a resonator of bamboo tuned to the same pitch (c) cymbals of various kinds (d) huge tenor & bass gongs hung each in a separate frame (e) drums. The woodwork of all these instruments is teak, carved & painted & gilt with inconceivable richness. An orchestra, which is called a gamelan, has anything from 20 to 30 performers. There are numerous different scales, and any one orchestra of instruments is permanently tuned to one scale; but all these scales are selections from the same scale which we recognize in Europe, so all Balinese music is perfectly intelligible to the European ear. Although every instrument is a percussion one, & all the melodic instruments are of metal, the tone hasn't got the jangling confused character of a chime of bells; the tone is both brilliant & soft, and the players can get such a perfect legato that I have often fancied I was listening to a flute. No music is written down, but a great deal is composed & there is also a great deal of 'classical' music which everyone knows by heart. I have heard a modern symphony in 3 movements, lasting 25 minutes, played by an orchestra which had been taught it by 3 of their own members who had visited the orchestra that had composed this symphony & had learnt it by heart in 3 days. The music is harmonic, or rather contrapuntal. The themes are given out, generally in 2-part harmony, by the gongs, & the other instruments come in with semiquaver accompaniment, figures which embroider the theme. I have heard this kind of music now every day for over a fortnight, sometimes all day, sometimes all night, sometimes both; and I have never heard anybody play a wrong note or come in wrong or (most difficult of all) fail to be dead on the 'beat' – although, as there isn't any conductor, there isn't any way of knowing when the beat happens except by having the music, as the Balinese say, in your belly. There is no European orchestra that could come anywhere near the standard of an ordinary Balinese village orchestra in the technical perfection of its playing. And this is not only my opinion, it is also that of European musicians who have been here.

The dancing is a little like our ballet work, only (a) as superior to our ballet in technique as Balinese orchestral playing is to ours (b) our ballet dancers begin thinking in their legs, Balinese dancers begin thinking in their hands. Most of their best work is done by movements of fingers, wrists, arms, heads, eyes, shoulders. They can do a long and first-rate dance without ever moving from a sitting posture. It will consist of movements most of which I can't do at all, however slowly – e.g. vibrating the second finger sideways between the first & the third, or moving the head from side to side keeping the chin-nose line vertical. This may sound comic; but out of such movements you can build up a very flexible dance-language, far richer than that which our ballet dancers have built up out of footwork. There are many kinds of dance, varying from a solo dance without any plot, 'interpreting' a symphony, to a concerted dance-drama with sung & spoken parts. As with musicians, there are no professional dancers; the people who dance are farmers, house-servants, chauffeurs, postmen & so forth. I have seen the greatest living Balinese dancer; he is the best dancer I have ever seen except Massine [*Leonide Massine, 1895–1979*], and although I don't think that he could do what Massine does, I am quite sure that Massine couldn't do what Gusti Raka does. I saw him dance an eagle attacking a man. He was dressed in scarlet & purple & green silks and cloth of gold, with an elaborate gold head-dress, and he had wings fastened to his wrists. The whole dance was done on a stage about 8 ft. square. Gusti Raka never rose from a squatting position, his legs concealed by his cloth-of-gold train. But his eagle, with furious screams (Gusti Raka of course never opened his mouth) rose again & again thousands of feet in the air and swooped again and again until I wanted to scream with terror. Unlike Massine, however, he didn't make me want to cry.

I will try to describe one modern Balinese drawing. It is by a young man of about 23, a farmer, who is also the leader of the orchestra in this village & therefore a very active composer. My host took me to call on him a few days ago, about sunset: he was out, but his beautiful little wife entertained us and showed us this drawing, unfinished; it hung in the veranda with a cloth over it.

It is on Whatman paper, done with pen & brush in diluted Chinese ink. As a first rough idea of its style, think of Chinese wash-drawing crossed with some Italian primitive. It is about 20 inches high by 14 wide. On the right is a mass of coconut-trees, lashed by a furious gale from the left; they are bending right over, & one has just broken off below the head. They stand just outside the mud wall of a village. Immediately to L. of them is a deep ravine with water raging down it; above that, you see a very peaceful landscape of rice fields stretching away miles & miles to a distant range of volcanoes. Above that, a stormy sky. Out of the ravine there has risen a demon, who is chasing a boy up one of the coconut palms. The demon must be about 20 ft. high, and he is hurling globes of flame at the boy; whose name we were told, is Manik (Itu Manik, said a small child, lending a hand to entertain the visitors. I didn't know what a Manik was; I thought it might be some kind of fairy, so I asked: apa manik? Oh, said the child patiently, itu anak bernama Manik. Manik is the name of that boy).

These people are tall and broad in the shoulder, strong & active. They don't run to fat, they run to muscle. They are a lovely golden brown colour, but that is only the sun; they are born white. They have extremely beautiful intelligent faces: at least, the men have; the women I don't find so exciting. They are very open & friendly, and make friends with you on the smallest provocation. I am living here with an elderly bachelor; and every evening, on our veranda, we are surrounded by a squatting crowd of boys & men, based on the 6 house-boys and extending to any number of their friends & relations and of callers from near or far, some of them coming to show a new statuette they have just finished & want sympathy about, others just looking in for a chat. They all sit around our feet and pet the dogs & chatter to us in Malay and make endless jokes. This morning, at 6.30, there turned up a small boy of 8 who had walked 60 kilometres in the last 12 hours from his home in the mountains, because he thought he would like to pay a morning call on his dear friend Tuan Bonnicker. So he sailed in, as fresh as paint, while we were drinking our morning coffee in our dressing-gowns, and was given breakfast. This (which is typical of the Balinese child, who is never beaten, is allowed to do exactly what he likes, & is never told to don't or to hush, & is in consequence always as good as gold, and as intelligent as they are made) brings me to food. Yesterday I lunched off boiled maggots. They looked like wasp-maggots but a bit larger. I ate them with cucumber salad & they were delicious. I dined off something whose bones slightly resembled those of a bird, but which in fact was in life a lizard about 2ft. 6″ long. It was a trifle tough. The Balinese eat practically everything except men & dogs, and all on a foundation of rice. They think it well to remember that they live practically <u>in</u> the Spice Islands, and a real Balinese dinner almost takes the skin off the inside of your mouth. I have eaten one, cooked by a real princess, and very good it was. But that is another story. I can't recapitulate even the highlights of my Bali life in a single letter. For example: the musical festival which accompanied the 25-year jubilee of the local prince, the Regent of Gianjar. The banquet at same (to which I procured an invitation). My acquaintance with Walter Spies,* the Swiss who, alone of Europeans, really knows Bali; he looks like Ruskin in youth. My stay with a Dutch artist & his Danish wife, who live in the palace of a native prince. Details of the various dances I have seen, and how I fell asleep in the middle of one which lasted from 11 PM to broad daylight, and nearly squashed a group of sleeping children who were leaning against my legs. No, I can't do it even in this headline style. I had better stop. When you get this, I shall be at sea, beginning a 6-weeks cruise round Celebes, Ternate, Amboina, Halmaheira, Banda Neira, Sumba, Sumbawa, Flores, Timor and the rest of them. I sail for home on 8 March. I am very well, and happier than I thought it possible for anybody to be who knows as much as I know about what sort of a world we have to live in.

Goodbye darling, & be careful of your gall-bladder, whatever a g.b is. R.

* *Note written down the margin*: Make your library lend you Spies and De Zoete's book, Dance & Drama in Bali (Faber). Quite new, & trustworthy.

INDEX

Note: Bold entries refer to illustrations.

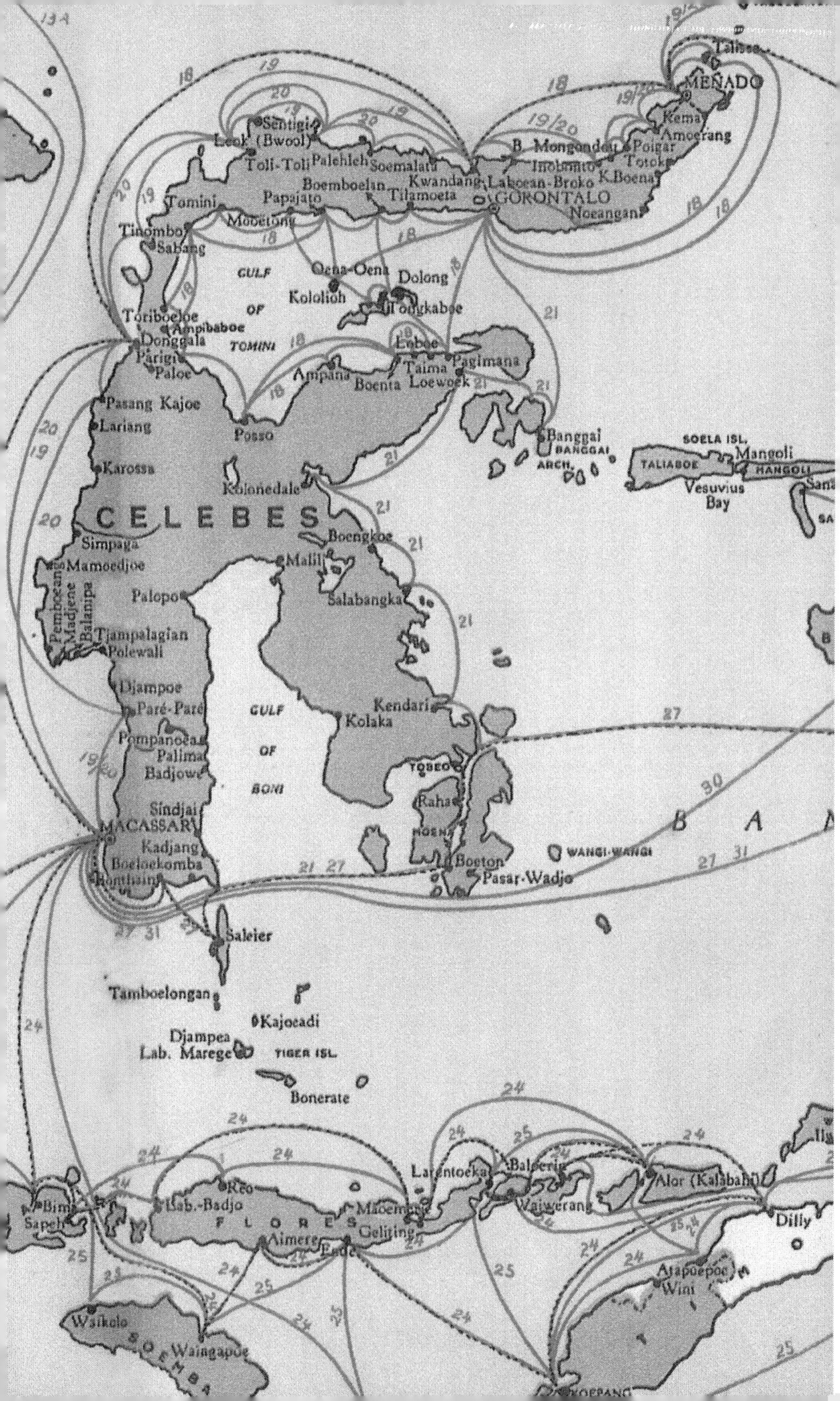

MENADO
Talisse
Kema
Amoerang
Poigar
Totok
K. Boena
B. Mongondou
Inobonto
Noeangan
GORONTALO
Lakoean-Broko
Kwandang
Tilamoeta
Soemalatu
Palehleh
Boemboelan
Papajato
Sentigi
Leok (Bwool)
Toli-Toli
Tomini
Moetong
Tinombo
Sabang
GULF OF TOMINI
Oena-Oena
Dolong
Kololioh
Tongkaboe
Toriboeloe
Ampibaboe
Donggala
Parigi
Paloe
Ampana
Loboe
Taima
Pagimana
Boenta
Loewoek
Pasang Kajoe
Lariang
Posso
Banggai
BANGGAI ARCH.
SOELA ISL.
TALIABOE
Mangoli
MANGOLI
Vesuvius Bay
Karossa
Kolonedale
CELEBES
Simpaga
Mamoedjoe
Pembocan
Madjene
Balampa
Boengkoe
Malili
Palopo
Salabangka
Tjampalagian
Polewali
Djampoe
Paré-Paré
GULF OF BONI
Kendari
Kolaka
Pompanoea
Palima
Badjowe
TOBEO
Raha
MOENA
Sindjai
MACASSAR
Kadjang
Boeloekomba
Bonthain
Boeton
Pasar-Wadjo
WANGI-WANGI
B A N
Saleier
Tamboelongan
Kajoeadi
Djampea
Lab. Marege
TIGER ISL.
Bonerate
Larantoeka
Balaerin
Waiwerang
Alor (Kalabahi)
Dilly
Reo
Lab.-Badjo
FLORES
Maoemere
Geliting
Aimere
Ende
Bima
Sapeh
Atapoepoe
Wini
Waikelo
SOEMBA
Waingapoe
KOEPANG

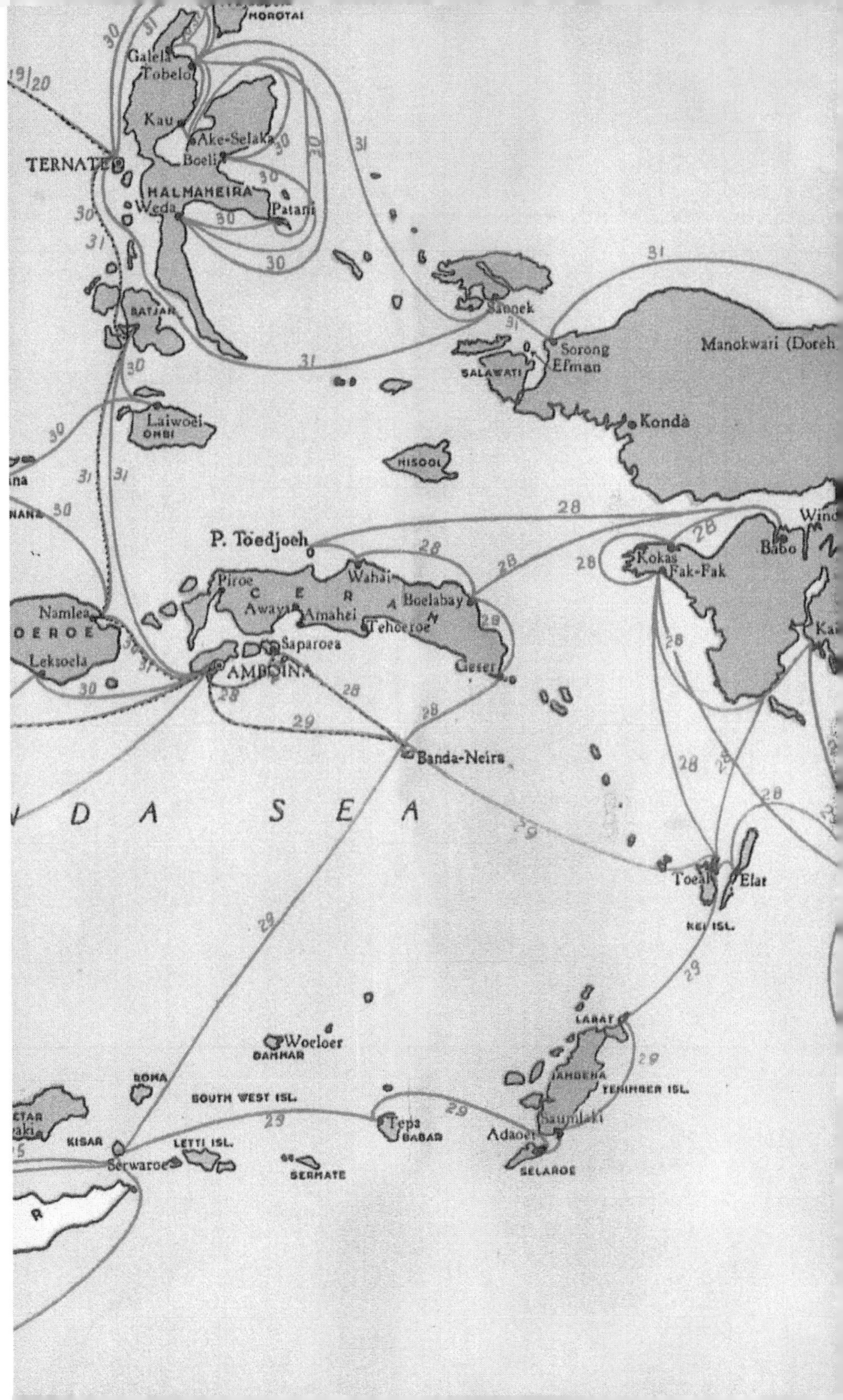
MOROTAI
Galela
Tobelo
Kau
Ake-Selaka
Boeli
TERNATE
HALMAHEIRA
Weda
Patani
BATJAN
Saonek
Sorong
Efman
SALAWATI
Manokwari (Doreh
Laiwoei
OMBI
Konda
MISOOL
P. Toedjoeh
Wahai
Piroe
C E R A M
Awaya
Amahei
Boelabay
Tehoeroe
Namlea
Leksoela
Saparoea
AMBOINA
Geser
Kokas
Fak-Fak
Babo
Banda-Neira
D A S E A
Toeal
Elat
KEI ISL.
Woeloer
DAMMAR
LARAT
ROMA
SOUTH WEST ISL.
JAMDENA
TENIMBER ISL.
KISAR
Serwaroe
LETTI ISL.
Tepa
BABAR
Adaoet
Saumlaki
SERMATE
SELAROE

Printed and bound by CPI Group (UK) Ltd, Croydon, CR0 4YY